LAST DAYS

NEW TESTAMENT

Everyday Dynamic Version (EDV)

Translation & Footnotes
by Rev. Stephen Henley

First published in Australia 2025 by Sid Harta Books & Pty Ltd.
This second edition published 2026 by Luke 21 Ministries.

Copyright © Luke 21 Ministries (www.luke21.com.au) (ABN: 63 492 528 870)
Cover design, typesetting: WorkingType (www.workingtype.com.au)

The right of Rev. Stephen Henley to be identified as the
Author of the Work has been asserted in accordance with the
Copyright, Designs and Patents Act 1988.

All rights reserved. No part of this publication may be reproduced, stored in a retrieval system, or transmitted, in any form or by any means without the prior written permission of the publisher, nor be otherwise circulated in any form of binding or cover other than that in which it is published and without a similar condition being imposed on the subsequent purchaser.

ISBN: 978-1-922958-95-2

About the Author

Steve was born in Perth, Western Australia. He achieved a Bachelor Of Engineering (Civil) at University of W.A. and became a Christian in 1984 whilst still studying at University. He met his wife Cathi in 1988. Cathi was born and raised in the western suburbs of Sydney where she began serving with the Youth for Christ singing band 'Travellers' for two years before she met Steve. They both felt the call to missions in 1988 and so after marrying went to New Tribes Mission Bible College in Sydney.

In 1995 Steve and Cathi and their three young boys went to the mountains of Papua New Guinea and planted and established 14 churches with over 500 believers in the West New Britain province. Their ministry was to plant churches and also to translate the New Testament in the local language. Steve and his team completed the Asengseng New Testament in March 2007.

From March 2010 to the end of 2019, Steve was the senior pastor at Minden Baptist Church and solo pastor at Churchill Baptist Church from May 2021 to October 2024 and has specialised in foundational chronological teaching in Genesis through to Christ with his special interest being in the end times.

"For if you keep silent at this time, relief and deliverance will rise for the Jews from another place, but you and your father's house will perish. And who knows whether you have not come to the kingdom for such a time as this?"
Esther 4:14 (ESV)

To the love of my life, Catherine Anne who is pure and gracious both in name and nature and who has helped and supported me every step of the way.

Acknowledgements

Special thanks to Renier van Rooyen for proofreading the entire EDV New Testament with also a special mention to Mick Alexander, Cathi Henley and Gordon Colledge for their valuable corrections and suggestions. A big thankyou also goes to those who contributed financially to making this project possible.

Abbreviations used in this translation:

(AD)	Anno Domini [date], the Year of Our Lord
(BC)	[date] Before Christ
(CJB)	Complete Jerusalem Bible
(DARBY)	Darby Translation
(DRB)	Douay Rheims Bible
(ESV)	English Standard Version
(JNT)	Jerusalem New Testament (Commentary)
(KJV)	King James Version
(LEB)	Lexham English Bible
(LGV)	Tim Warner's Last Generation Version
(LSV)	Literal Standard Version
(LXX)	Greek Septuagint Old Testament
(MSS)	Manuscripts
(NEB)	New English Bible
(NIV)	New International Version (1984)
(NKJV)	New King James Version
(NRSV)	New Revised Standard Version
(NT)	New Testament
(NWO)	New World Order
(OSAS)	Once Saved Always Saved
(OT)	Old Testament
(TH)	Bible Society's Translator's Handbook
(TR)	Textus Receptus
(YLT)	Young's Literal Translation

Preface

In 2018 when I began this translation project, it was my aim to put down in one place many of the things that I had learnt over the years as a cross cultural missionary with the Asengseng tribe in Papua New Guinea and as a Baptist pastor in Australia. And what better place than the New Testament with study notes! Of course this is not the first time that I have translated the New Testament. The first time was the Asengseng New Testament for the people living in that language group in West New Britain Province, Papua New Guinea. It was published in 2006 with 1500 copies being printed. I believe God inspired and challenged me with the idea to do it all again but this time in a new English version which utilizes all the translation knowledge and skills gained the first time around.

Why another English version when there are over 200 English translations? Good question. The simple answer... Languages are ever changing and English is the trade language of the world. And because new discoveries are being made all the time such as the Dead Sea Scrolls in 1947 and new insights into verses, I believe that a lot has been missed. I have always gone by the mantra since my missionary days that the best Bible translators are Bible teachers and the best Bible teachers are Bible translators of which I have had the privilege of doing both. So what am I saying? I am saying that translations need to be 'road-tested' so that the best translation can be achieved. My 'Everyday Dynamic Version' (EDV) is not just an academic translation but uses information gained from many years of Bible teaching experience both on the foreign mission field and in the local church context in Australia.

I remember teaching Bible translation principles to missionary training candidates in the 1990s saying to them that a translation is needed for each new generation because language is ever changing. How long is a generation? Anywhere from 20–40 years in languages. That's how fast things change! My vision for my new EDV translation is to capture the language of our day in this last generation in the days before Jesus returns.

At the end of the day, Bible Translation is interpretation and translations are highly vulnerable to the doctrinal stances and biases of the translators. In studying the Bible, one must use many different versions, I believe, to get different angles in arriving at the original meaning.

I have used the AGNT Plus (Analytical Greek New Testament Plus) 2015 version as my basis together with many English translations including ESV, KJV, ISV, NIV, Tim Warner's LGV, Good News, LEB and many others. Each has had a purpose in helping me to achieve a more up to date translation that tries to be dynamic and yet faithful to the original meaning. All translations have their pros and cons and each have different purposes and biases. There is no perfect translation except the original autographs and they do not exist. My translation is neither based on 'Textus Receptus' (KJV) or the 'critical text' (to the dismay of some) but uses both according to where I have seen the best interpretation. The experience gained in translating the New Testament into a tribal language group as well as the experiences in Bible teaching as a missionary in Papua New Guinea and as a pastor in Australia have certainly influenced me to make this translation very readable to the 21st century English reader.

The EDV has an 'end times' flavour because I believe that we are very near to the second coming of the Lord Jesus Christ. In fact, my belief is that we will see this 70th week begin before the end of this decade. Therefore, in my opinion, this translation fills a need in helping to navigate the coming 70th week known as the seven-year tribulation. See my website **https://luke21.com.au** for many articles concerning the coming last days. The Kingdom of God is coming and I believe that we will see the two witnesses of Revelation kick events off.

You will notice several differences including certain key biblical terms such as Christ, Holy Spirit, predestination, sanctification, justification, disciple, repent, redeem, and kingdom being some of them which are translated using terms or phrases that I feel are either more accurate or more dynamic or descriptive. There are also extensive footnotes which help explain hard to understand verses.

Please note that any word in *italics* in the main text has been added for clarification where necessary but is not in the original Greek.

I hope that the EDV is a blessing and thought provoking as you too use it as an inspiration for your own personal study and devotions.

Blessings

Rev. Stephen Henley

Table of Contents

Abbreviations viii
Preface 1

Matthew 5
Mark 83
Luke 127
John 199
Acts 257
Romans 323
1 Corinthians 355
2 Corinthians 383
Galatians 401
Ephesians 413
Philippians 425
Colossians 433
1 Thessalonians 441
2 Thessalonians 449
1 Timothy 455
2 Timothy 465
Titus 471
Philemon 477
Hebrews 481
James 507
1 Peter 515
2 Peter 527
1 John 533
2 John 541
3 John 543
Jude 545
Revelation 549

MATTHEW

Introduction

The first synoptic gospel written by Matthew with a Hebrew perspective written primarily for Jewish believers in the AD 60s. Matthew, also named Levi by Luke and Mark, was a tax collector in the town of Capernaum. The book is written in a concise way, although not a chronological way unlike Luke's Gospel.

Even though written for Jewish believers it is important to note that it is not exclusively Jewish but for the whole church which is important eschatologically. Otherwise Matthew 24 could be excluded for part of the church which is a dangerous position to take. If only taken to be for the Jewish section of the church, then one could surmise that the church does not need to 'become prepared' (Matt. 24:44) for the end times but that it will be taken out prior to the last seven years with a pre-tribulation rapture.

The Book of Matthew is the largest book of the New Testament (NT) and includes the Jewish lineage of Christ, the parables, Sermon on the Mount, the miracles of Jesus, Olivet discourse about the end times and the crucifixion and resurrection of Christ. It contains a bit of everything and is an excellent book for instructing new believers. The Book of Matthew in Matt. 28:19–20 contains the last command to believers to evangelise the world known as the 'Great Commission'.

The genealogy of Jesus through Joseph

(Luke 3:23–38)

1 ¹This is an account of the genealogy of Jesus Christ, the descendant of David who is the descendant of Abraham.

²Abraham fathered Isaac and Isaac fathered Jacob and Jacob fathered Judah and his brothers. ³Judah fathered Perez and Zerah by Tamar. Perez fathered Hezron and Hezron fathered Ram. ⁴Ram fathered Amminadab and Amminadab fathered Nahshon and Nahshon fathered Salmon. ⁵Salmon fathered Boaz by Rahab. Boaz fathered Obed by Ruth. Obed fathered Jesse. ⁶And Jesse fathered David the king.

David fathered Solomon by the wife of Uriah.¹ ⁷Solomon fathered Rehoboam and Rehoboam fathered Abijah and Abijah fathered Asa. ⁸Asa fathered Jehoshaphat and Jehoshaphat fathered Jehoram and Jehoram fathered Uzziah. ⁹Uzziah fathered Jotham and Jotham fathered Ahaz and Ahaz fathered Hezekiah. ¹⁰Hezekiah fathered Manasseh and Manasseh fathered Amon and Amon fathered Josiah. ¹¹Josiah fathered Jeconiah and his brothers at the time when *Israel* was deported to Babylon.

¹²After Israel was deported to Babylon, Jeconiah fathered Shealtiel and Shealtiel fathered Zerubbabel. ¹³Zerubbabel fathered Abiud and Abiud fathered Eliakim and Eliakim fathered Azor. ¹⁴Azor fathered Zadok and Zadok fathered Akim and Akim fathered Eliud. ¹⁵Eliud fathered Eleazar and Eleazar fathered Matthan and Matthan fathered Jacob. ¹⁶Jacob fathered Joseph, the husband of Mary. Mary gave birth to Jesus, the one who is called the Messiah.

¹⁷Therefore the number of generations in all from Abraham to David is fourteen and the number of generations from David to when *Israel* was deported to Babylon is fourteen and the number of generations from the deportation to the Messiah, fourteen also.

The birth of Jesus Christ

(Luke 2:1–7)

¹⁸Now the birth of Jesus Christ was like this: His mother Mary was engaged to be married to Joseph. Before the two of them came together she was found to be with child by means of Holy Breath. ¹⁹Now because Joseph her husband was a righteous man and did not wish to publicly disgrace her, he decided to divorce her in private. ²⁰However while he was still thinking about this an angel of *the* Lord appeared to him in a dream saying, "Joseph, son of David. Do not be afraid

---

1 Bathsheba. Cf. 2 Sam. 12:24.

to take Mary as your wife for that which has been begotten[2] in her from *God's Breath is holy.*[3] [21]She will give birth to a son and you are to name him 'Jesus' for he will save the people from their sins."

[22]Now all this took place that the thing spoken of by the Lord through the prophet might be fulfilled who said, [23]"The virgin will have a child in her womb and she will give birth to a son and they will call him Immanuel."[4] It means, "God with us."

[24]As Joseph arose from his sleep, he did as the angel of the Lord had commanded him in the dream and he took *Mary* to be his wife. [25]But he did not know her intimately until she had given birth to a son. And he named him 'Jesus'.

The magi visit Jesus

2 [1]Now after Jesus had been born in Bethlehem of Judea[5] in the days of King Herod, magi[6] from the east arrived in Jerusalem. [2]They arrived saying, "Where is the one who has been born of the Jews? For we saw the star of his *birth* as it was rising and we have come to worship him." [3]Now having heard this, King Herod was greatly troubled and many of the people of Jerusalem with him were troubled as well. [4]And so having assembled all the chief priests and scribes,[7] he enquired of them as to where the Messiah was supposed to be born. [5]And so they said to him, "In Bethlehem of Judea for it has been written through the prophet as such,

> [6]'And you Bethlehem in the land of Judah are by no means the least
>   among the rulers of Judah.
> For from you a ruler will come. And he will shepherd my people Israel.'"
>
> Micah 5:2

[7]Then Herod, having called for the magi secretly, he calculated exactly from

---

2   The male role in causing the conception of a child, i.e. 'fathered'. Cf. Heb. 1:5.
3   Cf. Luke 1:35.
4   Cf. Isa. 7:14. In Isaiah, the mother names the child. There is a dual focus in Isaiah's prophecy, the near fulfilment concerning how the land of Judah will be safe from the northern invaders and the other far fulfilment being how the virgin will give birth to the baby Jesus.
5   Rev. 12:1-2 tells us exactly when Jesus was born. The moon was under the feet of the woman (Virgo = Virgin) and she is clothed by the sun with twelve stars on her head. This only occurred between 6:15 pm-7 pm on the Jewish New Year (Rosh Hashanah), Sep 11th 3 BC.
6   The magi were astronomer-priests, perhaps Zorasters from Persia. Babylonians and later Persians were experts in the exact sciences such as astronomy and mathematics but many became infected by superstition with the belief that there were miraculous powers in numbers resulting in pursuits such as numerology, becoming more aligned with astrology. Astronomers were able to predict solar and lunar eclipses using mathematics and would scan the heavens at night on his ziggurat. Eclipses were considered to be omens of ill fate such as the imminent death of a ruler (Strathern, Paul, *Ten Cities That Led The World* (2022), pp. 7-12).
7   The scribes were the experts and teachers of the Jewish religious Law of Moses.

them the timing of the appearing of the star.⁸ ⁸And Herod sent them to Bethlehem instructing them saying, "Go and enquire carefully about the child. And when you find him, report back to me so that I too may come and worship him."

⁹And so having listened to the king the *magi* left and saw that the star which they had *previously* seen rising was going before them. It went before them until it came to the place where the child was.⁹ ¹⁰Seeing the star they were greatly overjoyed.

¹¹When the magi came into the house, they saw the child with his mother Mary and they fell down and worshipped him.¹⁰ And then they opened their treasures and they offered to him gifts of gold, frankincense and myrrh.¹¹ ¹²And having been warned in a dream not to return to Herod, they left going back to their country by another way.

Joseph, Mary and Jesus escape to Egypt

¹³Now after the magi had left, an angel of the Lord appeared to Joseph in a dream and the *angel* said to him, "Arise, take the child and his mother and flee to Egypt and remain there until I tell you. For Herod is about to search for the child to kill him." ¹⁴So *Joseph* arose and took the child and his mother during the night and left for Egypt. ¹⁵And he was there until the death of Herod in order that the thing spoken of by the Lord through the prophet might be fulfilled. He said, "Out of Egypt I called my son."

---

8   The magi had seen the signs in the stars that a king had been born. Over a period of 18 months or so from May 3 BC to December 2 BC there were about nine major conjunctions in the sky where planets or stars came together. In August 3 BC there occurred a conjunction of Jupiter and Venus visible from the eastern sky in modern-day Iraq or Babylon where the magi were situated. That would have particular significance to astrologers who knew about the Messiah or were familiar with the Jews. On that morning, they would have seen a conjunction of Jupiter and Venus taking place in the constellation Leo near the star Regulus (Regal) which is Latin for prince or little king. Venus is the feminine Ishtar or mother god.

9   The Star of Bethlehem that stopped stationary over the little city was none other than the king planet, Jupiter. In 2 BC as viewed from Jerusalem, Jupiter came to its normal stationary position directly over Bethlehem in late December. Just before dawn (the regular time the magi would have begun their normal observations of the heavens), Jupiter came to a 'stopped' position directly over Bethlehem as witnessed from Jerusalem. On this particular night when the magi visited the infant Jesus, the king planet Jupiter also stood still as the brightest object in the sky over the little city of Bethlehem. Christmas is the day that the magi came to visit the little child Jesus at the end of 2 BC.

10   Scholars say that the magi visit occurred anywhere between forty days and two years after Jesus was born. It didn't happen the same night where we get all these visitors as the picture perfect nativity scene shows us. The magi saw all these conjunctions and signs in the sky and they went searching for the king of the Jews. From the stars we now know that Jesus would have been an infant around fifteen months old when the Star of Bethlehem appeared.

11   Magi came bearing gifts around the very time of Hanukkah when it was custom to give gifts to children.

King Herod gives orders to kill

¹⁶Then Herod, having seen that he was tricked by the magi, he was extremely enraged. He sent orders to kill all the male children aged two years and under in Bethlehem and in all of its districts. This was exactly calculated according to what the magi had said. ¹⁷Then the thing spoken by the prophet Jeremiah was fulfilled which said,

> ¹⁸"A voice was heard in Ramah, great weeping, and mourning.
> It is Rachel weeping for her children.
> She refused to be comforted for her children because they were dead."
>
> Jeremiah 31:15

Joseph and Mary return to Nazareth

¹⁹Herod was now dead and an angel of the Lord appeared to Joseph in a dream in Egypt. ²⁰The angel said, "Arise, take the child and his mother and go into the land of Israel for the ones seeking the child's life have died." ²¹So *Joseph* arose and he took the child and his mother and entered into the land of Israel. ²²But *Joseph* having heard that Archelaus was reigning in Judea instead of his father Herod, he was afraid to go there. But having been warned in a dream, he left for the district of Galilee. ²³And having arrived, he settled in the city called Nazareth so that the thing spoken of by the prophets might be fulfilled saying, "He will be called a Nazarene."

John the Baptist prepares the way for the Lord
(Mark 1:2–8, Luke 3:1–18, John 1:19–28)

3 ¹Now in the days when John the Baptist came, he preached in the wilderness of Judea. ²He was saying, "Turn from your sins because Heaven's reign is coming soon."¹² ³For John is the one spoken of through Isaiah the prophet when he said,

> "A voice crying out in the desert saying, 'Prepare the way for the Lord.
> Straighten the way for him.'"
>
> Isaiah 40:3

⁴Now John's clothing consisted of the hair of a camel and a leather belt around his waist and his food was locusts and wild honey. ⁵Many of those from

---

12 This phrase is the term often translated as 'Kingdom of Heaven' in the Book of Matthew or 'Kingdom of God' in other gospels. Its primary meaning is God's activity of ruling rather than a literal land, country or territory that he rules. 'Heaven' in Matthew is often capitalised because it is a metaphor for God whereas in other places it means the sky or the abode where God lives.

Jerusalem and all over from Judea and the whole region of the Jordan *Valley* kept going out to him. ⁶And they were baptised by him in the Jordan River, confessing their sins.

⁷And seeing that many were coming to be baptised, John said to the Pharisees and Sadducees, "You nest of snakes! Who warned you to flee the coming wrath? ⁸Therefore you must produce fruit which shows that you have turned from your sins. ⁹And do not think that you can tell yourselves that you have Abraham as your father. Because I tell you that out of these stones God can raise up children for Abraham.¹³ ¹⁰God has the axe *ready* to cut down the trees at the root. Therefore every tree that is not producing good fruit is cut down and thrown into the fire.

¹¹"I, *John*, baptise you with water because you have turned away from your sins. But there is the one coming who is more important than me of whom I am not worthy to even remove his sandals. He will baptise you with Holy Breath and fire. ¹²And he has the winnowing fork in his hand *ready*. He will clear his threshing floor and he will gather his wheat into the shed. But he will burn up the chaff with an inextinguishable¹⁴ fire."

John baptises Jesus
(Mark 1:9–11, Luke 3:21–22)

¹³Then Jesus came from *the district of* Galilee to the Jordan to John to be baptised by him. ¹⁴But John tried to stop him saying, "I need to be baptised by you and yet you come to me? ¹⁵But answering, Jesus said to him, "Allow it to be so for now. It is proper for you and me to do what God requires." Then *John* allowed him *to be baptised*.

¹⁶Having been baptised, Jesus immediately came up out of the water and then the heavens were opened for him to see and he saw the Breath of God descending like a dove and it landed on him. ¹⁷Note this, a voice came out of the heavens saying, "This is my Son whom I love. I am very pleased with him."

The devil tests Jesus
(Mark 1:12–13, Luke 4:1–13)

4 ¹Then Jesus was led up¹⁵ into the desert by the Breath *of God* in order to be put to the test by the devil. ²And after having fasted for forty days and forty

---
13 In Hebrew there is a play on words between children (*banim*) and stones (*abanim*) (TH).
14 Interestingly the word "inextinguishable" is translated from the Greek adjective *asbestos* which is also an English word for the material now outlawed for its toxicity. It has nonflammable properties.
15 The Judean desert is in the Judean mountains which is at a higher altitude than the Jordan Valley hence the upwards direction.

nights, *Jesus* was hungry. ³The *devil* came to him and said, "If you are the Son of God, speak to these stones so that they may become bread." ⁴But he answered, "It has been written that man shall not live on bread alone but on every word that proceeds from the mouth of God."¹⁶

⁵Then the devil brought Jesus to the holy city and had him stand on the pinnacle of the temple. ⁶And he said to him, "If you are the Son of God, throw yourself down. For it has been written in the Scriptures,

'He will command his angels concerning you and they will lift you up in
   their hands, so that you will not hit your foot against a stone.'"

Psalm 91:11–12

⁷And Jesus said to him, "It has also been written in the Scriptures, 'Do not test the Lord your God.'"

⁸Again, the devil took him to a very high mountain¹⁷ and showed him all the countries and nations of the world and their wealth and magnificence. ⁹And the *devil* said to *Jesus*, "All these things I will give to you if you will bow down and worship me." ¹⁰And Jesus said to him, "Go away Satan.¹⁸ For it is written in the Scriptures, 'You are to worship the Lord your God and you are to serve him only.'"

¹¹Then the devil left him and angels came and ministered to him.

*Jesus begins his ministry year in Galilee*¹⁹
(Mark 1:14–15, Luke 4:14–15)

¹²Now having heard that John had been arrested, Jesus went to the *district* of Galilee. ¹³He left the *city* of Nazareth and he went and lived in Capernaum²⁰ *which was a city* by the sea in the district of the *descendants* of Zebulun and Naphtali. ¹⁴He did this so that the thing spoken of by the prophet Isaiah might be fulfilled who said,

---

16 Cf. Deut. 8:3.
17 Traditionally the 'Mount of Temptation' located at Jericho in the Judean wilderness. Today in Palestinian Arabic it is called 'Jebel Quruntul' (Mount Quarantine) after the forty day period of Jesus' temptation in the wilderness rising to 400 m (138 m above sea level) above Jericho. Its outlook faces the mountains (the world) on the other side of the Dead Sea in Jordan.
18 "Satan" is of Hebrew origin and wasn't originally used as a name for the serpent in the OT but had the definite article 'the' as in 'the satan' (Job 1:6) meaning the adversary or accuser. However by NT times during the intertestamental period Satan had become a proper noun and name of the devil. The Apostle John makes it clear that Satan, the devil and the dragon are the one and same being (Rev. 12:9).
19 The length of Jesus' public ministry was only 62 weeks. Cf. John 2:13 and related footnote.
20 Literally Capernaum means 'village of Nahum'.

¹⁵"Land of Zebulun and land of Naphtali, on the road to the *Sea of* Galilee on the other side of the Jordan,²¹ the *district* of Galilee where the Gentiles live.

¹⁶"The people²² living in darkness²³ have seen a great light.

To them living in the land and the shadow of death²⁴ a light has dawned."

Isaiah 9:1-2

Jesus calls his first four followers
(Mark 1:16–20, Luke 5:1–11)

¹⁷From this time on it was Jesus who began to preach saying, "Turn from your sins because the Heaven's reign is coming soon."

¹⁸Jesus was walking beside the Sea of Galilee and he saw two brothers, Simon called Peter and his brother Andrew, casting a net into the sea for they were fishermen. ¹⁹And Jesus said to the two of them, "Come, and follow me, and I will make you fishermen of men *to bring in people instead*." ²⁰Immediately they left their nets and followed *Jesus*.

²¹And going on from there, Jesus saw two other brothers, James the son of Zebedee and John his brother. He saw *the two of* them in a boat with their father Zebedee, mending their nets. Jesus called them, ²²and immediately *the two brothers* left the boat and they left their father and followed *Jesus*.

Jesus heals the sick
(Luke 6:17–19)

²³And Jesus went all over *the region of* Galilee teaching in their synagogues and preaching the good news²⁵ that God will soon reign. He healed every disease and every illness among the people. ²⁴And news of Jesus went all over the *province of* Syria.²⁶ The people brought to Jesus all who were sick with various diseases and those being tormented by pain, those who were demon-possessed, those having epileptic fits, the paralysed and Jesus healed them all. ²⁵And large crowds from Galilee, the Decapolis,²⁷ Jerusalem, Judea and the region beyond the Jordan *to the west* followed him *around*.

---

21   This is referring to the west side of the Jordan Valley.
22   This is the Jewish people.
23   This refers to spiritual darkness.
24   This refers to the condition of the people who are spiritually dead.
25   The good news is what is also known as the gospel.
26   To the Jew, Syria meant the region to the north of Galilee.
27   Literally 'ten cities' mainly situated west of the Jordan River. They were a league of ten Greek speaking cities. The only city in the Transjordan in the Decapolis was Bethshan (Scythopolis).

Jesus' sermon on the mount

(Luke 6:20–23)

5 ¹Now seeing the crowds, Jesus went up the mountain[28] and he sat down.[29] When he sat down, his followers[30] came to him, ²and he began to teach them saying,

> ³"Blessed are the poor in spirit[31] for they have a part in the realm of Heaven.
> ⁴Blessed are the ones who are mourning for they will be comforted.
> ⁵Blessed are the meek for they will receive what has been promised.
> ⁶Blessed are the ones who hunger and thirst for God's will to be done for they will be satisfied.
> ⁷Blessed are the merciful for they will be shown mercy.
> ⁸Blessed are the pure in heart for they will see God.
> ⁹Blessed are the peacemakers for they will be known as the sons of God.
> ¹⁰Blessed are the ones being persecuted because they are doing the will of God and they have a part in the realm of Heaven.

¹¹"Blessed are you when people verbally abuse you and persecute you and say all kinds of evil against you telling lies because of me. ¹²Rejoice and be glad for great is your reward in heaven. In the same way, people persecuted the prophets of long ago.

We are to be like salt and light

(Mark 9:50, Luke 14:34–35)

¹³"You are the salt of the earth. But if the salt becomes tasteless then how can it become salty again? It is no longer good for anything except to be thrown away and to be trampled upon by men.

¹⁴"You are the light of the world. A city situated on a mountain[32] is not able to be hidden. ¹⁵Nor do people light a lamp[33] and put it under a grain-bucket. But

---

28   Note that it is 'the mountain' meaning that it must have been a known mountain. Tradition has it that the mountain is on the western shore of the Lake of Galilee.
29   It was customary for the Jewish rabbis and teachers to teach their followers while sitting.
30   In Hebrew this word is *talmidim* (plural) or *talmid* (singular). The English words 'disciple' or 'follower' fail to convey the richness of the relationship between a Jewish rabbi and his talmidim. Followers of teachers gave themselves wholeheartedly over to their teachers. The essence of the relationship was one of trust in every area of living and the goal was that the talmid was to become exactly like his rabbi in knowledge, wisdom and ethical behaviour (Stern, David H, *JNT Commentary* (1992), p. 23).
31   I.e. the humble person.
32   Gk: *orous*. This means mountain not hill as translated in most English translations.
33   This is a light made by burning a wick saturated with oil contained in a relatively small vessel. The

they light it upon the lampstand and it gives light to everyone in the house.[34] [16]Therefore let your light shine before men so that they may see your good works and praise your Father in heaven.

Jesus came to give complete meaning to the Law and Prophets.

[17]"You must not think that I have come to abolish the Law *of Moses* or *the teachings of* the Prophets. I have not come to abolish but to give complete meaning *to them*. [18]For I am telling you all the truth, that not until heaven and earth disappear will the smallest letter *of the alphabet* or the smallest part of a letter be removed from the Law. Nothing will be removed until all things are accomplished. [19]Therefore anyone who breaks one of the least of these commandments and teaches others to do likewise, he will be called least in the realm of Heaven. [20]For I tell you all that unless your desire to do God's will surpasses that of the scribes and the Pharisees, you will never enter into the realm of Heaven.

Anger
(Luke 12:57–59)

[21]"You have all heard that it has been said to the people of long ago, 'You must not murder and that every one of you who murders will be brought to trial.' [22]But I say to you that every one of you who is angry with his brother will be brought to trial. Or if anyone insults his brother as being a 'numskull'[35] then he will be brought to the Sanhedrin council[36] for trial. And anyone who says, 'moron' will be in danger of the fire of hell.[37]

[23]"So if one of you brings your gift to the altar *in the temple* and while there you remember that your brother has something against you, [24]then you must leave your gift in front of the altar. First, go and make peace with your brother and then come and offer your gift.

[25]"Agree with your plaintiff quickly while you are with him on the way to court lest he hands you over to the judge and the judge then hands you over to

---

	closest modern equivalent would be a kerosene lamp not a torch or flashlight (Louw, J, & Nida, E, *Greek-English Lexicon of the New Testament based on Semantic Domains* (1988) 6.104).
34	More than likely a one room structure (TH).
35	This is most likely the Aramaic term *raca* with the root meaning 'empty'.
36	The Sanhedrin council was the supreme judicial body of the Jews consisting of 71 members including the High Priest.
37	Literally 'Gehenna'. Gehenna was the name of a valley southwest of Jerusalem, where human sacrifices had once been offered and where garbage from the city was constantly burning. Later this picture was combined with the idea of God's judgment, and so the notion of a fiery hell developed (TH). Hell has the idea of eternal torment and constant uncleanness. Gehenna/lake of fire/hell are all synonyms for the place where their occupants are separated from God for all eternity.

the bailiff who will throw you into prison. ²⁶I am telling you the truth, you will not get out of prison until you have paid the debt to the last cent.

Adultery

²⁷"You have all heard that it has been said, 'You must not commit adultery.' ²⁸But I say to you that every one of you who gazes with desire at a woman has already committed adultery with her in his heart.

²⁹"If your right eye causes you to sin then you must tear it out and throw it away. It is better for you that you lose one of the members of your body than for your whole body to be thrown into hell.³⁸ ³⁰And if your right hand causes you to sin then you must cut it off and throw it away. It is better for you that you lose one of the members of your body than for your whole body to be thrown into hell.

Divorce

(Matthew 19:9, Mark 10:11–12, Luke 16:18)

³¹"It has been said, 'Whoever divorces his wife, that he must give her a certificate of divorce.' ³²But I say to you that every one of you who divorces his wife except for sexual immorality, he is making her commit adultery and he is making the one in whom the divorced woman marries to commit adultery *also*.

Making oaths

³³"Again you have all heard that it has been said to the people long ago, 'You must not break your oath but you must keep your oaths made to the Lord.' ³⁴But I am telling you that you must not swear at all by heaven for it is God's throne. ³⁵And you must not swear by the earth for it is God's footstool nor swear by Jerusalem for it is the city of the great King. ³⁶And you must not swear by your head either for you cannot make even one hair white or black. ³⁷But simply let your 'yes' be 'yes' and your 'no' be 'no'. Anything beyond these words is from the evil one.

Revenge

(Luke 6:29–30)

³⁸"You have all heard that it has been said, 'An eye for an eye and a tooth for a tooth.'³⁹ ³⁹But I say to you all that you are not to oppose⁴⁰ the person who has

---

38   Cf. Matt. 5:22 footnote.
39   The law of an eye for an eye and a tooth for a tooth is mentioned in Exo. 21:24, Lev. 24:20 and Deut. 19:21; its original intent was humanitarian to prevent unrestrained blood vengeance (Gen. 4:23 is an example). However, later on it became more of an excuse to execute judgment on the wrongdoer rather than limit judgment on the offender (TH).
40   The context, as well as the parallels found in rabbinic sources, suggests that the word has a specifically

wronged you *in court*. Instead, if someone *insults you by* slapping you on the right cheek[41] then you must turn *and allow him to* slap you *on the other cheek*. [40]And if someone wants to sue you and take your shirt, let him take your *more valuable* coat as well.[42] [41]And if someone forces you to go one mile[43] then go with him two miles. [42]You must give to the one asking you. When someone asks if he can borrow something from you, don't refuse him.

Loving our enemies
(Luke 6:27–28, 6:32–36)

[43]"You have all heard that it has been said, 'You must love your neighbour and you are to hate your enemy.' [44]But I say to you all that you must love your enemies and you must pray for those who are persecuting you. [45]*Do this* so that it may show that you are true sons of your Father in the heavens. God causes his sun to rise on the evil person and the good person and he sends rain on those people who do the will of God and those who don't. [46]For if you *only* love those who love you then what reward is there in that? Do not even the tax collectors do the same? [47]If you greet and speak only to your own group of friends then how are you doing anything remarkable? Do not the Gentiles do the same thing? [48]Therefore you must be perfect *in your devotion to God* as your heavenly Father is perfect *towards you*.

Giving to the needy

6 [1]"You must be careful not to just practice your religion in front of men with the aim to be seen by them. If you do then you will have no reward from your Father in the heavens.

[2]"Therefore whenever you do give to the needy do not blow your own trumpet as the hypocrites[44] do in the synagogues and in the streets so that they are praised by men. I am telling you all the truth that they have already received their reward in full. [3]But when you do give to the needy, do not let your left hand know what your right hand is doing. [4]This is so that your giving may be

---

    legal connotation: 'resist' in a court of law, or 'oppose' before a judge (TH).
41   This has reference to an injury of insult, not of violence. In the near East, both in Jesus' day and in the present, the most insulting physical blow that one can give another is a slap with the back of the hand against the right cheek (TH).
42   The words rendered shirt and coat here require comment, since they reflect a unique aspect of Israelite Law. The outer garment (coat) was both an article of clothing and a covering for the night. Israelite Law did not permit it to be kept from its owner overnight; therefore the legal adversary was actually after the man's shirt, a garment worn under the outer coat.
43   This is literally a Roman mile which is 1000 steps and equates to 1.5 km. One mile was presumably the distance a Roman soldier could force a Jew to carry his equipment (TH).
44   Those who pretend to be believers and followers of God.

in secret. Then your Father, who sees what you are doing in secret, will reward you in the open.

Instructions in how to pray
(Luke 11:1-4)

⁵"And when you pray, you must not pray like the hypocrites for they like to pray as they are standing in the synagogues and on the street corners so that others will see them. I am telling you all the truth that they have already received their reward in full. ⁶However when you pray, make sure you go into your hidden room and having closed the door, pray to your Father secretly. Then your Father, when he sees what is done in secret, he will reward you in the open.

⁷"And when you all are praying, do not keep on babbling like the Gentiles do for they think they are heard because they pray with so many words. ⁸Therefore do not pray like they do for your Father knows what you need before you *actually* ask him.

⁹"So then, this is how you should all pray:

'Our Father in the heavens, may your name be revered.
¹⁰May your reign be established,
May your will on earth be done as it is in heaven.
¹¹Give us the food that we need this day.
¹²And forgive us our sins as we also have forgiven those who have
    sinned against us.
¹³May you lead us so we are not tempted to do wrong and rescue us
    from the evil one.'

¹⁴"For if you forgive others when they wilfully disobey[45] then your heavenly Father will also forgive you. ¹⁵But if you do not forgive others then your Father will not forgive you when you wilfully disobey.

Instructions in how to fast

¹⁶"When you all fast, you must not look miserable like the hypocrites do for they change their appearance[46] to show that they are fasting. I am telling you the truth that they have already received their reward in full. ¹⁷But when you fast, do your hair[47] and wash your face, ¹⁸so that it will not be apparent to others

---

45 This is the Biblical term 'transgress' which literally means 'stepping aside' or to make a false step. Basically it means to break a law wilfully or to intentionally disobey a standard.
46 This is literally 'disfigure their faces', which makes the modern reader mistakenly think that they have done some permanent disfigurement to their faces.
47 This is literally 'anoint your head with oil'.

that you are fasting, but only to your Father in secret. And when your Father who sees what is done in secret, he will reward you.

Having treasures in heaven
(Luke 12:32–34, 11:33–36, 16:13)

[19]"You must not store up for yourselves too much excess here on earth, where moth and rust destroy and where thieves can break in and steal. [20]But rather store up for yourselves treasures in heaven, where moth and rust cannot destroy and where thieves cannot break in and steal anything. [21]For, where your excess is, there the devotion of your heart, will be also.

[22]"The eye is the lamp of the body. Therefore if your eye is good then your whole body will be full of light. [23]But if your eye is evil[48] then your whole body is full of darkness. If then the light within you is in fact darkness then that darkness is very great.

[24]"No one is able to serve two masters. For either, he will hate the one and love the other, or he will hold onto one and despise the other one. You will not be able to serve both God and money.[49]

Do not worry
(Luke 12:22–31)

[25]"Therefore I am telling you, that you must not worry about your life. You must not worry about what you might eat or drink or worry about your body or what you might be wearing. Is not life itself more important than food and the body more important than clothing? [26]Look carefully at the birds of the air for they do not sow or reap or store *grain* in sheds and yet your heavenly Father feeds them. Are you not worth much more than the *birds*? [27]Who among you is able to add anything to his life by worrying?

[28]"And why do you all worry about clothing? Observe the lilies of the field and look at how they grow. They do not labour or spin *a wheel to make clothing for themselves*. [29]But I am telling you that not even the *magnificent King* Solomon in all his splendour and richness was dressed like one of these *flowers of the field*.

---

[48] An 'evil eye' is a Jewish metaphor for stinginess. Cf. Prov. 23:6 KJV. In ancient Egypt, the eye of Horus (blue iris) was a symbol representing protection, health, and restoration. According to Egyptian myth, Horus lost his left eye in a struggle with Seth. The eye was magically restored by Hathor, and this restoration came to symbolize the process of making whole and healing. (*Encyclopaedia Britannica* https://www.britannica.com/topic/Eye-of-Horus).

[49] Money here is personified as a god. Banker Mayer Amschel Rothschild (1744–1812) said, "Let me issue and control a nation's money and I care not who makes the laws." "All wars are banker's wars" (Michael Rivero). It is clear that money rules the unsaved world. There are only two masters: God or the god 'money'.

³⁰And if that is how God clothes the grass of the field, which is here today and thrown into the fire tomorrow, will he not much more *likely* clothe you, you ones of little faith? ³¹Therefore you must not worry, saying, 'What can we eat?' or 'What can we drink?' or 'What can we wear?' ³²For these things are the types of things that the Gentiles chase after. Your heavenly Father knows that you need all these things. ³³But above all else you must first look to allow God to reign in your life and to do his will. If you do so then all these things will be given to you. ³⁴Therefore you must not worry about what might happen tomorrow for there will be enough to worry about tomorrow. Each day has enough trouble and evil happening as it is.

Judging others
(Luke 6:37–38, 6:41–42)

7 ¹"You must not pass judgment on each other otherwise *God* will pass judgment on you. ²For in the way that you pass judgment on others, *God* will pass judgment on you. The standard that you use on others, *God* will use the same standard for you. ³Why do you see the speck of dust in your brother's eye and yet you pay no attention to the large beam of wood in your own eye? ⁴How can it be that you say to your brother, 'Let me remove the speck of dust out of your eye,' when there is already a beam of wood in your eye? ⁵You hypocrite! You must first take the beam of wood out of your own eye and then you will see clearly enough to be able to remove the speck of dust out of your brother's eye.

⁶"You must not give that which is sacred, to dogs⁵⁰ nor throw your pearls to pigs. Otherwise, they will trample them under their feet and then they will turn on you and tear you to pieces.

Ask, seek and knock
(Luke 11:9–13)

⁷"You must keep on asking *God* and it will be given to you, you must keep on seeking and you will find *what you are looking for* and you must keep on knocking and *the door* will be opened. ⁸For every one of you who keeps asking will receive and the one who keeps seeking will find and the one who keeps knocking on doors, it will be opened.

⁹"Which of you, if his son asks for bread, will give him a stone instead? ¹⁰Or if he asks for a fish, will give him a snake instead? ¹¹You are sinful⁵¹ and yet you know how to give good gifts to your children. Therefore how much more *likely*

---

50 Gentiles were commonly referred to as dogs by the Jews.
51 Literally 'evil' in the Greek but the sense here is more the comparison between God and man.

will it be that your Father in the heavens will give good gifts to those who ask him! ¹² "Therefore in all things, however you wish men to treat you, make sure that you treat them in the same way.

Enter through the narrow gate
(Luke 13:24)

¹³"You must enter through the narrow gate. For wide is the gate and roomy and easy is the way that leads to destruction and many people enter through and go this way. ¹⁴But small is the gate and constricted and full of difficulties is the way that leads to *eternal* life and only a few people find it.

Watch out for false prophets
(Luke 6:43–44, 13:25–27)

¹⁵"You must watch out for false prophets. They come to you as in sheep's clothing but inside they are really like vicious wolves. ¹⁶By their fruit you will know them. For people do not gather grapes from thornbushes or figs from thistles, do they? No! ¹⁷In the same way a healthy tree *in the orchard* produces useful fruit and a rotten tree produces bad fruit. ¹⁸A good tree is not able to produce bad fruit and a rotten tree is not able to produce useful fruit. ¹⁹Every tree that is not producing good fruit will be cut down and thrown into the fire *by the farmer*. ²⁰Therefore, in conclusion, you will recognise *false prophets*[52] by examining their fruit.

²¹"Not every one of you who says to me, 'Lord, Lord,' will become one of Heaven's subjects, but only he who does the will of my Father who is in the heavens. ²²Many people will say to me on the *judgment* day, 'Lord, Lord, did we not prophesy in your name and in your name did we not drive out demons and did we not perform many miracles in your name?' ²³Then I will tell them all quite openly, 'I never knew you. Get away from me you wicked people.'

There are two kinds of builders
(Luke 6:47–49)

²⁴"Therefore everyone who hears these words of mine and he *actually* does them, he will be compared to be like a wise man who built his house upon the *solid* rock. ²⁵For when the rain came down and the floodwaters rose and the winds blew and buffeted that house, it did not fall down because its foundation was on the solid rock. ²⁶But every one of you who hears these words of mine and he does not

---

52   In the Greek it has the plural 3rd person plural pronoun, 'them'. But I have made this explicit showing that this refers back to the false prophets not trees.

do them, he will be compared to be like a foolish man who built his house upon the sand. ²⁷For when the rain came down and the floodwaters rose and the winds blew and battered that house, it fell down and was totally destroyed."

²⁸When Jesus had finished saying all these things *to his followers on the mountain*, the crowd was astonished at the way he taught. ²⁹They were astonished because Jesus taught as one in whom he alone had the authority to teach not like their scribes.⁵³

A man with leprosy approaches Jesus
(Mark 1:40–44, Luke 5:12–14)

8 ¹As *Jesus* was coming down from the mountain, a large crowd followed him. ²All of a sudden a man with leprosy came to Jesus kneeling down low before him saying, "Lord, if you are willing, you can cleanse and *heal*⁵⁴ me." ³And so Jesus reached out his hand and touched the man. Jesus said, "I am willing. Be cleansed." And immediately the man was cleansed and healed of his leprosy. ⁴And Jesus said to the man, "Make sure that you do not tell anyone about this. Instead, go and show yourself to the priest *so he can examine you* and also offer the gift⁵⁵ that Moses commanded as proof to people *that you are cleansed*."

A Roman centurion shows that he has great faith
(Luke 7:1–10)

⁵When Jesus entered into the city of Capernaum, a *Roman* centurion⁵⁶ approached him needing his help. ⁶The centurion said to Jesus, "Lord, my servant boy is lying bedridden in the house unable to move and he is in terrible suffering." ⁷Jesus said, "I will come and heal him." ⁸The centurion answered, "Lord, I am not worthy for you to come *into my house* under my roof. But just say the word and my servant boy will be cured. ⁹For I myself am a man under

---

53 Teachers of the Jewish Law. The idea of teaching with authority has often been misunderstood. Many have translated it as 'he taught with power', for example. However, this verse is contrasting the way Jesus taught with the way the scribes taught. Their manner was to take a Scripture verse and cite what a variety of other rabbis or teachers had said about it. But Jesus taught directly without referring to other teachers (TH).

54 This is literally 'you can make me clean'. This refers to a ritual cleansing not a literal cleansing. A person with leprosy was considered to be 'unclean' in a spiritual sense and so wasn't allowed to mix with others or worship God properly because of their skin disease. If a person was healed then they were 'cleansed' after going to a priest and therefore able to be brought back into the community once again.

55 The gift that Moses commanded consisted of two birds. One of the birds was killed during the ceremony; the other was released (TH).

56 In the Roman army a man of this rank commanded one hundred men, and so the origin of the term centurion, which derives from a Latin noun meaning 'one hundred'. Centurions were career soldiers, and as such they were often the most experienced and most highly regarded men in the Roman army (TH).

authority, with soldiers under me. I say to this one, 'Go,' and he goes and to another, I say, 'Come,' and he comes. To my slave I say, 'Do this,' and he does it." ¹⁰Having heard this *from the centurion*, Jesus was amazed and he said to those following him, "I am telling you the truth, I have not found anyone in Israel with as such great faith as this *centurion*.

¹¹ "I am telling you that many people will come from the east and the west and they will recline at the table *to feast* with Abraham, Isaac and Jacob when the God of heaven establishes his reign. ¹²But the Jewish people *who were supposed to enjoy the blessings* of God's reign[57] will be thrown into the outer darkness where there will be weeping and gnashing of teeth."[58]

¹³Then Jesus addressing the centurion only said, "Go! Because you believed, it will be done for you as such." And his servant boy was healed at that very hour.

Jesus heals many sick people
(Mark 1:29–31, Luke 4:38–39)

¹⁴Upon coming into Peter's house, Jesus saw that Peter's mother-in-law was lying in bed with a fever. ¹⁵He touched her hand and the fever left her. And then she rose from the bed and began to attend to his needs.

¹⁶When evening arrived, many demon-possessed people were brought to him and Jesus cast out the spirits with a word and he healed all the sick. ¹⁷This was so that the thing spoken of by the prophet Isaiah could be fulfilled who said,

"He took away our sicknesses and removed our diseases."

Isaiah 53:4

The personal cost of following Jesus
(Luke 9:57–60)

¹⁸Seeing a crowd around him, Jesus commanded *his followers* to cross to the other side *of the lake*. ¹⁹Then a scribe[59] approached him and said, "Teacher, I will follow you wherever you go." ²⁰Jesus said to him, "Foxes have burrows and the birds of the air have nests, but the Son of Man[60] does not have a place to lay his head *down to rest*." ²¹Another one of his followers said to him, "Lord, first allow

---

57   This is literally 'the sons of the kingdom' which is a Semitic (Jewish) idiom meaning 'people (here, the Jewish people) who belong to the kingdom' (TH).
58   A favourite expression used by Matthew meaning great pain or rage.
59   The scribes were the experts and teachers of the Jewish religious Law of Moses.
60   This is a title that Jesus uses of himself in the third person. It is used almost entirely only in the Gospels except for Acts 7:56. Central to the meaning of this title is one who speaks and acts with divine power and authority. It is the one whom God himself has appointed or installed (TH).

me to go and bury my father." ²²But Jesus said to him, "Follow me, and let the dead bury their own dead."

Jesus calms the storm
(Mark 4:35–41, Luke 8:22–25)

²³And when Jesus got into a boat his followers went with him. ²⁴Then suddenly without warning, a huge storm came up on the lake so that the boat was about to be swamped by the waves but Jesus was asleep. ²⁵His followers went and woke him up and they said to him, "Lord, help! We're all about to die." ²⁶And he said to them, "You ones of little faith, why are you all so afraid?" Then Jesus got up and he rebuked the winds and the sea and it became completely calm. ²⁷The men were amazed, asking, "What kind of man is this? Even the winds and the sea obey him!"

Jesus heals two demon-possessed men
(Mark 5:1–17, Luke 8:26–37)

²⁸When Jesus reached the other side of the lake in the region of the Gergesenes,[61] two demon-possessed men met him. They had come out of the tombs.[62] These men were so dangerous that no one was able to go by that way. ²⁹They shouted out, "What do you want with us, Son of God? Have you come here to torture us before the time?"[63] ³⁰In the distance there was a large herd of pigs feeding. ³¹The demons pleaded with Jesus saying to him, "Since you are going to cast us out, send us into the herd of pigs."

³²And Jesus said to them, "Go!" So the demons came out of the men and went into the pigs. At once, the whole herd rushed down the steep bank and they all[64] died in the waters.

³³Those tending the pigs fled. Having gone into the city they reported all these things including what had happened to the demon-possessed men. ³⁴And

---

61 Some MSS have Gadarenes. Gergesenes is more likely as Gergesa was situated right on the eastern shore of the Lake of Galilee whereas Gadara was a city 8 km southeast of the lake. Nevertheless this was Gentile territory as evidenced by the herd of pigs in v. 30, which would not be found in a Jewish area as they were an unclean animal (Deut. 14:8).

62 The tombs were more specifically 'burial caves'. The dead were customarily placed in the rear of burial caves, leaving a small antechamber toward the front of the cave. It was there, in the front part of the cave, that these men would probably have lived. According to Jewish teaching, tombs were ritually unclean, but they would have been considered suitable homes for demons and demon-possessed people (TH).

63 Specifically this refers to the Day of Judgment.

64 The implication in the Greek here is that both the herd of pigs and the demons died in the waters of the lake. This is because the verb 'rushed' is in the singular and the verb 'died' is in the plural. This would then affirm that at the command of Jesus the demons met their destruction before the day of the final judgment (TH).

so the whole city went out to meet Jesus. When they saw him, they begged for him to pass by and to leave their region.

Jesus heals a paralysed man
(Mark 2:1–12, Luke 5:17–26)

9 ¹Then after this, Jesus got into a boat and crossed back over the lake and came back to his own city.⁶⁵ ²Without warning, a paralysed man lying on a makeshift bed was brought to Jesus. Having seen their faith, Jesus said to the paralysed man, "Take courage, child. Your sins are forgiven."

³At this, some of the scribes⁶⁶ said amongst themselves *about Jesus*, "He is blaspheming."⁶⁷

⁴Jesus could see what they were thinking and he said to them, "Why do you think such evil thoughts? ⁵For it's just as easy to say, 'Your sins are forgiven,' as it is to say, 'Get up and walk.'⁶⁸ ⁶But in order that you may know that the Son of Man has authority on earth to forgive sins…" Then Jesus turned to the paralysed man and said to him, "Get up, take your bed and go home." ⁷And so the man got up and went home. ⁸Having seen this, the crowds were afraid and they praised God, who had given such authority to mankind.

Jesus calls Matthew to follow him
(Mark 2:13–17, Luke 5:27–32)

⁹As Jesus left and went on from there, he saw a man whose name was Matthew sitting at the booth where taxes are collected. Jesus said to Matthew, "Follow me." Matthew rose and followed Jesus.

¹⁰Sometime later on, Jesus was reclining at the table having dinner in the house when all of a sudden many tax collectors and sinners⁶⁹ came and reclined at the table with Jesus and his followers to eat with them. ¹¹When the Pharisees saw this they *criticised* asking his followers, "Why does your teacher eat with tax collectors and sinners?"

¹²Having heard this, Jesus said, "Healthy people don't need a doctor, only

---

65   I.e. Capernaum. Cf. Matt. 4:13.
66   The scribes were the experts and teachers of the Jewish religious Law of Moses.
67   In this context blaspheming doesn't mean that Jesus was insulting the name of God but they are offended that Jesus was forgiving sins which only God could do. He was acting in the name and with the authority of God. And of course they didn't see Jesus as being the very Son of God.
68   In the NT era, Jews believed that the healing of a person's body was evidence that God had forgiven him, and so Jesus bases his remarks on that presupposition. He is not in any way intimating that the forgiveness of sin was less difficult for him than the healing of the man's body (TH).
69   The word "sinners" here must not be thought of in the way it is understood today. It probably means 'outcast Jews' who didn't keep the Law in the strictest sense like the Pharisees. Today we might call them secular or non-observant Jews as opposed to orthodox or religious Jews.

the sick. ¹³You need to go and learn what this means when *God* says, 'I desire mercy, not sacrifice.'⁷⁰ For I have not come to call righteous *people* but outcasts."

Jesus is asked about fasting
(Mark 2:18–22, Luke 5:33–39)

¹⁴Then *while Jesus was still there at the house,* some of John *the Baptist's* followers came and asked him, "Why is it that, we, the followers of John and the Pharisees, practice fasting, but your followers do not fast?"

¹⁵And Jesus answered them, "How can the wedding guests be sad and mourn while the bridegroom is still with them? The day will come when the bridegroom will be taken away from the guests and then they can fast *and mourn*."

¹⁶"No one patches up an old coat with a piece of new unshrunk cloth because the new patch will shrink resulting in an even worse tear. ¹⁷Also new wine is not poured into old wineskins otherwise the wineskin will burst and become ruined and the wine will be lost. New wine is put into a new wineskin and so then both are preserved."

Jesus raises a dead girl back to life and heals a sick woman
(Mark 5:21–43, Luke 8:40–56)

¹⁸While Jesus was still speaking to *John's followers*, a *Jewish* leader came and knelt before him *in respect* and said, "My daughter has just died. But come and lay your hand upon her and she will live." ¹⁹Jesus got up from the table and went with him, as did his followers.

²⁰And then at that time a woman who had been suffering from haemorrhages for 12 years⁷¹ came up behind Jesus and touched the edge of his garment. ²¹She was thinking to herself, "If only I can touch his garment then I will be healed." ²²And Jesus turned and upon seeing her he said, "Take courage daughter. Your faith has healed you." At that very moment, the woman was healed.

²³When Jesus arrived and entered the leader's house, he saw the flute players and the noisy crowd.⁷² ²⁴He commanded to all those present, "Everyone leave! The girl is not dead but asleep." But they laughed at him. ²⁵After he had sent the crowd outside, Jesus went into the room *where the girl lay* and took her by the hand and she got up. ²⁶News about this spread all throughout that region.

---

70   Quotation by Jesus from Hos. 6:6.
71   It seems quite likely that this woman would have been ceremonially unclean during these twelve years according to Lev. 15:25–30.
72   According to Jewish tradition, even the poorest of people were expected to have two flute players and a wailing woman for a funeral.

Jesus heals the blind and those who cannot talk

²⁷As Jesus was leaving there, two blind men followed behind him and they repeatedly shouted out, "Have mercy on us, Son of David!" ²⁸When Jesus had entered into the house, the blind men approached him and Jesus asked them, "Do you believe that I am able to do this?" They replied, "Yes, Lord." ²⁹Then Jesus touched their eyes and said, "Because of your faith, may it be done for you both as you wish." ³⁰And so their sight was restored. Jesus strictly warned them to make sure they told no one about this. ³¹But after they had left, they spread the news about Jesus all over that region.

³²As the two men were leaving, another man, who could not talk because he was demon-possessed, was brought to Jesus. ³³The demon was cast out and so the man who could not talk began speaking. The crowds of people watching were amazed saying, "Nothing like this has ever happened in Israel before." ³⁴But the Pharisees said, "It is because the leader[73] of demons gives him the power to do it that he is able to cast out demons."

Jesus says that the workers are few

³⁵Jesus went through all the cities and villages, teaching in their synagogues, preaching the good news that Heaven will soon reign and he healed every disease and sickness. ³⁶When he saw the crowds, Jesus was moved with compassion for them because they were troubled and defeated in their attitude. They were like sheep without a shepherd. ³⁷Then he said to his followers, "The harvest is plentiful but the workers are few in number. ³⁸Therefore ask the Lord of the harvest to send out workers into his harvest field."

Jesus chooses the Twelve Apostles
(Mark 3:13–19, Luke 6:12–16)

10 ¹Jesus called together his twelve *main* followers and gave them authority to cast out evil spirits and to heal every disease and sickness. ²These are the names of the twelve apostles: first Simon (who is called Peter) and his brother Andrew; James the son of Zebedee and his brother John; ³Philip and Bartholomew; Thomas and Matthew the tax collector; James the son of Alphaeus and Thaddaeus; ⁴Simon the Zealot and Judas Iscariot, who betrayed him.

Jesus sends out the Twelve
(Mark 6:6–13, Luke 9:1–5)

⁵Jesus sent out these twelve men with the following instructions: "You must

---
73 This is a reference to Satan himself.

not go to where the Gentiles live or enter any of the cities of the Samaritans. ⁶You must go rather to the lost sheep, the people of Israel. ⁷As you go, make sure you preach saying, 'Heaven will soon be reigning.' ⁸You are to heal the sick, raise the dead back to life, heal those with leprosy and cast out demons. Do these things without charge for you yourselves have received these gifts freely too.

⁹"Do not take with you any gold, silver or copper coins in your money-belts. ¹⁰Also do not take a bag for the journey or any extra clothes or sandals or a hiking pole. For the worker deserves to be given what he needs to live on.

¹¹"And whatever city or village you enter, look for somebody who is trustworthy and stay at his house until you leave. ¹²And upon entering the house you must be sure to give it your blessing. ¹³If the household receives you well then let your peace rest upon it. If they do not receive you well then let your blessing of peace return to you. ¹⁴And if no one in that household or city welcomes you or listens to your words then you are to shake the dust off your feet as you leave that household or city. ¹⁵I am telling you *men* the truth, that it will be more tolerable for *the wicked cities of* Sodom and Gomorrah on the Day of Judgment than for that city that rejects you."

Jesus warns his followers that they will suffer persecution
(Mark 13:9–13, Luke 21:12–17)

¹⁶Jesus warned his followers, "I am sending you all out like *helpless* sheep among *vicious* wolves. Therefore you must be as wary as snakes and as harmless as doves. ¹⁷Make sure that you be very careful of people for they will hand you over to the local councils[74] and they will flog[75] you in their synagogues. ¹⁸You will be brought *to trial* before governors and kings because of me so that you may be witnesses to them and to the Gentiles. ¹⁹But when they hand you over do not worry about what you will say or how to say it. At that time it will be given to you what to say. ²⁰For it is not you who is *really* speaking, but the Breath of your Father speaking through you.

²¹"Brother will hand over brother to death and a father will hand over his child. Children will rebel against their parents and have them put to death. ²²Everyone will hate you because you follow me. But he who endures to the

---

[74] This is not referring to the supreme Sanhedrin religious council which was presided over by the High Priest in Jerusalem but to the councils from local synagogues. These councils consisted of 23 influential members, and their responsibility was to keep peace among the members of the local Jewish community.

[75] Flogged means whipped. Normally the whip used by the Jews was made of calf skin and donkey hide woven together. The minister of the synagogue or the synagogue attendant administered the punishment, and it was limited to a maximum of 39 lashes. According to 2 Cor. 11:24, Paul suffered this punishment five times (TH).

end will be saved. ²³When they persecute you in one city then you must flee to the next city. I am telling you the truth, you will not finish going through the cities of Israel before the Son of Man comes.⁷⁶

²⁴"A student is not above his teacher, nor a servant above his master. ²⁵It is good enough for the student to be like his teacher and the servant like his master. If the head of the household is called Beelzebul,⁷⁷ then the members of his household will be called even worse.

God is the only one to be feared
(Luke 12:2-7)

²⁶"Therefore you must not be afraid of these people. For everything that is veiled will be revealed and everything that is hidden will be made known. ²⁷What I am saying to you in the dark, you must speak in the light and what you are hearing in private, you must proclaim it from the rooftops. ²⁸You must not be afraid of those who kill the body but cannot kill the soul. Rather, you must be afraid of God. He is the one who can destroy both soul and body in hell.⁷⁸

²⁹"Are not two sparrows sold for a penny?⁷⁹ Yet not one of them will fall to the ground *and die* unless your Father allows it. ³⁰And even the very hairs of your head are all numbered. ³¹Therefore you *men* must not be afraid. You are worth much more than many sparrows.

The followers of Christ must confess him openly
(Luke 12:8-9, 12:51-53, 14:26-27)

³²"So whoever professes *his belief in* me openly before men, I will also profess him and intercede on his behalf before my Father, the one who resides in the heavens, *on the Day of Judgment*. ³³But whoever denies me before men, I will also deny that he is my follower before my Father, the one who resides in the heavens, *on the Day of Judgment*.

³⁴"You followers must not think that I have come to bring peace to the earth. I have not come to bring peace, but I have come to bring division and strife. ³⁵For I have come to turn,

---

76 This most likely refers to the second coming of Christ when he comes in glory and explains the fact that the work of proclaiming the gospel to the Jews will not be complete until Jesus returns.
77 This is another name for Satan. This is similar to the name of the god of the Philistine city of Ekron (2 Kings 1:2).
78 Cf. Matt. 5:22 footnote.
79 The Greek word for "penny" refers to a Roman copper coin worth about one sixteenth of the coin that was the workman's average daily wage in the 1st century AD. So it is a very small denomination coin signifying that a pair of sparrows were not worth very much.

'a man against his father,
A daughter against her mother,
A daughter-in-law against her mother-in-law,
³⁶Your own family will become your worst enemies.'

Micah 7:6

³⁷"If any of you love your father or mother more than me then you are not worthy of me and if any of you love your son or daughter more than me then you are not worthy of me. ³⁸And the one who does not take up his cross and follow me, he is not worthy of me.[80] ³⁹Whoever tries to find *purpose in* his own life will fail and whoever pays no attention to his own life's *ambitions* for my sake will find *purpose in* life.

God gives rewards to those who receive his servants
(Mark 9:41)

⁴⁰"He who welcomes you, *it is as if* he is welcoming me, and he who welcomes me, he is *also* welcoming the one who sent me. ⁴¹He who recognises a prophet and welcomes him as such, he will receive the same reward as the prophet. And he who welcomes a righteous man because he is righteous, God will reward him the same way as he does for that righteous man. ⁴²And if someone even gives a drink of cold water[81] to one of you who are of least importance because you are my followers then I am telling you the truth, that person will certainly not go unrewarded by God."

Messengers from John the Baptist come to Jesus
(Luke 7:18–35)

11 ¹And when Jesus had finished instructing his twelve *main* followers, he went on from there and he taught and preached in their cities.

²Now at this time John was in prison and having heard about what the Messiah had been doing, he sent two[82] of his followers ³to ask him, "Are you the one whom John said was going to come, or should we expect someone else?"

⁴Jesus answered, "Go and report to John what you hear and see. ⁵Blind people receive their sight, lame people walk, those who have leprosy are cleansed and

---

80 Jesus gives this picture of taking up one's cross to show that as followers of him, we must suffer and be willing to sacrifice our lives in much the same way as Jesus did. The early Christians would have recognised that the cross was a Roman instrument of death and those that were about to die by crucifixion would have to carry their cross to their place of execution. The cross became a symbol of discipleship. Cf. Matt. 16:24, Mark 8:34, Luke 14:27.
81 A cup of cold water reflects the show of hospitality in first-century Palestine (TH).
82 Most MSS do not state John the Baptist's followers as being two in number. KJV and NKJV states that John sent two of his followers to Jesus.

healed, the deaf people are hearing, the dead are raised and the poor are being evangelised. ⁶Blessed is he who is not stumbled and offended because of me."

⁷As they were leaving, Jesus began to speak to the crowd about John, "What did you go out into the desert to see? Did you go out to see a reed shaken by the wind?⁸³ No! ⁸If not, what did you go out to see? A man dressed in soft and delicate clothing?⁸⁴ Of course not! Those who wear soft and delicate clothing are in the houses of kings. ⁹Therefore what did you go out to see? A prophet? Yes, I tell you. You saw more than a prophet. ¹⁰This is the one about whom it is written,

> "'I am sending my messenger ahead of you who will prepare your way before you.'
>
> Malachi 3:1

¹¹"I am telling you the truth that among those born of women there has not been anyone greater than John the Baptist. Yet he who is the least in Heaven's realm is greater than *John*. ¹²From the time when John the Baptist *appeared on the scene preaching* until now, there have been men who have tried to forcefully establish, by violence, the realm of Heaven.⁸⁵ ¹³For before John appeared, all the prophets of old and the Law *of Moses* prophesied about the coming time when God would establish his reign. ¹⁴And if you are willing to accept it, John the Baptist is Elijah who was prophesied to come. ¹⁵He who has ears to listen, let him pay attention.

¹⁶"But what can I say about today's generation? They are like children sitting in the marketplace. One group calls out to the other, ¹⁷'We played a *happy* wedding tune for you on our instruments but you did not dance! We sang *sad* funeral songs but you would not mourn!' ¹⁸*Today's generation is like these children* because John came neither eating nor drinking and yet they say, 'He has a demon.' ¹⁹And the Son of Man came eating and drinking, and they say, 'Here is a glutton and a drunkard, a friend of tax collectors and outcast Jews.'⁸⁶ But in the end wisdom is proved right by her actions."

---

83   Jesus has in mind the tall cane-grass which was found along the banks of the Jordan River. In other words John the Baptist wasn't a man swayed easily by the Romans or Jewish religious authorities but he preached the truth without compromise even though he was imprisoned and it would cost him his life.
84   This is best understood as a contrast between the luxurious clothes of the rich and the rough garments worn by John the Baptist (TH).
85   This is a hard verse to understand and there are a few interpretations followed by Bible scholars. The interpretation favoured is that there are violent men like the Zealots who were trying to bring about God's reign by violent means. They erroneously viewed that what John the Baptist and Jesus Christ were doing was to establish a political rule of Israel once again over its enemies such as the Romans.
86   This is literally 'sinners' in the Greek. Cf. Matt. 9:10 footnote.

The cities who would not turn from their sins
(Luke 10:13–15)

²⁰Then Jesus began to reprimand the cities in which most of his miracles had been performed because they did not turn from their sins. ²¹Jesus said, "What a disaster it is for you Chorazin! What a disaster it is for you Bethsaida! If the miracles that were done in you had been done in *the cities of* Tyre and Sidon,[87] they would have turned from their sins long ago and they would be *mourning* in sackcloth and ashes.[88] ²²But I am telling you, it will be more bearable for *the cities of* Tyre and Sidon on the Day of Judgment than it will be for you. ²³And you Capernaum, *do you think* you will be exalted up as high as heaven? No way, you will be brought down as far as Hades.[89] If the miracles that were done in you had been done in *the city of* Sodom then it would be still there today. ²⁴But I am telling you that it will be more bearable for Sodom on the Day of Judgment than for you."

Jesus invites the weary to come to him and he will give them rest
(Luke 10:21–22)

²⁵Then Jesus said, "I praise you, Father, Lord of heaven and earth. You have hidden these things from the wise and the learned and you have revealed them to the naïve.[90] ²⁶Yes Father. This was your good pleasure. ²⁷All things have been made known to me by my Father and have been committed to me by him. No one knows who the Son really is except the Father, and no one knows the Father except the Son and those to whom the Son chooses to reveal him.

²⁸"Come to me, all of you who are weary and being burdened *by the Law* and I will give you rest. ²⁹Take my yoke[91] upon yourselves and learn from me for I am gentle and humble of heart. Do this and you will find rest for your souls. ³⁰For my yoke is easy and my burden is light."

---

[87] Tyre and Sidon were cities along the Phoenician coastline in the modern-day country of Lebanon. Especially during OT times these two cities were notorious for their evil, and Israel's prophets regularly spoke against them.

[88] Sackcloth and ashes were signs of repentance and sorrow (Isa. 58:5, Dan. 9:3, Jonah 3:6). Sackcloth was a coarse cloth and was worn by those in repentance, but the ashes were sprinkled on the head as an additional sign.

[89] Hades also translated as hell by many, is the world of the dead.

[90] This is literally the Greek word meaning children or infants but the intent here is the uneducated or those who don't know much.

[91] A yoke is a heavy wooden bar that fits over the neck of an ox so that it can pull a cart or a plough. Jesus here uses yoke as a symbol of submission, and the most appropriate commentary is perhaps to be found in Jeremiah, chapters 27–28; there the prophet wears an ox yoke as a symbol of the nation's submission to the king of Babylonia (TH). Jesus wants us to submit ourselves to him and learn from him as his follower.

Jesus is master of the Sabbath
(Mark 2:23–28, Luke 6:1–5)

12 ¹Around this time Jesus was walking through the grain fields⁹² on the Sabbath Day.⁹³ His followers were hungry and so they began to pick heads of wheat and eat them. ²When the Pharisees saw this, they said to him, "Look! Your followers are doing what is not allowed on the Sabbath." ³Jesus answered the Pharisees, "Have you not read what David and his men did when they were hungry?⁹⁴ ⁴David went into the house of God, and he and his men ate the holy bread. This was not allowed, only the priests were supposed to eat this bread. ⁵Have you not also read in the Law *of Moses* that the priests work in the temple on the Sabbath Day thereby breaking the Law but they are not *considered* guilty. ⁶I am telling you there is something greater and more important than the temple here. ⁷*The Scriptures say about God,* 'I desire mercy, not sacrifice.' If you had known what these words mean then you would not have condemned the innocent. ⁸For the Son of Man is master of the Sabbath."⁹⁵

Jesus heals a man on the Sabbath
(Mark 3:1–6, Luke 6:6–11)

⁹Jesus left that place and came to a synagogue, ¹⁰where there was a man with a withered hand. Wanting to have a reason to accuse Jesus, the *Pharisees* there asked Jesus, "Does the Law of Moses permit to heal on the Sabbath?" ¹¹Jesus said to them in reply, "If any of you has a sheep and it falls into a pit on the Sabbath, will you not go and retrieve it and lift it out? ¹²A man is much more valuable than a sheep surely? Therefore it is permitted to do a good thing on the Sabbath." ¹³Then Jesus said to the man, "Put out your hand." So the man put his hand out *as Jesus had instructed* and it was completely restored and it was as healthy as his other hand. ¹⁴But the Pharisees went away and they planned on how they might kill Jesus.

Jesus is God's chosen servant

¹⁵And knowing about this plot to kill him, Jesus left from that place. Many people followed him and he healed all who were sick. ¹⁶He ordered them not to

---

92 In Palestine at this time, the only two grains grown were wheat and barley. It is more likely that they would have been walking through wheat fields as it is the more highly valued of the two grains. The Greek term however is a generic term which could mean either grain.
93 The weekly Sabbath began sunset Friday and finished sunset Saturday evening in Jewish reckoning.
94 I.e. King David. Cf. 1 Sam. 21:1–6.
95 Jesus is talking about himself in the third person using the title, the Son of Man, and is basically saying that he is the one who has the authority to say what may or may not be done on the Sabbath.

make it known who he was. ¹⁷This was in order to fulfil what was spoken of by the prophet Isaiah:

> ¹⁸"Look at my servant whom I have chosen, the one I love and with whom
>   I am very pleased.
> I will give him my Breath and he will proclaim justice to the peoples of
>   the nations.
> ¹⁹He will not argue or shout. No one will hear him making loud speeches
>   in the streets.
> ²⁰He will not break off a bent reed or put out a flickering lamp until justice wins.⁹⁶
> ²¹The people of the nations will put their hope in his name."
>
> Isaiah 42:1-4

The Pharisees accuse Jesus of working with Beelzebul
(Mark 3:20–30, Luke 11:14–23, 12:10)

²²Then they brought him a demon-possessed man who was blind and couldn't speak. Jesus healed him and so he was able to both talk and see once again. ²³The crowd was amazed and they said, "Could this be the Son of David *as was prophesied*?" ²⁴However when the Pharisees heard this, they said, "He casts out demons only because Beelzebul⁹⁷ is enabling him to do so."

²⁵Knowing their thoughts, Jesus said to them, "Every realm divided against itself will be laid to waste and ruined, and every city or family divided against itself will not be able to stand or survive. ²⁶If Satan casts out Satan then he is divided against himself. How then can his reign continue? ²⁷If that is the case that I drive out demons by the power of Beelzebul then by whose *power* do your people drive the demons out? So then, their actions show that your argument is wrong.⁹⁸ ²⁸But if I am casting out demons by God's Breath then you know that the reign of God has come upon you.

²⁹"To put it another way, how can a person enter into the house of the strong

---

96 Essentially this means that Jesus will continue to be the gentle and humble servant until justice is victorious. A possible interpretation would be that the world will receive the gospel of grace and Jesus will not be seen as the reigning king until the time of the Gentiles are complete when Jesus returns as the victorious king riding on the white horse (Rev. 19:11–21). Then the world will not see him as the humble servant but will see him as he really is, the King of Kings and Lord of Lords.
97 This is a reference to Satan. Cf. Matt. 10:25 footnote.
98 The followers of the Pharisees were also apparently doing similar sorts of miracles. Jesus' point is that this is sufficient evidence to prove that the Pharisees' argument is erroneous. If they were claiming that Jesus was casting out demons by the power of Satan then they would have to admit that they were doing the exact same thing.

man and carry away his possessions unless he first ties up the strong man? And then indeed he will completely plunder the strong man's house.

³⁰"He who is not with me is against me, and he who does not gather with me scatters.

³¹"Therefore I tell you, every sin and blasphemy[99] will be forgiven men, but blasphemy against the Breath *of God* will not be forgiven.[100] ³² Anyone who speaks a word against the Son of Man will be forgiven, but anyone who speaks against the Holy Breath will not be forgiven, either in this age or in the age to come.

A tree and its fruit
(Luke 6:43–45)

³³"A tree is known by its fruit. If a tree is good then its fruit will be good. If a tree is bad then its fruit will be bad. ³⁴You nest of snakes! You are not able to say anything good because you are evil. For out of the overflow of the heart the mouth speaks. ³⁵The good man brings good things out of the good riches in him and the evil man brings out evil things out of the evil riches in him.

³⁶"But I tell you that men will have to give an account on the Day of Judgment for every careless word they have spoken. ³⁷For by the words that you say, God will either declare you innocent or declare you guilty."

The sign of the prophet Jonah
(Mark 8:11–12, Luke 11:29–32)

³⁸Then some of the Pharisees and the scribes said to Jesus, "Teacher, we want you to show us a miraculous sign[101] to prove your authority."

³⁹Jesus answered, "You people these days are an evil and godless generation in asking for a miraculous sign. No sign will be given to you except the sign of the prophet Jonah. ⁴⁰For as Jonah was three days and three nights[102] in the belly of

---

99 Evil things that are said against God.
100 Blasphemy against the Holy Breath (Holy Spirit) is essentially unbelief and in the context here the Pharisees did not believe that Jesus had healed this man by the power of God's Breath. Attributing to Satan what the Holy Breath has done is blasphemy of the Holy Breath. Their unwillingness to acknowledge the presence of God in the ministry of Jesus means that they cannot be forgiven. If we do not believe what the Holy Breath reveals to us about Jesus then there can be no forgiveness.
101 Bible commentators are in unanimous agreement that "sign" here means more than a mere miracle. Jesus' opponents are not merely asking for another miracle; they have seen him perform many miracles, and they still refuse to believe. What they are seeking is an unambiguous demonstration that it is God himself who is at work in and through the miracles of Jesus. In other words, they are looking for 'a sign from heaven' (Matt. 16:1), a 'super miracle' that will serve to validate the divine origin of all Jesus' other miracles (TH).
102 This clearly refers to three periods of twenty-four hours each. This therefore is problematic for the traditional belief that Jesus was crucified at 3 pm Friday afternoon and rose early Sunday morning which only includes two nights, one full day and only a very small part of two other days. This problem is resolved if one takes the view that Jesus was crucified at 3 pm on the Thursday afternoon.

the sea monster,[103] so the Son of Man will be three days and three nights in the heart of the earth. [41]The people of the city of Nineveh will stand up as witnesses against you people of this generation and condemn you. For they turned from their sins when they heard Jonah preach and yet something far greater than Jonah is here. [42]The Queen of the South[104] will stand up as a witness against you people of this generation and condemn you. For she came from the ends of the earth to listen to the wisdom of Solomon and yet now something far greater than Solomon is here.[105]

An evil spirit returns to the person it leaves
(Luke 11:24–26)

[43]"When an evil spirit goes out of the man, it goes through arid places[106] looking for a home but it does not find one. [44]Then it decides to return to the house that it came from. When it arrives back, it finds the house vacant, swept clean and put in order. [45]Then it goes and brings with it seven other spirits more evil than itself, and they go in and live there. And the final condition of that man is worse than at first. That is how it will be with you evil people of this generation."

Jesus' mother and brothers come to see him
(Mark 3:31–35, Luke 8:19–21)

[46]While Jesus was still talking to the crowd, his mother and his brothers were standing outside, wanting to speak to him. [47]Someone told him, "Look, your mother and brothers are standing outside, wanting to speak to you." [48]Jesus answered him, "Who is my mother, and who are my brothers?" [49]And Jesus pointed to his followers and he said, "Here are my mother and brothers. [50]For whoever does the will of my Father in heaven is really my brother and my sister and mother."

The parable of the sower
(Mark 4:1–9, Luke 8:4–8)

13 [1]On this same day Jesus went out of the house and sat by the lake. [2]There were such large crowds of people gathering around him, that Jesus got into a boat and sat in it, while the people stood on the shore. [3]Then he set about telling

---

103   Most translations say huge fish or whale but the Greek literally says 'sea monster'.
104   Cf. 1 Kings 10:1–7.
105   While King Solomon was wise, Jesus Christ is wisdom incarnate (Prov. 8:22–36, 1 Cor. 1:24).
106   Arid, waterless places were thought to be favourite dwelling places of demons (TH). Cf. Isa. 13:21–22.

them many things in parables.[107] He said, "Once there was a farmer who went out to sow seed that he had. ⁴As he went scattering the seed, some of it fell along the pathway and the birds came along and ate it all up. ⁵Other seed fell on rocky ground, where there was little soil. The seed sprouted quickly because the soil was shallow.[108] ⁶However when the sun came up, the plants were scorched and they withered away because they had no root. ⁷Other seed fell among the thorn bushes, which subsequently grew up and choked the plants. ⁸Other seed fell on good soil where it produced a crop, some one hundred, some sixty, some thirty times *what was sown*. ⁹He who is listening, let him pay attention."

Why does Jesus speak in parables?
(Mark 4:10–12, Luke 8:9–10)

¹⁰Jesus' followers approached him and asked, "Why do you speak to the people in parables?" ¹¹Jesus replied, "The knowledge of the secrets of Heaven's coming realm has been given to you but not to them. ¹²God will give more *understanding* to those who already have so that they will have an abundance. Whoever does not have, even the little *understanding* that he has, God will take away from him. ¹³This is why I speak to the people in parables: Though seeing with their *eyes*, they do not really see. Though hearing with their *ears*, they do not really hear or understand. ¹⁴They are fulfilling the prophecy of Isaiah which says,

> "'You will be always hearing but never *really* understanding.
> You will be always seeing but never *really* perceiving.
> ¹⁵For this people's heart has become calloused and hardened.
>> They hardly hear with their ears at all and they have closed their eyes.
>> If they had not done this then they might have been able to see with their
>>> eyes, hear with their ears and understand with their hearts.
>> And so they would return to me and I would heal them.'

Isaiah 6:9–10

---

107 The Greek word translated parable literally means 'comparison', but its meaning is best derived from the Hebrew word which it translates in the LXX. Except in five instances, it always translates the same Hebrew word, which has a wide range of meanings: proverb, by-word, allegory, fable, comparison, riddle and parable. In recent years much scholarly research has been done on parables, and it is now the consensus that each parable is intended to convey only one point which concerns some aspect of the Kingdom of God. Cf. Matt. 3:2 footnote. Jesus was not alone in the use of parables. Jewish teachers often used them, but as a rule they place parable and interpretation side by side. But Jesus did not usually provide the explanation along with the parable; instead he demanded of his hearers that they discern the truth of what he was saying, and that they respond accordingly (TH).

108 Probably the thin layer of soil would have been warmed by the heated rock underneath resulting in quicker growth than in the other soil.

¹⁶"However you are all blessed because you see it and you are hearing. ¹⁷I am telling you the truth that many prophets and righteous men wanted to see what you are now seeing, but they did not see it, and to hear what you are now hearing, but they did not hear it.

The parable of the sower explained
(Mark 4:13–20, Luke 8:11–15)

¹⁸"Listen then, to what the parable of the sower means: ¹⁹Those who hear the news about Heaven's coming realm but do not understand it are like the seeds that fell along the pathway. The evil one comes and snatches away what was sown in their hearts. ²⁰The seed that fell on the rocky ground is like those who hear the news and receive it joyfully at once. ²¹But the seed does not take root and so they don't last long. So when trouble or persecution comes because of this news, they quickly fall into the trap of unbelief. ²²The seed that fell in the place of thorns are like those who hear the news, but the worries of this life and the deception that chasing after wealth brings, chokes this news, making it unfruitful. ²³However the seed that fell on the good soil is like those who hear the news and understand it. They produce a crop yielding one hundred, sixty or thirty times that which was sown."

The parable of the wheat and the tares

²⁴Jesus then told them another parable, "Heaven's coming realm can be likened to a man sowing good seed in the field *he owned*. ²⁵But while everyone was sleeping, the enemy came and sowed *poisonous* tares[109] among the wheat and then he went away. ²⁶Later when the *wheat* sprouted and formed heads, *it was noticed that* tares were also growing *in the midst of it*. ²⁷The owner's servants came to him and said, 'Sir, didn't you sow good seed in your field? How is it then that there are tares *growing amongst the wheat*?'

²⁸"The owner replied, 'An enemy did this.' Then the servants asked him, 'Do you want us to go and pull out the tares?' ²⁹The owner declined and said, 'No because while you are pulling out the tares, you might uproot the wheat with them. ³⁰Let both the wheat and the tares grow together until the harvest time. Then at that time, I will tell the harvest workers to first pull out the tares and tie them in bundles to be burned.[110] Then they must gather the wheat and bring it into my shed.'"

---

[109] I.e. Darnel, also known as tares or poison ryegrass, resembles wheat in its early stages of growth and is a poisonous weed. Its scientific name is *Lolium temulentum*. If eaten the plant can cause a drunken state of nausea and is sometimes fatal.

[110] The tares (those who do evil) are weeded out during the tribulation period, plague by plague, by

The parable of the mustard seed and the yeast
(Mark 4:30–34, Luke 13:18–21)

³¹Jesus told them another parable, "Heaven's coming realm can be likened to a mustard seed, which a man took and planted in his field. ³²Even though the mustard seed is the smallest of all seeds, when it grows it is the largest of all the vegetables growing into a tree so that the birds of the air come and nest in its branches."

³³Jesus told them still another parable, "Heaven's coming realm can be likened to yeast that a woman took and mixed into three large measures[111] of flour until it worked through all the dough."

³⁴Jesus spoke all these things to the crowds in parables. In parables only did he speak to them.[112] ³⁵This was to fulfil what was spoken through the prophet. The prophet said,

> "I will speak to them in parables.
> I will utter things that have been hidden since the overthrow of the world."
>
> Psalm 78:2

The parable of the wheat and the tares explained

³⁶Then having sent away the crowds, *Jesus* came into the house *where he was staying*. His followers approached him and said, "Please explain to us the parable of the tares in the field."

³⁷*Jesus* answered them, "The one who sowed the good seed is the Son of Man. ³⁸The field is the world and the good seed are the ones who come under the realm of God. The tares are the ones who belong to the evil one. ³⁹And the enemy who sows the tares is the devil. The harvest time is the end of the age and the harvest workers are angels. ⁴⁰So just as the tares are pulled up and consumed in the fire *at harvest time*, so it will be at the end of the age. ⁴¹The Son of Man will send out his angels and they will pull out from the realm of God those who cause others

---

the angels. Assuming a current world population of around 8 billion, perhaps half of the world's population will be 'weeded out' before the end. In fact, Jesus said that if he did not come back, then there would be no survivors (Matt. 24:22). After this weeding out of the wicked, the wheat (people of God) are gathered at the rapture. This parable supports the post-trib view rather than the pre-trib view because the people of God are gathered after the wicked are weeded out during the tribulation. Cf. Matt. 24:29–31, Rev. 14:14–20.

111   It is estimated that the bread baked from this amount of dough would be sufficient for more than 100 people and is equivalent to over 20 kg of wheat flour.

112   This verse represents a chiastic structure where a concept is repeated in reverse form to add emphasis or for clarification. An example used in English would be 'when the going gets tough, the tough get going'. The structure is A-B-B-A. There are probably over 2000 examples in the Bible.

to sin and those who do evil. ⁴²They will throw them into the furnace of fire, where there will be weeping and gnashing of teeth.*¹¹³* ⁴³Then the righteous ones will shine like the sun after the Father establishes his reign. He who is listening, let him pay attention."

Three more parables

⁴⁴Jesus said to his *followers*, "Heaven's coming realm can be likened to a treasure which has been hidden in the field. When a man came along and found it, he buried it again. And because he was elated with what he had found, he went and sold everything he owned and bought that field.

⁴⁵"Heaven's coming realm can also be likened to a business man who was looking for fine pearls *to buy*. ⁴⁶When he found one of great value, he went away and sold everything he had and bought it.

⁴⁷"And yet again Heaven's coming realm can be likened to a net that was lowered into the lake and all kinds of fish were caught. ⁴⁸When the net was full, the fishermen pulled it up onto the shore of the lake. Then they sat down and gathered the good fish in baskets and they threw the bad ones away. ⁴⁹This is how it will be at the end of the age. The angels will come and separate the wicked people from the good people. ⁵⁰They will throw the wicked people into the furnace of fire, where there will be weeping and gnashing of teeth."*¹¹⁴*

⁵¹Jesus asked his *followers*, "Have you understood everything I have told you in these *parables*?" "Yes," they replied. ⁵²He said to them, "Therefore every scribe who has learned the truth about God's reign is like the homeowner who brings out of storage new treasures as well as old treasures."

A prophet has no honour in his hometown
(Mark 6:1–6, Luke 4:16–30)

⁵³When Jesus had finished *telling* these parables, he moved on from this place. ⁵⁴Having arrived at his hometown, he began teaching the people in their synagogue and they were amazed. They were saying, "Where did this man get this wisdom and how does he do these miracles? ⁵⁵Isn't he the carpenter's son? Isn't his mother's name Mary? And aren't his brothers James, Joseph, Simon and Judas? ⁵⁶And do not all his sisters live amongst us? Where then did this man get such wisdom and power?" ⁵⁷And they took offense, rejecting him. But Jesus said to them, "A prophet is not usually dishonoured except in his hometown

---

113 Cf. Matt. 8:12 footnote.
114 Cf. Matt. 8:12 footnote.

and by his own people." ⁵⁸And Jesus did not do many miracles there because of their unbelief.

John the Baptist is beheaded
(Mark 6:14–29, Luke 3:19–20, 9:7–9)

14 ¹At this time Herod,[115] the ruler over the *district* of Galilee, heard the report about Jesus. ²He said to his court officials, "This Jesus must be John the Baptist. He has risen from the dead! That explains why he has such power working in him."

³Previously Herod had arrested John and bound him and put him in prison because of Herodias who had been the wife of his brother Philip. ⁴For John had been telling him repeatedly, "Our Jewish Law does not permit you to marry her." ⁵Herod wanted to kill John but he was afraid of the people because they believed him to be a prophet.

⁶However at the celebrations on Herod's birthday the daughter of Herodias danced for them and it pleased Herod so much ⁷that he made her a promise with an oath that he would give her whatever she asked for. ⁸So having been prompted by her mother, she said to Herod, "Give to me on a platter here, the head of John the Baptist."

⁹The king was sad because of this, but because he had made an oath and because of his dinner guests, he ordered that her request be granted. ¹⁰And so Herod had John beheaded in prison. ¹¹His head was brought in on a platter and it was given to the girl, who in turn carried it to her mother. ¹²John's followers came and took his body and buried it. Then they went and reported it to Jesus.

Jesus feeds five thousand men
(Mark 6:30–44, Luke 9:10–17, John 6:1–13)

¹³Having heard that John had died, Jesus took a boat and went by himself to a deserted place. Hearing of this, the crowds followed him from the various cities, on foot via land. ¹⁴When Jesus landed and saw the large crowd, he felt sorry for them and he healed those who were sick.

¹⁵That evening, his followers came to him and said, "This is a remote place and it's already getting late. Send the crowds away so that they can go to the villages and buy food for themselves. ¹⁶But Jesus replied, *"There is no need for them to go away. You men should give them something to eat."* ¹⁷"We only have

---

[115] Herod Antipas, the son of Herod the Great. Often he is described as Herod the tetrarch which transliterates a title meaning 'ruler of a fourth part'. Herod the tetrarch ruled only on the west side of the Lake of Galilee and he ruled from 4 BC to AD 39.

five *small* loaves of bread[116] and two fish,"[117] they answered. [18]Jesus said, "Bring the loaves and fish to me here."

[19]Then he instructed the people to sit down on the grass. Jesus took the five loaves and two fish and he looked up into heaven and he gave thanks, breaking the loaves of bread. Then he gave them to his followers and then they, in turn, gave them to the crowds of people. [20]All the people ate and were satisfied and the followers gathered up twelve basketfuls of broken pieces of bread that were left over. [21]The total number of people who ate was about five thousand men, not including women and children.[118]

Jesus walks on the water
(Mark 6:45–52, John 6:16–21)

[22]Immediately Jesus made his followers get into the boat and go on ahead of him to the other side, while he dismissed the crowds of people. [23]After he had dismissed the people, he went up the mountain by himself in order to pray. When evening came, Jesus was on the mountain alone, [24]but the boat was already a long way from land. The boat was being tossed about by the waves because the wind was against it. [25]During the fourth watch of the night[119] when it was nearly dawn, Jesus went out to his followers, walking on the lake. [26]When his followers saw him walking on the lake, they were terrified. They were so terrified that they cried out in fear. "It's a ghost," they said. [27]Straight away Jesus calmed them saying, "Take courage! It's me. Don't be scared."

[28]Peter answered, "Lord if it is really you, command me to come to you on top of the water." [29]"Come," Jesus commanded. And so Peter got out of the boat and walked on the water towards Jesus. [30]However when Peter saw the wind, he was afraid and began to sink. He called out saying, "Lord save me!"

[31]Immediately Jesus reached out his hand and caught him saying, "You have such little faith. Why did you doubt?" [32]And as they were getting into the boat, the wind died down. [33]Then those who were in the boat worshipped him saying, "It's true. You are the Son of God."

---

116   This is barley bread (John 6:9) instead of wheat bread because this with the small fish comprised the basic diet of the poor in Galilee. These are small round loaves so five loaves would be enough for two people at the most (TH).
117   The two fish would have been either smoked or pickled; these were considered a delicacy when eaten as a relish for the bread (TH).
118   If there were 5000 men who were fed then there would have been many more when including women and children perhaps as many as 15,000.
119   Roman custom divided the time between 6 pm and 6 am into four equal periods of three hours each. Each one of these time periods was called a 'watch'. The Jews and the Greeks, on the other hand, divided the night into three watches (TH).

Jesus heals the sick at Gennesaret
(Mark 6:53–56)

[34]When they had all crossed over the lake, they landed at Gennesaret.[120] [35]And when the men of that area recognised Jesus, they sent the word out to everyone in the region. The people brought everyone who was sick. [36]They were begging him to let the sick even just touch the tassels on the corner of his coat,[121] and all those who touched him were healed.

The traditional teaching of the Jewish elders
(Mark 7:1–13)

15 [1]Then Pharisees and scribes from Jerusalem came and asked Jesus, [2]"Why do your followers break the traditional teaching of our elders? For they are not washing their hands *in the correct way* before they eat!"[122]

[3]And Jesus replied, "And *I ask you* why do you break the command of God in favour of your tradition?[123] [4]For God said in the commandments, 'Honour your father and mother,' and he also said, 'anyone who curses his father or mother must be put to death.' [5]But you teachers *have a tradition that teaches* that if a man has something that could help his father or mother but then this man says that it is a gift dedicated to God then he doesn't have to honour his father with this gift. [6]Therefore you are nullifying the word of God on account of your tradition.

[7]"You are all hypocrites! The prophet Isaiah was right when he prophesied about you like this,

> [8]"'These are a people who honour me with their lips but their hearts are far from me.
>
> [9]They worship me in vain because their teachings are but mere traditions of men.'"

Isaiah 29:13

Jesus teaches what makes a person truly unclean
(Mark 7:14–23)

[10]Jesus called the crowd to himself and said, "Listen and understand this,

---

120   North-west corner of the Lake of Galilee in between Magdala and Capernaum.
121   Every Israelite man was obliged to wear tassels on the four corners of his outer garment.
122   This is not about hygiene. The Pharisees had a prescribed way of ceremonially washing of hands.
123   To answer a question with a question was a typical method of debate among the Jewish teachers. It is intended to imitate the form of the question which they asked of Jesus (TH). Although Jews tend to question their Rabbis and value difference of opinions summed up by the saying, "Ask two Jews, get three opinions," Jesus is saying here that they favour their own traditions rather than the commands of God.

¹¹"It is not what goes into a man's mouth that makes him unclean, but what comes out of his mouth."

¹²Then *Jesus'* followers came to him and asked, "Do you realise that the Pharisees were offended when you said that *about them*?"

¹³Jesus replied, "Every plant that my heavenly Father has not planted will be pulled out by the roots. ¹⁴Don't be worried about the *Pharisees*. They are blind guides. If a blind man leads a blind man then both will fall into a pit."[124]

¹⁵Peter said, "Can you explain the parable *you just told the crowd* to us?" ¹⁶And Jesus asked, "What!? You are my followers, yet you still don't understand? ¹⁷Can't you see that whatever goes into the mouth then goes down into the stomach and eventually out of the body? ¹⁸But the words that come out of the mouth come from the heart and it is this that makes a man 'unclean' so to speak. ¹⁹For out of the heart comes evil thoughts such as murder, adultery, sexual immorality, theft, false testimonies and slander. ²⁰These things are what make a man 'unclean' as such. But eating with unwashed hands does not make him unclean."

The faith of a Canaanite woman
(Mark 7:24–30)

²¹Jesus left there and went to the region *close to the cities* of Tyre and Sidon. ²²A Canaanite woman from around there came to him crying out, "Lord, Son of David, have mercy on me! My daughter is suffering immensely from demon possession." ²³But Jesus did not answer her a word. His followers came to him and urged him, "Send her away for she keeps calling out to us."

²⁴But Jesus answered, "I was sent only to the lost sheep of Israel." ²⁵The *Canaanite* woman came and pleaded before Jesus saying, "Sir, Please help me." ²⁶And he replied, "It is not right to take the children's bread and throw it to the dogs." ²⁷She said, "Yes Sir. But even the dogs eat the leftovers from their master's table." ²⁸Then Jesus answered, "Woman, your faith is huge! It must be done as you have requested." And her daughter was healed at that very hour.

Jesus heals many people in Galilee

²⁹Jesus left that region[125] and travelled along the Sea of Galilee. Then he went up on a mountainside and sat down. ³⁰A great many people came to him, bringing with them the lame, the blind, the crippled, those who couldn't speak and many others and they laid them at his feet. Jesus healed them all. ³¹The people were amazed when

---

124 The title 'leader of the blind' was a title enjoyed by Jewish teachers (Rom. 2:19). Jesus' accusation is that the Pharisees cannot lay claim to this title, because they themselves are blind and in need of someone to lead them (TH).

125 That is, the coastal regions of Tyre and Sidon, i.e. modern-day Lebanon.

they saw the non-verbal speaking, the crippled healthy, the lame walking and the blind able to see. And they praised the God of Israel.

Jesus feeds four thousand men
(Mark 8:1–10)

³²Jesus called his followers over and he said to them, "I feel sorry for the people here. They have already been with me for three days and they have nothing to eat. I don't want to send them away hungry or they may faint on the way back home." ³³And his followers answered him, "Where are we going to get enough loaves of bread to feed this large crowd in such a remote place as this?" ³⁴Jesus asked them, "How many loaves do you have?" And they replied, "We have seven loaves and a few small fish."

³⁵Jesus instructed the crowd to recline on the ground. ³⁶Then he took the seven loaves and the fish and after he had given thanks, he broke them. He then gave them to his followers and then they gave them to the crowds of people. ³⁷Everyone ate and was satisfied. Afterwards, Jesus' followers collected seven really large basketfuls[126] of broken pieces that were left over. ³⁸The number of those who ate was four thousand men, not counting women and children. ³⁹After Jesus had sent the crowds away, he got into the boat and went to the area of Magadan.

The Pharisees and Sadducees ask for a sign
(Mark 8:11–13, Luke 12:54–56)

16 ¹Pharisees and Sadducees came to Jesus to try and trap him so they asked him to show them a sign from heaven. ²Jesus replied, "When evening comes you say that it will be good weather the next day because the sky is red. ³In the morning you say that today will be stormy because the sky is red and overcast. So you know how to interpret the appearance of the sky, but you cannot interpret the signs of the times. ⁴An evil and faithless generation demand a miraculous sign, but no sign will be given to it except the sign of Jonah." Then Jesus left them and went away.

The 'yeast' of the Pharisees and the Sadducees
(Mark 8:14–21)

⁵Jesus' followers crossed over to the other side of the lake where he was, but they had forgotten to take any bread with them. ⁶Jesus said to them, "Be careful

---

126   Specifically a fisherman's basket woven from marsh grass. This is larger than the normal food baskets and is different than the one described in Matt. 14:20 (TH).

and be on your guard against the yeast of the Pharisees and Sadducees." ⁷His followers discussed amongst themselves about what Jesus had said about the yeast and reasoned that he said this because they had not brought any bread with them. ⁸Aware of their discussion, Jesus asked them, "You men have such little faith. Why are you still talking amongst yourselves about having no bread? ⁹Are you still not understanding? Don't you remember *how I fed* five thousand men with the five loaves and how many basketfuls you gathered? ¹⁰Or *how I fed* four thousand men with seven loaves and then also how many basketfuls you gathered after? ¹¹How come you do not understand that I was not talking to you about bread? I was talking to you about being on your guard against the yeast of the Pharisees and Sadducees."

¹²Then Jesus' followers understood that he was not telling them to guard against *literal* yeast used in bread but to be on their guard against the teachings of the Pharisees and Sadducees.

Peter reveals Jesus' identity
(Mark 8:27–30, Luke 9:18–21)

¹³When Jesus came to the region of Caesarea Philippi,[127] he asked his followers, "Who do the people say the Son of Man[128] is?" ¹⁴And they replied, "Some say John the Baptist, others say the *prophet* Elijah and still others say Jeremiah or some other prophet." ¹⁵Jesus asked them, "But who do you yourselves say that I am?" ¹⁶Simon Peter answered, "You are the Messiah, the Son of the living God."

¹⁷Jesus replied, "Blessed are you Simon son of Jonah for this was not revealed to you by flesh and blood, but by my Father in the heavens. ¹⁸So I am telling you that you are Peter the rock, and on this rock, I will build my church and the gates of Hades will not be strong enough to prevail against it.[129] ¹⁹I will give you the keys to the realm of Heaven.[130] Whatever *door* you close on earth will be closed in heaven and whatever *door* you open on earth will be opened in heaven."

²⁰Then Jesus warned his followers not to tell anyone that he was the Messiah.

---

127   A city (ancient name Paneas now named Banias) on the south-eastern slopes of Mt Hermon, the highest mountain in Israel located near the borders of Lebanon and Syria about 24 km north of the Sea of Galilee. It is one of the sources of the Jordan River. There is an adjacent grotto dedicated to the Greek god of shepherds, Pan. Earlier the Canaanites worshipped Baal at Banias and prisoners were thrown into the cave known as the 'Gates of Hades/Hell'.

128   Cf. Matt. 8:20 footnote.

129   This day at Caesarea Philippi is when Jesus founded his church. It would be symbolically built on the rock of Caesarea Philippi where the gates of Hades was located. No enemy would be able to withstand the advance of the church.

130   Jesus will give great authority to Peter and the church to carry out the Great Commission.

Jesus predicts his death
(Mark 8:31–9:1, Luke 9:21–27)

²¹From this time onwards Jesus began to explain to his followers that he must go to Jerusalem and suffer many things at the hands of the elders, chief priests and scribes. He explained that he must be killed and be raised to life on the third day.

²²Then Peter took Jesus aside and began to rebuke him saying, "God forbid Lord! This shall never happen to you!" ²³Jesus turned and said to Peter, "Get behind me, Satan! You are trying to trip me up. You do not have in mind the things of God but the things of men."

²⁴Then Jesus said to his followers, "If anyone wants to be my follower then he must disregard his own ambitions and take up his cross[131] and follow me. ²⁵For whoever tries to keep his own life safe will fail, but whoever pays no attention to his own life's *ambitions* for my sake will find *purpose in* life. ²⁶What benefit is it if a man gains the whole world, yet he loses his soul? Or what can a man give in exchange for his soul? ²⁷I tell you all this because the Son of Man will be coming in his Father's glory with his angels and he will reward each person according to what they have done. ²⁸I am telling you the truth, there are some standing here right now who will not die before they see the Son of Man coming as king."[132]

The transfiguration of Jesus
(Mark 9:2–13, Luke 9:28–36)

17 ¹After six days Jesus took with him Peter, James and John the brother of James, and took them up to the top of a high mountain[133] by themselves. ²And as they were there, Jesus' whole appearance completely changed before their very eyes. His face was shining like the sun, and his clothes became as a brilliant white light. ³At that moment Moses and Elijah appeared before them talking

---

131 Cf. Matt. 10:38 footnote.
132 This is a reference to the transfiguration. Peter, James and John would soon see Jesus on the high mountain as he will be in all his glory when he comes as king in his future millennial reign.
133 Christian tradition (Cyril of Jerusalem c. AD 348) tends to identify the mountain with Mt. Tabor (588 m), though Mt. Hermon (2,774 m) being higher and closer to Caesarea Philippi (Matt. 16:13) makes it a more logical choice. Jewish tradition says that Mt. Hermon (mountain of the oath) was the location of the descent of the watcher angels referred to in Gen. 6:1–4. In 1869, British explorer Charles Warren found an inscription or oath on top of Mt Hermon of Satan's actual command to the watcher angels to go ahead and corrupt mankind by taking the daughters of men as their wives. Doug Hamp gives his translation: "According to the command of the great bull god Batios (Satan), those swearing an oath in this place go forth." (Hamp, D, *Corrupting the Image 2: Hybrids, Hades, and the Mt Hermon Connection* chapter 8)

to Jesus. ⁴Peter said to Jesus, "It is so good that we are all here. If you like, I will set up three shelters[134] here: one for you, one for Moses and one for Elijah."

⁵While Peter was still speaking, a bright cloud covered them all and a voice spoke from the cloud saying, "This is my Son, whom I love. I am very pleased with him. Make sure you all listen to him!"

⁶When the followers heard this, they lay face-down to the ground as they were very afraid. ⁷But Jesus came over and putting his hand on them he said, "Get up. Don't be scared." ⁸When the three of them looked up, they saw no one but Jesus.

⁹As the four of them were coming down the mountain, Jesus instructed them saying, "You must not tell anyone about this vision[135] until the Son of Man has been raised from the dead."

¹⁰His followers asked him, "Why then do the scribes say that Elijah must come first?"

¹¹Jesus replied, "Indeed Elijah is coming and he will fulfil[136] all things.[137] ¹²But I am telling you the truth, Elijah has already come but the Jewish people did not recognise him, but have done to him everything they wished. In the same way, the Son of Man is going to suffer at their hands." ¹³Then the followers understood that he was talking to them about John the Baptist.

Jesus heals a boy possessed by a demon
(Mark 9:14–29, Luke 9:37–42)

¹⁴When Jesus and his followers returned *back down the mountain* to the crowd, a man approached Jesus and knelt before him saying, ¹⁵"Lord, have mercy on my son. For he is a lunatic[138] and is suffering greatly *with fits*. He often falls into the fire or into the water. ¹⁶I brought him to your followers, but they could not heal him."

¹⁷Jesus answered, "This generation has no faith and is seriously misguided. How long do I have to stay here with you? How long do I have to put up with

---

134   A tent which was a portable dwelling of cloth and/or skins, held up by poles and fastened by cords to stakes. The construction of portable shelters is something that the Jews did every year at the Feast of Tabernacles. But one must not think of a modern-day tent used on holidays.

135   Important to note here that Jesus calls this a 'vision'. Visions can take place at any time as opposed to dreams which take place only when a person is sleeping.

136   Greek = 'restore all things'. Aramaic = 'everything might be fulfilled' (Lamsa Bible). Possibly the Aramaic is a better translation here but in one sense the Elijah to come will restore relationships.

137   Cf. Mal. 4:5–6, Luke 1:16. Elijah will bring reconciliation perhaps between Jews and Christians at the end of the age, before the Day of the Lord. In the extra Biblical book Sirach 48:10, it says concerning Elijah: "At the appointed time, it is written, you are destined to calm the wrath of God before it breaks out in fury, to turn the hearts of parents to their children, and to restore the tribes of Jacob."

138   This Greek word literally means 'moonstruck' and is the origin of the English word 'lunatic'. It means to suffer epileptic seizures and in ancient times this was associated with the supernatural power of the moon (TH).

you? Bring the boy here to me." ¹⁸Jesus rebuked the demon, and it came out of the boy and he was healed from that moment.

¹⁹Then the followers came to Jesus in private and asked him, "Why weren't we able to cast out *the demon*?"

²⁰Jesus replied, "It is because you do not have enough faith. I tell you the truth that if you have faith as small as a mustard seed, you will be able to say to this mountain to move from here to there and it will move.¹³⁹ Nothing will be impossible for you. [²¹But this kind of demon does not come out except by prayer and fasting."]¹⁴⁰

Jesus predicts his death again
(Mark 9:30–32, Luke 9:43–45)

²²When later they all came together in Galilee, Jesus said to his followers, "The Son of Man is going to be betrayed into the hands of men. ²³They will kill him and on the third day he will be raised to life." And *upon hearing this* the followers were all filled with sadness.

The temple tax

²⁴After Jesus and his followers arrived in *the city of* Capernaum, the collectors of the temple tax came to Peter and asked him, "Doesn't your teacher pay the temple tax?"¹⁴¹ ²⁵Peter replied, "Yes, of course."

When Peter came back into the house, Jesus was the first to speak. He said, "I have a question for you Simon. From whom do the kings of the earth collect duty and taxes? Do they collect taxes from their own citizens or from foreigners?"¹⁴² ²⁶Peter answered, "From *foreigners*." Jesus stated, "So then the citizens are exempt. ²⁷But so that we may not offend them, go to the lake and throw out a line. Take the first fish you catch, open its mouth and you will find a shekel coin in it. Take it and give it to the collectors, *enough* for my tax and yours."

---

139 Jesus uses a common colloquialism of the day; to a Jew of Jesus' day, a mountain is a metaphor signifying a seemingly impossible task. Faith that can move mountains is not meant to imply a faith that can literally move literal mountains. The point Jesus was making is that even a little bit of faith—faith the size of a tiny mustard seed—can overcome mountainous obstacles in our lives.
140 Most translations omit this verse. It is the consensus of scholars that v. 21 was added to the gospel at a later date, perhaps under the influence of the parallel in Mark 9:29 (TH).
141 The temple tax was the amount of ½ shekel (literally 'the two-drachma coin'). It was a yearly tax levied on individuals for the upkeep of the temple. According to Exo. 30:13, this tax was required of every male Jew from the age of 20 onward. It is the equivalent of half a day's wages for a labourer at that time. After the destruction of the temple in AD 70, the Romans continued to collect this annual tax, but applied it to the support of the temple of Jupiter Capitolinus (TH).
142 In those days, kings normally taxed the people they had conquered, not their own citizens (TH).

Who will be the greatest?
(Mark 9:33-37, 42-48, Luke 9:46-48, 17:1-2)

18 ¹At that time the followers of Jesus came to him and asked, "Who will be the greatest in Heaven's realm?"

²Jesus called a little child over and had him stand in front of everyone. ³And he said, "I am telling you the truth, that unless you change *your whole outlook* and convert like the little children, you will never enter into Heaven's realm.¹⁴³ ⁴Therefore, whoever humbles himself like this child *standing here*, he is the greatest in Heaven's realm.

⁵"And whoever welcomes a little child like this one, in my name, welcomes me.

⁶"But if anyone causes one of these little ones who believe in me, to sin, it would be better for him to have a large millstone¹⁴⁴ hung around his neck and to be drowned in the depths of the sea.

⁷"The world is so bad because there are many things in it that cause people to sin! Things like this are bound to occur, but how bad will it be for the man who causes others to sin! ⁸If your hand or your foot causes you to sin, cut it off and throw it away. It is better for you to enter life maimed or crippled than to have two hands or two feet and be thrown into eternal fire. ⁹And if your eye causes you to sin, gouge it out and throw it away. It is better for you to enter life with one eye than to have two eyes and be thrown into hell where the fire never goes out.

¹⁰"Therefore make sure that you do not look down on one of these little ones for I tell you that their guardian angels in the heavens always have contact with my Father in the heavens. [¹¹For the Son of Man has come to save the lost.]¹⁴⁵

The parable of the one lost sheep
(Luke 15:3-7)

¹²"What would you do if you owned a hundred sheep and one of them wandered away and was lost? Would you not leave the ninety-nine remaining sheep on the

---

143 Jesus considered the little children before they reach an age when they can understand, to already be converted. In effect, Jesus was urging his followers to be converted as the little ones already were. Psa. 51:5 does not say that David was a sinner at conception rather he was recalling that his mother gave birth to him out of wedlock and that she was the one who committed the sin. David was an illegitimate child born to Jesse and another woman. Psa. 69:8 says that David was a stranger to his brothers and an alien to his mother's people, possibly the Moabites.

144 This refers to the large stone that was turned by a donkey, rather than to the smaller, lighter ones used by women. A natural rock found at Capernaum, where this conversation took place, is a type of basalt that has just the right texture for grinding grain. Many millstones, some unfinished, were found at Capernaum, suggesting that it may have manufactured them for export.

145 This verse is not found in some of the earliest MSS.

hills and go and search for the one that had wandered off and was lost? ¹³And if you found it, I am telling you the truth, you would be happier about that one sheep than the ninety-nine that hadn't wandered off. ¹⁴In the same way, your Father in the heavens does not want any of these little ones to be lost spiritually.

The Christian brother who sins against you

¹⁵"If your brother sins against you, go to him privately and talk to him about it. If he listens to you then you will have won over your brother. ¹⁶But if he will not listen then take one or two others along with you in order that *as the Scripture says*, 'the matter may be established by two or three witnesses.' ¹⁷However if he refuses to listen to them, bring the matter to the church. If he refuses to listen even to the church, treat him as you would a Gentile or a tax collector.

¹⁸"I am telling you all the truth, whatever *door* you close on earth will be closed in heaven and whatever *door* you open on earth will be opened in heaven.

¹⁹"And another thing I tell you that is the truth, that if there are two of you on earth in agreement about a matter that you are praying about, it will be done for you by my Father in heaven. ²⁰For where two or three come together in my name, I am with them right there."

The parable of the unmerciful servant

²¹Then Peter came to Jesus and asked, "Lord, how many times shall I forgive my brother when he sins against me? Should I forgive him up to seven times?"

²²Jesus said to him, "No, not seven times, but seventy times seven.[146]

²³"This is because the realm of Heaven can be likened to the parable of a king who wants to settle accounts with his servants. ²⁴As the king began to settle the accounts, a man who owed him ten thousand talents[147] *of money* was brought to him. ²⁵The man was not able to pay, so the king ordered that he and his wife and his children and all that he had must be sold to repay the debt. ²⁶The servant fell on his knees in front of the king begging him saying, 'Be patient with me and I will pay back everything.' ²⁷The king took pity on his servant and cancelled the debt and let him go.

²⁸"But when the servant departed, he went and found one of his fellow servants who owed him 100 denarii.[148] He grabbed him and began choking him saying, 'Pay back what you owe me!'

²⁹"His fellow servant fell to his knees and begged him saying, 'Be patient

---

146 There should be no limit to the number of times that we should forgive someone for an offence.
147 This is an extremely large sum of money. One talent was the equivalent of between 6–15 years' worth of wages.
148 One denarius was worth one day's wage so overall 100 denarii was a very small amount compared to ten thousand talents.

with me and I will pay you back.' ³⁰But he refused. Instead, he went away and had him thrown into prison until he could pay what was owing.

³¹"When the other servants saw what had happened, they were devastated and went and told the king everything that had occurred.

³²"And so then the king called the servant in and said, 'You wicked servant. I cancelled all of your debt because you begged me to. ³³Shouldn't you have had mercy on your fellow servant just as I had on you?' ³⁴The king was very angry and so he turned the wicked servant over to the torturers until he could pay everything that was owing.

³⁵"This then is how my heavenly Father will treat each of you unless you forgive your brother from your heart."

Jesus teaches about divorce
(Mark 10:1-12, Luke 16:18)

19 ¹When Jesus had finished saying these things, he left Galilee and went into the region of Judea to the other side of the Jordan.¹⁴⁹ ²Large crowds followed Jesus and he healed¹⁵⁰ them there.

³Some Pharisees came to him in order to try and trap him by asking, "*According to the Mosaic Law* is it allowable for a man to divorce his wife for whatever reason he wishes?" ⁴And Jesus answered, "Haven't you read *in the Scriptures* that in the beginning, the Creator 'made them male and female,' ⁵and that he said, 'For this reason, a man will leave his father and mother and be joined to his wife and the two will become one flesh'? ⁶So they are no longer two *separate people*, but one *person*. Therefore what God has joined¹⁵¹ together, man must not separate."

⁷"Why then," they *further tested*, "did Moses command that a man is to give his wife a certificate of divorce and send her away?"

⁸Jesus replied, "Moses did permit you to divorce your wives because of the hardness of your hearts. But it was not so in the beginning. ⁹I say to you that anyone who divorces his wife unless she has been unfaithful, this man commits adultery if he marries another woman."

¹⁰Jesus' followers said to him, "So if this is the situation between a husband and wife then it is better that the man¹⁵² does not marry *at all*."

---

149 This probably means the eastern end of the Jordan Valley in the Judean region but the western bank of the Jordan River. It can't be the other side of the Jordan River because that was the region of Perea. This is likely the town of Bethabara (John 1:28).
150 The parallel Mark verse says that Jesus taught them there.
151 This literally means yoked together like two oxen in a yoke.
152 This only reflects the case for a man as Jewish women were not allowed to divorce their husbands.

¹¹Jesus replied, "Not everyone can accept this teaching, but only those to whom God has allowed. ¹²Some are eunuchs from birth and so cannot marry but some have been made that way by other men and some others have renounced marriage because of the realm of Heaven. The one who can accept this teaching, let him accept it."

Jesus blesses the little children
(Mark 10:13–16, Luke 18:15–17)

¹³Some little children were brought to Jesus for him to place his hands on them and pray for them. But the followers strongly disapproved of those who brought them. ¹⁴However Jesus said, "Let the children come to me and don't stop them for Heaven will reign over people such as these." ¹⁵And after he had placed his hands on them, he departed from that place.

The rich young man
(Mark 10:17–31, Luke 18:18–30)

¹⁶It happened one time that a man approached Jesus and asked, "Teacher, what good must I do in order that I might have eternal life?"

¹⁷Jesus in reply said, "Good? Why would you ask me about what is good? There is only One who is good. But if you want to enter into *eternal* life then you must keep the commandments."

¹⁸The *young man* asked, "Which *commandments* must I keep?" Jesus answered, "'Do not murder, do not commit adultery, do not steal. Do not bear false witness. ¹⁹Honour your father and mother,' and 'love your neighbour as *you love* yourself.'"

²⁰And the young man said, "All these *commandments* I have kept. What must I still yet do?"

²¹Jesus answered, "If you want to be perfect then go and sell your possessions and give *the money* to the poor. Do this and Heaven will reward you with treasure. Then once you have done that, come and be my follower." ²²When the young man heard this, he went away sad because he had great wealth.

²³Then Jesus said to his followers, "I am telling you the truth, it is hard for a rich man to enter into Heaven's realm. ²⁴Again I am telling you, it is easier for a camel to go through the eye of a needle than it is for a rich man to enter into God's realm."[153]

---

[153] There is no convincing evidence that the expression "eye of a needle" in Matt. 19:24 and Luke 18:25 is a figurative name for a postern (narrow gate). Cyril of Alexandria (fragment 219) claimed that 'camel' was a Greek scribal typo where *kamêlos* (camel) was written in place of *kamilos* ('rope' or 'cable'). The reference to a camel passing through the eye of a needle is a case of rhetorical hyperbole, that is to say, a purposeful exaggeration to point out the extreme difficulty of the event referred to

²⁵When the followers heard this, they were completely astonished and they were saying, "Who then is able to be saved?" ²⁶Jesus looked at them intently and said, "With man this is impossible, but with God all things are possible."

²⁷Then Peter answered him saying, "We have left everything to follow you! What *reward* then will we receive?"

²⁸Jesus spoke to them all saying, "I am telling you the truth, in the new world, when the Son of Man is sitting on his glorious throne, you who have followed me will also sit on twelve thrones and you will rule over the twelve tribes of Israel. ²⁹And everyone who has left houses or brothers or sisters or father or mother or children or the land for my sake will receive a hundred times as much and will inherit eternal life. ³⁰But many who are first will be last and many who are last will be first."[154]

The parable of the workers in the vineyard

20 ¹Jesus told a parable saying, "Heaven's coming realm can be likened to a landowner who went out early in the morning to hire some men to work in his vineyard. ²He agreed with the men to pay them one denarius coin for the day and then sent them into his vineyard. ³Then at about the third hour, *nine in the morning,* he went out and saw other men standing around in the marketplace doing nothing. ⁴The *landowner* told these other men that they too should go and work in his vineyard and that he would pay them whatever was right. ⁵Upon hearing this the men went *and worked in the vineyard.* Then three hours later at about midday and again at three in the afternoon, the *landowner* went out and *said the* same thing *to yet other men.*

⁶"Then around five in the afternoon, the *landowner* went out and still found others standing around. He asked *the men,* 'Why have you been standing around here all day long doing nothing?' ⁷They replied, 'Because no one has hired us.' He said to them, 'You must also go and work in my vineyard.'

⁸"When the evening came, the owner of the vineyard said to his foreman, 'Call the workers and pay them their wages, beginning with the last ones hired and finishing with the first ones. ⁹The workers who were hired in the last hour came and each one of them received one denarius coin. ¹⁰So, when it came to pay the workers, hired first, they expected to receive more. But each one of them also received only one denarius coin each. ¹¹When they received their wage, they

---

(Louw, J, & Nida, E, *Greek-English Lexicon of the New Testament based on Semantic Domains* (1988) 6.215). Jesus is probably using humour and a proverbial expression well known to his hearers. This is one of the rare cases where Matthew employs "God" instead of "Heaven". But the proof that the two terms are synonymous is in Jesus' statement here in vv. 23–24.

154   This statement serves as a transition into the parable in the next chapter as Matt. 20:16 ends with the same statement but reversed.

began to complain against the landowner. ¹²'These men *who you* hired last, only worked for one hour and you have made them equal to us who have borne the burden of the work and the heat of the day,' they said.

¹³"But the owner answered one of them saying, 'My friend, I am not being unfair to you. Didn't you agree to work for one denarius coin? ¹⁴Take your pay and go! I want to give the man who was hired last the same as I gave you. ¹⁵Don't I have the right to do what I want with my own money? Or are you annoyed because I am generous?'

¹⁶"So the last will be first and the first will be last."

Jesus again predicts his coming death
(Mark 10:32–34, Luke 18:31–33)

¹⁷As Jesus was on his way up to Jerusalem, he said to his twelve *main* followers, ¹⁸"We are going on up to Jerusalem where the Son of Man will be betrayed to the chief priests and the scribes. They will condemn him to death. ¹⁹Then they will turn him over to the Gentiles in order to be mocked and flogged and crucified. On the third day, he will be raised to life."

A mother's request
(Mark 10:35–45)

²⁰It was then that the mother of Zebedee's sons came to Jesus along with her sons and knelt before him with a request. ²¹And so Jesus asked her, "What is your request?" She said, "Command that one of my two sons will sit at your right and the other at your left when the time comes for you to reign as king." ²²"You don't know what you are asking," Jesus answered the sons. "Are you able to drink the cup I am going to drink?" "We are able," they both answered. ²³And Jesus said to them, "You will indeed drink from my cup, but it is not up to me to grant who will be sitting at my right or left. These places belong to whom they are prepared by my Father *in heaven*."

²⁴Later when Jesus' ten other followers heard about this they were resentful of the two brothers. ²⁵Having called them all together, Jesus said, "You are aware that the world's strongmen lord it over their people and their rulers exercise complete authority. ²⁶But it must not be so with you. Instead, whoever amongst you wants to become great, he must serve the others. ²⁷And if one of you wants to be first then he must subject himself in service to the rest. ²⁸Just like the Son of Man did not come to be served, but to serve and to give his life in order to set many people free *from their sins*."

Two blind men receive back their sight

(Mark 10:46–52, Luke 18:35–43)

²⁹As Jesus and his followers were leaving the city of Jericho, a large crowd followed him. ³⁰And two blind men happened to be sitting by the roadside, and when they heard that Jesus was passing by, they shouted out, "Lord, Son of David, have mercy on us!" ³¹The crowd strongly disapproved and told them to be quiet. But they shouted even more loudly saying, "Lord, Son of David, have mercy on us!"

³²Jesus stopped and called them and asked, "What do you want me to do for you?" ³³"Lord," they answered, "we want to be able to see." ³⁴Jesus had compassion on them and so touched their eyes. Immediately they were able to see again and they followed him.

Jesus' triumphal entry into Jerusalem[155]

(Mark 11:1–11, Luke 19:29–40, John 12:12–19)

21 ¹As Jesus and his followers approached Jerusalem,[156] they came to the *village* of Bethphage[157] on the Mount of Olives. Jesus sent two of his followers on ahead ²with these instructions: "Go to the village ahead of you and immediately you will find a donkey tied there, with a colt by her. Untie them and bring them to me. ³If anyone says anything to you, tell him that the Lord needs them and then he will let them go at once."

⁴This took place to fulfil what was spoken through the prophet,

⁵"Say to the daughter of Zion,[158] 'Look, your king is coming to you,
gentle and riding on a donkey and on a colt, the foal of a donkey.'"

Zechariah 9:9

⁶So the two followers went and did as Jesus had instructed them. ⁷They brought the donkey and the colt and placed their coats on them and Jesus sat on them.[159] ⁸A very large crowd of people spread their coats on the road, while others cut branches from the trees and spread them on the road *in honour*.[160] ⁹The crowds that went ahead of him and those that followed shouted,

---

155 This occurred on Sunday which is now known as Palm Sunday.
156 Jesus and his disciples were approaching Jerusalem from the east, travelling on the road from Jericho in the Jordan Valley.
157 Bethphage was a small village which literally means 'house of figs'.
158 An idiom for the people of the city of Jerusalem.
159 Matthew does not explain how Jesus was able to sit on both donkeys.
160 This would be similar to the modern-day action of laying out the red carpet for a visiting dignitary.

"Hosanna to the Son of *King* David!"
"Blessed is he who comes in the name of the Lord."

Psalm 118:26

"Hosanna in the highest *heaven*!"
[10] When Jesus entered Jerusalem, the whole city was in an uproar and they were asking each other, "Who is this?" [11] The crowds answered, "This is Jesus, the prophet from the *city* of Nazareth in Galilee."

Jesus enters the temple
(Mark 11:15–19, Luke 19:45–48, John 2:13–22)

[12] Then Jesus entered the temple[161] and forced out all who were buying and selling there. He overturned the tables of the money changers and the stools of those selling doves. [13] Jesus said to them, "It is written *in the Scriptures*, 'My house will be called a house of prayer,'[162] but you are making it a 'hideout of robbers.'"[163]
[14] The blind and the lame came to Jesus at the temple, and he healed them. [15] But when the chief priests and the scribes saw the wonderful things that Jesus had done and they saw the children in the temple shouting, "Hosanna to the Son of David," they became resentful. [16] They asked him, "Do you hear what these children are saying?" And Jesus replied, "Yes. Have you *men* never read, 'From the lips of children and breastfeeding babies you have produced praise'?" [17] And Jesus left them and he went out of the city to the *village of* Bethany, where he spent the night.

Jesus curses a fig tree that has no figs
(Mark 11:12–14, 11:20–24)

[18] Early the next morning on his way back up to the city, Jesus became hungry. [19] Seeing a fig tree by the roadside, he went up to it but found nothing on it except leaves. Then he said to it, "May you never bear fruit again!" At once the fig tree withered.
[20] When Jesus' followers saw this, they were astonished. They asked, "How did the fig tree wither away so quickly?"
[21] Jesus replied, "I am telling you the truth, if you have faith and do not doubt, not only can you do what was done to the fig tree, but also you will be able to

---

161 The events described probably took place in the Court of the Gentiles, where money changers were allowed to set up their tables prior to the Festival of Passover (TH).
162 Cf. Isa. 56:7.
163 Cf. Jer. 7:11. The Greek word here for "hideout" is literally cave. It was customary in those days for thieves and robbers to store their stolen goods and hideout in caves.

say to this mountain, 'Go and throw yourself into the sea', and it will be so. ²²If you believe, you will receive whatever you ask for in prayer."

The authority of Jesus is challenged
(Mark 11:27-33, Luke 20:1-8)

²³Jesus entered the temple courts and began teaching. While he was teaching, the chief priests and the elders of the people came to him and asked him, "By what authority are you doing these things?[164] And furthermore who gave you this authority?" ²⁴Jesus replied, "I also have a question for you all. If you answer me then I will tell you by what authority I am doing these things. ²⁵My question is this. By what authority did John baptise? Was it from God, or did it come from men?" They discussed it among themselves and said, "If we say that John baptised by the authority of God then he will ask us why we didn't believe him. ²⁶But if we say that John acted on his own authority then we are afraid of the crowd for they are all convinced that John was a prophet." ²⁷Therefore they answered Jesus saying, "We don't know." Then he said, "Neither will I tell you by what authority I am doing these things."

The parable of the two sons

²⁸Jesus told a parable and asked, "What do you think about this? There was a man who had two sons. He went to the first son and said, 'Son, go and work today in the vineyard.' ²⁹At first he refused to go but later he changed his mind and went *and worked in the vineyard*. ³⁰Then the father went to the other son and said the same thing. The other son said, 'Yes father, I will go.' But he did not go. ³¹Which one do you think did what his father wanted?" They answered, "The first one."

Jesus said to them, "I am telling you the truth that the tax collectors and the prostitutes are entering the realm of God ahead of you all. ³²For John came to you to show you the right way that God requires and you did not believe him. But the tax collectors and the prostitutes did believe him. And even after having seen them do so, you still did not turn from your sins and believe him."

---

164 Probably referring to the previous day when Jesus had chased the merchants and the money-changers from the temple.

The parable of the vineyard
(Mark 12:1–12, Luke 20:9–19)

³³Jesus told another parable saying, "Listen again. There was a landowner who planted a vineyard. He put a wall around the vineyard, dug a winepress in it and built a watchtower. Then he rented out the vineyard to some farmers and left to go on a trip. ³⁴When the harvest time came, he sent his servants to the farmers to collect his share. ³⁵The farmers grabbed the servants. They beat one servant, killed another and attacked a third one with stones. ³⁶Then later the owner sent other servants to the farmers, more than the first time, and the farmers treated them the same way.

³⁷"Finally, the owner sent his son, thinking to himself that they will respect his son. ³⁸But when the farmers saw the son, they said to each other, 'This is the owner's heir. Come, let's kill him and take his inheritance.'[165] ³⁹So they took the owner's son and threw him out of the vineyard and killed him. ⁴⁰Therefore, when the owner of the vineyard comes, what will he do to these farmers?"

⁴¹They replied, "He will bring those evildoers to a sticky end and he will lease the vineyard to other farmers, who will give him his share of the crop at harvest time." ⁴²Jesus said to them, "Haven't you read this Scripture,

> "'The stone the builders rejected has become the cornerstone; the Lord has done this and it is amazing'?[166]

Psalm 118:22–23

⁴³"Therefore I say to you that the *privilege of being in* the realm of God will be taken away from you and given to a nation and peoples who will do the right thing. ⁴⁴The man who falls on this stone will be broken to pieces. But he on whom it falls will be crushed."

⁴⁵When the chief priests and the Pharisees heard Jesus' parables, they perceived that he was talking about them. ⁴⁶They searched for a way to arrest him, but they were afraid of the mob because the people were convinced that Jesus was a prophet.

---

165   In Galilee during the time of Jesus there was a law whereby under certain circumstances an inheritance could be considered ownerless property, and thus could be claimed by the persons who secured immediate possession of it. If this interpretation is correct then the tenants would have assumed that the owner of the property was dead, and that his son was now coming to take possession of the land. Therefore the reasoning would be that if they kill the son, the property would belong to them.

166   Both David and the Son of David, Jesus, were the stones that the builders rejected. The builders, the prophet Samuel and Jesse (Isa. 11:1), thought that the Lord's anointed would be amongst the seven brothers but the Lord rejected them all because God doesn't look at the outward appearance but the heart (1 Sam. 16:6–7). Instead the Lord chose the one that they the builders (Samuel and Jesse) rejected—the illegitimate son, David who was conceived in his mother's iniquity (Psa. 51:5).

The parable of the wedding reception
(Luke 14:16–24)

22 ¹Jesus spoke to those *who had been questioning his authority* again in parables saying, ²"Heaven's coming realm can be likened to a king who prepared a wedding reception for his son. ³When it was time for the reception *to begin*, he sent his servants to those who had been invited to tell them to come, but they did not want to come. ⁴Then the king sent some more of his servants telling them, 'Tell those who have been invited that I have prepared dinner. The oxen and specially fattened beef have been butchered and everything is ready. Come to the reception.'

⁵"But they paid no attention, instead they went off, one to his field and another to his business. ⁶The rest *of the invited guests* grabbed his servants, mistreated them and killed them. ⁷And so the king was furious. He sent his soldiers in and obliterated those murderers and burned their city *to the ground*.

⁸"Then he said to his servants, 'The wedding reception is ready, but those I invited did not deserve to come. ⁹Therefore go to the main street intersections in the city and invite to the reception anyone you can find.' ¹⁰So the servants went out into the streets and gathered as many people as they could find, both good and bad and the wedding reception hall was filled with guests.

¹¹"But upon entering the reception to see the wedding guests, the king noticed a man who was not wearing the appropriate dress standard. ¹²'Friend,' he asked, 'how did you get in without the proper dress standard for the wedding?' There was nothing the man could say. ¹³Then the king told the reception staff, 'Tie him hand and foot and throw him outside into the darkness where there will be weeping and gnashing of teeth.'[167]

¹⁴"For many *people* will be *there*[168] who have been invited but only a few of those will have been chosen ones."[169]

A question about who to pay taxes to
(Mark 12:13–17, Luke 20:20–26)

¹⁵Then after departing, the Pharisees sometime later conspired together in

---

167 Cf. Matt. 8:12 footnote.
168 Where is "there"? It is Heaven's coming realm – the kingdom of Heaven.
169 Bible scholars say that this verse is very difficult to translate and interpret. My opinion, also because of the context of the previous parable of the vineyard that Jesus is talking about the Jews and the Gentiles. The Jews are the chosen ones and have a seat at the table so to speak. Jesus came for the lost sheep of Israel (Matt. 15:24). Yet because the Jews rejected their Messiah, just like in this parable, an invitation was sent out to the world (city intersections) to invite anyone who would listen and respond.

order to trap Jesus in his words. ¹⁶They sent their followers to him along with the Herodians¹⁷⁰ and they asked him a question saying, "Teacher, we know that you are a man of integrity and that you teach the way of God according to the truth. You do not care what people think because you pay no attention to their status. ¹⁷Therefore tell us, what is your opinion? Is it right to pay Caesar's tax or not?"

¹⁸But Jesus knew their evil intentions. He replied, "You hypocrites, why are you trying to trap me? ¹⁹Show me the coin used for paying the tax." They brought to him a denarius coin. ²⁰Jesus asked them, "Whose image is this? Whose name is inscribed on the coin?" ²¹And they replied, "Caesar's." Then Jesus said to them, "You should pay Caesar what is due him and pay God what is due him also."

²²When they heard this, they were amazed and so they left him and went away.

The Sadducees test Jesus about the resurrection
(Mark 12:18–27, Luke 20:27–40)

²³On the same day the Sadducees, who believe that there is no resurrection, came to him with a question saying, ²⁴"Teacher, Moses taught us that if a man dies without having children then his brother must marry the widow and have children for him. ²⁵Now *once there was a case where* there were seven brothers living amongst us. The first one married and died and since he had no children, he left his wife to his brother. ²⁶Likewise, the same thing happened to the second and third *brother*, right down to the seventh *brother*. ²⁷Finally, the woman herself died. ²⁸Therefore the question is, in the resurrection, whose wife will she be of the seven brothers, since all of them were married to her *at one stage or another*?"

²⁹Jesus replied to them, "You have got it all wrong *about the resurrection* because you do not know the Scriptures or the power of God. ³⁰At the resurrection, people will not marry but they will be like the angels in heaven.

³¹"But concerning the resurrection of the dead, have you not read *in the Scriptures* what God says? ³²He says, 'I am the God of Abraham, the God of Isaac and the God of Jacob.' God is not the God of the dead but of the living." ³³When the crowds heard this, they were astonished at his teaching.

The greatest commandment
(Mark 12:28–31, Luke 10:25–28)

³⁴The Pharisees, having heard that Jesus had silenced the Sadducees, came together and went to Jesus. ³⁵One of them, an expert in the Law, tested him with this question: ³⁶"Teacher, which is the greatest commandment in the Law?"

---

170   A Jewish political group that supported Herod to be ruler.

³⁷Jesus replied, "'Love the Lord your God with all your heart and with all your soul and with all your mind.'¹⁷¹ ³⁸This is the first and greatest commandment. ³⁹And the second *greatest commandment* is like it: 'Love your neighbour *as much as you love* yourself.' ⁴⁰All the Law *of Moses* and the *teachings of the* Prophets hang on these two commandments."

A question about the Son of David
(Mark 12:35–37, Luke 20:41–44)

⁴¹While the Pharisees were still gathered together, Jesus asked them, ⁴²"What do you think about the Messiah? Whose son is he?" They replied, "The son of David." ⁴³He asked them again, "How then could David, inspired by *God's* Breath, call him 'Lord'? For David says,

⁴⁴"'The Lord *God* said to my Lord: "Sit at my right hand until I have put
   your enemies under your feet."'¹⁷²

Psalm 110:1

⁴⁵"So if David calls him 'my Lord,' how can the *Messiah* be his son?" ⁴⁶No one could say a word in reply, and from that day on no one dared to ask him any more questions *in order to trap him.*

Jesus warns against the sin of the Pharisees
(Mark 12:37–40, Luke 11:37–54, 20:45–47)

23 ¹Then after that, Jesus said to the crowds and to his followers, ²"The scribes and the Pharisees have inherited the authority of Moses. ³So you must obey them and do everything they tell you. But do not do what they do for they do not practice what they preach. ⁴They put heavy loads on people's shoulders but they themselves are not willing to lift a finger to help them carry those loads.

⁵"Everything that they do is so that others will see what they do. They make the small prayer boxes strapped to their foreheads and arms with Scriptures in them even larger and the tassels¹⁷³ on their garments even longer than normal. ⁶They love to sit in the place of honour *next to the host* at feasts and they love to sit in the most important seats in the synagogues.¹⁷⁴ ⁷They love to be greeted in the marketplace and to have men call them 'Rabbi'.¹⁷⁵

---

171   The command is to love God in all that we think, feel and do or our whole entirety of being.
172   David is calling the Messiah 'his Lord' in this verse.
173   Tassels worn by the Jews on the corners of their garments was a sign of their devotion to God.
174   The most important seats in the synagogue were seats on the elevated podium while the rest of the people sat on the floor (TH).
175   "Rabbi" is a transliteration of a Hebrew word which means 'my great one'. In Jesus' day it was used exclusively as an honourific for teachers.

⁸"But you must not be addressed as 'Rabbi', for you have only one Teacher and you are all brothers. ⁹And you must not address anyone on earth *with the honorary title*, 'father', for you have one Father, and he is in heaven. ¹⁰Nor are you to be addressed as 'interpreters', for you have one Interpreter, the Messiah. ¹¹The greatest among you all will be the one who serves. ¹²For whoever exalts himself will be humbled and whoever humbles himself will be exalted."

Jesus warns the Pharisees of seven disasters
(Mark 12:38–39, Luke 11:39–52, 20:47)

¹³Then Jesus spoke to the scribes and the Pharisees, "How disastrous it will be for you scribes and Pharisees, you hypocrites! You close the door in men's faces so they cannot enter into Heaven's realm. You yourselves do not enter nor are you allowing others to enter who are trying to. [¹⁴How disastrous it will be for you scribes and Pharisees, you hypocrites! For you rob widows of their houses and say long prayers to cover it up. Therefore you will receive greater judgment.][176]

¹⁵"How disastrous it will be for you scribes and Pharisees, you hypocrites! You travel great distances over land and sea to win a single convert to Judaism, and when he becomes one, you make him twice as much deserving to go to hell as you *deserve*.

¹⁶"How disastrous it will be for you, blind guides! You say, 'If anyone swears by the temple, it means nothing. But if anyone swears by the gold of the temple, he is bound by his oath.' ¹⁷You blind fools! Which is greater? The gold or the temple that makes the gold holy? ¹⁸You also say, 'If anyone swears by the altar, it means nothing. But if anyone swears by the gift *given to God* on it then he is bound by his oath.' ¹⁹You blind men! Which is greater? The gift? Or the altar that makes the gift holy? ²⁰Therefore, he who swears by the altar, in fact, swears by it and everything on *the altar*. ²¹And he who swears by the temple swears by it and by God who dwells in it. ²²And he who swears by heaven swears by God's throne and by God who sits on the throne.

²³"How disastrous it will be for you, scribes and Pharisees, you hypocrites! You give a tenth of your spices—mint, dill and cumin. But you have neglected the more important matters of the Law—justice, mercy and loyalty. You should have followed these important matters without neglecting the less important matters as well. ²⁴You are blind guides! You strain out a gnat but swallow a camel.

²⁵"How disastrous it will be for you, scribes and Pharisees, you hypocrites! You clean the outside of the cup and dish, but that which is inside the cup and

---
176 This verse is omitted by most modern translations.

on the plate is full of greed and violence. ²⁶Blind Pharisee! First, clean the inside of the cup and then the outside also will be clean.

²⁷"How disastrous it will be for you, scribes and Pharisees, you hypocrites! You are like whitewashed graves, which appear beautiful on the outside but on the inside are full of dead men's bones and every kind of filth and rottenness. ²⁸In the same way, on the outside, you appear to all as good people but on the inside, you are full of hypocrisy and sinfulness.

²⁹"How disastrous it will be for you, scribes and Pharisees, you hypocrites! You build *magnificent* tombs for the prophets *of old* and decorate the graves of those who lived good lives. ³⁰And you claim that if you had been alive in the days of your ancestors then you would not have done what they did and would not have murdered the prophets. ³¹So you are testifying against yourselves *in effect* saying that you are the descendants of those men who murdered the prophets. ³²Therefore *go on*, finish off what your forefathers started!¹⁷⁷ ³³You snakes! You nest of snakes! How are you going to avoid being condemned to hell?

³⁴"Because of this, I am going to send to you prophets, wise men and teachers *of God's way*. Some of them you will kill and crucify. Others you will flog them in your synagogues and chase them from city to city. ³⁵*I am going to send them* and so as a result, all the innocent blood that has been shed on the earth, from the blood of innocent Abel to the blood of Zechariah, the son of Berekiah, whom you murdered between the temple and the altar, will be on your heads. ³⁶I am telling you all the truth, all this will come upon this *present* generation.

Jesus' sorrow for Jerusalem
(Luke 13:34–35, 19:41–44)

³⁷"Jerusalem, Jerusalem, you have kept on killing the prophets and stoning those whom God has sent to you. How often I have wanted to gather your people together as a hen gathers her chicks under her wings *and protect you*. But you were not willing. ³⁸Well then, your temple is left to you desolate. ³⁹For I am telling you that you will not see me again until you can say, 'Blessed is he who comes in the name of the Lord.'"¹⁷⁸

---

177   This may be a reference to the murder of Jesus.
178   Cf. Psa. 118:26. There is uncertainty expressed here in the Greek that until the leaders of Israel can repent and acknowledge that Jesus was the promised Messiah, he will not return for a second time at the end of the age. This has huge implications because this is a conditional statement. If Satan and his Antichrist are successful in turning the entire humanity against God and Jesus then Satan knows that he can delay his punishment in the Lake of Fire. Therefore the time will be cut short (Matt. 24:22). Cf. 2 Thess. 2:7.

Jesus predicts the coming destruction of the temple in AD 70
(Mark 13:1-2, Luke 21:5-6)

24 ¹As Jesus was leaving the temple his followers came up to him to direct his attention to the temple buildings. ²Jesus asked them, "Do you see all these buildings? I am telling you the truth, not one stone here will be left on another. Every one of these buildings will be demolished."

The Olivet Discourse
(Mark 13:3-13, Luke 21:7-11)

³As Jesus was sitting on the Mount of Olives, the followers came to him privately[179] and said, "Tell us when these things will happen and what will be the sign of your coming and of the end of the age?"

⁴Jesus answered them, "Watch out that no one deceives you.[180] ⁵For many will come using my name *even admitting* by saying, "I am the Messiah," and will deceive many people.[181] ⁶You will hear wars close by and you will hear news of wars far away. But do not be alarmed. These things are going to happen, but that doesn't mean the end has come. ⁷For nation will rise against nation and kingdom against kingdom and there will be famines, epidemics and earthquakes everywhere. ⁸All these events are *just* the beginning of birth pains.

⁹"At that time you will be arrested to be persecuted and you will be put to death. The entire world will hate you because of me. ¹⁰At that time many *of you* will turn away from the faith and will betray and hate each other. ¹¹At that time many false prophets will rise up and they will deceive many people.[182] ¹²Lawlessness will increase which will result in the love of most *followers* growing cold. ¹³But the one who endures to the end will be saved. ¹⁴This good news of Heaven's coming realm will be preached in the whole world as a testimony to all peoples and then the end will come.

---

179 It is significant that it was only Jesus' disciples who were there when he was talking about the end times and not the public. Whenever Jesus spoke publicly, he never referred to his crucifixion or the coming church age. Therefore one cannot say that Jesus was addressing Jews only when he was warning them of the tribulation to come in this passage but to the whole church in a general sense.

180 Jesus is not just referring to his twelve main followers (disciples) here but to all of his followers in the end times in a generic sense.

181 This verse is not saying that men will come claiming to be Christ. They will admit that Jesus is the Messiah which makes their eschatological teaching even more deceptive in a way because Christians will trust their teaching. This is the first subtle stage of mass deception before the last seven years. The second stage of mass deception is described in Matt. 24:11.

182 The second stage of mass deception is more intense than stage 1 which was false teaching. During the first half of the 70th week Satan increases the deception by sending his false prophets saying that nothing bad is going to happen. This will lead to the great falling away described in 2 Thess. 2:3. This is similar to the false prophets in Jeremiah's day who were saying that no harm would come to Jerusalem (Jer. 5:12) from Babylon. The third stage of mass deception is described in Matt. 24:24.

Surviving the Great Tribulation (the last 1290 days)
(Mark 13:14-23, Luke 21:12-24)

¹⁵"So when you see 'the abomination of desolation,' the thing spoken about by the prophet Daniel, standing in the holy place, (Note to the reader: understand what this means) ¹⁶then those who are in Judea must flee to the mountains.¹⁸³ ¹⁷No one who is on the roof of his house must go down to get anything out of the house as he leaves. ¹⁸And anyone who is at work in the field must not turn back to get his coat *from the house*. ¹⁹It will be a disaster for women who are pregnant or breastfeeding in those days.¹⁸⁴ ²⁰You must pray that your escape does not take place in winter or on the Sabbath day.¹⁸⁵

²¹"For then there will be great tribulation, such as has never occurred before since the beginning of the world until now and it will never happen like this again. ²²If the number of those days had not been cut short, then no flesh would survive. But for the sake of the elect, the number of those days will be cut short.¹⁸⁶ ²³And at that time if anyone says to you, 'Look, here is the Messiah!' or, 'There he is!' do not believe it. ²⁴For false Messiahs and false prophets will appear and perform great signs and wonders so if it is possible *for them to do so*, they will deceive even the chosen ones.¹⁸⁷

²⁵"See, I have warned you all ahead of time. ²⁶Therefore if anyone tells you

---

183 This can only be a reference to the mountains of Jordan. Edom, Moab and Ammon are the only three places that will not be overrun by the so called 'King of the North' (Dan. 11:41). Interestingly Edom, Moab and Ammon are listed as three places that Jews fled to before the Babylonian army overran Jerusalem when the 1st temple was destroyed (Jer. 40:11-12). Petra in southern Jordan (Edom) is 167 km from Jerusalem 'as the crow flies'. Many see 'all those who are in Judea' as being a reference to Jews or Christians in Judea only but all believers are the 'true Israel' (Gal. 3:29). Cf. Rev. 12:1. Besides a 'mixed multitude' escaped Egypt with Israel (Exo. 12:38). Furthermore there is a historical precedence of believers fleeing across the Jordan to seek a place of safety during persecution (John 10:40).

184 "Those days" refers to the fact that it will be hard for pregnant woman and those who are breastfeeding for the whole second half (the Great Tribulation) period of 1290 days not just for those women who are fleeing to the safe place. Cf. v. 22.

185 This is because of the difficulty of travel at this time including the fact that Orthodox Jews walk on the road on Shabbat as opposed to the footpaths (sidewalks). In the winter there are often swollen rivers and flowing wadis and therefore there is the risk of flash flooding. The ancient Jews spoke of only two seasons, winter and summer (Psa. 74:17). 'Summer time' (Daylight Saving Time-DST) in Israel is calculated starting on the last Friday before the last Sunday in March. For example in 2033, DST begins at 2 am on Friday 25th March thus starting the beginning of summer.

186 Cf. 1 Cor. 7:29. The decision by God to shorten the days was made in the past (Mark 13:20) but obviously it will happen in the future. Cf. Matt. 23:39.

187 The third stage of mass deception involves both 'false prophets' and 'false christs' which is even more intense than the second stage. This occurs during the second half of the 70th week when Satan is allowed to empower his servants to perform great signs and wonders so that it might even be able to deceive the chosen ones. Notice how each stage of mass deception occurs in three different time periods with increasing intensity: stage 1 – before the tribulation; stage 2 – the first half of the tribulation; stage 3 – the Great Tribulation (second half). Cf. Matt. 24:4 for the first stage.

that he is out in the desert, you must not go out *there to look*. Or if anyone tells you that he is in the inner rooms, do not believe it. [27]For just as lightning that flashes across *the sky* from the east to the west, so will the coming of the Son of Man be. [28]For where the dead body is, there the eagles will be gathered together.[188]

The coming of the Son of Man after the tribulation
(Mark 13:24-27, Luke 21:25-28)

[29]"Immediately after the tribulation of those days,

"'the sun will be darkened and there will be no moonlight
and the stars will fall from the sky and the heavenly powers will be shaken.'[189]

Isaiah 13:10, 34:4

[30]"At that time the sign of the Son of Man[190] will appear in the sky, and all the peoples of the earth will mourn. They will see the Son of Man coming on the clouds of the sky, with power and great glory. [31]And he will send his angels with a loud trumpet call[191] and they will gather his elect from the four winds, from one end of the heavens to the other end.

The parable of the fig tree[192]
(Mark 13:28-31, Luke 21:29-33)

[32]"Now I want you to learn the lesson from the parable of the fig tree: When the branches on the fig tree become tender and its leaves come out, you know

---

188 This is most likely indicating that the coming of the Son of Man will be at the very place where the dead body is. The dead body referred to has the definite article 'the' meaning that the dead body was a known dead body or carcass. The most likely candidate is the body of Moses (Jude 9). The body of Moses was buried at Mt. Nebo opposite the Dead Sea in modern-day Jordan. The chosen ones or 'elect' (ones who survive the Great Tribulation by avoiding capture by the beast and don't take the mark of the beast) will be raptured into the air from the four corners of the earth at the end of the 1290 days and his angels will gather them to Mt Nebo. The dead in Christ will be waiting for the elect in the air and together they will gather to this point. It is at Bozrah (southern Jordan) where Jesus will first return and begin his final campaign, defeating the Antichrist and his forces. This is the winepress also known as the Valley of Jehoshaphat (Joel 3:12-16). Cf. Luke 17:37, Rev. 14:20.

189 Verse 29 clearly states that immediately after the tribulation the sun will darkened and there will be no moonlight. Acts 2:20 also says that the sun will be turned to darkness and the moon to blood before the coming of the great Day of the Lord which is a quote from Joel 2:28-32. Therefore one can deduce that the Day of the Lord itself will come after the Great Tribulation. To put it simply, if 'b' comes after 'a' and 'c' after 'b', then obviously 'c' comes after 'a'. This then supports the view of a post-tribulational coming of Christ. Pre-tribulation position believes that the Day of the Lord begins at the rapture before the last seven year tribulation period but these verses prove otherwise.

190 It is impossible to know what this sign is. Some have suggested the sign is Jesus himself when he returns or a cross like the Roman Emperor Constantine is reputed to have seen on 27th October AD 312. At any rate all peoples will recognise it and then mourn about the one in whom they have not believed or expected to come.

191 Cf. Zech. 9:14 where Yahweh sounds the shofar.

192 The fig tree represents unsaved Israel.

that the summer is near. ³³Therefore when you see all these things, you know that it is near, right at the door. ³⁴I am telling you the truth, this generation will certainly not pass away until all these things have happened. ³⁵Heaven and earth will pass away, but my words will never pass away.

No one knows the day and the hour
(Mark 13:32–37, Luke 17:26–30, 17:34–36)

³⁶"But concerning that day and hour, no one knows about it, neither the angels in heaven nor the Son, only the Father.[193] ³⁷The coming of the Son of Man will be like it was in the days of Noah. ³⁸For in the days before the flood, people were eating and drinking, marrying and being given in marriage[194] right up to the day that Noah entered the ark. ³⁹They did not realise what was happening until the flood came and swept them all away. That is how it will be at the coming of the Son of Man. ⁴⁰Two men will be working in the field; one will be received and the other left behind. ⁴¹Two women will be grinding grain together; one will be received and the other left behind. ⁴²Therefore you must keep watch because you do not know what day your Lord will come. ⁴³So keep this in mind: If the owner of the house had known what time of the night the thief was coming, he would have kept watch and he would not have let his house be broken[195] into. ⁴⁴Therefore you must also become ready because the Son of Man will come at an hour when you do not expect him.[196]

We must be loyal until the Master returns
(Luke 12:42–46)

⁴⁵"Who then is the loyal and wise servant? It is the one that his master has put in charge of the servants in his household to give them their food at the appropriate time. ⁴⁶Blessed is that servant whose master finds him doing this

---

193   Either a reference to the previous verse as to the timing of when heaven and earth will pass away or to the day when Christ will return on the Jewish New Year's Day—Rosh Hashanah. The exact day that Rosh Hashanah fell was not known because it depended on the sighting of the new moon by two reliable witnesses. It was known as the hidden day. Once the new moon was sighted and reported to the Sanhedrin, this would begin the blowing of 100 trumpets. The last trumpet (100th) was Tekiah Gedolah—a long uninterrupted shofar blast signifying the end. This verse indicates that some things were hidden from Jesus Christ and only revealed to him as revealed to him by God. He did everything only as enabled by the power of God and his Holy Breath. Cf. John 14:10, Acts 10:38, Phil. 2:7.

194   According to Jewish custom at the time men 'married' and women were 'given in marriage'.

195   This is literally 'dug through' because the houses were made of sun-dried brick.

196   Jesus did not say 'be ready' as though a believer must be in a continuous state of readiness. Rather to 'become ready' in this context means to learn or discover the timeframe of the tribulation events so that you know when to watch for his arrival. This is only possible when the events have been unsealed so to speak as Daniel prophesied in Dan. 12:9–10, closer to the time of the end. He says only the wise will understand. LSV & YLT translate this verse with 'become ready'.

work when he comes. ⁴⁷I am telling you the truth, he will put him in charge of all his possessions. ⁴⁸But suppose that the wicked servant says to himself, 'My master is staying away a long time,' ⁴⁹and then he begins to beat his fellow servants and he eats and drinks with drunkards then what? ⁵⁰⁻⁵¹Then the master of that servant will come on a day when he does not expect him and at an hour he does not know and he will severely punish him. He will assign him a place with the hypocrites, where there will be weeping and gnashing of teeth."¹⁹⁷

The parable of the ten young virgins

25 ¹And Jesus said to his followers, "At that time Heaven's coming realm can be likened to ten young virgins who went out to meet the bridegroom.¹⁹⁸ They had with them their torches.¹⁹⁹ ²Five of the virgins were foolish and five were wise. ³The foolish ones had taken their torches without any oil. ⁴However the wise ones had taken oil in containers along with their torches. ⁵Now the bridegroom was taking a long time to arrive and so they all became drowsy and fell asleep.

⁶"At the midpoint of the night there was a loud scream crying out,²⁰⁰ 'The bridegroom is coming! Go out and meet him!' ⁷Then all the young virgins woke up and trimmed their torches. ⁸The foolish ones said to the wise ones, 'Give us some of your oil! Our torches are going out.' ⁹But the wise virgins replied, 'No way! There will not be enough oil for both us and you. Instead, you must go to those who sell oil and buy your own.' ¹⁰But while they were away buying oil, the bridegroom arrived. The virgins who were ready went with him into the wedding and the door was shut.

¹¹"Later the other young virgins also arrived at the house and they cried out, 'Lord! Lord! Open the door for us!' ¹²But he replied, 'I am telling you the truth, I don't know you.'"

¹³And Jesus *concluded* by saying, "Therefore keep watch because you do not know the day or the hour."

197	Cf. Matt. 8:12 footnote.
198	The last generation of Christians are described in this parable as virgins. Cf. 2 Cor. 11:2–3.
199	These are not the small oil lamps (Gk: *luchnos*) but torches (Gk: *lampas*) meaning sticks wrapped with rags soaked in oil. *Lampas* here represents testimony. The foolish virgin's testimony at the darkest time of history (midnight) when the Abomination of Desolation appears on the scene fails. The wise virgins are those Christians who are ready and make the journey into the safe place (Petra).
200	At the midpoint of the 70th week a loud scream is heard that wakes up all the virgins (Christians) and shocks them making them realise that Jesus is actually coming back soon. What is this scream? The beast arises from the abyss at the midpoint—an evil dictator resurrected from a historical kingdom. Cf. Rev. 17:9–10. His resurrection astonishes the world and he sits in the rebuilt Jewish temple declaring to be God himself. Cf. 2 Thess. 2:4.

The parable of the talents
(Luke 19:11–27)

¹⁴Jesus said to his followers, "Again Heaven's coming realm can be likened to a man going on a journey and who calls his servants and puts them in charge of his possessions. ¹⁵He gave five talents[201] *of money* to one of them, two talents to another and one talent to the other servant. He gave to each of them according to their ability. Then the man went on his journey. ¹⁶The *servant* who had received the five talents went immediately and put his money to work and he gained five more talents. ¹⁷Likewise the *servant* who had received two talents gained another two talents. ¹⁸But the *servant* who had received one talent went and dug a hole in the ground and hid his master's silver.[202]

¹⁹"After a long time the master of those servants returned to settle accounts with them *and check on his money*. ²⁰The servant who had received five talents brought the other five and said, 'Master, you put me in charge of five talents and look, I have gained five more *talents*.' ²¹And his master replied, 'Well done, good and loyal servant! You have been loyal with a few things. Now I will put you in charge of many things. Come on in and share your master's joy.'

²²"Then the servant with two talents also came and said, 'Master, you put me in charge of two talents and look, I have gained two more *talents*.' ²³And his master replied, 'Well done, good and loyal servant! You have been loyal with a few things. Now I will put you in charge of many things. Come on in and share your master's joy.'

²⁴"Then the servant with one talent came and said, 'Master, I knew that you are a hard and shrewd man. You *expect to* harvest where you have not sown and gather where you have not scattered seed. ²⁵I was afraid *I might lose the money* so I went and hid your talent in the ground. Look, that which belongs to you *is safe*.'

²⁶"The servant's master replied, 'You evil and lazy servant! So you knew that I harvest where I have not sown and gather where I have not scattered seed? ²⁷Well, you should have put my money on deposit with the bankers. Then when I returned I could have received it back with interest.

²⁸"The servant's master said, 'Take the one talent from him and give it to the *servant* who has the ten talents. ²⁹For everyone who has will be given more, and he will have an abundance. Whoever does not have anything, even what he

---

201 A talent was a measure of weight not a specific unit of currency. A talent could be in either gold, silver or copper. One talent of gold was worth between 5 and 6 thousand denarii. One denarius was worth about one day's wage. A talent of gold is worth a huge sum of money.
202 It appears more likely that the talents referred to were talents of silver not gold.

has will be taken from him. ³⁰Throw that useless servant outside into the outer darkness, where there will be weeping and gnashing of teeth.'²⁰³

The judgment of the sheep and the goats

³¹"When the Son of Man comes with glory and splendour in the company of all the angels then he will sit on his royal throne *in judgment*.²⁰⁴ ³²All the nations will be gathered before him and he will separate the people from each other into two groups as a shepherd separates the sheep from the goats. ³³He will put the sheep on his right and the goats on his left.

³⁴"Then the King will say to those on his right, 'Come, you who are blessed by my Father. Receive your inheritance, and enter into the realm of Heaven which has been prepared for you because of the overthrow of the world *by Satan*. ³⁵For I was hungry and you gave me something to eat, I was thirsty and you gave me something to drink, I was a stranger and you invited me in. ³⁶I needed clothes and you clothed me, I was sick and you visited me, I was in jail and you came to see me.'²⁰⁵

³⁷"Then the good people who did the right thing will answer him, 'Lord, when did we see you hungry and feed you, or thirsty and give you something to drink? ³⁸When did we see you as a stranger and invite you in, or when did we see you as needing clothes and clothe you? ³⁹When did we see you sick or in jail and go and visit you?'

⁴⁰"The King will reply, 'I am telling you the truth, whatever you did for one of the least of these brothers of mine, *it was as if* you were doing it for me.'

⁴¹"Then he will say to those on his left, 'Leave me, you who are cursed, and go into the eternal fire having been prepared for the devil and his angels.²⁰⁶ ⁴²For I was hungry and you gave me nothing to eat, I was thirsty and you gave me nothing to drink. ⁴³I was a stranger and you did not invite me in, I needed clothes and you did not clothe me, I was sick and in jail and you did not help me.'

⁴⁴"They will also answer in a *similar way to the good people who did the right thing* and they will say, 'Lord, when did we see you hungry or thirsty or a stranger or needing clothes or sick or in jail and we did not help you?'

---

203   Cf. Matt. 8:12 footnote.
204   The implication is that this judgment of the sheep and the goats or in other words, the good and the evil, occurs after the seven year tribulation period but before Christ's earthly 1000 year millennial reign. At the time of Christ's coming, the saved and the lost who survived the tribulation are still mingled together and so they need to be separated.
205   This judgment will be based on how God's holy people (Christ's brethren) were treated during this difficult time of tribulation.
206   The original purpose of eternal punishment (Lake of Fire) was for the devil and his evil angels—the one-third that fell in the original rebellion. However mankind who refuses to repent and believe in the gospel will also be cast into the Lake of Fire.

⁴⁵"The King will reply, 'I am telling you the truth, whatever you did not do for one of the least of these, *it was as if* you did not do it for me.' ⁴⁶Then they will go away to eternal punishment, but the good people to eternal life."[207]

A plot against Jesus
(Mark 14:1-2, Luke 22:1-2, John 11:45-53)

26 ¹When Jesus had finished saying all these things, he said to his followers, ²"As you all know, the Passover *Feast* is only two days away and the Son of Man will be betrayed and handed over to be crucified."

³At that time the chief priests and the elders of the people assembled together in the palace of the high priest, Caiaphas. ⁴They plotted and planned in how they might arrest and trap Jesus in order to have him killed. ⁵They said, "We must not do it during the *Passover* Feast or there may be a riot among the people."

A woman pours perfume on Jesus' head
(Mark 14:3-9, John 13:1-17)

⁶Meanwhile Jesus was in the *village of* Bethany in the home of a man known as Simon the Leper. ⁷Whilst there, a woman[208] came to him with an alabaster[209] *stone* jar of very expensive perfume. As Jesus was reclining at the table, she poured *the perfume* onto his head. ⁸However when Jesus' followers saw this they were most displeased. They said, "Why this waste of *expensive* perfume? ⁹This perfume could have been sold at a high price and the money given to the poor."

¹⁰Jesus was aware of their displeasure and he said to them, "Why are you bothering this woman? She has done an appropriate thing for me. ¹¹You will always have the poor amongst you, but you will not have me for very much longer. ¹²When she poured this perfume on my body, she did it to prepare me for my burial. ¹³I am telling you the truth that wherever this good news is preached throughout the world, people will also be told about what she has done in memory of her."

---

207   This does not mean that salvation is by works by doing good deeds but that the people who survived the Great Tribulation and treated God's holy people with works of love and kindness during that period will enter into the 1000 year millennial reign of Christ on earth. In other words I believe that they will extend their stay of judgment and then be subject to the requirements of the new and final dispensation which is underpinned by the statement that Christ 'will rule with a rod of iron'. Salvation is always by faith in any dispensation.

208   Matthew doesn't identify the woman in this anointing however in the other anointing six days before the Passover, Mary, Martha's sister, anointed Jesus' feet with perfume (John 12:1-3).

209   A soft stone of creamy colour. The stone itself was imported from Egypt, and thousands of small alabaster perfume flasks have been excavated by archaeologists in Palestine (TH).

Judas agrees to betray Jesus
(Mark 14:10–11, Luke 22:3–6)

[14]At that time one of the twelve named Judas Iscariot went to see the chief priests. [15]He asked them, "What are you willing to give me if I hand Jesus over to you?" They weighed out 30 silver coins and gave them to him. [16]From then on Judas sought for a good opportunity to hand him over.

The Last Supper
(Mark 14:12–21, Luke 22:7–13, 22:21–23)

[17]Before the Feast[210] of Unleavened Bread, the followers came to Jesus and asked him, "Where do you want us to make preparations for you to eat the Passover *meal*?"[211]

[18]Jesus replied,[212] "Go into the city to a certain man and tell him, 'The Teacher says: My appointed time is close. I am going to celebrate the Passover *meal* with my followers at your house.'" [19]So the followers did as Jesus had directed them and they prepared the Passover *meal*.

[20]When evening came, Jesus was reclining at the table with the twelve. [21]While they were all eating, he said to them, "I am telling you the truth that one of you will betray me." [22]They were all very sad and began to say to him one after the other, "Surely not I, Lord?" [23]Jesus replied, "The one who dips his hand into the bowl with me is the one who will betray me.[213] [24]The Son of Man will die as the Scriptures say he will. But woe to that man who betrays the Son of Man! It would be better for him if he had not been born." [25]Then Judas, the one who would betray him, said, "Surely not me, Rabbi?" And Jesus replied, "You have said it yourself."

Jesus gives thanks for the bread and the cup
(Mark 14:22–26, Luke 22:15–20, 1 Corinthians 11:23–25)

[26]And while they were still eating, Jesus took some bread and gave thanks to God for it and broke it. Then he gave it to his followers, saying, "Take it and

---

210   The preparation for the meal in a private home occurred during the day on Wednesday, Nisan 13, the day before Jesus was crucified. The actual meal was eaten that night on Nisan 14 (Wednesday night) because it had become the custom for the Jews of Jesus' day to prepare and eat the Passover meal privately a day earlier than it was sacrificed and eaten at the temple by the priests. Cf. Mark 14:12 and footnotes, John 18:28 and footnote.
211   This refers to the sacrificial lamb that became the Passover meal (TH).
212   The Passover could be celebrated only in the city within the walls of Jerusalem (Deut. 16:5–8) and Jewish residents of Jerusalem were expected to make available spare rooms in their houses for Passover pilgrims (Edwards, James R, *The Pillar NT Commentary on Mark* (2002)).
213   This indicates a serious betrayal because it means that the one who dipped his bread into the bowl had close proximity and also was a close friend.

eat for this is my body." ²⁷Then he took the cup and gave thanks to God for it. Then he gave it to them saying, "Each one of you, drink from this cup. ²⁸This is my blood of the new covenant which is being poured out for many *people* for the forgiveness of sins. ²⁹I tell you the truth, I will not drink this fruit of the vine from now on until that day when I drink the new *wine* with you all once my Father has established his reign."

³⁰Then they sung a hymn and went out to the Mount of Olives.

Jesus predicts Peter's denial that very night
(Mark 14:27–31, Luke 22:31–34)

³¹Then Jesus told his followers, "This very night you will all stumble *in your faith* because of what will happen to me. For God has written it in the Scriptures,

"'I will strike the shepherd and the sheep of the flock will scatter.'

Zechariah 13:7

³²"But after I have risen back to life, I will go on ahead of you into *the district of* Galilee."

³³Peter replied, "Even if everyone stumbles because of what will happen to you, I myself won't stumble."

³⁴Jesus answered Peter, "I am telling you the truth, this very night, before the rooster crows, you will deny me three times."

³⁵But Peter said, "Even if I have to die with you, I will never deny you." And all the other followers said the same thing.

Jesus prays in the garden of Gethsemane
(Mark 14:32–42, Luke 22:39–46)

³⁶Then Jesus and his followers went to a place called Gethsemane²¹⁴ and he told them to sit down while he went and prayed a little way away. ³⁷He took with him Peter and the two sons of Zebedee. Jesus became sad and distressed. ³⁸Then he said to them, "The sadness that I am feeling in my soul is killing me. Stay here and keep watch with me."

³⁹Then Jesus went a little further on and he lay face down on the ground in prayer. He prayed, "My Father, if it is possible, please take this cup²¹⁵ from me. But it is not about what I want, but what you want."

⁴⁰Jesus went back to his followers and he found the three of them sleeping.

---

214 Gethsemane is the name of an olive orchard on the Mount of Olives and is a transliteration of the Hebrew phrase meaning '(olive) oil-press'.
215 The cup is a picture of the pain and suffering that Jesus was faced with.

He asked Peter, "Could you men not keep watch with me for just one hour? ⁴¹Watch and pray so that you don't enter into temptation. The spirit is willing but the flesh is weak."

⁴²Jesus went away a second time and prayed, "My Father. If it is not possible that this cup is taken from me unless I drink of it then I pray that your will is done."

⁴³When Jesus returned, once again he found them sleeping because they couldn't keep their eyes open. ⁴⁴So he left them and went away once again and prayed a third time, saying the same thing.

⁴⁵Then Jesus went back to his followers and said to them, "Are you still sleeping and resting? Look, the hour is near and the Son of Man is betrayed into the hands of sinners. ⁴⁶Get up! Let's go! Here comes my betrayer."

Jesus is arrested
(Mark 14:43–50, Luke 22:47–53, John 18:1–11)

⁴⁷And while Jesus was still speaking, Judas, one of the twelve, arrived and with him was a large crowd armed with swords and clubs. They were sent from the chief priests and the elders of the people. ⁴⁸Now previously the betrayer had arranged a signal with them: "The one I kiss is the man. Arrest him!" ⁴⁹Judas went immediately to Jesus saying, "Hello, Rabbi!" and he kissed him.

⁵⁰Jesus replied, "My friend, do what you came to do." Then the men stepped forward and seized Jesus and they arrested him. ⁵¹As this was happening, one of the men[216] with Jesus reached for his sword, drew it out and struck the servant of the high priest, cutting off his ear.

⁵²Jesus said to him, "Put your sword away for those who draw the sword will die by the sword. ⁵³Do you not think that I cannot call on my Father and then at once he could send me more than twelve legions[217] of angels? ⁵⁴But if I did that then how would the Scriptures be fulfilled that say that it must happen in this way?"

⁵⁵Then Jesus said to the crowd, "Am I a robber[218] that you have come out with swords and clubs to capture me? Every day I have been sitting in the temple teaching and you did not arrest me? ⁵⁶But this has all taken place so that what the prophets wrote in the Scriptures might be fulfilled."

Then all the followers deserted him and fled.

---

216 The parallel account in John 18:10 identifies this man as Simon Peter.
217 There were 6000 soldiers in a legion. Therefore 12 legions of angels would be equal to 72,000 if Jesus had needed them.
218 The Greek word here can mean a robber, thief, bandit, highwayman, insurrectionist or revolutionary. There is a wide range of English translations of this word but most have 'robber'.

Jesus is brought before the Sanhedrin council
(Mark 14:53-65, Luke 22:54-55, 22:63-71, John 18:12-14, 18:19-24)

⁵⁷Those men who had arrested Jesus took him to the high priest, Caiaphas where the scribes and the *Jewish* elders were gathered. ⁵⁸Peter however, had followed him at a distance, right up to the courtyard of the high priest. He entered and sat down with the guards to see what would happen *to Jesus*.

⁵⁹The chief priests with the rest of the whole Sanhedrin[219] council were looking for false evidence against Jesus so that they could put him to death. ⁶⁰Many false witnesses came forward but they were not able to find any *suitable* evidence. Finally, two witnesses came forward. ⁶¹They said, "This man said, 'I am able to destroy the temple of God and rebuild it in three days.'"

⁶²Then the high priest stood up and said to Jesus, "Do you have an answer? What do you say to the accusations of these men?" ⁶³But Jesus was silent.

The high priest said to him, "I command you under oath to God: Tell us if you are the Messiah, the Son of God."

⁶⁴Jesus replied, "It is as you say. But I am telling you the truth that in the future you will see the Son of Man sitting at the right hand of the Power and coming on the clouds of heaven."[220]

⁶⁵Then the high priest tore his clothes and said to the council, "He has blasphemed! Why do we need any further witnesses? See, you have heard the blasphemy. ⁶⁶What do you think?"

They answered, "He is worthy of death."

⁶⁷Then they spat in his face, struck him and slapped him. ⁶⁸They insulted him saying, "Prophesy to us, Messiah! Who hit you?"[221]

Peter disowns Jesus
(Mark 14:66-72, Luke 22:56-62, John 18:15-18, 18:25-27)

⁶⁹Now Peter was sitting outside in the courtyard when a servant girl came to him and said, "You also were with Jesus the Galilean."

⁷⁰But Peter denied this before them all saying, "I don't know what you're talking about." ⁷¹Then he went out to the entryway, where another girl saw him

---

219 The Great Sanhedrin was the supreme and highest court of ancient Israel. It had the final authority in matters governing the religion and life of the Jewish people. It was made up of 70 members and also the High Priest.

220 The two powers of heaven will be descending on the clouds, the Father and the Son (Rev. 6:16-17). Yahweh is declared to be the 'cloud rider' in the OT (Deut. 33:26, Psa. 68:4). Cf. Matt. 24:30, Mark 8:38, Rev. 1:7.

221 This might seem odd that they are commanding Jesus to "prophesy" but in Mark 14:65 we learn that Jesus was also blindfolded.

and said to the people there, "This man was with Jesus the Nazarene." ⁷²Again Peter denied it with an oath saying, "*I swear* that I do not know this man." ⁷³After a while, those standing around came up to Peter and said, "Surely you are one of them for your *Galilean* accent gives you away." ⁷⁴Then Peter called down curses on himself *from above* and he swore *by God* saying, "I do not know the man."

Immediately a rooster crowed. ⁷⁵Then Peter remembered what Jesus had said: "Before the rooster crows, you will deny me three times." And he went outside and wept bitterly.

Jesus is taken to Pilate
(Mark 15:1, Luke 23:1–2, John 18:28–32)

27 ¹Early the next morning, all the chief priests and the elders of the people decided together to put Jesus to death. ²They had him bound and he was led away and handed over to Pilate, the *Roman* governor.²²²

Judas hangs himself
(Acts 1:18–19)

³When Judas the betrayer, saw that Jesus was condemned to death, he was overcome with regret and he returned the 30 silver coins to the chief priests and the elders. ⁴Judas said, "I have sinned for I have betrayed innocent blood." The priests and the elders replied, "What is that to us? That's your problem."

⁵And so Judas threw the silver coins into the temple and left. Then he went and hanged himself.

⁶The chief priests picked up the coins and said, "It is against the Law to put this money into the temple treasury since it has the price of blood on it. ⁷So they decided together to use the money and to buy the potter's field as a burial place for foreigners.²²³ ⁸This is the reason why it has been called the Field of Blood to this day. ⁹This fulfils what the prophet Jeremiah said, "They took 30 silver coins, the price set on him by the people of Israel. ¹⁰And they used them to buy the potter's field, just as the Lord commanded me."

Jesus is questioned by Pilate
(Mark 15:2–5, Luke 23:3–5, John 18:33–38)

¹¹Meanwhile Jesus stood before the *Roman* governor, and the governor asked him, "Are you the king of the Jews?"

---

222   Pontius Pilate was the Roman governor of Judea during the period AD 26–36. The title "governor" describes Pilate's military authority and would not have been his official title (TH).

223   Interesting comment by one commentator: "The unclean money is used for an unclean purpose, the purchase of a cemetery for foreigners, presumably Gentiles."

"So you say," replied Jesus.

[12] But when he was accused by the chief priests and the elders, he gave no answer. [13] Then Pilate said to Jesus, "Don't you hear the accusations that they are bringing against you?" [14] But Jesus made no reply, not even to a single charge, which amazed the governor greatly.

Pilate sentences Jesus to death
(Mark 15:6-15, Luke 23:13-25, John 18:38-19:16)

[15] Now every year at the *Passover* Feast, it was the *Roman* governor's custom to release one prisoner as chosen by the crowd. [16] At this time there was a notorious prisoner named Jesus[224] Barabbas. [17] So when the crowd had gathered, Pilate asked them, "Which one do you want me to release to you: Barabbas or Jesus, the one they call the Messiah?" [18] For Pilate knew very well that the *Jewish leaders* handed over Jesus to him because they were jealous of him.

[19] While Pilate was sitting in judgment, his wife sent him a message saying, "Don't have anything to do with that innocent man for I have had a dream and have been bothered a great deal today because of him."

[20] But the chief priests and the elders persuaded the crowd to ask for Barabbas *to be released* and that Jesus should be executed. [21] The governor asked the crowd, "Which one of the two men do you want me to release to you?"

"Barabbas," they answered.

[22] "What shall I do then, with Jesus who is called the Messiah?" They all answered, "Crucify him!" [23] "Why? What crime has he committed?" asked Pilate. But they shouted even louder, "Crucify him!"

[24] When Pilate saw that he was getting nowhere and that a riot was beginning, he took some water and washed his hands in front of the crowd. He said, "I am innocent of this man's blood. It is your fault!" [25] All the people answered, "Let his blood be on us and our children!" [26] Then *Pilate* released Barabbas to *the crowd and their Jewish leaders*. But Pilate had Jesus flogged[225] first and then handed him over to be crucified.

---

224 Some translations have the name 'Jesus' along with Barabbas but some say that the textual evidence for its inclusion is slender. If true then this is extremely ironic as the translation of this man's name would be, 'Jesus son of the father'. This is incredible in the sense that the Jewish crowd would have to select between the actual Jesus, the Son of the Father or an alternative Jesus, the son of the father. The choice for all of mankind too is this stark, between truth and deception, light and darkness.

225 The Roman flogging consisted of the victim being stripped and stretched against a pillar or bent over a low post with the hands being tied. The instrument was a short wooden handle to which several leather strips were attached, with bits of iron or bone tied to the leather strips. The torture was carried out by two men, one on each side resulting in severe damage. Often the victim would die during the flogging.

The soldiers mock Jesus
(Mark 15:16–20, John 19:2–3)

²⁷Then the governor's soldiers took Jesus into the governor's palace and the whole cohort[226] of soldiers gathered around him. ²⁸They stripped him and put a scarlet robe on him. ²⁹They twisted together a crown of thorns and placed it upon his head. They then put a stick[227] in his right hand and knelt in front of him and mocked him saying, "Hail, king of the Jews!" ³⁰They spat on him and took the stick and repeatedly hit him on the head. ³¹After they had mocked him, they took off the robe and put his own clothes on him. Then they led him away to be crucified.

Jesus is crucified
(Mark 15:21–32, Luke 23:26–43, John 19:17–27)

³²As they were leading Jesus out *of the city,* they met a man from the *city of* Cyrene,[228] named Simon and they forced him to carry the cross beam.[229] ³³They came to a place called Golgotha[230] which means "Place of the Skull." ³⁴There they offered Jesus wine to drink mixed with a bitter substance.[231] But after tasting it he refused to drink it. ³⁵When the soldiers had crucified him, they divided up his clothes by casting lots. ³⁶They then sat down and kept watch over him at that place. ³⁷Above his head they placed *a sign with* the written charge against him:

THIS IS JESUS—THE KING OF THE JEWS

³⁸Two thieves were *also* crucified with him, one on his right and one on his left. ³⁹The passers-by blasphemed and hurled insults at him and shook their heads in derision. ⁴⁰They said, "You said that you will destroy the temple and rebuild it in three days. So save yourself! Come down from the cross, if you are the Son of God."

⁴¹The chief priests, the scribes and the elders mocked him in a similar way. ⁴²They said, "He saved others but he can't save himself! He's the King of Israel so he says. If so then let him come down from the cross and we will believe in him. ⁴³He trusts in God. Then let God rescue him now if he wants him for he said, 'I am the Son of God.'" ⁴⁴In the same way the thieves who were crucified with him also insulted him.

---

226   This was a Roman military unit of about six hundred soldiers, though only a part of such a cohort was often referred to as a cohort. It is unlikely that such a large number would be involved in the mockery of one man but it is possible.
227   Literally the stalk of a reed plant like a cane. It was not a walking stick.
228   Cyrene was a capital city on the north coast of Africa.
229   It was customary for the condemned man to carry the cross beam on his shoulder; the upright of the cross whether a tree or piece of wood would have remained in a stationary position at the site of execution.
230   Golgotha is an Aramaic word meaning 'skull'.
231   Literally gall.

Jesus dies

(Mark 15:33–41, Luke 23:44–49, John 19:28–30)

⁴⁵From the sixth hour to the ninth hour[232] there was darkness over all the land.[233] ⁴⁶At about 3 pm in the afternoon Jesus cried out in a loud voice, "Eli, eli, lama sabachthani?"—which means, "My God, my God, why have you abandoned me?"

⁴⁷When some of the people standing nearby heard this, they said, "He's calling for *the prophet* Elijah."[234]

⁴⁸Immediately one *of the soldiers* ran and got a sponge. He filled it with cheap sour wine,[235] put it on a stick,[236] and offered it to Jesus to drink. ⁴⁹However the others said, "Now leave him alone. Let's see if Elijah comes to save him."

⁵⁰Then Jesus cried out in a loud voice and he breathed his last breath. ⁵¹At that very moment, the curtain of the temple was torn in two from top to bottom,[237] the earth shook and the rocks[238] split apart. ⁵²The tombs broke open and the bodies of many holy people who had previously died were raised to life. ⁵³They came out of the tombs and after the resurrection of Jesus, they went into the holy city[239] and appeared to many people.

⁵⁴When the *Roman* centurion and the soldiers with him who were guarding Jesus saw the earthquake and all that was happening, they were terrified and they said, "Surely he was the Son of God!"

⁵⁵Many women were there, watching everything from a distance. They had followed Jesus, *accompanying him* since *he had been in the district of* Galilee *in the north* in order to take care of his needs. ⁵⁶Among the women there were Mary Magdalene, Mary the mother of James and Joseph, and also the mother of Zebedee's sons.

---

232 I.e. From noon to 3 pm in the afternoon. In Hebrew thinking they start counting the hours from 6 am at sunrise. The book of John uses the Roman method of calculating time (i.e. counting from midnight) hence the apparent contradiction.

233 Could mean darkness over just the land of Israel or possibly over the entire earth.

234 "Eli" (Hebrew) sounds very similar to 'Elijah' so maybe that's why the confusion.

235 This may have been a favourite beverage of poorer people and was relatively effective in quenching thirst. Many versions say vinegar or wine vinegar.

236 Literally the stalk of a reed.

237 This is the first of many bad omens according to the Talmud which kept occurring for 40 years before the destruction of the temple in AD 70. Other bad omens that were reported to have occurred include the huge double doors of the temple opening by themselves, the oil lamp of the menorah closest to the Holy of Holies refusing to burn and a white stone with the words 'For the Lord' not coming up in the right hand of the High Priest on the Day of Atonement. This is evidence that the crucifixion took place in AD 30 (Warner, T, *The Time of the End* (2012), pp. 315–317).

238 This means the foundational bedrock like rocky crags and mountain ledges not small little stones.

239 I.e. Jerusalem.

Jesus' body is placed in a tomb
(Mark 15:42–47, Luke 23:50–55, John 19:38–42)

⁵⁷When evening came, a rich man from the city of Arimathea²⁴⁰ went to Pilate. The man's name was Joseph and he was also a follower of Jesus. ⁵⁸Going to Pilate, he asked for Jesus' body and so Pilate ordered that the body be given to him. ⁵⁹Joseph took the body and wrapped it in a clean linen *sheet*. ⁶⁰He placed the wrapped body in his own new tomb that he had cut out of the rock. He then rolled a big stone in front of the entrance to the tomb and went on his way. ⁶¹Mary Magdalene and the other Mary were there sitting opposite the tomb.

The guard of soldiers at the tomb of Jesus

⁶²The next day, the one after the Preparation Day,²⁴¹ the chief priests and the Pharisees went to Pilate. ⁶³They said to Pilate, "Lord, we remember that while he was still alive that imposter said, 'After three days I will rise again.' ⁶⁴You must give the order for the tomb to be closely guarded until the third day. Otherwise, his followers might come and steal the body and tell the people that he has risen from the dead. This last deception will be worse than the first."

⁶⁵Pilate said to them, "You may have a guard. Go and secure the tomb as best as you know how." ⁶⁶So they went and made the tomb secure by putting a seal on the stone and placing the guard of soldiers.

Jesus is resurrected
(Mark 16:1–10, Luke 24:1–10, John 20:1–18)

28 ¹After the Sabbath days,²⁴² at dawn on the first day of the week of Sabbaths,²⁴³ Mary Magdalene and the other Mary went to check out the tomb. ²Suddenly there was a huge earthquake for an angel of the Lord came down from heaven. The angel went to the tomb and rolled back the stone and sat on it. ³His appearance was like that of lightning and his clothes were as white as snow. ⁴The soldiers guarding the tomb were so afraid of him that they were shaking and became like dead men.

---

240 A city in Israel believed to be about 16 km east of Joppa or modern-day Tel Aviv on the coast. The exact location is unknown but it was almost certainly a city in Judea northwest of Jerusalem.

241 This day was the day on which preparations were made for a sacred or feast day and eventually became synonymous with 'Friday'. It is the modern-day Greek term for Friday. However in AD 30 there were two Sabbath days in a row: Friday and Saturday. The chief priests and Pharisees went to Pilate with their request on the Friday, the special 'high' Sabbath day.

242 There were two Sabbath Days in a row in AD 30 that year: Friday, the special high Sabbath, and Saturday, the weekly Sabbath. Cf. John 19:31.

243 This was a title for the Feast of Firstfruits. It was literally day 1 of the next 50 days before Pentecost and literally seven weekly Sabbaths to follow. This day was Sunday, Nisan 17. Cf. John 20:1, Acts 20:7, 1 Cor. 16:2.

⁵The angel said to the women, "Do not be afraid for I know that you are looking for Jesus who was crucified. ⁶He is not here for he has been raised from the dead just as he said *he would be*. Come and see the place where he lay. ⁷Then you must go quickly and tell his followers that he has been raised from the dead and that he is going ahead of them to Galilee. There they will see him. Now I have told you."

⁸So the women quickly left the tomb and were filled with both fear and joy. They ran to tell the followers. ⁹Suddenly Jesus met them on the way and greeted them saying, "Hello!" They came up to him and held onto his feet and worshipped him. ¹⁰Then Jesus said to them, "Don't be afraid. You must go and tell my brothers[244] to go to Galilee. There they will see me."

The guard of soldiers give a report on what happened

¹¹While the women were on their way, some of the soldiers of the guard went into the city and reported to the chief priests everything that had happened. ¹²When the chief priests finished meeting with the elders and had made a plan, they gave the soldiers a large sum of silver money. ¹³They told the soldiers, "You are to say *to people* that his followers came during the night and stole him while you were asleep. ¹⁴If this report gets to the governor, we ourselves will convince him and keep you out of trouble." ¹⁵So the soldiers took the silver and did as they were instructed. And so the *chief priest's* story has been widely circulated among the Judeans to this very day.[245]

The Great Commission
(Mark 16:14–18, Luke 24:36–49, John 20:19–23)

¹⁶And so the eleven followers went to the Galilee *district* and to the mountain[246] where Jesus had told them to go. ¹⁷When they saw him, they worshipped him but they had their doubts *that it was actually Jesus*. ¹⁸Then Jesus came to them and said, "All authority in heaven and on earth has been given to me *by my Father*. ¹⁹Therefore go and make followers in all nations, baptising them in the name[247] of the Father and the Son and the Holy Breath[248] ²⁰teaching them to do everything that I have commanded. Be assured, I will be with you always to the very end of the age."

---

244 Not a reference to his literal brothers but a loving reference to his followers.
245 Matthew wrote this gospel in c. AD 60 so obviously this refers up to that point.
246 In Jewish thought hills and mountains are places of divine revelation. The actual mountain in question was not revealed by Matthew.
247 To baptise a person "in the name of" means 'by the authority of'.
248 Here the Holy Breath is in the neuter gender whereas the Father and the Son have masculine genders. Michael S. Heiser says, "Unlike the NT, the OT has no Trinitarian phrases (Father, Son and Holy Spirit). The triune godhead is never transparently expressed in the Old Testament" (Heiser, Michael S., *The Unseen Realm* (2015), p. 39n1). However Heiser argues that the Israelites and 1st century Jewish writers did discern a two-person Godhead and that this verse is the clearest Trinitarian phrase in the NT.

MARK

Introduction

The unanimous opinion of the early church was that the synoptic gospel of Mark was written by John Mark in the late AD 50s or 60s and probably predated the other three gospels. Mark was probably written with a Roman audience in mind, is precise, fast moving and the shortest of all four gospels. It emphasises what Jesus did rather than what Jesus said and explains Jewish customs. It excludes lengthy Jewish genealogies and begins abruptly. Mark often begins sentences with the word 'and'. He also uses the word 'immediately' some 42 times in the Greek.

The Book of Mark also includes the Olivet discourse about the end times in chapter 13 but only includes nine parables in comparison to Matthew's twenty three parables and Luke's twenty eight parables. Most scholars hold the view that both Matthew and Luke have made direct use of the Gospel of Mark as a source because it was composed first although ancient authors did not agree on the order. A remark by Augustine of Hippo at the beginning of the fifth century presents the gospels as composed in their canonical order (Matthew, Mark, Luke, John) and this view was not challenged until the late 18th century.

John the Baptist prepares the way for Jesus

(Matthew 3:1–12, Luke 3:1–9, 3:15–17, John 1:19–28)

1 ¹This is the beginning of the good news about Jesus Christ, the Son of God. ²It is just as Isaiah the prophet wrote,

"Look! I will send my messenger ahead of you and he will prepare your way."

Malachi 3:1

³"He is a voice of one calling in the desert,
'Prepare the way for the Lord and make his paths straight.'"

Isaiah 40:3

⁴John came to the desert, baptising and preaching. He preached to the people that they should turn to God and be baptised so that their sins could be forgiven. ⁵The whole Judean countryside and all the people of Jerusalem went out to him, confessing their sins. He baptised them in the Jordan River.

⁶And John wore clothing made of camel's hair and had a leather belt around his waist. He ate locusts²⁴⁹ and wild honey. ⁷And John preached saying, "After me will come one more powerful than me. I am not even worthy to stoop down and untie the straps of his sandals. ⁸I have baptised you in water, but he will baptise you in Holy Breath."

The baptism of Jesus

(Matthew 3:13–17, Luke 3:21–22)

⁹And it came about in those days that Jesus came from Nazareth in the *district* of Galilee and he was baptised by John in the Jordan. ¹⁰And immediately as Jesus was coming up out of the water, he saw the heavens being split apart²⁵⁰ and the Breath *of God* descending down on him like a dove. ¹¹And a voice came out of the heavens saying, "You are my beloved Son, and I am very pleased with you."

Satan tests Jesus

(Matthew 4:1–11, Luke 4:1–13)

¹²At once the Breath led *Jesus* out into the desert.²⁵¹ ¹³He was in the desert for forty days where Satan was trying to tempt him. *Jesus* was with the wild animals²⁵² and the angels ministered to him.

---

249 Cf. Lev. 11:22. Locusts were the only insects that were kosher according to the Jewish Law.
250 Mark wants his readers to see that a new exodus event is happening and that Jesus is leading a people out of slavery once again (Heiser, Michael S, *The Unseen Realm* (2015), pp. 273–274). Cf. Jude 5.
251 I.e. the Judean desert east of Jerusalem.
252 Animals such as hyenas, jackals, foxes and gazelles.

Jesus begins preaching the good news
(Matthew 4:12–17, Luke 4:14–15)

¹⁴After John was put in prison, Jesus went to the Galilee *district* preaching the good news of God. ¹⁵Jesus said, "The time has come! God's reign is close. Turn away from your sins and believe the good news."

Jesus calls his first four followers
(Matthew 4:17–22, Luke 5:1–11)

¹⁶As Jesus was walking beside the Sea of Galilee, he saw Simon and his brother Andrew casting a net into the lake for they were fishermen. ¹⁷Jesus said to them, "Come and follow me and I will make you fishers of men." ¹⁸Immediately they left their nets and followed him.

¹⁹When Jesus had gone a little further, he saw James son of Zebedee and his brother John in a boat fixing up their nets. ²⁰Straight away he called them and they left their father Zebedee in the boat with the hired men and they followed *Jesus*.

Jesus cast out an evil spirit
(Luke 4:31–37)

²¹*Jesus and his followers* entered into *the city of* Capernaum and when it was the Sabbath,²⁵³ Jesus went into the synagogue and began to teach. ²²The people were amazed at his teaching because he taught them as one who had authority, not as the scribes.²⁵⁴ ²³Immediately a man in the synagogue who was possessed by an evil spirit cried out, ²⁴"What do you want with us, Jesus the Nazarene? Have you come to destroy us? I know who you are—the Holy One of God!"

²⁵However Jesus rebuked him saying, "Be quiet! Come out of him!" ²⁶The evil spirit threw the man into convulsions and came out of the man with a loud shriek.

²⁷The people were all so amazed that they began asking each other, "What just happened? Is this some kind of new authoritative teaching? He even gives orders to evil spirits and they obey him." ²⁸News about Jesus went viral into all the surrounding district of Galilee.

Jesus heals Simon Peter's mother-in-law
(Matthew 8:14–15, Luke 4:38–39)

²⁹As soon as *Jesus and his followers* left the synagogue, they went with James and John to the home of Simon and Andrew. ³⁰Simon's mother-in-law was in bed

---

253   I.e. the weekly Sabbath day—Saturday.
254   I.e. the teachers of the Jewish Law.

with a fever and they told Jesus about her. ³¹So he went to her, took her hand and helped her up. The fever left her and she began to attend to their needs.

Jesus helps many people
(Matthew 8:16–17, Luke 4:40–41)

³²That evening after sunset the people brought to Jesus all the sick and demon-possessed. ³³The whole city gathered at the door ³⁴and Jesus healed many who had various diseases. He also cast out many demons but he would not let the demons speak because they knew who he was.

Jesus prays in a quiet and deserted place
(Luke 4:42–44)

³⁵Very early the next morning while it was still dark, Jesus got up, left the house and went off to a quiet and deserted place where he prayed. ³⁶Simon and those with him went to look for him. ³⁷And when they found him they said, "Everyone is looking for you."

³⁸And Jesus said, "Let's go somewhere else—to the neighbouring villages—so I can preach there also, for that is the purpose for which I have come." ³⁹So Jesus travelled throughout the whole region of Galilee, preaching in their synagogues and casting out demons.

Jesus heals a man with leprosy
(Matthew 8:1–4, Luke 5:12–16)

⁴⁰A man with leprosy came to *Jesus* and begged him on his knees saying, "If you are willing, you can cleanse me." ⁴¹Jesus was filled with compassion for the man and reached out his hand and touched the man and said to him, "I am willing. Be cleansed!" ⁴²Immediately the leprosy left him and he was cured.

⁴³Jesus sent him on his way with a stern warning, ⁴⁴"You are not to tell anyone about this. But go, show yourself to the priest[255] and offer the sacrifices that Moses commanded for your cleansing as a testimony to them." ⁴⁵But the man went and spoke openly about it, spreading the word. Consequently, Jesus could no longer enter a city openly but stayed outside in quiet and deserted places. Yet the people still came to him from everywhere.

Jesus heals a paralysed man
(Matthew 9:1–8, Luke 5:17–26)

2 ¹A few days later, when *Jesus* returned to Capernaum, the people heard that

---

[255] Cf. Lev. 14:2–32. This was probably the serving priest in Jerusalem that the man had to report to.

he had come home. ²There were so many who had gathered in his house that there was no room left, not even outside the door. As Jesus was preaching the word to them, ³some men arrived bringing a paralysed man to him. There were four men carrying him. ⁴But since they could not get the man to Jesus because of the crowd, they made an opening in the roof above Jesus. After digging through the roof, they lowered the mattress that the paralysed man was lying on. ⁵And when Jesus saw their faith, he said to the paralysed man, "Son, your sins are forgiven."

⁶Now there were some scribes who were sitting there thinking to themselves, ⁷"Why does this man say such things? He's blaspheming! Who can forgive sins but God alone?"

⁸And immediately Jesus knew within himself that this was what they were thinking in their hearts, and he said to them, "Why are you thinking these things in your hearts? ⁹Which is easier? Is it easier to say to the paralysed man, 'Your sins are forgiven,' or to say, 'Get up, take your mattress and walk?' ¹⁰But so that you may know that the Son of Man has authority on earth to forgive sins, ¹¹I say to the paralysed man, 'Get up, take your mattress and go home.'" ¹²The man got up, took his mat and walked out in full view of them all. Everyone was amazed and they praised God saying, "We have never seen anything like this!"

Jesus calls Levi (Matthew) to follow him
(Matthew 9:9–13, Luke 5:27–32)

¹³Jesus went back to the lake again and walked along the shoreline. A large crowd gathered and he began teaching them. ¹⁴And as he was walking along, he saw Levi, the son of Alphaeus sitting at the tax collector's booth. Jesus said to him, "Follow me." Levi got up and followed him.

¹⁵Later it came about that Jesus reclined in the house of Levi. There with many tax collectors and sinners²⁵⁶ reclining together at the table *eating* with Jesus and his followers. ¹⁶And when the scribes, who were Pharisees, saw him eating with the sinners and tax collectors, they asked his followers, "Why does he eat with tax collectors and sinners?

¹⁷And on hearing this, Jesus said to them, "It is not the healthy who need a doctor, but the sick. I have not come to call righteous *people*, but outcasts."

Jesus is asked about fasting
(Matthew 9:14–17, Luke 5:33–39)

¹⁸On one occasion John's disciples and the Pharisees were fasting when

---

256   Sinners were Jewish people in general who did not carefully observe the Law in the Pharisee way especially dietary laws.

some people came and asked Jesus, "Why is it that the followers of John and the Pharisees are fasting yet yours are not?"

[19]Jesus said to them, "How can the attendants of the bridegroom fast while he is with them? As long as they are with the groom they cannot fast. [20]But the days will come when the bridegroom will be taken from them, and on that day they will fast.

[21]"No one sews a patch of unshrunk cloth[257] on an old garment otherwise the new patch will pull away from the old resulting in a worse tear. [22]And no one puts new wine into old wineskins otherwise the wine will tear the wineskins and both the wine and the wineskins will be ruined. No, new wine is put into new wineskins."

Jesus is master of the Sabbath

(Matthew 12:1–8, Luke 6:1–5)

[23]One Sabbath Day Jesus was passing through the grain fields and as his followers were walking along, they began to pick some of the heads of wheat. [24]The Pharisees said to him, "Look, why are they doing what is unlawful on the Sabbath?"

[25]Jesus said to them, "Have you never read what David did when he and his men were hungry and in need? [26]In the days of Abiathar the high priest, he entered the house of God and ate the consecrated bread. Normally it is only permitted for the priests to eat. Furthermore he also gave some to his men."

[27]Then Jesus said to them, "The Sabbath was made for the man,[258] not the man for the Sabbath.[259] [28]So the Son of Man is master even of the Sabbath."

Jesus heals a man on the Sabbath

(Matthew 12:9–14, Luke 6:6–11)

3 [1]Another time *Jesus* went into the synagogue where there was a man with a withered hand. [2]Some of the Pharisees were looking for a reason to accuse Jesus, so they watched him closely to see if he would heal the man on the Sabbath. [3]Jesus said to the man with the withered hand, "Stand up where everybody can see you."

[4]Then he asked them, "Which is permitted on the Sabbath? To do good or to do evil, to save life or to kill?" But they were silent.

[5]Jesus looked around at them in anger and he was deeply grieved at their

---

257 I.e. a new piece of cloth.
258 I.e. Adam in the beginning.
259 God made the Sabbath as a day of rest for the good of man; man was not made to serve the Sabbath.

stubborn hearts. He said to the man, "Stretch out your hand." He stretched it out and his hand was completely restored. ⁶The Pharisees left and began to plot with the Herodians[260] how they might kill Jesus.

Large crowds followed Jesus
(Luke 6:17–19)

⁷Jesus withdrew with his followers to the lake and a large crowd followed him. They came from Galilee and Judea. ⁸When they heard all the things Jesus was doing, many people came to him from Judea, Jerusalem, Idumea, from beyond the Jordan and from around Tyre and Sidon.[261] ⁹Jesus told his followers to have a small boat ready for him because of the crowds so that they wouldn't press around him. ¹⁰*They got a boat ready* because he had healed many people, and those with diseases kept pushing their way forward in order to touch him. ¹¹Whenever the evil spirits saw him, they fell down before him and cried out, "You are the Son of God." ¹²And he gave them strict orders not to reveal who he was.

Jesus chooses the Twelve Apostles
(Matthew 10:1–4, Luke 6:12–16)

¹³Jesus went up a mountain and called to himself the men that he wanted and they came to him. ¹⁴He appointed twelve *men* and named them apostles that they might accompany him and that he might send them to preach ¹⁵and have the authority to cast out demons. ¹⁶These are the twelve men Jesus appointed: Simon (whom he gave the name Peter), ¹⁷James, the son of Zebedee and his brother John (to them he gave the name Boanerges which means "Men of Thunder"), ¹⁸Andrew, Philip, Bartholomew, Matthew, Thomas, James son of Alphaeus, Thaddaeus, Simon the Zealot ¹⁹and Judas Iscariot, who betrayed him.

The Pharisees accuse Jesus of working with Beelzebul
(Matthew 12:24–32, Luke 11:14–23, 12:10)

²⁰Then Jesus entered a house and again a crowd gathered so that he and his followers were not even able to eat. ²¹And having heard this, his family went to take charge of him and they said, "He is out of his mind."

²²And some of the scribes having come down from Jerusalem said, "He is possessed by Beelzebul! By the prince of demons he is casting out demons."

²³So Jesus called them and spoke to them in parables: "How can Satan cast

---

260   A Jewish political group that supported King Herod as ruler who was subservient to Rome.
261   Tyre and Sidon are located in modern-day Lebanon on the coast.

out Satan? ²⁴If a realm is divided against itself, that realm will fall apart. ²⁵If a family is divided against itself, that family will break up. ²⁶And if Satan opposes himself and is divided, he cannot stand – his end has come.

²⁷"No one can enter a strong man's house and take away his possessions unless he first ties up the strong man. Then he can rob his house.

²⁸"I am telling you the truth, all the sins and blasphemous things that men say will be forgiven them. ²⁹But whoever blasphemes against the Holy Breath will never be forgiven. He is guilty of an eternal sin." ³⁰Jesus said this because they were saying that he had an evil spirit.[262]

Jesus' mother and brothers come to see him
(Matthew 12:46–50, Luke 8:19–21)

³¹Then Jesus' mother and brothers arrived. They were standing outside and they sent someone in to call him. ³²A crowd was sitting around him and they told him, "Look, your mother and brothers are outside looking for you."

³³Jesus answered them, "Who is my mother and who are my brothers?" ³⁴And having looked around at those seated around him in a circle he said, "Look! Here are my mother and my brothers! ³⁵Whoever does God's will is my brother and sister and mother."

The parable of the sower
(Matthew 13:1–9, Luke 8:4–8)

4 ¹Again Jesus began to teach beside the lake and a large crowd gathered around him. It was so large that he hopped into a boat and sat in it out on the lake while the people stood on the shore. ²He was teaching them many things and talking to them in parables he said,

³"Listen. A farmer went out to sow seed that he had. ⁴As he was scattering the seed, some of it fell on the path and the birds came and ate it up. ⁵Some fell on rocky ground where there was not much soil. It sprang up quickly because the soil was shallow. ⁶But when the sun came up, the plants were scorched and they withered because they had no root. ⁷Other seed fell among the thorn bushes which grew up and choked the plants so that they did not bear grain. ⁸And still other seed fell on good soil. It came up, grew and produced a crop which multiplied thirty, sixty and even one hundred times."

⁹Then Jesus said, "He who has ears to hear, let him pay attention."

---

262   Cf. Matt. 12:31 footnote.

The parable of the sower explained
(Matthew 13:18–23, Luke 8:9–15)

¹⁰When Jesus was alone, the twelve and the others around him asked him about the parables. ¹¹He told them, "The mystery about God's coming realm has been given to you. But to those on the outside everything is said in parables ¹²so that,

> "'they may look and look but never really perceive.
> They may be hearing but never understand.
> If they did, they would turn and be forgiven.'"

Isaiah 6:9–10

¹³Then *Jesus* said to them, "Don't you understand this parable? How then will you ever understand any parable? ¹⁴The farmer sows the word. ¹⁵Some *people* are the ones on the path where the word is sown. When they hear it, immediately Satan comes and takes away the word that was sown in them. ¹⁶Some others are the ones on the rocky ground who hear the word and immediately receive it with joy. ¹⁷They do not have any root so they only last a short time. When trouble or persecution comes because of the word, they immediately become trapped. ¹⁸Still others are the ones among thorns who hear the word ¹⁹but the worries of this life, the seduction of wealth and the desires for other things come in and choke the word making it unfruitful. ²⁰Others are the ones on the good soil who hear the word, accept it, and produce a good crop—thirty, sixty or even one hundred times what was sown."

The lamp under a box
(Luke 8:16–18)

²¹Then *Jesus* said, "Is it normal for a lamp to be put under a box[263] or under the bed? Isn't it put on its stand? ²²For whatever is hidden is meant to be revealed and whatever is concealed is meant to be brought out into the open. ²³If anyone has ears, let him listen."

²⁴He continued, "Pay attention to what you are listening to. The same measure you use *to judge others*, it will be used to *judge* you but even more so. ²⁵Whoever has will be given more, and whoever does not have, even what little he does have will be taken away from him."

The parable of the sprouting seed

²⁶Then *Jesus* said, "This is what God's coming realm is like. A man throws seed on the ground. ²⁷Whatever the man does, night and day, whether he sleeps

---

263 '*modios*' – Technically a container or basket for grain measuring about 8–9 litres.

or gets up, the seed sprouts and grows even though the man does not know how it happens. ²⁸The soil itself produces grain—first the blade of grass, then the head of grain, then the full wheat kernel in the head. ²⁹As soon as the grain is ripe, the man uses the sickle because the *day of* harvest has come.

The parable of the mustard seed
(Matthew 13:31–35, Luke 13:18–19)

³⁰"What should we compare God's coming realm to be like or what parable can we use to describe it? ³¹It is like a mustard seed which is the smallest seed that is planted in the ground. ³²However when it is planted it grows and becomes the largest of all vegetables. It has such large branches that the birds of the air can nest under its shade."

³³Jesus spoke to them with many similar parables as much as they could take. ³⁴He did not say anything to them without using a parable. But when he was alone with his own followers, he explained everything to them.

Jesus calms the storm
(Matthew 8:23–27, Luke 8:22–25)

³⁵That very day when evening came, Jesus said to his followers, "Let's go over to the other side." ³⁶Leaving the crowd behind, they took him just as he was in the boat. There were also other boats with him. ³⁷And a fierce storm came up and the waves broke over the boat so that it was nearly swamped. ³⁸Jesus was in the stern of the boat asleep on a cushion. The followers woke him up and said to him, "Teacher, don't you mind if we drown?" ³⁹Jesus got up, rebuked the wind and said to the waves, "Be still! Quiet!" Then the wind died down and it was completely calm. ⁴⁰He said to them, "Why are you so afraid? Do you still have no faith?" ⁴¹They were terrified and asked each other, "Who is this? Even the wind and the waves obey him!"

Jesus casts out a legion of demons
(Matthew 8:28–34, Luke 8:26–39)

5 ¹Jesus and his followers arrived at the other side of the lake to the region of the Gerasenes. ²When he got out of the boat, immediately a man with an evil spirit came from the tombs to meet him. ³He had been living in the tombs and no one could bind him, even with a chain. ⁴For he had often been bound with shackles and chains but he was able to tear apart the chains and break the shackles. No one was strong enough to subdue him. ⁵And constantly, night and day he was among the tombs and in the mountains crying out and cutting himself with stones.

⁶And when the man *with the evil spirit* saw Jesus from a distance, he ran and bowed down before him. ⁷He screamed in a loud voice, "Jesus, Son of the Most High God. What do you want with me? In God's name, I beg you not to torment me." ⁸He said this because Jesus was saying to him, "Evil spirit, come out of him."

⁹Then Jesus asked him, "What is your name?"

The man answered, "My name is Legion for we are many."²⁶⁴ ¹⁰The man kept begging Jesus again and again not to send them out of the area.

¹¹Now there happened to be a large herd of pigs feeding on a nearby hillside. ¹²The evil spirits begged Jesus, "Send us to the pigs so that we may enter into them." ¹³Jesus permitted them and so the evil spirits left the man and went into the pigs. The herd, being about two thousand in number, rushed down the steep bank into the lake and drowned.

¹⁴Those looking after the pigs ran off and reported it in the city and in the countryside and the people came out to see what had happened. ¹⁵When they came to Jesus, they saw the man who had been possessed by the legion of demons, sitting down, clothed and in his right mind and they were afraid. ¹⁶Those who had witnessed the whole thing told the people what had happened to the demon-possessed man. They told them about the pigs as well. ¹⁷After this, the people began to beg Jesus to leave their region.

¹⁸And as Jesus was getting into the boat to leave, the man who had been demon-possessed begged to go with him. ¹⁹But Jesus did not let him and said, "Go home to your family and tell them about all the things the Lord has done for you and how he has had mercy on you." ²⁰So the man went away and began to proclaim in the Decapolis²⁶⁵ all the things Jesus had done for him and everyone was amazed.

Jesus raises a dead girl back to life and heals a sick woman
(Matthew 9:18–26, Luke 8:40–56)

²¹Having crossed back over to the other side by boat, a large crowd gathered around him while he was still beside the lake. ²²Then one of the synagogue leaders named Jairus came and upon seeing Jesus, fell down at his feet. ²³He begged him greatly saying, "My little daughter is dying. Please come and put your hands on her so that she will be healed and live." ²⁴So Jesus went with him.

A large crowd followed and pressed around him. ²⁵And there was a woman

---

264   The Tenth Roman Legion (Fretensis) was the legion that laid siege to Jerusalem in AD 70. One of the symbols of this legion was the boar. It was garrisoned in Judea in the 20s BC and in Jerusalem from c. AD 73–late third century.

265   The Decapolis was a group of ten cities located southeast of Lake Galilee mostly inhabited by Gentiles therefore having a strong Greek influence. Josephus lists the cities as Scythopolis, Philadelphia, Raphanae, Gadara, Hippos, Dios, Pella, Gerasa, Otopos and Damascus.

who had been suffering incurable haemorrhaging for twelve years. ²⁶She had suffered a great deal and had seen many doctors and had spent all *the money* she had yet instead of getting better the condition continued to worsen. ²⁷When she heard about Jesus, she came up behind him in the crowd and touched his coat ²⁸for she was saying to herself, "If I can just touch his clothes I will be healed." ²⁹Immediately the woman's bleeding stopped and she felt in her body that she had been cured of her disease.

³⁰Straight away Jesus realised that power had gone out of him. He turned around in the crowd and asked, "Who touched my clothes?"

³¹His followers said to him, "How can you ask, 'Who touched me?' when there are so many people crowding around you?"

³²But Jesus kept looking around to see who had done it. ³³The woman, trembling with fear and having realised what had happened to her, came and fell at his feet and told him the whole truth. ³⁴He said to her, "Daughter, your faith has healed you. Go in peace. Your suffering is over."

³⁵While Jesus was still speaking, some men came from the house of Jairus, the synagogue leader, and said to Jairus, "Your daughter is dead. Don't bother the teacher any further."

³⁶However Jesus overheard what they had said and said to the synagogue leader, "Don't be afraid, just believe."

³⁷Jesus did not let anyone follow him except Peter, James and his brother John. ³⁸When they arrived at the house of Jairus the synagogue leader, Jesus saw a commotion. There were people crying and wailing loudly. ³⁹He entered the house and said to them, "Why are you upset and crying? The child is not dead—she is sleeping."

⁴⁰However they were laughing at him. After he had expelled them all from the house, he took the child's father and mother and the followers present with him and they went into the room where the child was lying down. ⁴¹Jesus took the girl by the hand and said to her, "Talitha koum!" which means when translated, "Little girl, I say to you, get up!" ⁴²Immediately the girl stood up and walked around. (She was twelve years old.) When this happened, they were completely astonished. ⁴³He gave strict orders telling them not to let anyone know about this and he told them to give her something to eat.

A prophet has no honour in his hometown
(Matthew 13:53–58, Luke 4:16–30)

6 ¹Jesus departed there and went to his hometown²⁶⁶ and his followers went

---
266 I.e. Nazareth.

with him. ²Then on the Sabbath, he began to teach in the synagogue and many who were listening were amazed. They said, "Where did this man learn these things? What is this wisdom that has been given to him? How does he perform such miracles? ³Isn't he the carpenter, the son of Mary and the brother of James, Joseph, Judas and Simon? Aren't his sisters here with us now?" And they took offense at him.

⁴Jesus said to them, "Only in his hometown, among his relatives and in his own house is a prophet without honour." ⁵And he was not able to do any miracles there, except lay his hands on a few sick people and heal them. ⁶Jesus was very surprised because of their unbelief.

Jesus sends out the Twelve
(Matthew 10:5-15, Luke 9:1-6)

Then Jesus went around from village to village teaching. ⁷And he called the Twelve to himself and he sent them out two by two and gave them authority over evil spirits. ⁸He instructed them as follows: "You must not take anything with you on the road except a hiking pole—no bread, no bag, and no money on your person. ⁹You can wear sandals but do not take an extra shirt. ¹⁰And whenever you enter a house, stay there until you leave that city. ¹¹If any place does not welcome you or listen to what you have to say, shake the dust off of your feet when you leave as a testimony against them."

¹²And so they left and preached that the people should turn to God. ¹³They cast out many demons and anointed many sick people with *olive* oil and healed them.

John the Baptist is beheaded[267]
(Matthew 14:1-12, Luke 3:19-20, 9:7-9)

¹⁴Now King Herod[268] heard about all these things for Jesus' name had become well known. Some were saying, "John the Baptist has been raised from the dead and that is why miraculous powers are at work in him."

¹⁵Others were saying, "He is Elijah."

And still others were saying, "He is a prophet like one of the prophets of long ago."

¹⁶But when Herod heard this he said, "John, the man I beheaded, has been raised *from the dead!*"

---

267 According to the historian Josephus, John was imprisoned and finally beheaded at Machaerus, a hilltop palace and desert fortress in the region of Perea, on the eastern side of the Dead Sea.
268 This was Herod Antipas, tetrarch of Galilee and Perea, son of King Herod the Great.

[17]For Herod himself had ordered to have John arrested. He had him bound and put in prison. He did this because of Herodias, his brother Philip's wife, whom he had married. [18]For John had kept saying to Herod, "It isn't right for you to have your brother's wife." [19]Consequently Herodias had held a grudge against John and wanted to kill him. But she was not able to [20]because Herod feared John and was protecting him. Herod knew that John was a righteous and holy man and he was happy to listen to him, even though it disturbed him at what he was hearing.

[21]Then finally a suitable day came. It was Herod's birthday and so he gave a banquet for his important government officials, the top military commanders and the who's who of Galilee. [22]When Herodias' daughter came in and danced, she pleased Herod and his dinner guests.

The king said to the girl, "Ask me for anything you want and I'll give it to you." [23]He promised her with an oath saying, "Whatever you ask I will give it to you, up to half my kingdom."

[24]So she went out and asked her mother, "What shall I ask for?"

Her mother answered, "The head of John the Baptist."

[25]Immediately the girl hurried back in to the king and made her request: "I want you to give to me right now the head of John the Baptist on a platter."

[26]King Herod was greatly distressed but because of the oaths and his dinner guests present, he did not want to refuse her. [27]So immediately he sent an executioner with orders to bring John's head. The man went and beheaded John in the prison [28]and brought back his head on a platter. He presented it to the girl and she gave it to her mother. [29]When John's followers heard this, they came and took his body and laid it in a tomb.

Jesus feeds five thousand men
(Matthew 14:13–21, Luke 9:10–17, John 6:1–13)

[30]The apostles gathered around Jesus and reported to him all they had done and taught. [31]There were so many people who were coming and going that Jesus and his followers did not even have a chance to eat. So he said to them, "Let's go somewhere quiet where we can get some rest for a while."

[32]So they departed by boat and went to an uninhabited place. [33]But many who saw them leaving recognised them and ran on foot from all the cities and got there ahead of them. [34]And when Jesus got out of the boat and saw a large crowd, he had compassion for them because they were like sheep without a shepherd. So he began teaching them many things.

[35]It was getting late in the day so his followers came to him and said, "This

is a remote place and it's already getting very late. ³⁶Send them away so that they can go to the surrounding farms and villages that they may buy something to eat."

³⁷Jesus answered them and said, "You men give them something to eat!"

They said to him, "Do you mean for us to go and spend 200 denarii[269] on loaves of bread[270] to feed them?"

³⁸Jesus asked them, "How many loaves do you have? Go and check it out." When they found out they told him they had five loaves and two fish.

³⁹Then Jesus directed them to have all the people sit down in groups on the green grass. ⁴⁰So the people sat down in groups of hundreds and fifties. ⁴¹Jesus took the five loaves and the two fish and looking up to heaven, he gave thanks and broke the loaves. Then he gave them to his followers in order that they could place them before the people. He also divided the two fish among them all. ⁴²And everyone ate and were satisfied. ⁴³*Jesus' followers* carried away twelve baskets full of broken pieces of bread and fish. ⁴⁴The number of men who had eaten was five thousand.

Jesus walks on the water
(Matthew 14:22–23, John 6:16–21)

⁴⁵Immediately Jesus made his followers get into the boat and go on ahead of him to Bethsaida on the other side of the lake while he dismissed the crowd. ⁴⁶After leaving them, he went to the mountain to pray. ⁴⁷When evening came, the boat was in the middle of the lake while *Jesus* was alone on the land. ⁴⁸Jesus saw them straining at rowing because the wind was against them. Just before sunrise (after 3 am) he went out to them, walking on the lake. He was wanting to pass them by ⁴⁹but when they saw him walking on the lake, they thought he was a ghost. They cried out ⁵⁰because they all saw him and were terrified.

Immediately he spoke to them saying, "Take courage! It's me. Don't be scared." ⁵¹Then he climbed into the boat with them and the wind died down. They were completely amazed ⁵²because they had not really understood about the loaves. Their hearts were hard.

Jesus heals the sick at Gennesaret
(Matthew 14:34–36)

⁵³And when Jesus and his followers had crossed over, they landed at Gennesaret and anchored there. ⁵⁴As soon as they got out of the boat, the

---

269   One denarius silver coin is worth about one day's wage at the time so 200 denarii would be about eight months' wages.
270   Small round loaves more like our modern-day buns or rolls.

people recognised Jesus. ⁵⁵They ran throughout the whole region and carried the sick on mattresses to wherever they heard he was. ⁵⁶And everywhere Jesus went, to villages, cities, or countryside, the people would place the sick in the marketplaces and they begged him to let the sick at least touch the edge of his coat. And everyone who touched him were being healed.

The traditional teaching of the Jewish elders
(Matthew 15:1–9)

7 ¹The Pharisees and some of the scribes who had come from Jerusalem gathered around Jesus and ²saw some of his followers eating food with hands that were 'unclean'. They hadn't washed their hands. ³(The Pharisees and all the Judeans do not eat unless they have washed their hands in the prescribed manner according to the traditions of the elders. ⁴Also they do not eat anything from the market unless they wash it first. And they observe many other traditions such as the washing of cups, pots, copper vessels and couches used for dining.)

⁵And so the Pharisees and scribes asked Jesus, "Why do your followers eat food with 'unclean' hands rather than living according to the traditions of the elders?"

⁶Jesus replied, "Isaiah was right when he prophesied about you hypocrites! As it has been written,

"'These people honour me with their lips but their hearts are far from me.
⁷They worship me in vain and their teachings are merely rules taught by men.'

Isaiah 29:13

⁸You have rejected the commands of God and are holding onto the traditions of men."

⁹And he spoke to them saying, "You certainly have a way of setting aside the commands of God in order to observe your own traditions! ¹⁰For Moses said, 'Honour your father and your mother,' and 'Anyone who curses his father or mother must be put to death.' ¹¹But you all teach that if someone has something that could help his father or mother but then says, 'This is Corban' (meaning a gift devoted to God) ¹²then they are excused from helping their father or mother. ¹³In this way you are nullifying the word of God by your tradition that you have handed down. You do many things like that."

All food is acceptable and 'clean'
(Matthew 15:10–20)

¹⁴Jesus summoned the crowd again and said to them, "Listen to me everyone, and understand this: ¹⁵Nothing that goes into a man's *stomach* from the outside can make him 'unclean'. Rather, it is what comes out of a man's mouth *in speech and actions* that makes him 'unclean'. [¹⁶If anyone has ears to hear, let him listen."][271]

¹⁷And when *Jesus* left the crowd and entered the house, his followers asked him about this parable. ¹⁸He asked them, "Do you not understand? Can't you see that nothing that enters a man from the outside can make him 'unclean' as such? ¹⁹For it doesn't go into his heart but into his stomach and then out of his body." (In saying this, Jesus was declaring all foods 'clean.')

²⁰*Jesus continued on* by saying, "Only the things that come out of the man makes him 'unclean'. ²¹For from within, out of the heart of the man, comes evil thoughts, sexual immorality, theft, murder, adultery, ²²greed, malice, deceit, shameless lust, jealousy, slander, arrogance and foolishness. ²³All these evil things come from within and makes the man 'unclean.'"

The faith of a Syrophoenician woman
(Matthew 15:21–28)

²⁴Jesus left there and went to the region *close to the cities* of Tyre and Sidon. He entered a house there and did not want anyone to know it but he was not able to escape notice. ²⁵Immediately, having heard about him, a woman whose little daughter was possessed by an evil spirit came and fell down at his feet. ²⁶The woman was Greek, born in Syrian Phoenicia.[272] She kept asking Jesus to cast the demon out of her daughter.

²⁷And he said to her, "Allow the children to eat all they want first for it is not right to take the children's bread and throw it to the dogs."

²⁸But she answered him saying, "Lord, even the dogs under the table eat the children's crumbs."

²⁹Then he said to her, "Because of your answer, go! The demon has left your daughter."

³⁰She returned home and found her child lying on the bed and the demon was gone.

Jesus healed a deaf man who could hardly speak

³¹Again, having left the coastal regions of Tyre, *Jesus* came through Sidon

---

271   Verse 16 is omitted in most English translations but included in the KJV.
272   She was a Phoenician from the Levant as opposed to the Phoenicians of North Africa.

down to the Sea of Galilee and into the regions of the Decapolis. ³²There were some people who brought a deaf man to him there who had great difficulty in speaking. They begged *Jesus* to place his hand on the man.

³³After *Jesus* took him aside away from the crowd, he put his fingers into the man's ears. Then he spat into his hands and touched the man's tongue. ³⁴Jesus looked up to heaven and with a deep sigh said to the man, "Ephphatha," which means, "Open up!" ³⁵Immediately, the man's ears were opened, his tongue was loosened and he began to speak normally.

³⁶*Jesus* ordered them not to tell anyone. But the more he did so, the more they kept talking about it. ³⁷The people were amazed beyond all measure saying, "He has done everything well. He even makes the deaf hear and the non-verbal ones speak."

Jesus feeds four thousand people
(Matthew 15:32–39)

8 ¹In those days another large crowd gathered. Since they had nothing to eat, Jesus called his followers and said to them, ²"I feel sorry for these people because they have been with me for three days and they do not have anything to eat. ³If I send them away hungry, they will faint from exhaustion on the way home, because some of them have come a long way."

⁴His followers answered him, "Where in this deserted place will anyone get enough bread to feed them?"

⁵Jesus asked them, "How many loaves do you have?"

"Seven," they answered.

⁶Jesus ordered the crowd to sit down on the ground and took the seven loaves. Having given thanks, he broke them and gave them to his followers to give out. And so they served the crowd. ⁷They had a few small fish and having given thanks for them, he told them to serve out the fish also. ⁸The people ate and were satisfied and they picked up seven basketfuls of broken pieces left over. ⁹There were approximately four thousand people present.

Afterwards having sent them all away, ¹⁰*Jesus* got into the boat with his followers and went to the region of Dalmanutha.

The Pharisees ask for a sign
(Matthew 16:1–4)

¹¹The Pharisees came and began to argue with *Jesus*. They wanted him to produce a sign from heaven—they were testing him. ¹²And with a great sigh he said, "Why does this generation ask for a miraculous sign? I tell you the truth,

no sign will be given to them." ¹³Then he left them, got back into the boat and crossed to the other side *of the lake.*

The 'yeast' of the Pharisees and Herod
(Matthew 16:5-12)

¹⁴The followers had forgotten to bring bread except for one loaf that they had with them in the boat. ¹⁵Jesus warned them saying, "Be careful. Watch out for the yeast of the Pharisees and the yeast of Herod."

¹⁶They were arguing amongst themselves saying, "It is because we have no bread."

¹⁷Jesus was aware of the discussion and he asked them, "Why are you saying that you have no bread? Are you not understanding or able to see what I am talking about? Have your hearts become so hardened? ¹⁸You have eyes but you cannot see, you have ears but you cannot hear. Maybe you don't remember? ¹⁹When I broke the five loaves for the five thousand, how many basketfuls of pieces did you pick up?"

"Twelve," they replied.

²⁰"And when I broke the seven loaves for the four thousand, how many basketfuls of pieces did you pick up?"

"Seven," they answered.

²¹And he said to them, "You still don't see it do you?"

Jesus heals a blind man at Bethsaida

²²They came to Bethsaida and some people brought a blind man and begged Jesus that he might touch him. ²³Jesus took the man by the hand and led him outside the village. After spitting on his eyes and laying his hands on him, Jesus asked him, "Do you see anything?"

²⁴*The blind man* looked up and said, "I see people and they look like trees walking around."

²⁵Once again *Jesus* placed his hands on the man's eyes and he opened his eyes. His sight was restored and he could see everything clearly. ²⁶*Jesus* sent him home and said to him, "Don't go into the village."

Peter reveals Jesus' identity
(Matthew 16:13-20, Luke 9:18-21)

²⁷Jesus and his followers went on further to the villages around Caesarea Philippi. On the way there he asked them, "Who do people say I am?"

²⁸They replied to him, "Some say John the Baptist, others say Elijah and still others say that you are one of the prophets."

²⁹And he questioned them, "Yes, but what about you? Who do you say I am?" Peter said, "You are the Messiah."

³⁰*Jesus* warned them not to tell anyone about him.

Jesus predicts his death

(Matthew 16:21–28, Luke 9:21–27)

³¹He then began to teach them that the Son of Man must suffer many things and be rejected by the elders, chief priests and scribes and that he must be killed and after three days rise *from the dead*. ³²He spoke plainly about this and Peter took him aside and began to rebuke him.

³³But *Jesus* turned around, looked at his followers and rebuked Peter saying, "Get behind me, Satan! You do not have the things of God in mind, but the things of men."

³⁴And so *Jesus* called together the crowd along with his followers and said, "If anyone wants to be my follower, he must disregard his own ambitions, take up his cross and follow me. ³⁵For whoever tries to keep his own life safe will fail, but whoever pays no attention to his own life's *ambitions* for my sake and for the gospel will find *purpose in* life. ³⁶What benefit is it if a man gains the whole world, yet he loses his soul? ³⁷Or what can a man give in exchange for his soul? ³⁸If anyone is ashamed of me and my words in this adulterous and sinful generation, the Son of Man will be ashamed of him when he comes in his Father's glory with the holy angels."[273]

9 ¹Jesus said to them, "I am telling you the truth, some who are standing here right now will not die before they see the realm of God."

The transfiguration of Jesus

(Matthew 17:1–13, Luke 9:28–36)

²After six days Jesus took Peter, James and John with him and led them up a high mountain, where they were alone. Jesus was transfigured before them. ³His clothes became a brilliant and shining white, whiter than anyone could bleach them. ⁴Then Elijah and Moses appeared before them and they were talking with Jesus.

⁵Peter said to Jesus, "Rabbi, it is so good to be here. Let us put up three shelters—one for you, one for Moses and one for Elijah." ⁶Peter did not know what he was saying because they were terrified.

---

273   The Son of Man is coming with his Father. Cf. Matt. 26:64, Rev. 6:17.

⁷Then a cloud came and surrounded them, and a voice came from the cloud saying, "This is my Son, whom I love. Listen to him!"

⁸Suddenly as they were looking around, they could not see anyone with them except for Jesus.

⁹And as they were coming back down from the mountain, *Jesus* ordered them not to tell anyone what they had seen until the Son of Man had risen from the dead. ¹⁰They kept the matter to themselves, discussing what "rising from the dead" meant. ¹¹They asked *Jesus*, "Why do the scribes say that Elijah must come first?"

¹²*Jesus* answered them saying, "To be sure, Elijah does come first and he restores all things. Yet why then is it written that the Son of Man must suffer much and be rejected? ¹³But I tell you that Elijah has come, and they have done to him everything as they have pleased just as it has been written about him."

Jesus heals a boy with an evil spirit
(Matthew 17:14–21, Luke 9:37–43)

¹⁴When they joined the other followers, they saw a large crowd around them and the scribes arguing with them. ¹⁵As soon as all the people saw Jesus, they were amazed and ran up to greet him. ¹⁶Jesus questioned them, "What are you arguing with them about?"

¹⁷A man in the crowd answered, "Teacher, I brought you my son, who is possessed by an *evil* spirit and he cannot speak. ¹⁸Whenever it overpowers him, it throws him to the ground and he foams at the mouth, gnashes his teeth and becomes rigid. I asked your followers to cast out the spirit but they were not able to."

¹⁹Jesus answered saying, "O unbelieving generation, how long do I have to stay with you? How long do I have to put up with you? Bring him to me."

²⁰So they brought him and when the *evil* spirit saw Jesus, it immediately threw the boy into a convulsion. He fell to the ground and rolled around, foaming at the mouth.

²¹Jesus asked the boy's father, "How long has he been like this?"

"From childhood," the father answered. ²²"It has often thrown him into the fire or water to try and kill him. But if you can do anything, please help us and take pity on us."

²³Jesus said, "Why do you say, 'If you can?' All things are possible for the one who believes."

²⁴Immediately the boy's father cried out, and with tears he said, "Lord, I believe, help me overcome my unbelief!"

[25]And Jesus, having seen that a crowd was running to the scene, he rebuked the evil spirit saying, "Spirit that is causing the boy to be non-verbal and deaf, I order you to come out of him and never enter him again."

[26]The spirit made a loud shriek, threw the boy into a violent convulsion and came out. The boy looked so much like a corpse that many were saying that he was dead. [27]But Jesus took him by the hand and lifted him to his feet and he stood up.

[28]After Jesus had gone into a house, his followers asked him privately, "Why couldn't we cast it out?" [29]Jesus replied, "This kind can only come out by prayer and nothing else."

Jesus predicts his death for a second time
(Matthew 17:22–23, Luke 9:43–45)

[30]Jesus and his followers left that place and passed through Galilee. He did not want anyone to know where they were [31]because he was teaching his followers. He said to them, "The Son of Man is going to be betrayed into the hands of men. They will kill him and after three days he will rise." [32]But they did not understand what he meant and were too afraid to ask.

Who is the greatest?
(Matthew 18:1–5, Luke 9:46–48)

[33]They came to *the village of* Capernaum and when they were in the house Jesus asked his followers, "What were you all arguing about on the road?" [34]But they kept silent because they had been arguing about who was the greatest follower. [35]Sitting down, Jesus called the Twelve and said to them, "He who wants to be first, he must be the very last and the servant of all."

[36]He took a little child and had him stand among them. Taking him in his arms, he said to them, [37]"Whoever welcomes one of these little children in my name welcomes me. And whoever welcomes me does not welcome me only but also the one who sent me here."

He who is not against us is for us
(Luke 9:49–50)

[38]John said to Jesus, "Teacher, we saw a man cast out demons in your name and we told him to stop because he was not a follower like us."

[39]"Do not try to stop him," Jesus said. "No one who does a miracle in my name can in the next breath say anything bad about me, [40]for whoever is not

against us is for us. ⁴¹I tell you the truth, anyone who gives you a cup of water in my name because you belong to Christ will certainly not lose his reward."

The seriousness of sin
(Matthew 18:6–9, Luke 17:1–2)

⁴²Jesus continued by saying, "And if anyone causes one of these little children who believe in me to sin, it would be better for him to be thrown into the sea with a large millstone tied around his neck.²⁷⁴ ⁴³If your hand causes you to sin, cut it off. It is better for you to enter life maimed than with two hands to go into hell, where the fire never goes out. [⁴⁴This place is where the worms²⁷⁵ do not die and the fire is not put out.]²⁷⁶ ⁴⁵And if your foot causes you to sin, cut it off. It is better for you to enter life crippled than to have two feet and be thrown into hell. [⁴⁶This place is where the worms do not die and the fire is not put out.]²⁷⁷ ⁴⁷And if your eye causes you to sin, pluck it out. It is better for you to enter God's realm with one eye than to have two eyes and be thrown into hell. ⁴⁸This place is where

> "'the worms do not die and the fire is not put out.'
>
> Isaiah 66:24

⁴⁹For everyone will be salted with fire.

⁵⁰"Salt is good, but if it loses its saltiness, how can you make it salty again? Have salt in yourselves and be at peace with each other."

Jesus teaches about divorce
(Matthew 19:1–12, Luke 16:18)

10 ¹From there (*Capernaum*), Jesus left and went into the region of Judea to the other side of the Jordan. Crowds of people came to him again and as he was accustomed to doing, he taught them.

²Then some Pharisees came and tested him by asking, "Does our *Jewish* Law allow a man to divorce his wife?"

³Jesus answered saying, "What did Moses command you?"

⁴They said, "Moses permitted a man to write a certificate of divorce and send her away."

---

274   The millstone illustration is highly appropriate because Capernaum had a secondary industry after fishing in making millstones made out of the black volcanic basalt which was common in this area.
275   The reference is to worms that feed on decaying bodies in the original Gehenna (rubbish dump of Jerusalem) is a vivid image of hell being a place of unending torment.
276   This verse is not included in most modern translations.
277   Only KJV includes this verse.

⁵But Jesus replied, "Moses wrote this law only because of the hardness of your hearts. ⁶But from the beginning of creation, 'God made them male and female.'²⁷⁸ ⁷'For this reason a man will leave his father and mother and be adhered²⁷⁹ to his wife, ⁸and the two will become one flesh.'²⁸⁰ So they are no longer two, but one. ⁹Therefore what God has joined together, let man not separate."

¹⁰When they had returned to the house, Jesus' *main* followers asked him about this again. ¹¹He answered saying, "Anyone who divorces his wife and marries another woman commits adultery against her. ¹²And if she divorces her husband and marries another man, she commits adultery."

Jesus blesses the little children
(Matthew 19:13–15, Luke 18:15–17)

¹³And it so happened that people were bringing little children to Jesus to have him touch them, but his followers strongly disapproved of them. ¹⁴When Jesus saw this, he became angry and he said to them, "Permit the little children to come to me and do not stop them for God will reign over people such as these. ¹⁵I tell you the truth, anyone who does not welcome God's reign like a little child will by no means enter into it." ¹⁶Jesus took the children in his arms, put his hands on them and blessed them.

The rich young man
(Matthew 19:16–30, Luke 18:18–30)

¹⁷As Jesus set out on the road, a man ran up to him and knelt before him. He asked him, "Good teacher, what must I do to inherit eternal life?"

¹⁸Jesus answered, "Why do you call me good? No one is good except God alone. ¹⁹You know the commandments: 'Do not murder; do not commit adultery; do not steal; do not bear false witness; do not cheat; honour your father and mother.'"

²⁰"Teacher, all these commandments I have kept since I was young," he declared.

²¹Jesus looked at him with love and said, "There is one thing that you lack. Go and sell everything that you own and give it to the poor and you will have treasure in heaven. Then come and follow me."

²²When the man heard this he was shocked and he left very sad because he was very rich.

---

278 Cf. Gen. 1:27.
279 Literally means 'to glue to'.
280 Cf. Gen. 2:24. Eph. 5:31.

²³Jesus looked around and said to his followers, "It is extremely difficult for the rich to enter the realm of God!"

²⁴His followers were amazed at his words but Jesus said again, "Children, it is extremely difficult to enter the realm of God! ²⁵It is easier for a camel to go through the eye of a needle than for a rich man to enter the realm of God."

²⁶The followers were even more amazed *at Jesus' words* and said to each other, "Who then is able to be saved?"

²⁷Jesus looked at them and said, "With man this is impossible but not with God. All things are possible with God."

²⁸Then Peter spoke up saying, "Hey, we have left everything to follow you!"

²⁹Jesus replied, "I tell you the truth, those who leave their home or brothers or sisters or mother or father or children or the land for me and the gospel ³⁰will receive much more in this present age. They will receive a hundred times more than their homes, brothers, sisters, mothers, children and lands but it will be with persecutions. And in the age to come they will receive eternal life. ³¹But many who are first will be last and the last will be first."

Jesus speaks about his imminent death a third time
(Matthew 20:17–19, Luke 18:31–34)

³²They were on their way up to Jerusalem and Jesus was leading the way. His *main* followers were amazed while those who were coming behind were afraid. Then Jesus took the Twelve aside and told them what was going to happen to him soon. ³³Jesus said to them, "We are going up to Jerusalem and the Son of Man will be betrayed to the chief priests and scribes. They will condemn him to death and will hand him over to the Gentiles ³⁴who will mock him and spit on him, flog him and kill him and after three days he will rise again."

James' and John's unusual request
(Matthew 20:20–28)

³⁵Then James and John, the sons of Zebedee, came to him and said, "There is something that we wish you to do for us."

³⁶"What do you wish me to do for you?" he asked.

³⁷They replied, "Let one of us sit at your right and the other at your left in your glory."

³⁸But Jesus said to them, "You don't know what you are asking. Can you drink the cup I am drinking or be baptised with the baptism *of suffering and death* that I am being baptised with?"

³⁹"We can," they answered.

Jesus said to them, "You indeed will drink the cup I am drinking and be baptised with the baptism I am baptised with ^{40}but to sit at my right or left is not for me to grant but it is for the ones it has been prepared for."

^{41}When the ten other followers heard about this they became angry with James and John. ^{42}And so Jesus called them together and said, "You are aware that those who are seen to be rulers of the Gentiles lord it over them. Their high officials exercise authority over them. ^{43}However it is not the case with you. Instead whoever wants to become great among you must be your servant. ^{44}And whoever wants to be first must be your slave. ^{45}For even the Son of Man did not come to be served, but to serve and to give his life to set many people free *from their sins*."

Jesus heals blind Bartimaeus
(Matthew 20:29–34, Luke 18:35–43)

^{46}Jesus and his followers came to Jericho and as they were leaving with a large crowd with them, a blind man named Bartimaeus (the son of Timaeus), was sitting by the roadside begging. ^{47}When he heard that it was Jesus the Nazarene passing by, he began to shout out, "Jesus, Son of David, have mercy on me!"

^{48}Many of the people strongly disapproved and told him to be quiet, but he shouted even louder, "Son of David, have mercy on me!"

^{49}Jesus stopped and said, "Call him to come."

So they called to the blind man, "Cheer up! Hop up on your feet! He's calling for you." ^{50}So he threw off his coat, hopped to his feet and came to Jesus.

^{51}"What do you want me to do for you?" Jesus asked him.

The blind man said, "Rabbi, I want to see."

^{52}Jesus said to him, "Go, your faith has healed you." Immediately he could see again and he followed Jesus along the road.

Jesus' triumphal entry into Jerusalem
(Matthew 21:1–11, Luke 19:29–40, John 12:12–19)

11 ^{1}As they approached Jerusalem and were coming to *the villages* of Bethphage and Bethany at the Mount of Olives, Jesus sent two of his followers on ahead ^{2}with some instructions, "Go to the village ahead of you and as you enter it, you will find a colt tied there which no one has ever ridden. Untie it and bring it here. ^{3}And if anyone asks you, 'Why are you doing this?' say, 'The Lord needs it and will send it back again at once.'"

^{4}So they went and found a colt outside in the street, tied at a doorway. As they were untying it, ^{5}some bystanders asked, "What are you doing, untying that colt?" ⁶They answered as Jesus had told them to and the people let them go. ⁷When they had brought the colt to Jesus and threw their coats over it, he sat on it. ⁸Many people spread their coats on the road, while others spread leafy branches that they had cut *from trees* in the fields. ⁹And those who were in front *of Jesus* and those behind him were crying out,

"Hosanna!"
"Blessed is he who comes in the name of the Lord."

Psalm 118:26

¹⁰"Blessed is the coming realm of our father David!"
"Hosanna in the highest *heaven*!"

¹¹Jesus entered Jerusalem and went to the temple. He looked around at everything, but since it was already getting late, he went to Bethany with the Twelve.

Jesus curses a fig tree that has no figs
(Matthew 21:18–19)

¹²The next day as they were leaving Bethany, Jesus was hungry. ¹³He saw a fig tree in the distance that had leaves on it so he went to find out if it had any fruit. When he reached it, he found nothing but leaves because it was not yet the season for figs. ¹⁴Then he said to the tree, "No one will eat fruit from you ever again." And his followers heard him.

Jesus enters the temple
(Matthew 21:12–17, Luke 19:45–48, John 2:13–22)

¹⁵When they arrived in Jerusalem, Jesus entered the temple and began forcing out those who were buying and selling there. He overturned the tables of the money changers and the tables of those who were selling doves. ¹⁶He did not allow anyone to carry anything through the temple *courts*. ¹⁷As Jesus was teaching he said to them, "Is it not written in the Scriptures,

"'My house will be called a house of prayer for all nations'?

Isaiah 56:7

But you have made it 'a hideout of robbers.'"

¹⁸The chief priests and the scribes heard this and began to look for a way to kill him. They feared him because the whole crowd was amazed at his teaching.

¹⁹When evening came, they went out of the city.

The fig tree withered
(Matthew 21:20–22)

²⁰The next morning, as they were passing by, they saw the fig tree. It was withered from the roots. ²¹Peter remembered and said to Jesus, "Rabbi, look! The fig tree that you cursed has withered."

²²Jesus answered them saying, "Have faith in God. ²³I tell you the truth, if anyone says to this mountain, 'Get up and throw yourself into the sea,' and does not doubt in his heart but believes that what he says will happen, so it will be done for him. ²⁴For this reason I tell you, whatever you ask for in prayer, believe that you have received it and it will be yours. ²⁵And when you stand, praying, if you hold anything against anyone, forgive him, so that your Father in heaven may forgive you your sins. [²⁶But if you do not forgive, neither will your Father who is in heaven forgive your sins."]²⁸¹

The authority of Jesus is challenged
(Matthew 21:23–27, Luke 20:1–8)

²⁷They arrived again in Jerusalem and while Jesus was walking in the temple, the chief priests, the scribes and the elders came to him *with a question.* ²⁸They asked him, "By what authority are you doing these things? Who gave you this authority?"

²⁹Jesus replied, "I will tell you by what authority I am doing these things if you answer me this one thing. ³⁰John's authority to baptise—did it come from heaven or from men? Answer me!"

³¹They discussed it among themselves and said, "If we say, 'It came from heaven,' then he will ask, 'Then why didn't you believe him?' ³²But if we say, 'It came from men'…" (They were afraid of the people for everyone held that John really was a prophet.) ³³So they answered Jesus, "We don't know."

Jesus said, "Neither will I tell you, then, by what authority I am doing these things."

The parable of the vineyard
(Matthew 21:33–46, Luke 20:9–19)

12 ¹Jesus began to speak to them in parables, "There was a man who planted

---

281   Verse 26 is not in the modern Greek texts.

a vineyard. He put a wall around it, dug a pit for the winepress and built a watchtower. Then he rented out the vineyard to some farmers and left to go on a trip. ²At harvest time he sent a servant to the farmers to collect from them some of the fruit of the vineyard. ³But they grabbed him, beat him and sent him away empty-handed. ⁴Then he sent another servant to them. They struck this man on the head and abused him. ⁵The man sent yet another servant and that one they killed. He sent many others and some of them they beat and others they killed.

⁶"It got to the point that he had only one person left to send—his son, whom he loved. He sent him last of all saying to himself, 'They will respect my son.'

⁷"But the farmers said to one another, 'This is the heir of the property, Come, let us kill him and the inheritance will be ours.' ⁸So they took him and killed him, and threw him out of the vineyard.

⁹"So what then will the owner of the vineyard do? He will come and kill those farmers and give the vineyard to others. ¹⁰Haven't you read the Scripture,

"'The stone the builders rejected has become the cornerstone;
¹¹the Lord has done this and it is amazing'?"

Psalm 118:22-23

¹²Then they looked for a way to arrest him because they knew he had spoken the parable against them. But they were afraid of the crowd so they left him and went away.

A question about who to pay taxes to
(Matthew 22:15-22, Luke 20:20-26)

¹³Some of the Pharisees and Herodians were sent to Jesus to catch him out in his words. ¹⁴They came to him and said, "Teacher, we know that you are truthful and that you are not concerned about what people think. You pay no attention to their status in life but teach the way of God in accordance with the truth. *Therefore, is it right to pay taxes to Caesar or not?* ¹⁵Should we pay or shouldn't we?"

But Jesus could see through their hypocrisy and said to them, "Why are you trying to trap me? Bring me a denarius and let me look at it. ¹⁶They brought him a coin and he asked them, "Whose image and inscription is this on the coin?"

"Caesar's," they said.

¹⁷Then Jesus said to them, "Give to Caesar what is Caesar's and to God what is God's." And they were amazed at him.

The Sadducees test Jesus about the resurrection
(Matthew 22:23–33, Luke 20:27–40)

[18]Then the Sadducees, a group who say that there is no resurrection, came to him with a question saying, [19]"Teacher, Moses wrote for us that if a man's brother dies and leaves a wife but no children, the man must marry the widow and have children for his *dead* brother. [20]Now suppose that there were seven brothers. The first one married and died without leaving any children. [21]The second *brother* married the widow, but he also died leaving no child and likewise with the third one. [22]In fact, none of the seven brothers left any children. Finally, the woman died too. [23]So, at the resurrection whose wife shall she be since the seven were all married to her at some stage."

[24]Jesus replied, "You are so wrong! Do you not know the Scriptures or the power of God? [25]When the dead rise, they will neither marry or be given in marriage for they will be like the angels in heaven. [26]Now concerning the dead—have you not read in the book of Moses about the account of the burning bush? There God said to Moses, 'I am the God of Abraham, the God of Isaac, and the God of Jacob.' [27]He is not the God of the dead, but of the living. You are badly mistaken."

The greatest commandment
(Matthew 22:34–40, Luke 10:25–28)

[28]One of the scribes came and heard the discussion about the resurrection. Noticing that Jesus had given the Sadducees a good answer, he asked Jesus, "Which is the most important commandment out of all of them?"

[29]Jesus answered saying, "The most important one is this, "Hear, O, Israel, the Lord our God , the Lord is one.[282] [30]Love the Lord your God with all your heart and with all your soul and with all your mind and with all your strength.' [31]The second is this, 'Love your neighbour as *much as you love* yourself.' There is no commandment greater than these two."

[32]The scribe said, "Well said teacher! You are right in saying that God is one and there is no other God except him. [33]And to love him with all your heart, with all your understanding and with all your strength, and to love your neighbour as yourself is more important than all the burnt offerings and sacrifices."

[34]Having seen that he had answered wisely, Jesus said to him, "You are very close *in understanding what* the realm of God is all about." And from then on no one dared ask him any more questions.

---

282   This is the start of the Shema prayer. 'Shema' literally means 'hear' and it was repeated twice daily by pious Jews as the essence of their faith. The entire Shema prayer is found in Deut. 6:4.

A question about the Son of David
(Matthew 22:41-46, Luke 20:41-44)

³⁵While Jesus was teaching in the temple, he asked, "Why do the scribes say that the Messiah is the son of David? ³⁶For David himself, speaking by the Holy Breath, said,

> "'The Lord *God* said to my Lord: "Sit at my right hand until I have put your enemies under your feet."' [283]

Psalm 110:1

³⁷David himself calls him 'Lord'. How then can the *Messiah* be his son?" The large crowd listened to him with delight.

Jesus warns against the scribes
(Matthew 23:1-36, Luke 11:37-54, 20:45-47)

The large crowd listened to Jesus gladly ³⁸and as he was teaching he said, "Watch out for the scribes. They like to walk around in long flowing robes and be greeted in the marketplaces. ³⁹They like to have the most important seats in the synagogues and the places of honour at banquets. ⁴⁰They take advantage of widows and rob them of their homes, and then put on a show with their lengthy prayers. These men will receive greater judgment."

The widow's offering to God
(Luke 21:1-4)

⁴¹Jesus was sitting down opposite the place where the offerings were put and he was observing the crowd putting their money into the temple treasury. Many rich people threw in large amounts. ⁴²But there was a poor widow who came and put in two very small copper coins—the equivalent of a penny.[284]

⁴³Jesus called his followers together and said, "I tell you the truth, this poor widow has put more into the treasury than all the others. ⁴⁴They all gave out of their wealth but she gave out of her poverty. She put in everything that she had—all that she had to live on."

---

283   David is calling the Messiah (Christ) "my Lord" in this verse.
284   The lepton was the smallest coin in circulation worth 1/128th of a denarius.

Jesus predicts the coming destruction of the temple in AD 70
(Matthew 24:1–2, Luke 21:5–6)

13 ¹As Jesus was leaving the temple, one of his followers said to him, "Teacher! Look! What massive stones! What magnificent buildings!"

²Jesus replied, "Do you see all these great buildings? Not one stone will be left on another. Every stone will be thrown down."

The Olivet Discourse
(Matthew 24:3–14, Luke 21:7–11)

³Jesus was sitting on the Mount of Olives opposite the temple when Peter, James, John and Andrew asked him privately, ⁴"Tell us, when will these things occur? And what will be the sign that all these things are about to be fulfilled?"

⁵Jesus started by saying, "Watch out that no one deceives you. ⁶Many will come using my name, even admitting by saying, 'I am the *Messiah.*' They will deceive many people in this way.

⁷"And when you hear the news of wars and reports of wars do not be alarmed. Such things must happen, but that is not the end yet. ⁸Nation will rise against nation, and kingdom against kingdom. There will be earthquakes in various places and famines. These events are just the beginning of birth pains.

⁹"You must be on your guard. They will hand you over to the local councils and you will be beaten in the synagogues. You will stand before governors and kings and witness to them because of me. ¹⁰But the gospel must first be preached to all nations. ¹¹So whenever you are arrested and brought to trial, do not worry beforehand about what you will say. Just say whatever is given to you at the time, for it is not you speaking, but the Holy Breath. ¹²Men will betray their own brothers to death and fathers will betray their own children in the same way. Children will rebel against their own parents and have them put to death. ¹³Everyone will hate you because of me, but he who stands firm to the end will be saved.

Surviving the Great Tribulation (the last 1290 days)
(Matthew 24:15–28, Luke 21:12–24)

¹⁴"When you see the 'abomination of desolation' standing where he[285] does not belong, **(Note to the reader: understand what this means)** then those who are in Judea must flee to the mountains. ¹⁵No one who is on the roof of his house must go down or enter his house to get anything to take with him as he leaves.

---

285 In Matt. 24:15 the abomination of desolation is referred to in the neuter gender (a thing) whereas here in the Mark reference the abomination of desolation is referred to in the masculine gender.

¹⁶And the one who is in the field must not go back to get his coat. ¹⁷It will be a disaster for those women who are pregnant and who are breastfeeding in those days. ¹⁸You must pray that this will not take place in the winter.

¹⁹"For in those days there will be tribulation of such a kind that has not happened since the beginning when God created the world, until now. It will never be repeated like that again. ²⁰If the Lord had not decided to cut short the number of those days, no flesh would survive. But for the sake of the chosen, he has shortened them.

²¹"At that time if anyone says to you, 'Look, here is the Messiah!' or, 'Look, there he is!' do not believe it. ²²For false Messiahs and false prophets will appear and perform signs and miracles so if it is possible *for them to do so* they will deceive even the chosen ones. ²³Therefore you must be on your guard. I have told you everything ahead of time.

The coming of the Son of Man after the tribulation
(Matthew 24:29–31, Luke 21:25–28)

²⁴"But in those days, after the tribulation, *the Scriptures say,*

"'the sun will be darkened and there will be no moonlight,
²⁵and the stars will fall from the sky and the heavenly powers will be shaken.'[286]

Isaiah 13:10, 34:4

²⁶"At that time men will see the Son of Man coming on the clouds with great power and glory. ²⁷Then he will send his angels and gather his chosen ones from the four winds, from the ends of the earth to the ends of the heavens.

The parable of the fig tree
(Matthew 24:32–35, Luke 21:29–33)

²⁸"Now I want you to learn the lesson from the parable of the fig tree: When its branches get tender and its leaves come out, you know that summer is near.[287] ²⁹Therefore when you see all these things happening, you know that it is near, right at the door. ³⁰I tell you the truth, this generation will certainly not pass away until all these things have happened. ³¹Heaven and earth will pass away but my words will never pass away.

---

286   James R Edwards says, "In Mark's day (and for some in ours) stars were thought to be heavenly powers that influenced human affairs. At the end of time all such powers, real and imagined, will be obliterated. The picture is one of total cosmic collapse." (Edwards, James R, *The Pillar NT Commentary on Mark* (2002))

287   The fig tree was a picture of unsaved or wicked Israel (Hos. 9:10) whereas the olive tree was a picture of righteous Israel. Here the fig tree (unsaved Israel) will come back to life at the end.

No one knows the day or the hour
(Matthew 24:36–44)

³²"But concerning that day and hour, no one knows about it, neither the angels in heaven nor the Son, only the Father. ³³Watch and pray for you do not know when the time will come. ³⁴It's like when a man goes away on a long trip. He leaves his house and puts his servants in charge, each with his work to do. He commands the doorkeeper to be alert.

³⁵"Therefore you must keep watch because you do not know when the owner of the house will return. It might be in the evening, or at midnight, or when the rooster crows, or at dawn. ³⁶If he comes suddenly, do not let him find you sleeping. ³⁷What I say to you, I say to everyone, 'Watch!'"[288]

A plot against Jesus
(Matthew 26:1–5, Luke 22:1–2, John 11:45–53)

14 ¹Now the Passover and the Feast of Unleavened Bread were only two days away, and the chief priests and the scribes were looking for a way to entrap Jesus so they could arrest and kill him. ²They said, "We must not do it during the Feast otherwise the people might cause a riot."

A woman pours perfume on Jesus' head
(Matthew 26:6–13, John 13:1–17)

³While Jesus was staying in *the village of* Bethany, reclining at the table in the home of a man known as Simon the Leper, a woman came with an alabaster *stone* jar of very expensive perfume made of pure spikenard. She broke the jar and poured the perfume on his head.

⁴Now some of those present were angry saying to each other, "What is the reason for wasting this perfume? ⁵It could have been sold for more than 300 denarii and the money given to the poor."[289] And they were very critical of her.

⁶But Jesus said, "Leave her alone. Why are you bothering her? She has done an appropriate thing on me. ⁷You will always have the poor with you and you can help them anytime you want. But you will not always have me. ⁸She did what she could—she anointed my body with perfume ahead of time to prepare me for my burial. ⁹I tell you the truth, wherever the gospel is preached throughout the world, what she has done will also be told in memory of her."

---

288 Jesus says this to everyone (the whole church), not just the Jews. The Olivet Discourse (Matthew 24, Mark 13, and Luke 21) is addressed to all believers.
289 The denarius (sg) or denarii (pl) was the Roman unit of money. Typically one day's wages would be one denarius so 300 denarii would be equivalent to almost a year's average wage.

Judas promises to betray Jesus

(Matthew 26:14–16, Luke 22:3–6)

¹⁰Then Judas Iscariot, one of the Twelve, went to the chief priests to betray Jesus to them. ¹¹They were very happy to hear what he had to say and they promised to give him silver.²⁹⁰ So he watched for an opportunity whereby he could betray him.

The Last Supper

(Matthew 26:17–25, Luke 22:7–14, 22:21–23)

¹²On the first day of the Feast of Unleavened Bread, when it was the custom to sacrifice the Passover lamb,²⁹¹ Jesus' followers asked him, "Where would you like us to go and make preparations for you to eat the Passover *meal*?"²⁹²

¹³Jesus sent two of his followers telling them, "Go into the city, and a man carrying a jar of water will meet you. Follow him ¹⁴and say to the owner of the house, 'The Teacher says, "Where is my guest room where I may eat the Passover *meal* with my followers?"' ¹⁵He will show you a large upper room, furnished and ready. Make preparations for us there."

¹⁶The two followers left, went into the city and found things just as Jesus had told them. So they prepared the Passover *meal*.

¹⁷When it was evening, Jesus arrived with the Twelve. ¹⁸While they were reclining at the table eating, he said to them, "I tell you the truth, one of you will betray me—one who is eating with me."

¹⁹They became very sad and one by one they said to him, "Surely it's not me is it?"

²⁰Jesus said, "It is one of the Twelve, the one dipping *bread* into the bowl with me. ²¹The Son of Man will go just as it is written about him. But it is disaster for that man who betrays the Son of Man! It would have been better for him if he had not been born."

---

290   I.e. money.
291   James R Edwards says, "Even though Exo. 12:6 stipulated the sacrifice of the Passover lamb on the afternoon of Nisan 14, there is some rabbinic evidence that Passover lambs were regularly sacrificed earlier. Such latitude in sacrifice is hardly surprising given the vast numbers of pilgrims serviced by the temple at Passover." (Edwards, James R, *The Pillar NT Commentary on Mark* (2002)). Josephus reports that at the Passover in AD 70, the year the temple was destroyed, 256,500 lambs were slaughtered in the temple meaning that there would have been 2.7 million people present in Jerusalem (Josephus, *Wars of the Jews*, Book 6, chapter 9, 424–25). Casey, M, *The Date of the Passover Sacrifices and Mark 14:12*, Tyndale Bulletin 48 (1997), pp. 245–47, argues that sacrifice on Nisan 13 was an 'accepted practice'.
292   It appears that Jesus and his followers prepared the Passover lamb one day earlier on Wednesday, Nisan 13 and ate it on Wednesday night, Nisan 14 because of Jesus' desire to eat the Passover meal before he would suffer the next afternoon (Luke 22:15). Cf. Matt. 26:17 and footnote.

Jesus gives thanks for the bread and the cup
(Matthew 26:26–30, Luke 22:14–20, 1 Corinthians 11:23–25)

²²And while they were eating, Jesus took a piece of bread, gave thanks and broke it. He gave it to his followers saying, "Take it—this is my body."

²³Then he took a cup, gave thanks and handed it to them and they all drank from it. ²⁴Jesus said, "This is my blood of the covenant, which is being poured out for many *people*. ²⁵I tell you the truth, I will not drink again of the fruit of the vine until that day when I drink the new *wine* once God has established his reign."

²⁶Then they sang a hymn and went out to the Mount of Olives.

Jesus predicts Peter will deny him that very night
(Matthew 26:31–35, Luke 22:31–34)

²⁷Jesus told his followers, "All of you will stumble *in your faith* for it is written in the Scriptures,

> "'I will strike the shepherd and the sheep of the flock will scatter.'
>
> Zechariah 13:7

²⁸But after I have risen, I will go ahead of you into Galilee."

²⁹However Peter said to him, "Even if everyone stumbles in their faith, I will not."

³⁰Jesus answered saying, "I tell you the truth, before the rooster crows two times tonight, you will deny me three times."

³¹But Peter insisted emphatically saying, "Even if I have to die with you, I will never deny you." And all the other followers said the same thing.

Jesus prays in the garden of Gethsemane
(Matthew 26:36–46, Luke 22:7–14)

³²Jesus and his followers went to a place called Gethsemane. Jesus said to his followers, "Sit here while I go and pray." ³³He took Peter, James and John along with him and he began to be deeply distressed and troubled. ³⁴He told them, "The sadness that I am feeling in my soul is killing me. Stay here and keep watch."

³⁵Jesus went a little further on and he laid face down on the ground and prayed that if possible this hour might pass from him. ³⁶He prayed, "Abba,²⁹³ Father, all things are possible for you. Please take this cup from me. But it is not about what I want, but what you want."

³⁷Then Jesus returned to his followers and found them sleeping. He said to

---

293   "Abba" represents the Aramaic 'aba' meaning 'father'. This bilingual expression was apparently used in prayer. Cf. Gal. 4:6.

Peter, "Simon, are you asleep? Couldn't you keep watch for one hour? [38]Watch and pray so that you don't enter into temptation. The spirit is willing, but the flesh is weak."

[39]Once again Jesus went and prayed the same thing. [40]When he returned, again he found them sleeping because they couldn't keep their eyes open. They didn't know what to say to him.

[41]Jesus returned a third time and he said to them, "Are you still sleeping and resting? Okay that's enough! The hour has come. Look, the Son of Man is betrayed into the hands of sinners. [42]Get up! Let's go! Here comes my betrayer!"

Jesus is arrested
(Matthew 26:47–56, Luke 22:47–53, John 18:1–11)

[43]And just as Jesus was still speaking, Judas, who was one of the Twelve, arrived. And with him was a crowd armed with swords and clubs, sent from the chief priests, the scribes, and the elders. [44]Now the betrayer had previously arranged a signal with them: "The man I kiss is the man. Arrest him and lead him away under guard."

[45]Upon arrival, Judas immediately went up to Jesus and said, "Rabbi!" and kissed him. [46]The men seized Jesus and arrested him. [47]Then one of those standing nearby drew his sword and struck the servant of the high priest, cutting off his ear.

[48]Then Jesus said to them, "Am I a robber that you have come out with swords and clubs to capture me? [49]Every day I was with you, teaching in the temple and you did not arrest me. But it must be so in order that the Scriptures might be fulfilled." [50]Then everyone deserted him and fled.

[51]A certain young man, wearing nothing but a linen garment was following Jesus. When some young men laid hold of him, [52]he fled naked, leaving his linen garment behind.

Jesus is brought before the Sanhedrin council
(Matthew 26:57–68, Luke 22:54–55, 22:63–71, John 18:12–14, 18:19–24)

[53]Then they took Jesus to the high priest where all the chief priests, elders and scribes were gathered together. [54]Peter followed Jesus at a distance, right into the courtyard of the high priest. There he sat with the guards and warmed himself by the fire.

[55]The chief priests and the whole Sanhedrin were looking for evidence against Jesus so that they could put him to death but they did not find any. [56]Many testified falsely against him but their statements did not agree.

⁵⁷Then some men stood up and testified falsely against Jesus saying, ⁵⁸"We heard him say, 'I will destroy this man-made temple and after three days I will build another one not made by men.'" ⁵⁹But not even on this did their testimonies agree.

⁶⁰Then the high priest stood up in front of them all and asked Jesus, "Aren't you going to answer what these men are accusing you of?" ⁶¹But Jesus was silent and did not answer. Again the high priest asked him, "Are you the Messiah, the Son *of God*—the Blessed One?"

⁶²"I am," answered Jesus, *"and you will see the Son of Man sitting at the right hand of the Mighty One and coming with the clouds of heaven."*

⁶³The high priest tore his clothes. He asked, "Why do we need any further witnesses? ⁶⁴You have heard the blasphemy. What is your verdict?"

They all condemned him saying he deserved to die. ⁶⁵Then some of them began to spit at him. They blindfolded him, struck him with their fists and said, "Prophesy!" And the guards took him and slapped him.

Peter disowns Jesus

(Matthew 26:69–75, Luke 22:56–62, John 18:15–18, 18:25–27)

⁶⁶While Peter was below in the courtyard, one of the servant girls of the high priest came by. ⁶⁷And when she saw Peter warming himself, she looked closely at him and said, "You also were with the Nazarene, Jesus."

⁶⁸But Peter denied it saying, "I don't know or understand what you're talking about." And he went out into the entryway and a rooster crowed.

⁶⁹Then the same servant girl saw him there and she said to those standing nearby, "This man is one of them." ⁷⁰However again Peter denied it.

After a little while, those standing near said to Peter, "Surely you are one of them for you are a Galilean."

⁷¹Peter said, "May God curse me if I am lying. I swear by God that I don't know this man you're talking about."

⁷²Immediately a rooster crowed for the second time. Then Peter remembered what Jesus had said to him, *"Before the rooster crows twice you will deny me three times."* And he broke down and cried.

Jesus is taken to Pilate

(Matthew 27:1–2, 27:11–14, Luke 23:1–5, John 18:28–38)

15 ¹Very early the next morning, the chief priests, together with the elders, the scribes and the whole Sanhedrin, reached a decision. They bound Jesus, led him away and handed him over to Pilate.

²Pilate asked him, "Are you the king of the Jews?"
Jesus answered him saying, "Yes, it is as you say."
³The chief priests accused him of many things ⁴so Pilate asked him again, "Aren't you going to answer? Look at how many things they are accusing you of." ⁵But Jesus still did not reply and Pilate was amazed.

Pilate sentences Jesus to death
(Matthew 27:15–26, Luke 23:13–25, John 18:38–19:16)

⁶Now at every Feast *of Passover*, Pilate was in the habit of releasing one prisoner whom the people were pleading for. ⁷During this particular time there was a man called Barabbas in prison with fellow radicals who had committed murder in the uprising. ⁸The crowd went up and began asking for Pilate for him to do like he had done before.

⁹Pilate asked the crowd, "Do you want me to release to you the king of the Jews?" ¹⁰He well knew that the chief priests had handed Jesus over to him because they were envious. ¹¹But the chief priests stirred up the crowd to have Pilate release Barabbas to them instead.

¹²Pilate asked the crowd again, "What shall I do, then, with the one you call king of the Jews?"

¹³"Crucify him!" they shouted back.

¹⁴"Why? What crime has he committed?" Pilate asked.

But they shouted even louder, "Crucify him!"

¹⁵Pilate wanted to satisfy the crowd so he released Barabbas to them. He had Jesus flogged and handed him over to be crucified.

The soldiers mock Jesus
(Matthew 27:27–31, John 19:2–3)

¹⁶The soldiers led Jesus away into the palace courtyard (which is called the Praetorium[294]) and called together the whole cohort of soldiers. ¹⁷They put a purple robe on him, then twisted together a crown of thorns and placed it on his head. ¹⁸And then they began to call out to him, "Hail, king of the Jews!" ¹⁹Again and again they struck him on the head with a stick, spat on him and fell on their knees paying homage to him. ²⁰When they had finished ridiculing him, they took off the purple robe and put his own clothes on him. Then they led him out to crucify him.

---

294 I.e. Fort Antonia. The Praetorium was the residence of a provincial governor. There were two praetoriums in pre-war Jerusalem—the main camp where the general in charge of the legion had his command post (Fort Antonia) and an auxiliary praetorium in the upper city at Herod's palace (Martin, Ernest L, *The Temples that Jerusalem forgot* (2000), p. 76). Pilate stayed at Fort Antonia during the Passover season to be near the Jewish temple so as to control the huge crowds.

Jesus is crucified

(Matthew 27:32–44, Luke 23:26–43, John 19:17–27)

²¹On the way a certain man named Simon,²⁹⁵ who was passing by on his way from the country, was forced by the soldiers to carry Jesus' cross. (Simon was from the city of Cyrene and was the father of Alexander and Rufus).²⁹⁶ ²²They brought Jesus to the place called Golgotha (which means The Place of the Skull). ²³Then they offered him wine mixed with myrrh but he refused to drink it. ²⁴Then they crucified him and divided up his clothes among themselves, casting lots to see who would get what.

²⁵It was the third hour²⁹⁷ when they crucified him. ²⁶The written notice of the charge against him read:

THE KING OF THE JEWS

²⁷They crucified two thieves with him, one on his right and one on his left. [²⁸The Scripture was fulfilled which says,

"He was numbered with those who wilfully disobey."]²⁹⁸

Isaiah 53:12

²⁹Those who were passing by hurled insults at him, shaking their heads and saying, "Ha! You said you were going to destroy the temple and rebuild it in three days, ³⁰come down from the cross and save yourself!"

³¹Likewise the chief priests and the scribes mocked him among themselves saying, "He saved others but he cannot save himself! ³²Let the Messiah, this King of Israel, come down now from the cross so that we may see and believe." Those crucified with him also heaped insults on him.

Jesus dies

(Matthew 27:45–56, Luke 23:44–49, John 19:28–30)

³³At the sixth hour darkness came over the whole land until the ninth hour. ³⁴At the ninth hour Jesus cried out in a loud voice, "Eloi, eloi, lama sabachthani?"—which means, "My God, my God, why have you abandoned me?"

³⁵When some of those standing nearby heard this, they said, "Listen, he's calling for Elijah."

³⁶One man ran and filled a sponge with cheap vinegar wine. He put it on a

---

295 Simon was most likely travelling from Cyrene to attend the Passover feast in Jerusalem.
296 Evidently Alexander and Rufus were well known to the Christian community at the time.
297 I.e. 9 am. Three hours past sunrise. The trial ended at around 6 am. Cf. John 19:14.
298 This verse is omitted by many of the modern translations.

stick and offered it to Jesus to drink. The man said, "Now leave him and see if Elijah comes and takes him down."

³⁷And with a loud cry, Jesus breathed his last breath.

³⁸The curtain hanging in the temple was torn in two, from top to bottom. ³⁹And when the centurion, who was standing there in front of Jesus, heard his cry and saw the manner in which he died, he said, "Surely this man was the Son of God!"

⁴⁰There were some women who were watching from a distance. Among them were Mary Magdalene, Mary the mother of young James and Joseph and *another woman named* Salome. ⁴¹In Galilee these women had followed him and looked after his needs. Many other women who had come up with him to Jerusalem were also there.

Jesus' body is placed in a tomb
(Matthew 27:57-61, Luke 23:50-55, John 19:38-42)

⁴²It was Preparation Day²⁹⁹ which was the day before the Sabbath. As evening approached,³⁰⁰ ⁴³Joseph of Arimathea, a prominent member of the *Sanhedrin* council, who was himself waiting for the coming reign of God, went to Pilate with boldness and asked for Jesus' body. ⁴⁴Pilate was surprised to hear that Jesus had already died so Pilate summoned the *Roman* centurion and asked him if he had already died. ⁴⁵When Pilate found out from the centurion that this was the case, he allowed Joseph to take the body. ⁴⁶So Joseph bought some linen cloth, took down the body, wrapped it in the linen and placed Jesus' body in a tomb cut out of rock. Then he rolled a stone against the entrance of the tomb. ⁴⁷Mary Magdalene and Mary the mother of Joseph had been observing where he was laid.

Jesus is resurrected
(Matthew 28:1-8, Luke 24:1-12, John 20:1-10)

16 ¹After the Sabbath was over,³⁰¹ Mary Magdalene, Mary the mother of James, and Salome bought spices so that they might go and anoint Jesus' body. ²Very early on the first day of the week, just after sunrise, the women were on

---

299 Preparation Day was normally on Friday before the weekly Sabbath but this year there was a special Sabbath occurring on the Friday so the Preparation Day fell on a Thursday. Cf. John 19:31.
300 I.e. between 3 pm and 6 pm before the Sabbath commenced at sunset.
301 This would be any time after 6 pm on the Saturday evening. The women would have bought the spices at the Saturday evening market.

their way to the tomb ³and they were talking among themselves asking, "Who will roll away the stone for us from the entrance of the tomb?"³⁰²

⁴But when they looked up, they saw that the stone, which was very large, had been rolled away. ⁵And as they entered the tomb, they saw a young man dressed in a white robe sitting on the right side *of the tomb* and they were utterly amazed.

⁶The young man said, "Don't be alarmed. I know that you are looking for Jesus the Nazarene, who was crucified. He is risen! He is not here. Look, this is the place where they laid him. ⁷But go and tell his followers and Peter. He is going ahead of you into Galilee and there you will see him, just as he told you."

⁸The women were trembling and couldn't believe it. They came out and fled from the tomb. They said nothing to anyone because they were afraid.

Mary Magdalene sees Jesus
(Matthew 28:1-10, John 20:11-18)

[⁹When Jesus rose early on the first day of the week, he appeared first to Mary Magdalene, from whom he had previously cast out seven demons. ¹⁰She went and told those who had been with him and who were grieving and weeping for him. ¹¹When they heard that Jesus was alive and that she had seen him, they did not believe it.

Jesus appears to two of his followers
(Luke 24:13-35)

¹²Afterward Jesus appeared in a different form to two of them while they were walking in the country. ¹³They returned and reported it to the rest but they did not believe them either.

Jesus appears to the Eleven
(Matthew 28:16-20, Luke 24:36-49, John 20:19-23)

¹⁴Then later Jesus appeared to the Eleven as they were eating. He scolded them for their lack of faith and their stubborn refusal to believe those who had seen him after he had risen.

¹⁵He said to them, "Go into all the world and preach the gospel to the whole creation. ¹⁶The baptised believer will be saved but whoever does not believe will be condemned.³⁰³ ¹⁷And these signs will accompany those who

---

302 This would have been a legitimate concern for the women as the stone would have weighed between 1-2 metric tons. It was easier rolling the round tomb stone into place than rolling it away.

303 Mark here assumes that a believer under normal circumstances would be baptised. One might conclude from this verse that baptism is a requirement of salvation but that would be a 'negative inference fallacy'. The verse here makes it clear that the negative inference applies to belief not

believe: In my name they will cast out demons; they will speak in new languages; ¹⁸they will pick up snakes with their hands; and when they drink deadly poison it will not hurt them at all; they will place their hands on the sick and they will get well."

Jesus ascends into the sky
(Luke 24:50–53, Acts 1:9–11)

¹⁹After the Lord Jesus had spoken to them, he was taken up into the sky and he sat at the right hand of God. ²⁰The followers left *Jerusalem* and preached everywhere and the Lord worked with them and confirmed the word by the accompanying signs. Amen.]³⁰⁴

---

baptism (John 3:16, 6:29). To prove this point, there is the example of the thief on the cross who was not baptised but would be with Jesus in paradise that very same day (Luke 23:43).

304 Some MSS and ancient texts do not have from verses 9–20.

LUKE

Introduction

The Gospel of Luke is the first of two books written to a man named Theophilus. The author was Luke, a Gentile convert—the only non-Jew to author a book of the Bible. Interestingly, Luke claims to give a chronological account of the ministry of Jesus which fulfils the typical need of the Gentile mindset. It is the only gospel that claims to be chronological. Luke was a loyal co-worker of Paul and a doctor (Col. 4:14). The writings of Luke indicate that he was well educated, a careful historian and a theologian. The gospel was written between AD 60–63.

Luke is the longest NT book and the most comprehensive, recording events from the origins of John the Baptist before Jesus' birth to the ascension of Jesus. Luke demonstrates a rich vocabulary and an excellent command of Greek. Luke also shows that the gospel is for Jew and Gentile alike. Luke refers to Jesus most often as the "Son of Man".

The purpose of the Gospel of Luke

1 ¹Many people have attempted to compile an account of the events that have taken place among us. ²They have passed this on to us from those who were eyewitnesses of these things from the very beginning and who became servants of the Word.[305] ³Therefore, since I have carefully investigated everything from the beginning, it seemed appropriate for me also to write a chronological[306] account for you, your excellency, Theophilus, ⁴so that you may know with certainty about the things you have been taught.

The angel Gabriel appears to Zechariah the priest

⁵In the days of Herod king of Judea there was a priest named Zechariah, who belonged to the priestly division of Abijah.[307] His wife Elizabeth was also a descendant of Aaron. ⁶Both of them were righteous in the sight of God and observed all the Lord's commandments and regulations without fault. ⁷But they had no children because Elizabeth could not fall pregnant and they were also advanced in years.

⁸While Zechariah was performing his priestly duties with his division, ⁹he was chosen by lot, according to the custom of the priesthood, to go into the temple of the Lord and burn incense. ¹⁰And so when the hour came for the burning of incense, everyone who was gathered outside were praying. ¹¹And then an angel of the Lord appeared to him, standing at the right side of the altar of incense. ¹²Upon seeing the angel, Zechariah was terrified and fear fell upon him. ¹³But the angel said to him, "Do not be afraid, Zechariah. Your prayer has been heard. Your wife Elizabeth will bear you a son and you are to give him the name John. ¹⁴He will be a joy and he will make you very happy. Many people will rejoice because of his birth ¹⁵for he will be great in the sight of the Lord. He must never consume wine or any other strong drink. He will be filled[308] with Holy Breath even from birth. ¹⁶He will turn many of the children of Israel back to the Lord their God.[309] ¹⁷He will precede the Lord, *ministering* in the spirit and the power of Elijah, and he will turn the hearts of the

---

305 "Word" (*Logos*) here is capitalised to reflect that this is a title of Jesus in quite a few places including Heb. 4:12–16. John also used this title in his gospel (John 1:1,14), his first epistle (1 John 1:1–3), and in Revelation (Rev. 19:13). A few English translations (YLT) follow this exegesis.
306 Luke is the only one who claims to give a step by step account of Jesus' 62 week ministry.
307 Cf. 1 Chron. 24:10. David divided the sons of Aaron into twenty-four courses. All of the priests were required to serve during the Feasts. However, for the remainder of the year, each of the courses served for eight days (Sabbath through Sabbath) twice a year (there were two tenures). The first course began the first week of the month Nisan. Thus the first two courses served before the Passover on the 14th. The third course began the week after the seven days of Unleavened Bread following Passover. Since the course of Abijah was the eighth course, Zacharias was serving the week just prior to Pentecost (LGV footnotes on Luke 1:5). Cf. Luke 6:1.
308 Note that there is no definite article (the) before Holy Breath here. Cf. Acts 2:4.
309 Cf. Mal. 4:5–6, Sirach 48:10 (NRSV), Matt. 17:11.

fathers to their children and the disobedient to the wisdom of the righteous in order that he might make people ready to be prepared for the Lord."

¹⁸Zechariah said to the angel, "How can I be sure of this? I am an old man and my wife is well advanced in years?"

¹⁹The angel answered, "I am Gabriel. I continually stand in the presence of God and I have been sent to speak to you and to tell you this good news."[310] ²⁰But look! You will now be silent and not able to speak until the day that this happens because you did not believe my words which will be fulfilled at their proper time."

²¹Meanwhile, the people were waiting for Zechariah and wondering what was taking him so long in the temple. ²²When he came out, he could not speak to them. They realised that he had seen a vision in the temple. He was making signs to them and was non-verbal.

²³When Zechariah's time of service was completed, he returned home. ²⁴After this, sometime later his wife Elizabeth became pregnant and she hid herself for five months saying, ²⁵"The Lord has done this for me. In these days he has shown favour and taken away my disgrace among the people."

The angel Gabriel appears to Mary

²⁶In the sixth month *of Elizabeth's pregnancy*, the angel Gabriel was sent from God to Nazareth, a city *in the district* of Galilee. ²⁷He was sent to a virgin who was engaged to a man named Joseph, a descendant of David. The virgin's name was Mary. ²⁸The angel approached her and said, "Hello, you who are highly favoured! The Lord is with you. You are blessed among women!"[311]

²⁹However Mary was confused and troubled by this statement and wondered what kind of greeting this might be. ³⁰The angel said to her, "Mary, do not be afraid. You have found favour with God. ³¹You will become pregnant with child and give birth to a son, and you are to give him the name Jesus.[312] ³²He will be great and will be called the Son of the Most High. The Lord God will give him the throne of his father David. ³³He will rule over the house of Jacob as king forever and there will not be an end to his reign."

³⁴But Mary asked the angel, "How will this be since I am a virgin?"

³⁵The angel answered saying to her, "Holy Breath will come upon you and

---

310 Jewish tradition has it that angels had no knees and therefore were unable to sit based on the phrase in Eze. 1:7 which says their knees were straight. Jewish tradition has a widespread view that no one is permitted to sit in the presence of God. To stand before God is an idiom for serving God. Cf. Rev. 8:2.

311 The one desired by Jewish women for generations was to be the mother of the Messiah (Jamieson, R, Fausset, A R, and Brown, David, *A Commentary, Critical, Practical, and Explanatory on the Old and New Testaments* (1882), Dan. 11:37).

312 Jesus is a transliteration of the Greek *Yeshua*. The Hebrew equivalent is Joshua which means 'God saves'. Just as Joshua followed Moses (the Law), Jesus came to fulfil the Law of Moses.

power from the Most High will overshadow[313] you. Therefore the holy begotten thing will be called "Son of God".[314] [36]Even your relative Elizabeth is going to have a child in her old age. Everyone said she couldn't have children but she is now six months pregnant. [37]For nothing is impossible with God."

[38]Mary replied, "I am the Lord's servant. May it happen to me as you have said." Then the angel left her.

Mary visits Elizabeth

[39]At this time Mary rose and hurried off to a city in the hill country of Judea. [40]She entered into the house of Zechariah and greeted Elizabeth. [41]When Elizabeth heard Mary's greeting, the baby leaped in her womb and Elizabeth was filled with Holy Breath. [42]In a loud voice she cried out, "Blessed are you among women and blessed is the child in your womb. [43]Who am I that the mother of my Lord should come to me? [44]Look! At the sound of you greeting me, the baby in my womb leaped for joy. [45]You are blessed *Mary*, because you believed that it will come about as the Lord told you."

Mary's song of praise[315]

[46]Mary said,

"My soul glorifies the Lord and [47]my spirit rejoices in God my Saviour
   [48]for he has seen me, his humble servant.
Look! From now on all generations will consider me blessed [49]for the
   Mighty One has done great things for me—holy is his name.
[50]He shows mercy to those who fear him from generation to generation.
[51]He has done mighty deeds with his arm, he has scattered those who
   are proud in their hearts.
[52]He has brought down rulers from their thrones and he has lifted up the
   ones who are humble.
[53]He has filled the hungry with good things and he has sent the rich away
   empty handed.
[54]He has helped his servant Israel and remembered to be merciful [55]to
   Abraham and his descendants forever just as he promised to
   our fathers."

---

313   A figure of speech indicating how God would cause Mary to conceive. Note: not sexual intercourse.
314   The Son of God was begotten out of the Father and was his preincarnate title. Later the Son of Man became flesh (John. 1: 14). This was the title Jesus referred to himself while on earth.
315   Mary is probably singing this to Elizabeth (and her household) *about* the Lord (TH) not directly *to* the Lord.

⁵⁶Mary stayed with Elizabeth for about three months and then returned home.

The birth of John the Baptist

⁵⁷The time arrived for Elizabeth to give birth and she had a son. ⁵⁸Her neighbours and relatives heard how the Lord had shown great mercy to her and they rejoiced together with her.

⁵⁹On the eighth day they came to circumcise the child and they were going to name him after his father Zechariah, ⁶⁰but his mother spoke up and said, "No! His name is to be John."

⁶¹They said to her, "There is no one among your relatives who has that name." ⁶²Then they made signs to his father and asked him what he would like to name the child. ⁶³Zechariah asked for a writing tablet and to everyone's astonishment he wrote, "His name is John." ⁶⁴Immediately his mouth was opened and he began to speak, praising God. ⁶⁵All the neighbours were awestruck and throughout the entire hill country of Judea, this was all that was being talked about. ⁶⁶Everyone who heard this was wondering about it and asking, "What then is this child going to *grow up to* be?" For the Lord's hand was with him.

Zechariah's prophecy

⁶⁷His father Zechariah was filled with Holy Breath and prophesied saying,

⁶⁸"Praise be to the Lord, the God of Israel, because he has visited us
    and come to set his people free.
⁶⁹He has raised up a strong and mighty Saviour for us, a descendant of
    his servant David,³¹⁶ ⁷⁰just as he said this through his holy
    prophets long ago.
⁷¹He saved us from our enemies and from the hand of all who hate us.
⁷²He said he would show mercy to our fathers and remember his holy
    covenant.
⁷³⁻⁷⁴He swore an oath to our father Abraham to rescue us from the hand
    of our enemies and to allow us to serve him without fear ⁷⁵so
    that we might be holy and righteous before him all the days of
    our life.
⁷⁶And you, my child,³¹⁷ will be called a prophet of the Most High for you will
    precede the Lord in order to prepare the way for him.
⁷⁷You will tell his people how to be saved by having their sins forgiven.

---

316   Literally a 'horn of salvation'. A horn is a metaphor for something very strong. Cf. Rev. 5:6.
317   The second part of Zechariah's prophecy concerning his son, John.

[78] Through the tender mercy of our God, the Rising Sun will visit us from heaven.[318]

[79] It will shine on those living in darkness and in the shadow of death[319] to guide our feet into the path of peace."

[80] The child *John* grew and became strong in spirit and he lived in the desert until he appeared publicly to *the people of* Israel.

The birth of Jesus Christ
(Matthew 1:18–25)

2 [1] It came about in those days that Caesar Augustus issued a decree saying that a census should be taken of the entire Roman Empire. [2] This was the first census that took place while Quirinius was governor of Syria.[320] [3] Therefore everyone went back to register, each to his own city.

[4] Now Joseph also went up from the city of Nazareth in Galilee to Bethlehem in Judea, the city of David, because he was a descendant of the household of David. [5] He went there to register with Mary who had been engaged to him.[321] She was pregnant and [6] while they were there, the time came for the baby to arrive [7] and she gave birth to her firstborn, a son. She wrapped him in a swaddling band[322] and placed him in a manger because there was no place for them in the common lodge.[323]

The shepherds and the angels

[8] There were some shepherds camping out in the fields nearby keeping watch over their flocks at night. [9] An angel of the Lord appeared to them and the glory

---

318 Cf. Mal. 4:2. The 'Rising Sun' is Christ because he brings light to the world.
319 Literally *Thanatos*—the Greek god of death. Cf. Rev. 20:13 and related footnotes. Every human being alive on earth lives in the shadow of death in the sense that we could die at any time.
320 Luke being a good historian distinguishes this census from another that took place under Quirinius mentioned by Gamaliel in Acts 5:37.
321 Joseph and Mary were now a legitimately married couple when they were travelling although the marriage was not consummated until after she had given birth. Joseph took Mary to be his wife soon after he had woken from his dream. Cf. Matt. 1:24–25.
322 The swaddling band (note: singular) was made from linen or cotton material and was 5 m long and about 10–12 cm wide. This proved that Joseph and Mary were a legitimately married couple upon arrival in Bethlehem and that the baby Jesus was a legitimate child. Cf. Job 38:9 ESV. Jerusalem in the days of her abominable practices was considered an unswaddled child cast out in the field (Eze. 16:1–5). Swaddling a baby was proof that the child was legitimate.
323 "Common lodge" here is the Greek *kataluma*, i.e. 'a place to lodge', usually after a journey. In Luke 22.11, *kataluma* refers to a room, not a house. The usual word for 'inn' is not *kataluma* but *pandocheion* (Luke 10:34). *Kataluma* therefore may refer to a common lodging place for large travelling groups under one roof. Nevertheless Joseph and Mary found refuge not in this lodging place but likely in a lower room of relatives where the animals were kept probably because of the crowd there for the census. Mary gave birth to her baby between 6–7 pm on the 11th September, 3 BC on Rosh Hashanah (Jewish New Year's Day). She placed him in a manger (animal feeding trough).

of the Lord shone around them and they were terrified. ¹⁰The angel said to them, "Do not be afraid. I bring good news of great joy that will be for all the people. ¹¹Today in the city of David your Saviour has been born—he is Christ the Lord. ¹²And this will be a sign to you: you will find a baby in a swaddling band and lying in a manger."

¹³Suddenly, a great heavenly army appeared with the angel praising God and saying,

> ¹⁴"Glory to God in the highest!
> Peace be on the land among men whom he favours."

¹⁵When the angels had left the shepherds and gone to heaven, the shepherds said to one another, "Let's go to Bethlehem and see this thing that has happened which the Lord has told us about." ¹⁶So they hurried off and found both Mary and Joseph and the baby lying in the manger. ¹⁷Having seen them, the shepherds made it widely known the word that had been spoken to them about this child. ¹⁸And everyone who heard it were amazed at what the shepherds said to them. ¹⁹But Mary kept in mind all these things, pondering them in her heart. ²⁰The shepherds returned, glorifying and praising God for all the things they had heard and seen. It was just as the angel had told them.

The baby Jesus is presented in the temple to the Lord

²¹On the eighth day, when it was time to circumcise *the baby*, he was named Jesus. This was the name the angel had given to him before he had been conceived.

²²When the days of their purification[324] according to the Law of Moses had been completed, Joseph and Mary took him to Jerusalem to present him to the Lord ²³just as it is written in the Law of the Lord: "Every firstborn male is to be consecrated to the Lord." ²⁴They also offered a sacrifice as required by the Law of the Lord: "A pair of doves or two young pigeons."

Simeon and Anna praise God

²⁵Now at this time there was a man living in Jerusalem named Simeon who was righteous and devout. He was eagerly waiting for God to console Israel. *God's* Holy Breath was upon him.[325] ²⁶It was revealed to him by the Holy Breath

---

324 There were forty days of purification in total as prescribed in the Law (Lev. 12:2–4).
325 Cf. Isa. 40:1. God is called the God of all comfort (consolation) (2 Cor. 1:3). In the future God will console Israel and Jerusalem and her time of sin will be paid for.

that he would not die before seeing the Lord's Messiah. ²⁷Moved by the Holy Breath, he went into the temple. And when the parents brought in the child Jesus to do what the custom of the Law required concerning him, ²⁸Simeon took him in his arms and praised God, saying,

> ²⁹"Lord, you can now dismiss your servant in peace according to your promise.
> ³⁰For my eyes have seen your salvation which you have prepared in the presence of all the people.
> ³¹And you caused him to be ready by the eyes of them all.
> ³²He is a light to reveal *salvation* to the Gentiles and he is the glory of your people Israel."

³³His father and mother were amazed at the things being said about him. ³⁴Then Simeon blessed them and said to Mary, his mother, "Listen! This child is destined to cause many to fall and many to rise in Israel.³²⁶ He is a sign from God which many will oppose. ³⁵He will cause the inner thoughts of many hearts to be revealed. And a sword will pierce your own soul too."

³⁶There was also a prophetess, Anna, the daughter of Phanuel of the tribe of Asher. She was very old and had lived with her husband for only seven years *when he died*. ³⁷She had been a widow until she was 84. She never left the temple but worshipped night and day, fasting and praying. ³⁸She came up to them at this very moment and praised God. She spoke about the child to everyone who was waiting for God to set Jerusalem free.

³⁹When Joseph and Mary had done everything required by the Law of the Lord, they returned to Galilee to their own city of Nazareth.

Jesus at the temple at twelve years old

⁴⁰The child grew and became stronger and stronger. He was filled with wisdom and God's grace was upon him. ⁴¹Every year his parents went to Jerusalem for the Passover Feast. ⁴²When Jesus was twelve years old, they went up to the Feast as per usual. ⁴³After the Feast was over, they returned home but the boy Jesus remained *in Jerusalem*, but his parents were unaware. ⁴⁴They thought he was in the travelling group and they were already a day into the journey when they began looking for him amongst the relatives and friends. ⁴⁵When they did not find him, they went back to Jerusalem to look for him.

---

326   "Fall" and "rise" are used metaphorically here to mean that many will move towards God and many will move away from God because of his message.

⁴⁶After three days they found him in the temple. He was sitting among the teachers, listening to them and asking them questions. ⁴⁷Everyone listening to him was amazed at his intelligence and his answers. ⁴⁸When his parents saw him, they were astonished. His mother said to him, "Son, why have you treated us like this? Your father and I have been anxiously searching for you."

⁴⁹He said to them, "Why were you searching for me? Didn't you realise that I had to be in my Father's house?" ⁵⁰But they did not understand *the implication of* what he was saying to them.

⁵¹So he went back down with them to Nazareth and was obedient to them but his mother treasured all these things in her heart. ⁵²And Jesus was growing in wisdom and maturity, and in favour with God and men.

John the Baptist prepares the way for the Lord
(Matthew 3:1–12, Mark 1:2–8, John 1:19–28)

3 ¹In the fifteenth year of the reign of Tiberius Caesar, Pontius Pilate was governor of Judea, Herod was the tetrarch of Galilee, his brother Philip was tetrarch of Iturea and Traconitis, and Lysanias was tetrarch of Abilene. ²At this time during the high priesthood of Annas and Caiaphas, the word of God came to John, son of Zechariah, in the desert. ³John went throughout all the region of the Jordan, preaching that people should be baptised showing that they had turned to God for the forgiveness of sins. ⁴As is written in the book of Isaiah the prophet,

"A voice cries out in the desert and says, 'Prepare the way for the Lord.
    Straighten the way for him.
⁵Every valley must be filled in and every mountain and hill must be
    levelled off.
The crooked roads must become straight and the rough paths must be
    made smooth.
⁶And all mankind will see God's salvation.'"

Isaiah 40:3–5

⁷John said to the crowds coming out to be baptised by him, "You brood of vipers! Who warned you to flee from the coming wrath? ⁸Produce fruit that proves that you have really changed your ways. And do not start by saying to yourselves, 'Abraham is our father.' For I tell you that out of these stones God can raise up children for Abraham. ⁹The axe is already waiting at the root of the trees; every tree that does not produce good fruit will be cut down and thrown into the fire."

¹⁰The crowd asked him, "What should we do then?"

¹¹John answered by saying to them, "The man owning two shirts must give to the man who has none and whoever has food must share likewise."

¹²Now tax collectors also came to be baptised. They asked, "Teacher, what should we do?"

¹³John told them, "Do not collect more taxes than you are *legally* required to."

¹⁴Then some soldiers asked him, "And what should we do?"

He replied, "Don't extort money, don't slander and be content with your wages."

¹⁵The people were anticipating and all wondering in their hearts if John might possibly be the Messiah. ¹⁶John answered everyone saying, "I baptise you with water but there is one coming who is stronger than me of whom I am not even worthy to untie the strap of his sandals. He will baptise you with Holy Breath and with fire.[327] ¹⁷His winnowing fork is in his hand to clear his threshing floor and to gather the wheat into his barn. But he will burn up the chaff with fire that cannot be extinguished."

¹⁸John taught the people about many different things and preached the good news to them.

¹⁹But when John rebuked Herod the tetrarch because of Herodias, his brother's wife, and all the other evil things he had done, ²⁰Herod did an even worse thing by locking up John in prison.

John baptises Jesus
(Matthew 3:13–17, Mark 1:9–11)

²¹It came about that as all the people were being baptised that Jesus also was baptised. And as Jesus was praying, heaven was opened ²²and the Holy Breath descended in bodily form like a dove. And a voice came from heaven[328] saying, "You are my Son, whom I love. I am very pleased with you."

The genealogy of Jesus through Mary
(Matthew 1:1–17)

²³Now Jesus himself was about 30 years old when he began his ministry. He was the son, presumably,[329] of Joseph, who was of Heli, ²⁴of Matthat, of Levi,

---

[327] We are either immersed (baptised) with God's Holy Breath or immersed in unquenchable and everlasting fire. The choice is what we are to be immersed in – salvation or punishment.

[328] In Luke's account of Jesus' baptism heaven is singular referring to the domain of God, heaven itself, being opened whereas in Matthew and Mark's account it is 'the heavens' (plural) referring to the sky being split apart. It is referring to two different things.

[329] The Gospel of Luke follows Jesus' biological genealogy through Mary whereas Matthew follows Jesus' paternal genealogy through Joseph. Jesus' ancestry can be traced back both paternally (legally) and maternally (biologically) to King David. Cf. 1 Chron. 17:11, Psa. 132:11, Acts 2:30.

of Melki, of Jannai, of Joseph, ²⁵of Mattathias, of Amos, of Nahum, of Esli, of Naggai, ²⁶of Maath, of Mattathias, of Semein, of Josech, of Joda, ²⁷of Joanan, of Rhesa, of Zerubbabel, of Shealtiel, of Neri, ²⁸of Melki, of Addi, of Cosam, of Elmadam, of Er, ²⁹of Joshua, of Eliezer, of Jorim, of Matthat, of Levi, ³⁰of Simeon, of Judah, of Joseph, of Jonam, of Eliakim, ³¹of Melea, of Menna, of Mattatha, of Nathan, of David, ³²of Jesse, of Obed, of Boaz, of Salmon, of Nahshon, ³³of Amminadab, of Admin, of Arni, of Hezron, of Perez, of Judah, ³⁴of Jacob, of Isaac, of Abraham, of Terah, of Nahor, ³⁵of Serug, of Reu, of Peleg, of Eber, of Shelah, ³⁶of Cainan, of Arphaxad, of Shem, of Noah, of Lamech, ³⁷of Methuselah, of Enoch, of Jared, of Mahalalel, of Cainan, ³⁸of Enosh, of Seth, of Adam, of God.

Satan tests Jesus

(Matthew 4:1–11, Mark 1:12–13)

4 ¹Jesus, now being full of Holy Breath, returned from the Jordan and was being guided by the Breath in the desert ²where he was being tested for forty days by the devil. He had not eaten anything during those days and at the end of those days he was hungry.

³The devil said to him, "If you are the Son of God, tell this stone to become bread."

⁴Jesus said to him, "It is written, 'Man shall not live on bread alone but on every word from God.'"

⁵The devil led Jesus up to a high place and showed him in an instant all the countries and nations of the world. ⁶And he said to him, "I will give all their wealth and magnificence to you, for it has been given to me and I can give it to whomever I desire. ⁷So if you worship me, it will all be yours."

⁸Jesus answered him saying, "Get behind me Satan for it is written, 'Worship the Lord your God and serve him only.'"

⁹Then the devil led him to Jerusalem and had him stand on the highest point of the temple. He said, "If you are the Son of God, throw yourself down from here. ¹⁰For it is written,

> "'He will command his angels concerning you to watch over you.
> ¹¹"They will lift you up in their hands so that you will not hit your foot
>   against a stone.'"
>
> Psalm 91:11–12

¹²Jesus answered, "It has been said, 'Do not put the Lord your God to the test.'"

¹³Having completed every test, the devil left him until an opportue time.

Jesus begins his ministry year in Galilee[330]
(Matthew 4:12-17, Mark 1:14-15)

[14]Jesus, in the power of the Breath *of God*, returned to Galilee and a report went out throughout all the surrounding countryside about him. [15]He began teaching in their synagogues and they were all praising him.

Jesus is rejected by the people of Nazareth
(Matthew 13:53-58, Mark 6:1-6)

[16]Jesus went up to Nazareth, where he had been raised as a child, and on the Sabbath day he entered the synagogue as was the custom. [17]The scroll of the prophet Isaiah was handed to him and having unrolled the scroll he found the place *and read* where it is written,

> [18]"*His* Breath is upon me because the Lord God anointed me to preach good news to the poor.
>
> He has sent me to proclaim freedom for the prisoners and recovery of sight for the blind.
>
> Isaiah 61:1
>
> He sent me to set free the oppressed.
>
> Isaiah 58:6
>
> [19]He sent me to proclaim the year of the Lord's favour."[331]
>
> Isaiah 61:2

[20]Then Jesus rolled up the scroll, gave it back to the attendant and sat down. The eyes of everyone in the synagogue were fixed on him [21]and he began to say to them, "Today this Scripture has been fulfilled in your hearing."

[22]Everyone was speaking well of him and were amazed at the gracious words that came from his lips. They were saying, "Isn't this Joseph's son?"

[23]Jesus said to them, "No doubt you will quote this parable to me, 'Doctor, heal yourself! Do the same things in your hometown what we have heard that you did in Capernaum.'"

[24]Jesus added, "But I tell you the truth, no prophet is accepted in his hometown. [25]It is so true that there were many widows in Israel during Elijah's time, when the sky was shut for 3 ½ years and there was a severe famine throughout the land. [26]Yet Elijah was not sent to any of them, but to a widow in Zarephath in the region of Sidon.

---

330   The length of Jesus' public ministry was only 62 weeks. Cf. John 2:13 and related footnote.
331   The allusion is to the Year of Jubilee, a year when men were set free from slavery and debts. Ultimately, this will not be fulfilled until Jesus returns in the 6000th year after creation.

²⁷And there were many in Israel with leprosy in the time of Elisha the prophet, yet not one of them was cleansed—only Naaman the Syrian."

²⁸Everyone in the synagogue were furious when they heard this. ²⁹They got up, drove Jesus out of the city and took him to the brow of the hill on which the city was built, in order to throw him over the cliff. ³⁰But Jesus having slipped through the middle of them, went on his way.

Jesus casts out an evil spirit
(Mark 1:21–28)

³¹Then Jesus went down to Capernaum, a city of Galilee, and he began to teach the people on the Sabbath. ³²They were amazed at his teaching, because his message had authority. ³³In the synagogue there was a man possessed by a demon, an evil spirit. The man yelled out at the top of his voice, ³⁴"Go away! What do you want with us, Jesus of Nazareth? Did you come to destroy us? I know who you are—the Holy One of God!"

³⁵Jesus rebuked him saying, "Silence! Come out of him!" Then the demon threw the man down in the middle of everyone and came out without harming him.

³⁶Everyone was amazed and they said to each other, "What is this teaching? He gives orders to evil spirits with authority and power and they come out!" ³⁷Reports about him were spreading throughout the surrounding region.

Jesus heals Simon Peter's mother-in-law
(Matthew 8:14–15, Mark 1:29–31)

³⁸Jesus left the synagogue and went to Simon's house. Simon's mother-in-law was suffering from a high fever and they asked Jesus to help her. ³⁹Standing over her, he rebuked the fever and it left her. She got up at once and began to attend to their needs.

Jesus heals many sick people
(Matthew 8:16–17, Mark 1:32–34)

⁴⁰As the sun was setting, the people brought to Jesus everyone who had various kinds of sicknesses. He laid his hands on each one of them and healed them. ⁴¹And demons also came out of many people, shouting, "You are the Son of God!" But he rebuked them and would not allow them to speak, because they knew he was the Messiah.

Jesus looks for a quiet and deserted place
(Mark 1:35–39)

⁴²The next day at daybreak, Jesus went out to look for a quiet and deserted place. The people were looking for him and when they found him, they tried to stop him from leaving them. ⁴³But he said, "I must preach the good news about God's coming realm in other cities too, because I was sent here for this purpose." ⁴⁴And he kept on preaching in the synagogues of the Galilee region.³³²

Jesus calls his first four followers
(Matthew 4:18–22, Mark 1:16–20)

5 ¹It came about one day that Jesus was standing by the Lake of Gennesaret³³³ with the crowd pressing in upon him and they were listening to the Word of God. ²Jesus saw at the water's edge two boats, left there by fishermen, who were washing their nets. ³He got into one of the boats, the one belonging to Simon, and asked him to put out a little way from the shore. Then he sat down and taught the people from the boat.

⁴When he had finished speaking, he said to Simon, "Put out into the deep water and let down your nets for a catch."

⁵Simon answered by saying, "Master, we have laboured all night and haven't caught a thing. But because you say so, I will let down the net."³³⁴ ⁶Having done this, they caught such a large number of fish that their net³³⁵ began to tear. ⁷So they motioned for their partners in the other boat to come and help them and they came and filled both boats so full that they began to sink.

⁸When Simon Peter saw this, he fell down at Jesus' knees and said, "Go away from me Lord; I am a sinful man!" ⁹For he and all his companions were astonished at the catch of fish that they had taken. ¹⁰It was the same with James and John, the sons of Zebedee, Simon's partners.

Then Jesus said to Simon, "Don't be afraid; from now on you will be catching men." ¹¹So they pulled their boats up onto the shore, left everything, and followed Jesus.

Jesus heals a man with leprosy
(Matthew 8:1–4, Mark 1:40–45)

¹²While Jesus was in one of the cities, a man came along who was full of

---

332   Critical text has 'Judea'. Mark 1:39 has Galilee.
333   Sea of Galilee.
334   TR says 'net' (singular). Simon's lack of faith did not allow him to let down more than one net even though Jesus asked him to let down his nets (plural).
335   Singular in TR (KJV). Plural in most modern translations (Critical Text).

leprosy. When he saw Jesus, he fell with his face to the ground and begged him saying, "Lord, if you are willing, you can cleanse me."

¹³Jesus reached out and touched the man and said, "I am willing. Be cleansed!" And immediately the leprosy left him.

¹⁴Then Jesus ordered him not to tell anyone. He said, "Go and show yourself to the priest and make an offering as commanded by Moses for your cleansing.³³⁶ This will speak to the people."

¹⁵However the news about Jesus *went viral* spreading all over the place, so that crowds of people came to hear him and to be healed of their sicknesses. ¹⁶But Jesus often withdrew to quiet and deserted places to pray.

Jesus heals a paralysed man
(Matthew 9:1-8, Mark 2:1-12)

¹⁷It came about one day as Jesus was teaching, Pharisees and teachers of the Law were sitting nearby. They had come from every village of Galilee and from Judea and Jerusalem. The power of the Lord *God* was present in Jesus for him to heal the sick.³³⁷ ¹⁸Just then, some men came carrying a paralysed man on a makeshift bed and tried to take him into the house to put him in front of Jesus. ¹⁹But they couldn't find a way to do this because of the crowd, so they went up on the roof and lowered him down while still on his bed through the roof tiles³³⁸ into the middle of the crowd, right in front of Jesus. ²⁰And when Jesus saw their faith, he said, "Your sins are forgiven, my friend."

²¹The Pharisees and the scribes began to reason saying, Who is this who is speaking blasphemies? Who is able to forgive sin except God alone?"

²²But Jesus knew what they were thinking and he asked them, "Why are you thinking these things in your hearts? ²³Which is easier? Is it easier to say, 'Your sins are forgiven,' or to say, 'Get up and walk'? ²⁴But I want you to know that the Son of Man has the authority on earth to forgive sins." So he said to the paralysed man, "Get up, take your bed³³⁹ and go home." ²⁵Immediately the man stood up in front of them, took what he had been lying on and left for his house, glorifying God. ²⁶Everyone gasped in astonishment and they praised God. They were filled with fear and said, "Today, we have seen some very remarkable things."

---

336 Cf. Lev. 14:1–33.
337 This verse proves that Jesus relied on the power of God and the Holy Breath to perform miracles and healing. It wasn't his own inherent power. Cf. John 5:19,30, 14:10, Acts 2:22, 10:38.
338 Tiles were made of baked clay.
339 A relatively small and often temporary type of object on which a person may lie or recline – 'cot, pallet, stretcher' (Louw, J, & Nida, E, *Greek-English Lexicon of the New Testament based on Semantic Domains* (1988) 6.106).

Jesus calls Levi (Matthew)

(Matthew 9:9–13, Mark 2:13–17)

²⁷Then later after this, Jesus went out and saw a tax collector by the name of Levi sitting at his tax booth. Jesus said to him, "Follow me." ²⁸Levi left everything and followed him.

²⁹Levi arranged a great banquet for Jesus at his house and a large number of tax collectors and others dined³⁴⁰ with them. ³⁰The Pharisees and their scribes began complaining saying to his followers, "Why are you all eating and drinking with tax collectors and sinners?" ³¹Jesus answered saying to them, "It is not the healthy ones who need a doctor, but the ones who are sick. ³²I have not come to call righteous *people* to turn to God but outcasts."³⁴¹

Jesus is asked about fasting

(Matthew 9:14–17, Mark 2:18–22)

³³They said to him, "John's followers often fast and pray, as do the followers of the Pharisees, but yours go on eating and drinking."

³⁴But Jesus said to them, "Surely you do not think that the guests of the bridegroom should fast while he is with them? ³⁵But the days will come when the bridegroom will be taken from them and in those days they will fast.

³⁶"No one tears a piece off a new coat and sews it on an old one. If you do, you will tear the new garment, and the piece from the new one will not match the old. ³⁷And no one pours new wine into old wineskins. If you do, the new wine will burst the skins and the wineskins will be ruined. ³⁸No, new wine must be poured into new wineskins. ³⁹And no one after drinking old wine wants the new wine, for he will say that the old wine is better."

Jesus is master of the Sabbath

(Matthew 12:1–8, Mark 2:23–28)

6 ¹It came about on the second-first Sabbath³⁴² that Jesus was passing

---

340 Literally, reclined which also implies eating.
341 The 'righteous' were the law-abiding 'good' people who were accepted within the Jewish religious structure. There is perhaps an intent here meaning those who were self-righteous. The word here for outcasts is literally 'sinners'. Sinners were people who were not accepted within that structure – i.e. 'outcasts'.
342 The second-first Sabbath was the first weekly Sabbath day of the second yearly tenure beginning with Tishrei 1. DARBY, YLT, DRB, also have translated this correctly. The twenty-four priestly courses, lasted for eight days (from Sabbath to Sabbath). Their courses started with the Sabbath just before the beginning of Nisan in order for the priests to be on duty to perform their regular ceremonials on Nisan 1. The same procedure was also followed for their second yearly tenure commencing six months later on Tishri 1. Cf. Martin, Ernest L, *The Chronology of the Twenty-four Courses*' (https://www.askelm.com/star/star006.htm). Cf. Luke 1:5 and footnote.

through the grain fields, and his followers began to pick and eat the heads of grain, rubbing them in their hands. ²Now some of the Pharisees asked, "Why are you doing what is unlawful on the Sabbath?"

³Jesus answered them saying, "Have you not read what David did when he and his companions were hungry? ⁴He entered the house of God and having taken the loaves of presentation, he ate what is only lawful for the priests to eat and he gave some to his companions also." ⁵Then Jesus said to them, "The Son of Man is master of the Sabbath."

Jesus heals a man on the Sabbath
(Matthew 12:9–14, Mark 3:1–6)

⁶On another Sabbath, Jesus went into the synagogue and was teaching and a man was there whose right hand was shrivelled. ⁷The Pharisees and the scribes were watching him to see if he would heal on the Sabbath in order that they could find something to accuse him of. ⁸But Jesus knew what they were thinking and said to the man with the shrivelled hand, "Get up and stand in front of everyone." So the man got up and stood there.

⁹Then Jesus said to them, "I have a question for you. What is more lawful? To do good on the Sabbath or to do evil? To save a life or to destroy it?" ¹⁰He looked around at them all and then said to the man, "Stretch out your hand." The man did so and his hand was completely restored. ¹¹But they were furious and began to discuss with one another what they were going to do to Jesus.

Jesus chooses the Twelve Apostles
(Matthew 10:1–4, Mark 3:13–19)

¹²During these days, one time, Jesus went to the mountain to pray and spent the night praying to God. ¹³When morning came the next day, he called his followers to come to him and chose twelve among them and he named them apostles. ¹⁴He named, Simon (whom he named Peter), his brother Andrew, James, John, Philip, Bartholomew, ¹⁵Matthew, Thomas, James son of Alphaeus, Simon who was called the Zealot, ¹⁶Judas son of James and Judas Iscariot, who became a traitor.

Jesus teaches and heals
(Matthew 4:24–25, Mark 3:7–12)

¹⁷Jesus went down with them and stood on a level place. A large crowd of his followers were there and a great number of people from all over Judea, Jerusalem, and from the coast of Tyre and Sidon were there too. ¹⁸They had come to hear him and to be healed of their diseases. Those troubled by evil spirits were being

healed ¹⁹and everyone in the crowd was trying to touch him, because power was going out from him and healing them all.

Jesus' sermon on the level place[343]
(Matthew 5:1–12)

²⁰Jesus looked at his followers and began to talk saying,

"Blessed are you who are poor for you have a part in the realm of God.
²¹Blessed are you who hunger now for you will be satisfied.
Blessed are you who weep now for you will laugh.
²²Blessed are you when men hate you, when they exclude you, when they insult you and when they reject your name as being evil because of the Son of Man.

²³"Rejoice in that day and jump for joy, because great is your reward in heaven. For that is how their ancestors treated the prophets.

²⁴"But disaster to you who are rich for you having an easy life.
²⁵Disaster to you who are being well fed now for you will go hungry.
Disaster to you who are laughing now for you will mourn and weep.
²⁶Disaster to you when everyone speaks well of you for that is how their ancestors treated the false prophets."

Jesus says we must love our enemies
(Matthew 5:38–48)

²⁷"But I tell the ones who are listening, 'Love your enemies, do good to those who hate you, ²⁸bless those who curse you, pray for those who abuse you. ²⁹If someone strikes you on one cheek, offer him your other cheek also. If someone takes your coat, let him have your shirt as well. ³⁰Give to everyone whatever they ask of you, and if anyone takes what belongs to you, do not demand it back. ³¹Do to others as you would want them to do to you.

³²"And if you love those who love you, what credit is that to you? Even the sinners love those who love them. ³³If you do good to those who are good to you, what credit is that to you? Even the sinners do that. ³⁴If you lend to those from whom you expect repayment, what credit is that to you? Even the sinners lend to sinners expecting to be repaid in full. ³⁵But love your enemies,

---

343   In contrast to the 'sermon on the mount' the 'sermon on the level place' contains disasters as well as blessings.

do good to them, and lend to them without expecting to get anything back. Then your reward will be great, and you will be sons of the Most High *God*, because he is kind to the ungrateful and wicked. ³⁶Be merciful, just as your Father is merciful.

Jesus teaches about not judging others
(Matthew 7:1-5)

³⁷"Do not judge, and you will not be judged. Do not condemn *someone as guilty*, and you will not be condemned. Forgive, and you will be forgiven. ³⁸Give, and it will be given to you—a good measure, pressed down, shaken together and running over, will be poured into your lap. For with the measure you use, it will be also measured out to you similarly."

³⁹Jesus also told them this parable, "Can a blind man lead a blind man? Won't they both fall into a hole? ⁴⁰A student is not above his teacher, but everyone having been fully trained will be like his teacher.

⁴¹"Why do you see the speck of dust in your brother's eye but you don't notice the wooden beam in your own eye? ⁴²How can you say to your brother, 'Brother, let me take the speck of dust out of your eye,' when you yourself fail to see the wooden beam in your own eye? You hypocrite!, first take the wooden beam out of your eye, and then you will see clearly to take out the speck of dust from your brother's eye.

There are two kinds of fruit
(Matthew 7:15-20, 12:33-35)

⁴³"A good tree does not bear bad fruit, nor does a bad tree bear good fruit. ⁴⁴Each tree can be recognised by its fruit. One does not gather figs from thorns, or harvest grapes from a thorn-bush. ⁴⁵The good man brings good things out of the good stored up in his heart, and the evil man brings evil things out of the evil stored up in his heart. For out of the overflow of the heart a man's mouth speaks.

There are two kinds of builders
(Matthew 7:24-27)

⁴⁶"Why do you call me, 'Lord, Lord,' but you do not do what I say? ⁴⁷I will show you what he is like who comes to me and hears my words and puts them into practice. ⁴⁸He is like a man who builds his house by digging down deep and laying its foundation on bedrock. When a flood comes, the river of water hits the house but it cannot shake it loose because it is so well built. ⁴⁹But the man who hears my words and does not put them into practice is like a man who builds

his house on the ground without a foundation. The moment that the river hits the house, the house collapses and it is totally destroyed."

A Roman centurion shows that he has great faith
(Matthew 8:5–13)

7 ¹When Jesus had finished what he was wanting to say to the people, he entered Capernaum. ²Now there was a certain highly regarded slave of a centurion who was sick and about to die. ³Having heard about Jesus, the centurion sent some Jewish elders to him asking if he might come and heal his slave. ⁴When they came to Jesus, they pleaded with him earnestly saying, "This man deserves to have you do this, ⁵because he loves our nation and has built our synagogue."

⁶So Jesus went with them. He was not far from the house when the centurion sent friends to say to Jesus, "Lord, don't trouble yourself, for I do not deserve to have you come under my roof. ⁷That is why I did not even consider myself worthy to come to you myself. But just say the word, and my slave will be healed. ⁸For I too am a man under authority, having soldiers under me. I say to this one, 'Go,' and he goes and to that one, 'Come,' and he comes. I say to my slave, 'Do this,' and he does it."

⁹When Jesus heard this, he was amazed at him and he turned to the crowd following him and said, "I tell you the truth, I have not found such great faith even in Israel." ¹⁰Upon returning to the house the men who had been sent found the slave in good health.

Jesus raises a widow's son back to life

¹¹The next day, Jesus went to a city called Nain and his followers and a large crowd travelled with him. ¹²As he approached the city gate, a dead person was being carried out—the only son to his mother and she was *also* a widow. A large crowd from the city was with her. ¹³When the Lord saw her, he felt sorry for her and said, "Don't cry."

¹⁴Then he approached the coffin and those carrying it stood still. Jesus said, "Young man! Get up." ¹⁵The dead man sat up and began to talk, and Jesus gave him to his mother.

¹⁶Everyone there was struck with fear and they began praising God. They said, "A great prophet has been raised up among us. God has visited his people." ¹⁷News about Jesus spread out throughout all Judea and the surrounding countryside.

Messengers from John the Baptist come to Jesus
(Matthew 11:1–19)

[18]When John's followers told him about all these things *concerning Jesus*, he summoned two of them [19]and sent them to the Lord to ask, "Are you the one who was to come or should we expect someone else?"

[20]When the men came to Jesus, they said, "John the Baptist sent us to ask, 'Are you the one who was to come, or should we be looking for someone else?'"

[21]Right at that very time Jesus had healed many who had diseases, sicknesses and evil spirits and he had granted sight to many who were blind. [22]So Jesus answered them saying, "Go back and report to John what you have seen and heard. The blind receive sight, the lame walk, those who have leprosy are cleansed and healed, the deaf hear, the dead are raised, and the poor are being evangelised. [23]Blessed is he who is not stumbled and offended because of me."

[24]After John's messengers left, Jesus began speaking to the crowd about John. He said, "What did you go out into the desert to see? A reed being shaken in the wind?[344] [25]If not, what did you go out to see? A man dressed in fine clothes? No, those who wear expensive clothes and indulge in luxury are in palaces. [26]So what did you go out to see? A prophet? Yes, I tell you, and so much more than a prophet. [27]John is the one written about,

"'I am sending my messenger ahead of you who will prepare your way before you.'

Malachi 3:1

[28]"I tell you, among those born of women there is no one greater than John. But the one who is least in God's realm is greater than *John*."[345]

[29]And when everyone including the tax collectors, having heard what Jesus said, they declared God righteous because they had been baptised by John. [30]But the Pharisees and experts in the law regarded God's purpose for themselves as invalid because they had not been baptised by John.

[31]Jesus continued by saying, "To what, then, can I compare this generation to? What are they like? [32]They are like children sitting in the marketplace and calling out to each other, 'We played a *happy* wedding tune on the flute for you and you did not dance! We sang *sad* funeral songs and you did not cry!' [33]For John the Baptist came neither eating bread nor drinking wine and you say, 'He has a demon.' [34]The Son of Man came eating and drinking and you say, 'Here is

---

344 Cf. Matt. 11:7 and footnote.
345 Bible Commentator and Anglican Bishop J C Ryle (1816–1900) said concerning this verse, "The child who knows the story of the cross possesses a key to religious knowledge which patriarchs and prophets never enjoyed."

a glutton and a drunkard, a friend of tax collectors and sinners.' [35]But Wisdom[346] is proved right when we see her children."

A sinful woman pours perfume on Jesus' feet[347]

[36]Now a certain Pharisee invited Jesus to have dinner with him, so he went to the Pharisee's house and reclined at the table. [37]There was a woman who had lived a sinful life in that city and she learnt that Jesus was eating at the Pharisee's house. So she brought an alabaster jar of perfume [38]and as she stood behind him at his feet crying, she began to wet his feet with her tears. She wiped his feet with her hair, kissing them and pouring perfume on them.

[39]When the Pharisee who had invited him saw this, he said to himself, "If this man was a prophet he would know who is touching him and what kind of woman she is and the kind of sinful life she leads."

[40]Jesus had an answer for the Pharisee and said, "Simon, I have something to say to you."

"Teacher, tell me," he said.

[41]Jesus said, "There were two men who owed money to a certain money lender. One owed him 500 denarii and the other just 50 denarii. [42]Neither of the men had the money to pay him back, so he cancelled the debts of both men. Now which of them will love him more?"

[43]Simon answered, "I suppose the one who had the larger debt cancelled."

"You have judged correctly," Jesus said.

[44]Then turning towards the woman he said to Simon, "Do you see this woman? I came into your house. You did not give any water to me for my feet, but she wet my feet with her tears and wiped them with her hair. [45]You did not give me a kiss, but this woman, from the time I entered has not stopped kissing my feet. [46]You did not put oil on my head, but she has poured perfume on my feet. [47]Therefore, I tell you, her many sins have been forgiven—for she loved much. But he who has been forgiven little loves little."

[48]Then Jesus said to her, "Your sins have been forgiven."

[49]The others reclining at the table with him began saying among themselves, "Who is this man who even forgives sins?"

[50]Jesus said to the woman, "Your faith has saved you, go in peace."

---

346   "Wisdom" is another title for the preincarnate Son of God. Cf. 1 Cor. 1:24 and footnote.
347   Some commentators link this with the woman who anointed Jesus' head with perfume in Matt. 26:6–13 because in both accounts it mentions a man named 'Simon'. In Matthew's account, it is Simon the Leper whereas in Luke it is Simon the Pharisee. But there are several reasons why the two narratives cannot be the same including the different body parts that are being anointed and the timeframe involved. Luke says that he is giving a chronological account (Luke 1:3) and so the two accounts seem to be at different times in Jesus' ministry and at different locations. Simon the Leper's house was at Bethany near Jerusalem whilst Simon the Pharisee's house appears to be in the Galilean region (Luke 7:11 and 8:26). Therefore it seems likely that they are two different accounts.

The women who supported Jesus

8 ¹Afterwards, it came about that Jesus travelled through every city and village proclaiming and preaching the good news about the coming reign of God. The twelve followers were with him, ²and also some women who had been cured of evil spirits and diseases. They were Mary (who was called Magdalene) from whom seven demons had come out, ³Joanna, whose husband Chuza was the manager of Herod's household, Susanna and many others. These women were helping to support *Jesus and his followers* out of their own pockets.

The parable of the sower
(Matthew 13:1–9, Mark 4:1–9)

⁴A large crowd was gathering and people were coming to Jesus from every city. So Jesus told a parable:

⁵"A farmer went out to sow seed that he had and as he was scattering the seed, some fell along the path. It was trod on and the birds of the air ate it up. ⁶Some *of the seed* fell on rock and when it sprouted the plants withered because of lack of moisture. ⁷Other seed fell in the middle of the thorns however the thorns grew up with the plants and choked them. ⁸Still other seed fell on the good soil and the plants sprouted and producing a crop, a hundred times more *than was sown.*"

When he had said this, Jesus called out saying, "He who has ears to hear, let him hear."

Why does Jesus speak in parables?
(Matthew 13:10–17, Mark 4:10–12)

⁹Jesus' followers asked him what this parable meant. ¹⁰He said, "God has allowed you to understand the secrets of God's coming reign but to others I speak in parables, so that,

"'they look but they do not really see.
They hear but they do not understand what they are hearing.'"

_{Isaiah 6:9}

The parable of the sower explained
(Matthew 13:18–23, Mark 4:13–20)

¹¹Jesus said, "This is the meaning of the parable: The seed is the word of God. ¹²Those who are on the path are the ones who hear, then the devil comes along and takes away the word from their hearts, to prevent them from believing and

being saved. ¹³Those on the rock are the ones who receive the word with joy when they hear it, but they have no root. They believe for a limited time, but in a time of testing they fall away. ¹⁴Now that which falls among the thorns are those who hear, but while going along in life they are choked by worries, riches and pleasures and so they do not mature and bear any fruit. ¹⁵Now that which falls on the good soil are those with an honest and good heart because they hear the word, retain it, and by persevering they bear fruit.

The lamp on a stand
(Mark 4:21–25)

¹⁶"No one lights a lamp and covers it with a jar or puts it under a bed rather it is put on a stand, so that those who come in can see the light. ¹⁷For whatever is hidden will become evident and whatever is in secret will be brought out into the open. ¹⁸Therefore be careful in how you listen. Whoever has will be given more and whoever does not have, even what he thinks he has will be taken from him."

Jesus' mother and brothers come to see him
(Matthew 12:46–50, Mark 3:31–35)

¹⁹Now it came about that Jesus' mother and brothers came to see him but they were not able to get to him because of the crowd. ²⁰Someone told him, "Your mother and brothers are standing outside wanting to see you."

²¹However he answered them by saying, "My mother and my brothers are those who hear the word of God and do it."

Jesus calms the storm
(Matthew 8:23–27, Mark 4:35–41)

²²Now it came about one day that Jesus got into a boat with his followers and they set out and he said to them, "Let's go over to the other side of the lake." ²³As they were sailing, Jesus fell asleep and a gust of wind came down to the lake.³⁴⁸ The boat was being swamped by the waves and they were in danger. ²⁴The followers went and woke him, saying, "Master, Master, we're going to drown!"

Upon wakening, Jesus ordered the wind and the rough water to stop and it became calm. ²⁵He said to them, "Where is your faith?"

In fear and amazement they asked each other, "Who is this? Even the winds and the water he commands obey him."

---

348 This makes sense because the lake, the Sea of Galilee, is like a huge bowl surrounded by mountains on nearly all sides and so the squall or storm would descend from the surrounding mountains.

Jesus casts out a demon
(Matthew 8:28-34, Mark 5:1-20)

²⁶They sailed to the country of the Gerasenes which is opposite Galilee on the other side of the lake. ²⁷When Jesus stepped ashore, he was met by a demon-possessed man from the city. This man had not worn clothes for a long time or lived in a house instead living among the tombs. ²⁸When he saw Jesus, he cried out and fell down at his feet, saying in a loud voice, "What do you want with me, Jesus Son of the Most High God? I beg of you, do not torment me." ²⁹For Jesus had commanded the evil spirit to come out of the man. It had caused the man to have many seizures and even though the man was shackled and chained and kept under guard, he had broken his chains and was driven by the demon into the desert.

³⁰Jesus asked him, "What is your name?"

"My name is Legion," he said, because many demons had entered him. ³¹The demons kept begging him to not order them to go into the abyss.³⁴⁹

³²Now there was a large herd of pigs feeding right there on the hillside. The demons begged Jesus to let them go into them and he gave them permission to do so. ³³The demons came out of the man and went into the pigs. The herd rushed down the steep bank into the lake and they were drowned.

³⁴When those who had been tending the pigs saw what had happened, they ran off and reported this in the city and to the nearby farms. ³⁵The people went out to see what had happened and when they came to Jesus they found the man from whom the demons had come out of. He was sitting at Jesus' feet, dressed, and in his right mind and they were afraid. ³⁶Those who had seen it all told the people how the demon-possessed man had been cured. ³⁷Then all the people of the surrounding country of the Gerasenes asked Jesus to leave them because they were overcome with fear. So Jesus got into the boat and left.

³⁸The man from whom the demons had gone out of, was begging to go with Jesus, but he sent him on his way saying, ³⁹"Return home and tell everyone what God has done for you." So the man left and went throughout the whole city proclaiming what Jesus had done for him.

Jesus raises a dead girl back to life and heals a sick woman
(Matthew 9:18-26, Mark 5:21-43)

⁴⁰Now when Jesus returned *to the other side of the lake*, a crowd welcomed him for they were all expecting him. ⁴¹Then a man named Jairus, a leader in

---

349   Evidently not all evil spirits/demons had been locked in the abyss. Cf. Rev. 9:1-3.

the *local* synagogue, came and fell at Jesus' feet. He was pleading with him to come to his house ⁴²because his only³⁵⁰ daughter, a girl of about twelve years of age, was dying.

As Jesus was on his way, the crowds were pressing in around him from every side. ⁴³And a woman was there *in the crowd* who had been suffering from chronic haemorrhaging for twelve years. She had spent all her finances on doctors but no one was able to heal her. ⁴⁴She came up behind Jesus and touched the hem of his cloak, and immediately her bleeding stopped.

⁴⁵"Who touched me?" Jesus asked.

Once they had all denied it, Peter said, "Master, the people are crowding and pressing against you."

⁴⁶But Jesus said, "Someone touched me for I know that power has gone out from me."

⁴⁷Then when the woman, seeing that she could not go unnoticed, came trembling and fell at his feet. In the presence of all the people, she told him why she had touched him and how she had been instantly healed. ⁴⁸Then he said to her, "Daughter, your faith has healed you. Go in peace."

⁴⁹While Jesus was still speaking, someone came from the synagogue leader's *house* and said, "Your daughter is dead. Don't bother the teacher anymore."

⁵⁰But when Jesus heard this he said to Jairus, "Don't be afraid, just believe and she will be healed."

⁵¹When he arrived at Jairus' house, he did not let anyone go in with him except Peter, John and James, and the child's father and mother. ⁵²Meanwhile, everyone there was crying and mourning for her. Jesus said, "Stop crying, she's not dead, just sleeping."

⁵³They all began ridiculing him because they knew that she was dead. ⁵⁴But he took her by the hand and said, "Child, get up!" ⁵⁵Her breath returned and immediately she stood up. Then Jesus told them to give her something to eat. ⁵⁶Her parents were astonished, but he ordered them not to tell anyone what had happened.

Jesus sends out the Twelve
(Matthew 10:5–15, Mark 6:7–13)

9 ¹Jesus called the Twelve together and he gave them power and authority over all the demons and to cure diseases. ²He sent them out to preach about the coming reign of God and to heal those who were sick. ³He instructed them, "Do not take anything with you for the journey—no hiking pole, no bag, no bread,

---

350   This is the Greek word *monogenes* meaning unique or one and only. Cf. Heb. 11:17 and footnote.

no money, not even an extra shirt. ⁴And whenever you enter a house, stay there until you leave. ⁵And if people do not welcome you, shake the dust off your feet when you leave their city as a testimony against them." ⁶So they set out and went from village to village, evangelising and healing people everywhere.

Herod enquires about Jesus
(Matthew 14:1–2, Mark 6:14–16)

⁷Now when Herod the tetrarch heard about all the things happening he was perplexed because some were saying that John *the Baptist* had been raised from the dead. ⁸Others were saying that Elijah had appeared and still others that one of the prophets of long ago had come back to life. ⁹But Herod said, "I beheaded John. Who, then, is this that I hear such things about?" Herod was trying to see Jesus.

Jesus feeds five thousand men
(Matthew 14:13–21, Mark 6:30–44, John 6:1–13)

¹⁰When the apostles returned, they reported to Jesus what they had done. Then he took them with him and they withdrew privately to a city called Bethsaida. ¹¹But the crowds learned about it and followed him. He welcomed them and spoke to them about God's coming reign, and healed those who needed healing.

¹²Now it was getting to be late in the afternoon and the Twelve came to him and said, "Send the crowd away so they can go to the surrounding villages and farms and find food and lodging because we are in a remote place here."

¹³Jesus said, "Give them something to eat yourselves."

But they said, "We only have five loaves of bread and two fish unless we go and buy food for all the people." ¹⁴(There were about five thousand men there.)

So Jesus instructed his followers, "Have the people sit down in groups of about fifty each." ¹⁵The followers did so and everybody sat down. ¹⁶Taking the five loaves and the two small fish and looking up to heaven, Jesus gave thanks and broke them. Then he gave them to the followers and had them place the food before the people. ¹⁷They all ate and were satisfied and the followers picked up twelve basketfuls of leftover broken pieces.

Peter reveals Jesus' identity
(Matthew 16:13–19, Mark 8:27–29)

¹⁸And it came about one time while Jesus was praying alone and his followers were with him, he asked them, "Who do the crowds say I am?"

¹⁹They answered saying, "Some say you are John the Baptist, others say Elijah and still others say you are one of the prophets of long ago that has come back to life."

²⁰He asked them again, "But what about you? Who do you say I am?" Peter answered saying, "The Messiah of God."

Jesus predicts his death
(Matthew 16:21-28, Mark 8:31-9:1)

²¹Jesus warned them and gave strict orders for them not to tell this to anyone. ²²He told them, "The Son of Man must suffer many things and be rejected by the *Jewish* elders, chief priests and scribes and he must be killed and on the third day be raised to life."

²³Then he said to the wider group, "If anyone wants to be my follower, he must disregard his own ambitions, take up his cross daily and follow me. ²⁴For whoever tries to keep his own life safe will fail, but whoever pays no attention to his own life's *ambitions* for my sake will find *purpose in* life. ²⁵What benefit is it if a man gains the whole world, yet he loses his soul? ²⁶If anyone is ashamed of me and my words, the Son of Man will be ashamed of him when he comes in his glory and in the glory of the Father and of the holy angels. ²⁷I tell you the truth, there are some standing here right now who will not die before they see the realm of God."

The transfiguration of Jesus
(Matthew 17:1-13, Mark 9:2-13)

²⁸About eight days[351] after Jesus had said these words, he took Peter, John and James with him and went up to the mountain to pray. ²⁹And as he was praying, the appearance of his face changed and his clothes became a brilliant dazzling white. ³⁰Two men, Moses and Elijah, ³¹appeared in *heavenly* glory, talking with Jesus. They spoke about his soon departure which he was about to fulfil in Jerusalem. ³²Peter and his companions were very sleepy but when they became fully awake, they saw his glory and the two men standing with him. ³³As the men were leaving Jesus, Peter said to him, "Master, it is good that we are here. Let us put up three shelters—one for you, one for Moses and one for Elijah." (Peter didn't understand what he was really saying.)

³⁴While Peter was speaking, a cloud appeared and enveloped them and they were afraid while they were entering into the cloud. ³⁵A voice came from the

---

[351] Matthew and Mark have "after six days" which likely means that they were counting the days from the first day of the week—Sunday. Luke however was dating the event eight days after the time Jesus was making the prediction on the previous Friday. Therefore there is no discrepancy meaning that both passages have the Transfiguration experience occurring on the Sabbath day.

cloud saying, "This is my Son whom I have chosen. Listen to him." ³⁶When the voice had spoken, they found Jesus alone. The followers kept silent and told no one in those days of what they had seen."

Jesus heals a boy with an evil spirit
(Matthew 17:14–21, Mark 9:14–29)

³⁷The following day, when they had come down from the mountain, a large crowd met him. ³⁸Then at this time, a man in the crowd called out, "Teacher, I beg you to look at my son, for he is my only child. ³⁹An *evil* spirit seizes him and he suddenly screams. It throws him into convulsions so that he foams at the mouth. It hardly ever leaves him and it is wearing him out. ⁴⁰I begged your followers to cast it out, but they were not able to."

⁴¹Jesus answered by saying, "O unbelieving and depraved generation, how long will I be with you and put up with you? Bring your son here."

⁴²Even while the boy was coming, the demon threw him to the ground in a convulsion. But Jesus rebuked the evil spirit, healed the boy and gave him back to his father. ⁴³And they were all astonished at the greatness of God.

Jesus predicts his death again
(Matthew 17:22–23, Mark 9:30–32)

And while everyone was marvelling at all these things that Jesus was doing, he said to his followers, ⁴⁴"Listen carefully to what I am about to tell you: The Son of Man is going to be betrayed into the hands of men." ⁴⁵But his followers did not understand what this meant. It was hidden from them so that they did not grasp it and they were afraid to ask him about what he was saying.

Who will be the greatest?
(Matthew 18:1–5, Mark 9:33–37)

⁴⁶Now an argument arose among the followers as to which one of them would be the greatest. ⁴⁷Jesus, knowing what they were thinking in their hearts, took a little child and had him stand beside him. ⁴⁸Then he said to them, "Whoever welcomes this little child in my name welcomes me and whoever welcomes me welcomes the one who sent me. For he who is least among you all—he is the greatest."

He who is not against us is for us
(Mark 9:38–40)

⁴⁹John said, "Master, we saw a man casting out demons in your name and we tried to stop him because he is not one of us."

⁵⁰But Jesus said to him, "Do not stop him for whoever is not against you is for you."

The Samaritans reject Jesus

⁵¹As the time approached for his ascension *to heaven*, Jesus resolutely set his face towards Jerusalem.³⁵² ⁵²He sent messengers on ahead, who went into a Samaritan village to get things ready for him. ⁵³But the people there did not welcome him because he was heading for Jerusalem. ⁵⁴When the followers James and John saw this they asked, "Lord, do you want us to call down fire from heaven to destroy them?" ⁵⁵However Jesus turned to them and he rebuked them ⁵⁶and they went to another village.

The personal cost of following Jesus
(Matthew 8:19–22)

⁵⁷As Jesus and his followers were going on their way a man said to him, "I will follow you wherever you go."

⁵⁸Jesus said to the man, "Foxes have burrows and the birds of the air have nests, but the Son of Man has no place to lie down and rest."

⁵⁹And he said to another man, "Follow me."

But the man said, "Lord, let me first go and bury my father."

⁶⁰But Jesus said to him, "Let the dead bury their own dead, but you go and proclaim the coming reign of God."³⁵³

⁶¹And also another man said, "I will follow you Lord but first let me go back and say good-bye to my family."

⁶²But Jesus said to him, "No one who starts ploughing the field and looks back is fit for serving in the realm where God reigns."

Jesus sends out the seventy-two

10 ¹After these things, the Lord appointed seventy-two other men and sent them out two by two ahead of him to every city and place where he was about to go. ²He instructed them, "The harvest is plentiful but the workers are few. Ask the Lord of the harvest, therefore, to send out workers into his harvest field. ³Go! I am sending you all out as lambs among wolves. ⁴Do not take a wallet, backpack or sandals and do not greet anyone on the road.

⁵"And when you enter a house, first say, 'Peace to this house.' ⁶And if a peaceful man is there, your peace will rest on him. If not, it will return to you.

---

352   This is an idiom for Jesus' determination and conviction for what was ahead. In other words, nothing was going to stop Jesus from making his way to Jerusalem to die on the cross for mankind.
353   I.e. Let the spiritually dead bury the physically dead.

⁷You are to stay in that house, eating and drinking whatever they give to you, for the worker deserves his wages. Do not move around from house to house.

⁸"And when you enter a city and are welcomed, eat what is set before you. ⁹Heal the sick who are there and tell them, 'The reign of God is getting close. You are not far off.' ¹⁰However if you enter a city and you are not welcomed, go into its streets and say, ¹¹"Even the dust of your city that sticks to our feet, we shake off *as a testimony* against you. But know this: The reign of God is coming.' ¹²I tell you that it will be more bearable on that day for Sodom than for that city."

The cities who would not turn from their sins
(Matthew 11:20-24)

¹³Jesus said, "What a disaster it is for you, Chorazin! What a disaster it is for you, Bethsaida! For if the miracles that were performed in you had been performed in Tyre and Sidon, they would have turned from their sins long ago. They would be sitting around *mourning* in sackcloth and ashes. ¹⁴But it will be more bearable for *the cities of* Tyre and Sidon at the judgment than for you. ¹⁵And Capernaum, *do you think* you will be exalted up to heaven? No way, you will go down to Hades.

¹⁶"The one listening to you, listens to me, but the one rejecting you rejects me and the one rejecting me rejects him who sent me."

The seventy-two arrive back

¹⁷The seventy-two returned with joy and said, "Lord, even the demons submit to us in your name."

¹⁸And he said to them, "I saw Satan fall like lightning from heaven.[354] ¹⁹Look, I have given authority to you to trample on snakes and scorpions and to overcome all the power of the enemy and nothing will harm you.[355] ²⁰But do not rejoice that the evil spirits submit to you, but rejoice that your names are written in heaven."

The Holy Breath causes Jesus to be full of joy
(Matthew 11:25-27, 13:16-17)

²¹At that very moment Jesus, full of joy by the Holy Breath, said, "I praise you Father, Lord of heaven and earth, because you have hidden these things from the wise and learned, and revealed them to the innocent. Yes, father, for this was your good pleasure.

354　Satan and his angels are cast out of heaven at the midpoint of the final seven year tribulation after warring with Michael and his angels (Rev. 12:9).

355　Cf. Rev. 9:10.

²²"Everything has been handed over to me by my Father. No one knows who the Son is except the Father, and no one knows who the Father is except the Son and those to whom the Son chooses to reveal him."

²³Then Jesus turned to his followers and said privately, "Blessed are those who see what you see. ²⁴For I tell you that many prophets and kings wanted to see what you see but did not see it, and to hear what you hear but did not hear it."

The parable of the Good Samaritan

²⁵On one occasion an expert in the law[356] stood up to test Jesus and asked, "Teacher, what must I do to receive eternal life?"

²⁶Jesus said to him, "Tell me, what does the law say? How do you interpret it?"

²⁷*The expert* answered saying, "You must love the Lord your God with all your heart, with all your soul, with all your strength and with all your mind and you must love your neighbour as yourself."

²⁸Jesus said to him, "You have answered correctly. Do this and you will live."

²⁹But he wanting to save face, he asked Jesus, "And who exactly is my neighbour?"

³⁰Jesus replied *with a parable* saying, "A certain man was travelling from Jerusalem down to Jericho when he fell into the hands of robbers. They stripped him bare, beat him up and left him half dead. ³¹But it so happened that a priest was going down the same road, and when he saw the man, he passed by on the other side. ³²Likewise a Levite also when he came to the same place and saw the man, passed by on the other side. ³³But soon after, a certain Samaritan, as he was travelling also came to the place where the man was. When he saw him, he took pity on him. ³⁴So he went to him and bandaged his wounds and poured oil and wine on his wounds. Then he put the man on his own donkey and took him to an inn.[357] ³⁵The next day the Samaritan took two denarii and gave them to the innkeeper saying, 'Take care of him, and when I return I will reimburse you for whatever extra expense you may have.'

³⁶"Which one of these three, then, do you think was a neighbour to the man who fell into the hands of the robbers?"

³⁷The expert in the law said, "The one who took mercy on him."
Jesus said to him, "Go and do the same."

Jesus visits Martha and Mary

³⁸While Jesus and his followers were on their way, he entered a village where a woman named Martha welcomed him into her home. ³⁹She had a sister named Mary, who was sitting at the Lord's feet and listening to what he was saying.

---

356 Literally a lawyer who was an expert in the Jewish Law of Moses.
357 Cf. Luke 2:7 and footnote.

⁴⁰But Martha was being distracted by all the preparations that had to be made. She came to him and said, "Lord, don't you care that my sister has left me to do all the work by myself? Speak to her to come and help me!"

⁴¹The Lord answered her saying, "Martha, Martha. You worry and get upset about many things ⁴²but there is just one thing that you need to do. Mary has chosen what is best and I will not stop her."

Jesus teaches his followers how to pray
(Matthew 6:9–15, 7:7–11)

11 ¹One day when Jesus was praying in a certain place and had finished, one of his followers said to him, "Lord, teach us to pray just as John taught his followers."

²He said to them, "When you pray, say this,

"'Father, may your name be revered.
May your reign be established.
³Give food to us that we need this day.
⁴And forgive us our sins as we also have forgiven those who have
    sinned against us.
May you lead us so we are not tempted to do wrong.'"

⁵Then he said to them, "Let's suppose that one of you goes to your friend's house at midnight, and you say to him, 'My friend, could you lend me three loaves of bread, ⁶because another friend of mine has been away and he has come to me and I have nothing to give to him.'

⁷"Then suppose the friend inside answers and says, 'Don't bother me. The door is already locked and my children are with me in bed. I can't get up and I am not able to give you anything.' ⁸I tell you, even though he doesn't want to get up and give bread to you, despite being your friend, he will get up and give to you as much as you need because of your persistence.

⁹"Therefore, I tell you, keep on asking *God* and it will be given to you, keep on seeking and you will find *what you are looking for,* keep on knocking and *the door* will be opened to you. ¹⁰For every one of you who keeps asking will receive and the one who keeps seeking will find and the one who keeps knocking on doors, it will be opened.

¹¹"Which of you fathers, if your son asks for a fish, will give a snake to him? ¹²Or if he asks for an egg, will give a scorpion to him? ¹³If you then, though you are evil, know how to give good gifts to your children, how much more *likely*

would it be that your Father from heaven will give Holy Breath to those who ask him!"

The Pharisees accuse Jesus of working with Beelzebul
(Matthew 12:22–30, Mark 3:20–27)

¹⁴There was one time when Jesus was casting out a demon that stopped a man from speaking. Once the demon came out, the non-verbal man spoke and the crowds were amazed. ¹⁵But some of them said, "He is able to cast out demons because Beelzebul, the prince of demons, is enabling him to do so." ¹⁶Others tested him by asking for a sign from heaven.

¹⁷But Jesus knew what they were thinking and he said to them, "Every realm divided against itself will be ruined, and a family divided against itself will fall. ¹⁸If Satan is divided against himself, how can his reign continue? I say this because you are claiming that I am casting out demons by Beelzebul. ¹⁹But *if it is true* that I am casting out demons by Beelzebul, then by whom do your people cast them out? Therefore they themselves show that you are wrong. ²⁰However if I am casting them out by God's power,[358] then the reign of God has already come upon you.

²¹"Furthermore if a strong man,[359] fully armed, guards his own palace then his possessions are safe. ²²But when someone who is stronger comes and overpowers him, then he takes away the armour in which the man depended on and he divides up his plunder.

²³"He who is not with me is against me, and he who does not gather with me, scatters."

An evil spirit returns to the person it left
(Matthew 12:43–45)

²⁴Jesus continued, "When an evil spirit goes out of the man, it goes through arid places looking for a home and does not find one. Then it says, 'I will return to the house I came from.' ²⁵And when it comes back, it finds the house swept clean and put in order. ²⁶Then it goes and takes seven other spirits more evil than itself, and they go in and live there. The final condition of that man is worse than at first."

---

358 Literally 'finger of God'.
359 In Jesus' explanation, Satan is the strong man guarding his property—that is, the person possessed by a demon. Jesus is the one who is even stronger. Note that he doesn't attack the strong man's palace, but the strong man himself, with the result being that he frees the palace and returns the property to the person who had suffered under demonic rule.

True happiness

²⁷While Jesus was saying these things, a woman from the crowd called out saying, "Blessed is the mother who gave birth to you and breastfed you."

²⁸But Jesus said, "On the contrary. Blessed are those who hear the word of God and obey it."

The sign of the prophet Jonah
(Matthew 12:38-42, Mark 8:12)

²⁹As the crowds continued to gather even more, Jesus said, "This is an evil generation. It asks for a miraculous sign but none will be given to it except the sign of Jonah. ³⁰For just as Jonah was a sign to the Ninevites, so also will the Son of Man be a sign to this generation. ³¹On the judgment day, the Queen of Sheba will rise with the men of this generation and condemn them. For she came from the ends of the earth to listen to King Solomon's wisdom[360] and yet now one greater than Solomon is here. ³²The men of Nineveh will stand up at the judgment with this generation and condemn it for they turned from their sins when hearing Jonah preach[361] and yet now one greater than Jonah is here.

We are to be filled with light
(Matthew 5:15, 6:22-23)

³³"No one lights a lamp[362] and puts it in a place where it will be hidden, or under a bowl. Instead he puts it on the lampstand so that those who come in may see the light. ³⁴The eye is the lamp of your body. When your eyes are healthy then your entire body is full of light but when they are bad then your body is full of darkness. ³⁵See to it, then, that the light within you is not darkness.[363] ³⁶If therefore, your whole body is full of light and no part of it is dark, then everything in you will be full of light as when a lamp shines on you."

Jesus warns the Pharisees of six disasters
(Matthew 23:1-36, Mark 12:37-40, Luke 20:45-47)

³⁷When Jesus had finished speaking, a Pharisee invited him to eat with him so he went in and reclined at the table. ³⁸The Pharisee however was very surprised to see that he did not wash before the meal.

³⁹Then the Lord said to him, "Now you Pharisees clean the outside of the cup

---

360 Cf. 1 Kings 10:1-7.
361 Cf. Jonah 3:5.
362 These are the small oil lamps (*luchnos*) not the torches (*lampas*).
363 The eye is the conduit for light in the body. Jesus is talking about the attitude of the people, urging them to be teachable and accept the light of God's Word into their dark hearts.

and dish but inside you are full of greed and wickedness. ⁴⁰You people are foolish. Did not *God* who made the outside make the inside also? ⁴¹Give what is inside the cup and dish to the poor, then indeed everything will be clean[364] for you.

⁴²"How disastrous it will be for you Pharisees, because you give a tenth of all your herbs to God—such as mint and dill but you neglect justice and the love of God. You should have practiced the latter without neglecting the former.

⁴³"How disastrous it will be for you Pharisees, because you love the seat of honour in the synagogues and you love to be formally greeted in the marketplaces.

⁴⁴"How disastrous it will be for you Pharisees, because you are like unmarked graves, which men walk on without knowing it."

⁴⁵And one of the experts in the law answered him saying, "Teacher, when you say these things, you insult us also."

⁴⁶But Jesus said, "And how disastrous it will be for you experts in the law also, because you load people down with heavy burdens they find it difficult to carry yet you yourselves do not lift a finger to help them.

⁴⁷"How disastrous it will be for you, because you build monuments as a memorial to the prophets and yet it was your ancestors who killed them! ⁴⁸Therefore it is as if you approve of what your ancestors did—they killed the prophets and you build monuments.

⁴⁹"Therefore for this reason, God in his wisdom said, 'I will send them prophets and apostles, some of whom they will kill and others they will persecute.' ⁵⁰So the people of this generation will be held responsible for the blood of all the prophets that has been shed since the overthrow of the world.[365] ⁵¹That is, the blood of Abel[366] to the blood of Zechariah,[367] who was killed between the altar and the Holy Place.[368] Yes, I tell you, this generation will be held responsible for it all.

⁵²"How disastrous it will be for you experts in the law, because you have taken away the key *to the door* of knowledge. You yourselves have not entered, and you have hindered those who were entering."

⁵³When Jesus left there, the Pharisees and the scribes began to be extremely hostile and they bombarded him with questions about many things. ⁵⁴They were trying desperately to catch him out with something he might say.

---

364 I.e. ritually clean because that is what was important for the Pharisees. Jesus is saying that the heart attitude is more important than ritual and just being seen to be doing the right thing.
365 Cf. Eph. 1:4 and footnote.
366 Cf. Gen. 4:8.
367 Cf. 2 Chron. 24:20–21.
368 I.e. the temple or sanctuary.

Jesus warns about the hypocrisy of the Pharisees
(Matthew 10:26–27)

12 ¹Meanwhile, when a crowd of many thousands had assembled so that they were treading on each other, Jesus began speaking to his followers first, saying, "Be careful of the yeast of the Pharisees, which is hypocrisy. ²Everything that is concealed will be brought out into the open and every secret will be revealed. ³So then, whatever you have said in the dark will be heard in the broad daylight, and whatever you have whispered in private behind closed doors will be shouted from the rooftops.

Only God is to be feared
(Matthew 10:28–31)

⁴"I tell you my friends, do not be afraid of those who kill the body but cannot do anything worse after that. ⁵But I will show you whom to fear: fear *God*, who after killing the body, has the authority to throw one into hell. *Believe me*, he is the one to fear.

⁶"Are not five sparrows sold for two small coins? Yet not one of them is forgotten by God. ⁷Indeed, he has even counted all the hairs of your head. Don't be afraid as you are worth more than many sparrows.

Followers of Christ must confess him openly
(Matthew 10:32–33, 12:32, 10:19–20)

⁸"I tell you, whoever professes *his belief in* me openly before men, the Son of Man will also profess him openly before the angels of God. ⁹But he who disowns me before men will be disowned by me before the angels of God.

¹⁰"And every one of you who speaks a word against the Son of Man will be forgiven, but anyone who blasphemes against the Holy Breath will not be forgiven.

¹¹"And when you are brought before synagogues, rulers and authorities, do not worry about how you will defend yourselves or what you will say, ¹²for the Holy Breath will teach you at that time what you must say."

The parable of the rich fool

¹³A man in the crowd said to him, "Teacher, tell my brother to share our father's inheritance with me."

¹⁴But Jesus said to him, "Man, who appointed me as judge or executor over you two? ¹⁵Then he said to them all, "Watch out and be on your guard against

all kinds of greed. A man's life does not consist in the amount of material possessions that he has."

¹⁶Then Jesus told them a parable, "There was once a rich man who owned land that produced a good crop. ¹⁷He began thinking to himself, 'What shall I do? I have no place to store my crops.'

¹⁸"Then he said, 'This is what I will do. I will tear down my sheds and build bigger ones, and I will store all my grain and goods in them. ¹⁹And I'll say to myself, "You have plenty of good things stored up for many years. Take it easy. Eat, drink and be merry."'

²⁰"But God said to him, 'You fool! This very night your life will be up. Then who will get what you have reserved for yourself?'

²¹"This is how it will be with anyone who stores up things for himself but is not rich towards God."

Jesus teaches his followers not to worry
(Matthew 6:25–34)

²²Then Jesus said to his followers, "Therefore I tell you, do not worry about your life, what you will eat or about your body and what you will wear. ²³For life is more than about food and the body is more than about clothing. ²⁴Think carefully about the ravens:³⁶⁹ They do not sow or reap and they have no storeroom or shed yet God feeds them. And how much more valuable are you than birds? ²⁵Which one of you by worrying can add a single hour³⁷⁰ to his life? ²⁶Since you cannot do this very little thing, why do you worry about the rest?

²⁷"Think carefully how the lilies grow. They do not labour or make clothing for themselves. Yet I tell you, not even Solomon in all his splendour was dressed like one of these lilies. ²⁸And if that is how God clothes the grass in a field, which is here today and thrown into the fire tomorrow, how much more will he clothe you? You have such little faith! ²⁹So you must not be concerned about searching for what you will eat or drink—don't be anxious about it. ³⁰For the unbelieving world runs after all these things and your Father knows that you need them. ³¹But look to allow God to reign in your life and then these things will be given to you as well.

Having treasures in heaven
(Matthew 6:19–21)

³²"Do not be afraid, little flock, for your Father has been pleased to give the

---

369   This could be either crows or ravens as they are of the same corvid family. Interestingly, ravens are reputed to be the most intelligent of all birds with crows having an uncanny ability to remember faces. If the smartest bird does not sow or reap then we too shouldn't worry about our lives.
370   Literally cubit which is a small unit of measure. This could be an hour or a day.

realm where he rules, to you. ³³Sell your possessions and give them to the poor. Provide purses for yourselves that will not wear out, an inexhaustible treasure in heaven where no thief comes near and no moth destroys. ³⁴For your heart will also be in the thing that you treasure most.

We must become ready
(Matthew 24:42–44)

³⁵"Be dressed and ready for action, keeping the lamps[371] burning. ³⁶You should be like men waiting for their master when he returns from the wedding, so that when he comes and knocks they can immediately open the door for him. ³⁷Blessed are those servants whose master finds them watching when he comes. I tell you the truth, the master will put on his apron,[372] have them recline at the table and he himself will come and serve them. ³⁸Blessed are those servants whose master finds them ready, even if he comes in the second or third watch of the night.[373]

³⁹"But know this, that if the owner of the house had known at what hour the thief was coming, he would not have let his house be broken into. ⁴⁰You must also become ready because the Son of Man will come at an hour when you do not expect him.

The loyal and disloyal servants contrasted
(Matthew 24:45–51)

⁴¹Peter asked Jesus, "Lord, is this parable for us or for everyone?"

⁴²The Lord said, "Who, then, is the loyal and wise manager, whom the master puts in charge of the other servants to give them their food rations at the proper time? ⁴³Blessed is the servant whom the master finds working when he returns. ⁴⁴I tell you the truth, he will put him in charge of all his possessions. ⁴⁵But what if that *same* servant says to himself that his master is taking a long time to come back and he then begins to beat both the male and female servants and eats and drinks and gets drunk? ⁴⁶Then the master of that servant will come on a day when he does not expect him and at an hour he does not know and he will cut him to pieces[374] and his place will be with the unbelievers.

⁴⁷"The servant who knows his master's will and does not get ready or does not do what his master wants will receive a severe flogging. ⁴⁸But the one who does not know and does things deserving punishment will only receive a light flogging. Much is required from the person to whom much is given and much

---

371   I.e. the small oil lamps (*luchnos*) not the large torches (*lampas*) as in Matt. 25:1–13.
372   Literally, 'will dress himself'.
373   The second or third watches were the periods of deepest sleep.
374   In other words that servant will be severely punished.

more is required from the person who has been entrusted with much. Much more will be asked of him.

Jesus came to bring division not peace
(Matthew 10:34–36)

⁴⁹"I came to throw fire on the earth and how I wish it was already alight! ⁵⁰But I have a baptism *of suffering* ahead of me,³⁷⁵ and I am under a lot of stress until it is over! ⁵¹Do you think that I came to bring peace on earth? No, I tell you, I came to bring division. ⁵²From now on there will be five in one family divided against each other. Three against two and two against three. ⁵³They will be divided, father against son and son against father, mother against daughter and daughter against mother, mother-in-law against daughter-in-law and daughter-in-law against mother-in-law."

Understanding the times that we live in
(Matthew 5:25–26,16:2–3)

⁵⁴Jesus said to the crowds, "When you see a cloud rising in the west, immediately you say, 'It's going to rain,' and it happens. ⁵⁵And when the south wind blows, you say, 'It's going to be hot,' and it happens. ⁵⁶You hypocrites! You know how to interpret the appearance of the earth and the sky. Why is it then, that you do not know how to interpret this present time?

⁵⁷"Why is it that you cannot judge for yourselves what is the right thing to do *in a dispute*? ⁵⁸As you are on the way with your plaintiff to the court, try hard to receive a settlement from him while you are still on the way. Otherwise he may drag you off to the judge, the judge will turn you over to the bailiff, and the bailiff will put you in prison. ⁵⁹I tell you, you will not get out until you have paid the debt to the last cent."³⁷⁶

The choice: Turn away from sins or die

13 ¹At this same time, there were some there who told Jesus about the Galileans whom Pilate had killed while they were *at the temple* offering sacrifices. ²And Jesus asked, "What do you think? Were these Galileans worse sinners than all the other Galileans because they suffered this way? ³No, I tell you! But unless you turn from your sins, you too will all die as they did. ⁴And what about those eighteen people

---

375   Jesus is referring to the suffering on the cross still ahead of him.
376   We need to see that 'understanding the times we live in' means understanding that we need to settle our dispute (the sin issue) with God while we are on the way (still alive) to being judged by God lest we are thrown into hell. In this short parable, we are the accused, the plaintiff is Jesus, the bailiff is the angels and the judge is God. The debt to be paid is our sin and the prison is hell.

who died when the tower in Siloam fell on them? Do you think they were more guilty than all the others living in Jerusalem? ⁵Of course not! But unless you turn from your sins, you too will all die as they did."

The parable of the fig tree that didn't produce any fruit

⁶The Jesus told them the following parable: "There was once a man who had a fig tree that was planted in his vineyard and he came looking for fruit on it but he did not find any. ⁷So he said to the caretaker of the vineyard, 'I've been coming for three years now to look for fruit on this fig tree and I haven't found any. Cut it down! Why should it continue use up the soil?'

⁸"But the man replied saying, 'Boss, leave it for one more year, and I'll dig around it and throw some manure on it. ⁹If it bears fruit next year, fine! If not, then you can have me cut it down.'"

Jesus heals a crippled woman on the Sabbath

¹⁰Now Jesus was teaching in one of the synagogues on the Sabbath ¹¹and there was a woman there who had an evil spirit keeping her ill for eighteen years. She was bent over and could not straighten up at all. ¹²When Jesus saw her, he called her to come and he said to her, "Sister, you have been set free from your illness." ¹³Then he put his hands on her, and immediately she straightened up and gave God the glory.

¹⁴The synagogue leader however was indignant because Jesus had healed on the Sabbath. He said to the gathering, "There are six days for working. So come and be healed on those days, not on the Sabbath."

¹⁵The Lord answered him saying, "You hypocrites! Doesn't each of you on the Sabbath untie his ox or donkey from the manger and lead it out to give it water? ¹⁶Then should not this woman, a daughter of Abraham, whom Satan has kept bound for eighteen long years, be set free on the Sabbath day from what kept her in bondage?"

¹⁷When Jesus had said these things, all those opposed to him were put to shame, but the people were delighted with all the wonderful things he was doing.

The parable of the mustard seed and the yeast
(Matthew 13:31-33, Mark 4:30-32)

¹⁸Jesus asked, "What is the realm of God like? What shall I compare it to? ¹⁹It is like a mustard seed,³⁷⁷ which a man took and tossed into his garden. It grew and became a tree, and the birds of the air nested in its branches."

---

377   In Rabbinic literature the mustard seed was proverbial for an insignificant size or amount (TH).

²⁰And again Jesus asked, "What shall I compare the realm of God to? ²¹It is like yeast that a woman took and mixed into a large amount of flour³⁷⁸ until it worked through the whole batch of dough."

Enter through the narrow door
(Matthew 7:13-14, 21-23)

²²Jesus travelled throughout the cities and villages, teaching as he was making his way to Jerusalem. ²³Someone asked him, "Lord, are only a few people going to be saved?"

He said to them, ²⁴"Make every effort to enter through the narrow door, because many, I tell you, will try to enter and will not be able to. ²⁵Because once the owner of the house gets up and closes the door, you will stand outside and begin to knock, saying, 'Sir, open the door for us.'

"But he will answer, 'I don't know you or where you come from.'

²⁶"Then you will begin to say, 'We ate and drank with you, and you taught in our streets.'

²⁷"But he will reply, 'I don't know you or where you come from. Away from me, all you wicked people!'

²⁸"There will be weeping and gnashing of teeth when you see Abraham, Isaac and Jacob and all the prophets in the realm of God but you yourselves being thrown out. ²⁹People will come from the east and west, north and south, and they will recline at the table when God *begins to* reign.³⁷⁹ ³⁰Indeed there are those who are last who will be first, and first who will be last."

Jesus' sorrow for Jerusalem
(Matthew 23:37-39)

³¹At that very same hour some Pharisees approached Jesus and said to him, "Leave this place and go somewhere else because Herod wants to kill you."

³²Jesus said to them, "Go and tell that fox,³⁸⁰ 'I am casting out demons performing healings today and tomorrow and on the third day I will be finished.' ³³But it is necessary for me today and tomorrow and the one following to travel because it is unthinkable for a prophet to die outside of Jerusalem.

³⁴"Jerusalem, Jerusalem, you who are killing the prophets and stoning those

---

378   Literally three measures (*saton*) – the Hebrew measure of grain equivalent to 22 lbs or about 10 kg of wheat flour. The precise amount of flour is not important.
379   Cf. Rev. 19:9.
380   The metaphor of calling Herod the tetrarch a "fox" does not imply he is sly rather more probably treacherous as foxes would prey on hens. Jesus is not threatened by this threat rather he would continue on with his work and be killed in Jerusalem, ironically the centre of Jewish piety.

who are sent to you. How often I have wanted to gather your children together as a hen gathers her chicks under her wings, yet you were not willing! ³⁵Look! Your house is left to you desolate. I tell you, you will not see me again until you say, 'Blessed is he who comes in the name of the Lord.'"

Jesus heals a man suffering from oedema (dropsy)

14 ¹It came about on one Sabbath when Jesus went to eat in the house of a prominent Pharisee that he was being carefully watched. ²There in front of him was a man who was suffering from oedema.[381] ³And Jesus asked the experts in the law and the Pharisees, "Is it lawful to heal on the Sabbath or not?" ⁴But they remained silent. So taking hold of the man, he healed him and sent him on his way.

⁵Then he asked them, "If one of you has a son or an ox that falls into a well on the Sabbath day, will you not immediately pull him out?" ⁶And they had nothing to say in reply.

⁷When Jesus noticed how the guests were choosing the places of honour at the table, he told them this parable: ⁸ "When someone invites you to a wedding reception, do not take the place of honour, for a person more distinguished than you may have been invited. ⁹If so, the host who invited both of you will come and say to you, 'You'll have to move as this is his seat.' Then you will feel humiliated having to take your place at the least important position. ¹⁰But when you are invited, take the lowest place so that when your host comes, he will say to you, 'Friend, let's move you to a better seat.' Then you will feel honoured in the presence of your fellow guests. ¹¹For every one of you who honours himself will be humbled, and he who humbles himself will be exalted."

¹²Then Jesus said to the one who had invited him, "When you prepare a lunch or dinner, do not invite your friends, your brothers or relatives, or your rich neighbours. If you do, they will probably invite you back and so the gesture will be repaid. ¹³Instead when you give a banquet, invite the destitute, the disabled, the lame, and the blind, ¹⁴and you will be blessed. Although they cannot repay you, you will be repaid at the resurrection of the righteous."

The parable of the big dinner

¹⁵When one of the men reclining at the table with him heard this, he said to Jesus, "Blessed is the man who will eat in the coming reign of God."

¹⁶Jesus said to him, "There was a certain man who was preparing a big dinner and he invited many guests. ¹⁷And so when the day arrived for the dinner he

---

381 I.e. dropsy (obsolete) meaning swollen limbs due to fluid in the tissues of the body. Dropsy comes from the Latin *hydropsis* meaning 'water'. Alternative spelling 'edema' (American).

sent his servant to say to those who had been invited, 'Come, for everything is ready now.'

¹⁸"But everyone alike began to make excuses. The first one said, 'I have just bought some land and I have to go and check it out. Please excuse me.'

¹⁹"And another said, 'I have just bought five pairs of oxen, and I'm on my way to examine them. Please excuse me.'

²⁰"Still another said, 'I just got married, so I can't come.'

²¹"The servant came back and reported this to his master. Then the master of the house was very angry and ordered his servant, 'Go out quickly into the streets and alleys of the city and bring in the destitute, the disabled, the blind and the lame.'

²²"The servant answered, 'Boss, it has been already done what you have commanded but there are still places available.'

²³"Then the master told his servant, 'Go out to the roads and country lanes and make them come in so that my house will be full. ²⁴I tell you, not one of those men who had been invited will get to taste my dinner.'"

The cost of being a follower of Christ
(Matthew 10:37–38)

²⁵There were large crowds travelling with Jesus, and turning to them he said, ²⁶"If anyone comes to me and does not hate his father and mother, his wife and children, his brothers and sisters, and even his own life, he cannot be my follower. ²⁷Anyone who does not carry his cross and come after me cannot be my follower.

²⁸"Suppose that one of you wants to build a tower. Won't he first sit down and estimate the cost to see if he has enough money to complete the job. ²⁹Otherwise if he has laid the foundation but is not able to finish the job, everyone who sees it will ridicule him, ³⁰saying, 'This man began to build and was not able to finish.'

³¹"Or suppose a king is about to go to war against another king. Won't he first sit down and work out whether he is able with his ten thousand men to meet the one coming with twenty thousand? ³²If he is not able, he will send a representative while the other king is still a long way off and will ask for terms of peace."

³³In conclusion Jesus said, "Therefore if anyone among you does not give up everything he has, he cannot be a follower of mine.

The parable about salt
(Matthew 5:13, Mark 9:50)

³⁴"Salt is a good thing but if it loses its saltiness how can it be made salty

again? ³⁵It is neither useful for the soil nor useful for the manure pile rather it just has to be thrown away. He who has ears to hear this, let him really listen."

The parable of the one lost sheep
(Matthew 18:12–14)

15 ¹Now many tax collectors and outcasts³⁸² were gathering around to listen to Jesus. ²But the Pharisees and the scribes were complaining saying, "This man welcomes outcasts and eats with them."

³Then Jesus told them this parable: ⁴"Let's suppose that one of you has a hundred sheep and you happen to lose one of them. Will you not leave the ninety-nine in the open grassland and go after the one lost sheep until you find it? ⁵And when you find it, you will joyfully put it on your shoulder ⁶and go home. Then you will call your friends and neighbours together and say, 'Come and celebrate with me. I have found my one lost sheep.' ⁷I tell you that in the same way there will be more rejoicing in heaven over one sinner who turns to God than over ninety-nine righteous persons who do not need to turn to God.

The parable of the lost coin

⁸"Or let's suppose a woman has ten silver coins³⁸³ and she loses one. Will she not light a lamp, sweep the house and search carefully until she finds it? ⁹And when she finds it she calls her friends and neighbours together and says, 'Come and celebrate with me. I have found my lost coin.' ¹⁰In the same way, I tell you, there is rejoicing in the presence of the angels of God over one sinner who turns away from his sins and turns to God."

The parable of the prodigal son

¹¹Jesus continued, "There was a certain man who had two sons. ¹²The younger son said to his father, "Father, give me my share of the estate." So he divided his property between the two of them.

¹³"Not many days after that, the younger son gathered together all his things and set off for a distant country. It was there that he wasted his wealth in reckless living. ¹⁴After he had spent everything, there was a severe famine in that whole country and he was facing starvation. ¹⁵So he went and hired himself out to a citizen of that country, who sent him into his fields to feed pigs. ¹⁶He was so

---

382 Cf. Luke 5:32 and footnote.
383 Literally *drachma*, a Greek silver coin not worth very much. Ten drachmas is a very small possession (TH).

hungry that he began to wish that he could eat the carob pods[384] that the pigs were eating but no one was giving him anything to eat.

[17]"Having come to his senses, he said to himself, 'All of my father's employees have more than enough to eat and here I am starving to death! [18]I'm going to get up and go back to my father and say to him, "Father, I have sinned against heaven and against you. [19]I am no longer worthy to be called your son. Please make me like one of your employees."' [20]So he got up and went to his father.

"While he was still a fair way off, his father saw him and was moved with compassion for him. He ran to his son, threw his arms around him and kissed him.

[21]"The son said to him, 'Father, I have sinned against heaven and against you. I am no longer worthy to be called your son.' [22]But the father said to his servants, 'Quick! Bring the best robe and put it on him. Put a ring on his finger and sandals for the feet. [23]Bring the prize calf and slaughter it. Let's eat and celebrate, [24]because this son of mine was dead and is alive again. He was lost and now is found. So they began to celebrate.

[25]"Meanwhile the older son was in the field and as he was coming closer to the house he could hear music and dancing. [26]So he called one of the servants over and asked him what was going on. [27]And he said to him, 'Your brother is here and your father has sacrificed the fattened calf because he has received him back in good health.'

[28]"The older brother was angry and he refused to go in. So his father went out and pleaded with him *to come in*. [29]But he answered his father and said, 'Look! All these years I've worked for you like a slave and I never disobeyed your orders. Yet you never even gave a young goat for me so I could celebrate with my friends. [30]But when this son of yours who has wasted your property with prostitutes returns, you slaughter the prize calf for him!'

[31]"The father said, 'My son, you are always with me and everything I have is yours. [32]But we had to celebrate and be happy because your brother was dead and he is alive again. He was lost but now he is found.'"

The parable of the shrewd manager

16 [1]Jesus also said to his followers, "There was a certain rich man whose manager had a charge brought against him that he was wasting his boss' money. [2]So *the boss* called him in and asked him, 'What is this I hear about you? You

---

384 The husks in question were the long bean-shaped pods of the carob tree (*Caratonia siliqua*), commonly used for fattening swine in Syria and Egypt. They contain a proportion of sugar. The very poorest of the population occasionally use them as food.
Cf. https://biblehub.com/commentaries/pulpit/luke/15.htm

need to give an account of your management because you cannot be manager any longer.'

³"The manager said to himself, 'What am I going to do? My boss is firing me. I'm not strong enough to dig *ditches* and I'm not going to beg—that is shameful. ⁴I know what I'll do! Then when I am removed from the management position people will welcome me into their houses.'

⁵"So he called in each one of his boss' debtors. He asked the first one, 'How much do you owe my boss?'

⁶"He said, 'One hundred large jars of olive oil.'

"The manager told him, 'Take your bill, sit down quickly and make it just fifty.'

⁷"Then the manager asked the second debtor, 'And how much do you owe?'

"He replied, 'One thousand sacks of wheat.'

"He told him, 'Take your bill and let's make it eight hundred sacks of wheat that you now owe.'

⁸"Then later when the boss heard he commended the dishonest manager because he had acted shrewdly. For the people of this world are more shrewd in dealing with their own kind than are the people of the light. ⁹And so I say to you, make friends for yourselves using worldly wealth, so that when it is gone, you will be welcomed into eternal dwelling places.

¹⁰"And he who shows himself to be loyal in little *matters* will also be loyal when it comes to large *matters* and he who is dishonest in small *matters* will be dishonest in large *matters*. ¹¹So if you have not been loyal in handling worldly wealth, who will trust you to handle true riches? ¹²And if you have not been loyal with the thing belonging to someone else, who will give to you the thing that is yours?

¹³"No servant can serve two bosses. Either he will hate the one and love the other, or he will be devoted to the one and despise the other. You cannot serve both God and money."

¹⁴The Pharisees, who loved money, heard all this and were sneering at Jesus. ¹⁵He said to them, "You are the ones who make yourselves look right in other people's sight, but God knows your hearts because the thing that is highly sought after among men is an abomination[385] in God's eyes.

---

385 An "abomination" in the OT was usually used in reference to idol worship. It is that which is detestable or abhorrent and has the implication of the mixing of opposites together (i.e. good and evil). It comes from the Greek root *bdeo* that which emits a foul odour and hence is disgustingly abhorrent.

The Law will not disappear
(Matthew 11:12)

[16] "The Law and the Prophets[386] were in effect up to the time of John the Baptist. Since that time, the good news about the coming reign of God is being preached and everyone is trying to force their way into being a part of it.

[17] "It is easier for heaven and earth to disappear than for the least pen stroke in the Law to cease to exist.

Divorce
(Matthew 5:31–32, 19:9, Mark 10:11–12)

[18] "Every one of you[387] who divorces his wife and marries another woman commits adultery, and the one who marries a divorced woman commits adultery.

The rich man and Lazarus[388]

[19] "Now there was a certain rich man who clothed himself in purple[389] and fine linen and lived in luxury every day. [20] Laying at his gate was a poor man named Lazarus who was covered in sores. [21] He was hoping to eat what fell from the rich man's table. Even the dogs would often come and lick his sores.

[22] "It came about in the fullness of time that the poor man died and the angels carried him to be with Abraham. The rich man also died and was buried. [23] In Hades, where he was in torment, he looked up and saw Abraham far away with Lazarus by his side. [24] And so he called out to him, 'Father Abraham, have pity on me and send Lazarus to dip the tip of his finger in water and cool my tongue because I am in agony in this fire.'

[25] "But Abraham said, 'Son, remember that in your lifetime you received your good things, while Lazarus received bad things. But now he is comforted here and you are in agony. [26] Besides all these things, a great chasm has been fixed so that those who want to go from here to you are unable, nor can anyone cross over from there to us.'

[27] "The rich man answered, 'Then I beg you, father, send Lazarus to my

---

386   The "Law" is the first five books of the Bible (Torah) and the "Prophets" consisted of eight books: Joshua, Judges, Samuel, Kings, Jeremiah, Ezekiel, Isaiah and the Twelve (the Minor Prophets).
387   Jesus is specifically talking about the Pharisees as a group in this context.
388   The question here is whether this is a real story or a parable. A parable usually presented a spiritual truth using an earthly illustration. The story of the rich man and Lazarus presents spiritual truth directly, with no earthly metaphor. Secondly, the poor man is named (Lazarus) which is unusual for a parable. At any rate even if the story is not real, the inclusion of Lazarus' name makes it very realistic, the lesson being that there is an afterlife and the decisions made on earth have eternal and irreversible consequences.
389   The colour purple was hard to come by in the ancient times and very expensive as it was derived from the murex shellfish. It was usually only worn by kings and rich people.

father's house, ²⁸for I have five brothers. He could warn them so that they will not also come to this place of torment.'

²⁹"But Abraham said, 'They have Moses and the Prophets,³⁹⁰ let them listen to them.'

³⁰"But he said to him, 'No, father Abraham. However if someone from the dead goes to them, they will turn to God.'

³¹"But Abraham said to him, 'If they do not listen to Moses and the Prophets, they will not be convinced even if someone rises from the dead.'"

How to deal with sin
(Matthew 18:6–7, Matthew 18:21–22, Mark 9:42)

17 ¹Jesus said to his followers, "People will always be tempted to fall into sin but what a disaster it will be for him through whom it comes. ²It would be better for him to be thrown into the sea with a millstone around his neck than for him to cause one of these little ones to stumble. So be very careful and pay attention.

³"If your brother *in Christ* sins, rebuke him but if he turns from his sins, forgive him. ⁴If he sins against you seven times in one day, and seven times comes to you saying, 'I have changed my ways,' you are to forgive him."

Having faith as small as a mustard seed

⁵The apostles said to the Lord, "Help us to have even more faith." ⁶The Lord said, "If you have faith as small as a mustard seed, you can say to this mulberry tree, 'Be uprooted and be planted in the sea,' and it will obey you.

Doing one's duty as a servant of God

⁷"What if a man had a servant ploughing *a field* or looking after the sheep. Would he say to the servant when he comes in straight from the field, 'Come, recline and eat'? ⁸No. Wouldn't he rather say, 'Make my dinner, put an apron on and serve me until I have finished eating and drinking. After that you may eat and drink'? ⁹Would he thank the servant because he had done what he was told to do? Of course not! ¹⁰So you also, when you have done everything you were told to do, should say, 'We are useless servants; we have only done our duty.'"

Jesus heals ten men of leprosy

¹¹And it came about while Jesus was on his way to Jerusalem, he was travelling along the border between *the districts of* Samaria and Galilee. ¹²As he

---

390　I.e. They have the Law of Moses (Torah) and the writings of the prophets which were read out every Sabbath day in the synagogue. The Hebrew Bible has three divisions: the Law, the Prophets, and the Writings.

was entering a certain village, ten men who had leprosy met him. They stood at a distance ¹³and called out to him in a loud voice, "Jesus, Master, have mercy on us!"

¹⁴When he saw them, he said, "Go and show yourselves to the priests." And as they went, they were cleansed.

¹⁵One of them, having seen that he was healed, came back praising God in a loud voice. ¹⁶He threw himself down at Jesus' feet and thanked him—he was a Samaritan.

¹⁷Jesus asked, "Were not all ten healed? Where are the other nine? ¹⁸Why is this foreigner the only one who came back to give glory to God?" ¹⁹Then he said to him, "Rise and go; your faith has made you well."

The coming reign of God
(Matthew 24:23–28, 24:37–41)

²⁰Now having been asked by the Pharisees when God's coming reign would begin, Jesus answered them and said, "God's coming reign will not come in a way that you can see it necessarily, ²¹nor will people say, 'Here it is,' or 'There it is,' no! God's reign is in your midst."[391]

²²Then he said to his followers, "The days are coming when you will be wishing to see one of the days of the Son of Man, but you will not see it.[392] ²³And they will say to you, 'Look! There he is,' or 'Here he is!' Do not go out looking *for him* in pursuit." ²⁴For the Son of Man in his day will be like the lightning, which flashes and lights up the sky from one end to the other. ²⁵But first it is necessary for him to suffer many things and be rejected by this generation.

²⁶"And just as it was in the days of Noah, so will it also be in the days of the Son of Man. ²⁷In Noah's day, people were eating, drinking, marrying and being given in marriage right up to the day Noah entered the ark. Then the flood came and destroyed them all.

²⁸"It was also the same in the days of Lot. People were eating and drinking, buying and selling, planting and building. ²⁹But on the day Lot left Sodom, fire and sulphur rained down from heaven and destroyed everyone.

³⁰"It will be just like this on the day the Son of Man is revealed. ³¹On that day no one who is on the roof of his house,[393] with his belongings inside, should go down and get them. Likewise, anyone who is out in the field must not go back

---

391   God's reign has already commenced in a sense because Jesus is with them. Of course the physical millennial reign of Christ is yet to come.
392   This is referring to the last days during the tribulation period. Such will be the darkness of those days that believers will be wishing they could visibly see Jesus.
393   The flat rooftop of the Middle Eastern houses was where residents went to rest and talk after a day's work. They had stairways that led down the outside wall of the house meaning that one could make haste by fleeing and not having to go inside to collect one's belongings.

for anything. ³²Remember Lot's wife! ³³Those who try to save their own life will lose it, and those who lose their life will save it.

³⁴"I tell you, on that night two people will be sleeping in the same bed; one will be taken and the other left behind. ³⁵Two women will be grinding grain together; one will be taken and the other left. [³⁶Two men will be in the field; one will be taken and the other left."]³⁹⁴

³⁷They asked him, "Where, Lord?"

He answered them, "Where the body is, there the eagles will be gathered together."³⁹⁵

The parable of the persistent widow

18 ¹Jesus then told his followers a parable to show them that they should always pray and not give up. ²He said, "In a certain city there was a judge who neither feared God nor cared about what people thought. ³And there was *also* a widow in that city who kept coming to him saying, 'Grant me justice against my opponent.'³⁹⁶

⁴"At first for some time he refused. But finally he said to himself, 'Even though I don't fear God or care what people think ⁵yet because this widow keeps bothering me, I will see that she gets justice. Otherwise she will keep coming and wear me out!'"

⁶And the Lord said, "Listen to what the unjust judge says. ⁷Now will not God bring about justice for his chosen ones who cry out to him day and night? Will he delay in helping them? ⁸I tell you, he will bring about justice for them quickly. However, when the Son of Man comes, will he find the *Christian* faith³⁹⁷ on the earth?"

The parable of the Pharisee and the tax collector

⁹Jesus also had a message for some of them who were self-confident in their own righteousness and those who were arrogant. He told this parable: ¹⁰"Two men went up to the temple to pray, one a Pharisee and the other a tax collector. ¹¹The Pharisee, standing up, prayed silently, 'God, I thank you that I am not like the other men—robbers, unrighteous, adulterers, or even like this tax collector here. ¹²I fast twice a week and give a tenth of all I get.'

---

394   Only the TR (KJV) includes this verse indicating that there is some degree of doubt.
395   'Body' has the definite article (the) before it, indicating that it is a known body or corpse. Michael the archangel and the devil argued over the dead body of Moses (Jude 9) buried near Mt. Nebo, possibly indicating the gathering point for all the raptured. If so, the angels will gather the elect from the four winds taking them to this point (Matt. 24:31). Mt. Nebo is also the Valley of Hamon Gog which will block the way of the travellers (evil spirits). Cf. Eze. 39:11.
396   Gk: *antidikou*—technical term for opponent or other party in court proceedings; litigant.
397   The definite article (the) is present in the Greek which is missing in most translations.

¹³"But the tax collector stood at a distance and he would not even raise his eyes up to heaven, but he was beating his chest and said, 'God, have mercy on me, a sinner.'

¹⁴"I tell you, that this man, rather than the Pharisee, went home being declared righteous before God. For every one of you who lifts up himself will be humbled, and he who humbles himself will be lifted up."

Let the little children come
(Matthew 19:13–15, Mark 10:13–16)

¹⁵The people were also bringing babies to Jesus that he might touch them. When the followers saw this, they rebuked them. ¹⁶But Jesus beckoned the children to come to him and said, "Permit the little children to come to me, and do not try and stop them, for God will reign over people such as these ones. ¹⁷I tell you the truth, anyone who does not welcome God's reign like a little child will by no means enter into it."

The rich young leader
(Matthew 19:16–30, Mark 10:17–31)

¹⁸"A certain leader asked Jesus, "Good teacher, what must I do to inherit eternal life?"

¹⁹Jesus said to him, "Why do you call me good? No one is good except God alone. ²⁰You know the commandments: 'Do not commit adultery; do not murder; do not steal; do not bear false witness,³⁹⁸ honour your father and mother.'"

²¹The man said, "I have kept all of these from my youth."

²²When Jesus heard this, he said to him, "You still lack one thing. Sell everything you have and give the proceeds to the poor and you will have treasure in the heavens and then come and follow me." ²³But having heard these instructions, he became very sad for he was a very rich man.

²⁴Jesus looked at him and said, "How hard it is for the rich to enter into God's realm. ²⁵It is easier for a camel to enter through the eye of a needle than for a rich man to enter into God's realm."

²⁶Those who heard this said, "Who then is able to be saved?" ²⁷Jesus said, "What is impossible with men is possible with God."

²⁸Peter said to him, "We have left everything we have to follow you!"

²⁹And Jesus said to them, "I tell you the truth, no one who has left home or wife or brothers or parents or children because of God's reign ³⁰will fail to receive many times as much in this age and eternal life in the age to come."

---

398   I.e. telling lies.

Jesus again predicts his coming death
(Matthew 20:17–19, Mark 10:32–34)

³¹Jesus took the Twelve aside and said to them, "We are going up to Jerusalem, everything that has been written by the prophets about the Son of Man will be fulfilled. ³²For he will be handed over to the Gentiles and he will be mocked and mistreated by them. They will spit on him, ³³flog him and they will kill him and on the third day he will rise again."

³⁴They did not understand any of this. The significance of his words was hidden from them and they did not understand what was being said.

Jesus heals a blind man on the side of the road
(Matthew 20:29–34, Mark 10:46–52)

³⁵As Jesus was approaching Jericho, a blind man was sitting on the side of the road begging. ³⁶The man heard the commotion of the crowd going by and asked what was going on. ³⁷They told him that Jesus of Nazareth was passing by.

³⁸He cried out, "Jesus, Son of David, have mercy on me!"

³⁹Those who were in front of him told him off telling him to be quiet but he shouted even louder, "Son of David, have mercy on me!"

⁴⁰Jesus stopped and ordered the man to be brought to him. When he came near, Jesus asked him, ⁴¹"What do you want me to do for you?" "Lord, I want my sight to be restored," he said.

⁴²And Jesus said to him, "Recover your sight; your faith has healed you." ⁴³Immediately the blind man was able to see again and he followed Jesus, giving God the glory. Having seen this, all the people gave the praise to God.

Zacchaeus the tax collector

19 ¹Jesus entered Jericho and was only passing through. ²And there happened to be a man there named Zacchaeus who was a chief tax collector and wealthy. ³He was wanting to see who Jesus was, but he was not able to due to the crowd because he was a short man. ⁴Therefore he ran ahead and climbed a sycamore-fig[399] tree so that he might see him since Jesus was about to pass by that way.

⁵As Jesus approached he looked up and said to him, "Zacchaeus, come down quickly, for I must stay at your house today." ⁶So he hurried down and happily welcomed him. ⁷Everyone saw this and began complaining, saying, "He has gone to stay in the house of a sinner."

⁸Zacchaeus stood up and said to the Lord, "Hear me, Lord! I am going to give

---

399 A broad, heavy tree reaching a height of around 15 m with large strong branches low down on the tree. The fruit has an appearance of a small fig but with an unpleasant taste.

half of my possessions to the poor and if I have cheated anybody out of anything, I will pay him back four times the amount."

⁹Jesus said to him, "Today salvation has come to this house, because this man too, is a son of Abraham. ¹⁰For the Son of Man came to seek and to save the lost."

The parable of the ten gold coins
(Matthew 25:14–30)

¹¹While they were hearing these things, Jesus continued and told them a parable because he was now almost at Jerusalem and the people thought that they were going to see the reign of God right away.

¹²So then Jesus said, "A man of noble birth went to a distant country to have himself appointed king after which he would return. ¹³So he called ten of his servants and gave a gold coin[400] to each of them instructing, 'Put this money to work until I come back.'

¹⁴"But his citizens hated him and they sent a representative after him to say, 'We don't want this man to be our king.'

¹⁵"It came about that he returned after having been made king, and he called for his servants to whom he had given the money to. He wanted to know what profit they had made. ¹⁶The first man came and said, 'Lord, your gold coin has earned ten more.' ¹⁷The king said to him, 'Well done, good servant. Because you were loyal in a very small thing, you can be in charge over ten cities.'

¹⁸"The second man came and said, 'Lord, your gold coin has earned five more.' ¹⁹The king said to this man also, 'You can be in charge over five cities.'

²⁰"Then another man came and said, 'Lord, here is your gold coin. I have kept it safely hidden away in a napkin. ²¹For I was afraid of you because you are a hard man and you take what is not yours and you reap where you did not sow.' ²²The king said to him, 'I will judge you by your own mouth, you evil servant! You knew, did you, that I am a hard man, that I take out what I did not put in, and I reap what I did not sow? ²³Why then didn't you put my money on deposit, so that when I came back, I could have at least collected it with interest?'

²⁴"Then the king said to those standing nearby. 'Take this man's gold coin away from him and give it to the one who has ten gold coins.' ²⁵They said to him, 'Lord, he already has ten gold coins.'

²⁶"The king said, 'I tell you that to everyone who has, more will be given but as for the one who has nothing, even what he has will be taken away. ²⁷But as for those enemies of mine who did not want me to be king over them—bring them here and kill them in my presence.'"

---

400 I.e. *minas*. A Greek monetary unit worth one hundred denarii.

Jesus' triumphal entry into Jerusalem

(Matthew 21:1–11, Mark 11:1–11, John 12:12–19)

²⁸ After Jesus had finished this parable, he travelled ahead of them, going up to Jerusalem. ²⁹ As he approached Bethphage and Bethany at the hill called the Mount of Olives, he sent two of his followers ahead ³⁰ saying, "Go into the village opposite. Upon entering you will find a colt tied there, which no one has ever ridden before. Untie it and bring it here. ³¹ If anyone asks you, 'Why are you untying it?' tell him, 'The Lord needs it.'"

³² Those who were sent ahead found everything just as he had told them. ³³ While they were untying the colt, its owners asked them, "Why are you untying the colt?"

³⁴ They said, "The Lord needs it." ³⁵ They brought it to Jesus and threw their coats on the colt and helped Jesus on it. ³⁶ As he was going along, the people were spreading out their coats on the road.

³⁷ When Jesus came near the place where the road goes down the Mount of Olives, the whole crowd of the followers burst out in praise to God with joy for all the miracles they had seen, ³⁸ singing,

> "Blessed is the king who comes in the name of the Lord!
> "Peace in heaven and glory *to God* in the highest *heaven*!"

Psalm 118:26

³⁹ Then some of the Pharisees in the crowd said to Jesus, "Teacher. Rebuke your followers!"

⁴⁰ And Jesus answered saying, "I tell you, if they keep quiet, the very stones will cry out."[401]

Jesus weeps for Jerusalem

⁴¹ As Jesus approached Jerusalem and saw the city, he wept over it ⁴² and said, "If you had only known on this day—what you would just need to do to bring you peace. But now it is hidden from your eyes. ⁴³ The days will come upon you when your enemies will build a barricade against you and they will encircle you and hem you in from all sides.[402] ⁴⁴ And they will raze you to the ground, you and your children within your walls. They will not leave one stone on another, because you did not recognise the time of your visitation."[403]

---

401 Cf. Hab. 2:11.
402 This happened in AD 70 when Titus laid siege and surrounded Jerusalem for five months from April to October AD 70.
403 The people of Jerusalem did not recognise Jesus as the very Son of God and his coming to earth

Jesus enters the temple
(Matthew 21:12–17, Mark 11:15–19, John 2:13–22)

[45] And having entered the *outer court of the* temple Jesus began forcing out those who were doing a market there [46] saying to them, "It is written, 'My house will be a house of prayer',[404] but you have made it 'a hideout for robbers'." [405]

[47] Every day Jesus was teaching at the temple but the chief priests, the scribes and the leaders among the people were trying to kill him. [48] But they could not find a way to do it because all the people were hanging upon his every word.

The authority of Jesus questioned
(Matthew 21:23–27, Mark 11:27–33)

20 [1] One day when Jesus was teaching the people in the temple and preaching the gospel, the chief priests and the scribes together with the elders, came up to him and asked him, [2] "Can you tell us by what authority you are doing these things and who gave you this authority?"

[3] Jesus answered and said, "I have a question for you as well. Tell me, [4] where did John's authority to baptise come from? Did it come from heaven or from men?"

[5] And so they reasoned among themselves saying, "If we say, 'From heaven,' he will ask, 'Well, why didn't you believe him?' [6] But if we say, 'From men,' all the people will stone us, because they are persuaded that John was a prophet." [7] So they answered that they did not know where it came from.

[8] Jesus said to them, "Neither will I tell you by what authority I am doing these things."

The parable of the vineyard
(Matthew 21:33–46, Mark 12:1–12)

[9] Then Jesus began to tell the people this parable: "A man planted a vineyard and rented it out to some farmers and then went away for a long time. [10] At the harvest time he sent a servant to the farmers in order to collect his share of the harvest. But the farmers beat him up and sent him away empty-handed. [11] So the *owner* proceeded to send another servant but he also was beaten, treated shamefully and sent away empty-handed. [12] The *owner* tried a third time and they

---

from heaven to save them from their sins. Cf. Matt. 24:1–2. The point is that if they had accepted Jesus as Saviour then things would be very different and God's kingdom would have commenced back then. As it is the Jew's rejection of Jesus meant that the Gentiles could be grafted into the tree (Rom. 11:11–24).

404 Cf. Isa. 56:7.
405 Cf. Jer. 7:11.

also wounded him and forced him out. ¹³The owner of the vineyard said, 'What am I going to do? I will send my son, whom I love. Perhaps they will respect him.'

¹⁴"But when the farmers saw him, they talked the matter over and said, 'This is the heir. Let's kill him and then the inheritance will be ours.' ¹⁵So they forced him out of the vineyard and killed him.

"What then will the owner of the vineyard do to them? ¹⁶He will come himself and kill those farmers and give the vineyard to others."

When the people heard this parable, they said, "May it never be!"

¹⁷Jesus looked directly at them and asked, "Then what does this Scripture mean:

"'The stone the builders rejected has become the cornerstone'?

Psalm 118:22

¹⁸Every one of you who falls on that stone will be broken to pieces, but he on whom it falls will be crushed."⁴⁰⁶

¹⁹The scribes and the chief priests looked for a way to arrest him immediately because they knew he had spoken this parable against them. But they were afraid of the people.

A question about who to pay taxes to
(Matthew 22:15–22, Mark 12:13–17)

²⁰They were keeping a close watch on him, so they sent spies who pretended to be sincere, that they might catch Jesus out on something he said. Then they would be able to hand him over to the authority and jurisdiction of the *Roman* governor. ²¹The spies questioned him saying, "Teacher, we know that you speak and teach what is right, and that you do not show favouritism but teach the way of God in line with the truth. ²²Should we pay taxes to Caesar or not?"

²³However Jesus could see through their duplicity and he said to them, ²⁴"Show me a denarius. Whose face and inscription is on it?"

²⁵"Caesar's," they said.

He said to them, "Then give to Caesar what is Caesar's, and to God what is God's."

²⁶And they were not able to catch him out in what he said in the presence of the people instead they were astonished by his answer and kept quiet.

---

406   The lesson is that those who do not accept Jesus will be broken to pieces and those who fall under his judgment will be completely smashed. Cf. Dan. 2:34–35, 44–45. The Messiah is a rock that will eventually crush the Gentile kingdoms of the world.

The Sadducees test Jesus about the resurrection
(Matthew 22:23–33, Mark 12:18–27)

²⁷Some of the Sadducees, who speak against the resurrection, came to Jesus with a question asking, ²⁸"Teacher, Moses wrote to us that if a man's brother dies and leaves a wife but no children, then the man must marry the widow and have children for his brother. ²⁹Now suppose there are seven brothers and the first one died leaving his wife childless. ³⁰The second *brother died* and ³¹then the third *brother* married her, and in the same way all seven *brothers* died, leaving her no children. ³²Finally, the woman herself died too. ³³Therefore, in the resurrection, whose wife will she be, since all seven were married to her?"

³⁴Jesus said to them, "The people of this age marry and are given in marriage. ³⁵But those whom God considers worthy of taking part in the next age and in the resurrection from the dead will neither marry nor be given in marriage ³⁶and they can no longer die.⁴⁰⁷ For they are like angels and they are of God since they are children of the resurrection. ³⁷Furthermore, even Moses showed that the dead rise, for he calls the Lord 'the God of Abraham, the God of Isaac, and the God of Jacob.' ³⁸He is not the God of the dead, but the God of the living, for God sees everyone as being alive."

³⁹Hearing that answer some of the scribes said, "Well said teacher!" ⁴⁰No one dared ask him any more questions.

A question about the Son of David
(Matthew 22:41–46, Mark 12:35–37)

⁴¹Then Jesus said to them, "Why do they say that the Messiah is the Son of David? ⁴²For David himself says in the book of the Psalms,

'The Lord *God* said to my Lord, "Sit at my right hand.
⁴³*Sit* until I make your enemies as a footstool for your feet."'

Psalm 110:1

⁴⁴David called the Messiah, 'Lord.' Therefore how can the Messiah be David's descendant?"

---

407 This is not a proof text implying that angels are immortal rather it is saying in the next life believers will be like angels in the sense that they will not marry or procreate. This is often mistranslated saying that believers in the next world are like angels in the sense that they do not die like the angels. God alone is immortal (1 Tim. 6:16). Christians will be clothed with immortality, it is not something that we have intrinsic in ourselves (1 Cor. 15:54).

Jesus warns against the scribes
(Matthew 23:1–36, Mark 12:37–40, Luke 11:37–54)

⁴⁵While all the people were listening, Jesus said to his followers, ⁴⁶"Beware of the scribes. They like to walk around in flowing robes and love to be formally greeted in the marketplaces and have the most important seats in the synagogues and the places of honour at banquets. ⁴⁷And yet they take advantage of widows and rob them of their homes and then make a show of saying long prayers. These men will receive greater judgment."

The widow's offering to God
(Mark 12:41–44)

21 ¹Jesus looked up and saw the rich men putting their gifts into the temple treasury. ²He also saw a poor widow put in two very small copper coins. ³He said, "I tell you the truth, this poor widow has put in more than all the others. ⁴Everyone else gave their gifts out of their wealth but she gave out of her poverty, everything that she had to live on."

Jesus predicts the coming destruction of the temple in AD 70
(Matthew 24:1–2, Mark 13:1–2)

⁵Some of Jesus' followers were admiring the temple how it was decorated with beautiful stones and remarking about the gifts that had been dedicated to God. But Jesus said, ⁶"As for these things you are looking at, the days are coming when not one stone will be left on another. Every stone will be thrown down."

The Olivet Discourse
(Matthew 24:3–14, Mark 13:3–13)

⁷They asked Jesus, "Teacher, when will these things happen? And what will be the sign that they are about to take place?"

⁸He said, "Watch out that you are not deceived. For many will come in my name claiming that they are me and saying, 'The time is near.' Do not follow them. ⁹When you hear of wars and terrorist acts, do not be frightened. These things must happen first, but the end will not come right away."

¹⁰Then he said to them, "Nations will make war with each other and different alliances will attack each other. ¹¹There will be great earthquakes, famines and pestilences in various places and there will be horrors⁴⁰⁸ and great signs from the sky.

---

408   This is the Greek word *phobetron* essentially meaning things to be scared of that come from the sky.

Surviving the Great Tribulation (the last 1290 days)
(Matthew 24:15-28, Mark 13:14-23)

¹²"But before all these things, they will arrest you and persecute you. They will deliver you to synagogues and prisons, and you will be brought before kings and governors because *you believe in* my name. ¹³It will turn out that this will be an opportunity to give your testimony.[409] ¹⁴Be determined however not to prepare how to defend yourselves. ¹⁵For I will give you words and wisdom that none of you enemies will be able to refute or contradict.

¹⁶"You will be betrayed *to the authorities* even by parents, brothers, relatives and friends, and they will put some of you to death.[410] ¹⁷Everyone will hate you because *you believe in* my name. ¹⁸But not one hair on your head will be lost. ¹⁹By standing firm you will save your life.

²⁰"When you see Jerusalem being surrounded by armies, you will know that its devastation is near.[411] ²¹Then those who are in Judea must flee to the mountains.[412] Those in the city must get out and those in the countryside must not enter it. ²²For these are the days of vengeance to be fulfilled that has been written about. ²³What a disaster it will be in those days for pregnant women and breastfeeding mothers! There will be great distress in the land and his anger will be upon this people. ²⁴They will be killed by the sword and will be led captive as prisoners into all the nations. Jerusalem will be trampled on by the Gentiles until the times of the Gentiles are fulfilled.

	In Greek mythology, a phobetor was a god, the 'god of nightmares' personified as monsters. Perhaps Jesus was saying that there will be monster gods or aliens in the end times. Cf. Rev. 12:9.
409	A Christian's testimony about how and what God has done for him in saving him. It will be an opportunity to preach the gospel.
410	These are the left behind who become tribulation martyrs of Rev. 7:14 and refuse the mark of the beast. Note however that not all will be killed and these will be the elect, the survivors. These will be raptured at the end in the twinkling of an eye.
411	Many Bible commentators see vv. 20-21 as being primarily fulfilled in AD 70 when the Roman Army surrounded and laid siege to Jerusalem. They say that this is not the Olivet Discourse but the Temple Discourse earlier in the day (Luke 21:37) and therefore it is referring to different times and events. Also because v. 12 says "before all these things", the inference is drawn that this occurs nearly 2000 years earlier in AD 70. Even though many Christians fled to Pella because they apparently heeded this advice, its primary fulfilment is yet to come just before the midpoint of Daniel's 70th week. Note that it says armies (plural) whereas in AD 70, it was only the Roman Army (singular). Joel Richardson makes an interesting point too that "if Jesus' warning in Luke 21:20-21 concerned Titus' destruction of Jerusalem, as so many commentators argue, then he gave some truly poor advice. Anyone in Jerusalem who waited until the city was surrounded to attempt to flee would have been taken prisoner or killed." He says, "I am of the opinion that we must understand all of Luke 21 as yet to be fulfilled." Cf. https://joelstrumpet.com/?p=6920
412	The actual mountains that people must flee to and take refuge is not defined but the closest mountains are the mountains across the Jordan Valley. Crossing the Jordan has traditionally been a place of refuge over the millennia. Cf. Matt. 24:15-16, John 10:40.

The coming of the Son of Man after the tribulation
(Matthew 24:29-31, Mark 13:24-27)

²⁵"There will be signs in the sun, moon and stars. On the earth, nations will be very anxious and perplexed about the sound of the sea and the surging waves.[413] ²⁶People will be terrified at what they see the world coming to, for the powers of the heavens will be shaken. ²⁷At this time they will see the Son of Man coming on a cloud with power and great glory. ²⁸When these things start to occur, stand up straight and lift up your heads because your liberation is drawing near."

The parable of the fig tree
(Matthew 24:32-35, Mark 13:28-31)

²⁹Jesus continued by telling them this parable: "Look at the fig tree and every other tree. ³⁰When you see their leaves sprouting you realise that summer is already near. ³¹Therefore, when you see these things happening, you can know that God will be reigning soon.

³²"I tell you the truth, this generation will certainly not pass away until all these things have happened. ³³Heaven and earth will pass away, but my words will never pass away."

Christians must flee from all that is about to happen

³⁴"Be careful, or you may overindulge, gorging yourself on food and drink due to the worries of life and then that day will close on you unexpectedly like a trap. ³⁵For that day will come upon all those who live upon the whole face of the earth. ³⁶But be always watching and praying that you may be able to flee everything that is about to happen so that you may be strong enough to stand before the Son of Man."[414]

³⁷Each day Jesus was teaching at the temple and each evening he went out to spend the night on the hill called the Mount of Olives. ³⁸Early each morning all the people went to the temple to hear him *speak*.

---

413 This could mean massive tsunamis due to the earthquakes.
414 One might misinterpret this verse as saying that we passively avoid or escape the tribulation by being ready for a supposed imminent pre-trib rapture at any moment but this is not what this verse is saying. The verb from the Greek root *ekpheugo* is in the active voice. In other words it is something that Christians need to do, it is not something that passively happens to them. When the signal comes at the halfway point of the tribulation, when the armies surround Jerusalem (Luke 21:20-21) and the Abomination of Desolation is set up on the wings of the Jewish temple, (Matt. 24:15-16) then the instruction for believers is to flee to the mountains across the Jordan Valley to Petra, Bozrah and southern Jordan in general. There, protection and refuge is available under the wings of the Almighty (Psa. 91).

The plot against Jesus
(Matthew 26:1–5, 26:14–16, Mark 14:1–2, 10–11, John 11:45–53)

22 ¹The Feast of Unleavened Bread called the Passover[415] was approaching ²and the chief priests and the scribes were looking for some way how they might have Jesus put to death but they were afraid of the people.

³Then Satan entered Judas called Iscariot, one of the Twelve.[416] ⁴Having departed, Judas made his way to the chief priests and the officers of the temple guard and discussed how he might betray Jesus to them. ⁵They were delighted and agreed to pay him money. ⁶He consented and watched for an opportunity to hand Jesus over to them when no crowd was present.

The Last Supper
(Matthew 26:17–25, Mark 14:12–21, John 13:21–30)

⁷Then the day came during the Feast of Unleavened Bread when it was time for the Passover lamb to be sacrificed. ⁸Jesus sent Peter and John with the instructions, "Go and make preparations for us to eat the Passover meal."[417]

⁹They asked, "Where do you want us to prepare for it?"

¹⁰He said to them, "As you enter the city, a man carrying a jar of water will meet you. Follow him to the house that he enters, ¹¹and say to the owner of the house, 'The Teacher asks, "Where is the room where my followers and I will eat the Passover meal?"' ¹²And he will show you a large upper room that is furnished. Make preparations there." ¹³They departed and found things just as Jesus had told them and they prepared the Passover meal.

Jesus gives thanks for the bread and the cup
(Matthew 26:26–30, Mark 14:22–26, 1 Corinthians 11:23–25)

¹⁴When the hour came, Jesus and his apostles reclined at the table. ¹⁵And he said to them, "I have been really looking forward to eating this Passover meal with you before I suffer. ¹⁶For I tell you, I will not eat it again until it has its ultimate fulfilment in the coming reign of God."

¹⁷After taking the cup, he gave thanks and said, "Take this cup and share it among yourselves. ¹⁸For I tell you, I will not drink of the fruit of the vine again until God establishes his reign."

¹⁹Jesus took the bread, and having given thanks he broke it and gave it to

---

415   I.e. Pesach (Hebrew).
416   Satan did not enter Judas on the night of the Last Supper but this occurred two nights before. Cf. Matt. 26:6–13, John 13:27.
417   The Passover meal is known as a Seder (order) in Hebrew.

them saying, "This is my body which is being given for you. You must keep doing this so that you can remember me." ²⁰In the same way, after they had eaten, he took the cup, saying, "This cup is the new covenant in my blood, which is being poured out for you.

²¹"Nevertheless, look! The one who is going to betray me is with me here at this table. ²²For indeed, the Son of Man will go *to his death* as has been determined, but what a disaster for that man who betrays him."

²³Then they began to discuss among themselves which one of them it could be who was going to do this.

Jesus' followers argue over who is the greatest among them

²⁴A dispute broke out among Jesus' followers as to which one of them was to be regarded as the greatest. ²⁵He said to them, "The kings of the Gentile nations lord it over their people but they are dictators who like to think they are benevolent. ²⁶But you must not be like that. Instead, the greatest among you should be like the youngest and the one who leads must be like the one who serves. ²⁷For who is greater? The one who is reclining at the table or the one who is serving? Is it not the one who is reclining at the table? But I am among you as the one serving.

²⁸"But you have stood by me in all my trials. ²⁹And I decree that you may rule just as my Father decreed me to rule in his realm, ³⁰so that when I reign as king you may eat and drink at my table and sit on thrones, judging the twelve tribes of Israel.

Jesus says that Peter will deny him that very night
(Matthew 26:31–35, Mark 14:27–31)

³¹"Simon, Simon, Satan has asked permission to sift you like wheat. ³²But I have prayed for you, Simon, that your faith might not fail. And when you have turned back, strengthen your *fellow* brothers."[418]

³³But Peter said to him, "Lord, I am ready to go with you to prison and to death."

³⁴But Jesus said, "I tell you Peter, before the rooster crows today, you will deny that you know me three times."

³⁵Then he said to them, "When I sent you out before without a wallet, bag, or sandals, did you lack anything?"

"Nothing," they said.

³⁶And he said to them, "But now if you have a wallet. Take it, and also a bag. But if you do not have a sword, sell your coat and buy one. ³⁷For it is written, 'He

---

418   I.e. Jesus' ten remaining followers.

was numbered with those who broke the law, and I tell you that this must be fulfilled in me. Yes, what is written about me has an end *in sight*."

³⁸The followers said, "Lord, look! Here are two swords."

"Enough!" he said.

Jesus prays on the Mount of Olives
(Matthew 26:36–46, Mark 14:32–42)

³⁹As Jesus was in the habit of doing, he went out to the Mount of Olives, and his followers went with him. ⁴⁰Upon reaching the place, he said to them, "Pray that you will not fall into temptation." ⁴¹He withdrew about a stone's throw away and knelt down and prayed. ⁴²He said, "Father, if you are willing, take away this cup from me; yet not my will, but let your will be done."

⁴³An angel from heaven appeared to him and strengthened him. ⁴⁴Jesus was in agony so he prayed more fervently and his sweat became like drops of blood falling to the ground.

⁴⁵When he arose from prayer and went back to his followers, he found them asleep as they were worn out from the grief. ⁴⁶He said to them, "Why are you sleeping? Get up and pray because you don't want to fall into temptation."

Jesus is arrested
(Matthew 26:47–56, Mark 14:43–50, John 18:1–11)

⁴⁷While Jesus was still talking, a crowd happened to arrive and the man known as Judas, one of the Twelve, was in front. He approached Jesus to kiss him, ⁴⁸and Jesus said to him, "So Judas, are you betraying the Son of Man with a kiss?"

⁴⁹When Jesus' followers saw what was going to happen, they said, "Lord, should we use our swords?" ⁵⁰And then one of them struck the servant of the high priest and cut off his right ear.

⁵¹Jesus answered by saying, "Stop! No more of this!" And he touched the man's ear and healed him.

⁵²Then Jesus said to the chief priests, the officers of the temple guard, and the elders who had come for him, "Am I leading a rebellion that you have come with swords and clubs? ⁵³Every day I was with you in the temple courts, and you did not lay a hand on me. But this is your hour when darkness reigns."

Peter disowns Jesus
(Matthew 26:57–58,69–75, Mark 14:53–54,66–72, John 18:12–18,25–27)

⁵⁴They seized Jesus and led him away and took him into the house of the high priest. Peter was following at a distance. ⁵⁵A fire had been lit in the middle

of the courtyard and they were all sitting down together and Peter was sitting with them too. ⁵⁶A young servant girl saw Peter seated there in the light of the fire. She examined him more closely and said, "This man was with him." ⁵⁷But Peter denied it saying, "Woman, I do not know him."

⁵⁸A little bit later someone else saw him and said, "You are one of them!" "Man, I am not!" Peter said.

⁵⁹About one hour later someone else insisted saying, "This man was certainly with him for he is also a Galilean."

⁶⁰But Peter said, "Man, I don't know what you are talking about!" And immediately while he was speaking, a rooster crowed. ⁶¹The Lord turned and looked straight at Peter and then Peter remembered that the Lord had said to him: "Before the rooster crows today, you will deny me three times." ⁶²And Peter went outside and wept bitterly.

Jesus is mocked and beaten
(Matthew 26:67–68, Mark 14:65)

⁶³The men who were guarding Jesus began mocking and beating him. ⁶⁴They blindfolded him and they began asking him, "Prophesy! Who hit you?" ⁶⁵And they said many other blasphemous things against him.

Jesus is brought before the Sanhedrin council
(Matthew 26:59–66, Mark 14:55–64, John 18:19–24)

⁶⁶At dawn, the Sanhedrin council—the elders, the chief priests and the scribes gathered together and Jesus was led before them. ⁶⁷And they said, "If you are the Messiah, tell us."

He said, "If I tell you, you will not believe me, ⁶⁸and if I ask you a question, you will not answer. ⁶⁹But from now on, the Son of Man will be seated at the right hand of the Almighty God."

⁷⁰They all asked, "Are you then the Son of God?"

He said to them, "As you are saying, I am."

⁷¹Then they said, "Why do we need any more witnesses? We have heard it from his own lips."

Jesus is taken to Pilate
(Matthew 27:1–2, 11–14, Mark 15:1–5, John 18:28–38)

23 ¹The whole council stood up and led him off to Pilate. ²They began to accuse him *before Pilate* saying, "We have found this man subverting our nation. He opposes payment of taxes to Caesar and claims to be the Messiah, a king."

³So Pilate questioned him, "Are you the king of the Jews?"

"So you are saying," Jesus said.

⁴Then Pilate said to the chief priests and the crowds, "I find no fault in this man."

⁵But they insisted, saying, "He incites the people throughout all of Judea through his teaching. He begun in Galilee and now has come here."

Jesus is taken to King Herod[419]

⁶Having heard this, Pilate asked if the man was a Galilean. ⁷And having learned that Jesus was under Herod's jurisdiction, Pilate sent him to Herod, who happened to be in Jerusalem at that time also.

⁸When Herod saw Jesus, he was very thrilled because he had been wanting to see him for a long time. From what he had heard about him, he hoped to see him perform some miracle. ⁹Herod asked Jesus many questions but Jesus did not answer him. ¹⁰The chief priests and the scribes were standing there, vehemently accusing him. ¹¹Then Herod and his soldiers ridiculed and mocked him. They dressed him in a brilliant robe and sent him back to Pilate. ¹²And on this day Herod and Pilate became friends; before this they had been enemies.

Pilate sentences Jesus to death
(Matthew 27:15-26, Mark 15:6-15, John 18:38-19:16)

¹³Pilate called together the chief priests, the rulers and the people ¹⁴and said to them, "You brought this man to me as someone who was inciting the people to rebellion. I have cross-examined him in your presence and have found nothing in this man worthy of the crimes of which you accuse him of. ¹⁵And neither did Herod for he sent him back to us as you can see. He has done nothing to deserve death. ¹⁶Therefore, I will punish him and then I am going to release him." ¹⁷(He was obliged to release someone to them at the Feast).

¹⁸But everyone in unison cried out, "Take him away! Release Barabbas to us!" ¹⁹(Barabbas had been thrown into prison for an insurrection in the city and for murder.)

²⁰Pilate wanted to release Jesus so he appealed to them again. ²¹But they kept shouting, "Crucify him! Crucify him!"

²²And a third time Pilate spoke to them saying, "Why? What crime has he committed? I did not find in him any crime worthy of death. Therefore I will have him punished and then I will release him."

²³But they insisted with loud voices and demanded that he be crucified,

---

419 This is the same Herod that had John the Baptist beheaded.

and their voices prevailed. ²⁴So Pilate relented and granted their demand. ²⁵He released the man who had been thrown into prison for insurrection and murder, the one whom they were requesting, and he handed Jesus over to be done to him as they willed.

Jesus is crucified

(Matthew 27:32-44, Mark 15:21-32, John 19:17-27)

²⁶The *soldiers* led Jesus away and on the way, they seized Simon from Cyrene, who was coming from the country. They put the cross on him and made him carry it behind Jesus.

²⁷A large number of people were following him including women who were mourning and wailing for him. ²⁸Jesus turned and said to them, "Daughters of Jerusalem, do not weep for me rather mourn for yourselves and for your children. ²⁹Listen! For the days are coming in which they will say, 'Blessed are the barren women, those who never bore babies! Blessed are those who never breastfed!' ³⁰For that will be when they will say to the mountains, 'Fall on us!' and to the hills, 'Cover us!' ³¹For if men do these things when a tree is green, what will happen when it is dry?"⁴²⁰

³²And two other men, both of them criminals, were also being led away with him to be executed. ³³And when they came to the place called the Skull, there they crucified him along with the criminals—one on his right and the other on his left. ³⁴Jesus said, "Father, forgive them, for they do not know what they are doing." And they divided up his clothes by casting lots.

³⁵The people stood there watching while the authorities were sneering at him saying, "He saved others; let him save himself if he is really the Messiah of God, the Chosen One."

³⁶The soldiers also approached and ridiculed him. They offered him *cheap wine vinegar* ³⁷and said, "If you are the king of the Jews, save yourself."

³⁸There was a written notice above his head which read:

THIS IS THE KING OF THE JEWS

³⁹One of the criminals who was hanging there on the cross with Jesus blasphemed him saying, "Aren't you the Messiah? Save yourself and the two of us!"

⁴⁰But the other criminal rebuked him saying, "Don't you fear God? You

---

420   Cf. Hos. 10:8, Rev. 6:16. This refers to the Great Tribulation when the wrath of God and his judgments are so intense that people will just want to hide. The green tree represents when Jesus is with them and the dry tree is the last seven years when people will question whether God even exists because of all the calamities coming upon the earth.

are receiving the same sentence as him. [41]And we are getting justice for we are getting what we deserve. But this man has done nothing wrong."

[42]Then he said, "Jesus, remember me when you begin to reign."

[43]Jesus said to him, "Truly I say to you, today you will be with me in paradise."[421]

Jesus dies
(Matthew 27:45–56, Mark 15:33–41, John 19:28–30)

[44]It was already about the sixth hour[422] and darkness was over the whole land until the ninth hour.[423] [45]The sun had stopped shining and the curtain of the temple was torn in two.

[46]Jesus called out with a loud voice, "Father, I commit my spirit into your hands." Once he had said this, he breathed out *his last breath*.

[47]The centurion, seeing what had happened, praised God and said, "Surely this was a righteous man."

[48]When everyone in the crowds of people who had gathered saw what had taken place, they beat their breasts in sadness and they returned home. [49]But all those who had personally known him, including the women who had followed him from Galilee, stood at a distance watching everything.

Jesus' body is placed in a tomb
(Matthew 27:57–61, Mark 15:42–47, John 19:38–42)

[50]Now there was a man named Joseph who was a member of the Sanhedrin council and he was a good and righteous man. [51]He had not consented with their decision and action. He came from the Judean town of Arimathea and he was waiting for the coming reign of God. [52]He went to Pilate and asked for Jesus' body. [53]Then he took it down, wrapped it in linen cloth and placed Jesus' body in a tomb cut in the rock in which no one had been laid. [54]It was Preparation Day[424] and the Sabbath was about to begin.

[55]The women who had travelled with Jesus from Galilee followed Joseph and saw the tomb and how his body was laid in it. [56]Then they went back and prepared spices and perfumes. But they rested on the Sabbath in obedience to the commandment.

---

421 A clear indication that there is life after death and not soul sleep. "Paradise" was originally a Persian word meaning 'a walled garden' but it is used as a synonym of the good compartment of Hades where Abraham was with Lazarus (Luke 16:22).
422 I.e. six hours after dawn – 12 noon.
423 3 pm in the afternoon.
424 I.e. Preparation Day was normally Friday but this year it fell on Thursday because there was a special high Sabbath on the Friday followed by the normal weekly Sabbath on the Saturday.

Jesus is resurrected
(Matthew 28:1–10, Mark 16:1–8, John 20:1–10)

24 ¹On the first day of the week of Sabbaths,⁴²⁵ very early in the morning, the women took the spices they had prepared and went to the tomb. ²They found that the stone had been rolled away from the entrance of the tomb, ³but when they entered, they did not find the body of the Lord Jesus. ⁴And while they were wondering about this, suddenly two men in dazzling clothes stood beside them. ⁵Being very frightened, the women bowed down with their faces to the ground, but the men said to them, "Why are you looking for he who is alive among the dead? ⁶He is not here. He has risen! Do you remember how he told you, while he was still with you in Galilee that ⁷the Son of Man must be delivered into the hands of sinful men, be crucified and on the third day be raised again?"

⁸Then the women remembered his words.

⁹When the women came back from the tomb, they told all these things to the Eleven and to all the others. ¹⁰Those women who reported this to the apostles were Mary Magdalene, Joanna, Mary the mother of James, and some others with them. ¹¹But the apostles did not believe the women, because their words seemed like nonsense to them. ¹²Peter, however, got up and ran to the tomb. Bending down, he saw the strips of linen cloth but nothing else. He went away wondering to himself what had happened.

Jesus appears to two of his followers on the road to Emmaus
(Mark 16:12–13)

¹³Now on the very same day two of Jesus' followers were going to a village called Emmaus, 60 stadiums⁴²⁶ in distance from Jerusalem. ¹⁴They were talking to each other about everything that had happened. ¹⁵As they were talking and discussing these things with each other, Jesus himself came up and travelled with them. ¹⁶But they were kept from recognising him.

¹⁷Jesus asked them, "What are you talking about as you are walking along together?"

They stood still looking very sad. ¹⁸One of them named Cleopas, asked him, "Are you the only visitor in Jerusalem who doesn't know what has been happening there in the last few days?"

¹⁹"What?" he said.

---

425   This was a title for the Feast of Firstfruits. It was literally day 1 of the next 50 days before Pentecost and literally seven weekly Sabbaths to follow. This day was Sunday, Nisan 17.

426   A stadium is a Greek fixed unit of measure equalling the length of 600 human feet, about 180 m. So 60 stadiums equates to Emmaus being about 11 km from Jerusalem—a couple of hours walk.

They said to him, "About Jesus of Nazareth. He was a man who was a prophet mighty in deed and word both in the sight of God and all the people. [20]The chief priests and our rulers handed him over to be sentenced to death. They crucified him [21]but we were hoping that he was the one about to set Israel free.

"Besides all these things, today is the third day since all these things happened. [22]Furthermore, some of the women among us amazed us. They went to the tomb early this morning [23]but his body was not there. They came and told us that they had seen a vision of angels, who said he was alive. [24]Then some in our group went to the tomb and found it just as the women had said but they didn't see him."

[25]Jesus said to them, "How foolish you all are; you are so slow to believe everything the prophets said! [26]Did not the Messiah have to suffer these things and then enter his glory?"[427] [27]Beginning with Moses and all the Prophets,[428] he explained to them what was said in all the Scriptures concerning himself.

[28]And as they approached the village where they were travelling to, Jesus acted as if he were going further. [29]But they strongly urged him to stay saying, "Stay with us, for it is nearly evening and the day is almost over." So he went in to stay with them.

[30]It came about that while Jesus was reclining at the table with them, he took bread, gave thanks, broke it and began to give it to them. [31]Then their eyes were opened and they recognised him and he disappeared from their sight. [32]They said to each other, "Were not our hearts burning within us while he talked with us on the road and opened the Scriptures to us?"

[33]They got up and returned to Jerusalem at once. There they found the Eleven and those with them, gathered together [34]and saying, "It is true! The Lord has risen and has appeared to Simon." [35]Then the two men told what had happened on the road *to Emmaus* and how Jesus had been made known to them when he was breaking the bread."

Jesus appears to his followers
(Matthew 28:16–20, Mark 16:14–18, John 20:19–23)

[36]While they were all still talking about these things, Jesus himself stood among them and said to them, "Peace be with you."

[37]They were startled and terrified, thinking they had seen a ghost. [38]He said to them, "Why are you troubled? Why are you having doubts? [39]Look at my hands and my feet. It is really me. Touch me and see for yourself. A ghost does not have flesh and bones, as you can see I have."

---

427 Cf. Heb. 2:10.
428 I.e. the entire Hebrew Bible what we know as the OT.

⁴⁰When he had said this, he showed them his hands and feet. ⁴¹They still could not believe it because of all the joy and amazement so he said to them, "Do you have any food?" ⁴²They gave a piece of cooked fish to him ⁴³and he took it and ate it in their presence.

⁴⁴He said to them, "This is what I have been telling you when I was still with you. Everything must be fulfilled that is written about me in the law of Moses, the Prophets and the Psalms."

⁴⁵Then he opened their minds so they could understand the Scriptures. ⁴⁶He said to them, "It has been written that the Messiah was to suffer and rise from the dead on the third day. ⁴⁷If, in his name, people turn to God they will receive the forgiveness of sins.[429] This message will be preached to all nations, beginning at Jerusalem. ⁴⁸You are witnesses of these things. ⁴⁹I am going to send you what my father has promised but you must remain in the city until you have been clothed with power from on high."[430]

Jesus ascends into the sky
(Mark 16:19–20, Acts 1:9–12)

⁵⁰When he had led them out to the vicinity of Bethany, he lifted up his hands and blessed them. ⁵¹While he was blessing them, he left them and was taken up into the sky. ⁵²Then they worshipped him and returned to Jerusalem with great joy. ⁵³And they remained continually at the temple, praising God.

---

429 Mankind must turn to God through Jesus. They cannot come to God any other way or in any other name. Cf. John 14:6.
430 Cf. John 20:22.

JOHN

Introduction

The Gospel of John is very different than the other three synoptic gospels. It was the last gospel composed between AD 80-95. It includes many events in Jesus' ministry that the other three gospels omit. John referred to himself five times in his gospel as the "follower whom Jesus loved". The apostle John is the son of Zebedee and brother of James and a member of Jesus' inner circle (Peter, James and John).

According to several ancient sources, the aging apostle John, while residing in Ephesus, was requested by the elders of Minor Asia to write his 'Ephesian Gospel' in order to counteract the dangerous heresy concerning the nature, person and deity of Jesus. John has in mind the cosmopolitan world of the first and second century Ephesus in writing his gospel account taking into account the religiously minded public in this area of Asia Minor. It has been said that John's Gospel is a key that opens the door for understanding the other three synoptic gospels.

Jesus talks much about his Father and his relationship to his Father and the Holy Breath (Holy Spirit). It is known as the spiritual gospel and the word 'believe' occurs some 98 times. 'Eternal life' is a key concept in the book. Whereas Mark's Gospel is primarily in the active voice and presents much of what Jesus did, John's Gospel emphasises the Holy Breath behind the events. Some of the prominent words and concepts in John's gospel are 'light', 'darkness', 'truth', 'flesh', 'love', and 'word'.

The only miracle to be recorded in all four gospels is the feeding of the 5000: Matt. 14:13-21, Mark 6:30-44, Luke 9:10-17, John 6:1-13.

Perhaps the most significant finding in the Book of John however is Jesus' 62 week ministry from his first Passover in AD 29 to his final Passover in AD 30 when He was crucified. The progression of the feasts can be followed throughout the gospel which provides another timeline of Jesus' earthly ministry beginning in John 2:13.

In the beginning was the Word

1 ¹In the beginning was the Word,⁴³¹ and the Word was with God, and the Word was God.⁴³² ²He was with God in the beginning.

³Everything came into existence through him. Not even one thing came to be without him.⁴³³ ⁴The Word is the source of life and it is this life that brought about spiritual enlightenment to mankind. ⁵The light shines in the darkness, but the darkness has not been able to overpower it.

⁶There was a man who was sent by God—his name was John.⁴³⁴ ⁷He came so that he could testify concerning that light in order that through him⁴³⁵ all men might believe. ⁸John himself was not the light, rather he came only to tell *people* about the light. ⁹The true light that enlightens every man was coming into the world.

¹⁰The Word was in the world⁴³⁶ and though the world was made through him, the people of earth did not recognise him. ¹¹He came to his own place⁴³⁷ but his own people⁴³⁸ did not receive him. ¹²But to those who have received him and are believing in his name,⁴³⁹ he has given the right to become children of God.

¹³He was not begotten by natural means or by the will of the flesh or by the will of a husband. No, indeed, he was born of God.⁴⁴⁰ ¹⁴And the Word became

---

431 Another name for the Son of God is 'The Word of God'. Cf. Rev. 19:13.
432 John starts out with this cryptic statement. But the question remains, How can the 'Word' be <u>with</u> God and <u>be</u> God at the same time? It seems illogical until you realise that there must be two different ways that the word 'God' is used in this verse. 'God' doesn't always mean the eternal, immortal, invisible, only wise God. In the first instance it does refer to the Father God, the invisible Yahweh. I.e. in the beginning the Word (visible Yahweh) was with God (invisible Yahweh). In the second instance however, the word 'God' is used in a more general way to indicate that the Son was addressed as 'God' in the sense that he was God's agent in certain contexts often appearing as the Angel of the LORD in the OT. God is El/Elohim in the OT and *theos* in the NT but it can mean different people in different situations. It can mean: (1) the Creator himself; (2) the Angel/Messenger of Yahweh (Gen. 16:7-13, 22:1,11-18, 48:15-16, Exo. 3:2-7, Judg. 6:11-14, 13:22); (3) the Son reigning in his Kingdom (Psa. 45:6-7, Isa. 9:6); (4) pagan gods with supposed sovereignty over certain aspects of nature (Exo. 12:12); (5) Moses who was like God to Pharaoh (Exo. 7:1); (6) the divine council (ben-elohim) (Deut. 32:8, Psa. 82:1,6); (7) the Antichrist (2 Thess. 2:4); (8) Satan (2 Cor. 4:4). The Son of God was 'God' to Adam, Abraham, Moses, and others as 'the Angel of the LORD', because God's name was upon him (Exo. 23:20-23).
433 The Son of God was God's agent in creation. Cf. Prov. 8:30, Col. 1:16.
434 John the Baptist. According to Irenaeus (*Against Heresies*, Bk. I, ch. xxvi:3), John's Gospel was written in part to counter the teachings of the Nicolaitans who denied that the Word (*logos*) became flesh. The Platonic view also removed the necessity of the resurrection of the flesh. Plato believed in the immortality of the soul and that the flesh was evil and that upon death man would be freed from the flesh. Cf. Rev. 2:6 footnote.
435 I.e. Jesus Christ not John.
436 The Son of God was previously in the world as the preincarnate Christ but no one recognised him.
437 The land of the Jewish people.
438 The Jews.
439 This refers to the preincarnate name of Jesus—'the Word' or in the Greek, 'Logos'.
440 Tertullian quoted the 'Old Latin' MSS in his writings saying that the subject here is the 'Logos' (The Word—Christ) rather than 'those who believed'. Most modern MSS and English translations say

flesh and resided[441] among us. We have seen his glory,[442] the glory of the one and only Son[443] from the Father, full of grace and truth.

[15]John *the Baptist* spoke about him. He cried out saying, "This is the one I was referring to when I said, 'He who comes after me is greater than me because he existed before I was born.'"[444]

[16]Out of the fullness of his grace he has blessed us all, giving us one blessing after another. [17]For the law was given through Moses but grace and truth came through Jesus Christ. [18]No one has ever seen God. The one and only Son,[445] who is at the Father's side, has made him known.

John the Baptist denies that he is the Messiah
(Matthew 3:1–12, Mark 1:7–8, Luke 3:15–17)

[19]This is the testimony of John when the Judeans[446] sent priests and Levites from Jerusalem to ask him, "Who are you?" [20]John did not refuse to answer but he confessed clearly, "I am not the Messiah."

[21]They asked him, "Then who are you? Are you Elijah?"

"No, I am not Elijah," he answered.

"Are you the Prophet?"

He answered, "No."

[22]Then they asked, "Who are you? We have to take an answer back to those who sent us. What have you got to say for yourself?"

[23]John answered with the words of the prophet Isaiah,

"I am the voice of someone crying out in the desert saying, 'Straighten
 the way for him.'"

Isaiah 40:3

[24]Those who had been sent *to John* were from the Pharisees [25]and they asked him, "If you are not the Messiah or Elijah, or the Prophet,[447] then why do you baptise?"

---

that it is believers who are born of God. Richard Lenski also accepts this in his commentary on John (Lenski, R H, *The Interpretation of St. John's Gospel* (1942)).

441 This verb is literally 'to live in a tent'. In other words the idea is that the Son of God came to live only temporarily on this earth.

442 John saw Jesus' glory at the Mount of Transfiguration.

443 Cf. Heb. 11:17.

444 Evidence of the preincarnate Christ even though John was conceived six months before Jesus.

445 I have followed the TR here but some old Greek MSS have 'God' instead of 'Son'.

446 I have followed David H Stern's translation (CJB) here. He makes the case that Jews should be translated as Judeans in many cases (Stern, David H, *JNT Commentary* (1992), pp. 157–161) See his commentary for full list where it is appropriate.

447 These three are the principal eschatological figures in Jewish thinking. Cf. Acts 3:22.

²⁶John answered by saying, "I baptise in water however there is one among you whom you really do not know. ²⁷He is the one coming after me. I am not even worthy to untie the strap on his sandals."

²⁸This all happened at Bethabara⁴⁴⁸ on the other side of the Jordan⁴⁴⁹ where John was baptising *people*.

The Lamb of God

²⁹The next day John saw Jesus coming towards him and he said, "Look everyone! Here is the Lamb of God who takes away the sin of the world! ³⁰This is the one I was talking about when I said, 'A man who comes after me is greater than me because he existed before I was born.' ³¹I myself did not know who he would be, but the reason I came baptising in water was so that he might be revealed to Israel."

³²John testified by saying, "I saw the Breath *of God* come down from heaven like a dove and it remained on him. ³³I did not recognise him except the one who sent me to baptise in water told me, 'The man whom you see the Breath *of God* come down upon and remain on him, this is the one baptising in Holy Breath.' ³⁴I have seen and I have testified that he is the Son of God."

Jesus calls his first followers

³⁵The next day John was standing there⁴⁵⁰ again with two of his followers. ³⁶When John saw Jesus walking by he said, "Look, the Lamb of God!"

³⁷And when his two followers heard him say this, they followed Jesus. ³⁸Jesus turned around and saw them following and asked, "What do you want?"

They said, "Rabbi" (translation is 'teacher'), "where are you staying?"

³⁹"Come and see," he answered. So they went and saw where he was staying, and spent that day with him. (It was about the tenth hour).⁴⁵¹

⁴⁰Andrew, Simon Peter's brother, was one of the two who had heard what John had said and who had followed Jesus. ⁴¹The first thing Andrew did was to find his brother Simon and tell him, "We have found the Messiah (*in the Greek* it is translated, 'Christ'). ⁴²And Andrew brought Simon to see Jesus.

---

448 Most ancient MSS have Bethany beyond Jordan here. Only KJV, NKJV and YLT have Bethabara (place of the crossing). Bethabara was located on the western bank of the Jordan River according to the ancient Madaba tile map located at St. George church in Jordan.
449 Jordan Valley.
450 The verb here probably just means that John was present. It is not stated where John was but most likely he was in the same place as the previous day—Bethany beyond Jordan by the river.
451 This refers to the time when Jesus gives the invitation not the time when the two men left. John seems to use the Roman system of reckoning time so this was the tenth hour from midnight meaning 10 am. The Romans counted the hours from either midnight or midday. Cf. John 4:52, 19:14.

Jesus looked at him and said, "You are Simon son of John.[452] You will be called Cephas" (translation is 'Peter').[453]

Jesus calls Philip and Nathanael

[43]The next day Jesus decided to leave for the *district of* Galilee. He found Philip and said to him, "Follow me."

[44]Philip, like Andrew and Peter was from the city of Bethsaida. [45]Philip went and found Nathanael and told him, "We have found the one Moses wrote about in the Law. The prophets also wrote about him—it is Jesus the Nazarene, the son of Joseph."

[46]Nathanael said, "Can anything good come out of Nazareth?"[454]

"Come and see *for yourself*," said Philip.

[47]When Jesus saw Nathanael coming towards him, he said about him, "See this man! He is a true Israelite, in whom there is nothing false."

[48]Nathanael asked, "How do you know me?

Jesus answered him, "I saw you under the fig tree before Philip called you."

[49]Nathanael declared, "Rabbi, you are the Son of God, you are the King of Israel."

[50]Jesus said, "Do you believe just because I told you I saw you under the fig tree? You shall see greater things than this." [51]Jesus added, "I tell you the truth, you shall see heaven open and the angels of God ascending and descending on the Son of Man."[455]

Jesus performs his first miracle at Cana

2 [1]On the third day[456] a wedding took place at *the city of* Cana in Galilee. Jesus' mother was there, [2]and Jesus and his followers had also been invited to the wedding. [3]Then when the wine was finished, Jesus' mother said to him, "They have no more wine."

[4]Jesus said to her, "Mother.[457] Why are you involving me? My time has not yet come." [5]His mother said to the servants, "Do whatever he tells you."

---

452   Not John the Baptist.
453   Cephas is the Greek form of the Aramaic *kepa* which means stone.
454   This was a proverb used by the people of Cana in reference to the nearby city of Nazareth, noting that Nathanael was from Cana (TH). Cf. John 21:2.
455   Like in Jacob's dream, Nathanael would come to realise that Jesus is the symbolic 'ladder' extended between heaven and earth, the mediator between God and man. Cf. 1 Tim. 2:5.
456   Marriages in Jesus' day were typically celebrated on a Wednesday afternoon. The first three days (Sunday – Tuesday) were usually set aside for the bride to prepare. The Marriage Feast of the Lamb (Rev. 19:6–19) will be at the beginning of the Seventh-Day, the Millennial Sabbath.
457   Literally 'woman' however Jesus is not rebuking her merely stating that the time for him to begin his ministry has not yet come. Cf. John 4:21, 19:26.

⁶Nearby there were six stone⁴⁵⁸ water jars, the kind of jars used by the Jews for ceremonial washing.⁴⁵⁹ They could each hold between two and three measures.⁴⁶⁰

⁷Jesus said to the servants, "Fill the jars with water." They filled them to the top ⁸then he said to them, "Now draw some of the water out and take it to the master of ceremonies of the banquet."

They did as he said, ⁹and the master of ceremonies tasted the water that had been turned into wine. He did not know where it had come from however the servants who had drawn the water knew. Then he called the bridegroom aside ¹⁰and said, "Usually, everyone brings out the choice wine first and then the cheaper wine after the guests have become drunk but you have saved the best till last."

¹¹Jesus performed this first miraculous sign at Cana of Galilee. It was there that Jesus revealed his glory and his followers put their faith in him.

Jesus clears out the temple
(Matthew 21:12-13, Mark 11:15-19, Luke 19:45-48)

¹²After this he went down to Capernaum with his mother, brothers and his followers where they stayed for a few days.

¹³The Judean Passover Feast⁴⁶¹ was getting near, so Jesus went up to Jerusalem. ¹⁴Upon arrival he found those in the temple selling cattle, sheep and doves, and also the money-changers sitting *at their tables*. ¹⁵So he made a whip out of cords and forced everyone out of the temple. He drove out both the sheep and cattle and he scattered the coins of the money-changers and overturned their tables. ¹⁶And to those who were selling doves he said, "Take these things out of here! How dare you turn my Father's house into a market!"

¹⁷His followers remembered what was written, "Zeal for your house will consume me."⁴⁶²

---

458 The fact that the jars are stone, rather than earthenware, is important. According to Jewish law, earthenware jars, if contaminated, had to be broken, but contaminated stone jars could simply be washed (TH). Cf. 2 Cor. 4:7.
459 The washing done before a meal (Matt. 15:2).
460 This is between 80–120 litres of water.
461 This Passover Feast (Pesach) was the first feast in a series of five feasts mentioned throughout John's Gospel leading to the culmination in Jesus' final Passover at his crucifixion. The list as follows: 1) Initial Passover – Spring AD 29 (John 2:13-14); 2) Pentecost – Spring AD 29 (John 5:1); 3) Tabernacles – Autumn AD 29 (John 7:2,10,37); 4) Hanukkah – Winter AD 29 (John 10:22); 5) Final Passover – Spring AD 30 (John 13:1). These five feasts cover Jesus' entire public ministry of 62 weeks but does not include the doubtful Passover Feast mentioned in John 6:4. Also Dan. 9:26 states that the Anointed One (Messiah) will be cut off after 62 'sevens' (weeks). This has a double meaning of 62 weeks of seven years as well as 62 weeks of seven days.
Cf. https://luke21.com.au/christ-was-cut-off-after-62-weeks/
462 Cf. Psa. 69:9. "Consume" could also mean in the sense that this zeal would ultimately destroy him. John places this clearing of the temple at the beginning of Jesus' ministry whereas Matthew places

¹⁸Then the Judeans asked, "What sign can you show us to prove that gives you the right to do such a thing?"

¹⁹Jesus answered by saying, "Destroy this temple and I will erect it again in three days."

²⁰Then the Judeans said, "It has taken 46 years to build this temple and you are going to erect it in three days?"

²¹However the temple which Jesus was speaking about was actually his body. ²²When therefore after Jesus was raised from the dead, his followers recalled what he had said. Then they believed the Scripture and the word that Jesus had spoken.

²³Now while Jesus was in Jerusalem during the Passover Feast, many people saw the miraculous signs he was doing and they believed in his name. ²⁴But Jesus did not entrust himself to them because he knows what all men are really like. ²⁵He did not need anyone to tell him about what they were like because he already knew what was on their minds.

Jesus and Nicodemus

3 ¹Now there was a Jewish religious leader named Nicodemus who was a Pharisee. ²One night he came to Jesus and said, "Rabbi, we[463] know you are a teacher who has come from God. For no one could do these miraculous signs you have been doing unless God was with him."

³Jesus replied by saying, "I tell you the truth, no one can see the coming reign of God unless he is born again."

⁴Nicodemus asked, "How can a man be born when he is old? Surely he cannot enter a second time into his mother's womb to be born!"

⁵Jesus answered, "I tell you the truth, no one can enter into the realm of God unless he is born of water and Breath.[464] ⁶That which is born of the *human* flesh is flesh and that which is born of the *Holy* Breath is breath.[465] ⁷You shouldn't be surprised to hear me say to you that all of you[466] must be born again. ⁸The wind[467] blows wherever it wishes. You hear its sound, but you cannot tell where

---

the clearing of the temple at the end of his ministry. They are two separate events.

463   It is impossible to know who Nicodemus is including when he says, "we" but it is 1st person plural exclusive meaning that it excludes Jesus but likely includes the Pharisees and maybe a few others in the Sanhedrin.

464   I.e. the Breath that comes from God.

465   The noun "breath" is *pneuma* in the Greek. This is not talking about the literal physical breath in a man but a man's spiritual nature. In other words, a man can only be spiritually born by the power of the Breath of God (Holy Spirit).

466   I.e. those in the Sanhedrin particularly the Pharisees whom Jesus had been railing against.

467   The word for wind in the Greek (*pneuma*) is the same as the word for spirit or breath so there is a play on words that is missed in English. The analogy is that the wind is invisible yet we hear and see its effects and so it is when a man is born again. We see that a person is born again but it is hard to

it comes from or where it is going; so it is the same with every one of you[468] who is born of the Breath."[469]

⁹Nicodemus asked, "How does that work?"

¹⁰Jesus answered him by saying, "How is it that you are the teacher of Israel and yet you do not understand these things? ¹¹I tell you the truth *Nicodemus*, we[470] speak of what we know and we testify about what we have seen but still you *Pharisees* do not accept our testimony. ¹²If I told you about earthly things and you do not believe, then how will you people believe if I speak of heavenly things?[471] (¹³No one has ever ascended[472] into heaven except for the one who descended[473] from heaven—the Son of Man.) ¹⁴Just as Moses lifted up the snake in the desert, so the Son of Man must be lifted up ¹⁵so that every one of you believing in him may have eternal life. ¹⁶For God so loved the world that he gave his one and only Son so that every one of you[474] believing in him may not perish but have eternal life.[475]

¹⁷"For God did not send his Son into the world to condemn the world, but to save the world through him. ¹⁸He who believes in him is not condemned, but he who does not believe in him stands condemned already because he has not believed in the name[476] of God's one and only Son. ¹⁹This is how judgment works:

---

	understand how it happens hence Nicodemus' confusion.
468	The phrase "every one of you" is a unique clause in the Greek meaning the collective whole or a specific group. The KJV uses the word "whosoever" to translate this special Greek clause (πᾶς + singular articular participle). In this context, Jesus is referring to a definite subset group of people—the Pharisees. Other passages which use this construct are: 1 John 2:23,29; 1 John 3:3–15; 1 John 4:7; 1 John 5:1,18; 2 John 1:9. Cf. Tim Warner LGV John 3:8 footnote 91.
469	Cf. John 8:14.
470	The "we" here is 1st person plural exclusive meaning that Jesus is referring to himself and another person or persons but excluding Nicodemus. It is impossible to tell from the text who he is referring to but some possibilities include God his Father, John the Baptist or even perhaps the prophets and earlier church fathers such as Abraham and Moses (Stern, David H, *JNT Commentary* (1992), p. 166).
471	Some modern translations now have the quotation from Jesus ending after v. 15 instead of v. 21 (LEB, NIV). See the reasoning in v. 13 footnotes below why the dialogue should end after v. 12. Other MSS have footnotes indicating the alternative.
472	This verb is now in the perfect tense (a continued result of a past action) indicating that v. 13 is John's editorial commentary after the ascension not a part of Jesus' dialogue with Nicodemus. Cf. Matt. 24:15, Mark 13:14.
473	The verb "descended" is in the aorist tense (a completed action in the past). Cf. John 6:38 where the same verb is in the perfect tense because Jesus was still present on earth at the time. This is further proof that v. 13 is John's commentary not Jesus' dialogue.
474	Jesus is specifically talking about the Pharisees as a group.
475	This whole passage (vv. 10–16) is addressed specifically to Nicodemus and the Pharisees in the Sanhedrin because of the plural pronoun in v. 11. I believe Jesus is saying that if they would just accept his testimony and believe, then every one of them in the council would have eternal life. The whole reason God sent his Son into the world was so that all peoples everywhere could have eternal life. In vv. 17–21, Jesus generalises, moving away from speaking specifically about the Pharisees and perhaps a few others in the Sanhedrin.
476	Cf. John 1:12. Believing in the "name" infers that this is before Jesus was born as a human being. God's unique son was begotten in the beginning of time and so in the OT, the Jews had to believe in

Light has come into the world, but mankind loved the darkness instead of the light because their deeds were evil. ²⁰Every one of you who does evil hates the light and he will not come into the light for fear that his deeds will be exposed. ²¹But the honest man comes into the light so that it can be plainly seen that what he has done has been done in obedience to God."

Jesus and John the Baptist

²²After this, Jesus and his followers went out into the Judean countryside, where he spent some time with them, baptising. ²³John was also baptising at Aenon near Salim[477] because there was plenty of water there. People were constantly coming to be baptised. ²⁴(This was before John was put in prison.)

²⁵An argument arose between some of John's followers with the Judeans[478] over the matter of ceremonial washing. ²⁶They came to him and said, "Rabbi, that man who was with you on the other side of the Jordan, the one you spoke about, well he is baptising now and everyone is going to him."

²⁷John answered by saying, "A man can only receive *and do* what heaven allows him to do. ²⁸You yourselves are my witnesses when I said, 'I am not the Messiah but I was sent ahead of him.' ²⁹The bride belongs to the bridegroom but the best man[479] stands by and listens, and he is happy when he hears the bridegroom speak. That joy is mine and it is now fulfilled. ³⁰He must become more *important* and I must become less."

³¹The one who comes from above is superior to everyone and the one who is from the earth belongs to the earth and speaks as one from the earth. The one who comes from heaven is superior to everyone.[480] ³²He testifies to what he has seen and heard, but no one accepts his testimony. ³³The one who has accepted it has certified that God is true. ³⁴For the one whom God has sent speaks the words of God, for God gives his Breath *to him* without limit. ³⁵The Father loves the Son and has given him control over everything. ³⁶He who believes in the Son has eternal life, but the one disobeying[481] the Son will not see life but will continue to remain under God's punishment.

Jesus and the woman at the well

4 ¹The Pharisees heard that Jesus was making more followers and baptising

---

the Messiah or the name of the one who was promised only. In the NT period believers can believe in the person and works of the physical Son of Man.
477 Salim was in the Decapolis, where there are many springs and water enough for baptising.
478 Modern MSS have that the argument arose with only one not many.
479 Literally, 'the friend of the bridegroom'.
480 Evidence of the preincarnate Christ and that the Son of God originated in heaven.
481 This seems to imply that only those who wilfully reject the Son will not see life. It is not necessarily a condemnation of those who have never heard the gospel.

many more than John. ²(However Jesus did not baptise anyone himself, it was actually his followers *who did the baptising*). ³So when Jesus knew this, he left Judea and went back to Galilee. ⁴It was necessary for him to go through Samaria.

⁵Therefore he came to a city in Samaria called Sychar, near the plot of ground Jacob had given to his own son Joseph. ⁶Jacob's well[482] was there and Jesus having become tired from the journey, sat down by the well. It was about the sixth hour.[483]

⁷A Samaritan woman came to draw water and Jesus said to her, "Give me a drink of water." ⁸(His followers had gone into the city to buy food.)

⁹Then the Samaritan woman said to him, "Why is it that you ask me for a drink for you are a Jew and I am a Samaritan woman?" (For Jews do not associate with Samaritans.)

¹⁰Jesus answered by saying, "If only you knew what a gift from God this is and who it is that is asking you for a drink, you would have asked him and he would have given living water[484] to you."

¹¹ "Sir," the woman said, "you do not have a bucket and the well is deep. Where are you going to get this living water? ¹²Are you greater than our father Jacob, who gave us this well and drank from it himself, along with his sons and his flocks and herds?"

¹³Jesus answered by saying, "Every one of you[485] who drinks this water will be thirsty again, ¹⁴but whoever drinks the water that I am willing to give to him will never thirst again. In fact, the water I will give to him will become in him a spring of water bubbling up to eternal life."

¹⁵The woman said, "Sir, give me this water so that I won't get thirsty and have to keep coming here to draw water."

¹⁶Jesus told her, "Go and get your husband and come back."

¹⁷She said, "I don't have a husband."

Jesus said to her, "You are right when you say you do not have a husband. ¹⁸The fact is that you have had five husbands, and the man you are now with is not your husband. What you have said is true."

¹⁹The woman said to him, "Sir, I can see that you are a prophet. ²⁰Our fathers

---

482   Jacob's well is not mentioned in the OT but archaeologists place its location at the foot of Mount Gerizim (TH).
483   John used Roman time so this was six hours counting from midday or about 6 pm in the evening.
484   The concept of living water occurs quite a few times in John's Gospel. On one level living water was fresh running water that came from a spring as opposed to dead water that was stored in cisterns. D A Carson in his commentary says, "the living water in John's Gospel is a metaphor that speaks of God and his grace, the knowledge of God, life, and the transforming power of the Holy Spirit" (Carson, D A, *The Pillar NT Commentary on John* (1991)) Living water pertains to eternal life.
485   Jesus is probably addressing the Samaritans as a group.

worshipped on this mountain[486] but you Jews claim that the place we must worship is in Jerusalem."

²¹Jesus said to her, "Believe me, woman,[487] a time is coming when you will worship the Father neither on this mountain nor in Jerusalem. ²²You Samaritans worship what you do not know whereas we Jews worship what we do know, because salvation comes from the Jews. ²³But a time is coming, and in fact, the time is now, when the true worshippers will worship the Father in a spiritual way as he truly is. These are the kind of worshippers the Father is wanting.[488] ²⁴God is breath, and only in a spiritual way can people worship him as he truly is."

²⁵The woman said to him, "I know that a Messiah[489] is coming—the one who is called Christ. When he comes, he will explain everything to us." ²⁶Jesus said to her, "I am him—the one speaking to you now."

²⁷At that moment Jesus' followers returned and they were astonished to find that he was speaking with a woman. However no one asked, "What do you want?" or "Why are you speaking with her?"[490]

²⁸Then the woman left her water jar and went back into the city and said to the people there, ²⁹"Come! There's a man who told me everything I ever did. Could this be the Messiah?" ³⁰They came out of the city and went to Jesus.

³¹Meanwhile Jesus' followers urged him, saying, "Rabbi, have something to eat!"

³²But he said, "I have food to eat that you do not know about."

³³So the followers said to each other, "Could somebody have brought him food?"

³⁴Jesus said to them, "My food is to do the will of him who sent me and to finish his assignment for me. ³⁵Do you not have a saying, 'Four more months and then the harvest?'[491] Look, I tell you, open your eyes and see! The fields are white, ready for harvest. ³⁶Even now the person who reaps the harvest receives

---

486 I.e. Mt. Gerizim. Jacob's well was at the foot of this mountain where they were conversing. Geography is the fifth gospel! Cf. Deut. 11:29–30, 27:11–12, Josh. 8:33–35.
487 "Woman" here in English sounds like Jesus is being derogatory, but in fact it is a polite form of address. Cf. John 2:4, 19:26.
488 The time for worshipping God in a physical place like the temple, synagogue or a mountain has become obsolete. In the NT times God's people do not have to go to a physical place rather we worship him in the power of the Holy Breath because he dwells in us through his Breath. We are being built as his dwelling place (Eph. 2:22).
489 Ancient Judaism acknowledged multiple messiahs, the two most relevant being 'Messiah ben Joseph' and the traditional 'Messiah ben David'. Messiahs were not just Jewish either, as the OT refers to the Persian king, Cyrus the Great, as a messiah for his decree to rebuild the Jerusalem temple (Isa. 45:1).
490 It may be that the first question was directed at the woman. It is impossible to tell from the text but good translation theory says that when the original text is vague leave it as vague.
491 There were certain rabbinic writings indicating a four month period in between sowing and harvest.

a wage and he is gathering fruit for eternal life so that the sower and the reaper may rejoice together. ³⁷This saying is true: 'One sows and another reaps.' ³⁸I sent you to reap what you have not worked for. Others have done the hard work and you have reaped the benefits of all their hard work."

³⁹And many of the Samaritans in that city believed in him because of the woman's testimony when she said, "He told me everything I ever did." ⁴⁰Then when the Samaritans came to him, they kept asking him to stay with them and so he stayed two days. ⁴¹And because of his message, many more believed.

⁴²They said to the woman, "At first we only believed because of what you said but now that we have heard for ourselves we believe. We know that this man really is the Messiah—the Saviour of the world."

Jesus returns to Galilee

⁴³After the two days *with the Samaritans,* Jesus left for Galilee ⁴⁴for Jesus himself had said that a prophet has no honour in his own homeland.⁴⁹² ⁴⁵So when he arrived in Galilee, the Galileans welcomed him, having seen all the things he did in Jerusalem during the *Passover* Feast for they also went to the Feast.

⁴⁶Once again Jesus visited Cana in Galilee where he had turned water into wine. There was a certain government official whose son lay sick at Capernaum. ⁴⁷When this man heard that Jesus had arrived in Galilee from Judea, he went to him and begged him to come and heal his son, who was close to death.

⁴⁸Jesus said to him, "Unless you people see miraculous signs and wonders you will never believe."

⁴⁹The government official said, "Sir, please come now before my child dies."

⁵⁰Jesus replied, "You may go. Your son will live."

The man believed what Jesus said and left. ⁵¹While the man was on his way down, his servants met him with the report that his boy was alive and well. ⁵²When he inquired as to what time his son began to get better, they told him, "The fever left him yesterday at the seventh hour."⁴⁹³ ⁵³Then the father realised that this was the exact time at which Jesus had said to him, "Your son will live." So he and all his household believed.

---

492 Jesus in this instance seems to be referring to the land of his forefathers—Bethlehem. That is the reason he left Judea and went back to Galilee. Judea was the centre of hostility against Jesus. However in Matt. 13:57, Mark 6:4, and Luke 4:24, he seems to be referring to Nazareth where he grew up rather than his birthplace.

493 John uses Roman method of time so the seventh hour probably meant seven hours after midday. Therefore it was probably 7 pm in the evening when the boy was healed. At any rate it does not really matter. The important point is that the boy was healed at the very same time that Jesus had told his father that he would live. Cf. John 1:39, 19:14.

⁵⁴This was the second miraculous sign that Jesus had done after coming from Judea to Galilee.

Jesus heals a man on the Sabbath

5 ¹After these things, Jesus went up to Jerusalem for a Judean feast.⁴⁹⁴ ²Near the Sheep Gate⁴⁹⁵ in Jerusalem there is a pool with five covered walkways.⁴⁹⁶ In Hebrew it is called 'Bethesda'. ³At this pool, a large number of disabled people used to lie—the blind, the lame, and the paralysed.⁴⁹⁷ ⁵There was a man there who had been an invalid for 38 years. ⁶When Jesus saw him lying there and learned that he had been in this condition for a long time, he asked him, "Would you like to get better?"

⁷The disabled man replied, "Sir, I have no one to help me into the pool when the water bubbles up.⁴⁹⁸ While I am trying to get in, someone else goes down ahead of me."

⁸Jesus said to him, "Get up, pick up your mat, and walk." ⁹Immediately the man was cured. He picked up his mat and began walking around.

Now the day that this happened was a Sabbath day, ¹⁰and so the Judeans said to the man who had been healed, "It is the Sabbath and so it is against the law to carry your mat."⁴⁹⁹

¹¹But the man replied, "The man who made me well said to me, 'Pick up your mat and walk.'"

¹²They asked him, "Who is the man telling you to pick up your mat and walk?"

---

494 Even though this feast is not mentioned by name, the next logical feast that Jesus would have had to attend in John's Gospel would be Pentecost (Shavuot) as it was one of three pilgrim feasts in which all Jewish males were required to attend in Jerusalem. Some commentators say it refers to the Feast of Purim but this wasn't a 'Judean' Feast as such and Jesus would not be required to attend. This feast is therefore the second feast in a series of five feasts mentioned throughout John's Gospel leading to the culmination in Jesus' final Passover at his crucifixion. The list as follows: 1) Initial Passover – Spring AD 29 (John 2:13–14); 2) Pentecost – Spring AD 29 (John 5:1); 3) Tabernacles – Autumn AD 29 (John 7:2,10,37); 4) Hanukkah – Winter AD 29 (John 10:22); 5) Final Passover – Spring AD 30 (John 13:1). These five feasts cover Jesus' entire public ministry of 62 weeks but does not include the doubtful Passover Feast mentioned in John 6:4.
Cf. https://luke21.com.au/christ-was-cut-off-after-62-weeks/
495 The Sheep Gate was strategically located at the north-eastern corner of the City of David near the temple and Pool of Bethesda for easy access to the altar for the sacrificial animals such as sheep.
496 Gk: *staos*—a porch or covered colonnade or portico like a verandah which was open on one side where people could stand, sit, or walk, protected from the weather and the heat of the sun.
497 Part of v. 3 and v. 4 do not occur in the best Greek MSS and so have been omitted.
498 The water bubbled up due to the syphon effect of the Gihon Spring as many as five times a day when the water was plentiful. This water source was close to the temple. In my opinion the water wasn't stirred by an angel, it was the natural occurrence of the water springing up. There were superstitions around springs that would siphon up by themselves because they didn't know why it occurred—the people believed that a spirit lived in the spring and the spirit (angel/demon) would stir up the water.
Cf. https://www.nehemiaswall.com/john-6-4-new-testament-part-4
499 A Pharisaical law not a law in the Torah. I.e. It was only an interpretation by the Pharisees.

¹³But the man who had been healed had no idea who it was, for Jesus had slipped away into the crowd that was present.

¹⁴Later Jesus found the man at the temple and said to him, "See, you are well again. Stop sinning or something worse may happen to you." ¹⁵The man went away and told the Judeans that it was Jesus who had healed him.

¹⁶Therefore because Jesus was doing these things on the Sabbath, the Judeans persecuted him. ¹⁷But Jesus said to them, "My Father is always at work to this very day, and I too, am working."⁵⁰⁰ ¹⁸For this reason the Judeans tried all the harder to kill him because not only was he breaking the Sabbath but he was even calling God his own Father thereby making himself equal with God.

The authority of the Son

¹⁹Therefore Jesus answered them by saying, "I tell you the truth, the Son is not able to do anything of his own accord. He can only do what he sees his Father doing because whatever the Father does the Son also does likewise.⁵⁰¹ ²⁰For the Father loves the Son and shows him all that he does. You will marvel that he will show him even greater things than these. ²¹For just as the Father raises the dead and gives life to them, even so the Son gives life to whom he desires to give it to. ²²Furthermore, the Father judges no one, but has entrusted all judgment to the Son ²³so that everyone will honour the Son in the same way as they honour the Father. Whoever does not honour the Son does not honour the Father who sent him.

²⁴"I tell you the truth, he who is hearing my word and believing the one who has sent me has eternal life and does not come into judgment but has crossed over from death into life.

²⁵"I tell you the truth, a time is coming and has now come when the *spiritually* dead will hear the voice of the Son of God and those who hear will live. ²⁶For as the Father has life in himself, so also he has given the Son to have life in himself.⁵⁰² ²⁷And he has given authority to the Son to judge because he is the Son of Man. ²⁸Do not be amazed at this teaching for a time is coming when all those

---

500   There is the sense that the Father and the Son were working because it was still within the millennial week. The ultimate millennial Sabbath day occurs on the last seventh day, being the last one thousand years. The Talmud (the basic compendium of Jewish law and thought) says that the history of the world comprises six eras of one thousand years each.

501   As the Son was seeing what the Father was doing, he then acted accordingly in sync with him. For example, the healing of the disabled man at the pool of Bethesda was a case in point. The Son, understanding that the Father was about to heal the lame man, simply spoke the words telling him to get up, take up his mat, and walk. When Jesus performed a miracle it was the Father working through him by the power of the Holy Breath (Luke 5:17, John 14:10, Acts 10:38).

502   Cf. John 1:4, 1 John 1:2.

who are in their graves[503] will hear his voice ²⁹and they will come out. Those who have done good will experience a resurrection of life and those who have practiced evil will experience a resurrection to be judged."[504]

Testimonies about Jesus

³⁰Jesus continued, "I am not able to do anything of my own accord. I judge only as I hear *from God* and my judgment is just for I seek not to please myself but the will of the Father who sent me.

³¹"If I testify about myself, then my testimony cannot be accepted.[505] ³²However there is another who testifies on my behalf and I know that his testimony about me is true. ³³You *Judeans* have sent messengers to John and he has testified to the truth.[506] ³⁴It's not that I must have a human testimony but I say these things so that you may be saved. ³⁵John was a lamp[507] that burned and gave light, and you chose to be happy in his light for a time.

³⁶"However I have a testimony greater than John's. For the very work that the Father has given to me to finish, and which I am now doing, testifies that the Father has sent me. ³⁷And the Father who has sent me has himself testified about me. You *Judeans* have never heard his voice nor seen his form, ³⁸nor does his word remain in you, for you do not believe the one whom he sent.

³⁹"You *Judeans* search the Scriptures because you think in them you can have eternal life. These are what testify about me! ⁴⁰And yet you refuse to come to me that you may have life.

⁴¹"I do not accept praise from men, ⁴²but I know you *Judeans*. I know that you do not have the love of God in your hearts. ⁴³I have come in my Father's name, and you do not accept me. If another comes in his own name, you will accept him.[508] ⁴⁴When others praise you, you love it but you make no effort to receive praise that comes from the only God?[509] How, then, can you believe?

⁴⁵"But do not think that I will accuse you *Judeans* before the Father. Your accuser is Moses, in whom you have put your confidence in. ⁴⁶For if you really

---

503   This refers to all those who have died.
504   John is not preaching a salvation by works here because later in John 6:29 he says that the work of God is to believe in the one he sent. Rather it is a reminder of Dan. 12:2 that there will be two resurrections. Cf. Rev. 20:5.
505   Cf. Deut. 19:15.
506   Cf. John 1:19–34.
507   Gk: *luchnos*—the small lamp with a wick saturated with oil.
508   According to Josephus there were a string of false Messiahs before AD 70 and so this could be anyone who comes speaking on his own authority culminating in the ultimate imposter—the eschatological Antichrist who sits in the temple claiming to be God himself (2 Thess. 2:4).
509   Cf. Mark 12:29. Evidence that there is only one God.

do believe in Moses then you would believe me for he wrote about me.[510] [47]But since you do not believe what he wrote, why would you believe my words?"

Jesus feeds five thousand men[511]
(Matthew 14:13–21, Mark 6:30–44, Luke 9:10–17)

6 [1]After these things, Jesus crossed over to the far shore of the Sea of Galilee (also called Tiberias), [2]and a big crowd of people followed him because they had seen him perform miraculous signs healing the sick. [3]Jesus went up the mountain and he sat down with his followers. [[4]The Judean Passover was near.][512]

[5]When Jesus looked up and saw a large crowd coming towards him, he said to Philip, "Where can we buy bread for these people to eat?" [6]But Jesus said this just to test him for he already knew what he was going to do.

[7]Philip answered him, "Even if we had 200 denarii, it would not be enough to buy bread for everyone to have even a little bit each." [8]Another one of his followers, Andrew, Simon Peter's brother, spoke up, [9]"Here is a boy with five small barley loaves and two small fish, but how far will that go among so many people?"

[10]Jesus said, "Make the people sit[513] down." There was plenty of grass in that place and so they all sat down. There were about five thousand men in number. [11]Jesus then took the loaves and gave thanks *to God*. He distributed the loaves to the people who were sitting there. He did the same with the fish. They had as much as they wanted.

[12]When they were full, Jesus told his followers, "Gather up all the leftover pieces and make sure that nothing is wasted." [13]So they gathered them all up and they filled twelve baskets with the pieces that were left over from the original five barley loaves which the people had eaten.

[14]After the people saw what Jesus had done, they began to say, "Surely this is

---

510   Cf. Deut. 18:18–19, Acts 3:22–23.
511   The feeding of the five thousand is the only miracle recorded in all four gospels.
512   Although all modern English translations include v. 4 [The Judean Passover Feast was near], it is included here as being doubtful. Some of the earliest MSS do not have this verse (13th century manuscript called Minuscule 472 housed in the Lambeth Palace library in London). Furthermore if v. 4 re the Passover Feast is legitimate, then the question remains as to why Jesus is not attending the feast rather than being in Galilee. In addition, if this was before the Passover Feast, barley would not have been ripe to make bread as per v. 9 with the boy with five small barley loaves. The difficulty of this verse and the inclusion of the Passover here is recognised by some saying that chapters 5 & 6 if reversed, would greatly improve the geography of Jesus' movements because of the theory that scribes may have displaced passages when copying MSS (Hunter, A M, *The Cambridge Bible Commentary on the New English Bible* (1993), p. 2).
513   Literally the Greek says 'recline' as that is how the Israelites situated themselves when eating.

the Prophet[514] *whom Moses said* would come into the world." [15]Therefore Jesus, knowing that they were about to come and force him to become king, withdrew again to a mountain by himself.

Jesus walks on the water
(Matthew 14:22–33, Mark 6:45–52)

[16]As evening came, Jesus' followers went down to the sea [17]and got into a boat and set off across the sea to Capernaum. By this time darkness had already come and Jesus had not yet joined them. [18]A strong wind was blowing and the sea was getting rough. [19]When they had rowed 25 or 30 stadiums,[515] they saw Jesus approaching the boat. He was walking on top of the sea and they were afraid. [20]But he said to them, "It's me. Don't be afraid." [21]So they eagerly took him aboard, into the boat, and immediately the boat reached the land where they were going.

The people search for Jesus

[22]The next day the crowd that had remained on the opposite shore of the sea saw that Jesus' followers had only taken one boat and they realised that Jesus had not gone with them—they had left without him. [23]Meanwhile other boats arrived from *the city of* Tiberias landing where the people had eaten the bread after the Lord had given thanks. [24]Once the crowd realised that neither Jesus nor his followers were there, they got into the *other* boats and went to Capernaum looking for Jesus.

Jesus is the bread of life

[25]When the crowd found Jesus on the other side of the sea they said to him, "Rabbi, when did you get here?"

[26]Jesus answered them, "I tell you the truth, you are looking for me, not because you saw miraculous signs but because you ate the loaves of bread and were satisfied. [27]Do not work for food that spoils, but for food that lasts unto eternal life, which the Son of Man is willing to give to you. God the Father has placed his seal of approval on him."

[28]So they asked him, "What do we have to do to do the works of God?"

[29]Jesus answered and said, "The work that God wants you to do is to believe in the one whom he sent."[516]

---

514 Cf. John 1:21, Acts 3:22–23.
515 A stadium is a Greek fixed unit of measure equalling the length of 600 human feet, about 180 m. So 25–30 stadiums is about 5–6 km.
516 The people raise the question by asking in the plural ("works of God") but Jesus answers in the singular saying, "work", indicating that salvation is not based on a series of good works but just one

³⁰Therefore they asked him, "What miraculous sign will you do for us that we may see and believe you? What will you do? ³¹Our forefathers ate the manna in the desert just as it is written, 'He⁵¹⁷ gave bread from heaven to them to eat.'"⁵¹⁸

³²Jesus said to them, "I tell you the truth, it was not Moses who has given⁵¹⁹ the bread to you from heaven, but it is my Father who gives the true bread to you from heaven. ³³For the bread of God is he who comes down from heaven and gives life to the world."

³⁴They said to him, "Sir, from now on give us this bread."⁵²⁰

³⁵Then Jesus said to them, "I am the bread of life. He who comes to me will never go hungry and he who believes in me will never thirst. ³⁶But I have already told you, you have seen me and still you do not believe. ³⁷All that the Father gives to me will come to me and whoever comes to me I will never turn away. ³⁸For I have come down from heaven not to do my will but to do the will of him who sent me. ³⁹This is the will of him who sent me—that I should not lose even one of all those whom God has given to me, but raise them up *to life* on the last day.⁵²¹ ⁴⁰For my Father's will is that every one of you who looks to the Son and believes in him shall have eternal life. I will raise them up *to life* on the last day."

⁴¹The Judeans started to grumble about him because he said, "I am the bread that came down from heaven." ⁴²They said, "Is this not Jesus, the son of Joseph? We know his father and mother! How, then, can he now say that he came down from heaven?"

⁴³Jesus answered by saying, "Stop grumbling amongst yourselves. ⁴⁴For no one is able to come to me unless the Father who sent me draws him and I will raise him up *to life* on the last day. ⁴⁵It is written in the prophets, 'Everyone will be taught by God.'⁵²² Every one of you who listens to the Father and learns from him comes to me. ⁴⁶Not that anyone has seen the Father except the one who is from God—only he has seen the Father.⁵²³ ⁴⁷I tell you the truth, he who believes

---

        work—belief.
517   The people were quoting Scripture and interpreted the pronoun "he" to refer to Moses who gave them bread from heaven to eat. In v. 32 Jesus corrects them by saying that it was actually "my Father".
518   Cf. Psa. 78:24.
519   The word "given" here is in the perfect tense indicating a past action with ongoing effects. In other words, the Jews believed the Law to be bread that was given by Moses in the past but continues to be the source of life. But Jesus corrects them by saying that the Father "gives" (present tense) the true bread from heaven and v. 33 indicates that Jesus is that true bread from heaven.
520   The crowd had failed to understand what Jesus was really saying.
521   It is not the will of God that anyone should fall away from the grace of God and salvation but that doesn't abrogate man's responsibility to endure to the end and be an overcomer. Being raised up at the last day means that a believer takes the responsibility to persevere to the end of his life or till the Lord returns. The Lord never turns away or leaves anyone. It is man that turns away from God.
522   Cf. Isa. 54:13.
523   No one has ever seen God the Father except Jesus—God is the invisible one.
        Cf. John 1:18, 5:37, Col. 1:15, 1 Tim. 1:17, 6:16, 1 John 4:12. God's people (the pure in heart) will

has everlasting life. ⁴⁸I am the bread of life. ⁴⁹Your forefathers ate the manna in the desert, but they died. ⁵⁰But whoever eats the bread that comes down from heaven will not die. ⁵¹I am the living bread that came down from heaven. If anyone eats of this bread, he will live forever.⁵²⁴ Indeed, the bread is *also* my flesh and it is for the life of the world."

⁵²Therefore the Judeans became angry at this and began to argue with each other saying, "How can this man expect us to eat his flesh?"

⁵³So Jesus said to them, "I tell you the truth, unless you eat the flesh of the Son of Man and drink his blood, you have no life in you. ⁵⁴Whoever continues to feed on my flesh and drink my blood has eternal life, and I will raise him up *to life* on the last day. ⁵⁵For my flesh is truly food and my blood is truly drink. ⁵⁶Whoever continues to feed on my flesh and drink my blood remains in me, and I in him. ⁵⁷Just as the living Father sent me here and I live because of the Father, the one who continues to feed on me will live because of me. ⁵⁸This, then, is the bread that came down from heaven. It is not like the bread that your forefathers ate because they died. But the one who continues to feed on this bread will live forever." ⁵⁹Jesus said these things while teaching in the synagogue in Capernaum.

Many followers desert Jesus

⁶⁰Upon hearing *this teaching*, many of Jesus' followers said, "This is a hard teaching. Who can listen to this?"

⁶¹Knowing that many of his followers were grumbling about this, Jesus said to them, "Does this teaching offend you? ⁶²What if you see the Son of Man ascending to where he was before? ⁶³The Breath *of God* gives life but the flesh counts for nothing. The words I have spoken to you are breath and life. ⁶⁴But there are some of you who do not believe." For Jesus had known from the beginning which of them did not believe and who would betray him. ⁶⁵He continued by saying, "This is why I told you that no one can come to me unless the Father has granted him the opportunity."

⁶⁶From this time on, many of Jesus' followers turned back and no longer followed him.⁵²⁵ ⁶⁷Therefore Jesus asked the Twelve, "You don't want to leave too do you?"

⁶⁸Simon Peter answered him, "Lord, to whom shall we go? You have the words of eternal life. ⁶⁹We believe and know that you are the Holy One of God."⁵²⁶

---

see the image of the invisible God—Jesus in all his glory (Matt. 5:8, Rev. 22:4).

524 To eat the flesh of the Son of Man is to absorb his entire way on being and living and must not be taken literally. It must be taken in a symbolic sense otherwise it would imply cannibalism.

525 This refers to the wider group of Jesus' followers not his twelve main followers often referred to as 'the disciples'.

526 Cf. Mark 1:24. A Messianic title.

⁷⁰Jesus replied, "Have not I chosen you, the Twelve? Yet one of you is a devil!" ⁷¹He was referring to Judas, the son of Simon Iscariot, who, even though he was one of the Twelve, would later betray him.

7 Jesus goes up to the Feast of Tabernacles

¹After these things, Jesus travelled throughout *the district of* Galilee because he was not wanting to travel in Judea because the Judeans⁵²⁷ were trying to kill him. ²But when the Judean Feast of Tabernacles⁵²⁸ was near, ³Jesus' own brothers said to him, "You should leave here and go to Judea so that your many followers can see the works⁵²⁹ you are doing. ⁴For no one who wants to be in the public eye acts in secret. Since you are doing these things, show yourself to the world." ⁵(For even his own brothers did not believe in him.)

⁶Therefore Jesus said to them, "The right time for me has not yet arrived. But for you the time is always right. ⁷The world has no reason to hate you, but it hates me because I keep saying that its ways are evil. ⁸You go on up to the Feast. I'm not going up to the Feast yet because for me the right time has not yet come."⁵³⁰ ⁹Having said this, he remained in Galilee.

¹⁰But, after his brothers had already left for the Feast, he also went up, but he didn't go openly, but in secret. ¹¹The Judeans were looking for him at the Feast and they were asking *people*, "Where is that man?"

¹²There was much whispering going on about Jesus amongst the crowds. Some said, "He is a good man" but others were saying, "No, he deceives the people." ¹³But no one would dare say anything publicly about him for fear of the Judean *authorities*.

¹⁴The Feast was nearly halfway over when Jesus went up to the temple and began teaching. ¹⁵The Judeans were amazed and asked, "How did this man get such learning without having studied?"

¹⁶Jesus answered them saying, "My teaching is not my own but it comes

---

527   Most English translations have the Jews trying to kill Jesus but I have followed David H Stern's CJB translation and reasoning that it was specifically Judeans (Stern, David H, *JNT Commentary* (1992), pp. 157-161).
528   This Feast of Tabernacles (Sukkot) was the third feast in a series of five feasts mentioned throughout John's Gospel leading to the culmination in Jesus' final Passover at his crucifixion. The list as follows: 1) Initial Passover – Spring AD 29 (John 2:13–14); 2) Pentecost – Spring AD 29 (John 5:1); 3) Tabernacles – Autumn AD 29 (John 7:2,10,37); 4) Hanukkah – Winter AD 29 (John 10:22); 5) Final Passover – Spring AD 30 (John 13:1). These five feasts cover Jesus' entire public ministry of 62 weeks but does not include the doubtful Passover Feast mentioned in John 6:4. Cf. https://luke21.com.au/christ-was-cut-off-after-62-weeks/
529   I.e. the miracles he was doing.
530   This creates an apparent dilemma in which Jesus says one thing (v. 8) and does another (v. 10). But the thing to remember is that Jesus' itinerary is determined by the Father not 'the counsel of the wicked' (Psa. 1:1).

from the one who sent me. ¹⁷If anyone wants to do God's will, he will discover whether my teaching comes from God or whether I am just speaking on my own authority. ¹⁸He who speaks on his own authority does so to try and get the glory for himself, but he who wants glory for the one who sent him is a man of truth—there is nothing false about him. ¹⁹Has not Moses given you the Law? But there is not one of you who keeps the Law. Why are you trying to kill me?"

²⁰The people in the crowd said, "You have a demon in you! Who is trying to kill you?"

²¹Jesus answered saying, "I did one miracle and everyone is surprised.[531] ²²And yet Moses ordered you to circumcise, (even though it actually came from the forefathers and not Moses) and you circumcise your sons on the Sabbath. ²³So if a boy can be circumcised on the Sabbath and the Law of Moses is not broken, why are you angry with me because I made a man completely well on the Sabbath?[532] ²⁴Stop judging according to what appears right and judge on the basis of what is true."

The people ask whether Jesus is the Messiah

²⁵Therefore some of the Jerusalemites began to ask, "Isn't this the man they are trying to kill? ²⁶See! He is speaking openly and they are not saying anything to him. Perhaps the rulers truly knew that this man is the Messiah. ²⁷But we know where this man is from. However, whenever the Messiah comes, no one will know where he is from."

²⁸Then Jesus, while still teaching in the temple *grounds*, cried out, "Yes, you know me, and you know where I am from. I am not here on my own, but he who sent me is true. You do not know him, ²⁹but I know him because I am from him and he sent me."

³⁰Then they tried to arrest him but no one laid a hand on him because his time had not yet come. ³¹However many in the crowd believed in him and were saying, "When the Messiah comes, will he do more miraculous signs than this man?"

Temple guards are sent to arrest Jesus

³²The Pharisees heard the crowd whispering such things about him. Then the chief priests and the Pharisees sent temple guards[533] to arrest him. ³³Jesus

---

531 Jesus is most likely referring to the miracle he did by healing the disabled man at the pool of Bethesda on the Sabbath (John 5:1-9).
532 The Jews believed that circumcision had priority over keeping the Sabbath so Jesus was arguing how much more important is the healing of the man on the Sabbath because it involves his whole body not just a small part. So, in effect, he was asking them, "What's your problem with me healing on the Sabbath when you don't have a problem with circumcising on the Sabbath?"
533 Literally 'servants'. They were effectively security guards.

said, "I am only with you for a short time and then I am going away to the one who sent me.[534] [34]You will look for me but you will not find me and where I am, you are incapable[535] of coming."

[35]The Judeans said to themselves, "Where does this man intend to go where we cannot find him? Will he go to the Greek speaking Jews and teach the Greeks? [36]What did he mean when he said, 'You will look for me, but you will not find me,' and 'Where I am, you are incapable of coming'?"

Jesus speaks on Sh'mini Atzeret—the last great day of the Feast

[37]On the last and greatest day of the Feast,[536] Jesus stood up and said in a loud voice, "If anyone is thirsty, let him come to me. Let him drink, [38]the one believing in me. As the Scripture has said, 'Rivers of living water will flow from within him.'"[537] [39]Jesus was referring to the Breath *of God*, which those who believed were about to receive. Up to that time Breath[538] had not yet been given since Jesus had not yet been glorified.

[40]Upon hearing these words, some in the crowd said, "Surely this man is the Prophet *we have been waiting for.*"

[41]Others said, "He is the Messiah."

But still others asked, "How can the Messiah come from Galilee? [42]Does not the Scripture say that the Messiah will come from David's family and from Bethlehem, the village where David was?" [43]Therefore the people were divided because of Jesus. [44]Some wanted to arrest him, but no one dared layid their hands on him.

The unbelief of the Judean authorities

[45]The temple guards then went back to the chief priests and Pharisees who asked them, "Why didn't you bring him in?"[539]

[46]The temple guards answered, "No one has ever spoken like this man."

[47]The Pharisees replied, "Has he deceived you too? [48]Have any of the rulers

---

534 After Jesus' rejection here, he announces for the first time that he is going away in fulfillment of Hos. 5:15. This is on the Feast of Tabernacles, six months before his crucifixion in AD 30 and marks the end of the 69 weeks in Daniel's prophecy where it says the Messiah would be 'cut off'.
535 Comes from the Greek word *dunamai* which means power. In other words they are powerless to follow Jesus where he will be with the Father because they are powerless of ascending into the sky. Cf. John 3:13, 13:33.
536 Originally the Feast of Tabernacles was only a seven-day celebration then later an eighth day (Sh'mini Atzeret) was added. By the 1st century the Feast was thought of as an eight day feast. It was a day of great celebration and rest (i.e. a special Sabbath) distinguished by particular sacrifices, the joyful dismantling of the booths, and the repeated singing of the Hallel (Psa. 113–118).
537 The pronoun "him" could either be referring to Jesus or the believer here. The Greek is not clear.
538 Note there is no definite article (the) in Greek MSS before "Breath" here.
539 This was presumably still the last day of the feast so there was a gap of four days when the guards were initially sent out by the Pharisees until the last day of the feast.

or the Pharisees believed in him?[540] No! [49]But this crowd, knowing nothing about the Law, are cursed."

[50]Nicodemus, the one who had gone to Jesus earlier and who was one of their own, asked, [51]"Does our Law condemn a man without hearing from him first to find out what he is doing?"

[52]They responded by saying to Nicodemus, "Are you also from Galilee? Do your research and you will see that no prophet arises from Galilee."[541] [53]And then everyone went back to their own home.

The woman caught in adultery

8 [1]But Jesus went to the Mount of Olives. [2]At dawn the next morning Jesus came back to the temple *grounds* where all the people were gathered around him and he sat down and began teaching them. [3]The scribes and the Pharisees brought a woman who had been caught in adultery and made her stand in the middle of everyone. [4]They said to Jesus, "Teacher, this woman was caught in the act of committing adultery. [5]Now in our Law, Moses commanded us to stone such women. Therefore what do you say?" [6]They were saying this to try and trap him so that they might have something to accuse him of.

But Jesus bent down and started to write *in the dust* on the ground with his finger and ignored them. [7]As they were continuing on questioning him, Jesus straightened up and said to them, "If any one of you is without sin, let him be the first one to throw a stone at her." [8]And again he bent down and began writing on the ground.[542]

[9]When they heard this, one by one they began to leave, the older ones first, until only Jesus was left with the woman still standing there. [10]Jesus stood up and said to her, "Woman, where are they? Has no one condemned you?"

[11]She replied, "No one, sir."

---

540   This was not true as Nicodemus, a Pharisee, and Joseph of Arimathea of the Sanhedrin, believed.
541   The prophet Jonah came from Gath-Hepher in Galilee (2 Kings 14:25) but this may be a reference to the fact that no prophet was ever predicted to come from Galilee.
542   There is a lot of speculation as to what Jesus was writing in the ground with his finger. There is only one place in Jerusalem where there is a list of people starting from the oldest to the youngest—the Sanhedrin. So, Jesus was writing the names of the Sanhedrin starting with the oldest going down to the youngest hence they left one by one. By writing their names in the dust, Jesus was indicating that they had forsaken the LORD, the spring of living water (Jer. 17:12-13). There are four elements in Jer. 17:12-13 that become apparent: 'rejection'; 'shame'; 'names written in the dust'; and 'water'. Only one day before, the Jewish leaders had rejected him (John 7:32-33), the spring of living water—two of the elements. The very next day the Judean leaders were trying to shame the woman (third element) and so Jesus brought the fourth and final element by writing their names in the dust. Effectively, Jesus was saying that they would be shamed because they had rejected the spring of living water, so he wrote their names in the dust.

Jesus said, "Then neither do I condemn you. Go, and from now on don't sin anymore."

Jesus the light of the world

[12] When Jesus spoke again to the people, he said, "I am the light of the world. Whoever follows me will never walk in darkness, but will have the light of life."

[13] Therefore the Pharisees said to him, "You are testifying about yourself so your testimony is not true."

[14] Jesus answered by saying, "Even if I testify on my own behalf, my testimony is valid, for I know where I came from and where I am going.[543] But you have no idea where I come from or where I am going. [15] You make judgments based according to the flesh, I am not judging anyone. [16] But if I do judge, my judgments are right, because I am not alone, the Father who sent me is with me.[544] [17] It is written in your own Law that when two witnesses agree, their testimony is true. [18] I am one who testifies for myself and the Father who sent me also testifies on my behalf."

[19] Then they said to him, "Where is your father?"

Jesus answered, "You do not know me or my Father. For if you had known me, you would have also known my Father."

[20] Jesus spoke these words while teaching in the temple near the treasury[545] where the offerings were placed. No one arrested him because his time had not yet come.

Jesus says he is going away[546]

[21] Once again Jesus said to them, "I am going away and you will look for me and you will die in your sin. Where I go, you are incapable of coming."

[22] This therefore caused the Judeans to ask, "Is he going to kill himself? Is that why he says, 'Where I go, you are incapable of coming'?"

[23] Jesus said to them, "You are from here below but I am from above. You are from this world, I am not of this world. [24] I told you that you would die in your sins. If you do not believe that I am *he*, you will indeed die in your sins."

[25] So they started asking him, "Who are you?"

Jesus said to them, "The Beginning,[547] and also that which I have been

---

543 Jesus came from the Father (Heb. 1:5 – the begotten) as the firstborn over all creation. He came down from heaven (John 6:38) and he will ascend back up to the Father's side (John 6:62).
544 Any judgment that Jesus does make originates from God not in a humanly way.
545 The treasury was a number of small rooms in the temple where valuables were stored possibly in the court of the women. Cf. Mark 12:41–42.
546 This is a fulfilment of Dan. 9:26 ("The Messiah will be cut off and have nothing") and Hos. 5:15.
547 This refers back to the very beginning when Christ was the firstborn of all creation and when Yahweh 'brought forth' the Wisdom of God (Prov. 8:22 NIV) which is a title of Christ. Prov. 8:22 is also commonly translated as 'Yahweh possessed me'. Ontologically, Yahweh and his Son (Wisdom)

saying.[548] [26]I have much to say about you, much to condemn you of but the one who sent me is truthful and I tell the world what I have heard from him."

[27]They did not understand that the Father was speaking to them.[549] [28]So Jesus said, "When you have lifted up the Son of Man, then you will know that I am he, and that I do nothing on my own but just speak what the Father has taught me. [29]The one who sent me is with me. He did not leave me alone because I always do what pleases him." [30]As Jesus was saying these things, many believed in him.

The truth will set you free

[31]So Jesus said to the Judeans[550] who had believed in him, "If you continue in keeping to my teaching, you are truly my followers [32]and then you will know the truth and the truth will set you free."

[33]They replied, "We are Abraham's descendants and have not been enslaved ever. How can you say that we will become free?"

[34]Jesus replied, "I tell you the truth, every one of you who sins is a slave to sin. [35]But the slave does not remain in the household forever but the son stays forever. [36]Therefore if the Son sets you free, you will certainly be free. [37]I know that you are descendants of Abraham yet you are wanting to kill me because you make no room for my teaching. [38]I speak about the things I have seen while with the Father, and you do what you have heard from your father."

[39]They answered him saying, "Abraham is our father."

Jesus answered, "If you were truly Abraham's children then you would do the things Abraham did. [40]But now you are seeking to kill me, a man who has told you the truth that I heard from God. Abraham did not do such things. [41]You are doing the things your own father does."

Then they said, "We have not been born from fornication.[551] God is the only Father we have."

---

were the same hence the term 'possession' makes sense. In Col. 1:18 Paul describes Christ saying, "He is the Beginning." Cf. Heb. 1:5 footnote.

548 I.e. He who came down from heaven (John 3:13, 6:33, 38, 41–42, 50–51)

549 The Judeans missed the point that every word that Jesus speaks is in reality the word of the Father himself (Lenski, R H, *The Interpretation of St. John's Gospel* (1942)).

550 Although some of the Judeans do appear to believe in Jesus in this verse it is apparent that most of them turn out to be children of the devil in v. 44. A genuine believer is one who remains in Jesus and continues to obey his teachings.

551 Most commentators spiritualise this verse saying that it has nothing to do with biology but the Pharisees were obsessed with biology emphasising that they were the physical 'seed' of Abraham. Carson in his commentary on John comments that there is some evidence that the Samaritans thought Satan seduced Eve to produce Cain (Carson, D A, *The Pillar NT Commentary on John* (1991)). The Judeans may be thinking that Jesus is a Samaritan evidenced by their response in v. 48. It was also a widely held belief by the Jews that 200 watcher angels fornicated with the daughters of men producing the Nephilim (Gen. 6:1–4, 1 Enoch 6).

The Judeans are children of the devil

⁴²Jesus said to them, "If God were your Father, you would love me for I came forth out of God⁵⁵² and now I am here. I have not come on my own authority but the Father sent me. ⁴³Why can't you understand what I am saying? It's because you are incapable of hearing what I am saying. ⁴⁴You are the children of your father, the devil,⁵⁵³ and you want to carry out your father's evil desires. He was a murderer from the beginning, and he has never held to the truth for there is no truth in him. When he speaks the lie, he is speaking in character for he is a liar and the father of lies. ⁴⁵But because I speak the truth you do not believe me. ⁴⁶Can anyone among you prove that I am guilty of sin? If I am telling the truth, why do you not believe me? ⁴⁷He who belongs to God listens to what God has said. The reason you do not listen is that you do not belong to God."

Jesus is better than Abraham

⁴⁸The Judeans answered him saying, "Are we not right in saying that you are a Samaritan and demon-possessed?"

⁴⁹Jesus answered, "I am not possessed by a demon but I honour my Father and you dishonour me. ⁵⁰I am not trying to seek glory for myself however there is one who seeks it and he is the judge. ⁵¹I tell you the truth, if anyone keeps my word, he will never see death."⁵⁵⁴

⁵²Then the Judeans said to him, "Now we surely know that you have a demon. Abraham died and so did the prophets yet you say that if anyone keeps your word, he will never taste death. ⁵³Are you greater than our father Abraham? He died, and so did the prophets. Who do you think you are?"

⁵⁴Jesus answered, "If I glorify myself, my glory is nothing. The one who glorifies me is my Father whom you claim as your God. ⁵⁵And you have never known him, but I know him. If I was to say that I do not know him, I would be a liar like you. But I do know him and I keep his word. ⁵⁶Your father Abraham rejoiced at the thought of seeing my day. He saw it and was happy."

⁵⁷Therefore the Judeans said to him, "You are not even yet fifty years old and you claim that you have seen Abraham?"⁵⁵⁵

---

552 The point here is that this does not mean that Jesus simply 'came' from God in the sense that God sent him from his presence but the Greek demands that the Son 'came out of' the Father. It is the essence of what 'begotten' means (Heb. 1:5). Cf. Psa. 2:7, 110:3.

553 Once again Bible commentators insist that Jesus here is referring to an ethical and moral relationship between the Judean Pharisees and the devil but the Greek infers that it is talking about biology not just that they are reflecting the characteristics of the devil. I.e. Jesus is saying that the devil is their physical father hence their vehement response in v. 48. Cf. 2 Cor. 11:3, 1 John 3:12.

554 Death here is spiritual death—the second death. Here we see a further proof text that there is a requirement for the believer to keep persevering and keep in the faith thereby disproving OSAS.

555 The Judeans knew that Jesus was claiming to have seen Abraham face to face (Gen. 18:1–33). Jesus was represented as the LORD (YHWH)—the visible Yahweh. Cf. Col. 1:15, Heb. 1:3.

⁵⁸Jesus said to them, "I tell you the truth, before Abraham came into being, I exist."⁵⁵⁶

⁵⁹Then they picked up stones to stone him but Jesus hid himself and departed out of the temple *grounds*. He slipped through the midst of them and went on his way.

Jesus heals a man who was born blind

9 ¹And as Jesus was passing by, he saw a man who had been blind from birth. ²His followers asked him, "Rabbi, whose sin caused this man to be born blind? Was it him or his parents?"

³Jesus answered, "Neither this man nor his parents sinned but he was born blind so that the work of God might be revealed in him. ⁴As long as it is day, we must do the work of him who sent me. Night is coming when no one can work. ⁵While I am still in the world, I am the light of the world."

⁶Having said these things, Jesus spat on the ground, made some mud with the saliva, and applied it on the man's eyes. ⁷And he said to him, "Go and wash in the Pool of Siloam"⁵⁵⁷ (Siloam means 'having been sent'). So the man went and washed *his face* and came home seeing.

⁸The man's neighbours and those who had previously seen him begging all the time asked, "Isn't this the same man who used to sit and beg?" ⁹Some claimed that he was *the same man*. Others were saying, "No, it just looks like him." But the man himself said, "I am him."

¹⁰They were asking him, "So, how is it then that your eyes were opened?"

¹¹He replied, "The man they call Jesus made some mud and applied it to my eyes. He told me to go to Siloam and wash my face there. So I went and as soon as I washed, I could see."

¹²"Where is this man?" they asked.

"I don't know," he said.

The Pharisees investigate the healing of the blind man

¹³They took the man who had been born blind to the Pharisees. ¹⁴The day that Jesus made the mud and opened the man's eyes was a Sabbath. ¹⁵Therefore the Pharisees also asked him how was it that he could see. The man said to them, "He placed mud on my eyes then I washed *my face* and I could see."

---

556   Cf. 1 John 1:1–2.
557   The Pool of Siloam was the pool from which the water was drawn for the water libation ceremonies during the Feast of Tabernacles. It is located within the walls of the old city of David, at the southern extremity near the lowest point where the Kidron and Tyropean valleys came together. In Hebrew the pool is *shiloah* (Isa. 8:6), which is derived from the Hebrew verb 'to send'.

¹⁶Some of the Pharisees were saying, "This man is not from God, for he does not keep the Sabbath."

But others were saying, "How can a sinner do such miraculous signs?" So there was division among them.

¹⁷Therefore the Pharisees asked the blind man again, "What do you say about him? It was your eyes that he opened."

The man said, "He is a prophet."

¹⁸The Judeans still did not believe that he had been blind and that he had received his sight until they sent for the man's parents. ¹⁹And they asked them, "Is this your son? Is this the one whom you say was born blind? How is it that now he can see?"

²⁰His parents answered by saying, "We know that this man is our son and that he was born blind. ²¹But we do not know how he is able to see now or who opened his eyes. Ask him! He is of age, he is able to speak for himself." ²²His parents said this because they were afraid of the Judeans for the Judeans had already decided that anyone who acknowledged that Jesus was the Messiah would be expelled from the synagogue. ²³That is why his parents said, "He is of age, ask him."

²⁴Therefore they called back the man who had been blind for a second time and said, "Give glory to God. We know that this man is a sinner." ²⁵Therefore the man answered, "Whether he is a sinner or not, I do not know. I do know one thing—I was blind but now I see!"

²⁶Then they asked him, "What did he do to you? How did he open your eyes?"

²⁷He answered, "I have told you already and you did not listen. Why do you want to hear it again? You don't want to become his followers too do you?"[558]

²⁸Then they threw abuse at him saying, "You are this man's follower! We are followers of Moses! ²⁹We know that God spoke to Moses but as for this man *Jesus*, we don't even know where he is from."

³⁰The man answered by saying, "Now that is truly remarkable! You don't know where he is from, yet he opened my eyes. ³¹We know that God does not listen to sinners.[559] He listens to the godly man who does his will. ³²Nobody has ever heard of opening the eyes of a man born blind. ³³If this man was not from God, he would not be able to do anything."

³⁴The *Pharisees* answered by saying to him, "You were born and bred in sin and now you are trying to teach us!" And they threw him out.

---

558 In the Greek, a negative answer is expected.
559 God will not ordinarily answer the prayers of the unsaved except for the prayers of repentance. E.g. God spared the city of Nineveh when their people prayed (Jonah 3:5–10).

Spiritual blindness

³⁵When Jesus heard that the Pharisees had thrown the blind man out, he found the man and asked him, "Do you believe in the Son of God?"

³⁶The man asked, "Who is he, sir? Tell me so that I may believe in him."

³⁷Jesus said, "You have already seen him and, in fact, he is the one speaking with you right now."

³⁸Then the man said, "I believe, Lord," and he worshipped him.

³⁹Jesus said, "I have come into this world to judge⁵⁶⁰ it, so that the blind may see and the ones who can see may become blind."

⁴⁰Some of the Pharisees who were standing close by heard him say this and asked, "What? Are we blind too?"

⁴¹Jesus said, "If you were blind, you would not be guilty of sin, but now that you claim you can see, you are in sin."

Jesus the Good Shepherd

10 ¹Jesus said, "I tell you the truth, the man who does not enter the sheepfold by the doorway, but gets in some other way, is a thief and a robber. ²But the one who enters through the doorway is the shepherd of the sheep. ³The door-keeper opens the door for the shepherd and the sheep listen to his voice. He calls his own sheep by name and leads them out.⁵⁶¹ ⁴When he has taken out all his own sheep he goes ahead of them and the sheep follow him because they know his voice. ⁵They will never follow a stranger but they will run away from him because they do not recognise a stranger's voice." ⁶Jesus told them this parable but they did not understand what he was telling them.

⁷Therefore Jesus said again, "I tell you the truth, I am the door of the sheep. ⁸Everyone who has come in the past before me were thieves and robbers, but the sheep did not listen to them. ⁹I am the door and whoever enters by me will be saved. He will come in and go out and find pasture. ¹⁰The thief comes in only to steal and kill and destroy. I have come that they might have life and have it abundantly.

¹¹"I am the Good Shepherd.⁵⁶² The Good Shepherd is willing to give his

---

560 Not a reference to final end-times judgment but more a reference to exposing the distinctions between people and their actions.

561 Shepherds often had names for their sheep. Often, the youngest boy in the family served as a shepherd until he grew older and could do harder manual labour.

562 This is in contrast to the 'worthless shepherd' which has its ultimate and final fulfillment in the Antichrist (Zech. 11:16–17), the resurrected beast—Adolf Hitler. This 'worthless shepherd' prophesied in Zechariah has a withered arm and his right eye is totally blinded. Interestingly, Hitler when shooting himself on April 30th 1945, shot himself in the right temple with his right (good) hand. When alive he held his left arm behind his back due to uncontrollable shaking towards the end of his life. This seems to support the idea that the unsaved (including the beast) will be

life for the sheep. ¹²The hired worker is not the shepherd who owns the sheep. So when he sees the wolf coming, he abandons the sheep and runs away. Then the wolf attacks the flock and scatters it. ¹³He runs away because he is only a hired worker and it does not matter to him what happens to the sheep.

¹⁴"I am the Good Shepherd. I know my sheep and my sheep know me, ¹⁵just as the Father knows me and I know the Father. I am willing to give my life for the sheep. ¹⁶I have other sheep[563] that are not of this sheep pen. I must bring them also. They too will listen to my voice and there shall be one flock and one shepherd.[564] ¹⁷The reason my Father loves me is because I am willing to give my life in order that I may receive it back again. ¹⁸No one takes my life away from me. I give it up of my own free will. I have the right to give it up and I have the right to take it up again. This is the command I have received from my Father."

¹⁹Because of these words, the Judeans were again divided *in their opinion about Jesus.* ²⁰Many of them said, "He is demon-possessed and he is mad. Why do you listen to him?"

²¹Others said, "These are not the words of a man who is demon-possessed. Is a demon able to open the eyes of someone who is blind?"

The Judeans try to stone Jesus during Hanukkah

²²It was winter and so the Feast of Dedication was being celebrated in Jerusalem.[565] ²³Jesus was in the temple *area* walking in the colonnade known as Solomon's Colonnade. ²⁴The Judeans were gathered around him asking, "How long will you keep us in suspense? If you are the Messiah, tell us in plain words."

²⁵Jesus answered, "I did tell you and you don't believe me. The works which I do in my Father's name testify as to who I am, ²⁶but you do not believe because you are not my sheep.[566] ²⁷My sheep listen to my voice and I know them and they follow me. ²⁸I am giving eternal life to them and they shall never perish. No one will snatch them out of my hand.[567] ²⁹My Father, who has given them to me, is

---

resurrected in their sinful condition not with a new incorruptible body like the righteous.
563   The Gentile believers.
564   One new man—Jewish and Gentile believers together (Eph. 2:14–18).
565   The Feast of Dedication (Hanukkah) was the fourth in a series of five feasts mentioned throughout John's Gospel leading to the culmination in Jesus' final Passover at his crucifixion in April AD 30. The list as follows: 1) Initial Passover – Spring AD 29 (John 2:13–14); 2) Pentecost – Spring AD 29 (John 5:1); 3) Tabernacles – Autumn AD 29 (John 7:2,10,37); 4) Hanukkah – Winter AD 29 (John 10:22); 5) Final Passover – Spring AD 30 (John 13:1). These five feasts cover Jesus' entire public ministry of 62 weeks but does not include the doubtful Passover Feast mentioned in John 6:4.
      Cf. https://luke21.com.au/christ-was-cut-off-after-62-weeks/
566   Sheep is a metaphor for God's people.
567   John 10:27–28 is often used as a proof text by OSAS proponents to say that one cannot lose salvation but v. 27 says that the condition for not losing one's salvation is that they continue to listen to the master's voice and continue to follow him.

greater than all and no one is able to snatch them out of my Father's hand. ³⁰I and the Father are one."⁵⁶⁸

³¹Again the Judeans picked up stones to stone him, ³²but Jesus said to them, "I have shown you many good works from the Father. Now, for which of these do you stone me?"

³³The Judeans answered him, "We are not stoning you because of a good work but for blasphemy because you, being only a man, claim to be a god."⁵⁶⁹

³⁴Jesus answered them, "Has it not been written in your Law, "I said you are gods'?⁵⁷⁰ ³⁵If God called them 'gods,' to whom the word of God came—and the Scripture cannot be broken—³⁶what about the one whom the Father set apart as his very own and sent into the world? Why then do you accuse me of blasphemy because I said, 'I am the Son of God'? ³⁷Do not believe me unless I do what my Father does. ³⁸But if I do it, even though you do not believe me, believe the works in order that you may know for once and for all that the Father is in me and that I am in the Father."

³⁹Again they tried to arrest him but he escaped from their grasp.

⁴⁰Then Jesus went back across the Jordan to the place where John had been baptising in the early days and he remained there.⁵⁷¹ ⁴¹Many people came to him and they were saying, "Even though John never performed a miraculous sign, all that John said about this man was true." ⁴²Many people believed in him at that place.

---

568   Ontologically, God the Father and the Son of God are the same yet they are different persons because the Son was issued forth out of God in the beginning (Heb. 1:5). One is the visible Yahweh and the other the invisible Yahweh (Col. 1:15). The Son is the exact representation of the invisible God (Heb. 1:3). Jesus was the incarnation of God's essence and he did nothing on his own (John 14:10, Acts 10:38).

569   The Greek does not have the definite article 'the' before the Greek noun *theon* (god). Normally in the NT when God the Father is referred to, the definite article is used before the noun 'god' (TH). It also fits with the context of Jesus' answer in the next verse when Jesus quotes Psa. 82:6 referring to the divine council and the 'gods' or *elohim*. The New English Bible (NEB) translates it this way. The OT writers understood that Yahweh was an *elohim* but no other *elohim* was Yahweh.

570   Cf. Psa. 82:6 (LXX). The context here is the non-human sons of God—i.e. the *elohim*, the spirits of the divine council. In Psalm 82, God is not speaking to other members of the godhead or human judges in Israel rather the members of Yahweh's divine heavenly council. Jesus' point is that if the spirits (the *elohim*) of the divine council were called the sons of God, how much more should He, whom the Father set apart and sent into the world, be called 'the Son of God'.

571   Cf. John 3:22–23. I.e. John had been baptising at Aenon near Salim in the Roman region of Decapolis. Jesus went into hiding for his last few months in the last winter before his death in April AD 30 (John 10:22). James D Tabor says, "This tradition of fleeing the city and going across the Jordan and being nourished and fed just like Elijah in a safe area is a tradition that might have some historical validity" (Tabor, James D, *Wadi el-Yabis and the Elijah 'Wadi Cherith' traditions in Relationship to John and Jesus in the Gospel of John* (2011)). Elijah hid in this area, John the Baptist hid in this area, Jesus fled to this area in the winter before his death when his enemies are trying to kill him and then the followers of Jerusalem in AD 66 fled to Pella to escape the dangers of the Roman takeover of Jerusalem. In the future, followers of Jesus will also flee to the wilderness across the Jordan because it has historical precedence (Matt. 24:15–16).

The death of Lazarus

11 ¹Now a certain man named Lazarus was sick. He was from Bethany, the village of Mary and her sister Martha. ²This Mary, whose brother now lay sick, was the same Mary who had poured perfume on the Lord and wiped his feet with her hair.⁵⁷² ³Therefore the sisters sent a message to him saying, "Lord, the one whom you love is sick."

⁴When Jesus heard the message he said, "This sickness will not end in death but it is for the glory of God so that the Son of God may be glorified through it." ⁵Now Jesus loved Martha and her sister and Lazarus. ⁶Yet when he heard that Lazarus was sick, he remained where he was for two more days.

⁷Then he said to his followers, "Let's go back to Judea."

⁸The followers said to him, "Rabbi. Just a short while ago the Judeans tried to stone you and yet you are going back there?"

⁹Jesus answered, "Are there not twelve hours in a day? A man who walks around in the daytime will not stumble, for he sees by this world's light. ¹⁰But if anyone walks around in the night-time, he stumbles, because the light is not in him."⁵⁷³

¹¹After he had said this, Jesus added, "Our friend Lazarus has fallen asleep but I am going up there to wake him up."

¹²His followers said, "Lord, if he is sleeping, he will recover." ¹³But Jesus had been speaking of his death whereas his followers thought he meant natural sleep.

¹⁴Therefore Jesus told them plainly, "Lazarus is dead, ¹⁵and for your sake I am glad I was not there so that you may believe. But let us go to him."

¹⁶Then Thomas (the one called 'the twin') said to the other followers, "Let us also go so that we may die with him."

Jesus is the resurrection and the life

¹⁷Upon his arrival, Jesus found that Lazarus had already been in the tomb for four days. ¹⁸Bethany was about three kilometres away from Jerusalem, ¹⁹and many Judeans had come to Martha and Mary to console them concerning their brother.

---

572 Cf. John 12:3.
573 D A Carson in his commentary says, "These verses metaphorically insist that Jesus is safe as long as he performs his Father's will. The daylight period of his ministry may be far advanced, but it is wrong to quit before the twelve hours have been filled up. The time will come soon enough when he will not be able to work. But because his followers have been asked to accompany Jesus to Judea, there is an obvious application to them as well. Jesus himself is the light of the world who is still with them. As long as they have him for the full twelve hours of their 'daylight' they should perform the works assigned them. The time would come, all too soon, when the darkness of his departure would make such work impossible" (Carson, D A, *The Pillar NT Commentary on John* (1991)).

²⁰Therefore when Martha heard that Jesus was coming, she went out to meet him but Mary remained sitting[574] in the house.

²¹Martha said to Jesus, "Lord, if you only had been here, my brother wouldn't have died. ²²But I know that even now, whatever you ask of God, he will give it to you."

²³Jesus said to her, "Your brother will rise again."

²⁴Martha replied, "I know he will rise again in the resurrection on the last day."

²⁵Jesus said to her, "I am the resurrection and the life. He who believes in me will live even if he should die.[575] ²⁶And the group which is *spiritually* alive and continues believing in me will never die, ever.[576] Do you believe this?"

²⁷She said to him, "Yes, Lord. I believe that you are the Messiah, the Son of God, who was to come into the world."

Jesus weeps for Lazarus

²⁸And after Martha had said this, she went back and called her sister Mary privately and said, "The Teacher is here and he is asking for you." ²⁹When Mary heard this, she got up quickly and went to him. ³⁰Now Jesus had not yet entered the village, but he was still at the place where Martha had met him. ³¹So when the Judeans saw how quickly she got up and went out, they followed her. They had been with Mary in the house consoling her so when she left they presumed that she was going to the tomb to mourn there.

³²When Mary reached the place where Jesus was and saw him, she fell at his feet and said, "Lord, if you had been here, my brother would not have died."

³³Therefore when Jesus saw her crying and the Judeans who had come along with her also crying, he was deeply moved in spirit and troubled. ³⁴"Where have you laid him?" he asked.

"Come and see, Lord," they said.

³⁵Jesus wept.

³⁶Then the Judeans said, "Look how he loved him!"

³⁷But some of them said, "He opened the eyes of the blind man so couldn't he have kept this man from dying?"

---

574 The context suggests it was sitting **shi'vah** (seven)—the Jewish custom of sitting in mourning for seven days following the death of a family member such as a sibling (Stern, David H, *JNT Commentary* (1992), p. 190). Martha was in fact breaking with custom to go and meet Jesus.
575 This refers to physical death.
576 I.e. the second death. Cf. Rev. 20:14.

Jesus raises Lazarus from the dead

³⁸Jesus, therefore again being deeply moved, came to the tomb. It was a cave with a stone laid across the entrance. ³⁹Jesus said, "Remove the stone!"

Martha, the sister of the dead man said, "Lord, by this time there will already be quite a stench for it is the fourth day!"

⁴⁰Jesus said to her, "Didn't I tell you that if you believed, you would see the glory of God?"

⁴¹Therefore they lifted the stone and Jesus looked up and said, "Father, I thank you that you have heard me. ⁴²I knew that you always hear me, but I said this for the benefit of the people standing here so that they may believe that you sent me."

⁴³When Jesus had finished saying this, he called out in a loud voice, "Lazarus, come out!" ⁴⁴The dead man came out, his hands and feet still wrapped with strips of linen, and a cloth around his face. Then Jesus said, "Unwrap him and let him go."

The plot to kill Jesus

(Matthew 26:1–5, Mark 14:1–2, Luke 22:1–2)

⁴⁵Therefore many of the Judeans who had come to visit Mary and had seen the things Jesus did, believed in him. ⁴⁶But some of them went to the Pharisees and told them what Jesus had done. ⁴⁷So the chief priests and the Pharisees called a meeting of the Sanhedrin and said, "What are we going to do? This man is doing many miraculous signs! ⁴⁸If we let him go on like this, everyone will believe in him and the Romans will come and take away both our temple and our nation."

⁴⁹But one of them named Caiaphas, the high priest that year, said to them, "You don't know anything! ⁵⁰Don't you think that it's better for you to have one man die for the people, instead of having the whole nation being destroyed?"

⁵¹Yet Caiaphas did not say this on his own, but as high priest that year he prophesied that Jesus would die for the nation of Israel, ⁵²and not only for the nation, but also for the scattered children of God,⁵⁷⁷ to bring them together into one *family*. ⁵³So from that day on they plotted to take his life.

⁵⁴Therefore Jesus no longer moved about publicly among the Judeans instead he withdrew to a region near the desert, to a village called Ephraim, where he stayed with his followers.

⁵⁵When it was almost time for the Judean Passover, many went up from the

---

577   I.e. the non-Jews—the Gentile believers scattered in various places.

country to Jerusalem for their ceremonial cleansing before the Passover. ⁵⁶They kept looking for Jesus, and as they stood in the temple grounds they asked each other, "What do you think? Surely he won't come to the Feast will he?" ⁵⁷Now the chief priests and Pharisees had given orders that if anyone found out where Jesus was, he should report it so that they could arrest him.

Mary pours perfume on Jesus' feet

12 ¹Then six days before the Passover,⁵⁷⁸ Jesus arrived at Bethany, where Lazarus lived, whom Jesus had raised from the dead. ²A dinner was prepared for Jesus there. Martha served, while Lazarus was among those reclining *at the table* with him. ³Then Mary took a bottle of expensive pure spikenard perfume and she poured it on Jesus' feet and wiped his feet with her hair. The fragrance of the perfume filled the whole house.

⁴Then Judas Iscariot, one of his followers—the one who would later betray him—said, ⁵"Why wasn't this perfume sold for 300 denarii and given to the poor?" ⁶But he did not say this because he cared about the poor, rather it was because he was a thief and was in charge of the money-box. He would periodically help himself from it.

⁷But Jesus said, "Leave her alone. She has kept this for the day of my burial. ⁸You will always have the poor but you will not always have me."

The plot to kill Lazarus

⁹Meanwhile a large crowd of Judeans found out that Jesus was at Bethany, so they came, not only because of Jesus but also to see Lazarus, whom Jesus had raised from the dead. ¹⁰Therefore the chief priests made plans to kill Lazarus as well, ¹¹for on account of him many of the Judeans were leaving them and believing in Jesus.

Jesus' triumphal entry into Jerusalem
(Matthew 21:1-11, Mark 11:1-11, Luke 19:29-40)

¹²The next day⁵⁷⁹ the large crowd that had come for the Feast heard that Jesus was on his way to Jerusalem. ¹³They took palm branches and went out to meet him, shouting,

---

578 In AD 30, the year that Jesus died, Nisan 14 (Passover) began at sunset on Wednesday evening. It seems that Jesus arrived before sunset on Friday Nisan 8, six days before the Passover. Note that this is not the same dinner recorded in Matthew 26 or Mark 14 as that meal occurred at Simon the Leper's house two days before Passover (Matt. 26:1-2).

579 Palm Sunday, Nisan 10. The Israelites were required to select a lamb on Nisan 10, four days before the Passover so as to make sure they were without defect (Exo. 12:3-6).

"Hosanna!"[580]

"Blessed is he who comes in the name of the Lord!"

"Blessed is the King of Israel!"

Psalm 118:25–26

¹⁴Jesus went and found a young donkey and sat on it, just as it is written,

¹⁵"Do not be afraid, O daughter of Zion.

See, your king is coming seated on a colt of a donkey."

Zechariah 9:9

¹⁶His followers did not understand these things at first however later when Jesus was glorified they were reminded of the things that had been written about him and what they had done for him.

¹⁷The crowd who had been with Jesus when he called Lazarus from the tomb and had raised him from the dead continued to report what had happened. ¹⁸And because they had heard about the miraculous sign that he had done, many *other* people went out to meet him. ¹⁹So the Pharisees said to each other, "You can see that we are not getting anywhere. Look at how the whole world is following after him."

Some Greek speaking Jews wish to see Jesus

²⁰Now there were some Greeks among those who went up to worship at the Feast.[581] ²¹They came to Philip,[582] who was from Bethsaida in Galilee, with a request saying, "Sir, we would like to see Jesus." ²²Philip went to tell Andrew and then Andrew and Philip in turn told Jesus.

²³Jesus said, "The hour has come for the Son of Man to be glorified. ²⁴I tell you the truth, unless a kernel of wheat falls to the ground and dies, it remains only a single seed. But if it dies, it produces many seeds. ²⁵The man who loves his life will lose it while the man who hates his life in this world will keep it for eternal life. ²⁶Whoever serves me must follow me and where I am, my servant also will be there. My Father will honour the one who serves me."

Jesus speaks about his death

²⁷Jesus said, "Now my very soul is troubled and what can I say? Shall I say,

---

580 "Hosanna" is Hebrew for 'save' which became an exclamation of praise.
581 In this instance the reference is to Gentiles who have become proselytes to Judaism and so have come up to Jerusalem to worship during the festival (TH).
582 They approached Philip whose name is Greek and who was also probably a Greek speaking Jew. Cf. John 7:35.

'Father, save me from this hour'? No, it was for this very reason that I have come to this hour. ²⁸Rather, Father, glorify your name!"

Then a voice came from heaven saying, "I have glorified it and I will glorify it again." ²⁹The crowd that was there and heard it said it had thundered. Others said that an angel had spoken to him.

³⁰Jesus said, "This voice was for your benefit, not mine. ³¹Now is the time for this world to be judged, now the ruler of this world will be overthrown.[583] ³²But when I am raised up from the earth, I will draw all men to myself." ³³Jesus said this to indicate the kind of death he was about to experience.

³⁴The crowd answered, "We have heard from the Law that the Messiah will remain forever, so how can you say, 'The Son of Man must be raised up'? Who is this Son of Man?"

³⁵Then Jesus said to them, "You will have the light just a little while longer. Walk while you have the light, before darkness overtakes you. The man who walks in the dark does not know where he is going. ³⁶Put your trust in the light while you have it, so that you may become children of the light."

The Judeans continue in their unbelief

When Jesus had finished speaking, he left and hid himself from them. ³⁷Even after Jesus had done all these miraculous signs in their presence, they still did not believe in him. ³⁸This was to fulfil what the prophet Isaiah said,

"Lord, who has believed our message?
To whom did the Lord reveal his power?"

Isaiah 53:1

³⁹Therefore they could not believe, because Isaiah also said,

⁴⁰"He has blinded their eyes and hardened their hearts so that they
should not see with their eyes and could not understand in their
hearts and they could not turn so that I could heal them.

Isaiah 6:10

⁴¹Isaiah said this when he saw his glory and spoke about him.[584] ⁴²Even so, many of the rulers believed in him, but because of the Pharisees they would not

---

583 The word "judged" here is literally the Greek word *krisis* where the English word "crisis" is derived. The Greek means judgment, the result of a trial, to decide a legal question, to arrive at a verdict. Indeed, Jesus' crucifixion was a crisis, the event that splits history when the world has to decide what to do with the death of Jesus, whether to believe or not believe. "The ruler of this world" is the devil. He was defeated at Calvary yet he is still active today. Eventually he will be thrown into the lake of fire at the end of the Millenium Kingdom (Rev. 20:10).

584 Cf. Isa. 6:1–3. Isaiah literally saw the Son of God in his preincarnate form seated on a throne.

confess their faith for fear they would be expelled from the synagogue. ⁴³For they loved praise from men more than praise from God.

⁴⁴Then Jesus cried out in a loud voice, "Whoever believes in me does not only just believe in me but also him who sent me.⁵⁸⁵ ⁴⁵And whoever sees me sees the one who sent me. ⁴⁶I have come into the world as a light, so that the group who believes in me will not remain in darkness. ⁴⁷And if anyone hears my words but does not keep them, I do not judge him for I did not come into the world to judge the world but to save it. ⁴⁸There is something that will judge him who rejects me and does not receive my message—the word I have spoken will judge him on the last day. ⁴⁹For I did not speak of my own accord, but the Father who sent me commanded me what I may say and speak. ⁵⁰I know that this command leads to eternal life. So whatever I say is just what the Father has told me to say."

*Jesus washes his followers' feet*⁵⁸⁶
(Matthew 26:6–13, Mark 14:3–9)

13 ¹It was just before the Passover Feast.⁵⁸⁷ Jesus already knew that the time had come for him to leave this world and go to the Father. He had loved his own who were in the world, and he loved them to the very end. ²Dinner was taking place, and the devil had already put into the heart of Judas Iscariot, son of Simon, that he should betray Jesus.⁵⁸⁸ ³Jesus knew that the Father had put everything under his control, that he had come from God and that he was returning to God. ⁴Jesus got up from the dinner, took off his outer garment and wrapped a towel around his waist. ⁵After that, he put water into a basin and began to wash his followers' feet, drying them with the towel that was wrapped around him.

⁶Jesus came to Simon Peter who said to him, "Lord, are you going to wash my feet?"

⁷Jesus answered by saying, *"You do not know what I am doing right now but later you will understand."*

⁸Peter said, "I will never let you wash my feet."

---

585   A basic theme of John's gospel is the preincarnate Son of God who was sent from God.
586   The foot washing did not occur at the Last Supper, the night before the Passover but it most likely occurs at the dinner described in Matt. 26:6–13 at the home of Simon the Leper two days before the Passover on Monday night, Nisan 12.
587   This Passover Feast (Pesach) was the final feast in a series of five feasts mentioned throughout John's Gospel, Jesus' final Passover when he would be crucified. The list as follows: 1) Initial Passover – Spring AD 29 (John 2:13–14); 2) Pentecost – Spring AD 29 (John 5:1); 3) Tabernacles – Autumn AD 29 (John 7:2,10,37); 4) Hanukkah – Winter AD 29 (John 10:22); 5) Final Passover – Spring AD 30 (John 13:1). These five feasts cover Jesus' entire public ministry of 62 weeks but does not include the doubtful Passover Feast mentioned in John 6:4.
      Cf. https://luke21.com.au/christ-was-cut-off-after-62-weeks/
588   The implication here is that the devil had already put into the heart of Judas to betray the Lord prior to this 'foot washing dinner' possibly at the Friday evening dinner referred to in John 12:1–8 when he had had an issue with the money spent on the perfume.

Jesus answered him, "Unless I wash you, you have no part with me."

⁹Simon Peter said to him, "Lord, do not *wash* my feet only but *wash* my hands and my head as well!"

¹⁰Jesus said to him, "A person who has already bathed needs only to wash his feet because his whole body is clean. And you are clean, though not every one of you." ¹¹Jesus said this because he knew who was going to betray him and that was why he said not everyone was clean.

¹²After Jesus had washed their feet, he put back on his outer garment and returned to his place at the table. He asked them, "Do you understand what I have just done? ¹³You call me 'Teacher' and 'Lord,' and rightly so, for that is what I am. ¹⁴Now that I, your Lord and Teacher, have just washed your feet, you also should wash one another's feet. ¹⁵For I have set you an example that you should do as I have done for you. ¹⁶I tell you the truth, a servant is not greater than his master, nor is a messenger greater than the one who sent him. ¹⁷Now that you know these things, you will be blessed if you do them.

Jesus predicts his betrayal after washing his follower's feet

¹⁸"I am not talking about all of you for I know those whom I have chosen. But it is so that the Scripture may be fulfilled which says, 'The one eating bread with me has lifted up his heel against me.'[589]

¹⁹"I am telling you now before it happens, so that when it does happen you will believe that I am *he*.[590] ²⁰I tell you the truth, whoever welcomes the person I might send, welcomes me and whoever welcomes me welcomes the *Father* who sent me."

²¹After Jesus had said this, he became troubled in his spirit and declared, "I tell you the truth, one of you is going to betray me."

²²The followers stared at each other and were uncertain about whom Jesus was speaking about. ²³One of them, the follower whom Jesus loved, was reclining next to him *on his right*. ²⁴Simon Peter motioned to this follower and said, "Ask who he was speaking about."

²⁵Leaning back against the breast of Jesus, he asked him, "Lord, who is it?"

²⁶Jesus answered, "It is the one to whom I will give this piece of bread after I have dipped it in the dish." Then after dipping the piece of bread in, he gave it to Judas Iscariot, the son of Simon. ²⁷And as soon as Judas took the piece of bread, Satan entered into him.

---

589 Cf. Psa. 41:9. In the Near East to show the bottom of one's foot was a mark of contempt, or even possibly a threat of violence. It was an especially treacherous thing to do after eating at someone's table, because eating a meal with a superior was a pledge of loyalty to that person (TH).

590 I.e. the one spoken about in Psa. 41:9.

Jesus said to him, "What you are about to do, do it quickly," ²⁸but no one at the meal understood why Jesus said this to him.⁵⁹¹ ²⁹Since Judas was in charge of the money, some thought Jesus was telling him to go and buy what was needed for the Feast, or to give something to the poor. ³⁰As soon as Judas had taken the bread, he left and it was night-time.

Jesus gives a new commandment

³¹Once Judas had left, Jesus said, "Now the Son of Man is glorified and God is glorified in him. ³²If God is glorified in him, God himself will glorify the Son and he will do so immediately.

³³"Children, I will be with you only a little while longer. You will look for me, and as I said to the Judeans, 'Where I am going, you are incapable of coming.'⁵⁹²

³⁴"I am giving a new command to you all: Love one another. As I have loved you, so you must also love one another. ³⁵By this all men will know that you are my followers, if you love one another."

Jesus predicts that Peter will deny him

³⁶Simon Peter asked him, "Lord, where are you going?"

Jesus answered him, "Where I am going, you are incapable of following me now, but you will follow me later."

³⁷Peter asked him, "Lord, why am I incapable of following you now? I am ready to lay down my life for you."

³⁸Jesus answered, "Will you really lay down your life for me? I tell you the truth, before the rooster crows, you will disown me three times!"⁵⁹³

Jesus is the only way to God and salvation

14 ¹Jesus said to them, "Do not let your hearts be troubled. Believe in God but also make sure that you believe in me. ²In my Father's house there are many rooms.⁵⁹⁴ If it wasn't so, I would have told you. I am going there to prepare a place for you. ³And if I go and prepare a place for you, it means that I am coming

---

591   The question is what was Judas about to do? Even though it looks like it, this was not the Last Supper, the night before Jesus died, rather this was the meal two nights before the Passover, described in Matt. 26:6–13 at Simon the Leper's house. So Judas was not heading out to betray Jesus on Jesus' last night, rather Luke tells us that after Satan entered him, he went straight to the chief priests to discuss how he might betray Jesus late on the Monday night (Luke 22:4).

592   Jesus first said this to the Judeans six months earlier at the Feast of Tabernacles (John 7:33–34). This was the time that Jesus was 'cut off'. He is referring to his soon ascension to heaven.

593   Jesus' prediction of Peter's denial here is different than the denial predicted in Matt. 26:31, Mark 14:30, and Luke 22:34. The prediction here occurs two nights before on Monday night, Nisan 12 after the foot washing. Notice carefully in the predictions in all the other gospels, Jesus said that Peter would deny him that very night or day.

594   In John 2:16, Jesus calls the temple in Jerusalem, "My Father's house."

back[595] and I will gather you to be with me so that you may also be where I am. ⁴You know the way to the place where I am going."

⁵Thomas said to him, "Lord, we don't know where you are going, so how can we know the way?"

⁶Jesus answered, "I am the way, the truth, and the life. No one comes to the Father except through me. ⁷If you really knew me, you would know my Father as well. From now on, you do know him and have seen him."

⁸Philip said, "Lord, show us the Father and that will be enough for us."

⁹Jesus said to him, "Don't you know me, Philip, even after I have been with you all for such a long time? Anyone who has seen me has seen the Father. How can you say, 'Show us the Father'? ¹⁰Don't you believe that I am in the Father, and that the Father is in me? The words I say to you men are not from myself but it is the Father who lives in me, who is doing his work. ¹¹Believe me when I say that I am in the Father and the Father is in me, or at least believe on the evidence of the works[596] themselves. ¹²I am telling you the truth, the one who believes in me will do the works I have been doing. He will do even greater things than these, because I am going to the Father. ¹³And I will do whatever you ask in my name so that the Father may be glorified through the Son. ¹⁴If you men ask me for anything in my name, I will do it."

Jesus promises the Holy Breath

¹⁵Jesus continued, "If you love me, you will obey what I command. ¹⁶And I will ask the Father and he will give another advocate to you so that he[597] may be with you forever. ¹⁷That is the Breath of Truth, which the world is incapable of receiving because *the world* does not see it or know it. But you know it because it lives with you and it will be in you.[598]

¹⁸"I will not leave you as orphans, I am coming to you.[599] ¹⁹Very soon, the world will not see me anymore, but you will see me and because I *will continue to* live, you also will live. ²⁰On that day you will realise that I am in my Father, and you are in me, and I am in you. ²¹Whoever has my commands and keeps them, he is the one who loves me. He who loves me will be loved by my Father, and I too will love him and make myself known to him."

²²Then Judas (not Judas Iscariot) said, "But Lord, why do you intend to make yourself known to us and not to the world?"

---

595   This is the only place in the NT where Jesus specifically says that he is coming back.
596   I.e. the miracles that Jesus performed.
597   This is referring to the Father here not the Holy Breath.
598   In v. 17, the Holy Breath (Holy Spirit) is referred to in the neuter gender.
599   Jesus will come to them in a new way by means of the 'advocate' after he departs from the earth.

²³Jesus answered by saying to him, "If anyone loves me, he will obey my word. My Father will love him and we will come to him and abide with him. ²⁴He who does not love me will not obey my words. The word you hear is not mine but it is from the Father who sent me.

²⁵"I have told you these things while I am still here with you all. ²⁶However the advocate, the Holy Breath, which the Father will send in my name, will teach you all things and will remind you of everything that I have told you.

²⁷"Peace I leave you and my peace I give to you. I do not give to you as the world gives. Do not let your hearts be troubled and do not be afraid. ²⁸You have all heard me say that I am going away and I am coming back to you. If you loved me, you would be happy that I am going to the Father, for the Father is greater than I am. ²⁹I have told you these things now before it happens so that when it happens you may believe. ³⁰I will not be speaking with you for much longer, for the ruler of this world is coming. He has no hold over me ³¹but the world must know that I love the Father and that I do just as the Father has commanded me.

"Come, let us go now."⁶⁰⁰

The true vine, the branches and the gardener

15 ¹Jesus told *a parable* saying, "I am the true vine and my Father is the gardener. ²He cuts off every branch in me that bears no fruit, while every branch that does bear fruit he prunes so that it may bear even more fruit. ³You are already clean because of the word I have spoken to you. ⁴If you remain joined with me, I will remain joined with you. No branch can bear fruit by itself rather it must remain joined to the vine.

⁵"I am the vine, you are the branches. If a man remains joined to me and I to him, he will bear a lot of fruit because without me you can do nothing. ⁶Those who do not remain joined to me are like a branch that is thrown away and withers. These sorts of branches are picked up, thrown into the fire and burned.⁶⁰¹

---

600   This whole conversation in John 13–14, took place in the home of Simon the Leper on the Monday night, Nisan 12 during which many things happened: Jesus' head was anointed, he washed his disciple's feet, he identified Judas as his betrayer and Satan entered into him. Then Judas left the meal early and went to discuss with the chief priests how to betray Jesus (Luke 22:3–4). Jesus also predicted that Peter would deny him a couple of nights later. At this point in the narrative, Jesus instructs that they all leave Simon's house but John does not say where Jesus and his disciples went from there. However we know from Matt. 26 and Mark 14, the next day, that Jesus instructs his disciples to prepare the Passover meal. Jesus' words in chapters John 15–17 would have occurred in between leaving Simon's house and the Passover meal two evenings later.

601   John 15:1–6 is a proof text that one needs to remain or abide in Christ and endure to the end which completely opposes the principle of OSAS. Jesus will only remain in his followers if they remain in him. Without the sustenance of the vine, the branches wither. Believers always have the choice to stay with Jesus or leave him, to be in union with him or to depart. Case in point: Judas who had already betrayed Jesus in his heart prior to the Monday night 'foot washing dinner' (John 13:2).

⁷"If you remain joined to me and my words remain in you, you must ask for whatever you want and it will be done for you. ⁸This is all for my Father's glory when you bear a lot of fruit and it shows that you really do follow me.

⁹"As the Father has loved me, so have I loved you. Now make sure that you allow me to keep on loving you. ¹⁰If you keep my commands, you will remain in my love just as I have kept my Father's commands and remain in his love. ¹¹I have told you these things so that my joy may be in you and your joy may be full.

¹²"This is my command: Love each other as I have loved you. ¹³This is the greatest kind of love that there is: A man laying down his life for his friends. ¹⁴You are my friends if you do what I command. ¹⁵I no longer call you servants, because a servant does not know what his master is doing. Instead, I call you friends, for everything that I heard from my Father I have made known to you.

¹⁶"You did not choose me, but I chose you and appointed you to go and bear fruit, to bear fruit that will last. Then the Father will give to you whatever you ask in my name. ¹⁷This is my command: Love each other."

The world hates the followers of Jesus

¹⁸Jesus continued by saying, "If the world hates you, remember that it hated me first. ¹⁹If you belonged to the world, it would love you as one of its own. But I have chosen you out of the world. That is why the world hates you. ²⁰Remember what I have told you: 'No servant is greater than his master.' If they persecuted me, they will also persecute you. If they obeyed my teaching, they will obey yours also. ²¹They will treat you this way because of my name, for they do not know the one who sent me. ²²If I had not come and spoken to them, they would not have been guilty of sin. As it is now, they no longer have any excuse for their sin.[602] ²³He who hates me hates my father as well. ²⁴If I had not done the works among them that no one else did, they would not be guilty of sin. But now they have seen these *miracles*, and they have hated both me and my Father. ²⁵But this has come about to fulfil what is written in their Law: 'They have hated me without reason.'[603]

²⁶"When the advocate comes, whom I will send to you from the Father, the Breath of Truth which leaves from within the Father, he will testify about me. ²⁷And you also must testify about me, for you have been with me from the beginning.

16 ¹"I have told you these things so that you will not go astray. ²They will expel you out of the synagogues, and the time will come when anyone who kills you will think that he is doing God a service. ³They will do these things

---

602   If Jesus had not come into the world and spoke his message then the world would have an excuse for their sin but as it is, Jesus did come into the world and the world is now conscious of their sin.
603   Cf. Psa. 35:19.

because they have not known the Father or me. ⁴But I have spoken about these things so that when their hour comes you might remember that I have told you. I did not tell you this at first because I was with you.

The work of the Holy Breath

⁵"But now I am going to him who sent me, yet none of you asks me where I am going?[604] ⁶And now because I have said these things, you are filled with sadness. ⁷But I am telling you the truth that it is for your good that I am going away. Unless I go away, the advocate will not come to you, but if I go, I will send him to you. ⁸And when he comes, he will rebuke the world concerning sin, righteousness, and judgment: ⁹concerning sin, because they do not believe in me; ¹⁰concerning righteousness because I am going to the Father and you will not see me anymore; ¹¹and concerning judgment because the ruler of this world has been judged.

¹²"I have much more to tell you, but it is too much for you to bear now. ¹³But when the Breath of Truth comes, he will guide you into all truth, he will speak only what he hears,[605] and he will tell you what is yet to come. ¹⁴He will glorify me, because he will take what I say and reveal it to you. ¹⁵Everything that belongs to the Father is mine. That is why I said *the Breath* will take what I say and reveal it to you. ¹⁶In just a little while you will see me no more, and then a little while later you will see me again."[606]

Happiness will replace mourning

¹⁷Therefore some of his followers asked each other, "What does he mean when he says, 'In a little while you will see me no more, and then a little while later you will see me again,' and also when he says, 'It is because I am going to the Father'?" ¹⁸They kept asking, "What does he mean by 'a little while'? We don't understand what he is referring to."

¹⁹Jesus could see that they were wanting to talk to him about this so he said to them, "Are you asking each other what I meant when I said, 'In a little while you will see me no more, and then a little while later you will see me again'? ²⁰I am telling you the truth, you will weep and mourn while the world rejoices. You will grieve, but your grief will turn into great happiness. ²¹When a woman is

---

604 Peter does ask Jesus where he is going in John 13:36 and Thomas questioned Jesus regarding the way to where he was going in John 14:5. Peter and John's questions occurred on the Monday night, Nisan 12 however Jesus' speech in chapters 15–17 could have occurred at any time between their leaving the house of Simon and completing the Passover meal two evenings later.

605 Like the Son, the Holy Breath does not speak on his own authority but only what he hears. Cf. John 12:49, 14:10.

606 Jesus is referring to the fact that he will be in the tomb for three days and three nights and then after that they will see him again.

about to give birth she is anxious because her time has come but when her baby is born she forgets the trouble because of her joy that a child has been born into the world. ²²And so it is with you: Now is your time of grief, but I will see you again and you will be full of happiness and no one can take that happiness away from you. ²³And on that day, you will not ask me anything. I am telling you the truth when I say that the Father will give to you whatever you ask for in my name. ²⁴Up until now you have not asked for anything in my name. Ask and you will receive so that your happiness will be full.

Jesus has conquered the world

²⁵"Even though I have been speaking with figures of speech *up to this point*, a time is coming when I will no longer use this kind of language but I will speak to you plainly about my Father. ²⁶On that day you will ask in my name. I am not saying that I will ask the Father on your behalf. ²⁷No, for the Father himself loves you because you have loved me and have believed that I came forth out of God.⁶⁰⁷ ²⁸I came from the Father and I have come into the world; now I am leaving the world and I am going to the Father."

²⁹Then Jesus' followers said, "Now you are speaking clearly and without figures of speech. ³⁰We know now that you know all things and that you do not need to question anyone because of this.⁶⁰⁸ This makes us believe that you really did come forth out from God."

³¹Jesus answered them, "So, do you believe now? ³²But a time is coming, and has come, when you will be scattered, each to his own home. You will leave me all alone. Yet I am not alone, for my Father is with me. ³³I have told you these things so that you may have peace. In this world you will have trouble. But take courage! I have conquered the world."

Jesus prays for himself, his followers and for the world

17 ¹After Jesus had said these things, he looked up to heaven and said,

"Father, the time has come. Glorify your Son, that your Son may glorify you. ²For you granted him authority over all the people that he might give eternal life to all those you have given to him. ³Now this is eternal life: that they may know you, the only true God, and Jesus Christ whom you have sent. ⁴I have glorified you on the earth by finishing the work you have given to me that I

---

607 Cf. John 8:42 and footnote.
608 I.e. It is not necessary for Jesus to question people what they are thinking because of the fact that he has come from God and the Father shows him everything that he does (John 5:20).

should do. ⁵Father, glorify me in your presence with the glory I had with you before the world began.

⁶"I have revealed you to those whom you gave to me out of the world. They were yours; you gave them to me and they have obeyed your word. ⁷Now they know that everything you have given to me comes from you. ⁸For I gave the words you have given to me to them and they accepted them. They know that it is true that I came forth out of you[609] and they have believed that you sent me. ⁹I pray for them. I am not praying for the world, but for those you have given to me because they are yours. ¹⁰All I have is yours, and all you have is mine and I am being glorified in them. ¹¹I am no longer going to be in the world but they are still in the world and I am coming to you. Holy Father, protect them by the power of your name—the name you gave to me, so that they may be one as we are one. ¹²While I was with them, I protected them and kept them safe by that name that you gave to me. None of them perished except the man who was doomed to utter ruin[610] so that the Scripture would be fulfilled.

¹³"I am coming to you now, but I say these things while I am still in the world so that they can be filled with my joy. ¹⁴I have given your message to them and the world has hated them for they are not of this world any more than I am of the world. ¹⁵I am not asking that you take them out of the world but that you protect them from the evil one. ¹⁶They are not of the world, just as I am not of it. ¹⁷Set them apart[611] for yourself by means of the truth— your word is truth. ¹⁸As you sent me into the world, I have sent them into the world. ¹⁹And for their sake, I set myself apart so that they too may be truly set apart.

²⁰"I not only pray for them alone, but I pray also for those who will believe in me through their message. ²¹I pray that all of them may be one, Father, just as you are in me and I am in you. May they also be in us so that the world may believe that you sent me. ²²⁻²³I give them the glory[612] that you have given to me so that they may be one as we are one—I in them and you in me. May they be brought to complete unity so as to let the world know that you sent me and that you love them just as you love me.

---

609   Cf. John 8:42 and footnote.
610   Paul used the same expression of the coming Antichrist, literally 'the son of perdition' in 2 Thess. 2:3 but here it is used of Judas. The term son was given by the Hebrews to those who possessed the character described by the word or name following. Thus Judas is called a son of perdition because he had the character of a destroyer. He was a traitor and a murderer.
611   The words sanctify or consecrate are used here in many translations.
612   It is hard to understand what Jesus is referring to here by giving believers the 'glory'. Because of the context of Jesus' imminent death, the work of the message of the gospel is in the hands of his followers and it seems likely that glory here refers to the glory of fulfilling the mission that God first gave to his Son to the earth.

²⁴"Father, I want those you have given to me to be with me where I am⁶¹³ and that they may see my glory—the glory you have given to me because you loved me before the overthrow of the world.⁶¹⁴ ²⁵Righteous Father, even though the world does not know you, I know you, and they⁶¹⁵ know that you sent me. ²⁶I have made your name known to them and will continue to do so in order that they may love others in the same way you have loved me and in order that I may live in them."

Jesus is arrested

(Matthew 26:47–56, Mark 14:43–50, Luke 22:47–53)

18 ¹When Jesus had finished praying, he left with his followers and crossed the Kidron Valley. On the other side there was a garden, and he and his followers went into it.

²Now Judas, the one who betrayed him, knew the place, because Jesus had often met there with his followers. ³Then Judas went to the garden taking with him the cohort of Roman soldiers and some of the temple guards of the chief priests and the Pharisees. They were carrying torches, lanterns and weapons.

⁴Jesus, knowing all that was going to happen to him, went out and asked them, "Who is it you want?"

⁵"Jesus the Nazarene," they answered.

"I am he," Jesus said. (Now, Judas also, the betrayer, was there with them.) ⁶When Jesus said, "I am he," they went backwards and fell to the ground.

⁷Again he asked them, "Who is it you want?"

And they said, "Jesus the Nazarene."

⁸"I told you that I am he," Jesus answered. "If you are looking for me then let these men go." ⁹(This happened so that the words he had spoken would come true: "I have not lost one of those you have given to me.")

¹⁰Then Simon Peter, who had a sword, drew it and struck the high priest's servant and cut off his right ear. (The servant's name was Malchus).

¹¹Therefore Jesus said to Peter, "Put your sword back where it was! Should I not drink the cup of suffering which the Father has given to me?"

Jesus is taken to the high priest

¹²Then the cohort of Roman soldiers with its commander and the Judean officials arrested Jesus. They bound him and ¹³brought him first to Annas; (he was the father in law of Caiaphas who was the high priest that year. ¹⁴Caiaphas

---

613 Cf. John 14:3.
614 Cf. Eph. 1:4.
615 I.e. Jesus' followers (disciples).

was the one who had advised the Judeans that it would be good if one man died for the people).[616]

Peter's first denial

(Matthew 26:69–75, Mark 14:66–72, Luke 22:54–62)

[15] Simon Peter walked along behind Jesus, with another one of Jesus' followers who was known to the high priest. This other follower went with Jesus into the high priest's courtyard, [16] but Peter had to wait outside the door. Then the other follower, who was known to the high priest, came back, spoke to the female gatekeeper there and brought Peter in.

[17] The girl at the gate asked Peter, "Aren't you also one of his followers?"

Peter replied, "No, I am not."

[18] It was cold, so the servants and the guards stood around a fire[617] they had made to keep warm. Peter was also standing there with them, warming himself.

The high priest questions Jesus

(Matthew 26:57–66, Mark 14:53–64, Luke 22:66–71)

[19] Then the high priest questioned Jesus about his followers and his teaching.[618] [20] Jesus answered him, "I have always spoken publicly to the world and I have always taught in synagogues or at the temple, where all the Jews come together. I have said nothing in secret. [21] Why do you question me? Ask those who heard me. Surely they know what things I said."

[22] When he said these things, one of the temple guards standing nearby slapped Jesus in the face and said, "Is this the way you answer the high priest?"

[23] Jesus answered him, "If I have said something wrong, please tell me as to what was wrong. But if I spoke the truth, why did you hit me?" [24] Then Annas sent him, bound, to Caiaphas the high priest.

Peter's second and third denials

(Matthew 26:71–75, Mark 14:69–72, Luke 22:58–62)

[25] Now as Simon Peter was standing warming himself, they said to him, "Surely you are not one of his followers are you?"

Peter denied it, saying, "No, I am not."

---

616 Cf. John 11:49–52.
617 A charcoal fire as opposed to a wood fire. A wood fire would give off a lot of smoke which would not be suitable in a courtyard (TH).
618 Caiaphas was the high priest that year however here the high priest must be his father in law, Annas. He could loosely be referred to as the high priest since he had previously held that office. He was a highly influential man.

²⁶One of the high priest's slaves, a relative of the man whose ear Peter had cut off, spoke up, "Didn't I see you with him in the olive grove?" ²⁷Again Peter denied it, and immediately a rooster crowed.

Jesus is taken to Pilate
(Matthew 27:1-2, 11-14, Mark 15:1-5, Luke 23:1-5)

²⁸Then they led Jesus from Caiaphas to the Praetorium.[619] By now it was early morning and they did not enter into the Praetorium in case they might be defiled as they wanted to eat the Passover *meal*.[620] ²⁹So Pilate came out to them and asked, "What charges are you bringing against this man?"

³⁰They answered by saying to him, "If he wasn't a criminal, we would not have handed him over to you."

³¹Pilate then said to them, "Take him yourselves and judge him by your own law."

The Judeans said to him, "It is against Roman law for us to put someone to death." ³²This happened so that what Jesus had said indicating how he would die would be fulfilled.[621]

³³Pilate then went back inside the Praetorium, summoned Jesus and asked him, "Are you the king of the Jews?"

³⁴Jesus answered, *"Is this what you yourself are saying or have others told you about me?"*

³⁵Pilate answered, "Am I a Jew? It was your people and your chief priests who handed you over to me. What is it that you have done?"

³⁶Jesus said, *"My realm is not of this world. If it were, my servants would fight to prevent my arrest by the Judeans. But now my realm is from another place."*[622]

³⁷Pilate said, "So you are a king then!"

Jesus answered, *"You are right in saying that I am a king. In fact, for this* very reason *I was born, for this* reason *I came into the world, to tell the truth. Everyone belonging to the truth listens to me."*

³⁸Pilate said to him, "What is truth?"

---

619   I.e. Fort Antonia.
620   It was early Thursday morning, Nisan 14 and the high priest's servants and temple guards who had arrested Jesus had not yet eaten the Passover meal. If they had entered the praetorium, it meant they would be defiled and so not be able to eat the Passover meal (the Seder) later that night. D A Carson on this verse says, "Some forms of defilement could be removed by taking a bath at the end of the day (i.e. at sundown; cf. Lev. 15:5–11, 16–18; 22:5–7). If that were the case here, the Jews would then have been free to eat the Passover the 'next' day, i.e. after sundown on the same day, by our reckoning. We must therefore assume that the defilement in view is of a kind that cannot be removed until seven days have elapsed" (Carson, D A, *The Pillar NT Commentary on John* (1991)). Cf. Matt. 26:17 and footnote.
621   Cf. Matt. 20:17–19.
622   Matthew repeatedly described Jesus' realm as the 'realm of Heaven' (from another place).

Jesus is sentenced to be crucified

(Matthew 27:15–31, Mark 15:6–20, Luke 23:13–25)

Having said this, Pilate went out again to the Judeans and said, "I cannot find any fault in him. ³⁹But it is your custom for me to release to you one prisoner during the Passover. Therefore do you want me to release to you the king of the Jews?"

⁴⁰They shouted back, "No, not him but Barabbas!" (Barabbas was a radical.) **19** ¹Therefore Pilate took Jesus and had him flogged.⁶²³ ²The soldiers twisted together a crown of thorns and put it on his head. They clothed him in a purple robe ³and went up to him again and again, saying, "Hail, king of the Jews," and they began hitting him in the face.

⁴Pilate went back out again and said to them, "Look, I am bringing him out to you that you may know that I do not find any fault in him." ⁵When Jesus came out wearing the crown of thorns and the purple robe, Pilate said to them, "Here is the man himself!"

⁶Therefore when the chief priests and the temple guards saw him, they shouted, "Crucify! Crucify!"

But Pilate answered, "You take him and crucify him. As for me, I do not find any fault in him."

⁷The Judeans answered him, "We have a law and according to that law, he must die because he made himself out to be the Son of God."

⁸Therefore when Pilate heard this, he was even more afraid, ⁹and he went back inside the Praetorium and he asked Jesus, "Where are you from?" But Jesus did not answer him. ¹⁰Therefore Pilate said to him, "Do you refuse to speak to me? Don't you know I have the authority either to free you or crucify you?"

¹¹Jesus answered, "You do not have any authority over me at all if it wasn't given to you from above. Therefore the one who handed me over to you is guilty of a greater sin."

¹²From then on, Pilate tried to set Jesus free but the Judeans kept shouting, "If you let this man go, you are no friend of Caesar. Anyone who makes himself a king opposes Caesar."

¹³When Pilate heard this, he had Jesus brought out and he sat down on the judge's seat at a place known as the Stone Pavement (in Hebrew: Gabbatha). ¹⁴It was Preparation Day of the Passover about the sixth hour.⁶²⁴ "Here is your king," Pilate said to the Judeans.

---

623   Cf. Matt. 27:26 and footnote.
624   John uses the Roman method of time counting from midnight so the sixth was around 6 am Thursday morning, Nisan 14.

¹⁵But they shouted, "Away, away with him, crucify him!"

"Am I to crucify your king?" Pilate asked.

"We have no king but Caesar," the chief priests replied.

¹⁶Finally Pilate handed him over to them to be crucified and they took Jesus and led him away.

Jesus is crucified
(Matthew 27:32-44, Mark 15:21-32, Luke 23:26-43)

¹⁷Jesus himself carried his own cross and he went out and came to the 'Place of the Skull', which in Hebrew is called 'Golgotha'. ¹⁸It was at this place that they crucified him along with two others—one on each side and Jesus in the middle.

¹⁹Pilate had an inscription put on the cross. It read,

JESUS THE NAZARENE
THE KING OF THE JEWS

²⁰Many of the Judeans read this sign because the place where Jesus was crucified was near the city, and the sign was written in Hebrew, Latin and Greek. ²¹The chief priests said to Pilate, "Do not write 'The King of the Jews,' but that this man said I am king of the Jews."

²²Pilate answered, "What I have written, I have written."

²³When the soldiers crucified Jesus, they took his clothes and divided them into four piles, one for each of them but the shirt underneath was separate. The shirt was seamless, woven in one piece from top to bottom. ²⁴The soldiers said to one another, "Let's not tear it but let us cast lots to decide who will get it." This happened to fulfil the Scripture which said,

"They divided my clothing among themselves and they cast lots for my shirt."

Psalm 22:18

So this is what the soldiers did.

²⁵Near the cross of Jesus stood his mother, his mother's sister, Mary the wife of Clopas, and Mary Magdalene.[625] ²⁶Therefore when Jesus saw his mother there, and the follower whom he loved standing nearby, he said to his mother, "Dear woman, here is your son." ²⁷Then he said to the follower, "Here is your mother." From that time on, this follower took her into his own home.

---

625   Most take this to be four women who were standing nearby although it is grammatically possible that it could mean two or three women.

Jesus dies
(Matthew 27:45-56, Mark 15:33-41, Luke 23:44-49)

[28]After this, knowing that all was now completed, and so that the Scripture would be fulfilled, Jesus said, "I am thirsty." [29]A jar of wine vinegar was there, so they soaked a sponge in it, put the sponge on a stalk of the hyssop[626] plant, and lifted it up to Jesus' lips. [30]Once Jesus had received the vinegar Jesus said, "It is finished." He bowed his head and gave up his breath.

A soldier pierces Jesus' side

[31]Since it was the Day of Preparation, and the next day was to be a special Sabbath and because the Judeans did not want the bodies left on the crosses during the Sabbath, they asked Pilate to have the legs broken and the bodies taken down.[627] [32]So the soldiers came and broke the legs of the first man who had been crucified with Jesus, and then those of the other. [33]But when they came to Jesus and found that he was already dead, they did not break his legs. [34]Instead, one of the soldiers pierced Jesus' side with a spear and immediately blood and water came out. [35]The one having seen this, has testified to this fact and his testimony is true.[628] He knows that he speaks the truth in order that you also may believe. [36]For these things happened so that the Scripture would be fulfilled which says, "Not one of his bones will be broken,"[629] [37]and as another Scripture says, "They will look on the one whom they have pierced."[630]

Jesus' body is placed in a tomb
(Matthew 27:57-61, Mark 15:42-47, Luke 23:50-56)

[38]Now after these things, Joseph of Arimathea asked Pilate for the body of Jesus. (Joseph was a follower of Jesus, but secretly because he was afraid of the Judeans.) Pilate allowed him therefore he came and took the body away. [39]Nicodemus also came bringing about one hundred pounds of myrrh and aloes.[631] (He was the man who had earlier visited Jesus at night.)[632] [40]The two men took Jesus' body and wrapped it, with the spices, in strips of linen as is the custom of the Judeans when they bury a body. [41]Now at the place where Jesus

---

626 Hyssop was used for medicinal purposes.
627 The next day was Nisan 15, AD 30, the first day of Unleavened Bread which fell on a Friday. The Friday would be a special 'high' Sabbath and the weekly Sabbath would fall on the next day—Saturday as per normal. Therefore that year there would be two Sabbaths in a row. Cf. Matt. 28:1.
628 This is John speaking about himself, the one whom Jesus loved.
629 Cf. Exo. 12:46.
630 Cf. Zech. 12:10.
631 The Greek term (*litra*) refers to a Roman pound, 32.5 grams (approximately 12 ounces).
632 Cf. John 3:1.

was crucified, there was a garden, and in the garden a new tomb in which no one had ever been placed. ⁴²Therefore, since it was the Day of Preparation for the Judeans and since the tomb was nearby, they placed Jesus there.

The empty tomb
(Matthew 28:1-10, Mark 16:1-8, Luke 24:1-12)

20 ¹Early on the first day of the week of Sabbaths[633] while it was still dark, Mary Magdalene went to the tomb and saw that the stone had been removed from the entrance. ²So she ran to Simon Peter and the other follower, whom Jesus loved, and said, "They have taken the Lord out of the tomb and we don't know where they have put him!"

³Therefore Peter and the other follower went to the tomb. ⁴Both of them ran, but the other follower outran Peter and reached the tomb first. ⁵He bent down and looked in at the strips of linen lying there but he didn't go in. ⁶Then Simon Peter, who was behind him, arrived and went into the tomb. He saw the strips of linen lying there, ⁷as well as the face cloth that had been around Jesus' head. It was not with the linen strips but was separate having been folded up. ⁸Then the other follower who had reached the tomb first, also went inside. He saw and believed. ⁹(They still did not understand from Scripture that Jesus had to rise from the dead.) ¹⁰Then the followers went back to where they were staying.[634]

Jesus appears to Mary Magdalene
(Matthew 28:1-10, Mark 16:9-11)

¹¹Now Mary was standing outside the tomb crying. While she was still crying she bent down to look into the tomb and ¹²saw two angels in white. They were seated where Jesus' body had been lying, one at the head and one at the foot.

¹³They asked her, "Woman, why are you crying?

"They have taken my Lord away and I don't know where they have put him," she said. ¹⁴Having said these things, she turned around and saw Jesus standing there but she did not realise that it was Jesus.

¹⁵Jesus said to her, "Woman, why are you crying? Who is it that you are looking for?"

¹⁶Thinking that he was the gardener, she said, "Sir, if you have carried him away, tell me where you have put him, and I will go and get him."

Jesus said to her, "Mary!"

---

633 This was a title for the Feast of Firstfruits. It was literally day 1 of the next 50 days before Pentecost and literally seven weekly Sabbaths to follow. This day was Sunday, Nisan 17, AD 30. Cf. Matt. 28:1, Acts 20:7, 1 Cor:16:2.
634 I.e. in Jerusalem not Galilee.

She turned toward him and said, "Rabboni!" which means 'teacher'.[635]

[17]Jesus said to her, "Do not hold onto me for I have not yet returned to the Father.[636] Go instead to my brothers[637] and tell them, 'I am returning to my Father and your Father, to my God and your God.'"

[18]Mary Magdalene went and announced to the followers, "I have seen the Lord!" And she told them the things that he had said to her.

Jesus appears to his followers
(Matthew 28:16–20, Mark 16:14–18, Luke 24:36–49)

[19]In the late afternoon on the first day of the week of Sabbaths,[638] when the followers were together behind closed doors because of the fear of the Judeans, Jesus came and stood amongst them and said, "Peace be with you!" [20]After he said this, he showed them his hands and side. The followers were very happy having seen the Lord.

The followers receive Holy Breath

[21]Again Jesus said to them, "Peace be with you! As the Father has sent me, I am sending you also." [22]And having said this, Jesus breathed on them and said, "Receive Holy Breath.[639] [23]If you forgive anyone their sins, they are forgiven; if you do not forgive them, they are not forgiven."[640]

Jesus appears to Thomas

[24]Now Thomas (nicknamed the 'Twin'), one of the Twelve, was not present with the followers when Jesus came. [25]So the other followers told him, "We have seen the Lord!"

But he said to them, "Unless I see the nail imprints in his hands and put my finger where the nails were, and put my hand into his side, I will never believe."

[26]Eight days later his followers were in the house again and Thomas was with them. Even though the doors were closed, Jesus came and stood among

---

635 'Rabboni' is the Aramaic equivalent of the Hebrew 'rabbi'.
636 In the Law, a High Priest could not be touched by the people just before he entered into the Holy Place with the blood of animals. It was only after he had offered blood and been accepted before the mercy seat, that the common people could touch him. Likewise Jesus could not be touched by human hands until after he had ascended to his Father and offered his blood at the throne in heaven. It was probably done in the next few days because he told his disciples to touch him (Luke 24:39), (Whyte, Maxwell, *The Power of the Blood* (1973), p. 63).
637 Jesus is referring to his followers as "brothers". Cf. Rom. 8:29, Heb. 2:17.
638 I.e. It was late Sunday afternoon before sunset. Cf. John 20:1.
639 The term "Holy Breath" has no definite article (the) here. On the first day of Jesus' resurrection the followers received Holy Breath. Jesus gave them immediate power and authority to minister but they wouldn't receive 'the' Holy Breath of God until Pentecost some fifty days later. Cf. Acts 2:4. Only J B Phillips of all English translations translates v. 22 here without the definite article.
640 This privilege was granted to the Apostles only. Cf. Matt. 16:19.

them and said, "Peace be with you!" ²⁷Then he said to Thomas, "Come and put your finger here; look at my hands. Reach out and put your hand into my side. Stop doubting and believe."

²⁸Thomas said to him, "My Lord and my God!"[641]

²⁹Then Jesus said to him, "You have believed because you have seen me; blessed are those who have not seen, yet they have believed."

³⁰Jesus did many other miraculous signs in the presence of his followers, which are not recorded in this book. ³¹But these things have been written down that you may believe that Jesus is the Messiah, the Son of God, and that by believing[642] you may have life in his name.

Jesus appears to his followers in Galilee

21 ¹After these things Jesus appeared again to his followers by the Sea of Tiberias.[643] This is how it happened: ²Simon Peter, Thomas (nicknamed the 'Twin'), Nathanael from Cana in Galilee, the sons of Zebedee, and the two other followers were together. ³Simon Peter said, "I'm going fishing," and the others said, "We're coming too." So they all went out and got into the boat, but that night they caught nothing.

⁴Just as the sun was coming up, Jesus stood on the shore, but the followers did not realise that it was Jesus.

⁵Jesus called out to them, "Boys, did you get any fish?"

"No," they answered.

⁶He said to them, "Cast your net on the right side of the boat and you will find some." When they did so, they were unable to haul the net in because of the large number of fish.

⁷Then the follower whom Jesus loved said to Peter, "It is the Lord!" As soon as Simon Peter heard him say, "It is the Lord," he wrapped his outer garment around him (for he was half-naked) and jumped into the sea. ⁸But the other followers came in the boat, towing the net full of fish for they weren't very far from the shore, only about 90 metres away.[644] ⁹When they got to land they saw a

---

641   The definite article (my) is before both "Lord" and "God". The Granville Sharp grammatical rule which applies to all languages, states when two singular common nouns are used to describe a person, and those two nouns are joined by an additive conjunction (and), and the definite article precedes the first noun but not the second, then both nouns refer to the same person. Therefore in this case, Thomas is not referring to the same person. "My Lord" refers to Jesus and "my God" refers to the invisible Yahweh who had raised his Son from the dead. Thomas is acknowledging both Father and Son.

642   "Believing" here is in the present continuous tense. To be saved one must keep believing all of one's life and remain in the ship of salvation. Cf. John 3:16.

643   Tiberias was a city named by the Romans after the Roman Emperor Tiberius in around AD 20.

644   Gk: 200 cubits (1 cubit = 45 cm).

fire of burning coals with fish on it and some bread. ¹⁰Jesus said to them, "Bring some of the fish you have just caught."

¹¹Simon Peter climbed aboard and dragged the net ashore. It was full of large fish, some 153 in number, but even with so many the net was not torn. ¹²Jesus said to them, "Come and eat breakfast." None of the followers dared ask him, "Who are you?" They knew it was the Lord. ¹³Jesus came, took the bread and gave it to them, and did the same with the fish. ¹⁴This was now the third time Jesus appeared to his followers after having been raised from the dead.

Jesus reinstates Peter

¹⁵When they had finished eating, Jesus said to Simon Peter, "Simon son of John, do you truly love me more than these?"

"Yes Lord, you know that I love you as a brother," he said.

Jesus said, "Feed my lambs."

¹⁶Again Jesus said, "Simon son of John, do you truly love me?"

He answered, "Yes Lord, you know that I love you as a brother."

Jesus said, "Shepherd my sheep."

¹⁷The third time he said to him, "Simon the son of John, do you love me as a brother?"

Peter felt cut because Jesus had asked him a third time, "Do you love me as a brother?" He said, "Lord, you know all things and you know that I love you as a brother."

Jesus said, "Feed my sheep. ¹⁸I tell you the truth, when you were younger you dressed yourself and went wherever you wanted but when you are old you will stretch out your hands and someone else will dress you and lead you where you do not want to go." ¹⁹Jesus said this to indicate the kind of death by which Peter would glorify God. Then he said to him, "Follow me!"

The follower whom Jesus loved

²⁰Peter turned and saw that the follower whom Jesus loved was following them. (This was the one who had leaned back against Jesus at the supper and had said, "Lord, who is going to betray you?") ²¹When Peter saw him, he asked, "Lord, what about him?"

²²Jesus said to Peter, "If I want him to remain alive until I return, what is that to you? You must follow me." ²³Therefore a rumour spread among the Christian brothers that this follower would not die. But Jesus did not say that he would not die; he only said, "If I want him to remain alive until I return, what is that to you?"

²⁴This is the follower who testifies to these things, the one having written them down. We know that his testimony is true.

²⁵Jesus did many other things as well. If every one of them were written down, I suppose that even the whole world would not have enough room for the books that would be written. Amen.

ACTS

Introduction

The Book of Acts was written around AD 63 by Dr. Luke, the historian, who also wrote the gospel of Luke. Interestingly, it covers the first 33 years of the church's history from Jerusalem to Rome, from Jew to the centre of the Gentile world, Rome. As a church historian, Luke mentions 32 countries, 54 cities, nine Mediterranean islands, 95 different persons by name and many other important details. We know that Luke is in on the act as he travels with Paul and personally witnesses the travails, the persecution, the adventures and the miracles.

What is the purpose of the book of Acts? It gives teeth to the gospel and shows how the gospel moves from being a sect of Judaism to the start of being a worldwide influence. It records the transformation from the Gospels where it was a record of all that Jesus began to do and teach (Acts 1:1) to describing what Jesus continued to do through the Apostles by the power of the Holy Spirit. Acts 1:8 gives the church the key mandate and formula in how Christians are to reach the world for salvation through Jesus Christ. From chapters 1–12 we see Peter as the main actor with the church in Jerusalem whereas from chapters 13–28 Paul takes the lead with the church centred around Antioch in Syria where believers were first called Christians.

Gospel will go to the ends of the earth

1 ¹Dear Theophilus,

In my first book, I, *Luke*,[645] wrote about all the things that Jesus began to do and teach ²up until the day that he was taken up to heaven. Before that he gave specific instructions by Holy Breath to the apostles whom he had chosen. ³After his suffering, Jesus showed himself to these men and gave many convincing proofs that he was alive. He appeared to them over a period of forty days[646] and spoke about the time when God will reign *over his people*. ⁴While they were eating together Jesus gave them this command: "Do not leave Jerusalem, but wait for the gift that my Father promised which you have heard me speak about. ⁵For John baptised in water but in a few days you will be baptised in Holy Breath."

⁶When the apostles met together they asked him, "Lord, are you going to restore Israel to the position of ruling over other nations at this time?"

⁷Jesus replied to them, "It is not for you to know the times and dates the Father has set by his own authority. ⁸But you will receive power when the Holy Breath comes upon you. You will be my witnesses in Jerusalem, everywhere in the *province of* Judea, and *the province of* Samaria and to the ends of the earth."

Jesus ascends into the sky
(Mark 16:19-20, Luke 24:50-53)

⁹After *Jesus* had said this he was taken up before their very eyes and a cloud hid him from their sight. ¹⁰They were gazing up into the sky as he was going when all of a sudden two men dressed in white were standing beside them. ¹¹They said, "Men of Galilee, why are you standing there gazing up into the sky? This very same Jesus who has been taken from you into the sky, will come back in the same way that you have seen him go into the sky."

Matthias is chosen as a replacement for Judas

¹²Then *the apostles* returned to Jerusalem from the hill called the Mount of Olives which is a Sabbath day's walk from the city.[647] ¹³When they arrived they

---

645 Luke is the author of this book which covers some of the first 33 years of the church's history from Jerusalem to Rome.
646 The number '40' has a lot of significance in the Bible including when it rained for forty days and forty nights before the flood of Noah's day, Moses' forty days on Sinai and the forty days and nights in which Elijah travelled in the strength of the food given to him by an angel. In the NT, Luke himself records that Israel wandered in the for desert forty years (Acts 7:36) and Jesus was in the wilderness for forty days (Luke 4:2). Author Robert Smith says the figure is related to critical moments, turning points in the history of God's chosen people (Smith, Robert, *The Eschatology of the Book of Acts* (1958), p. 61).
647 The expression 'a Sabbath day's journey' is regarded as having originated during the time Israel was wandering through the desert. The calculation was ostensibly based on the distance from the place

went upstairs to the room where they were staying. Those present were Peter, John, James and Andrew, Philip and Thomas, Bartholomew and Matthew, James son of Alphaeus, Simon the Zealot and Judas son of James. [14]They all joined together constantly in prayer along with the women and Mary the mother of Jesus along with his brothers.

[15]In those days, Peter stood up among the believers in which there were about 120 people present [16]and he addressed them saying, "Brothers, the Scripture had to be fulfilled which the Holy Breath spoke long ago through the mouth of David concerning Judas who served as a guide for those who arrested Jesus. [17]*It says concerning Judas*, 'He was one of us and shared in this ministry.'"

[18](*Judas* bought a piece of land with the reward that he received for his evil act whereupon he fell headlong. His body burst open and all his intestines spilled out. [19]Everyone in Jerusalem heard about this and so they called that land Akeldama in *Aramaic* which means Field of Blood.)

[20]Peter said, "It is written in the book of Psalms,

"'May his place be deserted and let there be no one living on it.'

Psalm 69:25

and,

"'Let there be someone else who takes his position.'"

Psalm 109:8

[21]Peter continued saying, "Therefore it is necessary to choose one of the men who have been with us the whole time the Lord Jesus travelled with us, [22]beginning with John's baptism up to the time when Jesus was taken from us up *into heaven*. For one of these men must become a witness with us of his resurrection."

[23]So they proposed two men. One was Joseph called Barsabbas (also known as Justus) and Matthias. [24]Then they prayed, "Lord, you know everyone's heart. Show us which of these two men you have chosen [25]to take over this ministry and apostleship which Judas left to go where he belongs."[648] [26]Then they drew lots and the lot fell to Matthias so he was added to the eleven apostles.[649]

---

of worship to the tent in the camp farthest from it. In later times the phrase was often used merely as an expression of distance, and that is how Luke has used it in this passage (TH). It is about 800 metres or half a mile.

648 F F Bruce says, "It was Judas' apostasy, not his death that created the vacancy which had to be filled" (Bruce, F F, *The Acts of the Apostles (The Greek Text With Introduction And Commentary)* (1990), 1:16).

649 The choice was made in a manner similar to that in which the Urim and the Thummin were used in OT times. The names, written on stone, would have been placed in a vessel which was then shaken; the first stone to fall out would indicate the man chosen.

The Day of Pentecost

2 ¹When the day of Pentecost came they were all together in one place.⁶⁵⁰ ²Suddenly a sound like the blowing of a violent wind came from heaven and filled the whole house where they were sitting. ³They saw what appeared to be tongues of fire that separated and came to rest on each one of them. ⁴Everyone there was filled with Holy Breath and began to speak in other languages as the Breath enabled them.⁶⁵¹

⁵Now at this time there were God-fearing Jews from every nation under the sun⁶⁵² staying in Jerusalem.⁶⁵³ ⁶When they heard this sound a large crowd gathered and they were confused because each one of them heard their own languages being spoken by the believers. ⁷Astounded and totally amazed they asked each other, "Are not all of these men speaking Galileans? ⁸Then how come we can all hear them in our own mother tongues? ⁹There were Parthians,⁶⁵⁴ Medes and Elamites, residents of Mesopotamia, Judea and Cappadocia, Pontus and Asia, ¹⁰Phrygia and Pamphylia, Egypt and the parts of Libya near Cyrene. Also present were visitors from Rome ¹¹(both Jews and converts to Judaism), Cretans and Arabs. We hear them declaring the wonders of God in our own *mother* tongues!" ¹²Amazed and stunned by this they kept asking each other, "What does this mean?"

¹³However there were some who were making fun of them saying, "They have had too much to drink."

Peter explains to the crowd what is happening

¹⁴Then Peter stood up with the eleven *apostles*, raised his voice and addressed the crowd as follows, "*Fellow* Judeans and all of you who live in Jerusalem, let me explain what you are seeing. Listen carefully to what I am saying. ¹⁵These men are not drunk as you are supposing. It's only 9 o'clock in the morning!

---

650   Pentecost also known as the Feast of Weeks (Deut. 16:10) or Feast of Harvest (Exo. 23:16) was the second great Jewish festival of the year after Passover in which the main cereal grains, wheat and barley were harvested, celebrated and presented to God. Barley was harvested earlier than the wheat. Pentecost was the start of the church age and so represents the start of the great harvest of souls for God.

651   In this verse we see there is no definite article (anarthrous) in the first instance of "Holy Breath" but it exists in the second instance. William Mounce says, "When the article is present, it is emphasising *identity*. When the article is not present, it is generally emphasising the *quality* of the substantive" (Mounce, William D, *Basics of Biblical Greek Grammar* (2009), p. 334). Essentially this verse means that the Holy Breath as God's advocate or representative (*identity*) filled the believers with God's Breath (*quality*). Cf. John 20:22.

652   In the Greek it says 'heaven'.

653   Jews were required to attend each one of the three main festivals/feasts in Jerusalem every year and so there were many staying in Jerusalem because it was Pentecost.

654   The Parthians were very closely related to the Persians and their language was almost the same. Parthians were located in northern modern-day Iran.

¹⁶No, *in fact what you are seeing* is what was spoken of by the prophet Joel who prophesied as follows,

> ¹⁷"'In the last days God says, "I will pour out my Breath upon all people.⁶⁵⁵
> Your sons and daughters will prophesy and your young men will see
>   visions and your old men will have dreams.
> ¹⁸"In those days I will even pour out my Breath upon my servants, both
>   men and women and they will prophesy.
> ¹⁹"I will perform wonders in the heaven above and signs on the earth below.
> "There will be blood, fire and clouds of smoke.
> ²⁰"The sun will become dark and the moon blood *red* before the coming
>   of the great and glorious Day of the Lord.⁶⁵⁶
> ²¹"Everyone who calls on the name of the Lord will be saved."'"⁶⁵⁷

Joel 2:28–32

²²Peter continued, "Men of Israel, listen up now. Jesus the Nazarene was a man designated by God which was demonstrated by miracles, wonders and signs which God did among you through him, as you yourselves know. ²³God had already determined to hand this man over to you according to his plan and you, with the help of wicked men, killed him by nailing him to the cross. ²⁴However God raised him from the dead, freeing him from the agony of death, because it was impossible for death to retain its hold on him. ²⁵For David said about *Jesus* as follows,

> "'I saw the Lord right there before me at all times.

---

655 Peter says that this pouring out of God's Breath at Pentecost occurs in the last days. We think of the last days as the very last days before Christ returns in the 21st century however the last days can be considered to have begun at Pentecost in AD 30. We have been living in the last days before the Last Day (John 6:39).

656 This is an important eschatological verse as it helps to prove that the Day of the Lord occurs after the tribulation period when taken in conjunction with Matt. 24:29. Here the sun and moon signs occur before the Day of the Lord whereas in Matthew the same sun and moon signs occur after the tribulation. Therefore it follows that the Day of the Lord occurs after the tribulation hence disproving the pre-tribulation rapture theory and confirming a post-tribulational return of Christ.

657 The remainder of v. 32 in Joel has been left off by Peter which could possibly relate to the woman of Revelation 12 and the believers who escape to the safe place in the wilderness of Jordan. It says that deliverance will come on Mount Zion in Jerusalem for the survivors. The question is who are the survivors? The survivors could quite possibly be those who are called by the Lord to escape the Great Tribulation by fleeing firstly to Israel and then to Jordan. Notice that a call must come from the Lord to these survivors. Interestingly a related application comes in Isa. 1:9 which says unless the Lord leaves some survivors then we would become like Sodom and Gomorrah which were completely destroyed without a trace of any survivors except for Lot and his two daughters. The woman of Revelation 12 will survive by fleeing to the safe-place whereas most of the 'left-behind' will either be martyred or deluded into worshiping the image of the beast and by taking his mark. The left-behind will also include the 'elect' who will also survive and be raptured (Matt. 24:31).

> He is at my right hand and I will not be shaken.
> ²⁶That is why my heart is glad and my tongue rejoices. I am mortal but
> I live in hope.
> ²⁷This is because you, O God, will not abandon my soul in Hades
> nor will you let your Holy One see decay.
> ²⁸You have shown me the right path in life and you will fill me with the
> joy of your presence.'

Psalm 16:8–11

²⁹"Brothers *of Israel*, you can be sure that the patriarch David died and was buried and his tomb is here to this very day. ³⁰But he was a prophet and knew that God had promised him on oath that he would place one of his descendants on his throne. ³¹David could see what was ahead when he spoke of the resurrection of the Messiah in this psalm, in that he was not abandoned in Hades, nor did his body see decay. ³²God raised this Jesus to life and we are all witnesses of this fact. ³³He was exalted to the right hand of God and he has received from the Father the promised Holy Breath which he has caused to be poured out—you are seeing and hearing this right now. ³⁴For David did not ascend to heaven and yet he said,

> "'The Lord God⁶⁵⁸ said to my Lord, "Sit at my right hand ³⁵until I make your
> enemies a footstool for your feet."'

Psalm 110:1

³⁶"Therefore let all Israel be certain of this very fact: God has made this Jesus, whom you crucified, both Lord and Messiah."

³⁷When the people heard this they were extremely cut and they said to Peter and the other apostles, "Brothers, what should we do?"

³⁸Peter replied, "Each one of you must turn away from your sins and be baptised in the name of Jesus Christ, so that your sins will be forgiven and you will receive the gift of the Holy Breath. ³⁹This promise is for you and your children and for all who are far away,⁶⁵⁹ indeed for all whom the Lord our God will call."

⁴⁰With many other words Peter testified and appealed to them saying, "Save yourselves from this corrupt generation." ⁴¹Those who accepted his message were baptised and about 3000 were added to their number that very day. ⁴²They

---

658 In the Hebrew OT, Psa. 110:1 is literally Yahweh—the personal name of God. In other words David is saying, "Yahweh (God) told David's Lord (Jesus) to sit at his right hand," effectively proving that Jesus was the anointed Messiah that the Jews had been waiting for. In the English translations, Yahweh is nearly always written as "LORD" in capital letters.

659 Most likely a reference to the Gentiles. Cf. Eph. 2:13 footnote.

devoted themselves to the apostles' teaching and to the group, to the breaking of bread and to prayer.

Life in the group of the new believers

⁴³Everyone was in awe as they saw the many wonders and miraculous signs that were being done by the apostles. ⁴⁴All the believers were together and sharing everything with each other. ⁴⁵They were selling their property[660] and personal possessions, giving to anyone according to their needs. ⁴⁶Every day they continued to meet together in the temple courts. They broke bread in their homes and ate together with happy and sincere hearts. ⁴⁷They praised God and enjoyed the favour of all the people *in Jerusalem*. The Lord added to the group daily, the number of those who believed.

Peter heals a beggar with a disability

3 ¹One day Peter and John were going up to the temple at the time of prayer at 3 o'clock in the afternoon. ²There was a man who had been disabled from birth who was being carried to the temple gate called Beautiful. He was put there every day to beg from those going into the temple courts. ³When he saw Peter and John about to enter, he asked them for money. ⁴Peter and John looked straight at him and Peter said, "Look at us!" ⁵So the man paid attention, expecting to get something from them.

⁶Then Peter said, "I do not have any silver and gold but what I have I give to you. In the name of Jesus Christ of Nazareth, get up and walk." ⁷Taking the man by the right hand, Peter helped him up and instantly the man's feet and ankles became strong. ⁸He jumped to his feet and began to walk. Then he went with Peter and John into the temple courts, walking and leaping and praising God. ⁹When all the people saw him walking and praising God, ¹⁰they recognised him as the same man who used to sit begging at the temple gate called Beautiful. They were filled with wonder and amazement at what had happened to him.

Peter speaks to the onlookers

¹¹While the beggar was clinging onto Peter and John, all the people were astonished and came running to them in the place called Solomon's Colonnade.[661] ¹²When Peter saw this, he said to them all, "Men of Israel, why does this surprise you? Why do you stare at us as if by our own power or godliness we had made this man walk? ¹³The God of Abraham, Isaac and Jacob, the God of our ancestors has

---

660 Probably refers to real estate.
661 This was a covered walkway also described as a porch or colonnade which was on the east side of the temple overlooking the Kidron Valley.

glorified his servant Jesus. You handed him over to be killed and you disowned him before Pilate even though he had decided to let him go. ¹⁴You disowned the Holy and Righteous One and asked a murderer to be released to you instead. ¹⁵You killed the author of life but God raised him from the dead of which we are witnesses. ¹⁶By faith in the name of Jesus, this man was made strong. It is Jesus' name and the faith that comes through him that has made this man whole, as you can all see.

¹⁷"Now brothers, I know that you acted in ignorance as did your leaders. ¹⁸However God announced long ago through all the prophets saying that his Messiah would suffer and God made it happen in this particular way. ¹⁹Therefore I strongly urge you all to turn away from your old ways and turn to God so that your sins may be removed. ²⁰Do this and times of refreshing will come from the Lord and he will send the One whom he has chosen beforehand for you—the Messiah, Jesus. ²¹He must remain in heaven until the time comes for God to restore everything as he promised long ago through his holy prophets. ²²For Moses said, 'The Lord your God will raise up for you a Prophet⁶⁶² like me from among your own brothers.⁶⁶³ You must listen to everything he tells you. ²³Anyone who does not listen to him will be completely cut off from among his people.'

²⁴"Actually, all the prophets from Samuel onwards, as many as have spoken about this, have foretold about *the events of* these present days. ²⁵The promises of God through his prophets are for you and you share in the covenant that God made with your ancestors. He said to Abraham, 'Through your offspring all the peoples of the earth will be blessed.' ²⁶When God raised up his servant, *Jesus*, he sent him first to you *Jews* to bless you by making each one of you to turn from your wicked ways."

Peter and John are imprisoned

4 ¹While Peter and John were speaking to the people, the priests, the captain of the temple guard and the Sadducees came up to them. ²They were very concerned because the apostles were teaching and proclaiming to the people that because of Jesus there was a resurrection of the dead. ³They arrested Peter and John and because it was evening they put them in jail until the next day. ⁴But many who heard the message believed and the number of men *who believed* grew to about five thousand.

---

662   Cf. Deut. 18:15,18–19 (A prophecy concerning the Messiah as one of three eschatological figures in Jewish thinking). Cf. John 6:14.
663   The implication here is nation or the Jewish peoples not just one clan or tribe.

⁵The next day the Jewish leaders, elders and scribes[664] met in Jerusalem. ⁶Annas[665] the high priest was there and so was Caiaphas, John, Alexander and the other men of the high priest's family. ⁷They had Peter and John brought before them and asked, "By what power or what name did you make this *man walk?*"

⁸Then Peter, having been filled with Holy Breath, said to them, "Leaders and elders of the people! ⁹If we are being called to account today for the kindness shown to a man who is handicapped and are being cross-examined about how he was healed ¹⁰then you and all the people of Israel must know this: It is by the name of Jesus Christ of Nazareth, whom you crucified but whom God raised from the dead, that this man stands before you healthy. ¹¹The Scriptures say that Jesus is,

"'the stone that you builders rejected and he has become the cornerstone.'

Psalm 118:22

¹²Salvation is found in no one else for there is no other name under heaven which has been given to men by which we must be saved."

¹³When the *Sanhedrin* saw the courage of Peter and John and realised that they were unschooled, ordinary men, they were astonished and they took note that these men had been with Jesus. ¹⁴But since they could see the man who had been healed standing there with them, there was nothing that they could say. ¹⁵So they ordered them to withdraw from the Sanhedrin meeting room and then they conferred with each other. ¹⁶They said, "What are we going to do with these men? Everybody in Jerusalem knows that they have done an outstanding miracle and we cannot deny it. ¹⁷But to stop this thing from spreading any further among the people, we must warn these men not to speak anymore to anyone in this name."

¹⁸Then they called them in again and commanded them not to speak or teach at all in the name of Jesus. ¹⁹But Peter and John replied, "Determine for yourselves whether it is right in God's sight to obey you rather than God. ²⁰For we cannot help but speak about what we have seen and heard."

²¹After further threats they let them go. They could not decide how to punish

---

664 The scribes were the teachers of the Law.
665 Annas actually functioned as High Priest from AD 6–14, though he can be called the High Priest since it was customary for a man who had once held that position to maintain that title throughout life. Actually at this time Caiaphas, the son-in-law of Annas, was the High Priest, and held this office from AD 18–36 (TH). This would be similar to when a former U.S. president is still called president even after he has left office.

them, because all the people were praising God for what had happened. ²²For the man who had been miraculously healed was over forty years old.

The believers pray for boldness

²³As soon as they were released from jail, Peter and John returned to their own people and reported all that the chief priests and elders had said to them. ²⁴When the people heard this they raised their voices together in prayer to God saying, "Master, you made the heaven, the earth, the sea and everything in them. ²⁵You spoke by Holy Breath through the mouth of your servant, our ancestor David saying,

> "'Why are the nations angry at God?
> Why do they make their useless plots against him?
> ²⁶The kings of the earth take their stand and the leaders gather together
> against the Lord *God* and against his Messiah.'

Psalm 2:1–2

²⁷In fact *King* Herod and Pontius Pilate met together with the Gentiles and the people of Israel in this city to conspire against your holy servant Jesus, whom you anointed.[666] ²⁸However they only did what you had already determined in advance should happen by your power and will. ²⁹Now, Lord, *we ask that you might* consider their threats and enable *us*, your servants, to speak your word with great boldness. ³⁰Stretch out your hand[667] to heal and perform miraculous signs and wonders through the name of your holy servant Jesus."

³¹After they had prayed, the place where they were meeting shook[668] and they were all filled with the Holy Breath and spoke the word of God boldly.

The believers share their possessions

³²All the believers were one in heart and mind. No one said that any of his possessions was his own but they shared everything they had. ³³With great power the apostles continued to testify about the resurrection of the Lord Jesus and much grace was upon them all. ³⁴There were no needy persons amongst the group. From time to time those who owned lands or houses sold them and brought the money from the sales ³⁵and laid it at the apostle's feet. The money was distributed to anyone as they had need.

³⁶Joseph, a Levite from Cyprus, whom the apostles called Barnabas (which

---

666 The Greek word 'Christ' is equivalent to 'anointed' or 'Messiah'.
667 This is an idiom meaning for God to show his strength and power.
668 In the OT this was a sign of a theophany (appearance of God) showing that God was present. It was a divine response to the believers' prayers. Cf. Exo. 19:18, Isa. 6:4.

means a person who encourages), ³⁷sold a field that he owned and brought the money and laid it at the apostle's feet.

Ananias and Sapphira

5 ¹Now there was a man named Ananias together with his wife Sapphira, who also sold a piece of property. ²With his wife's full knowledge he kept back part of the money for himself, but brought the rest and laid it at the apostle's feet.

³Then Peter said, "Ananias, why have you allowed Satan to fill your heart in that you have lied to the Holy Breath and have kept some of the money that you received for the land for yourself? ⁴Did it not belong to you before it was sold? And after it was sold, wasn't the money at your disposal? What were you thinking? You have not lied to men but to God."⁶⁶⁹

⁵When Ananias heard this, he fell down and died. Then great fear came upon everyone listening. ⁶Then the young men came forward, wrapped up his body, and carried him out and buried him.

⁷About three hours later his wife came in, unaware what had happened. ⁸Peter asked her, "Tell me, is this the price you and Ananias got for the land?"

"Yes, that is the price," she replied.

⁹Peter said to her, "Why did you agree together to test the Breath of the Lord? Look! Those who buried your husband are standing at the door and they are going to carry you out also."

¹⁰At that very moment she fell down at his feet and died. Then the young men came in and finding her dead, they carried her out and buried her beside her husband. ¹¹Great fear seized the whole church and all who heard about these events.

The apostles heal many people

¹²The apostles performed many miraculous signs and wonders among the people who were all there together in Solomon's Colonnade. ¹³No one else dared join them even though they were highly regarded by the people. ¹⁴Nevertheless, more and more men and women believed in the Lord and were added to their number. ¹⁵As a result, people brought the sick into the streets and laid them on beds and mats so that at least Peter's shadow might fall on some of them as he

---

669   The Breath of God is equated with God here. The Breath of God is God's representative, the internal presence of God and Jesus in believers. At times the Holy Breath (Holy Spirit) is represented as a person and at other times in the Scriptures the Holy Breath is represented in the neuter gender. Cf. John 15:26, Eph. 1:14. Note: Caution is required because grammatical gender in the Greek does not always play out to agree with actual physical gender. Cf. 1 Cor. 2:11 footnote.

went by. ¹⁶Crowds of people from the cities surrounding Jerusalem gathered, bringing their sick and those tormented by evil spirits and everyone was healed.

The apostles persecuted

¹⁷Consequently the high priest and those from the Sadducee party who were with him were filled with bitter jealousy. ¹⁸They arrested the apostles and put them in the public jail. ¹⁹But during the night an angel of the Lord opened the doors of the jail and brought them out, saying to them, ²⁰"Go, stand in the temple and tell the people the full message of this new life."

²¹At dawn they entered into the temple as instructed *by the angel* and began to teach the people.

When the high priest and his group arrived, they called together the Sanhedrin—the full assembly of the elders of Israel, and sent word to the jail for the apostles to come. ²²But upon arrival at the jail, the temple guards did not find them there. So they went back and reported to the Sanhedrin saying, ²³"We found the jail securely locked with the guards standing at the doors but when we opened them we found no one inside." ²⁴On hearing this report, the captain of the temple guard and the chief priests were puzzled, wondering what they might do about it.

²⁵Then someone came and said, "Look! The men you put in jail are standing in the temple and teaching the people." ²⁶So the captain of the temple guard went with his men and brought the apostles without force because they feared that the people would stone them *to death*.

²⁷Having brought the apostles, they made them appear before the Sanhedrin to be questioned by the high priest. ²⁸The high priest said, "We gave you strict orders not to teach in this name, yet you have filled Jerusalem with your teaching and are determined to make us responsible for this man's blood."

²⁹Peter and the other apostles replied, "We must obey God rather than men! ³⁰The God of our ancestors raised Jesus from the dead who you had killed by hanging him on a tree.⁶⁷⁰ ³¹God exalted him to his own right hand as Prince and Saviour so that he might grant the people of Israel the opportunity to turn to God and have their sins forgiven. ³²We are witnesses to these things as is the Holy Breath, which God gave to those who obey him."

³³When the *Sanhedrin* heard this, they were furious and wanted to put them to death. ³⁴But there was a Pharisee named Gamaliel who was a teacher of the Law and who was honoured by all the people who stood up and ordered that the men be taken outside for a little while. ³⁵Then he addressed them all saying,

---

670   Cf. Gal. 3:13.

"Men of Israel, consider carefully what you intend to do to these men. ³⁶Some years ago there was a man named Theudas who appeared claiming to be a somebody and about four hundred men rallied to his cause. But eventually he was killed and all his followers dispersed and it all came to nothing. ³⁷After him, Judas the Galilean appeared in the days of the census[671] and incited a rebellion amongst the people. But he too was killed and all his followers were scattered. ³⁸Therefore in this present situation, I advise you to leave these men alone. Let them go for if their purpose or activity is of human origin, it will ultimately fail. ³⁹But if it is from God, you will not be able to stop these men. In fact you will only find yourselves fighting against God."

The *Sanhedrin* was persuaded by Gamaliel's speech. ⁴⁰They called the apostles in and had them whipped. Then they ordered them not to speak in the name of Jesus and let them go.

⁴¹The apostles left the Sanhedrin, rejoicing because they had been counted worthy of suffering disgrace for the name *of Jesus*. ⁴²Day after day, in the temple and house to house, they never stopped teaching and proclaiming the good news about Jesus the Messiah.

Seven men are chosen to serve

6 ¹In those days when the number of followers of Jesus was increasing, the Greek speaking Jews complained against the Hebrew Jews. The complaint was that their widows were being overlooked in the daily distribution of food. ²Therefore the twelve gathered all the followers together and said, "It would not be right for us to neglect the ministry of the word of God in order to wait on tables. ³Brothers, choose seven men from among you who have a good reputation, full of *God's* Breath and wisdom. We will turn this responsibility over to them ⁴and we will give our attention to prayer and the ministry of the word."

⁵This suggestion pleased the whole group and so they chose Stephen, a man full of faith and Holy Breath. They also chose Philip, Procorus, Nicanor, Timon, Parmenas and Nicolas[672] from Antioch. Nicolas was *a Gentile* who was a convert to Judaism. ⁶They presented these men to the apostles, who prayed and laid their hands on them.[673]

⁷So the word of God spread and the number of followers in Jerusalem

---

671 Cf. Luke 2:2.
672 Cf. Rev. 2:6 footnote.
673 This symbolised the imparting of strength and blessing upon the recipients as a sign of the community's support.

increased rapidly. A large number of priests became obedient to the faith as well.[674]

Stephen's ministry

[8]Stephen was a man full of God's grace and power. He did great wonders and miraculous signs among the people. [9]However opposition arose from the members of the Synagogue of the Freedmen (as it was so called). They were Jews of Cyrene and Alexandria as well as the provinces Cilicia and Asia. These men began to argue with Stephen, [10]but they could not stand up against his wisdom or the spirit with which he spoke.

[11]Then they secretly persuaded some men to say, "We have heard Stephen speak words of blasphemy against Moses and against God."

[12]So they stirred up the people and the elders and the scribes. They arrested Stephen and brought him before the Sanhedrin. [13]They produced false witnesses who testified saying, "This man never stops speaking against this holy place and against the law. [14]For we have heard him say that this Jesus the Nazarene will destroy this place and change the customs Moses handed down to us."

[15]All those who were sitting in the Sanhedrin looked intently at Stephen and they saw that his face was like the face of an angel.

Stephen makes a speech to the Sanhedrin

7

[1]Then the high priest asked *Stephen*, "Are these charges true?"

[2]*Stephen* answered, "Brothers and fathers, listen to me! The God of glory appeared to our father Abraham while he was still in Mesopotamia before he went and lived in Haran. [3]He said to *Abraham*, 'Leave your country and your people and go to the land I will show you.'

[4]"So he left the land of the Chaldeans and settled in Haran. After the death of his father, God sent him to this land where you are now living.[675] [5]God did not give Abraham any inheritance here, not even one square foot of ground. But God did promise him that he and his descendants after him would possess the land. This was even though at that time Abraham had no child. [6]God spoke to

---

674 Apparently there were about 8,000 priests in Israel at that time (TH).
675 Gen. 12:4 tells us that Abraham was 75 when he left Haran however Gen. 11:26 gives the impression that Abram (Abraham) was Terah's firstborn and that Terah was 70 years old when he became the father of Abram. Therefore when Gen. 12:4 is combined with Gen. 11:32 saying that Terah lived 205 years and that he died in Haran there appears to be a discrepancy of 60 years because 70 + 75 = 145 years. But the error is that Abram was not Terah's firstborn. He is listed first because he is the most important character in the narrative being in the line of Christ not because he was Terah's firstborn. Gen. 11:31 gives the proof that Abram was not the firstborn because Terah took Abram's nephew, Lot, making it most likely that Lot's father Haran at least, was older than Abram. Terah's correct age when becoming the father of Abram therefore is 130 years old (Warner, T, *The Time of the End* (2012), footnote p. 249).

Abraham in this way, 'Your descendants will be strangers in a country not their own and they will be slaves and mistreated for 400 years. ⁷But I will punish the nation they serve as slaves and afterwards they will leave that country and worship me in this place.' ⁸Then God gave Abraham the covenant of circumcision. And Abraham became the father of Isaac and circumcised him eight days after his birth. Later Isaac became the father of Jacob and Jacob in turn became the father of the twelve patriarchs.

⁹"And because the patriarchs were jealous of Joseph, they sold him as a slave into Egypt. But God was with him ¹⁰and rescued him from all his troubles. He gave Joseph wisdom and enabled him to gain the goodwill of Pharaoh the king of Egypt. Therefore Pharaoh made Joseph ruler over Egypt and his whole household.

¹¹"Then going forward, a famine struck the whole land of Egypt and Canaan, which brought great suffering in which our ancestors could not find food. ¹²When Jacob heard that there was grain in Egypt, he sent our ancestors there for the first time. ¹³On their second visit, Joseph told his brothers who he was and Pharaoh learned about Joseph's family. ¹⁴After this, Joseph sent for his father Jacob and his whole family, seventy five in total number.⁶⁷⁶ ¹⁵Then Jacob went down to Egypt where he and our ancestors ended up dying. ¹⁶Their bodies were brought back to Shechem and placed in the tomb that Abraham had bought from the sons of Hamor at Shechem for a certain amount of silver.

¹⁷"As the time drew near for God to fulfil his promise to Abraham, the number of our people in Egypt greatly increased. ¹⁸Then another king, who knew nothing about Joseph, became ruler of Egypt. ¹⁹This king took advantage of our people and oppressed our ancestors by making them place their newborn babies outdoors so that they would die *of exposure*.⁶⁷⁷

²⁰"At that time Moses was born and he was such a beautiful child in God's eyes. He was cared for in his father's house for three months. ²¹However he was placed outside and Pharaoh's daughter took him and raised him up as her own son. ²²Moses was educated in all the wisdom of the Egyptians and was powerful in speech and action.

²³"When Moses was forty years old, he decided to visit his fellow Israelites. ²⁴He happened to see one of them being mistreated by an Egyptian, so he went to his defence and avenged him by killing the Egyptian. ²⁵Moses thought that

---

676 Gen. 46:27 states that there were 70 people in total. Stephen here follows the LXX which states that there were 75 people. The Dead Sea scrolls also agree with the LXX that there were 75 people who went down to Egypt.

677 It was common practice for the surrounding pagan nations to abandon their babies to the elements and exposure which the Jews abhorred.

his own people would realise that God was using him to rescue them but they did not. ²⁶The next day Moses came upon two Israelites who were fighting. He tried to reconcile them by saying, 'Men, you are brothers, why are you trying to hurt each other?'

²⁷"But the man who was mistreating the other pushed Moses aside and said, 'Who made you ruler and judge over us? ²⁸Are you going to kill me as you killed the Egyptian yesterday?' ²⁹When Moses heard this he fled to Midian where he settled as a foreigner and had two sons.

³⁰"After another forty years had passed, the Angel of the Lord[678] appeared to Moses in the flames of a burning bush in the desert near Mt. Sinai. ³¹When Moses saw this, he was amazed at the sight. As he went closer to take a look, he heard the Lord's voice saying, ³²'I am the God of your ancestors, the God of Abraham, Isaac and Jacob.' Moses trembled with fear and did not dare to look.

³³"Then the Lord said to him, 'Take off your sandals. The place where you are now standing is holy ground. ³⁴I have seen the mistreatment of my people in Egypt. I have heard their groaning and have come down to set them free. Now come, I am sending you back to Egypt.'

³⁵"This is the very same Moses who they rejected with the words, 'Who made you ruler and judge?' He was sent to be their ruler and deliverer by God himself through the Angel who appeared to him in the *burning* bush. ³⁶*Moses* led the *Israelites* out of Egypt and performed wonders and miraculous signs in Egypt, at the Red Sea and for forty years in the desert.

³⁷"This is that Moses who told the Israelites, 'God will send you a prophet like me from your own people.' ³⁸Moses was with the church[679] in the desert when the Angel spoke to him on Mt. Sinai, and with our ancestors. It was there that he received living oracles[680] to pass on to us.

³⁹"But our ancestors refused to obey him. Instead, they rejected him and in their hearts they wished that they could go back to Egypt. ⁴⁰They told Aaron,[681] 'Make us *idol* gods who will go before us. As for this fellow Moses who led us out of Egypt—we don't know what has happened to him!' ⁴¹It was at this time that

---

678 The Angel of the Lord (Yahweh) who appeared to Moses in the burning bush, was the Son of God, the preincarnate Jesus. Cf. Exo. 3:2.
679 This is the Greek word *ekklesia* which means an assembly of believers. The very first act of Jesus after his crucifixion was to incorporate OT saints into the New Covenant. Eternal life for both Jew and Gentile from all dispensations is possible only under the New Covenant. OT saints looked forward to the cross and NT saints look back to the cross but it is always about the cross. The 'church' in reality therefore, includes all saints who possess eternal salvation. Paul wrote that all things are being joined together 'in Christ' (Eph. 1:9–10).
680 An oracle is a message from God. Moses received the 'Ten Commandments' or 'Ten Words' from God on Mt. Sinai which were written by God's own finger.
681 Aaron is Moses' brother.

they made an idol in the form of a bull calf.⁶⁸² They brought sacrifices to it and held a celebration in honour of what their hands had made.⁶⁸³ ⁴²But God turned away and gave them over to the worship of the heavenly stars as is written in the book of the prophets:⁶⁸⁴

> "'People of Israel! Did you bring me sacrifices and offerings forty years in the desert?⁶⁸⁵
> ⁴³You carried the canopy of Molech and the image of your star god Rephan—the idols you made to worship.⁶⁸⁶
> Therefore I will send you into exile beyond Babylon.'⁶⁸⁷

Amos 5:25–27

⁴⁴"Our ancestors carried the Tabernacle of God's presence with them in the desert. It had been made as God directed Moses according to the pattern he had seen. ⁴⁵Having received the Tabernacle, our ancestors under Joshua brought it with them when they took the land from the nations that God drove out before them. It remained in the land until the time of David, ⁴⁶who enjoyed God's favour. He asked God that he might provide a dwelling place for the God of Jacob. ⁴⁷But it was Solomon instead who built the house for *God*.

⁴⁸"However, the Most High God does not live in houses made by men. As the prophet *Isaiah* said,

> ⁴⁹"'The Lord says, "Heaven is my throne and the earth is my footstool.
> What kind of house will you build for me?
> Where will my resting place be?
> ⁵⁰Did I not make all these things?"'

Isaiah 66:1–2

⁵¹"You are such stubborn people! You have such pagan hearts and ears, refusing to listen! You are just like your ancestors in that you always resist the

---

682 This was the golden calf incident detailed in Exo. 32:4–6.
683 Interestingly the golden calf and the idol worship was the incident that Jewish rabbis were the most ashamed of in all of Israel's history because of its turn to idol worship virtually straight after its deliverance from Egypt and the Red Sea. Some several centuries later rabbis tried to explain this away by saying that it was the pagans who had accompanied the Israelites who had made the golden calf (Keener, Craig S, *IVP Bible Background Commentary* (1993)).
684 The book of the prophets was a single scroll which contained the text of all the Minor Prophets.
685 The expected answer here is no!
686 Molech/Moloch was the Canaanite god of sun and sky associated with child sacrifice and Rephan probably the Egyptian god of the planet Saturn. The canopy of Molech was literally a tent—it was common practice amongst societies to provide some sort of covering for the image of a god when carried in a public procession.
687 Amos both in the Hebrew and LXX passages have 'beyond Damascus' not Babylon.

Holy Breath! ⁵²Was there ever a prophet your ancestors did not persecute? They even killed those who predicted the coming of the Righteous One[688] of whom you have now betrayed and murdered. ⁵³You have received the Law that was put into effect by angels but have not obeyed it."

The stoning of Stephen

⁵⁴When the Sanhedrin heard this, they were furious and gnashed their teeth at him. ⁵⁵But Stephen, full of Holy Breath, looked up to heaven and saw the glory of God and Jesus standing at the right hand of God. ⁵⁶He said, "Look, I see the heavens open and the Son of Man standing at the right hand of God."

⁵⁷On hearing this *the members of the Sanhedrin* covered their ears and yelling at the top of their voices, they all rushed at him. ⁵⁸They dragged him out of the city and began to stone him *to death*. Meanwhile his accusers took off their garments and laid them at the feet of a young man named Saul.

⁵⁹While they were stoning him, Stephen prayed, "Lord Jesus, receive my spirit." ⁶⁰Then he fell on his knees and cried out, "Lord, do not hold this sin against them." When he had said this, he died.

8 ¹Saul was there, approving of his death.

Saul persecutes the church

On that very day a great persecution broke out against the church at Jerusalem and everyone except for the apostles were scattered throughout the regions of Judea and Samaria. ²Devout men *of God*[689] buried Stephen and mourned very loudly for him. ³But Saul began to destroy the church. He went from house to house, dragging both men and women off to prison.

Philip preaches the gospel in Samaria

⁴Those who had been scattered *by the persecution*, preached the word wherever they went. ⁵Philip went down to the main city of Samaria and preached *about* the Messiah there.[690] ⁶When the crowds heard Philip preach and saw the miraculous signs that he performed, they were paying close attention. ⁷Evil spirits came out of many people with loud screams and many of those who were paralysed and crippled were also healed. ⁸So there was great joy in that city.

---

688 I.e. Jesus.
689 These devout men of God could possibly mean pious Jews, Christians or both.
690 In NT times the OT city of Samaria was known as Sebaste, and the word Samaria referred to the province. The Samaritans, as the Jews, lived in the expectation of a coming Messiah; among the Samaritans he was known as Taheb, 'one who restores' (TH).

Simon the sorcerer

⁹Now there was a certain man named Simon who lived and practiced sorcery in the city and amazed all the people of Samaria. He boasted that he was someone great ¹⁰and all the people, from the least to the greatest, gave him their attention saying, "This man is called the Great Power of God." ¹¹They gave him their attention because he had amazed them with his magic tricks for a very long time. ¹²But when they believed Philip as he preached the good news that God will reign over his people and the name of Jesus Christ, both men and women were baptised. ¹³Simon, too, believed and was baptised. He followed Philip everywhere, astonished by the great signs and miracles that he was seeing.

Samaritans receive Holy Breath

¹⁴When the apostles in Jerusalem heard that Samaria had accepted the word of God, they sent Peter and John to them. ¹⁵When they arrived, they prayed for them that they might receive Holy Breath. ¹⁶This was because Holy Breath had not yet come upon any of them. They had simply been baptised into the name of the Lord Jesus. ¹⁷Then Peter and John placed their hands on them and they received Holy Breath.

Peter rebukes Simon

¹⁸When Simon saw that the Breath *of God* was given at the laying on of the apostle's hands, he offered Peter and John money ¹⁹and said, "Give me this ability also so that everyone on whom I lay hands on may receive Holy Breath."

²⁰Peter answered, "You and your money can go to hell, because you thought you could buy the gift of God with money. ²¹You have no part or share in this ministry, because your heart is not right before God. ²²Change your mind about this wickedness and pray to the Lord. Perhaps he will forgive you for having such a thought in your heart. ²³I can see that you are full of bitterness and captive to sin."

²⁴Then Simon said, "Pray to the Lord for me so that nothing you have said may happen to me."

²⁵When Peter and John had testified and preached the word of the Lord, they returned to Jerusalem, preaching the gospel in many Samaritan villages *along the way*.

Philip and the Ethiopian

²⁶Now an angel of the Lord said to Philip, "Go south to the road—the desert road that goes down from Jerusalem to Gaza." ²⁷So Philip started out on the road and on his way he met an Ethiopian eunuch who was an important power

in charge of all the treasury of Candace, the queen of the Ethiopians. This man had been to Jerusalem to worship God, ²⁸and was on his way back home. He was sitting in his chariot reading the book of Isaiah the prophet. ²⁹The Breath *of God* told Philip, "Approach that chariot and stay close by."

³⁰So Philip ran up to the chariot and heard the man reading Isaiah the prophet. Philip asked him, "Do you understand what you are reading?" ³¹The man replied, "How can I unless someone explains it to me?" So he invited Philip to come up and sit with him *in the carriage*.

³²The eunuch was reading the following passage of Scripture:

> "He was led like a sheep to the slaughter and as a lamb before the shearer is silent so he did not open his mouth.
> ³³In his humiliation he was deprived of justice.
> There is no one to speak of his descendants because his life was taken from the earth."

Isaiah 53:7-8

³⁴The eunuch asked Philip, "Can you please tell me who the prophet is talking about here? Is he talking about himself or someone else?" ³⁵Then Philip began with that very passage of Scripture and told him the good news about Jesus.

³⁶As they travelled along the road, they came to some water and the eunuch said, "Look, here is water. Is there any reason why I shouldn't be baptised?" [³⁷So Philip said, "If you believe with all your heart then you may be baptised." The eunuch said, "Yes, I do, I believe that Jesus Christ is the Son of God."]⁶⁹¹

³⁸So the Ethiopian eunuch gave orders to stop the chariot and then both Philip and the eunuch went down into the water and Philip baptised him. ³⁹When they had come up out of the water, the Breath of the Lord snatched⁶⁹² Philip away and the eunuch did not see him again but he went on his way rejoicing. ⁴⁰Philip, however, found himself to be in Ashdod⁶⁹³ and travelled around preaching the gospel in all the cities until he reached Caesarea.

Saul converted on the road to Damascus
(Acts 22:6-16, 26:9-18)

9 ¹Meanwhile, Saul was keeping up with his murderous threats against the Lord's followers. He went to the high priest ²and asked him for letters to the

---

691   The oldest Greek MSS do not contain v. 37 however it was quoted as Scripture by several early Christian writers including Irenaeus (*Against Heresies*, Bk. III, ch. xii:8).
692   Interestingly, this is the same root word *harpazo* that is used for the rapture in 1 Thess. 4:17.
693   Ashdod (Azotus) was an ancient Philistine city, 32 km north of Gaza. Caesarea was the chief city of Palestine and the residence of the Roman governor, on the north coast.

synagogues in Damascus, so that if he found any belonging to The Way[694] there, whether men or women, he might bring them back in chains to Jerusalem. ³As Saul was nearing Damascus, suddenly a light from heaven flashed around him. ⁴He fell to the ground and heard a voice say to him, "Saul, Saul, why are you persecuting me?"

⁵Saul asked, "Who are you, Lord?" The voice said, "I am Jesus, whom you are persecuting. ⁶Now get up and go into the city and you will be told what you must do."

⁷The men travelling with Saul stood there speechless. They had heard the voice but did not see anyone. ⁸Saul got up from the ground but when he opened his eyes he could not see anything. So they led him by the hand into Damascus. ⁹For three days he was blind and did not eat or drink anything.

¹⁰In Damascus there was a follower named Ananias. The Lord called to him in a vision, "Ananias!"

"Yes, Lord," he answered."

¹¹The Lord told him, "Go to the house of Judas on Straight Street and ask for a man from Tarsus named Saul, for he is praying. ¹²He has had a vision and he has seen a man named Ananias come and place his hands on him in order to restore his sight."

¹³Ananias said to the Lord, "Lord, I have heard many reports about this man and all the damage he has done to your people in Jerusalem. ¹⁴Furthermore he has come here with authority from the chief priests to arrest everyone who calls on your name."

¹⁵But the Lord said to him, "Go! This man is my chosen instrument to carry my name before the Gentiles and their kings and before the people of Israel. ¹⁶I will show him how much he must suffer for my name."

¹⁷Then Ananias went to the house and entered it and having placed his hands on Saul, he said, "Brother Saul, the Lord has sent me—Jesus himself who appeared to you on the road as you were coming here so that you may see again and be filled with Holy Breath. ¹⁸Immediately, something like fish scales fell from Saul's eyes and he could see again. He got up and he was baptised. ¹⁹After taking some food, *Saul* regained his strength.

Saul escapes from Damascus in a basket

Saul spent several days with the followers *of Jesus* in Damascus. ²⁰He immediately began to preach in the synagogues that Christ is the Son of God. ²¹Everyone who heard him were astonished and asked, "Isn't he the man in

---

694   From John 14:6.

Jerusalem who was attacking those who call on this name? Has not he come here to take them back in chains to the chief priests?" ²²Despite this, Saul grew more and more powerful and confounded the Jews living in Damascus by proving that Jesus was the Messiah.

²³After many days had passed, the *unbelieving* Jews conspired to kill Saul ²⁴but he learned of their plan. Night and day they kept close watch on the city gates in order to kill him. ²⁵But the followers took him by night and lowered him in a large basket through an opening in the city wall.

Saul returns to Jerusalem

²⁶When Saul arrived in Jerusalem, he tried to join up with the followers *of Jesus*. But they were all afraid of him, not believing that he was a true follower *of Jesus*. ²⁷However Barnabas took him and brought him to the apostles. He told them how Saul on his journey had seen the Lord and that the Lord had spoken to him, and how in Damascus he had preached without fear in the name of Jesus. ²⁸So Saul stayed with the apostles and moved about freely in Jerusalem, speaking boldly in the name of the Lord. ²⁹He spoke and debated with the Hellenistic Jews,[695] but they tried to kill him. ³⁰When the *Christian* brothers learned about this, they took him down to Caesarea *on the coast* and sent him to Tarsus.

³¹Then the church throughout Judea and Samaria enjoyed a time of peace. It was strengthened and encouraged by the Holy Breath, living in the fear of the Lord and increasing in number.

Peter heals a paralysed man at Lydda

³²As Peter travelled around the countryside, he went to visit the people of God in a village called Lydda.[696] ³³There he found a man named Aeneas who had been paralysed and bedridden for eight years. ³⁴Peter said to Aeneas, "Jesus Christ heals you. Get up and roll up your bed." Immediately Aeneas got up. ³⁵Everyone who lived in Lydda and *the Plain of* Sharon[697] saw him and turned to the Lord.

Peter raises Tabitha from the dead at Joppa[698]

³⁶In Joppa there was a follower *of Jesus* named Tabitha[699] (which, when translated is Dorcas), who was always doing good and helping the poor. ³⁷About this time she became sick and died. Her body was washed and placed in an upstairs

---

695   Greek speaking Jews.
696   Lydda (Lod-Hebrew) was a small village northwest of Jerusalem some 16 km southeast of Joppa/Jaffa and 20 km southeast of Tel-Aviv. Israel's international airport is located on the outskirts of Lod.
697   This is the coastal plain of Israel.
698   Joppa is the modern-day city of Jaffa, an important southern port.
699   Both Tabitha (Aramaic) and Dorcas (Greek) mean gazelle.

room. ³⁸The village of Lydda was close to Joppa so when Jesus' followers heard that Peter was in Lydda, they sent two men to him and urged him to come at once.

³⁹Peter went with them and upon arriving he was taken to the upper room. All the widows stood around him, crying and showing the garments and other clothing that Dorcas had made while she was still with them.

⁴⁰Peter sent them all out of the room and then got down on his knees and prayed. Turning to the dead woman, he said, "Tabitha, stand up." ⁴¹He took her by the hand and helped her to her feet. Then he called the believers and the widows and presented her to them alive. ⁴²This became known all over Joppa, and many people believed in the Lord. ⁴³Peter stayed in Joppa some time with a tanner named Simon.[700]

Cornelius calls for Peter to come

10 ¹Now there was a certain man in *the coastal city of* Caesarea named Cornelius who was a Roman centurion in what was known as the Italian cohort.[701] ²He and all his family were devout and God-fearing. He gave generously to those in need and he prayed to God regularly. ³One day at about three in the afternoon he had a vision. He distinctly saw an angel of God, who came to him and said, "Cornelius!"

⁴Cornelius stared at him and was afraid and asked, "What is it Lord?"

The angel answered, "Your prayers and gifts to the poor have been received by God as an offering. ⁵Now send men to Joppa to bring back a man named Simon who is called Peter. ⁶He is staying with Simon the tanner, whose house is by the sea."

⁷When the angel who spoke to him had left, Cornelius called two of his servants and a devout soldier who was one of his attendants. ⁸He told them everything that had happened and sent them to Joppa.

Peter's vision

⁹At about noon the following day as the men were on their journey and approaching the city *of Joppa*, Peter went up on the roof to pray. ¹⁰He became hungry and wanted something to eat. While the meal was being prepared, Peter fell into a trance. ¹¹He saw heaven opened and something like a large linen sheet being let down to the earth by its four corners. ¹²In the sheet there were various

---

700   This was a man who made articles out of leather such as a sandal maker. Interestingly, Peter was staying with a man whose trade was considered unclean by the Jews since it involved the handling of the skins of animals.

701   A cohort was one of the basic divisions of the Roman army consisting of 600 soldiers. There were ten cohorts in a legion and a centurion was in command of 100 men.

kinds of tetrapods,⁷⁰² as well as reptiles of the earth and birds of the sky. ¹³Then a voice told him, "Peter, get up, kill and eat."

¹⁴Peter answered, "Surely not Lord! I have never eaten anything common or unclean."⁷⁰³

¹⁵The voice spoke to Peter a second time and said, "Do not call anything unclean that God has made clean."

¹⁶This happened three times and then immediately the *sheet* was taken back up into heaven.

¹⁷While Peter was wondering about the meaning of the vision, the men sent by Cornelius found out where Simon's house was and stopped at the gate. ¹⁸They called out, asking if Simon who was known as Peter was staying there.

¹⁹While Peter was still thinking about the vision, the Breath *of God* said to him, "Simon, three men are looking for you. ²⁰Get up and go downstairs. Do not hesitate in going with the men for I have sent them."

²¹So Peter went down and said to the men, "I'm the one you are looking for. Why have you come?"

²²The men replied, "We have come from Cornelius the centurion. He is a righteous and God-fearing man, who is respected by all the Jewish people. A holy angel told him to have you come to his house so that he can hear what you have to say." ²³Then Peter invited them in to be his guests *for the night.*

Peter goes to Cornelius' house

The next day Peter started out with the men and some of the *Christian* brothers from Joppa went along. ²⁴The following day he arrived in Caesarea. Cornelius was expecting them and had called together his relatives and close friends. ²⁵As Peter entered the house, Cornelius met him and fell at his feet in reverence. ²⁶But Peter made him get up and said, "Stand up, I am only a man myself."

²⁷As Peter was talking with him, he went inside and found a large gathering of people. ²⁸Peter said to them, "I am sure that you know that it is against our Law for a Jew to associate with a Gentile or to visit him. But God has shown me that I should not call any man impure⁷⁰⁴ or unclean. ²⁹So when I was sent for, I came without raising any objection. May I ask you the reason why you asked me to come?"

³⁰Cornelius answered, "Four days ago I was in my house praying at this time, at three in the afternoon. Suddenly a man in shining clothes stood before me ³¹and said, 'Cornelius, God has heard your prayer and remembered your gifts to

---

702   I.e. four-footed animals.
703   This means something that was considered impure, common or defiled in the sense of the Jewish religion. Examples of unclean animals would be pigs, horses and camels.
704   Common or ritually unacceptable.

the poor. ³²Send someone to Joppa for Simon who is called Peter. He is staying in the home of Simon the tanner, who lives by the sea.' ³³Therefore I sent for you immediately and it was good of you to come. Now we are all here in the presence of God to listen to everything that the Lord has commanded you to tell us."

³⁴Then Peter began to speak, "I now realise how true it is that God does not show favouritism ³⁵but he accepts men from every nation who fear him and do what is right. ³⁶He has sent his message to the people of Israel and brought them the good news of peace through Jesus Christ who is Lord of all. ³⁷You know what has happened throughout Judea, beginning in Galilee after the baptism that John preached: ³⁸God anointed Jesus the Nazarene with Holy Breath and with power and he went all over the place doing good. He healed everyone who was under the power of the devil because God was with him.

³⁹"*In fact* we *apostles* are witnesses of everything that he did both in the Judean countryside and in *the city* of Jerusalem. They killed him by hanging him on a tree.⁷⁰⁵ ⁴⁰But God raised him from the dead on the third day and caused him to be seen. ⁴¹He was not seen by all the people but only by witnesses whom God had already chosen—those who had eaten and drank with him after he rose from the dead. ⁴²He commanded us to preach to the people and to testify that he is the one whom God appointed as judge of the living and the dead. ⁴³All the prophets testify to this fact that the group believing in him will receive the forgiveness of sins through his name."

⁴⁴While Peter was still speaking these words, the Holy Breath came upon all who heard this message. ⁴⁵The circumcised believers⁷⁰⁶ who had come with Peter were astonished that the gift of the Holy Breath had been poured out even on the Gentiles. ⁴⁶For they heard them speaking in different languages and praising God.

Then Peter said, ⁴⁷"Can anyone stop these people from being baptised with water? They have received the Holy Breath just as we have." ⁴⁸So Peter ordered that they be baptised in the name of Jesus Christ. Then they asked Peter to stay with them for a few days.

Peter explains to the church at Jerusalem what happened

11 ¹The apostles and the other believers in Judea heard that the Gentiles also had received the word of God. ²So when Peter went up to Jerusalem, the circumcised believers criticised him ³saying, "You went into the house of uncircumcised men and ate with them!"

---

705   Cf. Gal 3:13 and footnote.
706   Jewish believers. All male Jews were circumcised at eight days of age.

⁴Starting from the beginning, Peter explained everything as it had happened: ⁵"I was in the city of Joppa praying and in a trance I saw a vision. I saw something like a large linen sheet being let down from heaven by its four corners coming to a stop near me. ⁶I looked into it and saw tetrapods⁷⁰⁷ of the earth, wild beasts, reptiles and birds of the sky as well. ⁷Then I heard a voice which said, 'Peter! Get up, kill and eat!'

⁸"I said to the voice, 'Surely not, Lord! I have never eaten anything impure or unclean.'

⁹"The voice spoke from heaven a second time saying, 'Do not call anything impure that God has made clean.' ¹⁰This happened three times and then it was all pulled up to heaven again.

¹¹"Right at that moment, three men who had been sent to me from Caesarea stopped by at the house where I was staying. ¹²The Breath *of God* told me not to have any hesitation in going with them. These six brothers also went with me and we entered the man's house. ¹³He told us how he had seen an angel appear in his house saying, 'Send someone to Joppa for Simon who is called Peter. ¹⁴He will bring you a message through which you and all your household will be saved.'

¹⁵"As I began to speak, the Holy Breath came on them as he had come on us at the beginning. ¹⁶Then I remembered what the Lord had said: 'John baptised with water but you will be baptised with Holy Breath.' ¹⁷So if God gave to them the same gift as he gave to us who have believed in the Lord Jesus Christ, then who am I to think that I could prevent God?"

¹⁸When the *circumcised believers, who had been criticising*, heard this, they had no further objections and they praised God, saying, "So then, God has even allowed the Gentiles to turn to God and gain *eternal* life."

The church in Antioch

¹⁹Now those who had been scattered by the persecution when Stephen was killed, travelled as far as Phoenicia,⁷⁰⁸ *the island of* Cyprus, and Antioch,⁷⁰⁹ spreading the word to the Jews only. ²⁰Some of them, however, men from Cyprus and Cyrene, went to Antioch and began to speak to the Greek speaking Jews⁷¹⁰ also, telling them the good news about the Lord Jesus. ²¹The hand of the Lord was with them and a great number of people believed and turned to the Lord.

²²News of this reached the church at Jerusalem and they sent Barnabas to

---

707   I.e. four-footed animals.
708   Phoenicia was the coastal plain along northern Palestine including modern-day Lebanon.
709   Antioch was the capital of the imperial province of Syria; it was located about fifteen miles from the coast, and was the third city in the Empire, next only to Rome and Alexandria (TH).
710   This is literally 'Hellenists' whose mother tongue was Greek—they were Jews of the diaspora whereas Hebrews spoke Aramaic.

Antioch. ²³When he arrived and saw the evidence of the grace of God, he was happy and encouraged them all to remain true to the Lord with all their hearts. ²⁴*Barnabas* was a good man, full of Holy Breath and faith, and a great number of people came to the Lord.

²⁵Then Barnabas went to Tarsus to look for Saul, ²⁶and when he found him, he brought him to Antioch. So for a whole year Barnabas and Saul met with the church and taught a great number of people. The followers *of Jesus* were first called Christians at Antioch.[711]

²⁷During this time some prophets came down from Jerusalem to Antioch. ²⁸One of them named Agabus, stood up and by the Breath *of God* predicted that a severe famine would spread over the entire civilised world.[712] (This occurred during the reign of *Roman Emperor* Claudius.)[713] ²⁹The followers *of Jesus in Antioch* decided to provide help for the Christian believers living in Judea, each according to his own financial ability. ³⁰They sent their gift to the *church* elders via Barnabas and Saul.

Herod kills James and imprisons Peter

12 ¹During this period, King Herod[714] began to persecute certain members of the church. ²He had James, the brother of John, put to death by the sword. ³When Herod saw that this pleased the Jews, he proceeded to arrest Peter also. (This happened during the Feast of Unleavened Bread.) ⁴After arresting him, he put him in prison, handing him over to be guarded by four squads of four soldiers each. Herod intended to bring him out for public trial after the Passover.

⁵So Peter was kept in prison but the church was seriously praying to God for him.

⁶The night before Herod was to bring him to trial, Peter was sleeping between two soldiers, bound with two chains with guards keeping watch at the prison entrance. ⁷Suddenly an angel of the Lord appeared and a light shone in the jail cell. The angel struck Peter on the side and woke him up saying, "Quick, get up!" The chains fell off from his hands.

---

711   It is agreed by the commentators that "Christian" was a derogatory title given to the believers by the non-Christian community, perhaps because the believers said, "Christ is Lord" in contrast with the confession of the Roman world who would say, "Caesar is Lord." Thus the word "Christian" basically means 'one who is a follower of Christ'.

712   Literally this is 'inhabited earth'.

713   Claudius was emperor from AD 41–54, and evidently his reign was characterized by famines in various parts of the known world. In Palestine the famine was particularly severe around AD 46 (TH).

714   King Herod is Herod Agrippa the first, grandson of Herod the Great (Luke 1:5), who from AD 41–44 ruled over all the country of Palestine, with the title of 'King' (TH).

⁸Then the angel said to him, "Put on your clothes and sandals." Peter did so and the angel again said, "Put on your coat and follow me." ⁹Peter followed the angel out of the prison but had no idea that what the angel was doing was really happening. He thought that he was seeing a vision. ¹⁰They passed the first and second guards and came to the iron-gate leading into the city.[715] It opened for them by itself and they went through it. When they had walked the length of one street, suddenly the angel left him.

¹¹Then Peter came to his senses and said, "Now I know without a doubt that the Lord sent his angel and rescued me from Herod and from everything that the Jewish people were hoping for." ¹²After he had realised exactly what had happened, he went to the house of Mary the mother of John, also called Mark, where many people had gathered and were praying. ¹³Peter knocked on the door at the outer entrance and a servant girl named Rhoda came to answer. ¹⁴When she recognised Peter's voice, she was so excited that she ran back without opening the door and announced, "Peter is at the door!"

¹⁵"You're losing it," they said to her. When she kept insisting that it was true, they said, "It must be his angel."

¹⁶But Peter kept on knocking and when they opened the door and saw him they were astonished. ¹⁷Peter motioned with his hand for them to be quiet while he described how the Lord had brought him out of the prison. "Tell James and the *Christian* brothers about this," Peter said, and then he left for another place.

¹⁸The next morning, there was quite a stir among the soldiers as to what had become of Peter. ¹⁹After Herod had a thorough search made for him and did not find him, he interrogated the soldiers and ordered them to be put to death. After, Herod left Judea and went down to Caesarea and spent some time there.

Herod dies

²⁰Now Herod was very angry at the people of Tyre and Sidon. So they sent a delegation to gain an audience and make peace with him because their cities depended on Herod's country for their food supply. They had won the support of Blastus, King Herod's personal assistant.

²¹On the appointed day,[716] Herod, wearing his royal robes, sat on his throne and delivered a public address to the people. ²²They shouted, "This is the voice

---

[715] This is referring to the city of Jerusalem. The prison was most likely in Fort Antonia which was located within the outer city walls and the iron-gate was probably a gate that opened up internally into the rest of the city.

[716] According to the account of the Jewish historian Josephus, the appointed day was a celebration in honour of the Emperor (TH).

of a god, not of a man." ²³Immediately because Herod did not give praise to God, an angel of the Lord struck him down and he was eaten by worms and died.

²⁴Meanwhile the word of God continued to increase and spread.

²⁵When Barnabas and Saul had delivered their contribution *to the elders at Jerusalem* they returned to *Antioch*, taking John also called Mark with them.

The church at Antioch sends Barnabas and Saul off on mission

13 ¹In the church at Antioch there were prophets and teachers: Barnabas, Simeon called Niger, Lucius of Cyrene, Manaen (who had been brought up with Herod the tetrarch) and Saul. ²While they were worshipping the Lord and fasting, the Holy Breath said to them, "Set apart for me Barnabas and Saul for the work to which I have called them." ³So after they had fasted and prayed, they placed their hands on them and sent them off.

Barnabas and Saul go to the island of Cyprus

⁴Having been sent by the Holy Breath, *Barnabas and Saul* went down to the *port of* Seleucia[717] *from Antioch* and sailed from there to *the island of* Cyprus.[718] ⁵When they arrived at Salamis,[719] they preached the word of God in the Jewish synagogues. John Mark was with them to help.

⁶They travelled throughout the whole island until they came to Paphos. There they met a Jewish sorcerer and false prophet named Bar-Jesus. ⁷He was an attendant of the proconsul, Sergius Paulus. The proconsul was an intelligent man and sent for Barnabas and Saul because he wanted to hear the word of God. ⁸But Elymas the sorcerer (his name in Greek) opposed *Barnabas and Saul* and so tried to turn the proconsul away from the faith. ⁹Then Saul, who was also called Paul, having been filled with Holy Breath, looked straight at Elymas and said, ¹⁰"You are a child of the devil and an enemy of everything that is right! You are full of all kinds of dirty tricks and schemes. Will you never stop perverting the right ways of the Lord? ¹¹Now, look! The hand of the Lord is against you and you will become blind and for some time you will be unable to see the light of day."

Immediately a dark mist came over him and he groped about looking for someone to lead him by the hand. ¹²When the proconsul saw what had happened, he believed, for he was amazed at the teaching about the Lord.

---

717 Seleucia, on the coast 25 km west of Antioch, was the port city of Antioch (TH).
718 Cyprus, the home of Barnabas, was an island noted for its copper mines. In 57 BC, the island was taken over by the Romans, and in 22 BC it was made a senatorial province governed by a proconsul (TH).
719 Salamis, on the eastern coast of Cyprus, was the chief city of the island. It was the seat of the government for the eastern half of the island, although the capital was Paphos on the southwestern part of the island. The city had a rather large Jewish population, as is indicated by the mention of several Jewish synagogues (TH).

Barnabas and Saul go to Pisidian Antioch

[13]Paul and his companions set sail from Paphos to Perga in Pamphylia where John Mark left them and returned to Jerusalem. [14]From Perga they went on to Pisidian Antioch. On the Sabbath they entered the synagogue and sat down. [15]After the synagogue leaders had read portions from the Law and the Prophets,[720] they sent word to them, saying, "Brothers, if you have a word of encouragement for the people, please speak."

[16]Paul stood up and having motioned with his hand for quiet, said, "Men of Israel and you Gentiles who worship God, listen up now! [17]The God of the people of Israel chose our fathers. He caused the people to prosper during their stay in Egypt. He led them out of that country with incredible power. [18]He put up with them for about forty years in the desert. [19]He destroyed seven nations in the land of Canaan and gave their land to his people as their inheritance. [20]All of this took about 450 years.

"After this, God gave the people judges until the time of Samuel the prophet. [21]Then they asked for a king and so he gave them Saul, son of Kish, who came from the tribe of Benjamin. He ruled for forty years. [22]After removing Saul, God made David their king. This is what God said about him, 'I have found David son of Jesse a man after my own heart. He will do everything I want him to do.'

[23]"From *David's* seed God has raised up a Saviour for Israel, Jesus, as he promised. [24]However before the coming of Jesus, John *the Baptist* preached to all the people of Israel that they must turn to God and be baptised. [25]As John was finishing his *life's* work, he asked, 'Who do you think I am? I am not the one. No, he who is coming after me, I am not worthy to even untie his sandals.'

[26]"Brothers, descendants of the family of Abraham and also you God-fearing Gentiles, it is to us that this message of salvation has been sent. [27]The people of Jerusalem and their rulers did not recognise Jesus however they condemned him to death thereby fulfilling the words of the prophets that are read every Sabbath. [28]Even though they found no proper grounds for a death sentence, they asked Pilate to have him executed. [29]When they had carried out all that was written about him they took him down from the tree and placed him in a tomb. [30]But God raised him from the dead [31]and for many days he was seen by those who had travelled with him from Galilee to Jerusalem who are now witnesses to the people *of Israel*.

[32]"We are preaching the good news to you. God promised our ancestors

---

720 Basically this means the Hebrew Bible, what we call the OT with the Law being the first five books (Pentateuch) and the rest of the OT being the Prophets.

about this [33]which he has fulfilled for us, their descendants, by raising up Jesus. As it is written in the second psalm,

> "'You are my Son. Today I have begotten you.'"[721]
>
> Psalm 2:7

[34]"These words *in Isaiah* back up the fact that God raised Jesus from the dead, *his body* never to decay,

> "'I will give you the holy and sure blessings that I promised David beforehand.'
>
> Isaiah 55:3

[35]"And it is stated elsewhere too in the Psalms,

> "'You will not let your Holy one see decay.'"
>
> Psalm 16:10

[36]*Paul continued to speak in the synagogue,* "When David had served God's purpose in his own generation, he fell asleep and he was buried with his fathers and his body decayed. [37]But *Jesus* whom God raised from the dead did not see decay.

[38]"Therefore, my brothers, let it be known that the forgiveness of sins is proclaimed to you through Jesus. A man is set free and declared righteous in this way which could not be done by means of the Law of Moses. [39]Every one of you who believes in him is declared righteous. [40]Be careful that what the prophets have said does not happen to you as such,

> [41]"'Listen up, you scoffers, be amazed and perish.
> I am going to do something incredible in your days, something you will
> > hardly believe even if someone were to tell you.'"[722]
>
> Habakkuk 1:5

[42]As Paul and Barnabas were leaving the synagogue of the Jews, the people invited them to speak further about these things on the 'between Sabbath'.[723] [43]Once the meeting had finished many of the Jews and Gentiles who had

---

721 Cf. Heb. 1:5 footnote.
722 In their original setting these words referred to the Chaldean invasion which Habakkuk felt to be imminent; Paul applies the word to the final judgment (TH).
723 Most translations have "next Sabbath". However this is incorrect. The 'between' Sabbaths were the weekly Sabbaths that occurred inside the festival weeks of Passover, Pentecost and Tabernacles. The intervening Sabbaths which were not counted in the two cycles each year, were called the 'between Sabbaths'. Cf. Martin, Ernest L, *The Chronology of the Twenty-four Courses.* (https://www.askelm.com/star/star006.htm) Cf. Luke 6:1.

converted to Judaism[724] followed Paul and Barnabas outside. Paul and Barnabas talked with them and convincing them to continue in the grace of God.

⁴⁴Now on the coming Sabbath, almost the whole city gathered to hear the word of the Lord. ⁴⁵When the *unbelieving* Jews saw the crowds, they were filled with jealousy and they spoke against Paul, insulting him.

⁴⁶Then Paul and Barnabas answered boldly saying, "It was necessary to speak firstly to you Jews. But since you reject it and do not consider yourselves worthy of eternal life, we are now turning to the Gentiles. ⁴⁷For this is what the Lord has commanded us,

> "'I have made you a light for the Gentiles that you may bring salvation
>   to the ends of the earth.'"

Isaiah 49:6

⁴⁸When the Gentiles heard this, they were happy and they praised the Lord for this word and everyone who was proposed with eternal life, believed.[725]

⁴⁹The word of the Lord spread throughout the whole region. ⁵⁰But the *unbelieving* Jews incited the God-fearing women of high standing and the leading men of the city to persecute Paul and Barnabas and so they expelled them from their region. ⁵¹So Paul and Barnabas shook the dust off their feet in protest against them and went to *the city of* Iconium.[726] ⁵²The followers were filled with joy and with Holy Breath.

Paul and Barnabas go to Iconium

14 ¹The same thing happened in Iconium. Paul and Barnabas went into the Jewish synagogue where they spoke so powerfully that a great number of Jews and Gentiles believed. ²But the Jews who refused to believe stirred up the Gentiles and poisoned their minds against their fellow believers. ³So Paul and Barnabas spent considerable time there, speaking boldly about the grace of the Lord. The Lord confirmed that their message was true by enabling them to do miraculous signs and wonders. ⁴The people of the city were divided. Some sided with the *unbelieving* Jews and others with the apostles. ⁵There was an attempt among the *unbelieving* Gentiles and Jews, together with their leaders,

---

724 This is literally proselytes which means Gentiles who had become full converts to the Jewish religion, Judaism, including being circumcised. This is in contrast to verses 16 and 26 where the Gentiles had not become full Jews as such.

725 Arbitrary predestination was not in mind here since v. 46 clearly emphasises human responsibility in rejecting or accepting eternal life. Rather the sense here is to distinguish Christians from other hearers (Kittel, 1979, *Theological Dictionary of the NT*, Volume VIII, p. 28).

726 Iconium was a city about 128 km southeast of Antioch in the Roman province of Galatia, and it would probably have required four or five days' travel to arrive there (TH).

to attack them and stone them. ⁶But the *apostles* became aware of this and fled to the Lycaonian cities of Lystra and Derbe[727] and to the surrounding country, ⁷where they continued to preach the good news.

Paul stoned at Lystra

⁸In Lystra there was a man who was crippled in his feet and lame from birth and had never been able to walk. He was sitting there ⁹listening to Paul as he was speaking. Paul looked directly at him and saw that he had faith to be healed. ¹⁰Therefore Paul said to the man in a loud voice, "Stand up on your feet!" Immediately the man jumped to his feet and began walking.

¹¹When the crowd saw what Paul had done, they shouted in the Lycaonian language, "The gods have come down to us in human form!" ¹²They called Barnabas Zeus and Paul Hermes because he was the chief speaker.[728] ¹³The priest of Zeus, whose temple was just outside the city, brought bulls and wreaths to the *city* gates because he and the crowd wanted to offer sacrifices to the *apostles*.

¹⁴However when the apostles Barnabas and Paul heard of this, they tore their clothes and rushed out into the crowd, shouting, ¹⁵"Men, why are you doing this? We too are only men, just human like you. We are preaching the good news to you so that you'll turn away from these worthless things to the living God, who made heaven and earth and sea and everything in them. ¹⁶In the past, God let all nations go their own way. ¹⁷Yet he has not left them without evidence of himself. He has shown kindness by giving you rain from heaven and crops in their seasons. He provides you with plenty of food and fills your hearts with joy." ¹⁸Even with these words, they had difficulty in keeping the crowd from sacrificing to them.

¹⁹Then some *unbelieving* Jews came from Antioch and Iconium and won the crowd over. They stoned Paul and dragged him outside the city, thinking that he was dead. ²⁰But when the followers *of Jesus* gathered around him, he stood up and went back into the city. The next day Paul and Barnabas left for *the city of* Derbe.

Paul and Barnabas return to Antioch in Syria

²¹Paul and Barnabas preached the good news in Derbe and having made a large number of followers *to Jesus* there, they returned to Lystra, Iconium

---

727 Lystra was about 30 km southwest of Iconium and held the rank of a Roman colony. Derbe was a frontier city of the providence of Galatia, though its exact location has not been established. According to some it was about 48 km southeast of Lystra. Lycaonia was a district in the Roman province of Galatia (TH).

728 Zeus was the chief god of the Greek and Hermes was the messenger of the gods. A writer of the AD 400s refers to Hermes as 'the leader of the words' (the one who did the speaking). There was a local legend to the effect that an elderly and pious couple by the name of Philemon and Baucis had entertained Jupiter (Zeus) and Mercury (Hermes) without knowing that they were gods (TH).

and Antioch *in Pisidia*. ²²They strengthened the followers *in these places* and encouraged everyone that they must continue in the faith. They said, "We must go through many tribulations in order that we can enter into the coming realm of God." ²³Paul and Barnabas appointed elders for them in every church and with prayer and fasting, they recommended each one of them to the Lord, in whom they had put their trust. ²⁴After travelling through Pisidia, they came to Pamphylia, ²⁵and when they had preached the word in Perga, they went down to Attalia.⁷²⁹

²⁶From Attalia *Paul and Barnabas* sailed back to Antioch *in Syria*, where they had been committed to the grace of God for the work that they had now completed. ²⁷Upon arrival there, they gathered the church together and they reported all that God had done through them and how he had opened the door of faith to the Gentiles. ²⁸*Paul and Barnabas* stayed there a long time with the followers *of Jesus*.

The meeting in Jerusalem

15 ¹Some men came down from Judea to Antioch and began to teach the fellow believers. They were saying, "Unless you are circumcised according to the practice taught by Moses, you are not able to be saved." ²Paul and Barnabas got into a fierce debate and disagreement with them over this matter so Paul and Barnabas were appointed along with some other believers, to go up to Jerusalem to see the elders and the apostles about this issue.

³The church sent them on their way and as they travelled through Phoenicia and Samaria, they told how the Gentiles had turned to God. This brought great joy to all the fellow believers. ⁴When they arrived in Jerusalem they were welcomed by the church there and the apostles and the elders. They reported everything that God had done through them.

⁵Then some of the believers who belonged to the party of the Pharisees stood up and said, "The Gentiles must be circumcised and be required to obey the Law of Moses."

⁶The apostles and the elders met to consider this matter. ⁷After a lot of discussion, Peter stood up and addressed them all, "Men, brothers, you all know that some time ago God appointed me from among you to preach the good news to the Gentiles so that they could hear and believe. ⁸God, who knows the heart, showed that he accepted them by giving the Holy Breath to them, just as he did to us. ⁹He has not differentiated between us and them, for he has cleansed their hearts because they believed. ¹⁰Therefore why are you trying to test God by

---

729   Attalia was the chief seaport of Pamphylia.

putting a burden on the shoulders of the *Gentile* believers that neither we *Jews* nor our ancestors have been able to bear? ¹¹Ah, No! We believe it is through the grace of our Lord Jesus that we are saved, just as they are."

¹²The whole group was silent as they listened to Barnabas and Paul describe about the miraculous signs and wonders that God had done through them among the Gentiles. ¹³When these two had finished, James[730] spoke up saying, "Brothers, listen to me. ¹⁴Simon has just described to us about the time how God first showed his concern by taking a people for himself from the Gentiles. ¹⁵The words of the prophets agree with this when the Scriptures say,

> ¹⁶'At a later time, I will return and raise up the fallen tabernacle of David.[731]
> I will rebuild the ruins and I will restore it.
> ¹⁷I will do this so that the rest of the human race will search for me—all
>   the Gentiles whom I have called to be mine.'
> ¹⁸This is the word of the Lord who made this known ages ago."
>
> Amos 9:11–12

¹⁹James continued by saying, "Therefore, in my opinion, we should not make it difficult for the Gentiles who are turning to God. ²⁰Instead we should write to them, telling them to keep away from food polluted by idols, from sexual immorality, from the meat of strangled animals and from blood. ²¹For the *Law of* Moses has been preached in every city from ancient generations and is read in the synagogues on every Sabbath day."

The letter to the Gentile believers

²²Then the apostles and the elders together with the whole church, decided to choose some of their own men and send them to Antioch with Paul and Barnabas. They chose Judas (called Barsabbas) and Silas, two men who were leaders among the believers there. ²³They sent the following letter with them:

From the apostles and elders *in Jerusalem*, your brothers.

To the Gentile believers in Antioch, Syria and Cilicia,

---

730 James here is most likely Jesus' brother.
731 During David's time, the tabernacle housed the ark of the covenant and was a precursor to Solomon's temple. The prophet Amos says that God himself will restore and repair David's tabernacle tent in the last days so that his people may take possession of Edom (the ruins of ancient Petra). The reason Edom is mentioned is that of all nations they were the most hostile towards Israel. James applies this LXX quote from Amos to mean that God will save the Gentiles.

[24]We have heard that some men from here have troubled and unsettled you with their teaching, even though we did not authorise this. [25]Consequently we all agreed to appoint some men and send them with our dear friends, Barnabas and Paul. [26]These two men have risked their own lives for the name of our Lord Jesus Christ. [27]Therefore we are sending Judas and Silas to confirm by word of mouth what we have written *in this letter*. [28]It seemed appropriate to the Holy Breath and to us not to burden you with anything beyond the following requirements: [29]You are to keep away from food sacrificed to idols, from blood, from the meat of strangled animals and from sexual immorality. You will do well to keep away from these things.

Regards.

[30]The men were sent off and went down to Antioch *in Syria*, where they gathered the church together and delivered the letter. [31]Upon reading the letter the people were very happy with its encouraging message. [32]Judas and Silas, who themselves were prophets, said much to encourage and strengthen the *Christian* brothers. [33]After spending some time there, they were sent off by the *Christian* brothers with the blessing of peace to return to those who had sent them. [[34]But Silas decided to remain in *Antioch*.][732] [35]Paul and Barnabas remained in Antioch where they and many others taught and preached the word of the Lord.

Paul and Barnabas have a disagreement

[36]Some time later Paul said to Barnabas, "Let's go back and visit the *Christian* brothers in all the cities where we preached the word of the Lord and see how they are going." [37]Barnabas wanted to take John Mark with them, [38]but Paul preferred not to take him because he had deserted them in Pamphylia and had not continued with them in the work. [39]They disagreed so strongly that they parted ways. Barnabas took Mark and set sail for the island of Cyprus, [40]but Paul chose Silas and left having been commended by the *Christian* brothers to the grace of the Lord. [41]*Paul* went through Syria and Cilicia, strengthening the churches.

Timothy joins Paul and Silas

16 [1]Paul arrived in Derbe and then went on to Lystra, where a follower of Jesus named Timothy lived. His mother was a Jewess and a believer but his father was a Greek. [2]The *Christian* brothers at Lystra and Iconium spoke well

---

732 Most MSS do not have v. 34. It is thought that a scribe added this verse to get around the apparent contradiction in v. 40.

of *Timothy*. ³Paul wanted to take him along on the journey, so he circumcised him because of the Jews who lived in that area for they all knew that his father was a Greek. ⁴As they travelled from city to city, they passed on the decisions reached by the apostles and elders in Jerusalem to be kept. ⁵So the churches were strengthened in their beliefs and they grew daily in numbers.

Paul had a vision of a man in Macedonia

⁶Paul and the men travelled throughout the regions of Phrygia and Galatia having been prevented by the Holy Breath from preaching the word in Asia.⁷³³ ⁷When they came to the border of Mysia, they tried to enter Bithynia but the Breath of Jesus would not allow them to.⁷³⁴ ⁸So they passed by Mysia and went down to *the coast at* Troas.⁷³⁵ ⁹During the night Paul had a vision of a Macedonian man standing and pleading with him to come to Macedonia to help them. ¹⁰After Paul had the vision, we⁷³⁶ got ready immediately to leave for Macedonia. We concluded that God had called us to preach the gospel to them.

Lydia becomes a believer

¹¹From Troas we put out to sea and sailed straight for the *island of* Samothrace and then the next day on to Neapolis.⁷³⁷ ¹²From there we travelled to Philippi, an important city of the district of Macedonia—a *Roman* colony. We stayed there for several days.

¹³On the Sabbath day we went outside the city gate to the river, where we expected to find a place of prayer. We sat down and began to speak to the women who had gathered there. ¹⁴One of the women who was listening was a woman named Lydia. She was a dealer in purple cloth from the city of Thyatira and was a worshipper of God.⁷³⁸ The Lord caused her to have an open mind to what Paul was saying. ¹⁵When she and her household were baptised, she invited us into her home pleading, "If you consider me a believer in the Lord, come and stay at my house." And so she persuaded us.

---

733   This refers to Asia Minor (southwestern Turkey) not the modern-day continent of Asia.
734   Paul tried to go east into Bithynia from Mysia with the gospel but instead the Breath of Jesus (Holy Spirit) wouldn't allow them and since that time the gospel has travelled in a westerly direction.
735   Troas was a port on the Aegean Sea near ancient Troy.
736   Notice the change in the narrative from this point on with the inclusive "we" indicting that the author of Acts, Luke, is now part of the group travelling.
737   Evidently they had a favourable wind behind them because they sailed straight across to Samothrace. Samothrace was an island about 60 km from Troas; it was half way between Troas and Neapolis, the port city of Philippi, which was about 16 km south of Philippi (TH).
738   This means that she was a Gentile who participated in Jewish worship.

Paul and Silas flogged and thrown into prison

[16] Another time we were going to the usual place of prayer when we were met by a slave girl who had an evil spirit which enabled her to predict the future. She earned a lot of money for her owners by fortune-telling. [17] This girl followed Paul and the rest of us, shouting, "These men are servants of the Most High God who are telling you the way to be saved." [18] She repeatedly said this for many days. Finally Paul became so troubled by this that he turned around and said to the spirit, "In the name of Jesus Christ I command you to come out of her!" Immediately the evil spirit left her.

[19] When the owners of the slave girl realised that their hope of making money was gone, they grabbed Paul and Silas and dragged them into the marketplace[739] to face the authorities. [20] They brought them before the magistrates and said, "These men are Jews and are causing a lot of trouble in our city [21] because they are teaching customs that are against our Roman law and we cannot accept or practice it."

[22] The crowd joined in the attack against Paul and Silas and the magistrates ordered the men to be stripped and beaten. [23] After they had been severely flogged, they were thrown into prison and the jailer was ordered to guard them very closely. [24] When he received these orders, he put them in the inner cell and secured their hands and feet in the stocks.[740]

[25] About midnight Paul and Silas were praying and singing hymns to God and the other prisoners were listening. [26] Suddenly there was such a violent earthquake that the foundations of the prison were shaken. Immediately all the prison doors flew open and everybody's chains came loose. [27] The jailer woke up and when he saw the prison doors open, he drew his sword and was about to kill himself because he thought that all the prisoners had escaped.[741] [28] However Paul shouted, "Don't harm yourself! We are all here!"

[29] The jailer called for lights, rushed in and fell trembling *with fear* before Paul and Silas. [30] He then brought them out and asked, "Sirs, what must I do to be saved?"

[31] They answered, "Believe in the Lord Jesus and you will be saved—you and your family." [32] Then they spoke the word of the Lord to him and everyone in his house. [33] At that very hour of the night the jailer took them and washed their wounds and immediately after he and all his family were baptised. [34] The jailer

---

739. The marketplace was traditionally the public square where public courts were conducted because it is the place where people gathered.
740. Stocks are heavy blocks of wood with holes for hands and feet. Roman stocks had more than one pair of holes depending on the level of torture required.
741. In ancient times a jailer who allowed prisoners to escape would receive their punishment. The jailer assumed that he would be killed as punishment for allowing the prisoners to escape.

brought them into his house and prepared a meal for them. He was filled with joy because he had come to believe in God—he and his whole family.

³⁵When daylight came, the magistrates sent their officers to the jailer with the order: "Release those men." ³⁶The jailer told Paul, "The magistrates have ordered that you and Silas be released. Now you are free to leave. Go in peace."

³⁷But Paul said to the officers, "They beat us publicly without a trial even though we are Roman citizens. They threw us into prison and now they want us to go quietly? No way! They need to come themselves and escort us out."

³⁸The officers went back and reported this to the magistrates and when they heard that Paul and Silas were Roman citizens, they were afraid.⁷⁴² ³⁹They came and apologised to them and having escorted them from the prison they requested that they leave the city. ⁴⁰After Paul and Silas left the prison they went to Lydia's house and met with the *Christian* brothers and encouraged them. Then they left.

Paul and Silas go to Thessalonica

17 ¹When *Paul and Silas* had passed through the *cities of* Amphipolis and Apollonia, they⁷⁴³ came to Thessalonica where there was a Jewish synagogue. ²As usual Paul went into the synagogue and on three consecutive Sabbath days he reasoned with those *in attendance* from the Scriptures. ³He explained and proved that the Messiah had to suffer and rise from the dead saying, "This Jesus I am preaching to you about is the Messiah." ⁴Some of the Jews were persuaded and joined Paul and Silas as did a large number of God-fearing Greeks and also many prominent women as well.

⁵But the *unbelieving* Jews were jealous so they rounded up some bad characters from the marketplace and formed a mob and started a riot in the city. The *unbelieving* Jews and the mob attacked Jason's house in search of Paul and Silas in order to bring them out into the public. ⁶But when they did not find them, they dragged Jason and some other *Christian* brothers before the city officials shouting, "These men who have caused trouble all over the world have now come here ⁷and Jason has welcomed them into his house. They are all defying Caesar's decrees saying that there is another king—Jesus." ⁸When the

---

742　The Roman officials were afraid because severe penalties were often placed upon those who violated the rights of Roman citizens. Paul also enacted his rights as a Roman citizen in Acts 22:25–29. These examples by Paul illustrate the fact that Christians should be able to stand up for their legal rights when those rights are being trampled upon by the government. Submitting to the authorities does not mean submitting to their illegal acts.

743　Notice now the third person plural pronoun indicating that Luke is not included. Luke more than likely remained behind while Paul and Silas continued on in the journey.

crowd and the city officials heard this there was pandemonium. ⁹The authorities made Jason and the others post bail and then they let them go.

The Bereans believe Paul

¹⁰As soon as night fell the *Christian* brothers sent Paul and Silas away to Berea.⁷⁴⁴ Upon arrival they went straight to the Jewish synagogue. ¹¹In contrast to the Thessalonians, the Bereans were more open-minded for they received the message with great eagerness. They examined the Scriptures every day to see if what Paul was saying was true or not. ¹²Many *of the Jews* believed along with many prominent Greek women and many Greek men.

¹³However when the *unbelieving* Jews of Thessalonica learned that Paul was preaching the word of God at Berea, they went there too and agitated the crowds stirring them up. ¹⁴The brothers immediately sent Paul to the coast but Silas and Timothy stayed in Berea. ¹⁵The men who escorted Paul brought him to Athens and then left with a message from Paul instructing Silas and Timothy to join him as soon as possible.

Paul preaches at the Areopagus in Athens

¹⁶While Paul was waiting for *Silas and Timothy* in Athens, he was greatly distressed to see that the city was full of idols. ¹⁷So he reasoned with the Jews and other worshippers in the synagogue and with those that happened to be in the market place every day. ¹⁸A group of Epicurean and Stoic philosophers began to argue with him. Some of them asked, "What is this gas-bag trying to say?" Others said, "He seems to be advocating for foreign gods." They said this because Paul was preaching the good news about Jesus and the resurrection. ¹⁹Then they took him and brought him to a meeting of the Areopagus⁷⁴⁵ where they said to him, "Tell us about this new teaching that you are presenting. We want to know more? ²⁰You are bringing some strange ideas to our ears and we want to know what it all means." ²¹(As way of explanation—all the Athenians and the foreigners who lived there spent their time doing nothing but talking about and listening to the latest ideas.)

²²Paul then stood up in the meeting of the Areopagus and said, "Men of Athens! I can see that in every way you are very religious. ²³For I have been

---

744   Berea was a small city about 96 km west of Thessalonica in Macedonia north of Mt. Olympus.
745   The Areopagus was 'the hill of Ares'. Ares was the Greek god of war, equivalent to the Roman god Mars. It was on this hill that the Athenian Council met, and for this reason most Bible commentators understand the reference to the Areopagus to be to a meeting of Council rather than to the hill itself. In Athens there were several places where speakers might lecture to the public, and it was the responsibility of this council to hear and pass judgment on those lectures.

walking around and looking very carefully at your objects of worship. I even found an altar with the following description:

TO AN UNKNOWN GOD

But the God you are worshipping as something unknown I am going to tell you exactly who he is.

^{24}"The God who made the universe and everything in it is the Lord of heaven and earth. He does not live in temples built by human hands. ^{25}Furthermore he is not served by human hands as if he needed anything. In fact, he is the one who gives all men life and breath and everything else. ^{26}From one *person* he made every nation of men in order that they would inhabit the whole earth. He fixed beforehand the seasons and the boundaries of the places where they would live. ^{27}God did this so that it would be possible for men to reach out for him and find him. But in saying that he is not far from each one of us. ^{28}For we live and move and have our very existence in him as some of your own poets say, 'We also are his offspring.'

^{29}"Therefore since we are God's offspring, we should not think that the divine is like gold, silver or stone—an image made by man's design and skill. ^{30}In the past God overlooked such ignorance but now he commands all people everywhere to turn to God. ^{31}For he has set a day when he will judge the world with justice by the man he has appointed. He has proved this to all men by raising him from the dead."

^{32}When they heard about the resurrection of the dead some of them mocked him but others said, "We want to hear more from you about this." ^{33}Paul then left them. ^{34}A few of the men became followers of Paul and believed. Among them was Dionysius who was a member of the Areopagus and a woman named Damaris and a number of others as well.

Paul preaches in the city of Corinth

18 ^{1}After this Paul left Athens and went to *the city of* Corinth.[746] ^{2}At Corinth, Paul met a Jew named Aquila. He was from the province of Pontus and he had recently arrived from Italy with his wife Priscilla because of the order from *Emperor* Claudius that all Jews must leave Rome.[747] Paul went to see them ^{3}and because he was a tentmaker as they were, he stayed and worked with them. ^{4}Every Sabbath day he debated in the synagogue in an effort to persuade Jews and Greeks.

^{5}When Silas and Timothy arrived from Macedonia, Paul devoted himself

---

746 A commercial city in Greece known for its sexual immorality.
747 This occurred in AD 49 possibly due to a squabble between Christian Jews and non-Christian Jews.

solely to preaching, testifying to the Jews that Jesus was the Messiah. ⁶However when the Jews opposed Paul and became abusive, he shook out his clothes in protest and said to them, "Your blood be on your own heads! I am clear of any responsibility. From now on I will go to the Gentiles."

⁷Then Paul left the synagogue and went next door to the house of Titus Justus, a worshipper of God. ⁸Crispus, the synagogue ruler, and his entire household believed in the Lord. Many of the Corinthians who heard Paul also believed and were baptised.

⁹One night the Lord spoke to Paul in a vision as follows, "Do not be afraid, keep on speaking, do not be silent. ¹⁰For I am with you, and no one is going to attack and harm you, because I have many people in this city." ¹¹So Paul stayed for a year and a half, teaching them the word of God.

¹²While Gallio was proconsul of Achaia,[748] the *unbelieving* Jews made a concerted attack on Paul and brought him to the judgment seat. ¹³They said, "This man is trying to persuade people to worship God in ways contrary to the law."

¹⁴Just as Paul was about to speak, Gallio said to the Jews, "If you Jews were making a complaint about some wrong or serious crime, it would be reasonable for me to listen to you. ¹⁵But since it involves questions about words and names and your own law then go ahead and see to it yourselves. I am not going to judge such things." ¹⁶So he had them evicted from the judgment seat. ¹⁷Then all the Greeks turned on Sosthenes the synagogue ruler and beat him in front of the judgment seat. But Gallio showed no concern whatever.

Paul returns to Antioch

¹⁸Paul remained in Corinth for some time then he left the *Christian* brothers and set sail for Syria with Priscilla and Aquila. Before he left though, he had his head shaved at Cenchrea[749] because of a vow he had taken *to the Lord*.[750] ¹⁹They arrived at Ephesus where Paul later left Priscilla and Aquila. He himself went into the synagogue and debated with the Jews. ²⁰When they asked him to spend some more time with them, he declined. ²¹However as he was leaving, he promised saying, "I must attend the coming feast in Jerusalem[751] but I will

---

748   Gallio assumed the governorship of Greece around AD 51 and the author of Acts, Luke, has used the correct technical term to describe the office of Gallio. Greece is literally "Achaia", the Roman province that included the most important part of Greece (TH).
749   Cenchrea was the seaport of the city of Corinth.
750   This was probably the Nazarite vow which often ended with the long hair cut off and the shaving of the head. Originally this was a permanent vow but in later times it could be taken for a specific period of time.
751   Most likely the Passover in AD 51 or 52.

come back if it is God's will." Then he set sail again from Ephesus. ²²When Paul landed at Caesarea, he went up⁷⁵² and greeted the church *at Jerusalem* and then went down to Antioch *in Syria*.

²³After spending some time in Antioch, Paul set out from there and travelled from place to place throughout the region of Galatia and Phrygia, strengthening all the followers *of Jesus*.

²⁴Meanwhile a Jew named Apollos, an Alexandrian⁷⁵³ by birth, came to Ephesus. He was an eloquent speaker, with a thorough knowledge of the Scriptures. ²⁵He had been instructed in the way of the Lord, and he spoke with great enthusiasm and taught about Jesus accurately even though he only knew about the baptism of John. ²⁶He began to speak boldly in the synagogue when Priscilla and Aquila invited him to their home. They explained to him the way of God more accurately.

²⁷When Apollos desired to go to the *province of* Achaia, the *Christian* brothers encouraged him and wrote to the followers *of Jesus* there in order that they might welcome him. Upon arrival he was a great help to those who by grace had believed. ²⁸For he powerfully refuted the *unbelieving* Jews in public debate, proving from the Scriptures that Jesus was the Messiah.

Paul returns to Ephesus

19 ¹While Apollos was at Corinth, Paul took the road through the upper regions⁷⁵⁴ and arrived at Ephesus. There he found some followers *of Jesus* ²and asked them, "Did you receive Holy Breath when you believed?" They answered, "No, we have not even heard that there is Holy Breath." ³So Paul asked, "Then what baptism did you receive?" They replied, "John's baptism."

⁴Paul said, "John's baptism was about you changing your ways about your sin. He told people to believe in the one coming after him—Jesus." ⁵Upon hearing this, they were baptised into the name of the Lord Jesus. ⁶When Paul placed his hands on them, the Holy Breath came on them and they spoke in different languages and prophesied. ⁷There were about twelve men in all.

⁸Paul entered the synagogue and spoke boldly there for three months. He debated persuasively about God's reign. ⁹But some of them were stubborn and they refused to believe publicly speaking against the Way.⁷⁵⁵ So Paul left them taking the followers with him and held discussions daily in the lecture hall of

---

752 Jerusalem has an elevation of 785 m above sea level.
753 From the city of Alexandria on the north coast of Egypt.
754 Paul went through the interior land regions of Minor Asia not via the direct route on ship across the Aegean Sea.
755 "The Way" was a technical term for the Christian movement in the 1st century AD.

Tyrannus. ¹⁰This went on for two years, so that all the Jews and Greeks who lived in the province of Asia *Minor* heard the word of the Lord.

The sons of Sceva try to cast out demons

¹¹God performed some very unusual miracles through Paul. ¹²Even handkerchiefs and aprons that had only touched him were taken to the sick and their illnesses were cured and the evil spirits left them.

¹³Some Jewish exorcists were attempting this, invoking the name of the Lord Jesus over those who were possessed by evil spirits saying, "In the name of Jesus whom Paul preaches, I command you to come out." ¹⁴Seven sons of Sceva, a Jewish chief priest, were doing this. ¹⁵Eventually one of the evil spirits answered them saying, "Jesus I know and I know about Paul, but who are you?" ¹⁶Then the man who was possessed by the evil spirit jumped on them and overpowered them all. He attacked them with such force that they ran out of the house naked and bleeding.

¹⁷When this became known to the Jews and the Greeks living in Ephesus, everyone became struck with fear and the name of the Lord Jesus was held in high esteem. ¹⁸Many of those who believed now came and openly confessed their wrong actions. ¹⁹A number of those who had been into the occult gathered their books and burnt them in public. They calculated the value of these books to the sum of 50,000 silver coins. ²⁰Therefore the word of the Lord spread wider and wider and grew ever stronger.

The riot in Ephesus

²¹After all this happened, Paul felt compelled in his spirit[756] to go to Jerusalem via *the provinces of* Macedonia and Achaia saying, "I must visit Rome also." ²²He sent two of his helpers, Timothy and Erastus, to Macedonia while he stayed in the province of Asia *Minor* a little while longer.

²³About that time there arose a great disturbance in the Way. ²⁴A silversmith named Demetrius, who made silver models of the temple of Artemis,[757] was bringing in a huge amount of business for the craftsmen. ²⁵Demetrius called them all together along with workers in related trades and said, "Men, you know we receive a good income from this business. ²⁶And you see and hear how this Paul has been able to convince and lead astray large numbers of people here in Ephesus and in virtually the whole province of Asia *Minor*. He says that man-made gods are no gods at all. ²⁷There is a danger not only that our business will

---

756 <u>Alt</u>: Paul in the Breath *of God* felt led…
757 Artemis is the Greek equivalent to the Roman 'Diana', the goddess of the hunt, nature and fertility. Her temple was one of the seven wonders of the ancient world.

lose its good name but also that the temple of the great goddess Artemis will be discredited. Furthermore the goddess herself, who is worshipped throughout the province of Asia *Minor* and the world, will be robbed of her greatness and majesty."

²⁸When they heard this they were furious and began shouting, "Great is Artemis of the Ephesians!" ²⁹Soon the whole city was in an uproar. The people seized Gaius and Aristarchus, Paul's travelling companions from Macedonia, and rushed as one man into the theatre.[758] ³⁰Paul wanted to appear before the crowd, but the followers would not let him. ³¹Even some of the provincial officials who were friends of Paul, sent him a message begging him not to appear in the theatre.

³²The whole assembly was in complete confusion. Some were shouting one thing and some were shouting something else. Most of the people did not even know why they were there. ³³The Jews in the crowd pushed Alexander to the front telling him to explain the situation. He motioned for the crowd to be quiet in order that he might make a speech in defence of the Jews.[759] ³⁴But when they realised that he was a Jew, they all shouted in unison for about two hours: "Great is Artemis of the Ephesians."

³⁵The city clerk quietened the crowd and said, "Men of Ephesus. The whole world knows that the city of Ephesus is the guardian of the temple of Artemis and of the stone that fell from heaven,[760] don't they? ³⁶Therefore since these facts are undeniable, you should calm down and not do anything rash. ³⁷You have brought these men here even though they have not robbed temples or blasphemed our goddess. ³⁸Therefore if Demetrius and his fellow craftsmen have a grievance against anybody the courts are in session and there are proconsuls. Let them press charges. ³⁹If there is anything further you want to bring up, it must be settled in a legal assembly. ⁴⁰As it now is, we are in danger of being charged by the *Roman government* with rioting because of today's events. There is no excuse for this uproar and we would not be able to justify it *to them*." ⁴¹After he had said this, he dismissed the assembly.

758　The theatre in Ephesus was quite large-its seating capacity has been estimated at almost 26,000. The theatre in ancient Roman and Greek times was a large open air semi-circular stadium with tiered seating and a performance stage used for drama, dance and music and also for public events.

759　Since the Jews were known as opponents of idolatry, and since any riot in favour of Artemis might be interpreted by some people as an indirect attack upon the Jews, it may be that Alexander was put forward by Jews in order to explain to the crowd that the Jews themselves were not responsible for what had happened (TH).

760　The reference is to a stone, perhaps a fragment of a meteorite, which fell from the sky which the people of Ephesus looked upon as being the sacred representation of their goddess Artemis. The worship of a sacred stone thought as falling from the sky is not uncommon among religions (TH).

Paul goes to Macedonia and Greece

20 ¹When the uproar had finished, Paul sent for the followers *of Jesus* and after encouraging them, he said good-bye and set out for Macedonia. ²He travelled through that area and spoke many words of encouragement to the people and finally arrived in Greece. ³He stayed in Greece for three months. But because he discovered that the *unbelieving* Jews were plotting to kill him just as he was about to set sail for Syria, he decided to go back *inland* through Macedonia. ⁴He was accompanied by Sopater, son of Pyrrhus from Berea, Aristarchus and Secundus from Thessalonica, Gaius from Derbe, Timothy also and Tychicus and Trophimus from the province of Asia.⁷⁶¹ ⁵All these men went on ahead and waited for us at Troas. ⁶But we sailed from Philippi after the Feast of Unleavened Bread, and five days later we joined the others at Troas, where we stayed for seven days.

Paul raises Eutychus from the dead at Troas

⁷On the first day of the week of Sabbaths,⁷⁶² we gathered together to break bread. Paul spoke to the people and because he intended to leave the next day, he kept on talking until midnight. ⁸There were many lamps in the upstairs room where we were meeting. ⁹A young man named Eutychus was seated in a window and he was falling into a deep sleep as Paul kept talking for a long time. When he was sound asleep, he fell to the ground from the third story. When they picked him up they found that he was dead. ¹⁰Paul went down and stretched himself down over him and put his arms around him. Paul said, "Don't be alarmed, he is alive!" ¹¹Then Paul went back upstairs and broke bread and ate. He kept on talking until dawn and then he departed. ¹²The people took the young man home alive and were very relieved.

Paul's journey from Troas to Miletus

¹³We went on ahead to the ship and sailed for Assos, where we intended to take Paul aboard. He had made this arrangement because he was going there by land.⁷⁶³ ¹⁴When he met us at Assos, we took him aboard and sailed on to

---

761   This is the Roman province of Asia Minor (Turkey) not the modern-day continent of Asia.
762   Note here that Sabbaths is plural in the Greek. (The typical translation 'first day of the week' is incorrect). This was the annual Feast of Firstfruits, which was the Sunday after Passover, and was the first day of the 50-day (seven Sabbaths) countdown to Pentecost (Lev. 23:10–11, 15–16). Cf. Matt. 28:1, John 20:1, Acts 20:7, 1 Cor. 16:2. Since the new calendar day begins at sundown on the biblical calendar, this was Saturday evening just after sunset since probably Paul kept talking from after sundown until midnight.
763   It was a 32 km walk across the peninsula from Troas to Assos along a well paved road. It would have taken considerably longer to travel by ship around the coast. The famous temple of Athena was located in Assos.

Mitylene, *the main city on the island of Lesbos.* ¹⁵The next day we set sail from there and passed by *the island of* Kios. The day after that we crossed over to *the island of* Samos and on the following day we arrived at Miletus.⁷⁶⁴ ¹⁶Paul had decided to sail past Ephesus to avoid spending time in the province of Asia *Minor* for he was in a hurry to get to Jerusalem, if possible, by the day of Pentecost.

Paul farewells the Ephesian elders

¹⁷When Paul was at Miletus, he sent a message to the elders of the church at Ephesus for them to come. ¹⁸When they arrived, he said to them, "You are aware of the kind of life I lived the whole time I was with you, from the very first day that I arrived in the province of Asia Minor. ¹⁹I served the Lord in all humility and with many tears and trials because of the plots of the *unbelieving* Jews. ²⁰You know that I did not hold back anything that would be profitable to you but have taught you publicly and from house to house. ²¹I have revealed to both Jews and Greeks that they must turn from their sins to God and have faith in our Lord Jesus.

²²"I am now heading on to Jerusalem even though I don't know what will happen to me there as I am being compelled by the Breath *of God to do so.* ²³I only know that in every city the Holy Breath warns me that prison and troubles are waiting for me. ²⁴However, I am not worried about my life. *The only thing that concerns me is that* I might finish the race and complete the work that I have received from the Lord Jesus to testify about the gospel of God's grace.

²⁵"Now look, I know that none of you to whom I have preached about the reign of God, will ever see me again. ²⁶Therefore, I plainly state to you today that if any of you should be lost,⁷⁶⁵ then I should not be held responsible. ²⁷For I have not held back in informing you of all that God plans to do. ²⁸So make sure to keep watch over yourselves and all the flock of which the Holy Breath has made you overseers and shepherd the church of God which he bought with his own blood. ²⁹I know that after I leave, savage wolves will come in among you and will not spare the flock. ³⁰Even some from your own group of men will arise and distort the truth in order to draw followers. ³¹So be on your guard! Remember that for three years I never stopped warning each of you night and day with tears.

³²"Now I commit you to God and to the word of his grace, which can build

---

764 Miletus was a city and port about 48 km south of Ephesus.
765 Literally the Greek says here that Paul is innocent of the blood of all men probably meaning he is innocent of their death. The intent here is that if they should fall away after he has departed and thereby suffer eternal death because of their unbelief then he is not responsible because he has done his job.

you up and give you an inheritance together with all those who have been made holy. ³³I have not coveted anyone's silver or gold or clothing. ³⁴You yourselves know that these hands of mine have supplied the needs of myself and those with me. ³⁵Everything that I have done, I have shown you that by this kind of hard work we must help the weak, remembering the words of the Lord Jesus himself who said, 'It is more blessed to give than to receive.'"

³⁶When Paul had said this he knelt down with all of them and prayed. ³⁷They all wept as they embraced and kissed⁷⁶⁶ him good-bye. ³⁸What grieved the men most was his statement that they would never see him again. Then they went with him to the ship *to see him off.*

Paul sets out for Jerusalem

21 ¹After we had parted company from the men we put out to sea and sailed straight to the *island of* Cos. The next day we went to Rhodes and from there to the *port of* Patara. ²We changed ships and crossed over to Phoenicia. ³After sighting *the island of* Cyprus and passing to the south of it, we sailed on to Syria. We landed at Tyre where the cargo was unloaded from the ship. ⁴Having found the followers *of Jesus* there, we stayed with them for seven days. The Breath *of God* was telling them to urge Paul not to go on to Jerusalem. ⁵However when our time was up, we left and continued on our way and everyone together with their wives and children went with us out of the city where we knelt down to pray on the beach. ⁶Then we said our good-byes and boarded the ship while everyone else went back home.

⁷Having left Tyre, we ended our voyage at Ptolemais where we greeted the *Christian* brothers and stayed with them for a day. ⁸The next day we left and when we reached Caesarea⁷⁶⁷ we stayed at the house of Philip the evangelist who was one of the Seven.⁷⁶⁸ ⁹Philip had four unmarried daughters who were in the habit of prophesying.

¹⁰After we had been with Philip for a number of days, a prophet named Agabus came down from *the highlands of* Judea.⁷⁶⁹ ¹¹Agabus approached us, took Paul's belt, and tied his own hands and feet with it saying, "The Holy Breath says, 'In this way the Jews of Jerusalem will bind the owner of this belt and will hand him over to the Gentiles.'"

¹²When we had all heard this, we and the people there pleaded with Paul

---

766 This is the type of kissing even done nowadays in the Middle East on the cheeks.
767 The distance from Ptolemais to Caesarea was 64 km, more than one day's walk.
768 Luke is referring to the fact that Philip was one of the seven men who had been chosen to serve in Jerusalem (Acts 6:1–6).
769 Probably a reference to Jerusalem.

not to go up to Jerusalem. ¹³Then Paul answered saying, "Why are you crying like this and breaking my heart? I am more than willing and ready to not only be bound but also to die in Jerusalem for the name of the Lord Jesus." ¹⁴When Paul would not be dissuaded, we gave up and said, "The Lord's will be done."

Paul arrives at Jerusalem

¹⁵After this, we got ready and went up to Jerusalem. ¹⁶Some of the followers from Caesarea went with us and brought us to the home of Mnason, where we were to stay. He was a man from Cyprus and was one of the early followers *of Christ*.

¹⁷When we arrived at Jerusalem, the *Christian* brothers gave us a warm welcome. ¹⁸The next day Paul and the rest of us went to see James and all the elders of the church were present. ¹⁹Paul greeted them and reported in detail what God had done among the Gentiles through his ministry.

²⁰When they heard this they praised God. Then they said to Paul, "Brother, you can see that many thousands of Jews have believed and all of them are zealous for the Law. ²¹They have been told that you teach all the Jews who live among the Gentiles to turn away from the *Law of* Moses, instructing them not to circumcise their children or live according to our customs. ²²So what shall we do? They will certainly hear that you have come. ²³Therefore do what we tell you to do as follows: There are four men with us who have made a vow. ²⁴Take these men, join in with them in their purification rites and pay their expenses so that they can have their heads shaved. Then everyone will know there is no truth in these reports about you. But they will know that you yourself are in agreement with the keeping of the Law *of Moses*. ²⁵As for the Gentile believers, we have written to them about our decision that they should abstain from food sacrificed to idols, from blood, from the meat of strangled animals and from sexual immorality."

²⁶The next day Paul took the men and purified himself along with them. Then he went to the temple to give notice of the date when the days of purification would end and when the offering would be made for each of them.

Paul arrested at the temple

²⁷When the seven days were nearly over, some *unbelieving* Jews from the province of Asia *Minor* saw Paul at the temple. They stirred up the whole crowd and arrested him. ²⁸They shouted out loud saying, "Men of Israel, help us! This is the man who teaches all men everywhere against our people and our Law and this place. And also, he has brought Greeks into the temple area and defiled this

holy place."[770] [29](They had previously seen Trophimus the Ephesian in the city with Paul and had assumed that Paul had brought him into the temple area.)

[30]The whole city was in utter chaos and people came running from everywhere. The *mob* seized Paul and dragged him from the temple and immediately the *temple* gates were *shut behind him*.[771] [31]While the *mob* were trying to kill him, news reached the commander of the Roman cohort[772] that the whole city was in an uproar. [32]At once the commander took some centurions and soldiers and rushed down[773] to the crowd. When the mob saw the commander and his soldiers, they stopped beating Paul.

[33]The commander came up and arrested him and ordered him to be bound with two chains. Then he asked who he was and what he had done. [34]Some in the crowd shouted one thing and some another, and since the commander could not get a straight answer because of the noise, he ordered that Paul be taken into the soldier's barracks.[774] [35]When Paul reached the steps,[775] the violence of the mob was so great he had to be carried by the soldiers. [36]The crowd that followed were shouting, "Kill him!"

Paul speaks to the crowd in his defence

[37]As the soldiers were about to take Paul into the barracks, he asked the commander, "May I say something to you?"

"You know Greek then?" he replied. [38]"Aren't you the Egyptian who started a revolt and led four thousand men of the assassins out into the desert some time ago?"

[39]Paul answered, "I am a Jew, from Tarsus in the province of Cilicia, a fairly important city. Please let me speak to the people."

[40]Having received the commander's permission, Paul stood on the steps and motioned for the crowd to be silent. When they were all silent, he spoke to them in Hebrew saying,

22 [1]"Brothers and fathers, listen to me now in my defence." [2]When they heard him speaking to them in the Hebrew language, they became very quiet.

---

770   Gentiles were not allowed into the temple area proper and it was an offence punishable by death. There was even an inscription placed over the entrance warning that Gentiles took their lives into their own hands if they went beyond that point. A stone was found with this very inscription in 1871 by French archaeologist, Charles Simon Clermont-Ganneau.
771   This was to stop Paul from re-entering the temple for refuge.
772   A Roman military unit consisting of about 600 soldiers.
773   This indicates that the Roman military garrison was situated higher than the temple area proving that it looked down on the temple. The implication is that the temple was located in the lower City of David not the traditional temple mount as adhered to by current Jewish clerics.
774   Fort Antonia.
775   These are the southern steps which were uncovered in 1967 by archaeologist Benjamin Mazar. Cf. https://madainproject.com/southern_steps

Then Paul said, ³"I am a Jew, born in Tarsus of Cilicia, but I was brought up in this city. I was thoroughly trained under the teaching of Gamaliel in the Law of our fathers and was just as zealous for God as any of you are here today. ⁴In fact, I persecuted the followers of this Way to their death. I arrested both men and women and threw them into prison. ⁵The high priest and the whole council of elders can testify of this. I even obtained letters from them to give to their *Jewish* brothers in Damascus and went there to bring these people back as prisoners to Jerusalem in order to be punished.

Paul tells how he became a Christian
(Acts 9:3–19, 26:12–18)

⁶"About midday as I was approaching Damascus, suddenly a bright light from the sky flashed around me. ⁷I fell to the ground and heard a voice say to me, 'Saul! Saul! Why are you persecuting me?' ⁸I replied by asking, 'Who are you Lord?' Then the voice said, 'I am Jesus the Nazarene whom you are persecuting.' ⁹Those with me saw the light but they did not understand the voice of the one speaking to me.

¹⁰"And so I asked, 'Lord, what shall I do?' The Lord said, 'Get up and go into Damascus. There you will be told everything that has been assigned for you to do.' ¹¹Those with me led me by the hand into Damascus because the brilliance of the light had blinded me.

¹²"A man named Ananias came to see me. He was a devout observer of the Law and highly respected by all the Jews living there. ¹³He stood beside me and said, 'Brother Saul, receive your sight! At that very moment I was able to see him.'

¹⁴"Then Ananias said, 'The God of our ancestors has chosen you to know his will and to see the Righteous One and to hear words from his mouth. ¹⁵This is because you will be his witness to all men of what you have seen and heard. ¹⁶So what are you waiting for? Get up, be baptised and wash away your sins having called upon his name.'

The Lord sends Paul to preach to the Gentiles

¹⁷"When I returned to Jerusalem and was praying at the temple, I fell into a trance ¹⁸and I saw the Lord speaking and saying to me, 'Quick, leave Jerusalem immediately because they will not accept your testimony about me.' ¹⁹I replied, 'Lord, these men know very well that I went from one synagogue to another to imprison and beat those who believe in you. ²⁰Furthermore as the blood of your martyr Stephen was being shed, I was standing there in agreement guarding the

clothes of those who were killing him.' ²¹Then the Lord said to me, 'Go, I will send you far away to the Gentiles.'"

Paul informs the Roman soldiers that he is a Roman citizen

²²The crowd listened to Paul until he had said this then they raised their voices and shouted, "Rid the earth of him! He's not fit to live!"

²³As they were shouting and throwing off their coats and flinging dust in the air, ²⁴the commander ordered Paul to be taken into the barracks and he told them to flog him and question him in order to find out why the people were shouting at him like this. ²⁵As they were stretching out Paul to flog him, he said to the centurion standing there, "Is it legal for you to flog a Roman citizen who hasn't even been found guilty?"

²⁶When the centurion heard this, he went to the commander and reported it. He asked, "What are you going to do as this man is a Roman citizen?"

²⁷The commander went to Paul and asked, "Tell me, are you a Roman citizen?" Paul answered, "Yes I am." ²⁸Then the commander said, "I had to pay a big price for my citizenship." Paul responded, "But I was born a citizen."

²⁹Those who were about to question him withdrew immediately. The commander himself was afraid when he realised that he had put Paul who was a Roman citizen, in chains.

Paul appears before the Sanhedrin

³⁰The next day the commander released Paul because he wanted to find out exactly why Paul was being accused by the Jews. So he ordered the chief priests and all the Sanhedrin to assemble and then brought Paul and had him stand before them.

23
¹Paul looked straight at the Sanhedrin and said, "My Jewish brothers, I have lived before God with a clear conscience to this very day." ²At this the high priest Ananias ordered those standing near Paul to strike him on the mouth. ³Then Paul said to him, "God will strike you, you whitewashed wall! You sit there in judgment of me according to the Law, yet you yourself are violating the Law by commanding me to be struck!"

⁴Those who were standing near Paul said, "How dare you insult God's high priest!" ⁵Paul replied, "Brothers, I did not realise that he was the high priest for it is written, 'Do not speak evil about the ruler of your people.'"[776]

⁶Then Paul, knowing that some of them were Sadducees and the other

---

[776] It is possible that Paul is being sarcastic here because surely he would know who the high priest was and even the dress that he would be wearing. Another possibility is that Paul had poor eyesight (his thorn in the flesh) and couldn't see him very well.

Pharisees, called out in the Sanhedrin, "Brothers, I am a Pharisee, the son of a Pharisee. I stand on trial because of my hope in the resurrection of the dead." ⁷When he said this, a heated argument between the Pharisees and the Sadducees broke out and the assembly was divided. ⁸(The Sadducees believe that there is no resurrection, and that there are neither angels nor spirits, but the Pharisees believe in all three.)

⁹There was a huge raucous and some of the scribes who were Pharisees stood up and protested strongly saying, "We find nothing wrong with this man. What if a spirit or an angel has spoken to him?" ¹⁰The dispute became so violent that the commander was afraid that Paul would be torn to pieces by them. He ordered the soldiers to go down and take him away from them by force and bring him to the barracks.

¹¹The following night the Lord stood near Paul and said, *"Take courage! As you have testified about me in Jerusalem, so you must also testify about me in Rome."*⁷⁷⁷

The plot to kill Paul

¹²The next morning the Judeans banded together and swore an oath with each other that they would not eat or drink until they had killed Paul. ¹³More than forty men were involved in this plot. ¹⁴Then they went to the chief priests and elders and said, "We have taken a solemn oath not to eat anything until we have killed Paul. ¹⁵So then you and the Sanhedrin must petition the commander to bring him before you pretending to require more accurate information about his case. But we will be ready to kill him before he ever gets here."

¹⁶But when Paul's nephew—his sister's son—heard about this plot, he went into the barracks and told Paul.

¹⁷Then Paul called one of the centurions and said, "Take this young man to the commander, he has something to tell him." ¹⁸So he took him to the commander. The centurion said to the commander, "Paul, the prisoner, sent for me and asked me to bring this young man to you because he has something to tell you."

¹⁹The commander took the young man by the hand, drew him aside and asked, "What is it you want to tell me?"

²⁰He said, "The Jewish *leaders* have agreed to ask you to bring Paul before the

---

777 Rome is always the goal of Acts and the goal is never far from sight. Luke's nearly exclusive interest in the march of the gospel from Jerusalem to Rome is curious because surely the gospel went to many other regions. Yet Luke deliberately chose to narrate the progress from Jerusalem to Rome which testifies to the ultimate passing of salvation from Jew to Gentile. (Smith R, *The Eschatology of the Book of Acts* (1958), p. 82).

Sanhedrin tomorrow pretending to want to know more accurate information about him. [21]You must not be persuaded by them because there will be more than forty men waiting in ambush for him. They have taken an oath not to eat or drink until they have killed him. They are ready now to do it waiting for you to agree to their request."

[22]The commander dismissed the young man and cautioned him saying, "Do not tell anyone about what you have told me."

Paul is transferred to Caesarea on the coast

[23]The commander then called two of his centurions and ordered them as follows, "Go and prepare two hundred *foot* soldiers, seventy cavalry and two hundred spearmen ready to leave for Caesarea[778] at 9 pm tonight. [24]Provide some mounts[779] for Paul so that he may be taken safely to Governor Felix."

[25]The commander wrote the following letter:

[26]Claudius Lysias,

To His Excellency, Governor Felix:

Greetings.

[27]This man was seized by the Jews and they were about to kill him but I came with my soldiers and rescued him for I came to learn that he is a Roman citizen. [28]I wanted to know why they were accusing him so I took him down to their Sanhedrin.[780] [29]I found that the accusation had to do with questions regarding their Law but there was no actual charge against him that deserved death or imprisonment. [30]When I was informed of a plot to be carried out against the man, I sent him to you at once. I also ordered his accusers to present their case against him to you.

[31]Therefore the soldiers carried out their orders and took Paul with them during the night and brought him as far as *the city of* Antipatris.[781] [32]The next day

---

778   Caesarea Maritima.
779   Could either be mules or horses. The Greek is not specific.
780   Interesting point here that they lead him down to the Sanhedrin located in the Jewish temple perhaps indicating that the Roman fort was at a higher elevation than the temple. This would support my favoured theory that the Jewish temple was located in the old city of David and not the traditional so called temple mount near the Western Wall.
781   Antipatris was a city built during the 1st century BC by Herod the Great, who named it in honour of his father, Antipater. It was situated on the Roman road from Caesarea Maritima to Jerusalem, north

they let the cavalry continue on with him, while they returned to the barracks in Jerusalem.[782] ³³When they arrived in Caesarea, they delivered the letter to the governor and handed Paul over to him. ³⁴The governor read the letter and asked what province he was from. Upon learning that Paul was from *the province of* Cilicia, the *Governor Felix* said to him, ³⁵"I will hear your court case when your accusers get here." Then he ordered that Paul be kept under guard in Herod's palace.[783]

Paul's trial before Governor Felix

24 ¹Five days later the high priest Ananias went down to Caesarea with some of the elders and an orator named Tertullus.[784] They brought their charges against Paul before the governor. ²When Paul was called in, Tertullus presented his case before Felix saying, "We have enjoyed a long period of peace under you and your foresight has brought about reforms in this nation. ³Everywhere and in every way, most excellent Felix, we thank you with a deep gratitude. ⁴But in order not to weary you any further, I would request that you be kind enough to hear us briefly.

⁵"We have found this man to be a troublemaker, stirring up riots among the Jews all over the world. He is a ringleader of the Nazarene sect.[785] ⁶Once before he even tried to desecrate the temple so we seized him. We planned on judging him according to our law ⁷but the commander Lysias came and violently took him away from us. ⁸By examining him yourself you will be able to learn the truth about all these charges we are bringing against him." ⁹The Jews joined in on the accusations asserting that these things were true.

Paul defends himself before Felix

¹⁰When the governor motioned for Paul to speak he replied, "I know that you have been a judge over this nation for many years so I am happy to make my defence before you. ¹¹You can verify for yourself that it was no more than twelve days ago that I went up to Jerusalem in order to worship. ¹²Those accusing me did not find me arguing with anyone at the temple or stirring up a crowd in the synagogues or anyone else in the city. ¹³Furthermore they cannot prove to you the charges they are now making against me. ¹⁴However, I admit that I worship the God of our fathers as a follower of the Way, which they call a sect. But I also believe everything that is

---

of the city of Lydda where the road turned eastwards towards Jerusalem.

782   Since the road from Antipatris to Caesarea was in predominantly Gentile territory, and Paul would no longer have needed such a large guard to protect him (TH).

783   Herod the Great had several palaces including Jerusalem, Masada, Herodium and Caesarea Maritima, in this verse. Herod Antipas, his son, was the Herod who had John the Baptist beheaded and questioned Jesus when he was visiting Jerusalem at the Passover in AD 30 (Luke 23:7–11).

784   Tertullus was more than likely a specialist in Roman law rather than Jewish Law.

785   I.e. Christianity.

written in the Law and the Prophets. ¹⁵I have the same hope in God as these men, that there will be a resurrection of both the righteous and the wicked. ¹⁶So I strive always to keep a clear conscience before both God and man.

¹⁷"After being away *from Jerusalem* for several years, I came back to my people and brought gifts for the poor and to offer sacrifices *to God*. ¹⁸And so when *the Jews* saw me in the temple courts I had already completed my purification rites. There was no crowd with me nor any disturbance. ¹⁹However some of the Jews from Asia were there and they should be the ones here who should bring any charges if they have anything against me. ²⁰Also the Jews who are here should state what crime they found in me when I stood before the Sanhedrin. ²¹Unless it is for this one thing that I shouted out as I stood in their presence: 'It is concerning the resurrection of the dead that I am on trial before you today.'"

²²Then Felix, who was well acquainted with the Way, adjourned the proceedings and said *to Paul*, "When Lysias the commander comes, I will decide your case." ²³He ordered the centurion to keep Paul under guard but to give him some freedom and permit his friends to attend to his needs.

Paul speaks with Felix and his wife Drusilla

²⁴Several days later Felix came with his wife Drusilla who was a Jewess. He sent for Paul and listened to him as he spoke about faith in Christ Jesus. ²⁵As Paul talked about righteousness, self-control and the judgment to come, Felix became afraid and said, "That's enough for now! You may leave. When I find it convenient I will send for you." ²⁶However at the same time Felix was hoping that Paul would offer him a bribe. So he sent for him frequently and talked with him.

²⁷When two years had passed, Felix was succeeded by Porcius Festus. But because Felix wanted to grant a favour to the Jews, he left Paul in prison.

Paul's trial before Festus

25 ¹Three days after arriving in the province, Festus went up to Jerusalem from Caesarea. ²The chief priests and Jewish leaders appeared before him and presented the charges against Paul. ³As a favour to them they begged Festus to have Paul transferred to Jerusalem as they were preparing an ambush along the way in order to kill him. ⁴Festus answered, "Paul is being held at Caesarea and I am going there myself soon. ⁵Therefore if he has done anything wrong then let some of your leaders come down with me and press charges against the man there."

⁶After spending eight or ten days with them *in Jerusalem*, he went down to Caesarea. The next day *Festus* sat on the judgment seat and ordered for Paul to be brought before him. ⁷When Paul appeared, the Jews who had travelled down

from Jerusalem stood around him, bringing many serious charges against him that they were not able to prove.

⁸Then Paul made his defence by saying, "I have done nothing wrong against the Law of the Jews or against the temple or against Caesar."

⁹However Festus wished to do the Jews a favour and so said to Paul, "Are you willing to go up to Jerusalem and stand trial before me there on these charges?"

¹⁰Paul answered, "I am at this very moment standing before the judgment seat of Caesar where I should be tried. I have not done anything wrong to the Jews as you yourself very well know. ¹¹If, however, I am guilty of doing anything deserving of death, I do not refuse to die. But if the charges brought against me by these Jews are not true then no one has the right to hand me over to them. I appeal to Caesar!

¹²After Festus had discussed this with his council, he declared, "You have appealed to Caesar. To Caesar you will go!"

Festus consults King Agrippa about Paul

¹³Some time later King Agrippa[786] and *his sister* Bernice arrived at Caesarea to welcome Festus *to the area*. ¹⁴Since they spent many days there, Festus discussed Paul's case with the king. He said, "There is a man here whom Felix left as a prisoner. ¹⁵When I went to Jerusalem, the Jewish chief priests and elders brought charges against him and asked that he be condemned.

¹⁶"I told them that it is not the Roman custom to hand over any man before he has faced his accusers and has had an opportunity to defend himself against their charges.

¹⁷"When they came here with me, I did not delay the case but I sat down on the judgment seat the next day and ordered that the man be brought in. ¹⁸When his accusers stood up to speak, they did not charge him with any evil crimes I was suspecting. ¹⁹Instead, they had some points of dispute with him about their own religion and about a dead man named Jesus who Paul claimed was alive. ²⁰I was at a complete loss how to investigate such matters so I asked him if he would be willing to go to Jerusalem and stand trial there on these things. ²¹But when Paul appealed for the Emperor to make a decision, I ordered him to be held until I could send him to Caesar *in Rome*."

---

786   This is Agrippa II, son of Herod Agrippa I. He actually ruled over only a few small territories north of Palestine, though he did have the authority, given him by the Roman Emperor, to appoint the Jewish High Priest. Bernice, the oldest daughter of Herod Agrippa I, was not without her faults. She had been given by her father to his brother as a wife, and when he died she lived for a while in the home of her own brother, Agrippa II. After this she married the king of Cilicia, but then left him and came back to live with her brother. Later she became the mistress of the Roman general Titus, who felt it necessary to leave her when he was made Emperor (TH).

²²Then Agrippa said to Festus, "I would like to hear from this man myself." Festus replied, "Tomorrow you will hear from him."

Paul stands before King Agrippa

²³The next day Agrippa and Bernice came with great pomp and ceremony and entered the auditorium with the high ranking officers and leading men of the city. At the command of Festus, Paul was brought in. ²⁴Festus said, "King Agrippa, and all who are present with us, can you see this man standing here? The whole Jewish community has pleaded with me about him in Jerusalem and here in Caesarea. They shouted out that he must not live any longer. ²⁵I found that he had done nothing deserving of death but because he made his appeal to the Emperor I decided to send him to Rome. ²⁶But I do not have anything valid to write to our Majesty about him. Therefore I have brought him before all of you and especially before you King Agrippa so that as a result of this investigation I may have something valid to write. ²⁷For I think it is unreasonable to send a prisoner without specific charges."

Paul answers King Agrippa

26 ¹Then Agrippa said to Paul, "You have permission to speak for yourself."

So Paul motioned with his hand and began his defence by saying, ²"King Agrippa, I consider it a privilege to stand before you here today as I make my defence against all the accusations of the Jews ³and especially so because you are well acquainted with all the Jewish customs and *theological* issues. Therefore I beg you to listen to me patiently.

⁴"All the Jews know the manner in which I have lived since childhood, from the beginning of my life in my own country and also in Jerusalem. ⁵They have known me for a long time and can testify, if they are willing, that I have lived as a member of the strictest sect of our religion, the Pharisees. ⁶However today I am on trial because of my hope in what God has promised our ancestors. ⁷This is the very promise our twelve tribes are hoping to see fulfilled as they persistently and eagerly serve God day and night. O king, it is because of this hope that the Jews are accusing me. ⁸Why should any of you think it is unbelievable that God raises the dead back to life?

⁹"I too was convinced that I should be doing everything possible to oppose the name of Jesus the Nazarene. ¹⁰And that is exactly what I did in Jerusalem. On the authority of the chief priests I put many of God's holy people in prison and when they were put to death I voted in favour of this.⁷⁸⁷ ¹¹Many times I went

---

787 This seems to indicate that Paul was a member of the Sanhedrin (Jewish council of seventy) and voted for Christians to be put to death.

from synagogue to synagogue to have them punished and I tried to force them to blaspheme.[788] In my obsession against them, I even went to foreign cities to persecute them.

Paul testifies about his conversion to Christianity

[12]"On one such occasion I was on my way to Damascus with the authority and approval of the chief priests. [13]About midday, O king, as I was on the road, I saw a light from heaven, brighter than the sun, shining all around me and those travelling with me. [14]We all fell to the ground, and I heard a voice saying to me in Hebrew, 'Saul, Saul, why are you persecuting me? You are only hurting yourself by kicking against the *cattle* prod.'[789]

[15]"Then I asked, 'Who are you Lord?'

"The Lord replied, 'I am Jesus, whom you are persecuting. [16]Now get up and stand on your feet. I have appeared to you to appoint you as *my* servant. You are to testify about what you have seen today and what I will show you in the future. [17]I will rescue you from your own people and from the Gentiles. I am sending you to them [18]to open their eyes and turn them from darkness to light and from the power of Satan to God, so that they may receive forgiveness of sins and a place among those who have been made holy by having faith in me.'

Paul tells King Agrippa about his ministry work

[19]"So then King Agrippa, I did not disobey the vision I had from heaven. [20]First up I went to the people of Damascus, then to those in Jerusalem and in all Judea and I went to the Gentiles also. I preached that they must turn to God and prove it by their actions. [21]And that is the reason why the Jews seized me in the temple courts and tried to kill me. [22]However God has helped me to this very day and so I stand here and testify to small and great alike. I am saying nothing that goes beyond what the prophets and Moses said would happen. [23]They said that the Messiah would suffer and as the first who was to rise from the dead, he would proclaim light to his own people and to the Gentiles."

Paul appeals to King Agrippa to believe in Jesus

[24]At this point Festus interrupted as Paul was defending himself and shouted, "Paul, you are out of your mind. Your great learning is driving you mad."

[25]Paul replied, "I am not mad, Most Excellent Festus. What I am saying is true and reasonable. [26]The king is familiar with these things and I can speak

---

788   Probably Paul tried to make them curse Jesus and deny their faith.
789   This is referring to when a sharp-pointed stick (goad or prod) is used by a person goading an ox or a donkey while working.

freely to him. I am sure that none of this has escaped his notice because it was not done in a corner. ²⁷King Agrippa, do you believe in the prophets? I know that you do believe."

²⁸Then Agrippa said to Paul, "Do you think that in such a short time you can persuade me to become a Christian?"

²⁹Paul replied, "Whether it is a short time or long time, my prayer is that not only you but everyone who is listening to me today may become what I am, except of course to be chained *as a prisoner.*"⁷⁹⁰

³⁰The king rose along with the governor and Bernice and those sitting with them. ³¹They departed the room, and while talking with one another, they said, "This man has not done anything worthy of death or imprisonment."

³²Agrippa said to Festus, "This man could have been set free if he had not appealed to Caesar."

Paul is taken to Rome

27 ¹When it was decided that we⁷⁹¹ would sail for Italy, Paul and some other prisoners were handed over to a centurion. This centurion was named Julius and he belonged to the Imperial Regiment.⁷⁹² ²We boarded a ship from the *city* of Adramyttium which was scheduled to sail for various ports along the coast of the province of Asia *Minor*. We put out to sea along with Aristarchus, a Macedonian from Thessalonica, who was with us.

³The next day we landed at Sidon and Julius in kindness to Paul, allowed him to go to and see his friends so they might provide for his needs. ⁴From Sidon we put out to sea again and passed to the sheltered side of the island of Cyprus because the wind was against us. ⁵When we had sailed across the open sea off the coast of Cilicia and Pamphylia, we landed at Myra in Lycia. ⁶The centurion found an Alexandrian ship sailing for Italy and put us on board. ⁷However we made slow headway for many days and had difficulty in arriving at the *city* of Cnidus. When the wind did not allow us to hold our course, we sailed to the sheltered *southern* side of the island of Crete passing by Cape Salmone. ⁸We kept close to the coast and with great difficulty came to a place called Fair Havens,⁷⁹³ near the city of Lasea.

⁹Many days had passed and much time lost and sailing had already become dangerous because the Fast⁷⁹⁴ had already gone. Therefore Paul began warning

---

790 In other words, Paul would like everyone to become a Christian like he is.
791 Luke, the author of Acts, is including himself in this statement.
792 This army regiment was under the command of Rome and belonged to the Emperor.
793 A safe harbour for ships.
794 This refers to the Day of Atonement when all Jewish men were required to fast for 24 hours on the tenth day of the seventh month. If this was the year AD 59 as some suggest then the Day of

them saying, ¹⁰"Men, I can envisage our voyage being disastrous bringing great loss to ship and cargo and also endangering our lives." ¹¹But the centurion was persuaded by the captain and owner of the ship rather than what Paul was saying. ¹²Since the harbour was unsuitable to spend the winter in, the majority decided that we should keep sailing, hoping to reach Phoenix and spend the winter there. This was a harbour in Crete, facing both southwestern and northwest.

The storm

¹³When a gentle breeze from the south began to blow, the men saw their opportunity *to get to Phoenix* so they raised anchor and sailed close to the shore of Crete. ¹⁴But before long, a wind with cyclonic force called the "northeaster," swept down the island. ¹⁵The ship was caught in the storm and could not head into the wind so we gave up trying and allowed the ship to be driven along. ¹⁶As we passed to the sheltered side of a small island called Cauda, we barely managed to secure the lifeboat *being towed behind*.⁷⁹⁵ ¹⁷When the men had hoisted the lifeboat aboard, they passed ropes under the ship itself to try and hold it together. Fearing that they would run aground on the sandbars of Syrtis, they lowered the sea anchor and let the ship be driven along *by the wind*. ¹⁸We took such a beating from the storm that the next day they began to throw the cargo overboard. ¹⁹On the third day they even threw much of the ship's gear overboard with their own hands. ²⁰Neither the sun nor the stars were seen for many days and the storm continued raging until finally we gave up all hope of being saved.

²¹After the men had gone for a long time without food, Paul stood up in front of them and said, "Men, you should have taken my advice not to sail from Crete. If you had then you would have spared yourselves this damage and loss. ²²But now I urge you to keep up your courage because not one of you will be lost, only the ship will be destroyed. ²³Last night an angel of the God who I belong to and whom I serve stood beside me and said, ²⁴'Paul, do not be afraid. You are to stand trial before Caesar and God has graciously spared the lives of all those who are sailing with you.' ²⁵So take courage men, for I have faith in God that it will happen exactly as he told me. ²⁶Nevertheless, we must run aground on some island."

The shipwreck

²⁷On the fourteenth night we were still being driven across the Adriatric Sea,

---

Atonement would have fallen on the 5th October.

795 A small boat or skiff was normally kept aboard a larger ship and used by sailors in placing anchors, repairing the ship, or saving lives in the case of storms. The crew was barely able to hoist the small lifeboat aboard the ship such was the strength of the storm.

when about midnight the sailors sensed they were approaching land. ²⁸They took depth measurements and found that the water was 20 fathoms.⁷⁹⁶ A short time later they measured the depth again and the water was around 15 fathoms. ²⁹Fearing that we would be dashed against the rocks, the *sailors* dropped four anchors from the rear of the ship and prayed for daylight. ³⁰The sailors attempted to escape from the ship by letting the lifeboat down into the sea. They were pretending they were going to lower some anchors at the front of the ship. ³¹Then Paul said to the centurion and the soldiers, "Unless these men stay with the ship, you cannot be saved." ³²So the soldiers cut the ropes that held the lifeboat and let it fall away.

³³Just before dawn Paul urged them all to have something to eat as follows, "For the last fourteen days, you have been anxiously waiting and have had no food. You haven't eaten anything. ³⁴So I strongly urge you to eat something in order to survive. Not one of you will lose a single hair from your heads." ³⁵After he had said this, he took some bread and gave thanks to God in front of them all. Then he broke it and began to eat. ³⁶They were all encouraged and they also ate some food. ³⁷Altogether there were 276 of us on board. ³⁸After everyone had eaten as much as they wanted, they lightened the ship by dumping its cargo of wheat into the sea.

³⁹When daylight broke, they did not recognise the land but they saw a bay with a sandy beach where they decided to try and run the ship aground. ⁴⁰Cutting loose the anchors, they left them behind in the sea and at the same time untied the ropes that held the rudders. Then they hoisted the foresail to the wind and made for the beach. ⁴¹But the ship struck a sandbar and ran aground. The bow stuck fast in the sand and would not move while the stern was broken to pieces by the force of the waves.

⁴²The soldiers planned to kill the prisoners to prevent any of them swimming away and escaping. ⁴³But the centurion wanted to spare Paul's life and kept them from carrying out their plans. Instead he ordered those who could swim to jump overboard first and make it to land. ⁴⁴The rest were to get there on planks or on pieces of the ship. In this way everyone was brought safely to land.

---

796   They dropped a plummet line which is literally using a rope with a lead weight attached to it in order to measure the depth of water. A fathom was a standard measurement of ocean depth equivalent to six feet and is measured as being the distance between the two hands of outstretched arms.

Paul stays on the island of Malta for three months

28 ¹Once we arrived safely on shore, we found out that the island was called Malta.⁷⁹⁷ ²The indigenous people on the island were very friendly towards us and they built a fire and welcomed us all because it was raining and cold.⁷⁹⁸ ³Paul had been gathering firewood and as he placed it on the fire, a poisonous snake, driven out by the heat of the fire, attached itself onto his hand. ⁴When the people saw the snake hanging from his hand, they said to each other, "This man must be a murderer for even though he escaped from the sea, the *goddess that demands justice* has not allowed him to live. ⁵However Paul shook the snake off into the fire and suffered no ill effects. ⁶The people expected him to swell up or suddenly drop dead, but after waiting a long time and seeing nothing happen to him, they changed their minds and said he was a god.

⁷Now not very far from that place there was a property belonging to the chief of the island named Publius. He welcomed us and for three days we were his guests showing great hospitality. ⁸His father happened to be very sick in bed, suffering from fever and dysentery. Paul went in to see him and after prayer, placed his hands on him and healed him. ⁹When this had happened, the rest of the sick people on the island came and were being cured. ¹⁰The people honoured us in many ways and when we were ready to set sail, they gave us all the supplies that we needed.

Paul arrives in Rome

¹¹After three months we put out to sea in an Alexandrian ship that had spent winter on the island. The ship had the figurehead of the Twin Brothers—the gods Castor and Pollux.⁷⁹⁹ ¹²We then arrived at *the port of* Syracuse⁸⁰⁰ and stayed there for three days. ¹³From there we sailed on till arriving at Rhegium and the next day the south wind came up and on the following day we reached *the harbour of* Puteoli.⁸⁰¹ ¹⁴There we found some *Christian* brothers who invited us to spend a week with them. And so this is how we got to Rome. ¹⁵Other brothers *in Rome* had heard that we were coming and they travelled as far as the Forum of Appius and the Three Taverns to meet us. At the sight of these men Paul thanked God and was encouraged. ¹⁶When we got to Rome, Paul was allowed to live by himself, with a soldier to guard him.

---

797 Malta is a small island off the southern coast of Sicily meaning that the ship had travelled over 900 km across the open sea in two weeks in a westerly direction from Crete.
798 Obviously the storm must have still been ongoing.
799 Castor and Pollux were gods often worshipped by sailors being associated with the constellation Gemini. An image of the Twin gods were carved into the principal beam at the prow of the ship.
800 A port on the south-eastern coast of Sicily.
801 Puteoli was a natural harbour near the city of Naples.

Paul preaches in Rome under guard

[17] Three days later Paul called together the leaders of the Jews. When they had assembled, Paul addressed them saying, "I, my brothers, have done nothing against our people or against the customs of our ancestors, yet I was arrested in Jerusalem and handed over to the Romans. [18] They cross-examined me and wanted to release me because I was not guilty of any crime deserving death. [19] But when the Jews objected, I was forced to appeal to Caesar not that I had any charge to bring against my own people or anything. [20] For this reason I have asked to see you and talk it over with you. It is only because of the hope of Israel[802] that I am bound with this chain."

[21] They replied, "We have not received any letters from Judea concerning you and none of the brothers who have come from there has reported or said anything bad about you. [22] But we would like to hear what you think about this sect for we know that people everywhere have been speaking against it."

[23] So they arranged to meet Paul on a certain day, and came in even larger numbers to the place where he was staying. From morning till evening Paul explained and told them about God's *coming* reign and tried to convince them about Jesus from the Law of Moses and from the writings of the prophets. [24] And some of them were convinced by what he said, but others did not believe. [25] They disagreed amongst themselves and began leaving once Paul had said this one thing, "The Holy Breath spoke the truth to your ancestors when he said through Isaiah the prophet,

> [26] "'Isaiah, go to this people and say, "You are always hearing but never listening. You will always be looking but will never really see it or understand it."
> [27] For this people's heart has become calloused and they can hardly hear with their ears.
> They have shut their eyes.
> Otherwise they would be able to see with their eyes and hear with their ears and understand in their hearts.
> And if they turn to me I would heal them.'
>
> Isaiah 6:9–10.

[28] "Therefore I want you all to know that God's salvation has been sent to

---

802 Cf. Acts 23:6, 24:21. The hope of Israel is either the hope of resurrection or the Jewish Messianic hope. Commentators say both.

the Gentiles and indeed they will listen!" [²⁹After Paul had said these things, the Jews left, arguing vigorously among themselves.]⁸⁰³

³⁰For two whole years Paul stayed there in Rome in his own rented house and welcomed all who came to see him. ³¹He preached about the *coming* reign of God and taught about the Lord Jesus Christ with boldness and without hindrance.

---

803 Many modern translations omit this verse.

ROMANS

Introduction

Paul wrote his letter to the believers in Rome around AD 57. It is one of the heaviest books theologically and explains subjects such as justification and sanctification and how to be righteous in God's eyes. Paul had been ministering in the gospel for 25 years by the time he wrote this letter to the Roman church and he felt that they needed correcting and teaching especially in regards to the relationship between the Jews and Gentiles and the issues of sin, faith and grace.

The letter also details the gifts of the Holy Spirit and the downward regression of mankind ending up in homosexuality. The Romans road includes how a man progresses from sin (Rom. 3:23) towards salvation (Rom. 6:23) and thereafter the battle with sin that we all have (Rom. 7:21) when the Holy Spirit indwells new believers. Paul also talks about heavy subjects such as election, predestination and the redemption of Israel in the final days (Rom. 11:26).

1 ¹I Paul, a servant of Christ Jesus *have written this letter*. I was called to be an apostle and was set apart for the gospel of God. ²This gospel was promised beforehand through his prophets in the Holy Scriptures. ³This gospel is about *God's* Son. With respect to his human nature, Jesus was a descendant of David. ⁴However God powerfully demonstrated that Jesus Christ our Lord was the *very* Son of God when he was resurrected from the dead by means of his Holy Breath. ⁵Through him and for the benefit of Christ's name, God graciously allowed us *Jews* to become apostles so that people of all nations might come to faith and obey *the gospel*. ⁶You *people of Rome* also are amongst those whom *God* has called to belong to Jesus Christ.

⁷*I am writing this letter* to all of you in Rome who are loved by God and called to be his holy people:

Grace and peace to you all from God our Father and from the Lord Jesus Christ.

Paul wants to visit Rome

⁸First of all, let me give thanks to God through Jesus Christ for all of you *at Rome* because of your faith that is being reported all over the world. ⁹I serve God with my whole heart in preaching the gospel of his Son and God is my witness how constantly I remember you ¹⁰in my prayers at all times. I pray by God's will the way may be opened for me to finally come to you now.

¹¹I am really looking forward to seeing you all so that I might be able to impart to you some spiritual gift to make you strong. ¹²What I am meaning is that we will both be encouraged in our faith *by my visit*. ¹³I want you to know *Christian* brothers that I had planned many times to come to you but I have been prevented from doing so until now. I have wanted to come in order that I might see some *spiritual* fruit among you just as I have had among other Gentiles.

¹⁴I have an obligation *to preach* to both Greeks and barbarians, to the wise and the foolish. ¹⁵That is why I am so eager to preach the gospel also to you who are in Rome.

¹⁶I am not ashamed of the gospel because it is the power of God for the salvation of everyone who believes. Firstly it is for the Jew and then for the Gentile. ¹⁷For the gospel reveals how God allows a person to become righteous. It is by faith from start to finish just as it is written *in the Scriptures*,

"The righteous man lives by faith."

Habakkuk 2:4

The downward spiral of mankind

¹⁸God has revealed how, in his anger, he will judge men because of all of their godlessness and wickedness. They have been suppressing the truth about God from being known by means of their wickedness. ¹⁹*God punishes* them because he made it clear to them the truth about himself. ²⁰For since the creation of the world, God's invisible qualities—his eternal power and divine nature, have been clearly seen. These invisible qualities are known from what has been made *by God*. Therefore men are without excuse.

²¹For even though they have known about God, they neither glorified him as being God nor have they given thanks to him. Instead, their thinking has become purposeless and their foolish hearts are darkened. ²²Although they claim to be wise, they have become fools ²³and instead of worshipping the immortal God, they worship images made to look like mortal man and birds and animals and reptiles.

²⁴Therefore God has given them over to the sinful desires of their hearts to sexual depravity so that they do shameful things with each other.[804] ²⁵They have exchanged the truth of God for the lie and worshipped and served created things rather than the Creator himself who is to be forever praised.[805] Amen.

²⁶Because of this, God has given them over to shameful lust. Even females are exchanging their natural *sexual* relations for unnatural ones. ²⁷In the same way males are also abandoning natural sexual relations with females and are inflamed with lust for each other. Males are committing indecent acts with other males and so they bring upon themselves the due penalty for their *sexual* perversion.

²⁸Furthermore, since men are not thinking that it is worthwhile to retain the knowledge of God, God has given them over to a depraved mind so that they do what they shouldn't be doing. ²⁹They are filled with every kind of wickedness, evil, greed and depravity. They are full of envy, murder, strife, deceit and malice. They are gossips, ³⁰slanderers, God-haters, insulting of one another, proud and boastful. They invent different ways of doing evil and they disobey their parents. ³¹Furthermore they are foolish, faithless, heartless and ruthless. ³²Although they know God's right verdict that those who live this way deserve death, they continue to do these very things. Not only that, but they also approve of those who make a habit of doing these things as well.

---

804   I.e. God has deserted mankind and let them go their own way especially in these last days.
805   Cf. 2 Thess. 2:11.

God will judge all men

2 ¹So my friends, do you pass judgment on others? If you do then you have no excuse. For at whatever point you judge another person, you are passing judgment on yourself because you who pass judgment do the very same things. ²We all know that God's judgment against those who do such things is based on the truth. ³So when you, a mere man, pass judgment on someone else and yet you do the same things, do you think that you will escape God's judgment? ⁴Or perhaps you are just showing contempt for his rich kindness, his tolerance and his patience? Do you not realise that God's kindness should lead you to turn away from your sinfulness?

⁵But instead because of your stubbornness and your refusal to turn away, you are storing up more and more punishment against yourself for the day of God's great anger. This is the day when his right judgment will be revealed. ⁶God will repay each person according to what he has done.[806] ⁷To those *people* who seek glory, honour and immortality by striving to do good, God will give eternal life to them. ⁸But for those people who are self-seeking and who reject the truth and follow evil, there will be only the wrath and anger *of God*. ⁹There will be trouble and distress for every human being who does evil, firstly for the Jew and then for the Gentile. ¹⁰But there will be glory, honour and peace for everyone who does good, firstly for the Jew and then for the Gentile. ¹¹For God does not show any favouritism.

¹²The *Gentiles* who sin and do not have the Law *of Moses* will perish even though they don't have the Law. And the *Jews* who sin and do have the Law will be judged by the Law. ¹³For it is not those who just hear the Law who are declared righteous but it is those who actually obey the Law who will be declared righteous. ¹⁴When the Gentiles, who have never had the Law *of Moses*, do by very nature the things required by the Law, they show a kind of mindfulness of the Law. ¹⁵*Their behaviour* demonstrates that the requirements of the Law are written on their hearts. Their consciences also bear testimony to this fact since their thoughts at times accuse them and at other times their thoughts may excuse them.

¹⁶So all this will take place on that day when God will judge the secrets of all men through Jesus Christ as my gospel so declares.

The Jews and the Law of Moses

¹⁷Now to you who call yourselves Jews. You depend on the Law and even boast about your relationship with God. ¹⁸You know his will and because you

---

[806] The Greek here has the sense that God will reward according to what a person has done whilst on earth whether good or bad.

are instructed by the Law you know how to choose what is best. ¹⁹You have convinced yourselves that you are guides for the *spiritually* blind and like a light for those who are in darkness. ²⁰You *have convinced yourselves that you* are instructors of the foolish and teachers of immature infants *as it were* because you have the Law—the very embodiment of knowledge and truth. ²¹You *Jews* teach others so why do you not also teach yourselves? You preach against stealing so why do you steal? ²²You say that people should not commit adultery so why do you commit adultery. You detest *pagan* idols so why do you plunder *their* temples? ²³You boast about the Law so why do you dishonour God by breaking the Law? ²⁴As it is written, "God's name is blasphemed among the Gentiles because of you *Jews.*"⁸⁰⁷

²⁵Circumcision has value if you observe the Law but if you break the Law you might as well never have been circumcised. ²⁶Therefore if *Gentiles* who are not circumcised, keep the Law's requirements, then will not God regard them as though they are circumcised? ²⁷As a result, the *Gentiles* who are not physically circumcised and yet they keep the Law will bring judgment upon you *Jews* who have the written code and are physically circumcised and the reason is that you break the Law.

²⁸A person is not a Jew by appearance, nor is circumcision merely outward and physical. ²⁹No, a person is a Jew if he is one inwardly and circumcision is a change of heart produced by *God's* Breath not by merely obeying the letter of the law. That person will be praised by God, not by man.

What advantage is there in being a Jew?

3 ¹Are there any advantages of being a Jew? Is there any value in circumcision? ²Absolutely! There are many advantages. The first one is that God has entrusted his message to the *Jews.*

³But what if some of them have not been loyal? Does that mean God will not be loyal in return? ⁴Absolutely not! All humans are liars when compared to God who always keeps his word for as it is written *in the Scriptures* about him,

> "When you speak you will be proved right that you never lie.
> When you are accused in court you will always win."
>
> Psalm 51:4

⁵But if our wrong ways show all the more clearly God's right ways, can we argue that God is not justified⁸⁰⁸ in bringing his wrath upon us. (I am using

---

807   Cf. Isa. 52:5 (LXX) where the words "because of you" do not appear.
808   My use of the word "justified" here and in v. 8 is limited to its everyday use in the modern vernacular meaning 'deserved' or 'fair' and not the narrower theological term of justification meaning a

human logic.) ⁶Absolutely not! If that were the case then God could not judge the world. ⁷Suppose someone argues that their lies bring more honour to God by promoting his truthfulness then why should I be judged as a sinner? ⁸Why don't we just say, "Let's do evil that good may result"? Some people are accusing me of this very thing. God's judgment of them is justified.

No one on earth is righteous before God

⁹So therefore what conclusion can we come to? Are we *Jews* any better off *than the Gentiles*? Absolutely not! I have already said that Jews and Gentiles alike all live under *the influence of* sin. ¹⁰As the Scriptures say,

> "There is no one *on earth* who is righteous before God, not even one.
> ¹¹There is no one *on earth* who *really* understands and no one who seeks God.
> ¹²Everyone *on earth* has turned away from God and together everyone has gone wrong. There is no one on earth who does what is right, not even one *person*.
>
> Psalm 14:1–3
>
> ¹³"Men's throats are like open graves in that their mouths constantly speak deadly lies."
>
> Psalm 5:9
>
> "Their lips produce poison like the viper."[809]
>
> Psalm 140:3
>
> ¹⁴"Their mouths are full of cursing and bitterness."
>
> Psalm 10:7
>
> ¹⁵"Their feet are quick to shed blood.
> ¹⁶Their lives are characterised by ruin and misery.
> ¹⁷They are ignorant of how to follow the way that leads to peace."
>
> Isaiah 59:7–8
>
> ¹⁸"They do not fear God."
>
> Psalm 36:1

¹⁹Now we know that everything in the Law applies to the *Jews* who live under the Law in order to silence every excuse and to make the whole earth accountable to God. ²⁰Therefore no one will be declared righteous in *God's* sight by observing the Law. Rather the purpose of the Law is to bring about a consciousness of sin.

---

    declaration of righteousness.
809   Vipers are a group of snakes known for their long fangs and venomous bite including the rattlesnake.

Righteousness is only gained through faith

[21] But now in these days there is a way in which a person can gain righteousness and it is not through the Law *of Moses*. This *new* way was confirmed by the *Old Testament books of the* Law and Prophets. [22] And this new way of gaining righteousness from God comes through having faith in Jesus Christ—to everyone who believes. There is no difference *between Jew and Gentile,* [23] for all have sinned and fallen short of God's glorious *standard*. [24] And *all people are* declared righteous *by God the same way,* freely by his grace when he set us free through Jesus Christ. [25] God presented *Jesus* as an atoning sacrifice *for the forgiveness of our sins* when we have faith in his blood. He did this to show that what he was doing was right because in the past he was patient and had left everyone's sins unpunished. [26] But in the present time God is declaring *people* to be righteous so that we can see that he is fair and just. He declares *people* to be righteous when they believe in Jesus.

[27] Therefore how can there be any boasting? It is not possible. Why is it not possible to boast? It is because we are not declared righteous by observing the Law but by faith. [28] We hold the view that a person is not declared to be righteous by observing the Law but something quite separate—faith. [29] Is God the God of the Jews only? *Surely you can see* that God is the God of the Gentiles too? [30] The reason being is that there is only one God. He puts the circumcised (*Jews*) right with himself by faith and he puts the uncircumcised (*Gentiles*) right through that same faith. [31] Therefore is it the case that the Law *of Moses* is null and void because of this faith? Absolutely not! Rather, we must uphold the Law.

The example of Abraham and his faith

4 [1] What then did our forefather Abraham[810] discover about being declared righteous? [2] If God considered Abraham righteous because of his works, then he would have something to boast about. But of course, that is not the case. [3] What does the Scripture say? It says,

> "Abraham believed God which was counted as righteousness."
>
> Genesis 15:6

[4] Now, *let's think about this*: When a man works for a wage it is not regarded as a gift but as an obligation. [5] So therefore when a man does not work *for salvation* but he trusts God in being able to put the wicked person right with himself, then

---

810 Abraham was the father or progenitor of the Jewish nation and was looked upon as being acceptable in God's sight. So the reasoning is that if faith was good enough for Abraham then it should be good enough for the Romans and all of us.

that man's faith is regarded as being acceptable. ⁶David says the same thing when he speaks of the man who is blessed because God regards him as being righteous without working for it:

> ⁷"Blessed are they who are forgiven when they wilfully disobey and whose sins are covered.
> ⁸"Blessed is the man whose sin the Lord does not keep account of."
>
> Psalm 32:1–2

⁹Is this blessing only for the circumcised *(Jews)* or is it also for the uncircumcised *(Gentiles)* as well? For I have been saying that God regarded Abraham's faith as being acceptable to gain righteousness. ¹⁰When specifically did God regard Abraham's faith as being acceptable? Was it after he was circumcised or before? It was not after but before! ¹¹Abraham received the mark of circumcision as a sign after he already believed that God had accepted him and regarded him to be righteous. God had accepted Abraham even before he had been circumcised because he believed. ¹²Abraham is the father of the circumcised *(Jews)* not just because they have been *physically* circumcised but also in addition because they walk by faith like our father Abraham had been doing before he was circumcised.

Abraham receives a promise from God

¹³The promise to Abraham and his descendants that they would inherit the world was realised not because Abraham obeyed the Law *of Moses* but it was because Abraham believed and was accepted by God. ¹⁴But let us suppose that those who obey the Law do inherit *the world* then faith means nothing and the promise is worthless. ¹⁵The Law brings about the wrath of God but where there is no law or rules then there is no wilful disobedience.

¹⁶Therefore this promise *of inheritance* comes by faith and not by the Law. This is so that it may be by grace and that it may be guaranteed to all Abraham's descendants. That is, not only those who are under the Law but also to those who have the faith of Abraham. He is the spiritual father of us all, *both Jew and Gentile*. ¹⁷As it is written *about him in the book of Genesis,*

> "I have made you a father of many nations."
>
> Genesis 17:5

He is our father in the sight of God, in whom he believed—this is the God who gives life to the dead and can create something out of nothing.⁸¹¹

---

811   Paul reminds the Romans how powerful and omnipotent God is and that is the God that Abraham

[18]In spite of a seemingly hopeless situation, Abraham believed that he would become the father of many nations just as God had said to him, "You will have many descendants." [19]Abraham was nearing death being about 100 years old but despite this and the fact that Sarah's womb was lifeless, he did not waver in his faith of the promise. [20]*Abraham's* faith in the promise of God did not waver but instead, he was empowered by his faith and gave glory to God. [21]He was fully persuaded that God had the power to do what he had promised. [22]This is why his faith was regarded as being acceptable for righteousness. [23]The words written *in the book of Genesis*, "regarded as being acceptable" were not written for Abraham alone [24]but also for us. God who raised Jesus from the dead will regard us also as being righteous if we believe in him. [25]*Jesus* was sent to his death for our sins and was raised to life so that we could be accepted by God and have a right standing before him.

The benefits of being declared righteous

5 [1]Therefore since God has declared us to be righteous through faith we have peace with God through our Lord Jesus Christ. [2]Since we have believed in Christ we have entered into this environment of grace and we are now experiencing grace. We boast in the hope that one day we will share in God's glory. [3]Not only *do we boast in* that but we also boast about our troubles because we all know that trouble helps us to better endure. [4]And endurance, in turn, is character building and strong character underpins hope. [5]And when we hope, it does not disappoint us because God has poured out his love into our hearts by means of his Holy Breath which he has given to us.

[6]Realise this, that Christ died for the ungodly at the appointed time even while we were still powerless. [7]It is very rare that anyone will die for a righteous man, though for a good man someone might possibly dare to die.[812] [8]However God proves his absolute love for us all in this fact: While we were still sinners, Christ died for us.

[9]Since we have now been declared righteous by the blood *of Jesus*, how much easier will it be to be saved from God's wrath through him? [10]We were once

---

	believed in. This verse is often twisted by 'name it and claim it' preachers that we can speak dead things into existence but clearly the context here is that this is something that only God can do.
812	The sense here is that a good man is a man who is kind and is willing to show love and extend grace to others. An example of a good man is Barnabas in Acts 11:24. In contrast a righteous man is a law-abiding man, one who is more concerned about following the Jewish Law than extending love and grace to others. An example of a righteous man is Joseph, Mary's husband. It follows that a 'good' man would be more highly esteemed over a 'righteous' man who simply follows the rules. Therefore the point is that because a 'good' man would be more highly esteemed there might be the possibility of someone sacrificing himself for such a man. But what Christ has done is completely unheard of in that he died for sinners (v. 8).

enemies of God but our relationship with him has been restored through the death of his Son. Therefore how much more, having been reconciled, shall we be saved through his life? ¹¹Not only that but we are happy because our relationship with God has been restored because of what the Lord Jesus Christ has done.

Death came through Adam but life comes through Christ

¹²Therefore as sin entered into the world through one man and so death entered *the scene* through the sin *of that one man,* we can say that death has come to all of mankind because all have sinned.[813] ¹³For before the Law of Moses was given, sin was in the world. But sin is not taken into account when there is no law. ¹⁴Even though some did not wilfully break a command like Adam did, death still reigned from the time of Adam to the time of Moses.[814]

Adam was a pattern of the one who was to come later. ¹⁵But *the two men are not exactly the same because* the free gift *of God* is not like the trespass of *Adam.* For if the wilful disobedience of one man, *Adam,* caused the many to die how much more is it *true* that the gift that came by the one man, Jesus Christ, will flow through to the many also! ¹⁶Another reason why the gift of God is not like the result of Adam's sin is this: The judgment followed one sin and brought condemnation *to the many* whereas the *one* gift of Jesus Christ followed the many wilful disobediences of man and resulted in man being declared righteous. ¹⁷For if by the wilful disobedience of the one man, *Adam,* death reigned *over all people* through that one man, how much more *is it true that,* through the one man, Jesus Christ, life will reign in those who receive God's abundant provision of grace and the gift of righteousness.

¹⁸As a consequence it follows that just as the one act of wilful disobedience from Adam resulted in condemnation for all men, it so also follows that one righteous act by Jesus has meant that all men can be declared as righteous which brings life. ¹⁹For by through the disobedience of one man, mankind became sinners, but also through the obedience of the one man, mankind will be made righteous.[815]

---

813   Sin has not entered the world because of an inherited sin nature from man to man rather man sins according to his free will. David does not say in Psa. 51:5, "Behold, I was brought forth in iniquity, and in sin did my mother conceive me" (ESV) meaning that he himself was a sinner from birth but rather his mother committed some kind of sin, probably adultery, whilst conceiving David and so was brought forth as an illegitimate child. Many English versions mistranslate Psa. 51:5 including NIV which says, "Surely I was sinful at birth, sinful from the time my mother conceived me." Nowhere does Paul say that Adam's sin was imputed to his descendants rather all are guilty before God because of their own personal sin.

814   The implied conclusion here is that all men were still sinners because they died. Death is the ultimate proof that we are sinners by the logic presented by Paul in this passage.

815   Mankind became sinners because of Adam's sin but through the death of Jesus, mankind has the opportunity to be made right before God.

[20]The Law was introduced so as to increase man's wilful disobedience. But where sin increased, grace increased all the more. [21]So then because sin ruled it meant that all people had to die. But so also grace *now* rules through righteousness meaning that we have eternal life through Jesus Christ our Lord.

We are dead to sin and alive in Christ

6 [1]What are we to say then *about sinning*? Does it mean that we can go on sinning so that grace may increase all the more? [2]Not at all! We have died to sin so how can we live in it any longer? [3]And surely you must realise that when we were joined with Christ Jesus in baptism we were immersed[816] with him in his death? [4]In a sense, we died and were buried with him through baptism so that we may live a new life just as Christ was raised from the dead by the Father's glorious power.

[5]If we have been united with him like this in his death, then we will certainly also be united with him in his resurrection. [6]For we *all* know that our old self was crucified with him so that sin could become ineffective in our physical beings, thereby no longer being slaves to sin. [7]Because anyone who has died has been released from sin.

[8]If then we have died with Christ then we also believe that we will live with him. [9]For we know that since Christ was raised from the dead *by God*, he cannot die again. This is because death no longer has control over him. [10]*Jesus* died once and for all as far as the sin *issue* is concerned. But the life which he now lives he lives for God. [11]Therefore in the same way you should keep regarding yourselves dead to sin but you should see yourselves as being truly alive to God in Christ Jesus.

We are not slaves to sin any longer

[12]Therefore you must not allow sin to reign in your physical bodies any longer and so obey its evil desires. [13]Do not allow any part of your body to sin to be used for evil purposes. But rather allow yourselves to be used by God like as one who has passed from death to life. Allow your body parts to be used for doing what is right. [14]Sin must not be your master any longer because you are not under Law but under grace.

We are obligated to do what is right as Christians

[15]What then does this mean? Does it mean that we should keep sinning since we are not under Law but under grace? Not at all! [16]Do not you *people* realise

---

816   Literally immersion here is 'baptism' in the Greek but the sense here is that we identify or are joined with Christ very closely in his death.

that when you offer yourselves to somebody as a slave that you are actually a slave to the one you are obeying. This applies to whether you are a slave to sin which *ultimately* leads to death or whether you are obeying God which leads to righteousness. ¹⁷But thanks be to God that although you used to be slaves to sin, you have followed with all of your heart the kind of teaching you were subjected to. ¹⁸You have been set free from sin and have become subject to righteousness.

¹⁹Okay, let me use a common example because of the weakness of your *understanding*: Once upon a time, you allowed yourselves to be slaves, as it were, to *sexual* impurity and ever increasing lawlessness. But now you must offer yourselves to be slaves to righteousness which leads to holiness.

²⁰When you were slaves to sin, you were free from the control of righteousness. ²¹So when you did those things that you are now ashamed of, what benefit was that to you? Because as it is, those things only resulted in death! ²²But now that you have been set free from sin and have become slaves to God, the benefit that you reap leads to holiness which in turn leads to eternal life. ²³For the result of a sinful *lifestyle* is *ultimately* death but the gift of God is eternal life in Christ Jesus our Lord.⁸¹⁷

An illustration of the Law using marriage

7 ¹Are you aware *Christian* brothers—for I am speaking to men who know about law—that the law only applies to a man as long as he is still alive? ²For example with marriage, a woman is bound to her husband by the law only as long as he is alive. If her husband dies then she is released from the law as to her marriage. ³Therefore if she decides to go and sleep with another man while her husband is still alive, she will be called a cheat. But if her husband dies, she is released from that law and is not a cheat if she marries another man.

⁴So, my brothers, you also died to the Law through the body of Christ. This is so that you might be joined to another person. This person is the one who was raised from the dead and this is so that we might all be useful in our service for God. ⁵For when we were controlled by the flesh, the desire to sin was stirred up by the Law and so these desires were at work in our bodies which only caused us to die. ⁶But now, we have been released from the Law having died to that which was controlling us so that we can serve in a new spiritual way and not in the old way with the written code.

---

817 Many see this well-known verse as applying to non-Christians but the context is that Paul was addressing newly baptised Christians. So the intent here is that Paul was urging the Roman Christians not to go back to their old lifestyle as it will result in death and a loss of salvation.

The internal battle we all have with sin

⁷Well then, *because of all that I have said about the Law what* shall we say? Is the Law sinful? Absolutely not! *The fact is,* I would not have even known what sin was except through the Law. I would not have known what coveting really was if the Law had not said, "Do not covet." ⁸But the situation is that sin seized the opportunity that the commandment gave and it resulted in me having every kind of covetous desire. For if there is no law, sin has no power. ⁹Once upon a time I was alive yet not confronted by the Law. But when rules came, sin sprang to life and I died. ¹⁰I discovered that the very rule that was intended to bring life actually brought death.[818] ¹¹Sin seized its opportunity and deceived me and used the commandment to kill me.

¹²So then, the Law *of Moses* itself is holy and each commandment is holy, righteous and good. ¹³Does this then mean that the Law which is good caused me to die? Absolutely not! But rather sin caused me to die using that which is good—the Law, in order that sin might be recognised for what it actually is—sin. In other words, through the commandment, we see that sin is really sinful.

¹⁴We all know that the Law is spiritual but I am very human. In fact, I am sold-out to sin and am a slave to it. ¹⁵I do not understand why I do what I do. For the thing is that what I really want to do, I do not do it. And the thing that I really hate doing I find myself doing it. ¹⁶So if I know that I am doing the *wrong* thing I am really agreeing that the Law is right. ¹⁷So it is not really me who is doing the wrong thing but sin that lives in me *that is doing the wrong thing*. ¹⁸I know that nothing good lives in me, that is, in my flesh. For even though I have the desire to do what is good, I do not seem to be able to carry it out. ¹⁹I want to be able to do what is good but I am not doing it. I don't want to do evil but I keep doing it anyway. ²⁰So then if I am doing what I don't really want to do it is no longer me who is doing it but it is sin living in me that does it.

²¹So I find the following principle at work *in my life*: When I want to do what is good, evil is right there beside me. ²²For in my heart of hearts, I delight in the law of God, ²³but the thing is that I see another power at work in my body. It is at war with my mind thereby making me a prisoner of sin which is at work within my body. ²⁴Aargh! What a miserable man I am! Who will rescue me from this body of death? ²⁵I truly thank God through Jesus Christ our Lord.

So then, to sum up, I myself in my mind am a slave to God's law, but in the flesh, I am a slave to sin.

---

818   Cf. Luke 10:28.

Living according to the Holy Breath

8 ¹*The conclusion of this whole matter is that God* therefore does not now condemn those who are in Christ Jesus. ²This is because in Christ Jesus the law of the Breath *of God* that brings life has set me free from the law of sin and death. ³The Law *of Moses* was unable *to save us* because of the weakness of the flesh. But God was able to *save us* by sending his own Son in human form to be a sin offering thereby in the process condemning sin in sinful man and doing away with sin. ⁴This was so that the righteous requirements of the Law could be fully met in us, who do not live according to the flesh but according to *God's* Breath.

⁵Those who are controlled by the fleshly nature think about the things of the flesh but those who are controlled by the spiritual nature think about the things of the Holy Breath. ⁶The mind of sinful man *ultimately* results in death but the mind that is controlled by the Breath results in life and peace. ⁷The sinful mind is hostile to God. It does not submit to God's law nor is it possible. ⁸Those people who live according to *the* flesh are not pleasing to God.

⁹You, however, are not controlled by *the* flesh but by *his* Breath if indeed *the* Breath of God lives in you. If anyone does not have *the* Breath of Christ then he does not belong to Christ. ¹⁰Even though your body is dying because of sin, if Christ is in you then you have life-giving breath because you have been made righteous. ¹¹And if the Breath of the one who raised Jesus from the dead is living in you then *this same God* who raised Christ from the dead will also give life to your mortal bodies. He will do this through his Breath in you.

¹²Therefore, *Christian* brothers, we have an obligation but it is not to live according to the flesh. ¹³For if you live according to the flesh you will die but if by *God's* Breath you keep putting to death the misdeeds of the body, then you will live. ¹⁴For all those who are led by God's Breath, these are sons of God. ¹⁵For you have not received a spirit[819] of slavery that leads to fear but instead God has given you his Breath when he adopted you as his sons. You now call him, "Abba,[820] my Father." ¹⁶The Breath *of God* itself confirms with our breath—our spirit, that we are God's children. ¹⁷Now if we are his children then we are in fact heirs.[821] We are heirs and co-heirs with Christ. But if we are to share in his glory then we must also share in his sufferings too.

---

819 I.e. breath.
820 "Abba" is Aramaic language meaning father.
821 The question here is heirs of what? As children of God and descendants of Abraham by faith then we also inherit the Promised Land because of the Abrahamic Covenant (Gen. 17:8).

The future glory that awaits us

¹⁸I am absolutely certain that the sufferings that we are experiencing at this present time are not even worth comparing with the glory that he will reveal to us later. ¹⁹All of creation is waiting with eager anticipation for God's sons to be revealed. ²⁰For the creation was subjected to frustration not willingly but because it was God who decided it. Yet despite this, there was hope ²¹that the creation itself will be liberated from its bondage to decay and share in the glorious freedom with the children of God.

²²For we have observed that the whole of creation has been groaning as it were in the pains of childbirth right up to the present time.[822] ²³Not only that but we *as believers* who have received the Breath *of God*, the first-fruit of what is to come, we ourselves also groan inwardly as we wait eagerly for God to *fully* adopt us as his sons and to set us free with *new* bodies. ²⁴For we were saved with this exact same hope. But a hope that can be readily seen is not really hope at all because who hopes for something that they already have? *Nobody!* ²⁵But *in contrast* if we hope for what we do not yet have then we make sure that we wait for it with patience.

²⁶Similarly, the Breath *of God* helps us in our weakness for we do not know what we should pray for. The Breath *of God* intercedes for us with groans which no words can express. ²⁷And the One who searches our hearts knows the intent of the Breath because it intercedes for the holy people of God.

²⁸And we have observed that in all things God works with those who love him for the good. (Those who love him are those who have been called according to his plan.) ²⁹For those whom God previously knew,[823] he decided beforehand to fashion *their bodies* to be like that of his Son. In this way, his Son would be the first[824] among many brothers raised from the dead. ³⁰And those whom he decided beforehand *to be like his Son*, he also called and those whom he called, he also declared them to be righteous and those whom he declared to be righteous, he also gave them glory.

---

822   The creation both animate and inanimate has been undergoing suffering and physical consequences because of the sin of mankind.

823   This refers to people that God had known in previous times like Abraham and David. We are not to read this passage in a Calvinistic sense in that God has foreknowledge and determines something before it exists. Of course God does have foreknowledge but this is not the sense here. The meaning here is simply to have known someone previously. In v. 28–31 Paul is making an argument based on historical figures like Abraham whom God knew, that the predetermined plan was to give them new physical bodies like Jesus Christ who was the first to be resurrected with a new body. Furthermore Paul outlines the process involved for them from calling to justification to allowing them to share in the glory in the end. I believe this has nothing to do with Paul writing a short excursus on a general theology of salvation such as election and predestination for the individual.

824   Cf. Rev. 1:5

Nothing can separate us from God's love if we are in Christ

³¹What then shall we conclude concerning these things? If God is for us, who can be against us?⁸²⁵ ³²God did not spare his very own Son but he gave him up for all of us. He gave us his Son therefore will he not graciously give us all things? ³³Who will be able to bring any accusation against the chosen ones⁸²⁶ of God? Nobody *obviously* because God is the one who declares them to be righteous. ³⁴Who then is there who will condemn these *chosen ones*? Not Christ Jesus who died for them. More than that even—he was raised to life and is at the right hand of God and is pleading our case before him.

³⁵Who then can separate us from the love of Christ? What about the trouble *that we go through* or hardships *that we face* or persecution or famine or poverty or danger or a violent death? ³⁶As it is written,

> "For your sake, we are facing death all day long.
> We are seen merely as being sheep to be slaughtered."
>
> Psalm 44:22

³⁷But in all these *troubles of life* we have complete victory through him who loved us. ³⁸For I have become convinced that neither death nor life, nor angels, nor rulers,⁸²⁷ neither present nor future *circumstances,* nor any powers, ³⁹neither height nor depth, nor anything else in all creation, will be able to separate us from the love of God that is in Christ Jesus our Lord.⁸²⁸

God's chosen people—Israel

9 ¹I speak the truth in Christ—I am not lying and my conscience and Holy Breath confirm this ²how grieved I am and how the pain in my heart does not leave me ³⁻⁴for my people, my own flesh and blood, the people of Israel. How I wish that I myself was cursed and cut off from Christ for their sake for they

---

825   All opposition to God's holy people will eventually come to nothing not that there won't be opposition in the meantime especially as we move towards the final seven years tribulation period.
826   Here the Greek word is 'elect' in the plural which I believe is the correct way to see election by seeing us as chosen in a corporate body sense. God sees us as his holy group of people but only if we remain in Christ and we complete our faith journey with him until the very end. But in the meantime we are known collectively as the 'elect'. It's like a label encompassing all those who are in Christ. Of course some choose to reject Christ during this life and become apostate and fall away. They would then no longer be a part of the elect.
827   Principalities (KJV), demons (NIV). These are not earthly rulers.
828   Notice that all the things listed in vv. 38–39 are external influences that we have no control over. External forces cannot cause us to be separated from God or to lose our salvation however sin as the result of the internal influence of our own evil desires and sin can cause us to fall away (Jam. 1:14–15). The key is in the last phrase, "in Christ". If one chooses to remain "in Christ" then it is impossible for that person to become separated from God or lose his or her salvation.

are the adopted sons *of God*.[829] He revealed his glory to them, he made his covenants with them, they received the Law, they worshipped in his temple and *they received God's* promises. ⁵The patriarchs, *Abraham, Isaac and Jacob* are their ancestors and Christ can be humanly traced as one of them. May God who is over all people, be forever praised. Amen.

⁶I am not saying that God's word has failed *in terms of its promises about Israel*. For not everyone who is *physically* descended from Israel are *true* Israelites. ⁷And furthermore just because they might be *physical* descendants of Abraham does not mean that they are actually Abraham's children. On the contrary, God said *to Abraham*, "the only descendants that count are those through Isaac." ⁸In other words, it is not the natural children who are God's children, but it is only those whom God promised who are considered to be descendants. ⁹For this is how the promise was stated *to Abraham*: "At the right time I will return and Sarah will have a son."

¹⁰And here's something else. Rebekah gave birth to two children and they had the same father, Isaac. ¹¹⁻¹²Yet, before the twins were born or had done anything good or bad, she was told by God that the older one would serve the younger one. This was purely God's call and not anything that they did. It was in accordance with his plan. ¹³This is just as it is written, "Jacob I loved but Esau I hated."[830]

¹⁴What then can we say? Is God unfair? Absolutely not! ¹⁵For God said to Moses,

> "I will have mercy on whom I will have mercy and I will have compassion
>   on whom I will have compassion."
>
> Exodus 33:19

¹⁶Therefore it[831] does not depend on man's desire or effort but on God's mercy.

¹⁷For the Scriptures say to Pharaoh, "I raised you up for this very purpose,

---

829 Paul was willing to be separated from God in hell for his people which shows the extent of his love for his tribe so that they might be saved.

830 Cf. Mal. 1:2-3. It is important to realise that this was written by Malachi long after Jacob and Esau had become nations not before they were born. It does not mean that Jacob was elected to salvation whilst Esau was rejected before the boys were born thus supporting a Calvinistic election or predestination doctrine but rather it was a comment about the nations that they had become.

831 In the Greek it simply says 'it' and so the question becomes, "what is Paul referring back to?" The context makes it clear that Paul is referring back to v. 11 where it is talking about God's plan to use Jacob and not Esau and that he chooses whom he wants to for his purposes in fulfilling his promise to Abraham to bless all nations. He chose Isaac over Ishmael, Jacob over Esau and he has chosen to use the Gentile churches since AD 70 for the last 1960 years or so whilst Israel has been set aside for a time of punishment.

that I might show my power in you and that my name might be proclaimed in all the earth." ¹⁸Therefore God has mercy on whom he wants to have mercy on and he hardens the hearts of those he wants to harden.

¹⁹Yet one of you will say to me, "Then why does God still blame anyone? For who can resist his will?" ²⁰But *my response is,* "Who are you, man, to talk back to God? Can what is created say to him who creates, 'Why did you make me like this?'" ²¹Doesn't the potter have the right to make out of the same lump of clay some pottery for noble purposes and some for common use?

²²But what if God wants to demonstrate his anger and make his power known? He endured with great patience the objects of his anger who are prepared for destruction.⁸³² ²³He wanted to do this so as to make the riches of his glory known to the objects of his mercy who were prepared in advance for glory.⁸³³ ²⁴That is us, whom he also called, not only from the Jews but also from the Gentiles.

²⁵As it says in the book of Hosea,

> "I will call them 'my people' who are not my people and I will call her 'my loved one' who is not my loved one."⁸³⁴

Hosea 2:23

²⁶and,

> "At the very location where I said to them, 'You are not my people,' they will be called, 'sons of the living God.'"⁸³⁵

Hosea 1:10

²⁷Isaiah cries out on behalf of Israel,

> "Even though the number of the Israelites is like the sand on the seashore, only a *small* remnant will be saved.
> ²⁸"For the Lord will carry out his sentence on the earth without delay and sooner than expected."

---

832 The mistake here I believe is to individualise the objects of his anger as being those individuals who reject the gospel and consequently go to eternal destruction in hell. Seeing as this whole passage is talking about God's chosen people, Israel, perhaps a better and more accurate way to see the objects of his anger as being Israel. In other words God has been very patient with Israel but they were being prepared for destruction as a nation which was ultimately fulfilled in AD 70.

833 Just as the objects of his anger is Israel, the objects of his mercy is the church taken from both Jew and Gentile alike (v. 24). We live in the church age, approximately 2000 years (two days – Hos. 6:2) in which mercy is the key factor after which Israel will be revived in the third day.

834 In other words the Gentiles who were not originally God's holy people or his loved ones would now be included as part of God's plan.

835 In this context, "you are not my people" refers to Israel but in the future they will be restored.

Isaiah 10:22–23

²⁹It is just as Isaiah said previously,

"Unless the Lord of hosts[836] had left us descendants we would have become like Sodom and Gomorrah."

Isaiah 1:9

Israel stumbles over Christ

³⁰What does this all mean? Does it mean that the Gentiles who were not pursuing after righteousness have actually obtained it by faith? ³¹But Israel who were pursuing a law that would give them righteousness has not obtained it? ³²Why couldn't *they find such a law*? It is because they were pursuing it not by faith but as if it could be obtained by works. They stumbled over the "stumbling stone" so to speak. ³³As it is written,

"Look! I am laying in Zion a stone that causes men to stumble and a
    rock of offence.
But the one who trusts in him will never be ashamed."

Isaiah 8:14, 28:16

10 ¹*Christian* brothers, the deep desire of my heart and prayer to God *for my people, the Israelites*, is for their salvation.[837] ²I can testify about them that they are *in fact* very zealous for God but their zeal is *misplaced and* not based on *true* knowledge. ³This is because they did not know the righteousness that comes from God and they tried to establish their own righteousness. They did not submit to God's *way to gain* righteousness. ⁴For Christ has brought the Law to an end so that there may be righteousness for everyone who believes *in him*.

Salvation is for anyone who believes in Jesus

⁵Moses writes how righteousness is gained by the Law in that a man must obey all of its commandments so that he might live. ⁶But the righteousness that comes by faith says, "Do not say to yourselves, 'Who will ascend into heaven?' (which in effect is bringing Christ down *to earth*). ⁷Or do not say to yourselves, 'Who will descend into the abyss?'" (which in effect is bringing Christ up from

---

836   "Hosts" here is literally the Greek word *Sabaoth* which means the heavenly armies.
837   Paul begins this chapter with a prayer for the salvation of his own people, the Jews. Once again he details how the Jewish nation as a whole has sought salvation in the wrong way through the Law and not by faith in Jesus Christ. This continues a theme of Paul's throughout his letters—the discussion of the difference between Jews and Gentiles and how God is bringing the two groups of people together through faith in Jesus Christ. The mistake that is often made I believe is to make too much of the individual and not enough of how God is bringing two corporate groups together.

the dead).[838] [8]So what does *the Scripture* say? It says, "The Word of God is nearby, it is in your mouth and in your heart." In other words, what we are proclaiming is a message of faith and it says [9]that if you confess with your mouths that Jesus is Lord and you believe in your heart that God raised him from the dead then you will be saved. [10]For it is with our hearts that we believe and are declared righteous and it is through our mouths that we confess and are saved.

[11]As the Scriptures say, "The group believing in him will never be put to shame."[839] [12]For there is no difference between Jew and Gentile—the same Lord is Lord of everyone and he richly blesses all who call on him. [13]*For the Scripture says*, "Everyone who calls upon the name of the Lord will be saved."[840]

[14]How then can anyone call on the one in whom they have not believed in? And how can anyone believe in someone in whom they have not heard about? And how can anyone even hear without someone first preaching to them? [15]And how can they preach unless they are *first* sent? As it is written *in the Scriptures*, "How beautiful are the feet of those who bring good news!"

[16]But not all of the Israelites have accepted the good news *about Jesus*. For Isaiah says, "Lord, who has believed our message?"[841] [17]Faith then comes from hearing the message and the message is heard through the word of God.[842] [18]But I ask *myself*, "Didn't they hear *the message*?" Of course they did! The Scriptures say,

"Their voice has gone out into all the earth, their message to the ends of the world."[843]

Psalm 19:4

[19]And again I ask *myself*, "Did Israel not understand?[844] Firstly Moses says *about Israel*,

"I will make you jealous of those who are no nation at all and I will

---

838 Verses 6 and 7 are saying that the righteousness that comes by faith is not a difficult thing in that we have to go up to the heights of heaven or the depths of hell to try and find Christ in order to ask him. It is really close by on our lips and in our hearts.
839 Cf. Isa. 28:16.
840 In Jewish thought, calling upon the name of a person is the same as calling upon that person because the name encapsulates the essence of that person. Cf. Joel 2:32 where the reference is to calling upon the LORD (YHWH). In effect, Paul is equating Jesus with Yahweh.
841 Cf. Isa. 53:1. The implication to this question here is that the Jews have not called upon the name of the Lord or believed that Jesus was the Messiah.
842 Many versions have the word of Christ here instead of word of God.
843 Psalm 19 refers to the 'speech' of the stars in the heavens where everyone on earth has the ability to see and read this message in the signs of the constellations of the zodiac. The Bible refers to the zodiac in Job 38:32—it is the Hebrew word *mazzaroth*. So the implication is everyone is without excuse because this speech pours forth day and night (Psa. 19:2). Note that this is not the same as astrology which is of the devil.
844 The answer to this question is, "Yes, they did know." God had warned them through Moses and so the Israelites would be put to shame because they didn't believe but the Gentiles did.

provoke you to anger over a nation that has no understanding."

Deuteronomy 32:21

²⁰And *the prophet* Isaiah spoke fearlessly *for God* saying,

> "I was found by those who did not seek me.
> I revealed myself to those who did not ask for me."

Isaiah 65:1

²¹However when talking about Israel, Isaiah spoke for God saying,

> "All day long I have held out my hands to a disobedient and oppositional people *in hope of reconciliation with them.*"

Isaiah 65:2

God has mercy on Israel

11 ¹This, therefore, leads me to asking the question: Has God rejected his people? Absolutely not! I am an Israelite myself, a *physical* descendant of Abraham from the tribe of Benjamin. ²God did not reject his people whom he previously knew. Don't you know what the Scripture says in the passage about Elijah? He appealed to God against Israel saying, ³"Lord, they killed your prophets and have torn down your altars. I was left behind alone and they are trying to kill me." ⁴And what *do you think* was God's response? God said *to Elijah*, "I have reserved for myself seven thousand men who have not bowed the knee to *the false god*, Baal."

⁵So it is similar now in the present time. There are a small group of *Israelites* whom God has chosen by his grace. ⁶Since *God's choice* is by grace then it follows that it is no longer by works. If it were then grace would no longer really be grace.

⁷So what then *is the conclusion*? Israel was searching earnestly *for God's favour* but they did not obtain it yet a small group of chosen ones did. The others were hardened. ⁸As it is written,

> "God has put them into a deep sleep. To this very day, their eyes are
> not seeing and their ears are not hearing.⁸⁴⁵

Isaiah 29:10

⁹David also says,

> "May they be caught and trapped by their feasts.

---

845   In other words Paul makes the case saying that most of Israel is not perceiving what God is really doing especially with respect to the fact that their Messiah has come into the world.

May their feasts become a stumbling block and a punishment for them.[846]

¹⁰May their eyes become blind so they cannot see and may their backs be bent forever."[847]

Psalm 69:22-23

The Gentiles are grafted into the olive tree

¹¹Again I ask another question: Did *Israel* stumble as to fall beyond recovery? Absolutely not! Rather, because Israel wilfully disobeyed the Law, salvation has come to the Gentiles in order to make them jealous. ¹²However if Israel's wilful disobedience means abundance for the world and their loss means abundance for the Gentiles, how much more will their full inclusion mean?

¹³I speak now to you Gentiles: Since I am an apostle to the Gentiles, I take great pride in my ministry ¹⁴so that it may somehow make my own people jealous and thereby save some of them. ¹⁵For if God rejecting them resulted in the world being reconciled to God, wouldn't then the result of them being accepted be *as wonderful* as if the dead came back to life!

¹⁶If the first part of the bread dough is holy then the whole batch is holy too. If the root of a tree is holy then so are the branches.[848]

¹⁷⁻¹⁸If some of the *olive tree* branches have been broken off and you, though you are a wild olive shoot, have been grafted in among the other branches, do not boast about this. You now share in the rich nourishment from the olive tree root. If you do boast then consider this: You are not the one supporting the root but in fact, the root supports you. ¹⁹You might then say, "Branches were broken off so that I could be grafted in." ²⁰This is correct. But they were broken off because of unbelief but you remain only because of faith. Do not be arrogant but be afraid. ²¹For if God did not spare *the Jews who are* the natural branches, he will not spare you either.

²²Notice how God can be both kind and severe. He is severe on those who have fallen *into sin* but kind to you on the proviso that you continue in his kindness.[849] If you don't then you also will be cut off. ²³If Israel doesn't persist in unbelief then they will be grafted in, for God is able to graft them in again. ²⁴You *Gentiles* are cut out of an olive tree that is wild by nature. But contrary to nature you were grafted into a cultivated olive tree. So then how much more readily will *the Jews who are* the natural branches be grafted into their own olive tree?

---

846   The punishment is in retaliation for Israel's stubbornness and refusal to accept Jesus as Messiah.
847   Because of their troubles and suffering. The Jews have almost become synonymous with suffering throughout the ages. This will reach a climax during the last seven year tribulation period known as 'Jacob's trouble' (Jer. 30:7).
848   Paul is making the point here that the Gentiles ultimately owe their salvation to the Jews.
849   I.e. Believers need to remain in Christ.

The whole of Israel will eventually be saved

[25] Brothers, I do not want you *Gentiles* to be ignorant of this profound hidden truth so that you may not become arrogant: Israel has experienced a partial hardening[850] until the full number of the Gentiles has come in.[851] [26] And so all Israel will be saved for as it is written,

> "The deliverer will come from Zion.
> He will remove ungodliness from *the descendants of* Jacob.
> [27] I made a covenant[852] with them to take away their sins."
>
> Isaiah 59:20–21, 27:9

[28] *Israel* are now enemies concerning the gospel to your advantage. But *God still loves Israel* because he chose their ancestors, the patriarchs, *Abraham, Isaac and Jacob.* [29] For God does not change his mind about whom he chooses or blesses. [30] In the past, you *Gentiles* have not believed in God but now you have received mercy as a result of *Israel's* unbelief. [31] In the same way, Israel's unbelief has now come about so that they too may receive mercy as a result of God's mercy to you. [32] For God has caused all men to be imprisoned by their unbelief so that he may have mercy on them all.

Praise be to God

[33] Wow! How extensive are the riches of the wisdom and knowledge of God! How unsearchable are his judgments and his ways beyond working out! [34] *The Scriptures say,*

> "Who has known the mind of the Lord?
> Or who has ever given him advice?"
>
> Isaiah 40:13

> [35] "Who has ever been able to give anything to God so that he is obligated to that man?"[853]
>
> Job 41:11

[36] For he is the source of all things and all things exist through him and for him. To him be the glory forever. Amen.

---

850   A refusal or stubbornness to believe the gospel.
851   Cf. Gen. 48:19. Jacob prophesied that Ephraim would become a multitude of nations (Gentiles).
852   Cf. Gal. 4:24 footnote.
853   The expected answer is "nobody" because God owns everything and he is indebted to no one.

We must live for God

12 ¹Therefore brothers, in light of the many times God has shown mercy to us, I urge you to offer your physical bodies as living sacrifices, holy and acceptable to God. This is the logical way to worship him. ²You must not conform any longer to the way that the world thinks and acts but you are to be transformed by being renewed in your mind. Then you will be able to discern what God's will is—his good, pleasing and perfect will.

We must live for the body of Christ

³Because God has been so gracious to me,[854] I say to every one of you: Do not think of yourselves more highly than you should but rather think of yourselves realistically according to the measure of faith that God has given to you.

⁴Every one of us has a body with many parts but these parts do not all have the same function. ⁵So also in Christ we are like the body parts making up the one body. Each part belongs to all the other parts. ⁶We all have different gifts according to how God has been gracious to us. If a man's gift is to prophesy, then let him use that gift in proportion to his faith. ⁷If a man's gift is to serve, then let him serve. If a man's gift is to teach, then let him teach. ⁸If a man's gift is to encourage, then let him encourage. If it is to help others financially, then let him give generously. If it is to lead, then let him lead well. If a man's gift is to show mercy to others, then let him do it happily.

We must love each other

⁹When you love others, make sure it is sincere. Hate what is evil and cling to what is good. ¹⁰Love each other as a family remembering that you are brothers and respect each other even above yourselves. ¹¹Don't be lazy in the work but do it with enthusiasm. Be on fire for the Lord and serve him. ¹²Be happy in your confident hope, be patient in your troubles and remember to keep praying. ¹³Make sure that you are sharing with God's holy people who are in need and practise hospitality.

¹⁴Ask for God's blessing on those who are persecuting you. Make sure you are asking him to bless them and not curse. ¹⁵Be happy for those who are happy and cry with those who are crying. ¹⁶Make sure that you are of one mind in your thinking and do not be proud but be willing to do the humble thing. Do not become conceited.

¹⁷You must not get back at anyone when they do evil towards you. Be careful to do what is right in everybody's eyes. ¹⁸If it is possible, as far as it depends on

---

854 Paul is probably referring to his status as an apostle here.

you, live at peace with everyone. ¹⁹My dear friends, do not take revenge but leave room for God's wrath, for the Lord says, "It is my place to take revenge, I will repay." ²⁰On the contrary, *the Scriptures say,*

"If your enemy is hungry, feed him.
If your enemy is thirsty, give him something to drink.
In doing this, you will be heaping burning coals on his head."[855]

Proverbs 25:21-22

²¹You must not allow yourselves to be overcome by evil but make sure that you overcome evil by *doing* that which is good.

We must submit to the civil authorities

13 ¹Everyone must submit himself to the civil authorities for there is no authority except that which God has established. The existing authorities have been put there by God. ²Therefore the person who rebels against the authority is rebelling against what God has instituted. Those who do so will only bring judgment upon themselves. ³For the rulers hold no terror for those who do what is right but rather for those who do what is wrong. Do you want to be free of fear from the civil authorities? Then do what is right and they will praise you. ⁴For they are God's servants for your good. But if you do wrong, be afraid, for they hold the power to punish. They are God's servants, agents of his wrath to bring punishment on the wrongdoer. ⁵Therefore you must submit to the civil authorities not only to avoid possible punishment but also as a matter of conscience.

⁶This is also the reason why you pay taxes for the civil authorities are God's servants who are working full-time on this very thing. ⁷Therefore you must pay everyone what you owe them. If you owe taxes then pay taxes, if you owe any kind of duties then pay the duties, if respect then pay respect, if honour then pay honour.

⁸You must make sure that you do not have any outstanding debts except for this one ongoing debt: to love one another, for he who loves his fellow man has indeed fulfilled the Law. ⁹The commandments, "Do not commit adultery," "Do not murder," "Do not steal," "Do not covet," and whatever other commandments there may be, can all be summed up in this way: "Love your neighbour as yourself." ¹⁰Love does not harm its neighbour. Therefore love is the fulfilment of the Law.

---

855   This is an idiom which could possibly mean a couple of different things including causing your enemy to be 'burnt' in his conscience by the shame of his behaviour or marking him for the heat of God's judgment (1 Tim. 4:2, Num. 12:9).

¹¹You must do this,⁸⁵⁶ understanding the *critical* time that we are in. The hour has come for you to wake up from your sleep because our salvation is nearer now than when we first believed. ¹²The night is nearly over and the day *of Christ* is drawing near. Therefore let us put away the works of darkness and let us put on the weapons of the light. ¹³We must all behave decently as in the daytime not wild partying and drunkenness, sexual immorality or complete sexual indecency and no fighting or jealousy. ¹⁴Rather we should put on, as it were, the Lord Jesus Christ, not being obsessed with the desires of the flesh in self-gratification.

Christians must not judge each other

14 ¹Make sure that you accept the person who does not have a strong faith without passing judgment if they have a different opinion. ²For instance one person's faith allows him to eat anything whilst another person whose faith is weak may only eat vegetables. ³The person who eats anything must not look down on the person who does not and the person who only eats some things must not condemn the person who eats *anything*, because God has accepted this person. ⁴Who are you to judge someone else's servant? He stands or falls before his own master and he will stand because God enables him to stand.

⁵One person considers one day more sacred than another *day* and yet another person considers every day the same.⁸⁵⁷ The point is that each person should be fully convinced in his own mind *about what is right*. ⁶The person who regards one day as special, observes it as unto the Lord. The one who eats whatever, eats it as unto the Lord for he gives thanks to God. And the one who abstains does it for the Lord also and he also gives thanks to God.

⁷We do not live as our own *masters* and we do not die as our own *masters*. ⁸If we live, we live because of the Lord and if we die, we die because of the Lord. So, whether we live or die we belong to the Lord.

⁹For this very reason Christ died and returned to life so that he might be the Lord of both those who have died and those who are still living. ¹⁰So if this is the case why do you then, *who eats only vegetables,* judge your brother *who eats anything*? Or why do you *who eats anything,* look down on your brother *who eats only vegetables*? For we will all stand before God's judgment seat.⁸⁵⁸ ¹¹It is written,

---

856   This refers to what Paul was previously saying that we must get out of debt and exercise love because a crisis or critical time is coming upon the world—the impending tribulation period known as the night.
857   Paul continues the comparison between the person of weak faith versus the person of strong faith. In vv. 2–3 the person with a strong faith is listed first in the comparison whereas in v. 5 here the person with a weak faith is listed first.
858   The '*bema*' seat—a raised platform mounted by steps and usually furnished with a seat, used by officials in addressing an assembly, often on judicial matters - judgment seat, judgment place. This is not a judgment determining salvation but a judgment of believers being rewarded based on how

"The Lord says, 'As surely as I live everyone will kneel before me and everyone will say openly *that I am God.*'"

Isaiah 45:23

¹²Therefore each one of us will have to give an account of himself to God.

We must not cause other believers to sin

¹³Therefore let us stop passing judgment on one another. Instead, you must ensure that you do not hinder or put any obstacle in the way of a brother *in Christ*. ¹⁴As one who is in the Lord Jesus, I am sure that no food in and of itself is wrong[859] to eat. But if someone regards something as wrong then for him it is *clearly* wrong. ¹⁵If your *Christian* brother *or sister* is upset because of what you are eating, you are no longer acting in love. Do not let what you are eating destroy someone for whom Christ died. ¹⁶Do not let what you consider as good to be spoken of as evil.[860] ¹⁷For God's coming reign is not about eating and drinking but about righteousness, peace and joy that we have in union with *his* Holy Breath. ¹⁸Anyone who serves Christ in this way is pleasing to God and approved by men.

¹⁹Therefore we must make every effort to live in peace *with our fellow man* doing that which builds each other up. ²⁰Do not destroy the work of God for the sake of food. All foods may be eaten but it is wrong for a person to eat anything that causes someone else to stumble. ²¹It is better not to eat meat and drink wine or do anything else that causes your brother or sister to fall *into sin*. ²²So whatever you believe about these things keep it between yourself and God. Happy is the person who does not condemn himself when he does what he thinks is right. ²³But the person who has doubts is condemned if he eats because his eating is not based on faith. The point is that everything that is not based on faith is sin.

Let us please our neighbours rather than ourselves

15 ¹Those of us who are strong in the faith should bear with the failings of those whose faith is weak. We are not to just please ourselves. ²Instead each one of us should please his neighbour for his good in order to build him up in the faith. ³For even Christ did not please himself but as it is written *in the Scriptures,*

---

loyally they have served Christ.
859 Literally means 'common' which is the opposite of holy which means something that is set apart for a special unique purpose. So here the sense of common foods is the Jewish term "non-kosher" foods which Jews were not permitted to eat under the Law. However it doesn't mean unclean foods in the sense of meat sacrificed to idols. That was clearly forbidden even for the Gentiles (Acts 15:29) by the Jerusalem Council.
860 Probably the good things that Paul is talking about here are the freedoms that we have in Christ.

"They have insulted you but what they have said has in effect insulted me." ⁴For everything that was written in the past *in the Old Testament* was written to teach us so that through endurance and the encouragement of the Scriptures we might experience the hope.[861]

⁵I pray that God who gives endurance and encouragement give you a spirit of unity amongst yourselves as you follow Christ Jesus. ⁶In this way with one heart and one mouth you might be able to glorify the God and Father of our Lord Jesus Christ.

⁷You must accept one another just as Christ has accepted you. This will bring praise to God. ⁸For I declare that Christ has become a servant of the Jews[862] to confirm that God's promises made to the patriarchs,[863] *Abraham, Isaac and Jacob* are true. ⁹This is so that the Gentiles might be able to glorify God for his mercy. For it is written,

> "Therefore I will praise you among the Gentiles.
> I will sing hymns to your name."
>
> Psalm 18:49

¹⁰And again,

> "Join in with God's holy people and be happy Gentiles."
>
> Deuteronomy 32:43

¹¹And again,

> "Praise the Lord, all you Gentiles!
> Sing praises to him, all you peoples!"
>
> Psalm 117:1

¹²And yet in another place Isaiah says,
> "The root of Jesse will spring up.
> He is the one who will rise up to rule over the nations.
> The Gentiles will put their hope in him."
>
> Isaiah 11:10

¹³I pray that the God of hope might fill you with much happiness and peace

---

861 The word "hope" here has the definite article suggesting that Paul is referring to a particular hope. The question is what hope is he referring to? This is the hope of the promises first made to Abraham and ultimately fulfilled in Christ in that all nations of the earth will be blessed through Abraham (Gen. 12:3).
862 Literally 'the circumcision'.
863 These promises are the covenants God made with Abraham and confirmed with Isaac and Jacob.

as you trust in him. In this way, by the power of Holy Breath you will overflow with the hope.[864]

Paul is the minister to the Gentiles

[14]Brothers, I am quite convinced that you yourselves are good people and that you are knowledgeable enough and quite competent to instruct each other on all these matters. [15]However I have written this letter and have not held back on certain points because of the grace that God has given to me [16]to be a minister of Christ Jesus to the Gentiles. I have the priestly duty of proclaiming the gospel of God so that the Gentiles might become an offering acceptable to God having been set apart by Holy Breath.

[17]Therefore because I am in Christ Jesus I have so many reasons to be proud of what I am doing for God. [18]I am not going to go too far in talking about anything beyond that which Christ has accomplished through me in leading the Gentiles to obey God. He has done this through my words and deeds [19]by the power of signs and miracles, by the power of God's Breath. I have fully proclaimed the gospel of Christ starting from Jerusalem all the way around to Illyricum.[865] [20]It has always been my aim and desire to preach the gospel where Christ was unknown so that I would not be building on someone else's foundation. [21]Rather, as it is written,

> "The people who were not told about him will see and those who have
> not heard will understand."
>
> Isaiah 52:15

Paul plans to visit the city of Rome

[22]Circumstances have prevented me from coming to see you all many times. [23]But now because I have finished my work here in these regions and since I have been really wanting for many years to come and see you, [24]I am planning to do so when I go to Spain. I hope to visit you all while passing through and hope that you can assist me on my journey after I have enjoyed your company for a while. [25]At this time, however, I am on my way to Jerusalem to help God's holy people there. [26]For the *people of* Macedonia and Achaia were pleased to take up an offering for the poor among God's holy people in Jerusalem. [27]They were pleased to do it and indeed they owe it to them. For

---

864 Not a generic hope but the hope that comes when the Gentiles are blessed through the promises made to Abraham because the definite article "the" is placed here.
865 A Roman province northwest of Macedonia adjacent to the Adriatic Sea across from Italy. The Adriatic Sea is the body of water separating Italy from Greece and the Balkans.

if the Gentiles have shared in the Jew's spiritual blessings, they owe it to the Jews to share with them their material blessings. ^{28}So after I have completed this task and have made sure that they have received what has been raised for them, I will go to Spain and visit you on the way. ^{29}I know that when I come, I will come with the full blessing of Christ.

^{30}Brothers, I urge you because of *our faith in* the Lord Jesus Christ and because of the love that comes from the Breath *of God*, that you might join with me in my struggle by praying to God for me. ^{31}Pray that I might be rescued from the unbelievers in Judea[866] and that my service in Jerusalem may be acceptable to God's holy people there. ^{32}Therefore by God's will I might be able to come to you with great joy and together we will be refreshed. ^{33}May God's peace be with you all. Amen.

Paul finishes his letter with personal greetings

16 ^{1}I commend to you our sister Phoebe,[867] being a deaconess[868] of the church in *the harbour city of* Cenchrea.[869] ^{2}I ask that you receive her in the Lord as one who is worthy as one of God's holy people and that you might give her any help that she may need from you for she has been a great help to many people including myself.

^{3}Please give my greetings to Priscilla and *her husband* Aquila, my fellow workers in Christ Jesus. ^{4}They risked their lives for me and not only am I grateful for them but all the churches of the Gentiles are grateful too. ^{5}Make sure that you also give my greetings to the church that meets at their house as well.

Greetings to my dear friend Epenetus who was the first convert to Christ in the province of Asia.

^{6}Greetings to Mary who worked very hard for you.

^{7}Greetings to Andronicus and Junias, my fellow Jews who have been in prison with me. They are very well known among the apostles and they were in Christ before I was.

^{8}Greetings to Ampliatus whom I love in the Lord.

^{9}Greetings to Urbanus, our fellow worker in Christ and also to my dear friend Stachys.

---

866   This is a reference to the non-Christian Jews.
867   Phoebe was probably the one who delivered the letter from Paul to the Romans.
868   The feminine form of the word deacon—this is the only place in the NT where this form is used. Many translators say that this should be translated as 'servant' because this is too early for the office of deaconess having been established. But the present participle, "being" indicates that this was an ongoing role possibly showing that this was an office even at this early time. This verse in my opinion supports the role of women in the church in an official sense.
869   Cenchrea was a small harbour city for the city of Corinth, one of the largest and most important cities in ancient Greece. Paul wrote two letters to the Corinthians.

¹⁰Greetings to Apelles who has been tested and approved in Christ. Greetings to those who belong to the household of Aristobulus.

¹¹Greetings to Herodion, a fellow Jew. Greetings to those in the household of Narcissus who are in the Lord.

¹²Greetings to Tryphena and Tryphosa, two women who work hard in the Lord. Greetings also to my dear friend Persis, another woman who has worked very hard in the Lord.

¹³Greetings to Rufus, chosen in the Lord and to his mother who has been like a mother to me, too.

¹⁴Greetings to Asyncritus, Phlegon, Hermes, Patrobas, Hermas and all the brothers with them.

¹⁵Greetings to Philologus, Julia, Nereus and his sister and Olympas and all God's holy people with them.

¹⁶Make sure that you greet one another with a holy kiss. All the churches of Christ send you their greetings.

Final thoughts from Paul

¹⁷Brothers, make sure that you take note of those who cause divisions and put traps in your way that are contrary to the teaching you have learned. Keep away from them. ¹⁸For such people are not serving our Lord Jesus Christ but only their own desires. They deceive the minds of naïve people by their smooth-talking and flattery. ¹⁹Everyone has heard about your obedience, so I am very happy with you. Nevertheless, I want you to be wise about what is good and innocent towards what is evil.

²⁰The God of peace will crush Satan under your feet quickly. May our Lord Jesus Christ continue to show you grace.

²¹Timothy, my fellow worker, sends you all his greetings as do Lucius, Jason and Sosipater, my fellow Jews.

²²I, Tertius, the one who has written this letter for Paul, greet you in the Lord. ²³My host Gaius, in whose house the church meets, sends you his greetings. Erastus, the city treasurer, and our *Christian* brother Quartus, send you their greetings also. [²⁴May the grace of our Lord Jesus Christ be with you all. Amen.]⁸⁷⁰

²⁵Now all glory goes to God who is able to strengthen you according to my gospel and the preaching of Jesus Christ. The plan for you *Gentiles* has been revealed which has been kept hidden for a very long time. ²⁶But now it has been made known to all the Gentiles through the prophetic writings by the command

---

870   The earliest MSS do not have v. 24 but the TR (KJV) does.

of the eternal God so that all nations might believe and obey him. ²⁷To the only wise God be glory forever through Jesus Christ. Amen.

1 CORINTHIANS

Introduction

The Book of 1 Corinthians is an extensive letter from Paul to the church at Corinth, an ancient city in Greece, as it covers a myriad of subjects including marriage, divorce, the Lord's Supper, tongues, prophecy, spiritual gifts and the resurrection. It also presents the possibility of falling away in the faith for those who do not hold on firmly to the faith. It was written around AD 55–56 while Paul was serving a three year ministry at Ephesus.

The Corinthian church was having problems with sin in the church and so Paul writes this letter as a correction in how to deal with this sin. In a way this letter provides a template for the modern-day church in how to deal with all sorts of issues that arise.

1

¹From Paul, called to be an apostle of Christ Jesus by the will of God, and from the brother Sosthenes,

²To the church of God in Corinth.⁸⁷¹ God has made you holy in Christ Jesus and he has called you to be his holy people together with all those everywhere who call on the name of our Lord Jesus Christ. He is their Lord and our Lord too.

³Grace and peace to you all from God our Father and the Lord Jesus Christ.

Paul's initial blessings to the Corinthian church

⁴I am always thanking my God for you all because of the grace given to you in Christ Jesus. ⁵For in him you have been enriched in every way including all kinds of speaking *gifts* and all kinds of knowledge.⁸⁷² ⁶Our testimony concerning Christ was confirmed in this way in you ⁷so that you are not lacking in any spiritual gift as you eagerly wait for the revelation of our Lord Jesus Christ.⁸⁷³ ⁸He will keep you strong to the very end so that you may be blameless on the Day of our Lord Jesus Christ.⁸⁷⁴ ⁹And God, who has called you into fellowship with his Son Jesus Christ our Lord, is loyal.

Divisions in the church

¹⁰I am appealing to you, *Christian* brothers, in the name of our Lord Jesus Christ, to be in agreement so that there may be no divisions among you and that you may be united in mind and thought. ¹¹For some of Chloe's people have informed me, my brothers, that there are some serious arguments going on amongst you all. ¹²What I have heard is this: One of you says, "I follow Paul" and another says, "I follow Apollos" and another says, "I follow Peter"⁸⁷⁵ and yet another says, "I follow Christ."

¹³Is Christ divided? Was it Paul who was crucified for you? Were you baptised into the name of Paul? ¹⁴I thank God that I did not baptise any of you except Crispus and Gaius ¹⁵so that no one can say that you were baptised into my name. ¹⁶(Now, *I do recall that* I also baptised the household of Stephanas. Beyond that I can't remember if I baptised anyone else.) ¹⁷For Christ did not send me to baptise as such but to preach the gospel. And I do not preach by wisdom of my own words lest the cross of Christ be emptied of its power.

---

871   Paul wrote this letter just before Pentecost during his three-year ministry in Ephesus (1 Cor. 16:8).
872   Cf. 1 Cor. 13:8.
873   The early Christians in the 1st century fully expected that Christ would be returning very soon.
874   Cf. 2 Thess. 2:2.
875   Literally, 'Cephas' which is the Aramaic name for Peter.

Christ—the Power and Wisdom of God

¹⁸For the message of the cross is foolishness to those who are perishing but to us who are being saved it is the power of God. ¹⁹For it is written,

> "I will destroy the wisdom of the wise and I will reject the understanding of the intelligent."
>
> Isaiah 29:14

²⁰So where does that leave the wise man? Or the scholar? Or the debater of this age? Has not God *proven* that the wisdom of the world is foolishness? ²¹For God, in his wisdom, did not allow the world to know him by means of their own wisdom. Instead, by means of the so-called "foolish" message that we preach, God saved the believing ones. ²²The Jews keep asking for signs and the Greeks keep seeking wisdom ²³but we[876] preach Christ crucified. This *message* is a stumbling block to Jews and foolishness to Gentiles ²⁴but to those who are called, both to Jews and to Greeks, Christ is the Power of God and the Wisdom of God.[877] ²⁵For the foolishness of God is wiser than man's wisdom and the weakness of God is stronger than man's strength.

²⁶*Christian* brothers, *try and* think back to what you were when you were first called. There were not many of you who were wise by worldly standards, not many were that influential, and not many of you were from a well-to-do family. ²⁷But God chose the foolish things of the world in order to shame the wise and God chose the weak things of the world to shame the strong. ²⁸He chose what the world looks down on and the things that the world despises and the things that are not *important* to negate the things that are *important*. ²⁹This means that no one is able to boast in God's presence. ³⁰And it is because of him that you are in Christ Jesus, who has become for us wisdom from God. God has also made us righteous, holy and has set us free from evil. ³¹Therefore as it is written, "Let him who boasts boast in what the Lord has done."[878]

2 ¹Brothers, when I came to you to proclaim to you the mystery[879] of God, I did not come to you speaking in a superior way or with superior wisdom. ²For while I was with you, I decided to forget everything except Jesus Christ and *concentrate* especially on his death on the cross. ³I came to you in weakness, with fear and trembling. ⁴My teaching and preaching was not based on wise and

---

876 "We" here is 1st person plural exclusive meaning Paul and his crew but not his readers.
877 Christ is the "Power of God" for the Jews and the "Wisdom of God" for the Gentiles which are titles of Christ relevant to each group in a way. Cf. Prov. 8:22.
878 Cf. Jer. 9:23–24.
879 Some MSS have 'testimony'. The mystery of God is the gospel revealed through his Son, Jesus Christ.

persuasive words, but was a demonstration of power and *God's* Breath. ⁵This is so that your faith might not be based on human wisdom but on God's power.

The wisdom that comes from the Holy Breath

⁶Yet I am speaking about a wisdom for those who are *spiritually* mature, not a worldly wisdom or a wisdom that belongs to the powers that rule this current world for the worldly powers are coming to nothing. ⁷But I am speaking about a mystery—the Wisdom of God.⁸⁸⁰ This has been hidden but whom God predetermined to be for our glory even before time began. ⁸None of the rulers of this world understood it, for if they had, they wouldn't have crucified the Lord of glory.

⁹However, as it is written,

"No eye has seen, no ear has heard, no mind has conceived what God
 has prepared for those who love him."

Isaiah 64:4

¹⁰But God has revealed it to us by his Breath.

For the Breath searches all things, even the deep things of God. ¹¹For who really knows what a man is thinking except the breath—the spirit of the man—that is within him? In the same way no one knows what God is thinking except the Breath of God.⁸⁸¹ ¹²We have not received worldly thinking⁸⁸² but *we have received* the Breath that comes from God *in order* that we may understand what God has graciously given to us.

¹³We, *who are spiritually mature*, do not speak in words taught by human wisdom but in words taught by *God's* Breath explaining spiritual *truths* to those who are spiritual. ¹⁴But the natural man does not accept the things that come from the Breath of God because for him it is utter foolishness. He is not able to understand them because they need to be spiritually discerned. ¹⁵The spiritual man however is able to judge all things, but he is not judged by anyone. ¹⁶*It is written,*

"Who knows the mind of the Lord so that he can give him advice?"

Isaiah 40:13

---

880   'Wisdom' is the preincarnate Son of God, concealed in a mystery in Proverbs 8, but identified as God's 'Son' in Prov. 30:2–4.
881   Is the breath (the spirit within a man) a separate person from the man himself or a part of the man? In the same way we can ask the question is the 'Breath' or Spirit of God a distinct person? Cf. Acts 5:4 footnote.
882   Literally the breath (spirit) of the world.

We who are spiritual, however, have the mind of Christ.

Divisions in the church

3 ¹*Christian* brothers, I could not address you as spiritual men but as carnal[883] men as if I am speaking to baby Christians. ²I gave you milk, not solid food, because you were not ready for it. And in fact you are still not ready for solid food. ³You are still carnal. For since there is jealousy and arguments among you, are you not carnal? Are you not acting like the world? ⁴For when one of you says, "I follow Paul," or another, "I follow Apollos," are you not being worldly?

⁵Who after all is Apollos? And who is Paul? We are only servants through whom you came to believe. Each of us only does the work which the Lord assigns us. ⁶I planted the seed, Apollos watered it, but God made it grow. ⁷So neither he who plants nor he who waters is anything, but only the one who makes things grow *is important*—God. ⁸There is no difference between the one who plants *the seed* and the one who waters *the plant*, each will be rewarded according to his own labour. ⁹For we are God's co-workers, and you are God's field.

Rewards for Christian service

You are God's building.[884] ¹⁰God has gifted me *the ability* to lay a foundation as an expert builder and someone else is now building on *this foundation*.[885] But each person must be careful how he builds. ¹¹For no one can lay any foundation other than that which has already been laid—Jesus Christ. ¹²And whatever someone uses to build on this foundation whether it is gold, silver, precious stones, wood, hay or straw, ¹³the quality of his work will become clear because the Day[886] will make it plain. It will be revealed by fire and the fire will test the quality of each man's work.[887] ¹⁴And if anyone's work which he has built remains, he will receive a reward. ¹⁵However if anyone's work is consumed *by the fire* then he will suffer loss but he himself will be saved like one escaping through the flames.

¹⁶Are you not aware that you yourselves are God's temple and that the Breath of God lives in you? ¹⁷If anyone destroys the temple of God then God will destroy him, for the temple of God is holy and you are that temple.

The wisdom of the world

¹⁸Let no one deceive himself. If anyone thinks he is wise by the world's

---

883 A carnal man is a man who has an animal like nature who is controlled by his soulish and/or fleshly instincts as opposed to the man of God whose thoughts, speech and actions are controlled by the Holy Breath of God.
884 The local church assembly is effectively the house or building of God.
885 Paul is talking about his apostolic task of founding, planting and building of churches.
886 The Day of Christ.
887 The fire of tribulation will be the ultimate test in the years before Christ returns (Rev. 3:10).

standards, he should become a fool so that he may become wise. ¹⁹For the wisdom of this world is just foolishness with God. As it is written,

> "He catches the wise in their cleverness."

Job 5:13

²⁰And again *it is written*,

> "The Lord knows that the thoughts of the wise are empty."

Psalm 94:11

²¹So, let no one boast about men for everything belongs to you ²²whether Paul or Apollos or Peter or the world or life or death or the present or the future—everything is yours.⁸⁸⁸ ²³And you are of Christ and Christ is of God.

Paul's authority is challenged

4 ¹So then, you should be regarding us as servants of Christ and as those who have been put in charge of the mysteries of God.⁸⁸⁹ ²And it is required that those who have been put in charge must prove to be loyal. ³It's not a big thing to me if I am judged by you or by any human court. I'm not even judging myself. ⁴My conscience is clear but that doesn't make me innocent. It is the Lord who judges me. ⁵Therefore make sure that you do not judge anyone ahead of time—before the Lord comes. He will bring to light what is hidden in darkness and he will expose the motives of *men's* hearts. At that time each person will receive his due praise from God.

⁶*Christian* brothers, in order to help you, I have applied all this to myself and Apollos figuratively so that you may learn not to go too far and beyond what is written lest you take pride in one man over another. ⁷For what makes you different from anyone else? Didn't you receive everything that you have? Well then, you have no reason to boast since *God* has given all these things to you.

⁸You are already full! You have already become rich! You have become kings and what's more, you have done it without us! How I wish that you really had become kings so that we could be kings together.⁸⁹⁰ ⁹For I feel that God has appointed us apostles to the very lowest rank like people condemned to die *in the public arena*. We have become a spectacle⁸⁹¹ for the whole world including

---

888   Instead of being proud that they belong to a follower/disciple of Christ, the Corinthian Christians should realise that everything belongs to them anyway. We all have direct access to God.
889   The mysteries of God is essentially the Christian message centred on Christ. Christ was concealed in the OT but revealed in the NT. Cf. 1 Cor. 2:1.
890   In this verse Paul is employing sarcasm.
891   Spectacle refers to the entertainment which takes place in a Roman theatre specifically the contests between gladiators and wild animals.

both angels and human beings. ¹⁰We *apostles* are fools for Christ, but you are *so* wise in Christ! We are weak but you are *so* strong! You are *most* honoured but we are dishonourable!⁸⁹² ¹¹Up until this very moment we *apostles* have gone hungry and thirsty, we are dressed in rags, we are brutally treated and we are homeless. ¹²We work hard with our own hands. When we are abused, we only bless in return and when we are persecuted we endure it. ¹³When we are slandered we answer kindly in return. Up to this point in time we have become the scum of the earth, society's garbage.

Paul urges the Corinthians to follow his example

¹⁴I am not writing this letter to shame you, but to warn you like you are my own dear children. ¹⁵Even though you have ten thousand guardians in Christ, you do not have many fathers, for in Christ Jesus I fathered you through the gospel. ¹⁶Therefore I urge you to follow my example. ¹⁷And it is for this reason I am sending to you Timothy, my son whom I love, who is loyal to the Lord. He will remind you of my way of life in Christ Jesus, which is what I teach everywhere in every church.

¹⁸Some of you *in the church* have become arrogant, thinking that I am not going to come and visit. ¹⁹But I intend on coming to you very soon, Lord willing. Then I will find out for myself how these people in their arrogance are speaking and if there is any power *in what they are saying*. ²⁰For God's realm is not a matter of talk but of power. ²¹What do you prefer? When I come to visit you, will it be necessary to punish you, or will I be able to come to you in love and in a spirit of gentleness?

Sexual immorality in the Corinthian church

5 ¹It is actually being reported that there is sexual immorality going on in *your church* and it is of a kind that does not even occur amongst the pagans.⁸⁹³ *They are saying* that a man is having *sexual relations with* his stepmother. ²Are you proud of this? Shouldn't you rather be devastated and remove this man from your fellowship? ³Yes, indeed, I am not physically present with you but I am with you in spirit and I have already judged the man having done this thing. ⁴Therefore when you next meet together in the name of the Lord Jesus, I will be with you there in spirit and the power of our Lord Jesus will be there too. ⁵*So when you do meet,* hand this man over to Satan that his flesh may be destroyed and his spirit saved on the Day of the Lord.

---

892   In these three statements, Paul is using sarcasm again to highlight the arrogance of some who considered themselves superior to the apostles.
893   Pagans is a negative reference to non-Jews, i.e. 'unbelievers'.

⁶Your boasting is not good. Don't you know that a small amount of yeast spreads throughout the whole lump of dough? ⁷Get rid of the old yeast so that you may become new dough without yeast as indeed you really are. For Christ, our Passover *lamb* has been sacrificed. ⁸Therefore let us observe the *Passover* feast not with malice and evil that is like bread made with yeast, but with sincerity and truth which is like bread made without yeast.[894]

⁹In the letter that I wrote to you previously I told you not to associate with sexually immoral people.[895] ¹⁰I am not meaning that you must disassociate from the sexually immoral people of this world, or from greedy people, robbers or idol worshippers. If that were the case then you would have to leave the world. ¹¹However I am prohibiting you from associating with anyone who calls himself a *Christian* and is sexually immoral, greedy, into idol worship, slanders others, is a heavy drinker or robs people. Do not even have a meal with such a person.

¹²Far be it for me to judge someone outside of the church. Are we not to judge those inside the church? ¹³God will judge those outside the church. *It is written*, "Remove the evil man from among you."[896]

Lawsuits among believers

6 ¹If any among you has a dispute with someone else *in the church* how dare you go before the ungodly to be judged instead of God's people? ²Don't you know that God's people[897] will judge the world? And since you will judge the world, are you not competent enough to judge small matters? ³Don't you also know that we will judge angels? How much more then are we able to judge the things of this life? ⁴If then you have disputes about such matters, how is it that you can justify taking them to be settled by people who have little regard in the church? ⁵I speak this to your shame! Isn't there not someone amongst you who is wise enough to judge a dispute between *Christian* brothers? ⁶But instead, a brother goes to court against another brother and what's more they do it in front of unbelievers!

⁷The very fact that you have lawsuits with each other shows that you have completely failed. Wouldn't it be better for you to be wronged and to be cheated?

---

894   Paul makes a highly figurative comparison between bread with and without yeast meaning that Corinthian church must lead lives in a different manner than the Jews. Their Christian lives are to be like the Jewish Feast of Passover when they searched their houses high and low for any scrap of yeast. Similarly the Corinthians and all Christians are to be scrupulous in the purging out of sin in our lives.
895   It seems most likely that Paul had written to the Corinthians on a previous occasion.
896   Deut. 17:7.
897   The church not Israel.

⁸Instead, you yourselves cheat and do wrong and furthermore you do it to your brothers *in Christ*.

⁹Surely you know that the ungodly will not take their place in the realm where God reigns. Don't be deceived: Neither the sexually immoral nor those who worship idols nor adulterers nor effeminate nor homosexuals ¹⁰nor thieves nor the greedy nor heavy drinkers nor those who slander others nor robbers will take their place in the realm where God reigns. ¹¹And this is what some of you were previously.[898] But you have washed these things away and you have been made holy. You were declared righteous in the name of the Lord Jesus Christ and by the Breath of our God.

The Body of Christ is the temple of the Holy Breath

¹²*People say*, "I am allowed to do anything I want." Yes, but not everything is good for you. Everything is permissible but I for one will not be enslaved by anything. ¹³*People say*, "Food is for the stomach and the stomach is for food." Yes, but *in the end* God will destroy them both. The Body *of Christ* is not meant *to be* for sexual immorality, but for the Lord and the Lord for the Body.[899] ¹⁴God raised the Lord from the dead and he will raise us up also by his power. ¹⁵Do you not know that your bodies are members of Christ himself? Shall I then take the members of Christ and make them members of a prostitute? May it never be so! ¹⁶Or do you not know that he who joins himself with a prostitute is one with her in body? It says, "The two will become one flesh."[900] ¹⁷But the one who joins himself with the Lord has one breath.

¹⁸Run away from sexual immorality! Every time a man commits a sin it is independent of the Body *of Christ* but when someone commits a sexual sin he sins against his own Body.[901] ¹⁹Do you not know that the Body *of Christ* of which you are all a part of, is a temple of the Holy Breath that is in you all? You are not your own ²⁰for you were bought for a price therefore honour God by honouring the Body of Christ and the Holy Breath. They are both from God.

Instructions about marriage

7 ¹Now to the things which you wrote about: It is better that a man does not get married.[902] ²But since there is so much sexual immorality, each man

---

898 This verse proves that homosexuality can be overcome and that a person is not born as a homosexual but is a choice.
899 The context suggests that the "Body" (sg) here is taken to mean the 'Body of Christ'. Body is capitalised whenever it refers to the Body of Christ.
900 Cf. Gen. 2:24.
901 Sexual sin is against the corporate Body of Christ, his own group as a whole.
902 Celibacy is the preferred state not that marriage is wrong.

should have his own wife and each woman her own husband. ³The husband should fulfil his marital duty to his wife and likewise the wife to her husband. ⁴The wife does not have claim over her own body, it is her husband's. In the same way, the husband does not have claim over his own body, it is his wife's. ⁵Do not deprive each other of *sexual relations* except by mutual consent and for a time, so that you may devote yourselves to prayer. Then come together again so that Satan does not tempt you because of your lack of self-control. ⁶I say this as a concession, not as a command. ⁷I actually wish that all men were able to remain *celibate* as I am. But each man has his own *particular* gift from God. Someone has this gift and another has that gift *so to speak*.

⁸However in my opinion, it is better that the unmarried and the widows remain *unmarried* as I am. ⁹But if they cannot control themselves, they should marry for it is better to be married than to burn with passion.

¹⁰But to the married I give this command (not I but the Lord): A wife is not to be separated from her husband.⁹⁰³ ¹¹But if she is, she must remain unmarried or otherwise be reconciled to her husband. And a husband must not divorce his wife.

¹²To the rest I say this (not the Lord but me): If any *Christian* brother has an unbelieving wife and she is willing to live with him, he must not divorce her. ¹³And if a woman has an unbelieving husband and he is willing to live with her, she must not divorce him. ¹⁴For the unbelieving husband has been made holy through his wife and the unbelieving wife has been made holy through the Christian brother. Otherwise your children would be as the pagans, unclean, but as it is, God has accepted them.⁹⁰⁴

¹⁵But if the unbelieving one leaves then let them do so. The Christian brother or sister is not bound in such circumstances. God has called us to live in peace. ¹⁶How can you know, *Christian* wife, whether you will save your husband? Or, how will you know, *Christian* husband, whether you will save your wife?

The true Christian life

¹⁷Regardless, each one should lead the life that the Lord has assigned to him and to which God has called him. This is my rule in all the churches. ¹⁸*So, to make my point,* if a man was a Jew⁹⁰⁵ when receiving God's call *to faith* then

---

903   The sense here is that the action of separation has been done to the wife, rather than her having performed the action of separation herself.
904   The point here is that God is able to raise up godly offspring with one faithful parent who can instruct and pass on God's Word to the children even within a mixed marriage. Timothy is a good example of this (Acts 16:1–3). Unclean here means that if this wasn't the case then the children would be like pagan children not knowing God at all.
905   Literally 'circumcised' which is a metaphor for a Jew.

should he become uncircumcised? Or if a man is a Gentile[906] when God calls him *to faith* then should he get circumcised?[907] ¹⁹No, circumcision is nothing and uncircumcision is nothing. Keeping God's commands is what counts. ²⁰Each person should remain in the situation in which he was when God called him. ²¹Were you a slave when you were called? Let it not be a concern to you. But if you are able to be free then do so. ²²For he who was a slave when he was called by the Lord is the Lord's free man. Similarly, he who was a free man when he was called is Christ's slave. ²³You were bought for a price, so do not become slaves of men. ²⁴Brothers, each man should remain in the circumstance when God called him.

Advice for the unmarried in times of trouble

²⁵Now concerning what you wrote about young unmarried virgin women, I have no command from the Lord. But I will give you my opinion as one who the Lord by his mercy has deemed to be trustworthy. ²⁶Considering the impending distress,[908] I think that it is better for a man to remain as he is. ²⁷In other words, are you married? Do not seek a divorce. Are you unmarried? Do not look for a wife. ²⁸But if you do indeed marry, you have not sinned and if a young unmarried virgin woman marries, she has not sinned. But those who marry will face many troubles in this life and I am trying to spare you this *trouble*.

²⁹*Christian* brothers, the time that has been shortened[909] is just ahead. So, those who have wives should live as though they do not have wives.[910] ³⁰And those who are wailing for the dead should live as if they were not wailing and those who are rejoicing as if they were not rejoicing.[911] Those who are buying things should live as if it is not really theirs to keep.[912] ³¹Those who *live for*[913] the things of the world must not be taken up by them for this world is passing away in its present form.

---

906 Literally 'uncircumcised' which is a metaphor for a non-Jew.
907 Obviously it is not physically possible to become uncircumcised, rather Paul is emphasising and making the point that a Jew does not have to abandon his customs and traditions once becoming a Christian. The opposite is true also—a Gentile does not have to adopt Jewish customs such as circumcision just because he becomes a Christian. The Judaizers were trying to make the young Gentile church get circumcised and follow the Mosaic Law. Cf. Gal. 5:2.
908 The tribulation period specified in Matthew 24.
909 Cf. Matt. 24:22. The implication is that God has already shortened the time of the Great Tribulation to be 3 ½ years.
910 Jesus instructed believers during the tribulation when they will be fleeing to remember Lot's wife whom Lot had to leave behind in his haste (Luke 17:32).
911 The thought is that there is little time left to be engaging in the activities of life such as being married, mourning for the dead and the celebration of childbirth. Christians need to have the attitude that there is no time for the normal activities of life because of the proximity of the Great Tribulation.
912 Ownership of goods seems pointless when one considers how close we are to the end and how so much more now in the 21st century.
913 Literally 'use'.

³²I would like you all to be free of any concerns. An unmarried man is concerned about the things of the Lord and how he may please the Lord. ³³But a married man is concerned about the things of the world and how he can please his wife ³⁴which causes his interests to be divided. The same applies to the young single virgin and the unmarried woman—she is concerned about the things of the Lord and her aim is to be devoted to the Lord in both body and spirit. But a married woman is concerned about the things of the world and how she can please her husband. ³⁵I say this for your own good, not to put a noose around your neck but that you may do what is right and proper and be devoted to the Lord and not distracted.[914]

³⁶If a man feels that he is acting inappropriately toward the virgin he is engaged to and she is getting past her prime[915] then let them marry. He is not sinning. ³⁷But for the man who is firm in his own mind and feels under no compulsion but has control over his own will and has made up his mind for her to remain a virgin then he has also done the right thing. ³⁸Therefore he who marries the virgin does what is right, but he who does not marry her does even better.

³⁹A woman is bound to her husband as long as he lives. But if her husband dies, she is free to marry anyone she wishes but only if he is in the Lord. ⁴⁰In my opinion, she is happier if she remains as she is and I think that I too follow the Breath of God in this.

What to do about food offered to idols

8 ¹Now concerning what you wrote about food sacrificed to idols, we all know something about this. I would say though that knowledge puffs up but love builds up. ²The one who thinks he knows something really does not know as he should know. ³But the one who loves God is known by God.

⁴So then, concerning the matter of eating food that has been sacrificed to idols. We do know that an idol is nothing at all in the world and that there is only one God. ⁵For even if there are so-called gods either in heaven or on earth (as indeed there are many "gods" and many "lords"), ⁶yet to us there is only one God the Father from whom all things came and who we live for. There is only one Lord Jesus Christ, through whom all things came to be and through whom we live.

---

914   The context of these instructions from Paul is that the time that has been shortened mentioned in v. 29 is coming and he is trying to spare believers any unnecessary distraction. This is especially relevant in light of the fact what Jesus says that there will be betrayal at this time even from within families. Cf. Matt. 10:21, 24:10, Luke 21:16.

915   The average age at which young women were married in Roman and Greek times in the 1st century was between 14 and 17 soon after reaching puberty (Winter, Bruce W, *Roman Wives, Roman Widows* (2003), pp. 163–164). A young woman in her 20s would be considered past her prime.

⁷But not everyone knows this. Some *Christians* are so used to idols that when they eat such food they think of it as having been sacrificed to an idol. Their conscience is weak and they think they are being defiled by the food. ⁸But food does not bring us near to God. We are no worse if we do not eat and no better if we do.

⁹Be careful, though, that the exercise of your freedom does not become a stumbling block to the weak *Christian*. ¹⁰For if anyone with a weak conscience sees you who has this knowledge eating in an idol's temple, won't he think that it is okay to eat what has been sacrificed to idols? ¹¹Therefore your knowledge in effect has destroyed the weak brother for whom Christ has died. ¹²When you sin against your brothers in this way and wound their weak conscience, you are sinning against Christ. ¹³Therefore, if food causes my brother to stumble in this way, I should never eat meat again so that I will not cause him to stumble.

Paul—a true apostle

9 ¹Am I not free? Am I not an apostle? Have I not seen Jesus our Lord? Are you *Corinthians* not the result of my work in the Lord? ²Even though some do not consider me to be a true apostle, surely you do? For you yourselves are proof of my apostleship in the Lord.[916]

³This is my defence to those who are criticising me: ⁴Don't we[917] have the right to food and water? ⁵Don't we have the right to take our wives along with us as do the other apostles and the Lord's brothers[918] and Cephas? ⁶Or is it only Barnabas and myself who must work for a living? ⁷What soldier serves at his own expense? Who plants a vineyard and does not eat of its grapes? Who tends a flock and does not drink of the milk of his own flock?[919] ⁸Am I saying this from a merely humanistic point of view? Doesn't the Law say the same things? ⁹For it is written in the Law of Moses, "Do not muzzle the ox while it is treading out the grain."[920] Is God concerned about oxen in this case? ¹⁰Surely he is saying this for us? Yes, this was written in the Law for us because when a man ploughs and someone threshes the grain, they should do so in hope that they will share in the harvest. ¹¹And if we[921] have sown spiritual seed among you, is it not too

---

916 Paul was being challenged that he wasn't a true apostle. Paul was a true apostle because he met all three conditions: The person had to have been an eyewitness of Jesus after his resurrection (Acts 9:3); had to have been chosen by the Holy Spirit (Acts 9:15); and had to have ministered with miraculous signs and wonders (2 Cor. 12:12).
917 Paul is likely referring to himself and Barnabas.
918 James and Jude.
919 Either sheep or goats.
920 Cf. 1 Tim. 5:18.
921 Paul is excluding his readers but including himself and Barnabas but also could mean apostles and workers of the gospel in general.

much to expect if we reap material benefits from you? ¹²If others have this right of support from you, shouldn't we have it all the more?

But we have not used this right. On the contrary, we have put up with everything rather than hinder the gospel of Christ. ¹³Don't you know that the men who work in the temple get their food from the temple and those who officiate at the altar share in what is offered on the altar? ¹⁴In the same way, the Lord has commanded that those who preach the gospel should receive their living from the gospel.

¹⁵But I myself have not used any of these rights. And furthermore I am not writing this in the hope that you will do such things for me. I would rather die than have anyone deprive me of this boast. ¹⁶However if I do preach the gospel, it is not about boasting for I am compelled to preach. But how terrible it would be for me if I do not preach the gospel. ¹⁷If I preach willingly, I have a reward, if not voluntarily, I am simply fulfilling a task that I have been entrusted with. ¹⁸What then is my reward? It is the privilege of preaching the gospel without charging for it, without claiming my rights in doing so *to be paid*.

Paul is all things to all men

¹⁹Even though I am a free man and nobody's slave, I make myself a slave to everyone *in a way* so as to win as many people as possible *to Christ*. ²⁰To the Jews I became like a Jew in order to win the Jews. To those living under the Law *of Moses* I became like one living under the Law (even though I myself am not under the Law), in order to win those under the Law. ²¹To those not having the *Jewish* Law I became like one not having the Law (even though I am not free from God's law but am living under the law of Christ[922]), in order to win those not having the *Jewish* Law. ²²To those *whose faith is* weak I became weak in order to win the weak. I have become all things to all men in order by all possible means I might save some of them. ²³I do all this for the sake of the gospel in order that I may share in its blessings.

The race

²⁴Do you not know that in a race all the runners run but only one *runner* receives the prize? Therefore run in such a way as to obtain the prize. ²⁵Everyone who competes in the games goes into strict training. They do it to get a *victor's* wreath[923] that will not last but we do it to get one that will last forever. ²⁶Therefore I do not run like a man running without focus and I do not box like a man

---

922   The Bible nowhere specifically defines what precisely is the law of Christ but can be summed up loving God with all our being and loving our neighbours as we love ourselves. Cf. Gal. 6:2.
923   *Stephanon* not *diadem*. Wreath of eternal life. Cf. Jam. 1:12, Rev. 2:10.

punching the air. ²⁷No, I discipline[924] my body and make it my slave so that after I have preached to others, I myself will not be disqualified.

Warnings from Israel's history to Christians

10 ¹*Christian* brothers, do you remember what happened to our forefathers? They were all under *the protection of* the cloud and they all passed *safely* through the Red Sea. ²In the cloud and in the sea they were all baptised, *in a sense*, in *union with* Moses. ³They all ate the same spiritual food[925] ⁴and drank the same spiritual drink[926] for they drank from the spiritual rock that went with them. That rock was Christ himself! ⁵But God was not pleased with most of the Israelites and consequently their bodies were scattered all over the desert.[927]

⁶Now these things happened as examples to warn us from desiring evil things as they did.[928] ⁷Do not worship idols as some of them did for as it is written in the Scriptures, "The people sat down to eat and drink and got up to play."[929] ⁸We must not commit sexual immorality as some of them did when 23,000 men fell dead in one day. ⁹We must not put Christ to the test as some of them did who were killed by snakes.[930] ¹⁰Also remember not to grumble as some of them did who were killed by the destroyer.[931]

¹¹These things happened to our forefathers as examples and were written down as a warning to us for we are coming towards the end of the ages. ¹²So, if you think you are standing firm, be careful that you don't fall. ¹³No temptation has gripped you except what is common for everyone. But God is loyal to his promises and he will not let you be tempted beyond what you can bear, but will provide the way out with that temptation for you to be able to endure it.

Conclusion: idolatry prohibited

¹⁴Therefore my dear friends, flee from idolatry. ¹⁵I speak to you all as sensible people therefore judge for yourselves what I say. ¹⁶When we bless the cup of blessing *at the Lord's table*, are we not sharing in the blood of Christ? And when we break bread, are we not sharing in the body of Christ? ¹⁷And because there

---

924 The Greek word here is *hypo-piazo* which means to pummel one's body, hitting oneself under the eye.
925 I.e. manna.
926 I.e. water from the rock. Cf. Exo. 17:6. Israel was being nourished in the wilderness by the preincarnate Christ himself also identified as the Angel of the Lord in Exo. 23:20–23.
927 Cf. Num. 14:16.
928 Paul's point in all of this is that just as God did not tolerate Israel's idolatry, so he will not tolerate the Corinthians' idolatry either.
929 Cf. Exo. 32:6,19. This refers to the golden calf incident. The feast and the dancing took place to honour a pagan god.
930 Cf. Num. 21:5–6. This verse gives absolute proof of the preincarnate existence of Christ.
931 The Angel of Death who killed the firstborn of the Egyptians (Exo. 12:23, Heb. 11:28).

is only one loaf, we, who are many, are in effect one body for we all partake of the one loaf. ¹⁸Observe the people of Israel: Do not they who eat the sacrifices share with one another in the sacrifice to God made on the altar?⁹³²

¹⁹Am I saying that a sacrifice offered to an idol is important or an idol is important? ²⁰*No, but what I am saying is that* the sacrifices offered on pagan altars are offered to demons not to God. And I am not wanting you to be sharing anything with demons. ²¹You cannot drink the cup of the Lord and the cup of demons too. You cannot eat at the Lord's table and the table of demons. ²²Do you want to make the Lord jealous? Do you think that you are stronger than he is?⁹³³

Freedom in Christ

²³They say that we can do anything we like.⁹³⁴ That is true but not everything that we do is good for us. They say that everything is permitted but not everything builds up *the church*. ²⁴Nobody *in the church* should work for his own good rather for the good of others.

²⁵You are free to eat anything sold in the meat market without asking any questions in all good conscience. ²⁶For, as the Scripture says, "The earth and everything in it belongs to the Lord."⁹³⁵

²⁷If an unbeliever invites you for a meal and you decide to go, eat whatever is put before you without raising any questions of conscience. ²⁸But if anyone says to you, "This food has been offered in sacrifice," then do not eat it, both for the sake of the man who told you and for the sake of conscience—²⁹the other man's conscience, I mean, not yours. For why is my freedom to do or not do something limited by another person's conscience? ³⁰If I take part in the meal with thankfulness, why am I denounced because of something I thank God for?

³¹So whatever you do, whether you eat or drink, do it all for the glory of God. ³²You must be inoffensive both to the Jews, Greeks and the church of God. ³³This is how I try to be in order to please all men in everything that I do. I am not seeking to do things for my own advantage but for the advantage of the many so that they may be saved.

11 ¹Imitate my example, as I imitate the example of Christ.

---

932   When an animal was sacrificed by the people of Israel to God, part of it was burned on the altar and part of it was eaten by the people who were performing this act of worship indicating that they were entering into relationship with God.
933   <u>Alternative</u>: "Do you think that you are strong enough to defy the Lord without being punished?"
934   Probably a reference to the fact that Gentiles had freedom and were not required to eat according to the Jewish Law.
935   Cf. Psa. 24:1.

Head coverings for women in the worship service

²Now I commend you all for remembering my way of life and for sticking close to the teachings that I have passed on to you.

³However I want you to understand that the head of every man is Christ and the head of every woman is the man and the head of Christ is God. ⁴*So* every man who prays or prophesies with his head covered dishonours his head (*Christ*). ⁵But every woman who prays or prophesies with her head uncovered dishonours her head (*her husband*)—she is like a woman whose head has been shaved.⁹³⁶ ⁶For if a woman has not covered her head she should have her hair cut off. If it is a disgrace for a woman to have her hair cut or shaved off then her head must be covered. ⁷A man should not cover his head since he reflects the image and glory of God but the woman reflects the glory of the man.

⁸For man did not come from woman but woman from man. ⁹Nor was man created for the woman but woman *was created* for the man. ¹⁰Therefore because of this the woman must have *a symbol of* authority on her head to show the angels *that she is under her husband*.⁹³⁷

¹¹As we *live our life* in the Lord, though, the woman is not independent of man nor is man independent of woman.⁹³⁸ ¹²For as woman came from man, so also man is born of woman but really everything comes from God. ¹³Judge for yourselves. Is it proper for a woman to pray to God *in the worship service* with her head uncovered?⁹³⁹ ¹⁴Does not nature herself teach you that if a man has long hair, it is a disgrace to him ¹⁵but if a woman has long hair it is her glory? For long hair is given to her as a covering. ¹⁶But if anyone wants to be contentious about this issue, we nor any of the local churches have any other practice *than this*.

Corinthian church celebrate the Lord's supper wrongly

¹⁷In what I am about to say I am not commending you because when you meet you are doing more harm than good. ¹⁸Firstly, I hear that when you come together as a church there are divisions among you and I am inclined to partly believe it. ¹⁹There is no doubt that there must be some heresies among you so that the ones who are in the right may be clearly seen. ²⁰Therefore when you

---

936 Part of the punishment for adultery in 1st century Roman times was cutting off the offender's hair. If a wife will not wear her marriage veil, then she should cut off or crop her hair (Winter, Bruce W, *Roman Wives, Roman Widows* (2003), pp. 82–83).
937 When a woman willingly wears a scarf or head covering it shows the angels that she is not falling into the same sin of pride that the devil and his angels did.
938 This is because God views the husband and his wife as one flesh (Gen. 2:24).
939 The expected answer is "no". The principle behind this still holds today that a Christian woman should dress modestly. In Paul's day the dress code meant that a married woman wore a veil otherwise it indicated that she was a prostitute or an adulteress. Young women married soon after reaching puberty between the ages of 14 and 17 to ensure that they were virgins.

all come together it is not the Lord's supper you are eating. ²¹For when you are eating each one goes ahead without waiting for anyone else. While one remains hungry, another is getting drunk. ²²Don't you have homes to eat and drink in? Or do you prefer to despise the church of God and instead humiliate those who have nothing? What can I say? Shall I commend you for this? Not likely!

The right way to celebrate the Lord's supper
(Matthew 26:26–29, Mark 14:22–25, Luke 22:14–20)

²³In fact, I passed on to you what I received from the Lord which is that on the night he was betrayed, the Lord Jesus took some bread ²⁴and once having given thanks for it, he broke it and said, "This is my body broken for you. When you do this remember me." ²⁵In the same way after he had eaten, he took the cup saying, "This cup is the new covenant in my blood. Whenever you drink *the wine in* this cup, remember me." ²⁶For whenever you eat this bread and drink *the wine in* this cup you are proclaiming the Lord's death until he comes.

²⁷Therefore whoever eats the bread or drinks from the cup of the Lord in an unworthy manner he will be guilty of sinning against the body and the blood of the Lord. ²⁸So then, before anyone eats the bread and drinks of the cup, they should examine themselves first. ²⁹For anyone who eats and drinks without discerning the meaning of the Lord's body, they are eating and drinking judgment on themselves. ³⁰That is the reason why so many among you are weak and sick and some have even died. ³¹However if we had judged ourselves properly then we would not come under God's judgment. ³²But when we are judged by the Lord, we are being disciplined so that we will not be condemned with the world.

³³So then my *Christian* brothers, when you come together to eat *the Lord's supper*, wait for each other. ³⁴If anyone is hungry, he should eat at home so that when you meet together you will not bring judgment upon yourselves.

As for the remaining matters, I will give further instructions when I come.

Spiritual gifts

12 ¹Now about spiritual gifts, brothers, I want you to know the truth. ²You are aware that when you were unbelievers,⁹⁴⁰ you were led astray and influenced in many ways to worship dumb idols. ³Therefore I can tell you that no one who *is led* by God's Breath will curse Jesus and no one is able to say, "Jesus is Lord," except by Holy Breath.

⁴There are different kinds of *spiritual* gifts⁹⁴¹ but it is the same Breath *working*

---

940   Literally 'when you were Gentiles'.
941   The word "gift" here is the Greek *charismata* meaning an extension of grace. God's grace is extended throughout the world through the spiritual gifts he gives to believers.

in everyone. ⁵There are all sorts of ministries but *we all serve* the same Lord. ⁶There are different ways to do things but the same God works in us all to do it.

The local church has many parts but is one body

⁷Now to each person God gives his Breath in some way for the benefit of everyone. ⁸To one person there is given through the Breath *of God* the message of wisdom, to another *person* the message of knowledge by means of the same Breath, ⁹to another faith by the same Breath, to another gifts of healing by that one Breath, ¹⁰to another miraculous powers, to another prophecy, to another the ability to distinguish between *whether a message is from* the Breath *of God* or from another spirit. There is also the gift of speaking in other languages and the gift in translating these languages. ¹¹All these gifts are the work of the one and same Breath *of God* and he gives these gifts to each person as he so desires.

¹²The body is one although it is made up of many parts. Even though there are many parts they form one body. So it is with Christ. ¹³For we were also all baptised into the one Breath into one body—whether Jews or Greeks, slave or free and God has made us drink in that same Breath.

¹⁴Now the body is not made up of one part but of many. ¹⁵If the foot was to say, "I am not a hand therefore I do not belong to the body," it doesn't mean that it stops being part of the body. ¹⁶And if the ear was to say, "I am not an eye therefore I do not belong to the body," it doesn't mean that it stops being part of the body. ¹⁷If the whole body were an eye, where is the sense of hearing? If the whole body were an ear, where is the sense of smell? ¹⁸But in fact God has arranged each body part just as he wanted it to be. ¹⁹Because if each part were equal then the body wouldn't exist. ²⁰But as it is, there are many body parts but only one body.

²¹The eye cannot say to the hand, "I don't need you!" And the head cannot say to the feet, "I don't need you!" ²²On the contrary, the body parts that appear to be weaker are absolutely necessary ²³and the body parts we think are worthless we value them more. And our private parts we clothe them with greater modesty. ²⁴However our presentable body parts have no need of modesty. But God has arranged the body parts in such a way that gives greater honour to the parts that lack *dignity.* ²⁵God has done this so that there should be no division in the body but that all its body parts may have an equal concern for each other. ²⁶If one body part is suffering in pain then every body part suffers with it. If one body part is honoured then every body part rejoices with it.

²⁷Now *the point I am making is that* all of you *in Corinth* together are Christ's body and each one of you is a part of it. ²⁸God has appointed everyone in their place: First of all apostles, second prophets, third teachers, then those who

perform miracles, also those who have gifts of healing, helps, administration, and those able to speak in different languages. ²⁹Not everyone are apostles, prophets, teachers, or able to work miracles! ³⁰Not everyone has gifts of healing, able to speak in other languages or able to translate from one language to another. ³¹But the thing is that you should desire the greater gifts.⁹⁴²

Love is more important than spiritual gifts

However I will show you a better way.

13 ¹If I speak in human languages or *even* that of angels but I do not have love then I am nothing but a noisy brass gong or a reverberating cymbal.⁹⁴³ ²If I have the gift of prophecy, can fathom all mysteries, have great knowledge and have a faith that can move mountains but I do not have love, I am nothing. ³And if I give away all my possessions and sacrifice my body to the flames but I do not have love it is of no benefit to me.

⁴Love is patient, love is kind. It does not envy, it does not brag, and it is not inflated with pride. ⁵It is not rude, it is not self-seeking, it is not easily angered and it keeps no record of wrong done. ⁶Love does not delight in evil but rejoices in the truth. ⁷It always protects, always trusts, always hopes, and always perseveres.

⁸Love never fails but as for prophecies they will be abolished, *the gift of languages will cease in and of itself* and knowledge will pass away. ⁹For we only know partially and we only prophesy partially ¹⁰but when that which is complete comes, that which is partial will cease.⁹⁴⁴ ¹¹When I was a child I talked like a child, I thought like a child, and I reasoned like a child. When I became a man, I put childish ways behind me. ¹²What we see now is but a poor reflection like *what we see* in a mirror⁹⁴⁵ but later we shall see everything with great clarity. The knowledge I have at present is incomplete but then⁹⁴⁶ I shall know fully even as I am fully known.

---

942   The question is what are the greater gifts? The greater gifts presumably are the ones mentioned first in the list: prophecy and Bible teaching.
943   This is clearly hyperbole despite some claiming that the spiritual gift of tongues was an angelic language. Paul uses exaggeration to make the point about how important love is, even more important than having the most amazing abilities and gifts.
944   That which is "complete" is John's vision in the Book of Revelation in AD 96. This is the last example of direct revelation and prophecy until the two witnesses appear in the first 1260 days in the tribulation period. That which is "partial" is referring to knowledge and prophecy not the gift of tongues because that had already ceased before the destruction of the Jewish Temple in AD 70.
945   Paul had no idea of the modern highly reflective glass mirror but is thinking of the ancient mirrors which were made of polished metal and therefore gave a generally less clear reflection.
946   I.e. when perfection comes from v. 10.

¹³Yet these three *things* remain: faith, hope and love.⁹⁴⁷ But the greatest of these is love.

The gift of prophecy is better than the gift of languages

14 ¹Pursue love but it is also good to eagerly desire the spiritual gifts especially the gift of prophecy. ²For the one who speaks in a foreign language is not speaking to anyone but to God. In fact no one can understand him—he is speaking mysteries in his spirit. ³But everyone who prophesies, speaks to men to help them, encourage them and comfort them. ⁴He who speaks in another language edifies himself but he who prophesies edifies the whole church *with his words*.⁹⁴⁸ ⁵I wish that you could all speak in another language but I would rather that you prophesy because he who prophesies is greater than the one who speaks in another language unless he translates so that the church can be edified *by what he is saying*.

⁶Now *Christian* brothers, if I come to you and speak in other languages, how am I helping you? I am of no help unless I bring you some revelation from God or some knowledge or prophecy or some teaching. ⁷Even in the case of inanimate objects such as the flute or harp, how can anyone know what is making that sound⁹⁴⁹ unless there is a distinction in the notes? ⁸Again if the trumpet does not make a clear sound, who will get ready for battle? ⁹So it is with you. Unless you are speaking with intelligible words how can it be known what you are saying? You will be speaking into thin air. ¹⁰There are many different kinds of sounds in the world and yet none of them is without meaning. ¹¹If then I cannot understand what someone is saying, I am a foreigner⁹⁵⁰ to the speaker and he is a foreigner to me. ¹²Since you are so eager for spiritual *gifts*, try to be eager for gifts that help the church.

¹³For this reason anyone who speaks in another language should pray that he is able to translate what he is saying. ¹⁴For if I pray in another language, it is my spirit praying but my mind takes no part in it. ¹⁵So what am I to do? I will pray with my spirit, but I will also pray with my mind. I will sing with my spirit but I

---

947   Paul is likely referring to the time period after these gifts had ceased but before Christ returns because he is the one we are hoping for (Col. 1:27). Hope will then be fulfilled and realised and there will be no need for hope (Rom. 8:24–25). Also faith will not be needed then because we shall see him as he is (1 John 3:2). In contrast, love is the greatest concept because it will last forever.
948   It's important to note here that Paul was not necessarily supporting the Corinthian's use of the gift of languages rather he was stating a fact of how it was actually being used for self-edification. Self-edification was not the true purpose of languages rather it was a sign for unbelieving Jews that judgment was coming (1 Cor. 14:22).
949   This is the Greek word *phonen* from where we get the English word *phonetics*. Phonetics is the area of linguistics that deals with the identification and recording of different sounds made in all the different languages by means of the phonetic alphabet.
950   The Greek word here is literally *barbarian*.

will also sing with my mind. ¹⁶If you are praising in your spirit only, how can the outsider who finds himself in your presence say, "Amen" to your thanksgiving if he does not understand what you are saying? ¹⁷Fair enough, you may be giving thanks, but the other man is not being edified.

¹⁸Don't get me wrong. I thank God that I can speak in more languages than all of you. ¹⁹But in the church I would rather speak five intelligible words to instruct others than ten thousand words in another language.

The real purpose of the gift of languages

²⁰*Christian* brothers, you must stop thinking like children. In regard to evil be child-like but in your understanding be mature. ²¹In the Law it is written,

> "I will speak to my people through the mouths of men with other languages and through the lips of foreigners but even then they will not listen to me."
>
> Isaiah 28:11–12

²²*The gift of* languages therefore is a sign for unbelievers, not for those who believe whereas prophecy is not for the unbelievers but for the ones who believe.[951] ²³Therefore if the whole church comes together and everyone is speaking in other languages and there are outsiders or unbelievers who come in, will they not say that you are out of your mind? ²⁴But if an unbeliever or an outsider comes in while everybody is prophesying, he is convicted *of sin* and called to account *by what everyone is saying.* ²⁵The hidden things of his heart will become apparent and so he will fall down and worship God declaring, "God is really among you!"

Orderly worship in the church meeting

²⁶What shall we say then, brothers? When you come together to meet, one person has a hymn, another a word of instruction, another a message in another language, another a revelation, and another a translation. All of these gifts must be done for the building up *of the church.* ²⁷If someone does speak in another language only two or at most three should speak and they must speak one at a time but somebody must translate. ²⁸If there is no one to translate, the speaker should keep silent in the church and just speak to himself and God.

²⁹Let the prophets speak—two or three, while the others should weigh up

---

951 In light of Isaiah's prophecy here in the text, the gift of speaking in foreign languages was a sign specifically to unbelieving Israel that they were about to be judged in AD 70 with the impending destruction of Jerusalem by the Romans. In its original context it was a warning to unbelieving Israel when the Assyrians came with their strange language that judgment was also coming.

what is being said. ³⁰If however something is revealed to someone sitting close by, then the first speaker should stop. ³¹For you can all prophesy one by one in turn so that everyone may learn and be encouraged. ³²It is for the *group of* prophets themselves to control the spiritual gift of prophecy.⁹⁵² ³³For God is not a God of disorder but a God of peace.

And as in all the congregations of God's people, ³⁴women should remain silent in the churches.⁹⁵³ They are not allowed to speak during church *meetings* but they must be in submission as the Law says.⁹⁵⁴ ³⁵If the women want to inquire about something then they should ask their own husbands at home because it is disgraceful for a woman to speak in the church *meeting*.

³⁶Or perhaps the word of God originated with you *Corinthians*? Perhaps you are the only people it has reached?⁹⁵⁵ ³⁷If anybody thinks he is a prophet or is spiritual then let him acknowledge that what I am writing to you is the Lord's command. ³⁸But they who ignore this *command*, they themselves will be ignored.

³⁹So then, my brothers, be eager to prophesy and do not forbid speaking in other languages. ⁴⁰But everything should be done in a proper and orderly way.

The gospel according to the Scriptures

15 ¹Now *Christian* brothers, I want to remind you of the gospel I preached to you which you received and stand *firmly* in. ²It is this gospel which has saved you and that I preached to you, if you hold firmly to it—otherwise you have believed it in vain.⁹⁵⁶

³For what I received I passed on to you as of prime importance that Christ died for our sins according to the Scriptures, that he was buried, ⁴that he was raised on the third day according to the Scriptures,⁹⁵⁷ ⁵and that he appeared to

---

952 In other words, each prophet who prophesies is subject to examination, correction or rebuke by the other prophets.
953 This implies that there was a problem with women talking and possibly interjecting during the church meetings.
954 The Jewish Law does not specifically prohibit women from speaking but women and men were segregated into the court of the men and the court of the women in the temple and they were also kept separate in the synagogue as well. The Christian assemblies did not segregate the women and men.
955 Paul is being sarcastic here because obviously the Corinthian church had no right to decide independently of other Christian communities how Christians should conduct their meetings. What Paul is saying here is that the Christian message neither began or ended in Corinth so they had no right to do as they pleased.
956 Further proof that OSAS is a false doctrine. One needs to hold firmly to one's belief in the gospel to the very end to be saved. David Pawson when speaking of the Corinthians says, "Their initial faith was real enough but would be useless to them if not backed up with continual faith." (Pawson, D, *Once Saved Always Saved?* (1996), p. 58)
957 There are no OT Scriptures that specifically outline that the Messiah would be raised on the third day except a prophecy in Hos. 6:2 where it says that the Jews would be restored on the third day. Jonah was inside the fish for three days and three nights (Jon. 1:17) but Jesus used this as a sign for

Peter and then to the twelve.[958] ⁶After this he appeared to more than five hundred *Christian* brothers at the same time. Most of these are still living although some have already died. ⁷Then he appeared to James and then to all the apostles.[959] ⁸Last of all Jesus appeared to me like someone who was born abnormally late.[960] ⁹For I am the least of all the apostles and do not even deserve to be called an apostle because I persecuted the church of God. ¹⁰But by the grace of God I am what I am, and his grace to me was not in vain. No, I worked harder than all of them even though it wasn't really my own doing but God's own doing by his grace. ¹¹Therefore whether it was from me or them, you believed in the message that we continue to preach.

The resurrection is paramount

¹²Now since it is preached that Christ has been raised from the dead, how can some of you say that there is no resurrection of the dead?[961] ¹³If there is no resurrection of the dead, then that means that not even Christ has been raised. ¹⁴And it follows that if Christ has not been raised, our preaching is useless and so is your faith. ¹⁵And that means that we are found out to be lying about God since we have testified about God that he raised Christ from the dead. But if *it is true that* the dead are not raised *to life*, then he did not raise Christ either. ¹⁶For if the dead have not been raised then Christ has not been raised. ¹⁷And if Christ has not been raised, your faith is futile and you are still *lost* in your sins. ¹⁸Then *this means* that those also who have died in Christ are lost. ¹⁹If we have hope in Christ for this life only then we are to be pitied more than anyone else *on earth*.

²⁰But the truth is that Christ has indeed been raised from the dead—he is the firstfruits of those who have died. ²¹For since death came through a man, the resurrection of the dead also comes through a man. ²²For just as every person in Adam all die, so in Christ all will be made alive. ²³But each person will be raised in the proper order: Christ the firstfruits, then when he comes, those who belong to him. ²⁴After this the end *of the world* will come. He will destroy every ruler, authority and power and after that he will hand the rule over to God

---

	the Jews only in the NT (Matt. 12:40).
958	Even though by this time Judas was dead, 'The twelve' became a technical name for the original twelve main followers (disciples) of Jesus.
959	A group larger than the original twelve apostles although Paul is not included in this group.
960	Here Paul is self-deprecating, calling himself a freak compared to the other apostles because all the other apostles saw Jesus immediately but Paul didn't have his vision of Christ on the road to Damascus until some years later.
961	The Sadducees did not believe in the resurrection of the body neither did many Greeks who were influenced by the teaching of Plato's immortality of the soul and not the body. The body was seen to be something corrupt and almost despised so the resurrection of the body would be hard for the Greeks to accept. Jewish teachers often used the particular example to prove a general principle.

the Father. ²⁵For *Christ* must reign until *God* has put all the enemies under his feet.⁹⁶² ²⁶The last enemy to be destroyed is death. ²⁷For *the Scripture says, "God has put everything under his feet."*⁹⁶³ Now when it says, "everything" has been put under him, it is clear that this does not include God himself because he put everything under Christ. ²⁸When *God* has done this, then the Son himself will be made subject to him who put everything under him, so that God may be in control over everything.

²⁹But what if there is no resurrection? What would that mean for those who are being baptised for those who have died? If the dead are not raised, then why are people being baptised for them?⁹⁶⁴ ³⁰Why do we *Christians* endanger ourselves every hour *if there is no resurrection*? ³¹I face death every day! I say that brothers because I take great pride in you all in our Lord Jesus Christ. ³²I have fought wild beasts in Ephesus but what is the point of this if I have done it for merely human reasons? What have I gained from this? If the dead are not raised, then, as the saying goes, "Let us eat and drink for tomorrow we will all die."⁹⁶⁵

³³Do not be deceived, bad company corrupts good morals. ³⁴Wake up to yourselves and stop sinning. I say this to your shame because there are some who do not know God.⁹⁶⁶

Believers will receive a new resurrection body

³⁵But someone no doubt will ask, "How are the dead raised? What kind of body will they have? ³⁶You foolish man! The seed that is scattered does not come to life unless it first dies. ³⁷When you scatter, you don't scatter the body of the plant but you scatter the naked kernel, perhaps wheat or something else. ³⁸But God gives it a body as he has so determined and to each kind of seed he gives its own body. ³⁹The flesh of all living things is not the same. Human beings have one kind of flesh, animals another kind, birds another and fish another kind again. ⁴⁰And there are also heavenly bodies and there are earthly bodies. But the beauty of the heavenly bodies is one kind and the beauty of the earthly bodies is another. ⁴¹The sun has one kind of beauty and the moon another and the stars another again and even the stars differ in their beauty from each other.

⁴²And so it will also be with the resurrection of the dead. When the body is

---

962 Cf. Psa. 110:1.
963 Cf. Psa. 8:6.
964 Apparently there were some false Gnostic groups who were practicing baptism on behalf of the dead to aid their immortal souls in their journey to the higher planes. Paul was mocking them for this syncretistic practice because Christian baptism symbolises the resurrection of the body for believers yet the body was abhorrent to the Gnostics.
965 Cf. Isa. 22:13.
966 The sins of the Corinthian believers was a bad witness to those who did not know God.

planted *in the ground* it decays, but when it is raised *it will not be subject to decay* rather it will be immortal. ⁴³When the body is buried it is ugly and weak but when raised it will be beautiful and strong. ⁴⁴When buried it is a physical body but when raised it is a spiritual body.⁹⁶⁷

And because there is a physical body then *it follows that* there must also be a spiritual one. ⁴⁵So as it is written, "The first man Adam became a living being and the last Adam, a life-giving spirit.⁹⁶⁸ ⁴⁶The spiritual does not come first, but the physical and after that the spiritual. ⁴⁷The first man was formed from the dust of the earth but the second man came from heaven. ⁴⁸Those who belong to the earth are like the one who was made of earth and those who are of heaven are like the one who came from heaven. ⁴⁹And just as we bear the likeness of the earthly man, so shall we bear the likeness of the man who came from heaven.

⁵⁰I am telling you *Christian* brothers, that flesh and blood cannot take its place in the realm where God reigns⁹⁶⁹ neither does the perishable inherit the imperishable. ⁵¹Listen up, I tell you a secret. We will not all die but we will all be changed. ⁵²When the last trumpet⁹⁷⁰ sounds we will all be changed in the blink of an eye. For the trumpet will sound and the dead will be raised imperishable and we will be changed. ⁵³For that which perishes must be clothed with the imperishable, that which is mortal must be clothed with immortality. ⁵⁴So, when the perishable has been clothed with the imperishable and the mortal with immortality, then the word will come true, "Death has been swallowed up in victory."⁹⁷¹

⁵⁵"Where, O Death,⁹⁷² is your victory?
Where, O Death, is your sting?"

Hosea 13:14

⁵⁶The sting of death is sin.⁹⁷³ And the power of sin is the law.⁹⁷⁴ ⁵⁷But thanks be to God who gives us the victory through our Lord Jesus Christ.

---

967   The spiritual body is still a body, it is not immaterial or ghostly but a body which is fit for purpose and has been transformed at the resurrection for the believer's new heavenly life.
968   I.e. Jesus who imparts life in the resurrection. Cf. John 11:25.
969   Cf. Gal. 5:21.
970   What is the last trumpet? Some say the last trumpet is the Jubilee Trumpet blown on the fiftieth year on the Day of Atonement or that it is the seventh and last trumpet judgment in the series of seven. The last trump has to be the one hundredth and final trumpet blast blown on the Feast of Trumpets known as Tekiah Gedolah. Cf. https://luke21.com.au/what-exactly-is-the-last-trumpet.
971   Cf. Isa. 25:8.
972   Death is personified and capitalised here because in Greek mythology, *Thanatos* (Death) was the god that carried the soul of the deceased to *Hades*. Cf. Rev. 20:13-14 and related footnotes.
973   In Pauline theology sin is the deadly poison that leads to death.
974   Sin is energised in our lives when we are exposed to the Law. So in effect, the Law, even though it is good in and of itself, it acts as an agent of sin revealing the depth of one's depravity and rebellion

⁵⁸Therefore, my dear brothers, stand firm and do not be moved by anything. Keep busy always in the work of the Lord because you know that nothing you do in your service for the Lord is in vain.

The Corinthian believers take up an offering

16 ¹Now, I need to speak to you all about the collection for God's people *at* Jerusalem. Do what I told the churches in *the province of* Galatia to do. ²Every first day after the Sabbath,⁹⁷⁵ each one of you should set something aside in proportion to your income and save it up so that when I come no collections will have to be made. ³Then when I arrive, I will give letters of introduction to the men you approve and send them with your gift to Jerusalem. ⁴And if you think that it is appropriate for me to go also, they can go with me.

Paul's personal requests

⁵I will come to you whenever I pass through *the province of* Macedonia since I do intend to pass through Macedonia. ⁶And possibly I will stay with you awhile, or even spend the winter so that you may send me on my way, wherever that is. ⁷I do not want to just spend a short time with you in passing but I hope to remain with you for some time, Lord permitting. ⁸But I will remain in Ephesus until Pentecost ⁹because a door *of opportunity* has opened up for me to have great effect where there are many who are opposing.

¹⁰If Timothy comes, see to it that he has nothing to fear while he is with you, for he is doing the work of the Lord just as I am. ¹¹Make sure that no one looks down on him rather send him on his way in peace so that he may return to me for I am expecting him along with the *Christian* brothers.⁹⁷⁶

¹²Now, about the brother Apollos. I strongly urged him to come to you with the *Christian* brothers. He was quite unwilling to come now but he will come when he has the opportunity.

¹³Be alert and stand firm in the faith. Be men of courage and be strong. ¹⁴Let everything be done in love.

¹⁵I really urge you brothers, (you all know that the household of Stephanas were the first converts in the province of Achaia and they have devoted themselves to the service of God's people) ¹⁶to submit to such men as these and to everyone who joins in the work and serves with them.

---

      against God. Before the Law came, a person was ignorant to some degree of their sin.

975   This was a technical term for the Feast of Firstfruits which was literally the first day after the Passover—i.e. Sunday. It was one day in the year like when churches today take up a special offering on Easter Sunday. Paul was indicating that they take up a special one-off offering to be held for when he comes back. Cf. Matt. 28:1 and explanation in footnote where the same term was used.

976   They may have looked down on Timothy because he was a young pastor. Cf. 1 Tim. 4:12.

¹⁷I was glad when Stephanas, Fortunatus and Achaicus arrived *from Corinth*, because they have made up for your absence. ¹⁸For they refreshed my spirit and yours also. Such men deserve recognition.

Final greetings

¹⁹The churches in *the province of* Asia send you their greetings. Aquila and Priscilla greet you warmly in the Lord and so does the church who meet in their house. ²⁰All the *Christian* brothers here send you their greetings. Greet one another with a holy kiss.

²¹I, Paul, write this greeting in my own hand.

²²If anyone does not love the Lord let there be a curse on him. *Marana tha*—Our Lord, come!

²³The grace of the Lord Jesus be with you all. ²⁴My love to you all in Christ Jesus. Amen.

2 CORINTHIANS

Introduction

The Book of 2 Corinthians is the most autobiographical of all Paul's letters containing many transparent, honest and open references to his personal character and life. He did this because of his deep love and concern for the church. This letter contains a lot of theology concerning Christian suffering and reveals Paul's dramatic visit to the third heaven (2 Cor. 12:1–4) which is only otherwise seen in the Book of Revelation.

Paul wrote his second letter to the church at Corinth around AD 55–56 to encourage the majority of those at Corinth who were remaining faithful to him as their spiritual father. But he also addresses the false apostles in order to expose them and to reprimand the minority in the church who were being influenced by Paul's enemies.

1 ¹From Paul, an apostle of Christ Jesus by the will of God, and Timothy the brother,

To the church of God in Corinth, together with all the people of God throughout *the province of* Achaia.⁹⁷⁷

²Grace and peace to you all from God our Father and the Lord Jesus Christ.

Paul gives thanks to God who comforts

³Praise be to the God and Father of our Lord Jesus Christ, the Father of mercy and the God of all comfort. ⁴He comforts us in all our troubles enabling us to comfort those in any trouble with the comfort we ourselves have received from God. ⁵Since Christ's sufferings are abundant for us, so is Christ's comfort abundant for us also. ⁶If we⁹⁷⁸ are distressed, it is for your comfort and salvation.⁹⁷⁹ If we are comforted then it is for your comfort producing in you resilience to endure the same sufferings that we ourselves also suffer. ⁷So our hope for you is on solid ground because we are confident that just as you share in our sufferings, so also you share in our comfort.

⁸We do not want you to be ignorant, brothers, about the hardships we suffered in the province of Asia.⁹⁸⁰ We were under a great deal of pressure, far beyond our ability to cope with, even to the point where we were worried for our lives. ⁹Indeed, in our hearts we felt the sentence of death. But this occurred so that we might not rely on ourselves but on God, the one who raises the dead. ¹⁰He has rescued us from certain death and will rescue us again. Indeed we hope that he will continue to rescue us in the future. ¹¹You are helping by praying for us which will result in many people thanking God on our behalf. The grace shown to us through the answer to prayer will mean many giving thanks for us.

Paul explains his change of plans

¹²Now this is our boast: We can testify in all good conscience that we have conducted ourselves in the world, and especially towards you all *at Corinth*, with holiness and a sincerity that is from God. We have done so not according to worldly wisdom but according to God's grace. ¹³For we do not write anything you are not able to read or that is beyond your understanding. I hope that one day you will be able to understand us completely, ¹⁴even if you only understand

---

977 Paul expected this letter, like 1 Corinthians, to be read by Christians not only in the city of Corinth but also in other Roman cities in the province. Achaia was southern Greece including Athens.
978 "We" here is referring to Paul and Timothy not his readers.
979 Not salvation in the eternal sense but for their present spiritual well-being or protection.
980 This is Asia Minor not to be confused with the modern continent of Asia. In modern geography Asia Minor corresponds to the southwestern corner of Turkey of which Ephesus was the chief commercial centre at the time.

us in part at this time so that in the Day of our Lord Jesus[981] you can be proud of us just as we are proud of you all.

¹⁵I was sure that I would have visited you first in order that you might be blessed twice.[982] ¹⁶For I planned to visit you on my way to Macedonia and to come back to you from Macedonia, and then have you send me on my way to Judea. ¹⁷Do you think when I planned this that I was being fickle?[983] Or do I make my plans according to the flesh saying, "Yes, yes" but then, "No, no"?

¹⁸But just as God is trustworthy, my word to you is not yes and no. ¹⁹For the Son of God, Jesus Christ, who was preached among you by me and Silas and Timothy, was not "Yes" and No," but always "Yes" in him. ²⁰For there are many promises of God and they are always, "Yes" in Christ. That is why we always say, "Amen" through him to the glory of God. ²¹However it is God himself who causes both us and you all to stand firm in Christ. God has anointed us, ²²and set his seal of ownership on us, and put his Breath in our hearts as a deposit guaranteeing what is to come.[984] ²³I now call God as my witness that it was in order to spare you all that I did not return to Corinth. ²⁴It's not that we are being bossy about your faith but we are your co-workers for your happiness, for it is by faith that you have stood firm.

2 ¹Therefore I made up my mind not to make you another painful visit. ²For if I am the one who causes you pain, then who is the one who can encourage me except you whom I have pained? ³The reason I wrote to you all is so that when I come I will not be distressed by the very ones who should be making me happy. Surely you all know that I am happy when you are happy. ⁴For when I wrote to you it was with great conflict and anguish of heart and many tears, not to cause you pain but so as to let you know the depth of the love that I have for you all.

Forgiving each other

⁵Now there is a man amongst you who has caused grief but he has not done it to me only but he has grieved all of you to some extent. (I don't want to overstate the problem.)[985] ⁶This man has been sufficiently disciplined by the majority in the church. ⁷However now you should forgive him and encourage him so that

---

981 Cf. 1 Cor. 1:8.
982 Cf. 1 Cor. 16:5.
983 The Corinthian church were disappointed when Paul didn't show up questioning his sincerity because they had made preparations for his arrival to stay with them for the winter. Paul remained in Ephesus because a door of opportunity for effective ministry had opened up (1 Cor. 16:8-9).
984 Cf. Eph. 1:13-14.
985 Paul is most likely referring to the man in the church at Corinth who had been sleeping with his father's wife. Paul rebuked the elders for not immediately excommunicating him (1 Cor. 5).

he will not be swallowed up by despair. ⁸I urge you, therefore, to reaffirm your love for him. ⁹I wrote that *earlier* letter⁹⁸⁶ to you because I wanted to find out how committed you were to my instructions. ¹⁰If you forgive anyone, I also forgive him. And what I have forgiven, if indeed there was anything to forgive, I have forgiven in Christ through you in the presence of Christ⁹⁸⁷ ¹¹in order that Satan might not outsmart us. For we are not unaware of his schemes.

Paul was hoping to meet Silas in Troas

¹²Now previously when I went to *the city of* Troas to preach the gospel of Christ and found that the Lord had opened a door for me, ¹³I still had no peace of mind because I didn't find my *Christian* brother Titus there. So, having farewelled them, I went on to Macedonia.

The smell of death and the fragrance of life

¹⁴Thanks be to God, the one who through Christ always leads us in triumphal procession. We are making known the fragrance of the knowledge of him in every place. ¹⁵For we are like a sweet smelling aroma of Christ to God among those who are being saved and among those who are perishing. ¹⁶To the latter we are the smell of death leading unto death but to the former, we are the fragrance of life leading unto life. Who is qualified for such a task as this? ¹⁷Unlike so many, we are not trying to make a profit from the word of God. On the contrary, in Christ we speak before God with honesty, as men sent from God.

The apostles are ministers of the new covenant

3 ¹You may think we *apostles* are beginning to commend ourselves again. Or perhaps, like for some, you think we need letters of recommendation to you or from you?⁹⁸⁸ ²No, you yourselves are our letter, written on our hearts, being known and read by everyone.⁹⁸⁹ ³It has been shown that you are a letter of Christ, the result of our ministry, written not with literal ink but with Breath of *the* living God. It has not been written on stone tablets but on tablets of human hearts.

⁴We say this because we are confident in God through Christ. ⁵It's not that

---

986   The same letter referred to in verses 3 and 4. Paul is not likely referring to 1 Corinthians but to another intermediate letter because the context doesn't seem to fit what he wrote in 1 Corinthians.
987   Paul is acknowledging that the Corinthian church had the presence of Christ through the Holy Breath also and since they did then he would also trust that their forgiveness of the man was good enough for him to forgive the man also.
988   Letters of recommendation were common in the ancient world to introduce someone and to give approval to that person. Apparently some in the church at Corinth were opposed to Paul.
989   Paul does not need a written letter from human authorities to establish his apostolic authority. The existence of the church at Corinth which was the result of Paul's missionary work was proof enough that Paul was a genuine apostle.

we are saying that we have the necessary qualifications and capability, but our ability comes from God. ⁶It is he who has made us capable as ministers of a new covenant⁹⁹⁰ which is not the letter *of the Law* but of the Breath. For the letter *of the Law* kills, but the Breath gives life.⁹⁹¹

⁷Now since the dispensation of death, which was letters engraved in stone, came with glory so that the Israelites could not gaze into the face of Moses because of its glory (which was fading), ⁸does it not follow that the dispensation of the Breath will be even more glorious? ⁹So, if it is true that the dispensation that condemns men is glorious, how much more glorious is the dispensation that brings righteousness? ¹⁰For what was glorious before has no glory when compared with the *present* surpassing glory. ¹¹For if that which was fading away came with glory, how much greater is the glory of that which lasts *forever*?

¹²Therefore since we have such a hope, we speak with boldness. ¹³We are not like Moses who put a veil over his face so that the people of Israel could not see the glory of that which was fading away.⁹⁹² ¹⁴However God caused their minds to be made dull, for to this day the same veil remains when the old covenant is being read. The veil has not been removed, because only in Christ is the veil removed. ¹⁵Even today when the Law of Moses is read, it's as if there is a veil keeping them from truly understanding. ¹⁶But whenever someone turns to the Lord, the veil is taken away.⁹⁹³ ¹⁷Now the Lord *in that passage* is the Breath⁹⁹⁴ and where the Breath of the Lord is, there is freedom. ¹⁸All of us, then, with unveiled faces, reflect the glory of the Lord. We are being transformed into his likeness with ever-increasing glory which comes from the Lord, who is the Breath.

Treasure in clay pots

4 ¹Therefore, since we *apostles* are in this dispensation because of God's mercy, we do not lose heart. ²Rather, we have renounced the secret and shameful ways. We do not act with deceit and we do not water down the word of God. On the contrary, by presenting the truth plainly we commend ourselves to everyone's conscience as God is our witness. ³And even if the gospel we preach is hidden to some, it is hidden to those who are on the road to ruin. ⁴The god

---

990   I.e. The NT.
991   The contrast here is between the Mosaic Jewish Law and all its 613 written commandments and laws and the gospel of grace of the NT.
992   Because of the necessity to align genders, it appears possible that Paul is referring also to the Jewish Law as the thing which would fade away (TH).
993   Cf. Exo. 34:34. Moses removed his veil when he went into the presence of the LORD (YHWH).
994   Paul is equating 'the Lord' in Exo. 34:34 with the Breath of God (Holy Spirit). In other words, now in the NT, we are in the presence of God with our metaphorical veils removed because we have the Breath of God bringing us freedom.

of this age has blinded the minds of unbelievers, so that the light of the gospel (the glory of Christ, who is the image of God), does not shine on them.

⁵For our preaching is not about us, but we are preaching that Jesus Christ is Lord, and that we ourselves are your servants for Jesus' sake. ⁶The God who once said, "Let the light shine out of darkness," is the same God who made his light shine in our hearts, in order that we might have the enlightening knowledge of the glory of God *seen* in the face of Jesus Christ.

⁷But we are just clay pots[995] holding this treasure to show that this extraordinary power is from God and not from us *apostles*. ⁸We are being oppressed on every side, but not crushed. We are perplexed but not despairing. ⁹We are being persecuted but not abandoned. We are being knocked down but not destroyed. ¹⁰Everyday we carry around in our bodies the death of Jesus, so that the life of Jesus might also be seen in our bodies. ¹¹Everyday we who are alive are being exposed to death for Jesus' sake so that his life might be seen in our mortal bodies. ¹²So then, death is at work in us, but life is at work in you all.[996]

¹³And in that same spirit of faith as it is written, "I believed, therefore I have spoken" we also believe and therefore we speak.[997] ¹⁴We know that God, who raised the Lord Jesus from the dead will also raise us with Jesus and take us with you into his presence. ¹⁵All of this is for your sakes, so that as God's grace reaches more and more people, thanksgiving may increase to the glory of God.

Living by faith

¹⁶For this reason we do not lose heart. Even though outwardly we are wasting away, inwardly we are being renewed day by day. ¹⁷For our light and momentary troubles are achieving for us an eternal glory that far outweighs any problems that we might be having. ¹⁸Therefore we are not to focus on the things that we can see, but on the things that we cannot see. For the things we can see are only temporary, but the things we cannot see are eternal.

5 ¹For we know that if the earthly tent we live in is destroyed, we have a building from God, an eternal house in the heavens not built by human hands. ²Meanwhile here and now *on earth* we groan, looking forward to being clothed with our heavenly dwelling, ³because when we are clothed we will not be found naked.[998] ⁴For while we live in this tent, we groan and are burdened because

---

995 The point here is that clay pots are very fragile and easily broken indicating human frailty.
996 Paul and his co-workers suffer and are in danger of being put to death. Tradition holds that only the Apostle John died peacefully in his old age with many if not all of the others except Judas being martyred.
997 Paul is quoting from Psa. 116.10.
998 The Christian hope is that we will receive a new body whereas the hope of Greek philosophy is that a person's immortal soul will be finally rid of its body.

we do not wish to be unclothed but to be clothed with our heavenly dwelling so that which is mortal may be changed into that which is totally permanent. ⁵God himself has prepared us for this very thing and has given to us the Breath as a deposit, guaranteeing what is to come.

⁶Therefore at all times we are confident, *even* though we are away from the Lord, knowing that we are present in the Body.⁹⁹⁹ ⁷For we live by faith, not by sight. ⁸I am confident that we would all prefer to leave the Body *here* and to be present with the Lord. ⁹Therefore we should make it our goal to please him, whether we are present with the Lord or away from him. ¹⁰For we must all appear before the judgment seat of Christ so that each one may receive the rewards due for the things they have done through the Body, whether good or worthless.¹⁰⁰⁰

The ministry of reconciliation

¹¹Since then we *apostles* know what it is to fear the Lord, we try to persuade men accordingly. It is clear to God what we are *doing* and I hope that it is clear in your consciences also. ¹²We are not trying to commend ourselves to you again but we are giving you an opportunity to be proud of us so that you can answer those who boast about outward appearances rather than what is in the heart. ¹³If it seems that we are being paranoid¹⁰⁰¹ then that is for God to decide but if we are in our right minds then it is for your own good. ¹⁴Either way the love of Christ leaves us no choice. We have concluded that if one died for all, then all died.¹⁰⁰² ¹⁵*Christ* died for all so that the ones living must no longer live for themselves but for him who died for them and who was raised again.

¹⁶As a result, we no longer evaluate anyone according to the flesh. Even if we have known Christ in this way we do not anymore. ¹⁷Therefore if anyone is in Christ, he is a new creation. The old things have passed away and look, all things have become new!

¹⁸All of this is done by God, who through Christ changed us from enemies into his friends and has given us the ministry of reconciliation: ¹⁹God was in Christ, reconciling all human beings to himself, not counting their sins against them. He has appointed us to the message of reconciliation. ²⁰Therefore we are Christ's ambassadors, as if God himself were making his appeal through us.

---

999 "Body" here is the corporate Body of Christ not the individual fleshly body. Cf. 1 Cor. 6:12–20. In contrast Paul refers to the human body as a tent in verses 1,4 of chapter 5.
1000 Earliest MSS have worthless rather than 'bad' or 'evil' referring to the works of wood, hay and straw in 1 Cor. 3:12.
1001 Cf. Acts 26:24–25. Paul was repeatedly accused of being insane when he told of his encounter with Jesus on the road to Damascus.
1002 Christ died for all mankind consequently every person has died including Elijah and Enoch although Enoch didn't experience death in the same way as everyone else. Cf. Heb. 11:5.

We plead on Christ's behalf that you be reconciled to God. ²¹He made him who committed no sin to be a sin *offering* for us so that in him the righteousness of God might be produced in us.

6 ¹As God's co-workers we urge you not to receive God's grace in vain. ²For this is what he says,

"At the appropriate time I heard you and in the day of salvation I helped you."

Isaiah 49:8

Listen up! Now is the appropriate time, now is the day of salvation.

³We are putting no obstacle in anyone's way in case our ministry will be blamed. ⁴Instead, in every possible way it is shown that we are God's servants by our great endurance, by the troubles, hardships, difficulties, ⁵the beatings, imprisonments, riots, hard work, sleepless nights, and hunger *that we faced*. ⁶We *ministered* in purity, in understanding, in patience, in kindness, in Holy Breath and in genuine love. ⁷We spoke the word of truth, *acting* in the power of God with righteousness as our weapon in the right hand and the left.[1003]

⁸We *have been treated* with honour and disgrace, we have been defamed and praised. We are considered to be liars yet we are genuine. ⁹We are not recognised by some yet we are well-known. They say we were dying yet look, we live on. We are being punished but we do not die. We are poor yet we make many rich. We have nothing yet we possess everything *in the Lord*.

¹¹My dear Corinthians, we have been very straight with you all and our hearts have been very open. ¹²We are not holding back in any way from you but you have been holding out on us. ¹³To be fair, I speak to you as I would speak to my children: you must open your hearts also.

Believers are not to be yoked with unbelievers

¹⁴Do not be yoked together with unbelievers.[1004] For what does righteousness and lawlessness have in common? Or what fellowship can light have with darkness? ¹⁵What harmony is there between Christ and Belial?[1005] What does a believer[1006] have in common with an unbeliever? ¹⁶What agreement is there between the temple of God and idols? For you all are the temple of the living

---

1003 The right hand typically holds a spear as a weapon of attack whilst the left hand typically holds a shield for protection. Right living or goodness is our metaphorical armour. Cf. Eph. 6:10–17.
1004 In the Jewish Law (Deut. 22:10) it was prohibited for an ox and donkey to be yoked together for ploughing as they were too different. Similarly the idea is that believers should not be yoked (in partnership) with unbelievers. This could include marriage and business partners.
1005 "Belial" is a transliterated word from the Hebrew meaning 'wickedness'. In writings during the period between the Old and New Testament, Belial is often the name given to Satan.
1006 I.e. A Christian.

God. As God himself has said, "I will live with them and walk among them. I will be their God and they will be my people."[1007] The Lord says,

> [17]"Therefore you must come out from among them and separate yourselves from them.
> Do not touch anything unclean[1008] and I will receive you."
>
> Isaiah 52:11, Ezekiel 20:34,41

[18]The Lord Almighty says,

> "I will be a Father to you and you will be my sons and daughters."
>
> 2 Samuel 7:14

7 [1]My dear friends, since we have these promises *from God*, let us purify ourselves from everything that contaminates body and spirit and let us perfect holiness by living in the fear of God.

Paul is happy

[2]Please be open! We have not wronged anyone, ruined anyone or manipulated anyone. [3]I am not saying this to condemn you, for, as I have previously said, you are in our thoughts and you will always be so whether we live or die. [4]I have a lot of confidence in you and I take great pride in you. I am very encouraged and despite all of our troubles I am filled with happiness.

[5]Even after we arrived in Macedonia, we did not have any rest. There were troubles everywhere—battles on the outside and fears within. [6]But *God*, the one who comforts the downcast, comforted us by the arrival of Titus. [7]It was not only his arrival that encouraged us but also the report of how you encouraged him. He told us how much you want to see me, how sorry you all are and how eager you are to support me. This made me even more happy.

[8]Even if I did cause you some grief with my letter, I do not regret it. Actually I did regret it in some way because I see that it did cause you some grief albeit only for a short time. [9]Now, I am happy, not because I caused you grief, but because your grief led to you changing your ways. For that grief was as God intended and so really we did not cause you any harm. [10]Godly grief leads to a turning away from one's sins that leads to salvation and no regret. But worldly grief leads only to death.[1009] [11]Think about what Godly grief has produced in you. It has made you diligent and eager to prove yourselves innocent. You have

---

1007 This quotation is a combination of two verses in the OT, Lev. 26:12 and Eze. 37.27.
1008 Cf. Acts 10:14.
1009 Judas Iscariot is an example of how worldly grief only led to death.

become indignant in the matter, alarmed even and you have a longing to see me. You have an eagerness to see justice done. At every point you have shown yourselves to be innocent in the whole matter. [12]So, even though I wrote that letter, it was not about that the person who did wrong or about the one who was wronged. But I wrote it to make it clear to you, before God, how devoted you were to us. [13]Therefore we are so encouraged by this.

Not only that but we were also encouraged to see how happy Titus was because his spirit has been refreshed by all of you. [14]I boasted to him about you and you have not embarrassed me. We have always spoken to you with truthfulness and so our boasting about you to Titus also proved to be true. [15]And so his affection for you all is even greater when he remembers that you were obedient and how you welcomed him with fear and trembling.[1010] [16]It makes me happy that I have complete confidence in you.

Paul encourages the church to be generous

8 [1]*Christian* brothers, we want you to know about the grace God has shown the Macedonian churches. [2]They have been severely tested but their happiness is abundant and the extreme depth of their poverty has overflowed into rich generosity. [3]I can testify that the Macedonians gave as much as they could, and even beyond their ability. Entirely of their own accord, [4]they pleaded with us, requesting that they could participate in the contribution of the ministry to God's people *in Jerusalem*. [5]Furthermore they gave in a way that we had not even expected. They gave themselves firstly to the Lord and then to us in keeping with God's will. [6]So we urged Titus, as he had done previously, to complete this act of grace among you.[1011] [7]Just as you excel in everything—in faith, in speech, in knowledge, in your zeal *for the Christian cause* and in your love for us, see that you also excel in this grace of giving also.

[8]I am not commanding you in this, but I am testing how genuine your love really is when compared to the eagerness shown by others *in giving*.[1012] [9]For you know the grace of our Lord Jesus Christ—even though he was rich, yet for your sakes he became poor so that through his poverty you might become rich.

[10]In my opinion, this is the best thing for you to do: Last year you were the first not only to give but the first willing to do so. [11]Now finish what you have started so that your eager willingness may be matched by your actual completion

---

1010 It is likely from the context here that Titus was the person who delivered Paul's first letter to the Corinthians—hence their fear and trembling of Titus.
1011 Titus was assigned the responsibility to help the Corinthian church complete the raising of the collection for the Jerusalem church.
1012 Paul is referring to the generosity shown by the Macedonians.

of it, according to what you have. ¹²For if the willingness is there, the gift is acceptable according to what one has, not according to what one does not have.

¹³It is not our desire that others might be relieved while you are burdened, but that there might be equality. ¹⁴At this present time, your excess will supply what they need. Then later on their excess will supply what you need so that there will be equality. ¹⁵As it has been written, "The one who gathered a lot did not have too much and the one who only gathered a little was not lacking."¹⁰¹³

Paul sends Titus to Corinth

¹⁶Thanks be to God, who put into the heart of Titus the same devotion that I have for you all. ¹⁷Because Titus not only welcomed our request, but he is coming to you voluntarily and with much enthusiasm. ¹⁸We are also sending with *Titus*, the brother who is praised by all the churches for his service to the gospel. ¹⁹Furthermore, he was selected by the churches to travel with us as we carry this offering, which is being managed by us in order to honour the Lord himself and to show that we are eager to help.

²⁰We are being really careful to avoid any criticism of the way we are managing this generous gift. ²¹For we are trying to do what is right, not only in the eyes of the Lord but also in the eyes of men.

²²So we are sending with these *two men another* brother who has proven himself to be diligent many times and in many ways especially now that he is even more confident *that you will help.*¹⁰¹⁴

²³As for Titus, he is my partner and co-worker for you. As for our *Christian* brothers, they represent the churches and bring glory to Christ. ²⁴Therefore make sure that you show these men your love so that the churches can see why we boast about you.

The Corinthians are an example to the Macedonians

9 ¹Indeed, there is really no need for me to write to you about the gift that you are wanting to send for God's people *in Jerusalem*. ²For I know that you are very eager to help and I have been boasting about it to the Macedonians. I have been telling them that the believers in Achaia¹⁰¹⁵ have been ready to help since last year. Your eagerness to help has really stirred up many of them there *to also give*. ³However I have sent the brothers in order that our boasting about you in this matter should not be an empty boast so that as I have been saying,

---

1013 Cf. Exo. 16:8. This refers to the gathering of manna sent by God to the Israelites in the wilderness.
1014 The other brother (not Titus and the one mentioned in v. 18) was becoming more confident that the Corinthian church would help the Christians in Jerusalem financially.
1015 Corinth was located in the province of Achaia.

you have been ready *to give*. ⁴For if any Macedonians should come with me and find that you are not prepared, we would be most ashamed of having been so confident, not to mention the shame that you also would feel. ⁵Therefore I thought it was necessary to urge the brothers to visit you in advance and to complete the arrangements for the generous gift you have promised. Then it will be a blessing, not something done under compulsion.

⁶Remember, whoever sows sparingly will also reap sparingly and whoever sows generously will also reap generously. ⁷Each one should give what he has decided in his heart to give, not reluctantly or under compulsion, because God loves a cheerful giver. ⁸And God is quite able to provide in abundance for you, so that you will always have all that you need for yourselves and more than enough for every good cause. ⁹As it has been written,

"He gives generously to the poor and his righteousness endures forever."

Psalm 112:9

¹⁰Now the one who supplies seed to the sower and bread for food will also supply and multiply your store of seed and will increase your harvest that results from your righteousness. ¹¹*God* will make you rich in every way so that you can be generous at all times so that many will thank God for your gifts which they in turn receive from us.

¹²The doing of this ministry not only meets the needs of God's people but it also produces an outpouring of thankfulness to God. ¹³As a result of your ministry, many will give glory to God because your generosity is proof to them and to everyone that you are obedient to the gospel of Christ. ¹⁴They will pray for you with a deep affection because of the extraordinary grace that God has shown you. ¹⁵Thanks be to God for his gift which words cannot describe.

Paul defends his ministry

10 ¹You all know that Christ is meek and gentle. Therefore I, Paul, who am timid when I am with you, but hard when absent, appeal to you *on this basis of meekness and gentleness*. ²I appeal to you that when I come I may not have to be as hard as I could be with those who think that we are living according to fleshly motives. ³For even though we live in the flesh, we do not wage war according to the flesh.¹⁰¹⁶ ⁴The weapons that we fight with are not fleshly weapons rather that which have power through God to bring down strongholds. ⁵We tear down arguments and every pretentious obstacle that sets itself up against the knowledge of God. We take every captive thought to make it obedient to Christ.

1016   I.e. the old nature or a worldly way.

⁶And we stand ready to punish every act of disobedience. But first you must prove your complete obedience.¹⁰¹⁷

⁷You are judging by what you are seeing on the outside. If someone is sure that he belongs to Christ, he should recognise that we belong to Christ just as much as they do. ⁸For even if I have boasted too much about the authority the Lord has given us, it has only been to build you up, not to tear you down. So I will not be ashamed of using my authority. ⁹It is not my intention to seemingly frighten you with my letters. ¹⁰For they say, "His letters are weighty and forceful, but in person he is unimpressive and his speaking is despised. ¹¹Such people should realise that what we are in our letters when we are absent *from them in Corinth*, we will also be in our actions when we are present *there*.

¹²Of course we do not dare to classify or compare ourselves with those who rate themselves so highly.¹⁰¹⁸ When they measure themselves by themselves and compare themselves with themselves, they are not being wise. ¹³We, however, will not boast beyond the proper limits, but will confine our boasting according to the area that God has deemed to be appropriate. And that area certainly includes you Corinthians. ¹⁴We do not think that our boasting has been inappropriate about you as if we had never visited you. For we were the first ones who came to you with the gospel of Christ. ¹⁵Neither do we go beyond the proper limits in boasting about the work done by others. Rather our hope is that, as your faith continues to grow, that we may be able to do an even much greater work among you. ¹⁶This will mean that we can preach the gospel in regions beyond you. We do not want to boast about work already done in someone else's area. ¹⁷But let him who is boasting, boast in the Lord.¹⁰¹⁹

¹⁸For it is not the one who recommends himself who is approved, but the one whom the Lord recommends.

Paul is different than the false apostles

11 ¹I hope that you will bear with me as I engage in a bit of foolishness and indeed please do bear with me! ²I am jealous for you with a jealousy that comes from God. I promised you to one husband, to present you as a pure virgin to Christ. ³But I am afraid that just as the serpent completely seduced Eve by his cunning,¹⁰²⁰ your minds might somehow be led astray from the simplicity and

---

1017 Paul is referring to the gift that they had promised for the believers in Jerusalem.
1018 Paul is being sarcastic here referring to himself and his co-workers.
1019 Cf. Jer. 9:24.
1020 The complete seduction (*exepatesen*) or beguiling (KJV) of Eve by the serpent seems to have a sexual connotation according to some Jewish traditions (Keener, Craig S, *IVP Bible Background Commentary* (1993)). The Greek OT (LXX) also uses the same base word (*epatesen*) in Gen. 3:13. Cf. 1 Tim. 2:14.

purity *we have* in Christ. ⁴You seem to tolerate it so easily when someone comes and preaches another Jesus different from the Jesus we preached, and to receive a different spirit from the one you already received, and a different gospel from the one you already accepted.

⁵I do not think that I am the least bit inferior to those "super apostles." ⁶I am an untrained speaker but I do have knowledge. We have made this very clear to you in every way.

⁷I preached the gospel of God to you free of charge. I humbled myself in order that you might be lifted up. Did I commit a sin in doing so? *Hardly.* ⁸I "robbed" other churches by receiving support from them so that I could be of service to you. ⁹Furthermore when I was with you and needed something, I was not a burden to anyone; the *Christian* brothers who came from Macedonia supplied what I needed. I have kept myself from being a burden to you in any way, and I will continue to do so. ¹⁰As surely as the truth of Christ is in me, nobody in the whole of Achaia[1021] will be able to stop me boasting in this way. ¹¹Why *won't I ask you to help me*? Is it because I do not love you? God knows that I do! ¹²But I will keep on doing likewise so that I may stop the "super apostles" from having any opportunity to boast saying that they are our equals.[1022]

¹³For these men are false apostles. They are deceitful workmen, disguising themselves as apostles of Christ. ¹⁴And it is no wonder, for even Satan disguises himself as an angel of light. ¹⁵Therefore it is not surprising if his servants disguise themselves as servants of righteousness. In the end they will get what their actions deserve.

Paul boasts about his sufferings

¹⁶I will say it again: Let no one take me for a fool. But if you do, then receive me just as you would a fool, so that I also, like the others, may boast a little. ¹⁷The way in which I am now speaking is not as the Lord would speak but in such boasting I am speaking like a fool. ¹⁸Since there are many[1023] who are boasting according to the flesh, I too will boast. ¹⁹You are happily putting up with fools— being so wise as you are. ²⁰In fact, you even put up with those who enslave you or prey upon you, those who take advantage of you, put it over you, look down on you or face up to you. ²¹I am ashamed to admit that we have been too weak to do such things![1024]

But if anyone dares to boast (I am speaking as a fool), I also dare to boast

---

1021 I.e. southern Greece including the Isthmus of Corinth and all the land south of it including Athens.
1022 I.e. Paul and his co-workers will continue to refuse financial help from the Corinthian Christians.
1023 I.e. 'the super apostles'.
1024 Paul is being extremely sarcastic. He means the opposite of what he is saying.

about the same thing. ²²Are they Hebrews? So am I. Are they Israelites? So am I. Are they Abraham's descendants? So am I. ²³Are they servants of Christ? (I am out of my mind to speak like this.) I am more so. I have worked much harder, been in prison more frequently, been flogged more severely, and have been close to death often. ²⁴Five times I was given forty lashes less one by the Jews.[1025] ²⁵On three occasions I was beaten with rods, once I was stoned, three times I was shipwrecked. I also spent a night and a day in the open sea. ²⁶In my many travels I have been in danger from rivers, in danger from robbers, in danger from my own people and from Gentiles, in danger in the city, in the desert, and on the high seas. I have also been in danger from those who have pretended to be Christians. ²⁷I have laboured and toiled and have often gone without sleep. I have been hungry and thirsty and have often gone without food, have been cold and without enough warm clothing. ²⁸And besides all these things, I have the pressure of the day to day needs of all the churches. ²⁹When someone is weak then I too feel weak. When someone is led into sin, then I burn *with anger*.

³⁰If I must boast, I will boast of the things that show my weakness. ³¹The God and Father of the Lord Jesus, who is to be praised forever, knows that I am not lying. ³²While I was in Damascus, King Aretas' governor had guards surround the city of the Damascenes in order to try and arrest me.[1026] ³³But I was lowered in a basket from a window in the wall and escaped from his hands.

Paul is caught up to the third heaven

12 ¹I must continue to boast even though it doesn't do any good. So I will talk about visions and revelations given to me from the Lord: ²I know a man in Christ who fourteen years ago was snatched[1027] up to the third heaven.[1028] (I don't know whether he was in the body or out of the body—God knows). ³⁻⁴I know that this man was snatched up to paradise. (Again, I don't know whether this man was in the body or outside the body—God knows). He heard inexpressible things, things that man is not permitted to tell. ⁵I will boast about a man like that, but I will not boast about myself. I will only boast about my weaknesses. ⁶However even if I wanted to boast, it would not be foolish because I would be telling the truth. But I will refrain from boasting, because I do not want any of you to give me credit beyond what you have seen me do or heard me say.[1029]

1025 Cf. Gal. 6:17. Forty lashes of the whip was considered to be the maximum number that could be given to a guilty person when punished by a Hebrew court. To ensure there wasn't a miscalculation, tradition limited the maximum to one less—39. Cf. Deut. 25:1–3.
1026 Aretas IV died in AD 39, which places Paul's conversion previous to this.
1027 This is the Greek root *harpazo* where the term rapture is used. Cf. 1 Thess. 4:17.
1028 This probably occurred when Paul went down to Arabia (Gal. 1:17).
1029 Paul refrained from disclosing all that he heard and saw during his encounters with Jesus.

Paul's 'thorn in the flesh'

⁷But in order that I don't become too proud because of the exceptional revelations given to me, there was given to me a thorn in the flesh, a messenger¹⁰³⁰ of Satan, that he might beat me. It was given to me lest I became too proud. ⁸Three times I pleaded with the Lord to take it away from me. ⁹But he said to me, "My grace is sufficient for you for my power is made perfect in weakness." Therefore I will boast even more about my weaknesses so that Christ's power may take up residence in me. ¹⁰So then, I delight in weaknesses, in insults, in hardships, in persecutions, and in difficulties because I do it for Christ. For when I am weak, then I am strong.

Paul's concern for the Corinthian church

¹¹I have acted the fool but you made me do it. I should have been commended by you for I am not inferior to the "super-apostles" even though I am nothing really. ¹²Indeed, I did many signs, wonders and miracles of an apostle and I did these very patiently. ¹³Were you treated any worse than the other churches? I was never a burden to you! Please forgive me this wrong!¹⁰³¹

¹⁴Look, I am now ready to visit you for the third time and I will not make any demands of you because I do not want your possessions but you yourselves. After all, children should not have to provide for their parents, but parents for their children. ¹⁵Therefore I will gladly spend everything I have on you and I will give myself completely to you as well. Do you love me less because I love you so much?

¹⁶Be that as it may, I have not been a burden to you. But no doubt someone will say that I was being sneaky and I trapped you with lies. ¹⁷Did I manipulate you through those I sent to you previously? ¹⁸I urged Titus to go to you and I sent our brother with him. Would you say that Titus manipulated you? Of course not. Did we not act in the same spirit and behave the same way?

¹⁹Have you been thinking all along that we have been defending ourselves to you? We have been speaking as Christ would have us speak in the presence of God. Everything that we do, my dear friends, is to build you up. ²⁰For I am afraid that when I do come I may not find you to be as I expected and you may not find me to be as you expected. I fear that I might find quarrelling, jealousy, outbursts of anger, factions, slander, gossip, arrogance and disorder. ²¹I am afraid that when I do come again my God will humble me, in that I will be grieved over many

---

1030   I.e. *angelos* = angel.
1031   Paul is intentionally being sarcastic here.

who have sinned earlier and have not turned from their impure ways—sexual sin and indecent sexual depravity in which they have indulged.

Paul's final warnings

13 ¹This is now the third time that I am coming to you. The Scripture says, "Every matter must be established by the testimony of two or three witnesses."¹⁰³² ²I already gave you a warning when I was with you the second time. I now repeat it while absent: on my return I will not spare those who sinned earlier or any of the others, ³since you are demanding proof that Christ is speaking through me. When he deals with you, he is not weak, instead he is powerful among you. ⁴Indeed, Christ was crucified in weakness, yet he now lives by the power of God. Likewise we are weak in him, yet we will live with him by the power of God to serve you.

⁵Examine yourselves to see whether you are in the faith—test yourselves. Do you not realise that Christ Jesus is in you, unless of course you fail the test? ⁶But I hope that you will know that we have not failed the test. ⁷Now we pray to God that you will not do anything wrong and it's not to show that we have passed the test but to get you to do what is right, even though we seem to be failures. ⁸For we cannot do anything against the truth but only for the truth. ⁹We are happy whenever we are weak but you are strong. Our prayer is that you may become complete.¹⁰³³ ¹⁰This is why I write these things when I am absent so that when I arrive I may not have to be so harsh in the use of my authority. The Lord gave me this authority for building you up, not for tearing you down.

Final greetings

¹¹Finally brothers, rejoice! Become complete *Christians*! Listen to my encouragements! Be of one mind! Live in peace! And the God of love and peace will be with you.

¹²Greet one another with a holy kiss. ¹³All of God's people send their greetings.

¹⁴May the grace of the Lord Jesus Christ and the love of God and the fellowship of the Holy Breath be with you all.

1032   Cf. Deut. 17:6, 19:15. The meaning here by Paul quoting Deuteronomy is that the three witnesses may be the three visits.
1033   Paul's desire was that the Corinthians become complete in the sense of maturity. Cf. Gal. 6:1.

GALATIANS

Introduction

Pisidian Antioch is the city in the southern region of the province of Galatia where Paul wrote his letter to the Galatian churches in about AD 49. The issue here was that the Jewish believers were upsetting the new Gentile converts requiring them to be circumcised and putting other unnecessary Mosaic Law requirements on them. This letter is all about the freedom we have in Christ (Gal. 5:1) and that we need to be careful not to chase after another gospel which restricts (Gal. 1:6). One of the key verses in this letter is Gal. 5:22-23 which demonstrates the evidence of the kind of life when we live by the power and control of the Holy Spirit.

An important eschatological verse in this letter is Gal. 4:31 which describes the church as being the children of the free woman (Sarah). Importantly in Rev. 12:6 the woman (the church) flees into the desert for a time, times and half a time (1290 days). Sometimes the woman is Mary, sometimes Israel and as here in Galatians sometimes Sarah but importantly the woman is always a metaphor for those who have faith and believe in Christ. This letter to the Galatian churches is most likely the first letter that Paul wrote.

1 ¹From Paul, an apostle—sent not from men or by human source, but by Jesus Christ and God the Father who raised him from the dead ²along with all the brothers,

To the churches in Galatia.*¹⁰³⁴*

³Grace be to you all and peace from God our Father and the Lord Jesus Christ. ⁴Christ gave himself for our sins to rescue us from this present age and all of its evil. He did this according to the will of our God and Father, ⁵to whom be glory forever and ever. Amen.

There is only one gospel

⁶I am absolutely astonished that you *Galatians* are so quickly abandoning *God* who called you by the grace of Christ and are turning to a different gospel. ⁷But this *different gospel* is really, in fact, no gospel at all. It seems evident that some people are unsettling you and are trying to distort the gospel of Christ. ⁸But *hypothetically* even if we*¹⁰³⁵* or an angel from heaven*¹⁰³⁶* was to preach a gospel that was not the same as we preached to you, may he be cursed. ⁹As we have said before, so now I say it again that if anybody is preaching to you a gospel that is different than the one you originally accepted, may he be cursed.

¹⁰Does it sound like I am now trying to win the approval of men? Not at all! I want God's approval! Or *maybe you think* I am trying to be a man-pleaser? If I were trying to please men, then I would not be a servant of Christ.

God himself chose Paul to be an apostle

¹¹I want you to know brothers, the gospel I preach is not of human origin. ¹²I did not receive it from any person, nor was it something that I was taught, rather, I received it by a revelation of Jesus Christ. ¹³For you have heard of my former way of life in Judaism, how intensely I kept on persecuting the church of God and was attacking it. ¹⁴I was making progress in Judaism beyond many Jews of my own age and I was extremely enthusiastic for the traditions of my forefathers.

1034 Galatia is located in modern-day central Turkey. Some say that the letter to the Galatian churches was the first letter that Paul wrote c. AD 49. Paul wrote this letter in response to learning that there were certain Jewish teachers who were imposing circumcision and the Mosaic Law on the new Gentile converts. Paul writes this letter to reassure that salvation is by grace and to emphatically deny that any legal requirements such as circumcision are necessary in the new spiritual life in Christ.
1035 Probably meaning Paul alone or Paul and his companions, possibly Silas and Timothy.
1036 This piece of information from Paul gives us a hint at the type of Jewish false teaching that was around in the 1st century AD. There was a great Jewish fascination with angels in the period around the time of Christ in the centuries before and after.

¹⁵But God reserved me from the day of my birth and called me by his grace. And when it pleased him, ¹⁶God revealed his Son to me so that I might preach *the gospel* to the Gentiles. I did not consult anyone, ¹⁷nor did I go up to Jerusalem to *see* those who had become apostles before me but I went immediately into Arabia and then later I returned to Damascus.

¹⁸Then three years later, I went up to Jerusalem to become acquainted with Peter and I stayed with him for fifteen days. ¹⁹I did not see any of the other apostles except James, the Lord's brother. ²⁰Before God I am not lying, the things that I am writing to you are true.

²¹Then later I went to the regions of Syria and Cilicia. ²²The *members of the churches in Judea* did not personally know me. ²³They only heard the report about me saying, "The man who formerly persecuted us is now preaching the very faith that he was once attacking." ²⁴And they praised God because of me.

Paul is accepted by the apostles

2 ¹Fourteen years later I went back up to Jerusalem again with Barnabas and I brought Titus along also. ²I went back up because of a revelation from God. I met with the leaders privately to explain the gospel that I preach among the Gentiles. I did this to make sure that what I had done in the past and what I was doing now was acceptable to them. ³And even though Titus my companion was a Greek, they did not force him to be circumcised. ⁴This came about because some false brothers had slipped into the group in order to spy on the freedoms we have in Christ Jesus and to make us slaves. ⁵But we did not give in to them for even a moment so that the truth of the gospel might remain with you.

⁶As for those who seemed to be important leaders, those men had nothing to add to what I was already doing. Whether they were important or not makes no difference to me because God does not judge by external appearances. ⁷On the contrary, *rather than trying to change what I was already doing,* they could see that *God* had entrusted me with the task of preaching the gospel to the uncircumcised,[1037] just as Peter had been preaching to the circumcised.[1038] ⁸For God, who was at work in making Peter an apostle to the Jews, was also at work in making me an apostle to the Gentiles. ⁹James, Peter and John, the ones being seen as pillars of the church, gave to me and Barnabas the right hand of fellowship[1039] when they recognised *God's* favour in giving to me *this task*. ¹⁰The

---

1037 This is a figure of speech (metonym) meaning the Gentiles.
1038 This is a figure of speech (metonym) meaning the Jews.
1039 Fellowship indicates partnership in this great task of sharing the gospel. The leaders were indicating that they were behind and partnering with Paul and Barnabas in their ministry to the Gentiles.

only thing that they asked of us was that we must continue to remember the poor, the very thing that I was eager to continue in doing.

Paul and Peter have a disagreement

[11]When Peter came to Antioch, I opposed him to his face because clearly what he had done was wrong. [12]James had sent certain men to Antioch but before they had arrived Peter had been in the habit of eating with the Gentiles there. But after they had arrived, Peter began to withdraw and he separated himself from the Gentiles because he was afraid of those who were insisting on circumcision. [13]The other Jews joined him in his hypocrisy and even Barnabas was led astray as well.

[14]But when I saw that they were not following the truth of the gospel, I said to Peter in front of everyone, "You are a Jew, yet you have been living like a Gentile, not like a Jew. Why then do you force Gentiles to live as Jews *and follow their customs?*"

God saves both Jews and Gentiles by faith

[15]Indeed I say to you Galatians that we who are Jews by birth and not "Gentile sinners" as such, [16]know that God does not declare a man to be righteous[1040] because he observes the Law, but because he believes in Jesus Christ. So we *Jews* too, believe in Christ Jesus so that God may declare us as being righteous by having faith in Christ and not by observing the Law. *The fact is that* God does not declare any human being as being righteous by observing the Law.

[17]If we seek to be declared righteous by God through Christ and it so happens that we ourselves are found to be sinners, does that mean that Christ, in fact, encourages sin? Absolutely not! [18]It is only if I return to the system of Law that I had previously torn down that shows that I am in fact a lawbreaker. [19]For through the Law I died to the Law[1041] so that I might live for God. [20]In effect, I was crucified with Christ. And I am not *really* the one still living but Christ is living in me. The way that I am now living in the flesh, is based on my faith in the Son of God. He was the one who loved me and gave himself for me. [21]I am not setting aside the grace[1042] that God has shown me for if I could have obtained righteousness through the Law, then Christ has in effect died for nothing.

1040   This is the technical term often translated 'justified' in English translations. It basically means to be put in a right relationship with God. Note that God is the one who justifies and God is the one who we are put in the right relationship with. So justification essentially is God putting man right with himself.

1041   This means that the Law was the catalyst in Paul discovering that the Law was ineffective in being able to help him or save him. He was in a sense dead to its power. This led him to understand the true power of the gospel through the work of Jesus Christ and so he could now live for God effectively meaning that he could be put right with God. So again we see that God is the author and end goal of justification.

1042   Grace here probably means the unmerited gift of God sending his son, Jesus Christ, to die for mankind.

Obedience to the Law or trusting in Christ?

3 ¹You foolish Galatians! Who has bewitched you? I so clearly described to you how Jesus Christ was crucified. ²And I would like to know just one thing from you: Did you receive the Breath *of God* by observing the Law or by hearing *the gospel* and believing it? ³How can you be so foolish? You started out with the spiritual and now you are trying to be perfected *by acting* in the flesh. ⁴Have you suffered so much for no reason? I think not! Surely it was for a reason? ⁵Why is it that God gives you the Breath and works amazing miracles in your midst? Is it because you observe the Law or because you believe *the gospel*?

⁶Now consider *what the Scriptures say about* Abraham, "He believed God and so because of his faith, God considered him to be righteous." ⁷You need to understand then, that those who believe are the true children of Abraham.[1043] ⁸The Scripture foresaw that God would cause the Gentiles to be declared righteous by means of faith. In fact, God made known the gospel to Abraham in advance when he said to him, "All nations will be blessed through you." ⁹Therefore those people who believe are blessed along with Abraham, the man of faith.

¹⁰However those people who depend on observing the Law *to be declared righteous* are under a curse.[1044] For it is written *in the Scriptures*, "Cursed is everyone who does not continue to do everything that is written in the book of the Law." ¹¹Clearly God declares no one to be righteous by the Law because *as the Scriptures says*, "The righteous will live because they believe in him." ¹²But obedience to the Law is not the same as having faith. Rather, the Scripture explains the Law like this, "The man who has life is the one who does everything according to the Law."

¹³Christ set us free[1045] from the curse of the Law by actually becoming a curse for us, for it is written *in the Scriptures*, "Cursed is everyone who is hanged on a tree."[1046] ¹⁴He set us free in order that the blessing[1047] given to Abraham might

---

[1043] This is not meaning that those ones who have faith are literally the children of Abraham in a genealogical sense but in a spiritual sense because they share what was most important about Abraham – his faith in God.

[1044] This of course does not mean that they are under a spell. It means that those who try to obtain salvation or be righteous by means of trying to obey the Law stand condemned by God. They stand condemned because no one is able to obey the Law perfectly and persevere in it even if they are able to observe the Law.

[1045] The term 'set us free' is the theological word 'redeem' that is often used in translations. It has the dual meaning of 'to buy' but also 'release'. Christ paid for our release by his own death on the cross.

[1046] Cf. Deut. 21:23. In its original context the verse refers to the practice of hanging the bodies of criminals on trees and leaving them there; the Jews believed that to do so would defile their land (TH). The Roman practice of crucifying criminals was commonplace in the 1st century and was used as a deterrent for insubordination of its subjects. The term "tree" here does not necessarily mean a live green tree but it could mean a post or simply timber. Of course Jesus wasn't put to death by a rope around the neck as the word 'hanged' seems to infer in our modern-day way of thinking but he was nailed to the crossbar and upright post. Cf. Acts 10:39.

[1047] The blessing is that the Gentiles would come into a right relationship with God and that it would

come to the Gentiles through Christ Jesus. In this way, it became possible that we might all[1048] receive the promise of the Breath *of God* by believing in him.

God's promise cannot be changed by a later law

[15]*Christian* brothers. Let me give you an example from everyday life. Once an agreement has been drawn up and ratified between two parties, no one can break it or add anything to it. [16]Now *God* made promises to Abraham and in effect to his descendant. The Scripture does not say to 'his descendants' in the plural meaning many people but to 'his descendant' meaning only one person—Christ. [17]What I am saying is this: The Law which was introduced 430 years later does not break the agreement ratified by God and so invalidate the promise. [18]For if the inheritance depends on the Law then it no longer depends on a promise. But God in his grace gave the inheritance[1049] to Abraham by means of a promise.

[19]Therefore what was the purpose of the Law? The Law was added so that wilful disobedience[1050] could be recognised. It remained valid until the descendant[1051] came. He was the one referred to in the promise. The Law was handed down with the help of angels by the hand of a Mediator.[1052] [20]Now the mediator is not *needed for just* one *party* but God was only one *when he made his promise to Abraham*.[1053]

The purpose of the Law

[21]Does that mean that the Law is opposed to the promises of God? Absolutely not! For if a law had been given that could impart life, then man could be declared righteous by *obeying* the Law. [22]However the Scripture says that the whole world is imprisoned by sin. Therefore the *blessing* that was promised was by means of faith, *specifically* to those who believe in Jesus Christ.

[23]Before this *period of* faith came, we were held prisoners by the Law and it was as if we were being locked up until *the time of* faith was revealed. [24]Therefore the Law was our guardian to lead us to Christ so that God might declare us to

---

1048 fulfil the promise God gave to Abraham in Gen. 12:3 that all nations would be blessed through him. All Christians both Jews and Gentiles.
1049 "The inheritance" here implies all that God had promised Israel through Abraham including the land of Canaan, known as the Promised Land.
1050 This is the Biblical term 'transgression'. Cf. Matt. 6:14 footnote.
1051 Literally 'the seed' meaning Christ.
1052 The intermediary is Yahweh in human form as there is only one mediator between God and man—Christ (1 Tim. 2:5). This verse shows the inferiority of the Law over the promise because it was not administered directly by God.
1053 The inference here is that God acted alone without a mediator when giving his promise to Abraham therefore the promise is superior to the Law. The whole point of this letter to the Galatian church was to show them the inferiority of the Law. It had a place, to be sure, in showing sin in the life of the believer but it was an inferior mechanism to the work of grace through Christ. Cf. Mark 12:28-30.

be righteous by means of faith. ²⁵Now that the time of faith has come, we are no longer under the guardianship of the Law.

We are all sons of God through faith in Jesus Christ

²⁶You are all sons of God by having faith in Christ Jesus. ²⁷For all of you who were baptised into Christ have become like Christ himself.¹⁰⁵⁴ ²⁸So in light of this, there is neither Jew nor Greek, slave nor free, male or female, for you are all the one and the same in Christ Jesus.¹⁰⁵⁵ ²⁹If indeed you belong to Christ, then you are a descendant of Abraham and you thereby inherit whatever God promised to Abraham.¹⁰⁵⁶

4 ¹I will further explain what I am saying: As long as the heir is still a child, he is in fact no different than a slave, even though he owns the whole property. ²As a child he is subject to guardians and those who manage his financial affairs until the time set by his father. ³So also, when we were children, we were in slavery to worldly principles. ⁴But when the time had come, God sent his Son. He was born of a woman and he lived subject to *the Jewish* Law. ⁵*He was born* to set free those who were under the Law in order that God might adopt us as his sons.

⁶And because you are sons, God sent the Breath of his Son into our hearts, the Breath who causes us to cry out, "Abba,¹⁰⁵⁷ Father." ⁷So then, you are no longer a slave *to worldly principles or the Law* but a son and since you are a son, you are also to inherit *the blessing* through God.

Paul's concern for the Galatian church

⁸However in the past when you did not know God, you were enslaved to beings¹⁰⁵⁸ that were not really gods at all. ⁹But now that you actually know God or rather should I say you are known by God, why is it that you are turning back to those powerless and miserable worldly principles? Are you wanting to be enslaved by them all over again? ¹⁰You are observing *particular special* days

---

1054 In the Greek, the metaphorical expression 'putting on' as in putting on a garment or piece of clothing is used to convey the idea that we 'put on Christ' like we have taken on his character and qualities when we are baptised. Water baptism is an immersion into a new way of life and an acknowledgment to go forth and proceed in a new way.
1055 A beautiful picture of how we are to live together in Christ. There is no racism (Jew nor Greek), no classism (slave nor free) nor sexism (male or female). All are considered to be one in Christ.
1056 Believers are the 'true Israel' but that doesn't mean that God will not keep his promises to physical Israel as well. Cf. Rev. 12:1.
1057 Jesus spoke Aramaic, and he may have started the Lord's Prayer with the Aramaic *"Abba"*. This liturgical formula suggests a passionate and intimate cry addressed to God in recognition of his fatherhood and in gratitude for the gift of sonship (TH). Cf. Mark 14:36.
1058 It is unclear to what Paul was referring to here. It could be that he was referring to idols that the Galatians had previously worshipped before becoming Christians or to pagan deities or even demons. Most translations are vague on this as it is difficult to be definitive.

and months and seasons and years.*¹⁰⁵⁹* ¹¹I am worried for you *Galatians*. Maybe I have wasted my time with you.*¹⁰⁶⁰*

¹²Brothers, please, I'm begging you, put yourselves in my place as I have put myself in your place.*¹⁰⁶¹* You haven't done me any wrong. ¹³As you well know, it was because of an illness that I first preached the gospel to you. ¹⁴Even though my illness was a trial for you, you did not treat me with contempt or reject me. Instead, you welcomed me the same way as you would welcome an angel of God or as you would welcome Jesus Christ himself. ¹⁵So where has your happiness gone? I can vouch that if you could have done so, you would have plucked out your eyes and given them to me. ¹⁶Have I now become your enemy by telling you the truth?

¹⁷Those *Judaizers* are keen to win you over but their intentions are not good. What they actually want is to alienate you from us so that you may be passionate for them. ¹⁸It is fine to be passionate for a good cause. But be *passionate* always, not just when I am with you. ¹⁹My dear little children, I am in great pain as if I am in childbirth as *I wait for* you to mature in Christ. ²⁰Oh how I wish I could be with you all right now and change the tone *in which I have had to write to you* because you perplex me greatly.

The example of Hagar and Sarah

²¹Tell me something, you who desire to be under *the rule of* the Law: are you not aware of what the Law says? ²²It is written that Abraham had two sons, one by the slave woman and the other by the free woman. ²³His son by the slave woman was born in the way that children are normally conceived but his son by the free woman was born as the result of a promise.

²⁴These events may be taken allegorically, for the women represent two covenants.*¹⁰⁶²* One covenant is from Mount Sinai and bears children who are to be slaves: This is Hagar. ²⁵Hagar stands for Mount Sinai in Arabia and she also can be compared to the present city of Jerusalem. This is because the people that live in Jerusalem are in slavery to the Law. ²⁶But the Jerusalem which is

---

1059   Paul probably has in mind the Jewish system of religious feast days and weeks as it was the religious Judaizers who were trying to influence the young Gentile Galatian church to follow the Mosaic Law.
1060   Paul was worried for the Galatian church because they had begun to observe the Jewish legalistic system and for all intents and purposes they had turned their backs on the gospel of grace.
1061   Paul is pleading with his Galatian brothers in Christ to abandon the Jewish Law as a means of gaining acceptance before God.
1062   A covenant is a verbal pact or agreement between two parties which describes the reciprocal benefits and responsibilities of both sides. It is important to note that a covenant is not the result of negotiation or compromise but is initiated by one of the parties.

above[1063] is free and she is our[1064] mother. ²⁷For as it is written *in the Scriptures about Jerusalem,*

> "Be happy, childless woman, you who bears no children.
> Sing and cry out loudly, even though you have not felt labour pains.
> The reason is that more are the children of the woman who was
> abandoned than of her who has a husband."[1065]

Isaiah 54:1

²⁸Now, therefore, brothers, you are like Isaac, children of promise. ²⁹At the time, *Ishmael* the natural-born son persecuted the spiritual son, so it is today. ³⁰But what does the Scripture say? "Get rid of the slave woman and her son, for the slave woman's son will never share in the inheritance with the free woman's son." ³¹Therefore it can be said brothers, that we are not children of *Hagar*, a slave woman, but we are children of *Sarah*, the free woman.

Freedom in Christ

5 ¹Christ has freed us so that we might live freely.[1066] Therefore stand firm *in that freedom* and you must not allow yourselves to be subjected again by a yoke[1067] of slavery.

²Pay attention to me! I, Paul, am telling you that if you allow yourselves to be circumcised,[1068] then Christ will be of no profit to you whatsoever. ³Again I assert to every man who allows himself to be circumcised that in fact he is obligated to obey the whole Law. ⁴You who are trying to be declared righteous by God through the means of the Law have actually separated yourselves from Christ. You have put yourselves out of the reach of God's grace. ⁵But by faith we are eagerly waiting for *God's* Breath to put us right with him—that is our hope. ⁶For in Christ Jesus, whether you are circumcised or not circumcised, it

---

1063 The New Jerusalem coming down from heaven. Cf. Isa. 2:2–3, Rev. 21:2.
1064 Believers will be inhabiting the New Jerusalem which is above.
1065 Specifically this quote in context from Isa. 54:1 is referring to Jerusalem before the Babylonian exile and after in that Jerusalem would have greater prosperity after their return than before the exile. So it follows that the Christian Church, which corresponds to Sarah and the Jerusalem above (v. 26), would be more fruitful than Judaism, which corresponds to Hagar and 'the Jerusalem of today' (v. 25) whereas Judaism, in which the Law held sway, limited God's holy people to the Jews, the Church, through the preaching of the law-free gospel, embraced Gentiles and Jews alike within the one chosen people of God (Fung, Ronald Y K, *Commentary on Galatians (NICNT)* (1998)).
1066 Freedom here is in the sense that Christians are free from the requirements of the Mosaic Law.
1067 Cf. Matt 11:29 footnote.
1068 Apparently the Judaizers, through their false teaching, were trying to enforce the Gentile Galatian believers to go through the Jewish rites of circumcision before they could become Christians. In other words they must become Jews before they could become believers in Christ.

does not matter. It has no value. The only thing that really counts is when we exercise faith *in Christ*. And faith in turn expresses itself as *we show* love *for others*.

⁷You *Galatians* were running such a good race. Who obstructed you from obeying the truth? How did he persuade you? ⁸That kind of persuasion is not of God, the one who calls you. ⁹As the saying goes, "A small amount of yeast works itself through the whole batch of dough."¹⁰⁶⁹ ¹⁰I am confident in the Lord that you will take no other view *than mine*. But he who is troubling you will be judged and punished, whoever he may be.

¹¹Brothers, if they say that I am still preaching circumcision then why am I still being persecuted? If that were true *that I was preaching that one must be circumcised* then my preaching about the cross of Christ would not be causing any offence. But it is! ¹²As for those who are troubling you, I wish that they would *not only circumcise themselves but go the whole way and* castrate themselves completely!

¹³You, my *Christian* brothers, were called *by God* to be free. But do not use your freedom as an opportunity to indulge the flesh. Rather, serve one another, loving each other. ¹⁴For the Law can be summed up in a single command: "Love your neighbour in the same way that you love yourself." ¹⁵But if you continue on biting and devouring each other, you must be warned because you will end up completely destroying each other.

Living by God's Breath

¹⁶So what I am saying is that you must continue to live by *God's* Breath. Do this and you will not gratify the desires of the flesh. ¹⁷For the flesh desires what is contrary to the Breath and the Breath desires what is contrary to the flesh. The two are in opposition to each other so that *in effect* you end up losing your freedom to do what you want to do. ¹⁸But if you are being led by *God's* Breath, then the Law has no hold over you.

¹⁹The works of the flesh are rather obvious: sexual immorality, filthy sexual behaviour and indecent sexual depravity; ²⁰idolatry and witchcraft; hatred towards one another, bickering, jealousy, outbursts of anger, selfish ambition, cliques, and factions. ²¹Also it includes envy, drunkenness, orgies and the like. I am warning you now as I have done before that those who live like this will not take their place in the realm where God reigns.

²²But the fruit that comes from the Breath *of God* is love, joy, peace, patience, kindness, goodness, loyalty, ²³gentleness and self-control. The Law isn't needed

---

1069 In the Bible, yeast or leaven as it is also known is often used as a picture of how sin or evil spreads because the amount of yeast is small but its eventual influence is large. Here Paul is saying that the false teachers were few in number but their evil influence had affected the whole church.

when we live this way. ²⁴But those who belong to Christ Jesus have crucified the flesh with its passions and evil desires.

²⁵And since *God's* Breath has given life to us, let us also keep in step with *his* Breath. ²⁶We must not become conceited, provoking each other and being jealous of each other.

Believers must help each other

6 ¹Brothers, if someone has been detected wilfully disobeying *God*, then you who are spiritual should restore¹⁰⁷⁰ him in a spirit of meekness. But watch out that you yourselves are not also tempted. ²Help carry each other's burdens. By doing so you are fulfilling the law of Christ.¹⁰⁷¹ ³For if anyone thinks that he is something but really he is nothing, then he is deceiving himself. ⁴Each man should judge his own actions. If his actions are good then he can be satisfied. He should not compare himself to anyone else. ⁵Each man will have to bear his own load *in this matter*.¹⁰⁷²

⁶And *by the way*, if you receive instruction in the word then you must share and contribute materially with your instructor.

⁷Do not be misled: God cannot be mocked. Whatever a man sows, he will reap accordingly. ⁸For the man who sows to please his flesh will reap moral decay from that flesh. But the man who sows to please the Breath *of God* will reap eternal life from *his* Breath. ⁹Let us not be weary in doing good, for at the appropriate time *in the future* we will reap a harvest if we do not become discouraged and give up. ¹⁰Therefore, as the opportunity arises, let us do good to all people but especially let us do good to those who belong to the household of faith.

Paul's final warning

¹¹Look now at the large letters that I am using as I write to you with my own hand.

¹²There are *false teachers* who are wanting to show off by trying to make you be circumcised.¹⁰⁷³ The only reason that they are doing this is that they wish

---

1070 The Greek word here for "restore" is *kartartizo* which is the same word used in Matt. 4:21 for the mending of the fishing nets. It also has the sense as in here in Gal. 6:1 in restoring a person which means to lead that person back to a full commitment to Christ which involved true repentance.
1071 I believe that Paul is saying that if the whole Law can be summed up by the concept of love as mentioned in 5:14, then when we help carry one another's burdens it is like we are being obedient to that law of love or if you like, that law of Christ. Cf. 1 Cor. 9:21.
1072 Verse 5 is a hard verse to understand as it seems to contradict v. 2 where we are encouraged to bear each other's burdens or load. So why the paradox? One possible reason is that in v. 5, Paul might be referring to v. 4, not v. 2, where each man has enough of his own difficulties and problems to sort through so effectively, don't compare yourselves to others.
1073 The false teachers or Judaizers were keeping a foot in both camps and trying to remain in good

to avoid being persecuted for preaching about *the death of* Christ on the cross. ¹³Not even those who are circumcised obey the Law and yet they want you to be circumcised so that they can boast that you have submitted to this physical ceremony of the flesh. ¹⁴May it never be that I would boast. Absolutely not! The only exception would be that I would speak without reservation about the cross of our Lord Jesus Christ. Because of Jesus, the *things of this* world have become, as it were, dead to me and likewise, I have become dead to *the things of* the world. ¹⁵It does not matter whether someone is circumcised or not circumcised. What really matters is becoming a new creation. ¹⁶May there be peace to everyone who walks according to this principle and may there be mercy upon the Israel of God.

¹⁷The last thing I want to say is this: Let no one give me any more trouble for I bear the marks on my body because of Jesus. ¹⁸May the grace of our Lord Jesus Christ be with your spirit, brothers. Amen.

---

standing with the Jewish community.

EPHESIANS

Introduction

Paul wrote his letter to the Ephesian church in about AD 62 most likely when he was at Rome. It is thought that this letter was a circular letter with a wider readership in mind than just Ephesus. Ephesus was the mother church in Asia Minor with Jesus writing his first letter to Ephesus in Rev. 2:1–7 in his seven letters to the seven churches of Revelation. An important theme in the book of Ephesians is the phrase "in Christ" which is repeated numerous times. This ties in with the idea of corporate election with the only truly chosen people being the Jewish race. Election is Christocentric and only makes sense as we are found in Christ.

The letter explores the idea that the Gentiles have come into the household of God and now the two have become one. The Gentiles are also now called the elect because they have come by God's grace through the means of faith. Ephesians is heavy on the doctrines of predestination, corporate election and spiritual blessings in chapters 1 to 3 and concentrates on practical Christian living in chapters 4 to 6 including unity, marriage and spiritual warfare.

1

¹From Paul, an apostle of Christ Jesus by God's will,

To God's holy people at Ephesus, the loyal ones in Christ Jesus.

²May God our Father and the Lord Jesus Christ grant you grace and peace.

Every spiritual blessing for those in Christ

³Praise be to the God and Father of our Lord Jesus Christ, who has blessed us all, *both Jews and Gentiles,*[1074] with every spiritual blessing in the heavenly places in Christ. ⁴But before the overthrow[1075] of the world, he chose us in him, *the Jews*, to be holy and blameless in his sight. Because of his love, ⁵God predetermined that we, *the Jews*, were to be adopted as his sons through Jesus Christ according to his good pleasure and will. ⁶This is to the praise of the glory of his grace, which he has freely given to us by means of his beloved Son. ⁷In him, we have been bought back by means of his blood in which we all receive the forgiveness of sins. This is in accordance with the riches of God's grace ⁸that he lavished on us with all wisdom and understanding.

⁹And he made known to us, *the Jews*, a hidden truth which he desired and intended to make happen in Christ. ¹⁰The hidden truth is that God plans in the final dispensation to bring all things in heaven and on earth together in Christ.[1076]

¹¹God also chose us, *the Jews*, to be in Christ because it was determined in advance according to his plan. He works out everything to conform with the intentions of his will, ¹²in order that we *Jews*,[1077] who were the first to hope in Christ, might be to the praise of his glory.

1074 This first passage from vv. 3–14 is just one contiguous sentence in the Greek, therefore in my opinion, is including the one thought of contrast between the Jews and Gentiles. This has major theological implications in that Jews are chosen but the Gentiles were merely included in God's plan as per v. 13. This thought is further developed, I believe, by Paul in chapter 2.

1075 The significant Greek word which is typically translated as 'foundation' or 'creation' is from *kataballo* which is from *kata* and *ballo*; meaning to throw down. Strong's 2602. The overthrow of the world occurred when Adam and Eve listened to Satan and ate the fruit from the Tree of the Knowledge of Good and Evil. The overthrow of the world refers to the overthrow of God's established order when Adam sinned. Cf. Luke 11:50.

1076 Progressive dispensationalism as opposed to classic dispensationalism does not see that God has a separate purpose and salvation plan for Israel and the Gentiles but rather he has a single unfolding plan to redeem mankind by grace through faith. It does not believe however that Gentile believers replace Israel rather the promises made to Israel will still be literally fulfilled in the millennial kingdom. "All things in heaven and on earth" here means all of saved mankind and angels too.

1077 TH agrees that the 1st person plural pronoun here is exclusive not inclusive. In other words "we" here excludes someone. In my opinion, Paul here is excluding the Gentiles and just talking about himself and his people, the Jews. This gives weight to the theory that in this whole passage from vv. 3–14, Paul sometimes includes the Gentiles and sometimes excludes them in his thinking. But to be clear, the Greek does not demand inclusive/exclusive 1st person plural pronouns as per the English.

¹³And you *Gentiles*[1078] were also included in Christ when you heard the word of truth, the gospel of your salvation. Having believed, you were marked in him with a seal, which is the promised Holy Breath. ¹⁴It is a deposit guaranteeing our inheritance which remains until those who are God's possession will be set free. Praise be to his glory!

Paul gives thanks to God for the believers

¹⁵For this reason, ever since I heard about your[1079] faith in the Lord Jesus and your love for all of God's holy people, ¹⁶I have not stopped giving thanks for you and remembering you in my prayers. ¹⁷*I keep asking God*, the glorious Father of our Lord Jesus Christ, that he may give you the spirit of wisdom and revelation so that you may know him in a fuller way. ¹⁸*I pray* also that your eyes will be open and you will have insight so that you may understand the hope to which he has called you. *I pray* that you might know how rich the glorious inheritance is which he has promised to his people. ¹⁹And *I pray* also that you might know his immeasurably great power for us who believe. That power working in us is the same as the mighty strength ²⁰which he exerted when he raised Christ from the dead and seated him at his right hand in the heavenly places. ²¹Christ's rule is far above all *angels* who rule and have authority and every power and dominion. His rule is above every title that can be given, not only in this present age but also in the age to come. ²²And God placed everything under his feet and appointed him to be head over everything in the church. ²³The church is his body which he himself completes as he completes everything in every way.

The Gentiles are saved by grace through faith

2 ¹As for you *Gentiles*, you were dead in your disobedience and sins. ²You used to live according to the ways of this world and the prince of the power of the air.[1080] He is the spirit who is now at work in those who are disobedient. ³Actually, all of us *Jews* also lived just like the disobedient, satisfying the cravings of our flesh and following its desires and thoughts. Like the rest of *humanity*, we *Jews* were by nature people subjected to God's anger *because of sin*.

⁴But because of God's great love for us, God, who is rich in mercy, ⁵made us alive with Christ. He did this despite the fact that we were spiritually dead

---

But many languages do, which makes translating this passage very difficult.
1078 TH says that this could refer to either Gentile Christians or the readers of the letter (the Ephesians), so this seems to support the fact that Paul is speaking about two different people groups in this passage—the Jews and the Gentiles.
1079 Paul seems to be referring to the faith of the Ephesian Christians here as this is to whom he is addressing this letter. There is also the possibility that again he is referring to the Gentiles as opposed to the Jews.
1080 I.e. Satan.

in our disobedience. (It is by grace that you *Gentiles* have been saved.) ⁶He raised us *all up from spiritual death* with Christ and he seated us with him in the heavenly places because we are in Christ Jesus. ⁷He did this in order that in the coming ages he might demonstrate the immeasurable riches of his grace. This is seen by his generosity towards us in Christ Jesus. ⁸For it is by grace that you *Gentiles* have been saved, through faith.*¹⁰⁸¹* This is not your doing but *salvation is God's gift.¹⁰⁸²* ⁹*Salvation is* not by works so that no one can boast. ¹⁰For we are his masterpiece having been created in Christ Jesus to do good works. God prepared these good works in advance for us to do.

Jews and Gentiles are one in Christ

¹¹Therefore, you who are Gentiles by birth and who are called "uncircumcised" by those who call themselves "the circumcised," you must remember what you were in the past. (Circumcision refers to what is done to the body by the hands of men.) ¹²At that time in the past, you were separate from Christ. You were foreigners and had no citizenship in Israel. The covenants of promise*¹⁰⁸³* were foreign to you. You were without hope and without God in the world. ¹³But now in Christ Jesus you who were once far away*¹⁰⁸⁴* have been brought near through the blood of Christ.

1081   In my opinion there is a huge misunderstanding of this verse and in general, Ephesian chapters 1 and 2, in the sense that election is on an individual basis and that individuals are chosen by God. The corporate election view is a much better fit which comprehends individuals only in association with a group of people and for those 'in Christ'. Election is Christocentric and only makes sense as we are found 'in Christ'. In other words, Christ is really the only chosen individual apart from his twelve main followers (disciples). The Jews were chosen corporately as a race or people (Amos 3:2). In these first two chapters, Paul is comparing the salvation of the Jews with the Gentiles corporately as peoples, stating that it is only by grace that the Gentiles receive salvation and it is through the mechanism of faith in what Christ has done on the cross. Whilst it is true that each person has to make an individual choice to get aboard the 'ship of salvation' with Christ as their captain, God sees believers as a group called 'the elect' only if they come aboard and stay aboard and complete their faith journey with him until the end. 'He who endures to the end will be saved' (Matt. 24:13). Furthermore the Gentiles get to come aboard the 'ship of salvation' only because of the Jew's rejection of their Messiah, Jesus of Nazareth. To summarise, the Jews were chosen before the overthrow of the world by Satan. They were predestined to be adopted as sons (1:1,4) whereas the Gentiles are 'included' as part of the elect and receive salvation by grace through faith. This doesn't preclude the fact that God of course had foreknowledge and he knew that the Gentiles would come on board or be grafted into the tree using another metaphor. Ephesians chapter 2 states that both Jew and Gentile believers are now one people in Christ. Failure to see these things comes about because of the failure to see the difference between 1st person exclusive and inclusive plural pronouns (we, us) in chapter 1.

1082   Faith is not the gift because the genders do not agree. It means that the Gentiles didn't earn their salvation but God gave it to them because of his grace and their faith.

1083   Israel was brought into being by the covenants that God made with the patriarchs (Abraham, Isaac, Jacob) and with the people of Israel at Mount Sinai. The Biblical 'covenant' was not the result of a bargaining session between God and Israel; it was completely God's act, God's decision. The OT covenants were based on God's promises to his people (TH).

1084   The Gentiles were literally "far away" from Zion, the visible dwelling of God with his people but

¹⁴For Christ himself has caused us to be at peace with each other and he has made *both Jews and Gentiles*, the two *peoples*, one. He has broken down the dividing wall, the hostility between us and he accomplished it by what he did in the body.*¹⁰⁸⁵* ¹⁵He annulled¹⁰⁸⁶ the Jewish Law with its rules and regulations. His purpose in doing so was to create in himself one new race out of the two, thereby making peace. ¹⁶By his death on the cross, Christ killed their hostility with each other and he made one new race of people, reconciling them to God. ¹⁷He came and preached the good news of peace to you *Gentiles* who were far away and peace to the Jews who were near. ¹⁸For through him, we both have access to the Father by his one Breath.

¹⁹As a result, you *Gentiles* are no longer foreigners or temporary residents, but you are fellow citizens with God's holy people and *you are* members of God's household. ²⁰And you too are built on the foundation of the apostles and prophets with the cornerstone¹⁰⁸⁷ being Christ Jesus himself. ²¹In him every part of the building is joined together and keeps increasing until it becomes a holy temple in the Lord. ²²And in him also you are being built together to become a dwelling in which God lives by *his* Breath.

Paul explains his ministry to the Gentiles

3 ¹It is for this reason that I Paul, a prisoner because of how I have served Christ Jesus for the sake of you Gentiles, *am praying for you all*. ²I am assuming of course that you have heard that God has given to me, by his grace, the responsibility to help you all. ³In fact, God revealed to me a hidden truth which I now know and I have already written briefly about. ⁴So when listening to this being read, you will be able to understand my insight into this hidden truth concerning Christ. ⁵This was not made known to men in other generations as it has now been revealed by *God's* Breath to his holy apostles and prophets. ⁶The hidden truth is that the Gentiles are joint-heirs of the blessings with Israel, they are members of the one body *with Israel* and they share in the promises that come in Christ Jesus through the gospel.

---

    now they are "near" like the Jews. In Rabbinic teaching 'to come near' was used of the reception of a Gentile convert into the Jewish faith.

1085 I.e. By his crucifixion.

1086 This means to render ineffective the power or force of something. For example when a marriage is annulled, it is when a judge decides that there was no legal marriage. If a judge grants an annulment, the marriage is void. It doesn't deny that a ceremony took place. In the same way the Jewish Law is now void and it is rendered invalid in this NT period. In other words the Jewish Law does not need to be obeyed anymore. It still has a purpose in making a person conscious of sin and showing them that they are sinners and fall short of God's glory (Rom. 3:20,23).

1087 It is unclear what actual stone in a building is meant by the cornerstone but what is clear is that Christ is called the most important stone in the building, the one that provides cohesion and support for the whole structure.

⁷It is of this gospel that I became a minister which God gave to me by his grace through the working of his power.*1088* ⁸I *myself*, am less than the least of all God's holy people, yet this grace was given to me: to preach to the Gentiles the unsearchable riches of Christ, ⁹and to make plain to everyone my responsibility in this truth which was kept hidden with God, the one who created all things. ¹⁰God's intention was that now, by means of the church, the multi-faceted wisdom of God should be known to the angelic rulers and authorities in the heavenly places. ¹¹God did this according to his purposes ages ago and he accomplished this in Christ Jesus our Lord. ¹²We may approach God with boldness and confidence because we are in *Christ* and have faith in him. ¹³Therefore I ask you not to be discouraged because of my sufferings for you all. It is all for your benefit.

Paul prays for the Ephesian church

¹⁴For this reason on bended knees I kneel before the Father, ¹⁵from whom every family in heaven and on earth is derived and receives its name.*1089* ¹⁶I pray that he may strengthen you with power out of his glorious riches through his Breath in your inner person. ¹⁷In this way Christ will dwell in your hearts by faith. And I pray that you may have your roots and foundation in love, ¹⁸so that you might be able to completely understand together with all of God's holy people just how wide and long and high and deep is the love of Christ. ¹⁹I pray that you will experience this love that far exceeds knowledge and that you all may be completely filled with all the fullness of God.

²⁰Now to him who is able to do exceedingly more than all that we ask or can even imagine according to his power that is at work in us, ²¹to him be the glory in the church and in Christ Jesus to all generations for ever and ever! Amen.

Believers must have unity

4 ¹Therefore I greatly urge you all to live up to the standard when God called you *in salvation*. ²Be always humble, gentle and patient, forbearing one another in love. ³Do your very best to have unity which comes from the Breath *of God* and find the peace that keeps you together. ⁴There is one body and one Breath *of God* just like there is also one hope in which you were called to have. ⁵There is one Lord, one faith, one baptism, ⁶one God and Father of all people. God is over all *mankind*, works through all *mankind* and he is in all *mankind*.

1088 "Power" here is derived from the Greek root *dunamis* of which we get the English transliteration 'dynamite' which is of course a powerful explosive material.

1089 This means that every animate being whether in heaven or on earth owes its existence to God and he is the Father in a sense to every living being.

⁷But Christ has gifted to each one of us *a portion of* his grace as he has so determined. ⁸This is why it says *in the Scriptures,*

"When he ascended to the highest *place*, he led those whom he had
captured and he gave gifts to people."¹⁰⁹⁰

Psalm 68:18

⁹What does it mean that "he ascended" *in this quote*? If he ascended, does it not follow that he must have *previously* descended to the lowest parts of the earth as well? ¹⁰He who descended is actually the very one who has also ascended higher than all the heavens.¹⁰⁹¹ He did this in order that he might fill the whole universe with his presence. ¹¹It was *Christ* himself, who was the one who gave gifts to people gifting some to be apostles, some to be prophets, some to be evangelists and some to be pastors and teachers. ¹²He did this in order to equip God's holy people for works of service so that the body of Christ may be strengthened. ¹³*This will keep happening* until together we all reach unity in the faith and are experiencing the power of the Son of God. We shall keep maturing until we measure up to the standard of Christ.

¹⁴Then we will no longer be like *immature* children who are tossed back and forth *like a boat* in the waves of the sea and blown here and there by every wind of doctrine. Crafty men with their cunningness are scheming, trying to lead people astray. ¹⁵Rather, as we hold to the truth, we must grow up becoming mature in all things in him, who is Christ the head *of the church*. ¹⁶It is from him that the whole body comes together. The body is joined by supporting ligaments that provide in helping the body to grow in love as each part functions properly.

Believers are to live in a new way

¹⁷Therefore I say to you *all* and insist strongly on the Lord's *authority* that you must no longer live like the Gentiles in their mindless behaviour. ¹⁸Their reasoning is darkened and the life of God is totally foreign to them. This is because of their ignorance which has come about because they are stubborn. ¹⁹They show no empathy or remorse for others and are completely lacking in moral restraint, indulging themselves in every kind of indecent sexual depravity.

1090   This is a direct quote from Psalm 68 which is referring to a typical procession when a victorious king returns from battle to the heights of Mt. Zion in Jerusalem. The major difference here though is that in the original Psalm the king was to receive tribute from his enemies whom he had captured not to give gifts away. This is not an error or mistranslation but one assumes that this is what Paul intended. In other words, Jesus defeated the devil at Calvary and his response was to give gifts, namely gifts of the Spirit to the church.

1091   This reflects the Jewish belief that there are up to seven heavens of which God lives in the highest one.

²⁰But you did not come to learn that Christ was like that in any way. ²¹There is no doubt that you heard about him and were taught by him as truth is in Jesus. ²²*You were taught*, concerning the old manner of life, to put off your old ways. For you were being corrupted by deep desires which were deceitful. ²³*You were taught* to be spiritually transformed in your mind, ²⁴and that you must become a new person created to be like God, truly good and holy.

²⁵Therefore each one of you must stop lying but speak truthfully to his fellow believer[1092] for we are all members of the one body. ²⁶In your anger, do not sin.[1093] Do not let the sun go down while you are still angry and ²⁷make sure that you do not let the devil have any opportunity. ²⁸The man who has been constantly stealing must steal no longer but he must work, doing something useful with his own hands that he may have something useful to share with those who are in need.

²⁹There must not be foul language that comes out of your mouths, but only what is helpful for building others up according to what they need, so that it may strengthen and give grace to those who listen. ³⁰And do not sadden the Holy Breath of God which is your identifying mark of ownership in readiness for the day that you will be set free.[1094] ³¹You must rid yourselves of bitterness, rage, anger, quarrelling, insults and all kinds of evil. ³²You are to be kind and compassionate to each other making sure that you forgive each other just as God forgave you in Christ.

Believers are to live in the light

5 ¹You must be imitators of God since you are his dearly beloved children. ²You are to live a life of love just as Christ has loved us all and given himself up for us like an offering and sacrifice which is pleasing to God.[1095]

³But there must not be even the slightest hint of sexual immorality, any kind of sexual perversion or lust amongst you *believers* because these *sins* are improper for God's holy people. ⁴Nor should there be any sexual obscenities, foolish talk or joking with double meanings, which are inappropriate but instead there should be thanksgiving. ⁵You can be very sure of this: No one who is sexually immoral, perverted or lustful (which is *actually* idolatry) has any part with those whom

---

1092 This is literally 'neighbour' in the Greek but it has the meaning of fellow Christians or believers.
1093 This appears to be a quote from Psa. 4:4 (LXX).
1094 This refers to that day when Christ returns and sets us free and releases us from earthly limitations and sin in a complete and final sense. It will usher in the Messianic age and the renewal of all things.
1095 The phrase that modifies offering and sacrifice is literally 'fragrance of a sweet smell'. On the contrary, offerings and sacrifices would have a burning flesh odour, which is hardly a fragrant or perfume like smell. But in the OT, God some 40 times indicates his pleasure at sacrifice by indicating that it is like a sweet smelling fragrance.

Christ and God reign over. ⁶And you must not let anyone deceive you with empty arguments. Because of these very *sins*, God is angry with those who are disobedient. ⁷Therefore do not associate with such people.

⁸For you were once *upon a time living* in darkness *as it were* but now since you are in the Lord, you are *living* in the light. Therefore you must *live as though you are* of the light. ⁹(For light results in people doing every kind of goodness, following the will of God in their lives and being genuine and truthful.) ¹⁰*Live as though you are of the light* and examine that which pleases the Lord. ¹¹You must not participate in unproductive works of darkness but rather instead you should expose them. ¹²It really is very shameful to even mention what people do in secret. ¹³But everything exposed by the light becomes visible. ¹⁴And anything that becomes visible becomes light as has been written *in a hymn*,

> "Rise and shine, O sleeping one.[1096]
> You must rise from the dead.
> And so Christ will shine *a light* on you."

¹⁵Therefore you are to be very careful in how you live, not unwisely, but you are to live wisely. ¹⁶Take advantage of every opportunity because these are evil times. ¹⁷Do not act foolishly but you must try and understand what the Lord's will is. ¹⁸Stop getting drunk on wine because drunkenness only leads to ruin but be full of *God's* Breath, ¹⁹which means speaking to each other with psalms, hymns and spiritual songs[1097] singing and making melody in your hearts to the Lord, ²⁰ensuring that you are always giving thanks to God the Father for everything, in the name of our Lord Jesus Christ.

Instructions for wives and husbands
(Col. 3:18–19)

²¹Submit yourselves to each other because of the reverence you have for Christ. ²²The wife is to submit to her husband *in the same way* as *she would submit* to the Lord. ²³For the husband is the head of the wife as Christ is the head of the church. And it is he who is the Saviour of the body. ²⁴Just as the church submits to Christ, so wives also should submit to their husbands in everything.

²⁵Husbands, you should love your wives, just as Christ loved the church and

---

1096 This is addressed to someone who is actually dead not asleep as such. Sleep is often a euphemism for death in the Bible. But it is probably referring to the person who is spiritually dead.

1097 This seems a little strange that one would be instructed to speak to each other with songs when one would assume that they should be sung or chanted. It is possible that the verse could be translated as "speak to each other with the words of psalms, hymns and spiritual songs".

gave himself up for her. ²⁶*He did this* in order to dedicate her to God, having her cleansed by the washing with water in the word¹⁰⁹⁸ ²⁷so that he might present her to himself a radiant and clean church that has no wrinkle or stain or any other blemish. She may, therefore, be holy and faultless. ²⁸In this same way therefore, husbands must love their wives like they do their own bodies. He who loves his wife loves her like she is his own body. (²⁹For I have never heard of anyone hating his own body, but instead he feeds and cares for it just like Christ cares for the church. ³⁰For we are members of his body.) ³¹*As the Scripture says,*

> "So a man will leave his father and mother and be adhered to his wife
> and the two of them will become as one body."¹⁰⁹⁹

Genesis 2:24

³²There is a profound hidden truth here. I am talking about Christ and the church. ³³However each one of you also must love his wife as he loves himself and the wife must respect her husband.

Instructions for children and parents
(Col. 3:20–21)

6 ¹Children, because you are the Lord's, obey your parents for this is right. ²*The Scripture says,* "Honour your father and mother." (This is the first commandment with a promise.) ³*Do this so* "that it may go well with you and that you may enjoy a long life on the earth." ⁴Fathers, you must not provoke your children to anger instead you should bring them up in the training and instruction of the Lord.

Instructions for slaves and masters
(Col. 3:22–4:1)

⁵Slaves, you must obey your earthly masters with respect and fear. Do this with a sincere heart just as you would obey Christ. ⁶Do not obey them just to be man-pleasers when they are watching you, but you must obey them as slaves of Christ doing the will of God from your heart. ⁷You must serve enthusiastically as if you are serving the Lord himself, not *merely* men. ⁸Do this because you

---

1098 This is a very difficult verse to understand where it refers to "in the word". Interestingly, the context may suggest of the bath that a Jewish bride would take before her wedding as she dedicated herself to her husband. The word may refer to the gospel, the words that a Jewish bridegroom would address to his bride at their wedding, the baptismal formula that a minister would speak at a baptism or either the confession of faith spoken by a person receiving Christian baptism. There is no way of really knowing and translators have used all of the above.
1099 Cf. Mark 10:7.

know that the Lord will reward everyone for whatever good he does, whether he is a slave or a free person.

⁹Masters, you must treat your slaves in the same way and stop threatening them. You must bear in mind that they have the same Master in the heavens as you do and that he shows no favouritism.

The armour of God

¹⁰In concluding *I say to you all that* you must be continually empowered in the Lord by his mighty strength. ¹¹You must put on the weapons and armour[1100] of God so that you may be able to withstand the devil's scheming methods. ¹²For we are not fighting against flesh and blood but against the authorities, against the worldly powers of these dark times and against the spiritual forces of evil in the heavenly places. ¹³Therefore you must put on both the weapons and the armour of God so that when the hour of evil comes, you may be able to stand your ground. And after having done everything possible you have remained standing.

¹⁴So stand ready, having truth fastened around your waist like a belt and having put on integrity like body armour that protects your chest. ¹⁵And having put on readiness like shoes meaning that you are ready to *go and* share the gospel of peace. ¹⁶Above all this, ensure that you take up faith which is like the long shield[1101] which can help extinguish the flaming arrows of the evil one. ¹⁷And take hold of salvation like the helmet that protects the head and also receive the sword of the *Holy* Breath which is the word of God. ¹⁸And make sure that you pray at all times as *God's* Breath leads, with all kinds of prayers and petitions. Keeping this in mind, be alert and always keep praying for all of God's holy people.

¹⁹And pray also especially for me, that whenever I open my mouth, that God might give me the words to say so that I will make known the hidden truth of the gospel without fear. ²⁰It is for this hidden truth that I am an ambassador in prison. Pray that I might be able to speak boldly *about the gospel* as is fitting.

Final greetings

²¹Tychicus, our dear brother and loyal servant in the Lord's *work*, will tell you everything so that you may also know how I am and what I am doing. ²²And

---

1100 The phrase here represents a single Greek word which means the equipment and weapons worn by a soldier into battle both offensive and defensive.

1101 According to the ancient historian Polybius, this was probably the large oblong shaped shield that was taken by soldiers in their left hand to protect them in battle. Before a battle the soldiers would soak the leather and canvas covered shield in water to extinguish the flaming darts and arrows of the enemy (TH).

this is why I have sent him to you so that you all may know how we are here and that he may encourage you as well.

²³May God the Father and the Lord Jesus Christ grant peace to all the *Christian* brothers and may you love each other and trust *in them*. ²⁴May God's grace be with all those who love our Lord Jesus Christ with undying love.

PHILIPPIANS

Introduction

The church at Philippi was founded by Paul and his associates on his second missionary journey in the early 50s of the first century. He wrote this letter a decade later around AD 62–63 to them because of the division that was occurring in the church because of two warring women. This is one of Paul's four prison letters (Phil. 1:7, 13–14). He was facing many hardships of his own, being under house arrest himself continuously chained 24/7 to four squads of two soldiers. Despite this, Paul was able to find joy in his circumstances. He received very little help but knew how to trust God in all circumstances and he wanted to encourage the Philippian church likewise.

Like in many other churches of the time, Judaizers were like dogs nipping at the heels trying to convert the young believers to Judaism once again. Judaizers and false teachers were trying to get Christians to look backwards into the past. They were saying to be real believers Christians must keep the Sabbath, be circumcised, follow dietary laws and keep the Jewish feast days. But Paul emphasises in this letter that Christians live in the future tense as we look forward to our Lord and Saviour returning and the transformation of our lowly bodies.

Unlike many of Paul's letters which were written to address problems in the church, this letter is primarily about joy and appreciation for the congregation. Paul explains that joy is found in the Lord (Phil. 4:4) whereas happiness comes from favourable, temporary and external factors. That means that happiness comes and goes whereas joy should be continuously present despite the surrounding circumstances that can rob us of joy in life—people, things and worry.

1

¹From Paul and Timothy, as servants of Christ Jesus,

To God's holy people in Christ Jesus at Philippi as well as the church leaders and deacons.

²Grace and peace to you all from God our Father and the Lord Jesus Christ.

Paul's prayer for the church at Philippi

³I thank my God every time I remember you. ⁴Every time I pray for you all, I pray with joy ⁵because of your partnership in the gospel from the very first day until now. ⁶I am so sure that the One having begun a good work among you all will see it through to completion until the day of Christ Jesus.[1102] ⁷It is right for me to think this way about you all because you are all close to my heart. For whether I am in chains or defending and confirming the gospel you have all shared with me in this God-given privilege. ⁸God is my witness to how deeply I feel for you all which comes from the love Christ Jesus himself has shown.

⁹I especially pray that your love may keep on growing with every spiritual concept and right judgment ¹⁰so that you may be able to discern what is best. Then you will be pure and blameless until the day of Christ.[1103] ¹¹You will be filled with the fruit of righteousness that comes through Jesus Christ for the glory and praise of God.

Paul's imprisonment advances the Gospel

¹²Now I want you to know *Christian* brothers, that what has happened to me has really served to advance the gospel. ¹³As a result, it has become well known throughout the whole palace guard[1104] and to everyone else that I am in chains for Christ. ¹⁴Because of my chains, most of the brothers have become confident enough in the Lord to willingly speak the word of God without fear.

¹⁵Indeed, some are even preaching Christ out of envy and rivalry but others are preaching with good intentions. ¹⁶These ones *preach* out of love knowing that I am put here for the defence of the gospel. ¹⁷However the others preach Christ out of selfish ambition and they are not sincere, supposing that they can stir up trouble for me while I am in chains. ¹⁸It doesn't really matter. The important

---

1102 Paul was confident that God who began a good work at the first European church at Philippi in c. AD 50, would continue on and bring the work of world-wide evangelism to completion not stopping until the very end—the day of Christ Jesus. This does not refer to the inner work of sanctification in the individual.
1103 Cf. 2 Thess. 2:2.
1104 Literally 'praetorium', i.e. the imperial guard in Rome. Paul was under house arrest for two years awaiting trial in Rome. This letter was written in c. AD 62–63 whilst imprisoned in his house.

thing is that in every way, whether from false motives or true, Christ is being preached and because of this I will rejoice and I will continue to rejoice.

Paul faces two possibilities: death or release

¹⁹For I know that through your prayers and because of the help given to me by the Breath of Jesus Christ, what has happened to me will turn out to be for my own good.[1105] ²⁰Seriously, my expectation and hope is that I will not be ashamed but that as always but especially at this time, I will have enough courage with every ounce of my being to allow Christ to be magnified whether I live or I die. ²¹For to me, life means I keep living for Christ but if I die that is even better. ²²If I am to go on living in the body this means I can keep on being fruitful in my work. So, what will I choose? I don't really know. ²³I am torn between the two *choices*: I desire to depart *this life* and be with Christ which is better by far; ²⁴but for your sakes it is better that I remain alive in the body. ²⁵And having been persuaded that this is best, I know that I will remain and continue on with all of you for your progress and joy in the faith. ²⁶Therefore when I come to you all again you will have even more reason to take pride in Christ Jesus.

God allows the Philippian church to suffer

²⁷Above all, make sure that you conduct yourselves as citizens of heaven in a manner worthy of the gospel of Christ. Then, whether I come and see you or only hear about you in my absence, I will hear that you are standing firm in one spirit and one soul. I will hear that you are striving together for the faith of the gospel ²⁸and not being frightened in any way by those who oppose you. This is proof to them that they will be destroyed, but that you will be saved—indeed saved by God. ²⁹For it has been granted to you on behalf of Christ not only to believe in him but also to suffer for him. ³⁰You are going through the same struggle as you saw that I had in the past and that now you are hearing that I am still going through.

Be humble like Christ

2 ¹You are surely encouraged by being in Christ and comforted by the love that he has for you all. You are in partnership with *God's* Breath and you are kind and showing compassion for each other. ²Therefore I would ask that you would make me completely happy by being like-minded, sharing the same love and being one in spirit and purpose. ³Don't be selfish or try to impress others in

---

1105   Literally the Greek word here for "good" is 'salvation'. The intent here is that Paul is happy whether he is released from prison or martyred for his faith and both would be a deliverance or salvation in that sense from his current bondage.

your vanity, but be humble and consider others better than yourselves. ⁴Don't be just interested in yourselves but take an interest in others.

⁵Your attitudes should be the same as that of Jesus Christ:

> ⁶Who, despite being in very nature God, did not consider that he should try to hold onto being equal with God.[1106]
> ⁷Instead he emptied himself[1107] taking the nature of a slave having been born in appearance as a man.
> ⁸He humbled himself and became obedient to death—even death on a cross!
> ⁹Therefore God exalted him to the highest place and gave him the name that is above every other name,
> ¹⁰so that when Jesus' name *is called* every knee should bow in air, land and sea,[1108]
> ¹¹and every tongue confess that Jesus Christ is Lord to the glory of God the Father.

An early Christian hymn

Making our salvation complete

¹²Therefore my dear *Christian* friends, just as you have always obeyed in my presence and also more importantly, in my absence, continue to work out your salvation with fear and trembling.[1109] ¹³For God is the one who is working in you to make you willing and able to do what pleases him.

¹⁴Make sure that you do everything without complaining or arguing, ¹⁵so that you may become blameless and pure—children of God without fault in a crooked and depraved generation. You will shine like stars in the universe ¹⁶as you offer *them* the word of life. And in doing so, I will be able to boast on the day of Christ that I have not run *the race* or laboured in vain.

1106 Ontologically, the Father and the preincarnate Christ, the Son of God, are the same. In the OT they were equal with one being invisible (the Father) and one being visible at specific times (the Name, Angel of the LORD, Son of Man).

1107 The Son of God completely divested himself of his equality with God by being willing to become a man thereby fully experiencing what it was to be human, and to suffer temptation and finally death. This divestment may even relate to the prerogative of knowing some things such as the day and hour when he would return (Cf. Matt. 24:36).

1108 An expression borrowed from Exo. 20:4 meaning all living creatures, including the birds of the sky, land animals, and sea creatures which are beneath the land (below sea level).

1109 The primary interpretation here is about logistics and not speaking to their individual sanctification. Most of Paul's letters were written to encourage Christians who were far away from him. Likewise here, Paul was absent in the body but present with them in the spirit, in his thoughts. The Philippian church was finding things tough because Paul, as their main spiritual mentor, wasn't with them to help them in person. They needed to work out things by themselves for a while and walk with God in his absence.

¹⁷But even if I am being poured out like a drink offering[1110] as part of the sacrifice and service I offer for your faith, I am happy and rejoice with you all. ¹⁸Similarly you also should be happy and rejoice with me.

Paul sends Timothy to Philippi

¹⁹If the Lord Jesus allows it, I hope to send Timothy to you soon so that I also may be encouraged upon hearing what's going on there. ²⁰Timothy is the only one I have who is likeminded and who genuinely cares for you. ²¹For everyone looks out for their own interests and not the things of Jesus Christ. ²²However you know that Timothy has proven his worth because he has served with me in the work of the gospel like a son with his father. ²³I hope, therefore, to send him as soon as I see how things turn out here on my end. ²⁴I am also confident in the Lord that I myself will come soon.

Paul also sends Epaphroditus to Philippi

²⁵But I am thinking that it is necessary that I send Epaphroditus back to you. He is my brother *in Christ*, co-worker and fellow soldier and has served as your messenger whom you sent to take care of my needs. ²⁶He is anxious to see you all and has been feeling down because you heard that he has been ill. ²⁷And indeed he was very ill and almost died. But God had mercy on him and not on him only but on me too in order to spare me a great deal of worry *in losing him*. ²⁸Therefore I am actually very keen to send him back to you so that when you see him again you may be glad and I might not be as worried. ²⁹Make sure that you welcome him in the Lord with great joy. Honour men like him ³⁰because he almost died for the work of Christ risking his life to make up for the help that you were not able to give me.

Beware of the false teachers

3 ¹In conclusion, my *Christian* brothers, make sure that you are rejoicing in the Lord. It is no bother for me to write to you about the same issues again.[1111] In fact, I think that it will be for your safety to do so.

²Watch out for the dogs, those evil workers, the ones who mutilate the flesh.[1112] ³However we *Christians* are the truly circumcised because we worship

---

1110   The drink offering was usually a cup of wine poured out on the ground to honour a deity meaning that there is a possibility of martyrdom in Paul's mind. This possibility for Paul is not a cause to be concerned but a cause to rejoice.

1111   Paul is probably talking about warning the Philippian church against the false teaching of the Judaizers which the apostle has written about in previous letters such as his letter to the Galatians.

1112   Ironically Paul is using extremely strong language by turning the usual term for the Gentiles as in "Gentile dogs" (Matt. 7:6) on its head by referring to the Judaizers. That is, those Jews who require that the Gentiles must be circumcised in order to be saved.

by means of the Breath of God and we glory in Christ Jesus and furthermore we put no confidence in the *state of the external* flesh. ⁴I *of all men* would be fully justified in putting confidence in such things. If anyone else thinks he has good reason to put his confidence in *the status of* his *external* flesh then I have even more. ⁵For I was circumcised on the eighth day and am an Israelite by birth from the tribe of Benjamin. I am a Hebrew of Hebrews and in regards to the Law *of Moses*, a Pharisee. ⁶I was so zealous *for God* that I persecuted the church and as far as keeping the commands of the Law, I was without fault.

⁷But all those things which I might have previously considered as profitable, I now reckon they are worthless because of what Christ has done. ⁸What is more, I reckon everything is completely worthless when compared to the infinite greatness of knowing Christ Jesus my Lord for whose sake I have lost all things. Actually I consider them as rubbish*¹¹¹³* in order that I may gain Christ ⁹and be found in him. That means not having a righteousness of my own that comes from obeying the Law but that which comes through faith in Christ. That righteousness comes from God and depends on faith. ¹⁰I want to know Christ and experience the power of his resurrection, to share in his sufferings and become like him in his death ¹¹in the hope that somehow I myself will be resurrected from the dead as well.*¹¹¹⁴*

We must press on towards the goal

¹²It's not that I have already obtained all of this or that I have already been made perfect, but I keep pressing on to win *the prize* just as Christ Jesus has won me. ¹³*Christian* brothers, I do not consider myself yet to have won it but the one thing that I do is to forget what is behind me and reach toward what is ahead. ¹⁴I press on toward the goal to win the prize of the calling of God from on high in Christ Jesus.*¹¹¹⁵*

¹⁵All of us who are spiritually mature should take such a view of things. And if on some point you think differently, that too God will make clear to you. ¹⁶However be that as it may be, we must all behave and live up to the standard that we have lived by before.

¹⁷Brothers, join with others in following my example and take note of those who live according to the pattern we gave to you. ¹⁸I have mentioned this to you many times before and now I say it again with tears, many *so-called Christians* live as enemies of the cross of Christ. ¹⁹Their destiny is destruction,*¹¹¹⁶* their god

---

1113   The Greek word means the scraps and food thrown to dogs.
1114   Paul was hoping that he might take part in the first resurrection (Rev. 20:1–5).
1115   Our prize is to be resurrected when we hear the shout and trumpet call of God (1 Thess. 4:16).
1116   The ungodly are destroyed by being sent to hell (Matt. 10:28).

is their stomach and they take pride in what they should be ashamed of. Their minds are on worldly things. ²⁰But our citizenship is in heaven and we are eagerly awaiting a Saviour from there—the Lord Jesus Christ. ²¹He will transform our lowly bodies so that they will be like his glorious body by the power that enables him to bring everything under his rule.

Instructions to the church in Philippi

4 ¹Therefore my *Christian* brothers, you whom I love and long for. You are my joy and my wreath *of victory*, so stand firm in the Lord, dear friends.

²Euodia and Syntyche, I plead with you, try to agree with each other in the Lord. ³Yes, and I ask you loyal Suzugos, to help these women who have strived with me in the cause of the gospel. They, along with Clement and the rest of my fellow workers whose names are written in the book of life[1117] *have strived hard*.

⁴Rejoice in the Lord and again I say rejoice!

⁵Let your gentle attitude be evident to all. The Lord is near.[1118] ⁶Do not be anxious about anything but in everything with prayer and by pleading, let your requests be made known to God. ⁷And the peace of God which surpasses all *human* understanding will guard your hearts and minds in Christ Jesus.

⁸In closing brothers, I urge you to think about things that are true, things that are noble, things that are right, things that are pure, things that are lovely and things that are spoken well of. If something is excellent or praiseworthy, think about these kinds of things. ⁹Put into practice what you have learned and received from me, both words and actions. Do this and the God of peace will be with you.

Paul thanks the Philippian church for their gifts

¹⁰It gives me great joy in the Lord that after such a long time you have the opportunity once again to show that you care for me, not that you had stopped caring for me, but you were lacking the opportunity to do so. ¹¹And I am not saying this because I am in need for I have learned to be content whatever the circumstances are. ¹²I know what it is to be in need and I know what it is to have more than enough. I have learned the secret of being content in any and every situation, whether well fed or hungry, whether I have more than enough or I am lacking somewhat. ¹³I can do all things through him who gives me strength.

¹⁴But it was so good of you all to share in my troubles. ¹⁵You Philippians

---

1117 Cf. Rev. 3:5, Rev. 20:12.
1118 This word could mean either near in time or near in proximity (space). It is impossible to tell what is meant here. The early church believed and expected the Lord's early return so most think that Paul means the Lord is coming soon.

know very well in the early days of the gospel after I departed Macedonia that not one church helped me financially except you only. ¹⁶And even when I was in Thessalonica you helped me *financially* more than once. ¹⁷It's not that I am looking for a gift, but I am looking for ways in which you can increasingly benefit.[1119] ¹⁸I have received everything I need and it is more than enough, having received the things you sent from Epaphroditus. They are a sweet aroma, a sacrifice that is acceptable and pleasing to God. ¹⁹And so my God will meet every need of yours according to his glorious riches in Christ Jesus. ²⁰To our God and Father be glory forever and ever. Amen.

Paul's final greetings

²¹Please give my greetings to all God's holy people who belong to Jesus Christ. The *Christian* brothers who are with me send their greetings. ²²All God's holy people *here* send you greetings, especially those who are in Caesar's household.[1120]

²³May the grace of the Lord Jesus Christ be with you all. Amen.

1119 Paul was wanting that the Philippian church could benefit by adding spiritual rewards to their account. When we serve God it is a profitable investment in the kingdom of God.
1120 Nero was Caesar at the time. His "household" here probably refers to the Imperial Praetorian Guard, many of whom had become Christians listening to his preaching while being chained to him under house arrest (Phil. 1:13).

COLOSSIANS

Introduction

The city of Colossae was located only 16 km from Laodicea in southwestern Minor Asia yet it wasn't included in the letters to the seven churches in John's Book of Revelation. The Colossian church was founded in Paul's three year ministry in Ephesus (Acts 20:31) even though he probably never visited Colossae in person. The letter is one of Paul's four prison letters written when he was in prison in Rome in about AD 62.

The letter contains some really important doctrines regarding the Son of God and where he came from. He states that there are two divine powers of heaven who are ontologically the same—the visible Yahweh (Son of God—Jesus) and the invisible Yahweh (Father in heaven).

Paul's letter to the Colossians is sometimes regarded as a 'twin letter' with Ephesians because of its similarity in content and that it was written about the same time. Like the letter to the Ephesians, Paul first focusses on doctrine and then later on in the letter he focusses on practical relational issues for Christians like marriage, children and slaves or bosses in the modern context.

1 ¹From Paul, an apostle of Christ Jesus by God's will, and Timothy our *Christian* brother,

²To the holy and loyal brothers in Christ at Colossae.

May God our Father grant you grace and peace.

A prayer of thanksgiving for the Colossian church

³We[1121] always thank God, the Father of our Lord Jesus Christ, when we pray for you all, ⁴because we have heard of your faith in Christ Jesus and of the love that you have for all of God's holy people. ⁵This faith and love spring from the hope that came when you first heard the true message—the gospel. God is keeping safe for you in heaven that which you are hoping for.[1122] ⁶This gospel has now come to you which has been all over the world bearing fruit and growing just like it has been doing amongst you since the day you heard it and understood God's grace in all its truth. ⁷Epaphras, our dear fellow co-worker, was the one from whom you learnt *about God's grace*. He is a loyal servant of Christ on our behalf. ⁸He was the one who also told us of your love of spiritual things.[1123]

Continual prayer for the Colossian church

⁹Because of all that you have experienced, we have never stopped praying for you since we heard about you. We have not stopped asking God to fill you with the knowledge of his will through all spiritual wisdom and understanding. ¹⁰This is so that you may be able to live a life worthy of the Lord and may please him in every way, bearing fruit in every good work and grow in the knowledge of God. ¹¹We pray that you will be strengthened with all power according to his glorious might so that you may have great endurance and patience with joy. ¹²Give thanks to the Father, who has made it possible for you to share in the allotment[1124] of his people who live in the light.

1121 Paul is including Timothy in the 1st person exclusive plural here but also likely including others in his group as well. Paul wrote this letter from prison in Rome (Col. 4:3,10,18).

1122 The hope being reserved in heaven for Christians is the resurrection to immortality receiving new bodies and sharing in the Son's inheritance in the millennial kingdom (Rom. 8:24).

1123 Hard to understand verse. Most take this to be the Holy Breath (Spirit). It could mean the love that the Holy Spirit gives the believers or could possibly also mean the love for spiritual things that the Colossians had (Lamsa Bible). Commentators point out that Paul does not refer to the Holy Breath in this letter so it is unlikely that the Breath of God (Holy Spirit) is meant here.

1124 The Greek word here is literally allotment originally used to mean the territory allotted by God to the Israelites as their exclusive possession. Some suggest that this refers to a generic or unspecified 'inheritance' rather than specifically to the Land inheritance promised to Abraham and his descendants (Gal. 3:29). But all those of faith including Christians are Abraham's descendants and so we are all to receive a permanent land inheritance in the resurrection.

¹³He has rescued us from the powerful domain of darkness and transferred us into the realm of the one he loves, his Son ¹⁴by whom God bought us back through his blood and forgave us our sins.[1125]

The Son of God explained

¹⁵*The Son* is the image of the invisible God, the firstborn[1126] of all creation. ¹⁶For by him all things were created—things in heaven and on earth, visible and invisible (thrones, dominions, rulers and authorities). *In fact*, all things were created through him and for him.[1127] ¹⁷He existed before all things and he is the one who holds everything together. ¹⁸And he is the head of the body—the church. He is 'The Beginning'[1128] and the firstborn Son, who was raised from death in order that he alone might hold the pre-eminence in all things. ¹⁹For God was pleased to have all his fullness dwell in his Son.[1129] ²⁰And through him, *God was pleased* to reconcile to himself all things, the things on earth and the things in the heavens having made peace through his Son's blood on the cross.[1130]

²¹At one time you were far away from God and were enemies because of your evil behaviour and thinking. ²²But now he has reconciled you by Christ's physical body through his death to present you holy and faultless without blame in his sight. ²³But you must continue in your faith becoming established and firm in your faith and not be moved from the hope[1131] that you have heard in

---

1125 Cf. Eph. 1:7.
1126 Pertaining to being a firstborn child. It is the Greek word *proto-tokos* meaning 'first-to produce'. Literally the first in a sequence pertaining to the production of both humans and animals from the male. In the OT, Yahweh is often portrayed as being two persons or two powers: one the invisible and transcendent Yahweh and the other the visible Yahweh (Angel of the LORD, son of man, i.e. two persons of the Godhead). Cf. Dan. 7:13. Ontologically they are both exactly the same. They are both Yahweh but represented in two different ways—the invisible and the visible. Cf. Gen. 19:24 (LORD (YaHWeH) is referring to two different persons). Cf. Gen. 22:12 (The angel of the LORD equates himself with God).
1127 The Son is both the agent through whom all things were created and the heir of all things created. The Son of God (Wisdom of God) was the 'master craftsman' at God's side at creation (Prov. 8:30). Clearly God is the ultimate source of creation and the Son was present at his side as his agent.
1128 In John 8:25 when the Judeans asked Jesus, "Who are you?" Jesus said to them, "The Beginning!" (DRB). In most translations this has not been translated. This is a title of the Son of God in Prov. 8:22 (LXX). Ontologically, the Father and the Son were the same because the Son was issued forth out of the Father. In the OT, the Jews believed in two powers in heaven, one invisible (Yahweh) and one visible (Son of Man, Angel of the LORD) but later in the 1st century this was believed to be heresy partly to combat the rise of Christianity. Cf. Heb. 1:5 footnote.
1129 Cf. Eph. 3:19. The fullness of God is his full nature—undiminished, undiluted and unshared. It is his complete divinity and authority. The Greek verb '*eudokesen*' (was pleased) is an aorist indicative verb which points to a completed action in the past.
1130 The whole creation will eventually be reconciled to God which will be completed at the end of the 1000 year reign of Christ on earth. At this point all rebellion will be defeated and the last enemy (death) will be destroyed (1 Cor. 15:26).
1131 Cf. footnote in Col. 1:5.

the gospel. This is the gospel that I, Paul have become a minister of and is being proclaimed to every creature under heaven.[1132]

Paul's ministry in the church

[24]I am happy at this time to physically suffer for you all for I am taking part in the sufferings of Christ that continue for his body, the church, [25]of which I have been given the responsibility by God to minister to you all by proclaiming the word of God fully.[1133] [26]This was a mystery hidden for ages and generations but has now been revealed to God's holy people. [27]God has wanted them to know that the glorious riches of this mystery is for the Gentiles too. The mystery is that Christ lives in you which gives us the hope that we will share in his glory *one day*.

[28]So we proclaim Christ, warning and teaching everyone with as much wisdom as possible. We do this in order that we might present each person *to God* in relationship with Christ. [29]I toil to this end, striving hard according to his mighty power which is working in me.

The deception of the Jewish mystics

2 [1]I want you to know how hard I have worked for you all and for those in Laodicea[1134] and for all those who have not met me personally. [2]My aim is that everyone may be encouraged in heart and united in love and so have all the wealth of complete assurance which true understanding brings. In this way they will know the mystery of God—Christ.[1135] [3]In him are hidden all the treasures of wisdom and knowledge. [4]I am telling you this so that no one may delude you with what seems like a plausible argument. [5]For even though I am absent from you in body, I am with you in spirit, and I am glad to see how well disciplined you are and how firm your faith in Christ is.

[6]So then, just as you have received Christ Jesus as Lord, make sure that you continue to live in him, [7]having been grounded and built up in him and having firm foundations in the faith. You were taught this way and so be very thankful.

[8]Be alert in case you are taken captive by some empty and deceptive philosophy according to the traditions of men and according to worldly values and not according to Christ.

1132   Hyperbole—gospel was being preached to everybody in the Roman Empire at the time.
1133   Paul is saying here that suffering is an integral part of the ministry of Christ's followers and we are called to suffer just as if it was Christ himself.
1134   Colossae and Laodicea were only 16 km apart. Take note of what Paul wished for the church at Laodicea and their actual state as described by Jesus only three decades later (Rev. 3:14–22).
1135   The mystery or hidden truth is that Christ was concealed in the OT but revealed in the NT by the Holy Breath and that salvation is for the Gentiles as well-being joint-heirs of the blessings with Israel. Cf. 1 Cor. 2:7–10, Eph. 3:4–6.

⁹For all the fullness of the divine nature dwells in his physical body[1136] ¹⁰and you have experienced this completeness in Christ—the head over every ruler and authority.[1137] ¹¹In him you were also circumcised in the stripping off of the flesh not by a *physical* circumcision done by men but with a *spiritual* circumcision done by Christ. ¹²For when you were baptised you were buried with Christ but you were also raised with Christ through your faith in the power of God, who raised him from the dead.

¹³You were at one point in time, *spiritually* dead in your sins and your *old nature*, the flesh, was uncircumcised but God made you alive with Christ having forgiven all of our sins.[1138] ¹⁴God cancelled the written code with all of its regulations that stood opposed to us. He took it away having nailed it to the cross as it were. ¹⁵And having disarmed the powers and authorities *in the spiritual realm*[1139] he made a public spectacle of them by leading them as captives in triumph.[1140]

¹⁶Therefore you must not let anyone judge you by what you eat or drink, or with regards to a religious festival, a new moon celebration or Sabbath days.[1141] ¹⁷These matters are a shadow of the things to come. The reality however is found in Christ. ¹⁸Do not let anyone who delights in false humility and the worship of angels deprive you of the prize. Such a person goes into great detail about what he has seen. He has an inflated opinion of himself. ¹⁹He has lost all connection

---

1136   This was a direct affront to the Jewish mystics and Gnostics whose ultimate hope was to escape the prison of the body.
1137   Paul prayed that the Ephesians would be completely filled with all the fullness of God (Eph. 3:19).
1138   God forgave us our sins but he also defeated the works of the devil (the powers and authorities in the spiritual realm) in v. 15. So Christ accomplished two things: victory over Satan and redemption. Gustav Aulen draws attention to the victory aspect in his classic work *Christus Victor*. Cf. 1 John 3:8.
1139   The evil **ben-elohim** (sons of god) who really are the evil angels in charge of nations have been stripped of their former powers having been withdrawn and nullified (Psa. 82). The Most High God initially gave this authority to the sons of God at the Tower of Babel when the nations were divided amongst them (Deut. 32:8). The Dead Sea scrolls has the correct translation 'sons of God' rather than most modern translations which have 'sons of Israel'. Their total final destruction and handover by Jesus does not occur until the very end of the age (1 Cor. 15:24).
1140   Victorious Roman generals such as Julius Caesar led their captives in triumphal procession in Rome with the captives walking behind being chained to the chariot wheels. The triumph of Vespasian and his son Titus in AD 71 for their victory in Judea was notable for its display of the riches from the temple at Jerusalem (https://www.worldhistory.org/Roman_Triumph/).
1141   The three types of religious celebrations seem to cover the seven yearly Jewish feasts (Passover, Unleavened Bread, Firstfruits, Pentecost, Atonement and Tabernacles), the monthly new moon celebrations and the weekly Sabbaths. In other words, the sense here is no matter what you celebrate or don't celebrate and whatever you do or don't drink, Paul is emphasising that the Christian is freed from such ceremonial obligations. The Jewish mystics including the Essenes and later on the Gnostics believed they were the only true believers and that they were the chosen ones, that they had special knowledge, kept a better calendar and ate a stricter diet. This all resulted in a false sense of humility.

with the head[1142] from whom the whole body, supported and held together by its joints and ligaments, grows as God causes it to grow.

[20]When Christ died, you were set free[1143] from the elemental spirits of the world. Therefore why do you still subject yourselves to its rules: [21]"Do not handle! Do not taste! Do not touch!"? [22]These rules all deteriorate with use because they are based on human commands and teachings. [23]Such rules do initially appear to be wise, with their self-imposed worship, their false humility and their punishing treatment of the body, but they lack any real value in restraining one's carnal[1144] desires.

Taking off the old and putting on the new

3 [1]Since then you have been raised with Christ[1145] seek those things which are above, where Christ is seated at the right hand of God. [2]Seek those things which are above, not on earthly things. [3]For you died, and your *new* life is now hidden with Christ in God. [4]And when Christ who is your true life, appears, then you also will appear with him in glory.[1146]

[5]Therefore put to death whatever belongs to your earthly nature. This includes sexual immorality,[1147] sexual impurity, lust, evil desires, and greed which is in fact idolatry. [6]It is because of these things that the wrath of God is coming upon those who are disobedient. [7]At one time you used to walk in these ways, when you were living like that. [8]But now you must ensure that you get rid of all these things: anger, rage, malice, slander and a dirty mouth. [9]Do not lie to each other, for you have put off the old self with its practices [10]and have put on the new self. The Creator is constantly renewing you in his own image in order to bring you to a full knowledge of himself. [11]Accordingly, *this new situation means that* there is no such thing as Greek or Jew, circumcised or uncircumcised, barbarian,[1148] Scythian,[1149] slave or free, but Christ is all that matters since he is in everyone.

1142 Some translate this with a capital 'H' specifying that it is Christ. At any rate the meaning is clear that the Jewish mystics and Gnostics have lost all connection with reality and the truth that comes from the pure gospel of Christ.
1143 Literally 'died to'.
1144 Cf. 1 Cor. 3:1 footnote.
1145 The imagery here is likened to believer's baptism when they are raised out of the water identifying with Christ who was raised to life from the grave.
1146 This refers to the second future coming of Christ, at which time we will share in his glory.
1147 Cf. Heb. 12:16.
1148 'Barbarian' is the name that the Greeks applied to all other races (TH).
1149 'Scythian' is in some ways a metaphor for savagery. They were an ancient Eastern Iranian equestrian nomadic people who had migrated from Central Asia to the Pontic Steppe in modern-day Ukraine and southern Russia. The Scythians were reputed by the Romans to be the wildest, most uncivilised people alive (TH). The Jewish historian Josephus said that they were little better than wild beasts. The Apocryphal book 4 Macc. 10:7 (NRSV) describes how a young Hebrew man was scalped by

Christian virtues to be pursued

¹²Therefore as God's chosen people,*¹¹⁵⁰* holy and dearly loved, clothe yourselves with humility, gentleness and patience. ¹³Try and be tolerant with each other and forgive one another when you have complaints. Forgive just as Christ has forgiven you. ¹⁴And above all you must *clothe yourselves with* love which binds all these things together in perfect unity. ¹⁵You must allow the peace of Christ to rule in your hearts, since as members of one body you have been called to live in peace. And be thankful. ¹⁶You must allow the word of Christ in all its richness, to dwell in you as you teach and admonish one another with all wisdom. Make sure that you sing psalms, hymns and spiritual songs with thankfulness in your hearts to God. ¹⁷And whatever you do, whether in word or actions, do it all in the name of the Lord Jesus and give thanks to God the Father through him.

Instructions for Christian households and the workplace
(Eph. 5:22–6:9)

¹⁸Wives, submit to your husbands since that is the proper thing to do in the Lord. ¹⁹Husbands, love your wives and do not treat them harshly.

²⁰Children, obey your parents in everything, for this pleases the Lord. ²¹Fathers, do not provoke your children, or they will become disheartened.*¹¹⁵¹*

²²Slaves,*¹¹⁵²* obey your earthly masters in everything and do it not only when they are watching in order to please them but obey them with a pure heart out of respect for the Lord. ²³Whatever you do, work at it with all your heart, as if working for the Lord and not man. ²⁴Do this knowing that you will receive an inheritance from the Lord as a reward. *Remember,* it is the Lord Christ you are serving. ²⁵Anyone who does what is wrong will be repaid for his wrongdoing—there are no favourites.

4 ¹Masters, provide your slaves with what is right and fair, knowing that you also have a Master*¹¹⁵³* in heaven.

---

the guards of the tyrant Antiochus Epiphanes for refusing to eat pork. He was scalped 'with their fingernails in a Scythian fashion'. The last remnants of the Scythians were conquered by the Goths (German tribe) in the third century AD and were largely assimilated by the early Middle Ages.

1150 'Chosen' (the elect) is a term originally used of Israel but now also applied in the NT to the church in a corporate sense as a group. Cf. Eph. 2:8 footnote.

1151 Do not constantly correct, reprimand or criticise your child for every little wrong thing or imagined wrong that they do so that the child feels that he can never do anything right and so gives up trying.

1152 Literally slaves (*doulos*). The modern-day application would be the workplace with instructions for employers (bosses) and their employees (workers).

1153 Lord.

Further instructions

²Be persistent in prayer, being watchful and thankful. ³And pray for us too, that God might open a door for us for the word so that we may speak about the mystery of Christ—the reason that I am in chains.[1154] ⁴Pray that I might explain it clearly as I should.

⁵Be wise in the way that you act towards outsiders making the most of every opportunity. ⁶Your speech should always be full of grace, seasoned with salt,[1155] so that you may know how to answer everyone.

Final messages to the church at Colossi

⁷Tychicus will tell you all my news. He is a dear *Christian* brother, a loyal minister and fellow servant in the Lord's *work*. ⁸I have sent him to you for this very thing that you may know how we are going and that he may encourage you all. ⁹And with him will be your loyal Onesimus[1156] whom you all love. They will tell you everything that is happening here.

¹⁰Aristarchus, my fellow prisoner, says hello as does Mark, the cousin of Barnabas. (You already received instructions about Mark that if he should come to you, welcome him.) ¹¹Jesus, who is called Justus, also says hello. These are the only Jewish believers among my co-workers who work for the time when God will reign. They have been an encouragement to me.

¹²And Epaphras who is one of you and a servant of Christ Jesus, says hello. He is always wrestling in his prayers for you, that you may be able to stand as mature *Christians* having every confidence to do God's will. ¹³I can vouch for him that he is working hard for you all and for those at Laodicea and Hierapolis.[1157] ¹⁴Our dear friend Luke, the doctor, and Demas also say hello. ¹⁵Please give my regards to the *Christian* brothers at Laodicea and to Nympha and the church *meeting* in her house too.

¹⁶Please ensure that after this letter has been read to you all, that it is also read in the church of the Laodiceans and that you read the letter from the Laodiceans also.[1158]

¹⁷Tell Archippus as follows, "Pay attention to the work you have received in the Lord that you might finish it." ¹⁸I, Paul, write this greeting in my own hand.[1159] Remember my chains. Grace be with you all.

1154 The mystery of Christ is another way of saying the message of the gospel.
1155 Salt is a natural, non-toxic food preservative. It stops food from spoiling by drawing moisture out of food. "Seasoned with salt" here means that their speech was to reflect the fact that they were citizens of heaven, to the point, gracious and clean. Cf. Phil. 3:20.
1156 Onesimus had become a Christian in Rome through Paul's outreach. He encouraged Philemon to receive him back without punishment for his escape. Cf. Phm. 1:10–21.
1157 Hierapolis, Laodicea and Colossae were all within 20 km of each other.
1158 The letter referred to here is likely the Book of Philemon.
1159 Paul had dictated the letter but he himself writes the final greeting in his own hand.

1 THESSALONIANS

Introduction

Paul wrote this first letter to the church in Thessalonica situated in the harbour city in the Roman province of Macedonia in about AD 51. It was a large city with a large Jewish population. Unfortunately Paul received strong opposition to his teaching from the Jews there and so had to hurriedly leave before moving on to Berea (Acts 17:1–9). Paul wrote this letter because it was a young church and they had minimal instruction. One of the key things that Paul wrote about was Christ's return and how God's people need to be prepared and ready when he comes. Paul talks about the Day of the Lord and the so-called rapture of believers. All five chapters contain some reference to Christ's return and what it means for believers.

1 ¹From Paul, Silas and Timothy.

To the church of the Thessalonians who belong to God the Father and the Lord Jesus Christ.

Grace and peace to you all.

²Silas, Timothy and I are always giving thanks to God for you all, continually making mention of you in our prayers. ³We continue to remember your faith and how it has outworked, your love and how you have laboured and your hope in the Lord Jesus Christ and how it has enabled you to stand firm. ⁴Brothers, we know that God loves you and that you are his chosen ones.[1160] ⁵For we did not bring the gospel to you with words only, but also with power, with Holy Breath and with an absolute assurance of its truth. You know how we lived among you. It was for your benefit. ⁶As for you, you followed our example and the Lord's example. And despite suffering so much, you welcomed the message with joy *that comes by* Holy Breath. ⁷In doing so, you became a model to all the believers in the *provinces of* Macedonia and Achaia.[1161] ⁸The message about the Lord reverberated out from you not only in Macedonia and Achaia—your faith in God has become known everywhere. There is nothing more to be said. ⁹For they themselves report what effect our coming had on you when we came to you. They report how you turned to God from idols to serve the true and living God. ¹⁰They report how you are waiting for his Son from the heavens whom he raised from the dead. This is Jesus who rescues us from the coming wrath.[1162]

Paul's ministry in Thessalonica

2 ¹Brothers, our visit to you has not been in vain. ²Having previously suffered and having been insulted in Philippi, as you well know, we nevertheless took courage from God and told you the good news from God and we did this despite the opposition. ³For the appeal we made to you *Thessalonians* was not with error or with impure motives, nor are we trying to trick anyone. ⁴On the contrary, we speak as men approved by God who are entrusted with the good news. We are not trying to please men but God. He is the one who tests our

---

1160 'Chosen' (the elect) is a term originally used of Israel but now also applied in the NT to the church in a corporate sense as a group. Cf. Eph. 2:8 footnote.
1161 At the time Paul wrote, Macedonia and Achaia were two Roman provinces whose boundaries corresponded to those of no modern state. Together, they covered almost the whole area of modern Greece and Albania, and also the southern part of Yugoslavia, which is still called Macedonia (TH).
1162 "Wrath" here is not referring to the emotion of anger. It more refers to the punishment coming from God towards mankind as a result of their sin.

motives and intentions. ⁵As you all well know, we never used flattery, nor was our motive greed—God is our witness to this. ⁶We were not looking for praise from men, not from you or anyone else.

⁷Even though as apostles of Christ we could have made demands on you, we didn't. We were gentle with you, like a breastfeeding mother who takes care of her children. ⁸Because of our great affection for you, we were not only pleased to share the good news of God with you, but we did everything possible to help you. We did this because we loved you so much. ⁹Surely you remember brothers, how we toiled and the hardship we endured! We worked night and day in order not to be a burden on anyone while we preached God's good news to you all.

¹⁰You yourselves are our witnesses, as is God, of how pure, how right and how faultless our conduct was towards you who believe. ¹¹And as you know, we related to each one of you as a father relates to his own children, ¹²encouraging, comforting and urging you all to live lives worthy of God. For he is the one who calls you to share in his glorious reign as king.

¹³And another reason why we are always giving thanks to God is that when you received the word of God, which you heard from us, you accepted it. You accepted it not as a word from men, but as it actually is, the word of God, which is at work in you who believe. ¹⁴For the same things that happened to you, brothers, also happened in God's churches in the province of Judea, those who are in Christ Jesus. You suffered from your own people[1163] in the same way that the churches in Judea did from the Judeans ¹⁵who killed the Lord Jesus and *long ago*, the prophets.[1164] They have also persecuted us. They are most displeasing to God and are against all men ¹⁶in their effort to prevent us from speaking to the Gentiles so that they can be saved. In doing this they are continually heaping up their sins to the very limit. The wrath of God has finally caught up with them.

Paul desires to see the Thessalonians again

¹⁷But, brothers, having been separated from you for a short time, physically, not in our thinking, we realised how much we missed you all![1165] We tried very hard to see you face to face again. ¹⁸For we wanted to come to you many times but Satan stopped us. Well, certainly I, Paul did. ¹⁹For what is our hope, our joy, or the *victor's* wreath in which we will take pride in, in the presence of the Lord Jesus when he comes? Is it not you? ²⁰Yes, indeed you are. You are our pride and joy.

1163   Literally their own countrymen or compatriots.
1164   The Judeans (the leaders and the chief priests in Jerusalem) were the ones primarily responsible for Jesus' death however the people of Israel were complicit as well by agreeing to it by shouting, "Crucify him, crucify him!" The Romans were complicit in the fact that they actually were the ones who crucified him. Cf. Matt. 20:17–19, Acts 2:22–23.
1165   Paul and Silas were forced to leave the Thessalonians due to persecution. Cf. Acts 17:10.

3 ¹So when we could bear it no longer, we were happy to remain in Athens by ourselves ²and we sent Timothy, who is our brother and fellow co-worker of God in the gospel of Christ. We sent him to strengthen and encourage you all in your faith, ³in order that no one would turn back *from the faith* because of these persecutions. You yourselves know very well that *God's* plan for us includes persecution. ⁴Even when we were with you, we kept telling you that we would be persecuted. And as you well know, it, in fact, did turn out that way. ⁵For this reason, when I could bear it no longer, I sent Timothy to find out about your faith. I was fearful that somehow the devil had tempted you and our efforts might have been in vain.

Timothy brings good news regarding the Thessalonians

⁶But Timothy has just now returned from you and he has brought good news about your faith and love. He has told us that you always have pleasant memories of us[1166] and that you want to see us just as much as we would like to see you. ⁷Therefore brothers, we were very encouraged *by this report* concerning your faith despite all of the distress and persecution that we were going through at the time. ⁸Because you are standing firm in the Lord, we can now live and breathe again. ⁹How can we thank God enough for you all? We have received so much joy in the presence of our God because of you. ¹⁰Night and day we are praying with great determination that we might be able to see you again and that he might supply you with what is needed in your faith.

¹¹Now may our God and Father himself and our Lord Jesus make the way clear for us to come to you. ¹²May the Lord make your love increase and overflow for each other and everyone else, just as our *love overflows* for you. ¹³This will strengthen you and you will be perfect and holy before our God and Father when our Lord Jesus comes with all his holy ones.[1167] Amen.

Living to please God

4 ¹Brothers, in conclusion, we ask and encourage you, in the Lord Jesus, to live in a way that pleases God. In fact, you already received *instruction* from us in how to please him and you are actually doing just that. But we urge you to keep doing even better. ²For you know what instructions we gave you by the authority of the Lord Jesus.

³It is God's desire that you should be holy[1168] and that you should avoid sexual

---

1166   It is important to note that it was only months since Paul and Silas had seen the Thessalonians, not years.
1167   It is not clear whether "holy ones" here means Christians, angels or both.
1168   Here "holy" means that the Thessalonians should be set apart for God's purposes and service.

immorality. ⁴It is his desire that each one of you should know how to control his own body[1169] in a holy and honourable way, ⁵not in a passionate lustful way like the Gentiles, who do not know God. ⁶In this matter *of how a man conducts himself towards women* then, no one should wrong his fellow *Christian* brother or take advantage of him. The Lord will punish men for all such sins. We have previously told you and warned you about this. ⁷For God did not call us to live immoral lives but to live in holiness. ⁸Therefore, he who rejects this *teaching* does not reject man but God, the one who also gives you his Holy Breath.

⁹Now about the importance of loving each other we do not need to write to you, for you yourselves have been taught by God to love each other. ¹⁰And indeed, you have loved all the *Christian* brothers throughout the province of Macedonia. Yet we are urging you, brothers, to keep doing even better in this regard.

¹¹Make it your goal to lead a quiet life, to mind your own business and to earn your own living just as we have already instructed you *when we were in Thessalonica*. ¹²In this way your daily life may win the respect of non-believers[1170] and you will not be dependent on anyone for anything.

The coming of the Lord

¹³Brothers, we do not want you to be in any doubt about those *Christians* who have died.[1171] Also, we do not want you to grieve like the rest of men who have no hope. ¹⁴We believe that Jesus died and rose again. Therefore we also believe that God will bring with Jesus those who have died. ¹⁵Here is a word from the Lord: we who are still alive, those who are left behind until the coming of the Lord, they will certainly not precede those who have already died. ¹⁶For the Lord himself will come down from heaven with a loud command, with the voice of an archangel and with the trumpet call of God. Those who have already died *having believed* in Christ will rise to *new* life first. ¹⁷Then after that, we who are still alive and are left behind will be snatched up[1172] together with them in the clouds to meet the Lord in the air. And so then we will be with the Lord forever. ¹⁸Therefore you must encourage each other with these words.

5 ¹Now brothers, I do not need to write to you exactly when these things will occur. ²For you all know very well that the Day of the Lord will come like a thief

---

1169 It is possible that this verse means something completely different: '…each one of you should know how to live with his own *wife* in a holy and honourable way.'
1170 Literally the Greek here is 'outsiders' but the inference is those 'outside' of the Christian faith.
1171 This is literally 'those who have fallen asleep'. But that is more than likely a euphemism for those who have died. The euphemistic 'those who have fallen asleep' is not included here because some groups use verses such as this to promote the false doctrine of 'soul sleep'.
1172 This is where the term "rapture" first originated. The Latin Vulgate Bible used the word *raptu* which led to the transliterated word, "rapture". The Greek word is *harpazo*. Cf. 2 Cor. 12:2–4.

in the night. ³While they are saying, "Peace and security," sudden destruction will come upon them, like when labour pains come upon a pregnant woman.*¹¹⁷³* They certainly will not escape.

⁴But you brothers, are not in the dark regarding these matters that this day should surprise you like when a thief comes. ⁵Rather, you are all children of the light and day. We have nothing to do with the night or darkness. ⁶So then, we must not be asleep *at the wheel* as the rest but we must be awake and keep a clear head. ⁷For those who sleep, sleep at night and those who get drunk, get drunk at night. ⁸But since we belong to the day, we must keep a clear head. We must put on faith and love like a breastplate and we must put on hope of salvation like a helmet. ⁹For God did not put us here to suffer under his fury but to receive salvation through our Lord Jesus Christ.*¹¹⁷⁴* ¹⁰He died for us so that *when he comes,* whether we are alive or dead, we may live together with him. ¹¹Therefore you must continue to encourage each other and help each other just as you have been doing.

Final instructions

¹²Now we ask you brothers, that you must respect those who work hard among you. These are the men who exercise leadership over you in the Lord and instruct you. ¹³You are to hold them in the highest regard and *treat them* in love because of the work that they do. Be at peace amongst yourselves. ¹⁴And these are the things that we urge you, brothers, to do: you must warn those who are idle and refuse to work, console those who are discouraged, help those who need help and you must be patient with everyone. ¹⁵See to it that no one pays back wrong for wrong. *Regardless of what may happen* always try to be kind to each other and all people.

¹⁶Be happy always. ¹⁷Never give up praying. ¹⁸Be thankful to God in all situations and times, for this is God's will for you in Christ Jesus.

¹⁹Make sure that you do not extinguish the Holy Breath. ²⁰Do not despise prophecies thinking they have no value. ²¹But make sure that you test them all

---

1173　The United Nations (UN) was created in 1945, following the Second World War, with one central mission: the maintenance of international 'peace and security'. The UN Security Council has the primary responsibility for international peace and security. https://www.un.org/en/our-work/maintain-international-peace-and-security

1174　Pre-tribulation and pre-wrath supporters use this verse to incorrectly support the view that Christians will not go through the tribulation or Great Tribulation and that believers will be raptured prior to either the seal or trumpet judgments or both. However Paul is saying that we haven't been put on earth merely to be judged on the final day of judgment (Day of the Lord). In history the precedent is that God has always been able to supernaturally and adequately preserve his people while they remain on earth including the Flood, the early warning given to Lot and the Passover.

and hold onto those *prophecies* which are good. ²²You must avoid every kind of evil.

²³Now may God himself, the God of peace, make you holy in every way, keeping your whole being—spirit, soul and body—faultless when the Lord Jesus Christ comes. ²⁴He who has called you is loyal and he will be sure to do it.

²⁵Brothers, pray for us. ²⁶Greet all the *Christian* brothers with a holy kiss. ²⁷I order you by the Lord that this letter has to be read to all the *Christian* brothers.

²⁸The grace of the Lord Jesus Christ be with you.

2 THESSALONIANS

Introduction

Paul wrote a follow up letter to the church in Thessalonica, the harbour city in the Roman province of Macedonia, around AD 51–52 maybe only a few months after he wrote his first letter. Again Paul encourages the young believers with the signs that will accompany the coming Man of Lawlessness or Antichrist. In 2 Thess. 2:1–3, Paul warns them that the Day of the Lord will not come until first there is a great falling away and the Antichrist is revealed. Therefore they must not remain idle but continue on strongly until these signs are first seen. This was an error in their thinking that Christ would return at any moment so they were not working. This proves the point that even though Jesus Christ's return is getting extremely close it has never been imminent in the sense that he could come at any moment but that there are certain prophecies that must be fulfilled first. For the church today this letter continues to warn us not to be deceived (2 Thess. 2:3).

1 ¹From Paul, Silas and Timothy.

To the church of the Thessalonians who belong to God the Father and the Lord Jesus Christ.

²Grace and peace to you all from God the Father and the Lord Jesus Christ.

Thanksgiving and prayer

³Silas, Timothy and I must continually thank God for you all, brothers. And rightly so, because your faith is growing more and more, and the love that you all have for each other is increasing. ⁴That is why we ourselves speak with pride about you in all the churches of God. We speak to them about your perseverance and faith and about all the persecutions and trials you are patiently enduring. ⁵All of this *suffering* goes to prove that God's judgment of people will be appropriate. As a result, you will be counted worthy to enter into God's *future* reign for which you are currently suffering. ⁶God always does what is right. He will pay back trouble to those who are troubling you ⁷and give relief to you who are troubled and to us as well. This will occur at the revelation of the Lord Jesus from heaven when he comes in power with his angels in a flaming fire. ⁸God will punish those who do not know him and also those who do not obey the gospel of our Lord Jesus. ⁹They will be punished with everlasting utter ruin and they will be shut out from the presence of the Lord and they will never experience how wonderful he is. ¹⁰When he comes he will receive glory among his holy people and all those who believe will marvel at him on that Day. You too will be among them because you have believed what we told you.

¹¹With all of this in mind, we constantly pray for you that our God may make you worthy of the life that he has called you all to live. We pray that he might powerfully fulfil all of your good intentions and every act that comes as a result of your faith. ¹²We pray these things so that the name of the Lord Jesus may be honoured by you and that he may cause you also to be honoured, according to the grace of our God and the Lord Jesus Christ.

Man of Lawlessness

2 ¹*Christian* brothers, concerning the coming of our Lord Jesus Christ and our gathering together to him,¹¹⁷⁵ I plead with you ²not to become easily rattled or alarmed by some prophecy, report or letter that has supposedly come from us,

---

1175   I.e. the first resurrection of all past believers and rapture of believers alive at the time. The coming of the Lord Jesus and the gathering together is talking about the one and same event because of the Granville Sharp grammar rule.

saying that the Day of the Lord has arrived.[1176] ³You must not let anyone deceive you in any way *for that day will not come* until the apostasy occurs first and the Man of Lawlessness is revealed—the one who is doomed to utter ruin.[1177] ⁴He will oppose everything and exalt himself over every so-called god or anything that is worshipped. He will even sit in the temple of God[1178] claiming that he is God. ⁵I am sure that you remember that I told you all of this when I was still there with you *in Thessalonica*.

⁶Yet at this present time there is something[1179] that is restraining *the Man of Lawlessness* so that he may be revealed at the proper time. ⁷For the secret power of lawlessness[1180] is already at work but he[1181] who is at present restraining will continue to do so until he comes out at the middle. ⁸And then the lawless one will be revealed, whom the Lord Jesus will *ultimately* consume by the breath of his mouth. The Lord will destroy him by the *mere* appearance of his coming. ⁹The coming of the lawless one will be associated with the working of Satan who will demonstrate all kinds of power, performing all kinds of fake signs and wonders. ¹⁰He will deceive people in every way, ruining them in the process because they refused to love and accept the truth and so be saved. ¹¹The reason

---

1176 The Thessalonians were worried that they had missed the Day of the Lord. The pre-tribulational position says that the Day of the Lord begins with the rapture before the seven years and extends through the tribulation period and that the Antichrist will be revealed at the beginning of the seven years. However from both Matt. 24:29 and Acts 2:20, we know that the Day of the Lord does not occur until after the tribulation. One can conclude, therefore, that they were not worried about missing a pre-tribulational rapture because it is simply not true. The beast does not arise out of the abyss until it is opened at the fifth trumpet judgment at the mid-point (Rev. 11:7). After he appears he will sit down in the reconstructed temple and declare himself to be God. The rapture occurs 1290 days later on the Feast of Trumpets (Yom Teruah, Rosh Hashanah).

1177 I.e. The Antichrist. Literally 'the son of perdition' meaning the one who is to be destroyed. Its origin is from the Greek *apollumi*, the same as the king of the abyss, Apollyon (Rev. 9:11). In John 17:12, John calls Judas the 'son of perdition' also.

1178 This is the Jewish temple in Jerusalem which obviously implies that there must be a temple for him to be able to do this. This will happen in the second half of the seven-year tribulation period.

1179 There is much conjecture to what that something is that is holding back the Man of Sin or Antichrist from beginning his work in the second half of the tribulation. In the Greek in v. 6, "something" is in the neuter tense indicating that the restraining influence is not a person but an object or a force.

1180 This hidden power of lawlessness is hidden to the world but not to Christians, who know that the forces of evil are always at work in the current world that we live in. This is in the neuter tense correlating with the "something" in v. 6.

1181 There is a male behind the hidden power of lawlessness—Satan. Up to the midpoint of the final seven-year tribulation it has been the secret power of lawlessness that has been restraining the Antichrist from coming but at the halfway mark Michael the Archangel removes Satan and casts him down to the earth (Rev. 12:7-9). Satan has been trying to delay this as long as possible via his secret power of lawlessness (plan A) because he knows that he is ultimately doomed to destruction but once he is cast down to the earth he then reverts to plan B knowing that his time is short. He is likely the star (Rev. 9:1) that opens the seal over the abyss and releases his demonic forces. Satan's plan B during the Great Tribulation will be once again to try and prove that God is a liar just as he tried with Adam and Eve (Gen. 3:1) and try and turn all humanity against him. How will he do this? By getting everyone to believe once again the original lie that they will not surely die if they partake of the mark of the beast. Cf. Matt. 23:39.

that people will be deceived in every way is that God has been sending them a power that deludes[1182] in order that they will believe the lie.[1183] ¹²The result is that all who have not believed the truth but have taken pleasure in their sin will be condemned.

Standing firm

¹³But we must always thank God for you, *Thessalonian* brothers, whom the Lord dearly loves. For God has determined that you, *as a church*, would be the first saved among many, by the separating and purifying work of *his* Breath as you have believed the truth. ¹⁴He called you to this *salvation* through our gospel so that you might share in the glory of our Lord Jesus Christ. ¹⁵Therefore, brothers, you must stand firm and hold to the teachings that we have passed on to you, whether by word of mouth or by letter.

¹⁶Now may our Lord Jesus Christ himself and God our Father, who has loved us, *encourage you all*. May God who by his grace, gave us eternal encouragement and good hope, ¹⁷encourage your inner resolve and strengthen you in every good work and word.

3 ¹Now finally I ask you brothers that you must pray for us that the message of the Lord may continue to spread rapidly and that it may be received with due honour, just as it was with you. ²And also pray that we may be delivered from the wicked and evil men, for not everyone is of the faith. ³But the Lord is loyal, and he will strengthen and protect you from the evil one. ⁴We have confidence in the Lord that you are doing and will continue to do the things that we are commanding. ⁵We pray that the Lord will guide you into a greater understanding of God's love and that he may cause you to wait patiently for Christ's *coming*.

Believers should not be idle

⁶*Christian* brothers, we command you in the name of the Lord Jesus Christ that you are to keep away from every brother who is idle and refuses to work and those who do not live according to the teaching that you have received from

---

1182 Cf. Rev. 18:23.
1183 "Lie" here has the definite article so it must be a well-known lie. The delusion is not the lie but it enables people to believe the lie. The original lie the serpent told Eve is that mankind can be as the gods (*elohim*), knowing both good and evil and that dying they will not die (Gen. 3:4–5 KJV). The sense in Gen. 3:4 in the Hebrew is that there are two deaths. In other words, they would have control over their own destiny meaning that God was lying to her and Adam and that they wouldn't experience the second death. Cf. Rom. 1:25. The delusion, reinforced by a myriad of fake signs and wonders, most likely involves the most significant event of that time—the mark of the beast. If people take the mark (delusion) then the promise (lie) is that they will be like gods and be in control over their own destiny including life itself.

us. ⁷For you yourselves know how you must follow our example. We were not idle when we were with you, ⁸nor did we eat anyone's food without paying for it. On the contrary, we worked night and day, labouring and toiling so that we would not be a burden to any of you. ⁹We did this, not that we don't have the right *to ask this of you all*, but so that we ourselves would be an example for you to follow. ¹⁰For even when we were with you, we had this rule: "If a man refuses to work, he shall not eat."

¹¹We say this because we hear *reports* that there are some among you who are idle and refuse to work instead being busybodies. ¹²Such people, we command and urge in the Lord Jesus Christ to live their lives in a quiet and peaceful manner and earn their keep. ¹³And as for you, brothers, don't ever lose heart in doing what is right.

¹⁴And if there is anyone who does not obey our instructions in this letter, take note of this man. Do not associate with him, so that he may be put to shame. ¹⁵Yet do not consider him as an enemy but warn him as a brother *in Christ*.

Final Greetings

¹⁶I pray that the Lord of peace himself may give you peace at all times and in every way. The Lord be with you all. ¹⁷I Paul, am writing this greeting in my handwriting, which is the way I sign every letter.

¹⁸The grace of the Lord Jesus Christ be with you all.

1 TIMOTHY

Introduction

Paul wrote this letter to young Pastor Timothy at Ephesus to encourage him in his ministry to combat against the false teaching that was cropping up. He also instructed Timothy about the kind of people who should be leaders in the church and how one should relate to various groups within the church such as widows, young women, older men, younger men, slaves, rich people and false teachers. 1 Timothy is one of three letters known as the pastoral epistles and was written in about AD 65 after the events written in the Book of Acts. Paul was very emotional in this letter towards young Timothy and regarded him as his son in the faith. Ephesus was probably one of the most modern cities in the first century after Rome and there was a large Jewish population.

1 ¹I Paul, an apostle of Christ Jesus by the command of God our Saviour and of Christ Jesus our hope, *have written this letter.*

²*I am writing this letter* to you Timothy, my true son in the faith.

Grace, mercy and peace from God the Father and Christ Jesus our Lord.

Warnings against false teaching

³When I was on my way to Macedonia I urged you to remain in Ephesus.[1184] Stay there and tell certain men there that they must not teach false doctrine any longer. ⁴Tell them that they must not devote themselves to myths and endless genealogies. These promote controversies rather than God's work which is rather centred on *the life of* faith. ⁵The reason I am ordering you to do this is to stimulate love *amongst the believers,* which comes from a pure heart, a good conscience[1185] and a sincere faith. ⁶However some of them have wandered off instead turning to meaningless talk. ⁷They want to be teachers of the Law but really they do not know what they are talking about or about the matters about which they speak so confidently.

⁸We know that the Law is good if one uses it correctly. ⁹We also know that laws exist for those who break the law and for rebels not for those who do the right thing. The law is for the ungodly and sinners, the unholy and non-religious, for those who kill their fathers or mothers, for murderers, ¹⁰for the sexually immoral and homosexuals, for perverts, slave traders, liars and for those who commit perjury in court. In fact, the law is for anyone who does what is contrary to sound doctrine. ¹¹Sound doctrine is in accordance with the glorious gospel of the blessed God, which he entrusted to me.

Paul is thankful to the Lord

¹²I thank Christ Jesus our Lord, who has given me strength *to do his work.* I *am thankful* that he sees me as being loyal having appointing me to his service. ¹³Even though I was once a blasphemer and a persecutor and a violent man, *God* showed me mercy because I acted in ignorance and unbelief. ¹⁴The grace of our Lord was poured out on me with great abundance along with the faith and love that are in Christ Jesus.

¹⁵Here is a dependable statement that deserves our full acceptance: "Christ Jesus came into this world to save sinners." (I am surely the worst.) ¹⁶But because *I am the worst of all sinners,* I was shown mercy so that in me Christ Jesus might

---

1184   Paul is referring to the time seven years previously when he warned the Ephesian elders of the church that false teachers would come in as wolves and not spare the flock (Acts 20:29).
1185   Cf. 1 Tim. 3:9 footnote.

display his inexhaustible patience as an example for those who might believe in him resulting in eternal life. ¹⁷Now unto the King who is eternal, immortal, and invisible—the only God, be honour and glory forever and ever. Amen.[1186]

¹⁸Timothy, my son, I have some instructions for you in keeping with the prophecies once made about you. If you follow them then you may be able to fight the good fight ¹⁹with faith and a good conscience. Some people[1187] have not listened *to their conscience* and have ship-wrecked their faith.[1188] ²⁰Among them are Hymenaeus and Alexander, whom I have given over to Satan in order to be taught not to blaspheme.[1189]

Instructions on conduct at the worship service

2 ¹Therefore the most important thing that I urge you to do is that you make requests, pray, intercede and give thanks to God for everyone. ²*Pray* for kings and all those in authority so that we may live peaceful and quiet lives in all godliness and dignity. ³This is good and pleases God our Saviour, ⁴who wants everyone to be saved and to come to a knowledge of the truth. ⁵For there is one God and one mediator between God and mankind—the man Christ Jesus ⁶who gave himself in order to release all people *from their sin*. This was the proof at exactly the right time *that God wants everyone to be saved.* ⁷It was for this very purpose that I, *Paul*, was appointed as a preacher and an apostle. (I am absolutely telling the truth, I am not lying.) I am a teacher of the true faith to the Gentiles.

⁸Therefore, *as an apostle,* I would like the men in every place *of meeting* to lift up holy hands[1190] to God in prayer without anger or argument. ⁹I would also like the women to dress modestly, sensibly and with decency, and not to beautify themselves with elaborate hairstyles or gold, pearls or expensive clothing. ¹⁰But rather *they must beautify themselves* with good deeds which are appropriate for women who claim that they worship God.

¹¹*I also think that* a woman should learn quietly and in submission.[1191] ¹²I do

---

1186 Verse 17 is what is called a doxology which is a liturgical formula or short hymn for praising God. Liturgy is a form of public worship which is scripted and follows a definite pattern that is repeated. In other words this doxology would be a standardised short form of praise.
1187 These "some people" are the false teachers referred to in vv. 3–7.
1188 Paul reminds Timothy to be careful because some of these teachers who once taught the truth have turned away from Christ and have abandoned their faith.
1189 This probably means that the two men were excommunicated from the church with the aim of trying to bring them back to repentance.
1190 "Holy hands" here is a reference to the way that people in the 1st century church prayed both Jew and non-Jew. They lifted up their hands toward God. Paul is not commanding that we necessarily lift up our hands to the heavens today when we pray but it is included because that is the way prayer was done.
1191 "Quietly" is a good translation here not 'silence' as in some translations. It's not that Paul is saying

not allow a woman to teach or to have authority over a man. She must remain silent.[1192] [13]For Adam was formed first and then Eve. [14]And Adam was not the one seduced. It was the woman who was completely seduced[1193] and wilfully disobeyed.[1194] [15]However womankind will be saved through childbearing if they continue in faith, love and holiness with decency.[1195]

Leaders in the church

3 [1]Here is a dependable statement: If anyone aspires to being a leader in the church, he desires a very respectable task. [2]The church leader must be without fault and be faithful to his wife. He must be a man who has self-control, is restrained and one who is respected. He must be hospitable, able to teach [3]and not a heavy drinker or violent. But he must be gentle, non-contentious and not a lover of money. [4]He must be able to manage his own household well and see that his children obey him with proper respect. [5]For if he does not know how to manage his own family, how can he take care of God's church? [6]*The leader* must not be a new Christian otherwise he may become arrogant and fall under the same judgment as the devil.[1196] [7]He must also have a good reputation with the outside world so that he is not insulted by them and fall into a trap of the devil.

Helpers in the church

[8]Deacons likewise, must be men worthy of respect. They must be sincere, not addicted to wine and not greedy for money. [9]*Deacons* must *be men who* firmly

---

	that a woman can never speak but the theme of chapter 2 is that there has to be order in the church service. Some of the women were apparently abusing their new found freedoms in Christ and creating disturbances in the services. Church services in the 1st century were more than likely house meetings and there were interruptions occurring. Paul wrote something similar in 1 Cor. 14:34 that women were to be silent in the churches. Putting these two admonitions together the conclusion is that the women were talking and being noisy in the churches whilst meetings were going on. We must have order in the church and things must not get out of hand. The main activities in the church service are worship, prayer, learning and having communion. There must not be noisy interruptions.
1192	This verse often offends our modern-day sensibilities that women should be quiet, be submissive and not be allowed to teach. Even though Christianity was born out of Judaism and the early meetings often took place in the synagogue, the early Christian movement was a lot different in that women were included in instruction classes together with the men. But there was one condition: the women should learn in silence, which means that women were not allowed to speak at church meetings. The men were the main teachers and the women had to submit to the authority of the men as teachers and accept with humility and obedience what was taught them.
1193	Cf. 2 Cor. 11:3, 1 John 3:12.
1194	Cf. Matt. 6:14 and footnote.
1195	The female gender will always be secure as the survival of the human race is dependent on their role in giving birth and raising children in the home. The main issue of this whole passage is that a healthy church sees men and women working together in their God-given roles. The main issue here is decency and order in the worship service.
1196	Satan's downfall was arrogance and pride wanting to take the place of God. Arrogance and pride has no place in the life of the church leader.

hold to the profound truth of the *Christian* faith with a clear conscience.[1197] [10]They must first be tested and if there is nothing that can be held against them then let them serve as deacons.

[11]Likewise, deaconesses[1198] must be women worthy of respect as well. They must not be gossips but restrained and loyal in all things. [12]A deacon must be faithful to his wife and he must manage his children and his household well. [13]Those *men and women* who have served well achieve a good standing and a lot of confidence in their faith in Christ Jesus.

Paul's reasons for writing to Timothy

[14]I am writing to you these instructions as I am hoping that I will be able to come to you soon, [15]but if I am delayed, you will know how everyone should conduct themselves in the household of God. They are the church of the living God which is the pillar and foundation of the truth. [16]It is beyond question that our religion is very profound:

He was made to appear in the flesh and shown to be right in spirit.[1199]
He was seen by angels and was proclaimed amongst the nations.
He was believed throughout the world and was taken up to heaven in glory.

Coming apostasy in the end days

4 [1]The Breath *of God* explicitly says that in the end times some *believers* will abandon the faith and follow deceiving spirits and things taught by demons. [2]Teachings like these come from liars who are hypocrites. Their consciences have been seared as with a hot iron. [3]They forbid people to get married and order them to abstain from certain foods. But God created these foods to be received and eaten with thanks by believers who know the truth. [4]For everything that God created is good and nothing should be rejected if it is received with thanks. [5]This is because it is made to be holy by the word of God and prayer.

[6]*Timothy*, if you point out these things to the *Christian* brothers, you will be a good servant[1200] of Christ Jesus, one who is nourished in the truths of the

---

1197 Cf. 1 Tim. 1:5 where the translation is "a good conscience" not "a clear conscience" as in here. A good conscience enables one to make good decisions whereas a clear conscience is when you feel cleared of any wrongdoing.
1198 Bible translators are divided how this should be translated here. Some have 'deacon's wives' and others deaconesses. The problem is that this is the Greek word *gunaikas* which simply means 'woman'. Considering the context in that in 1 Tim. 3:1-7 there is no restriction placed on the wives of leaders in the church then it seems unlikely that there would be a separate special category for deacon's wives. Cf. Rom. 16:1.
1199 KJV has, "God was manifest in the flesh".
1200 This is literally the word 'deacon' here but here it is more in the general sense of a servant or minister and not the official office of deacon.

faith and the good teaching which you have followed. ⁷Make sure that you have nothing to do with godless myths and old wives' tales. Instead, train yourself to be godly. ⁸For physical training definitely has some profit but godliness is profitable in every way. It holds promise for both the present life and the life to come.

⁹Here is a dependable statement that deserves our full attention: ¹⁰(and for this, we work towards and really make an effort). We have put our hope in the living God, who is the Saviour of all men, particularly those who believe.[1201]

Personal advice to Timothy from Paul

¹¹*Timothy*, command and teach the *following* things. ¹²Make sure that you don't let anyone look down on you just because you are young. But set an example for the believers in speech, in life, in love *for others*, in faith and in purity. ¹³And until I come, I want you to devote yourself to the reading of Scripture *aloud*, to the preaching and to the teaching. ¹⁴Do not forget your *spiritual* gift which was given to you through a prophetic message when the group of elders laid their hands on you.

¹⁵Put into practice these things and give yourself completely to them so that your progress may be evident to everyone. ¹⁶Watch your life and doctrine closely and persevere in them. In doing this you will save both yourself and your hearers.

Instructions on different groups in the church

5 ¹Make sure that you do not rebuke an older man harshly, but appeal to him as if he was your father. *Treat* younger men as brothers, ²the older women as mothers and younger women as your own sisters, with absolute purity.

³Honour the widows *in the church* who have no one to support them. ⁴But if a widow has children or grandchildren, then they should learn to first of all practice godliness at home by caring for their own family. They should repay their parents and grandparents for this is pleasing to God. ⁵The widow who has no one to support her and is left all alone puts her hope in God and continues to pray and ask God for help. ⁶But the widow who is living in *the lap of* luxury is as good as dead even though physically she is still living. ⁷Command the people with these things so that no one may be criticised. ⁸If anyone does not provide for his relatives, especially for his immediate family, he has denied the faith and is worse than an unbeliever.

⁹You must not put the names of any widows on the list unless they are over the age of sixty. In addition, she must have been faithful to her husband, ¹⁰and be

---

1201 Theologically the Bible is clear that Christ died for all mankind but only those who believe and stand firm until the end are actually saved.

1 TIMOTHY

well known for her good deeds such as bringing up children, showing hospitality, washing the feet of God's holy people, helping those in trouble and devoting herself to all kinds of good deeds.

[11] But as for younger widows, do not *put them on the list* because when their sexual desires cause them to want to marry they turn away from Christ. [12] This then brings judgment upon them because they have broken their earlier promise. [13] Furthermore they get into the habit of being idle and going about from house to house and even worse, they become gossips and busybodies saying things they shouldn't be saying. [14] Therefore I counsel the younger widows to remarry, to have children, to manage their homes in order to give the enemy no opportunity for slander. [15] For some widows have in fact already turned away *from God* to follow Satan. [16] If any woman[1202] who is a believer has widows in her family, she should help them and not let the church be burdened with them. This is so that the church can help those widows who really do need help.

[17] The elders of the church who direct the affairs of the church well are worthy of double honour, especially those whose work is preaching and teaching. [18] For the Scripture says, "Do not muzzle the ox while it is treading out the grain,"[1203] and "The worker deserves his pay."[1204] [19] Do not accept an accusation brought against an elder unless there are two or three witnesses. [20] Those who are sinning must be rebuked publicly so that the rest will also be afraid *to sin*.

[21] As God is my witness and in the presence of Jesus Christ and the chosen angels, I command you to keep these instructions without discrimination, making sure that you do nothing out of favouritism.

[22] Do not be hasty in the laying on of hands[1205] and make sure that you do not share in the sins of others. Keep yourself pure.

[23] Timothy, you must stop drinking water only. Use a small amount of wine because of your stomach issues and frequent illnesses.[1206]

[24] Some people's sins are totally obvious easily pointing to judgment however the sins of others come behind later. [25] Similarly good deeds are obvious and even those *good deeds* which are not *obvious* cannot remain hidden.

6 [1] As for those who are under the yoke of slavery,[1207] they should consider

---

1202 TR MSS (KJV & NKJV) have 'any believing man or woman' here.
1203 Deut. 25:4.
1204 Luke 10:7. This quote from a saying of Jesus proves that Luke is part of Scripture and that the NT is equally as valid as the OT.
1205 The laying on of hands occurred when certain people were set apart for certain church offices such as an elder. The laying on of hands has become an important part of the rites of ordination.
1206 Important to remember that elders and deacons were not to be heavy drinkers of alcohol but a small amount of wine is okay.
1207 A slave is a person who is owned by someone else and effectively has no rights. They must show complete submission and loyalty to their masters. A yoke was a wooden frame placed over two

their masters worthy of full respect so that God's name and our teaching may not be discredited in any way. ²Those who have believing masters are not to show less respect for them because they are *Christian* brothers. Rather, they should serve them even better because those who benefit from their service are believers who are loved dearly. *Timothy*, these are the things which you must teach and urge them to do.

The love of money is a reason for all kinds of evil

³If anyone teaches contrary to what I have instructed you to teach and does not agree with the sound words of our Lord Jesus Christ and to godly teaching ⁴then he is arrogant and understands nothing. Rather, he has an unhealthy interest in controversies and arguments about words. This produces envy, rivalry, slander and evil suspicions ⁵and constant conflict between men who have corrupt minds. They have become devoid of the truth and they think that godliness is a way to become wealthy.

⁶But having godliness with contentment is of great value. ⁷For we bring nothing into this world and we can take nothing out of it. ⁸But if we can have food and clothing, we are to be content with that. ⁹The thing is that people who want to get rich fall into temptation and a trap. They fall into many foolish and harmful desires which plunges these people into ruin and destruction. ¹⁰For the love of money is a reason and source for all kinds of evil. Some people who are eager for money have wandered away from the faith and have caused themselves a lot of pain.

Paul gives further instructions to Timothy

¹¹But you, Timothy, man of God, make sure that you flee from all these things that I have mentioned. Instead, you must pursue righteousness, godliness, faith, love, endurance and gentleness. ¹²Put up a good fight for the faith and grab hold of the eternal life to which you were called to when you made your good confession in the presence of many witnesses. ¹³I am giving you this order in the sight of God, the one who gives life to everything, and in the sight of Christ Jesus, the one who made the good confession of the truth before Pontius Pilate. I order you ¹⁴to keep this command without spot or blame until the appearing[1208]

---

animals joining them to increase the pulling power either for ploughing or a cart. In the 1st century there were many slaves who became Christians. It is important to note that Paul does not condone slavery but rather to help them make the best of what situation they find themselves in. It is rather the present reality of 1st century under Roman rule. The main point is that we should not bring Christ's name into disrepute.

1208   This is the Greek word which we get the English word 'epiphany' from. It definitely means the second coming of Christ. Interestingly this command, by extension, is for all Christians not just Timothy. We keep the faith and endure until the Day of the Lord, the second coming of Christ.

of our Lord Jesus Christ. ¹⁵God will reveal *this appearing* in his own time.¹²⁰⁹ He is the blessed and sole Power, the King of kings and Lord of lords. ¹⁶He alone is immortal and lives in unapproachable light. No one has seen him or is able to see him.¹²¹⁰ To him be honour and might forever. Amen.

¹⁷*Timothy*, command those *Christians* who are rich in this present world not to be arrogant nor to put their hope in riches which is so uncertain. Instead, *tell* them to put their hope in God who generously provides us with everything for our enjoyment. ¹⁸Command them to do good, to be rich in good deeds and to be generous and willing to share with others. ¹⁹*If they do this* they will be laying up treasure for themselves as a firm foundation for the future so that they may experience the real life.

²⁰Timothy, guard what God has entrusted to your care.¹²¹¹ Turn away from godless chatter and the contradictory ideas of what is falsely called knowledge. ²¹Some people have wandered away from the faith by supporting this so-called knowledge.

Grace be with you.

1209   Not that God will reveal Jesus himself because Jesus will come publicly with power and glory upon the clouds. Rather, this is a revealing of Jesus' coming to his people, those who are eagerly waiting for his return and love his appearing (2 Tim. 4:8)—faithful servants like Daniel. In other words God will unseal the words of the book of Daniel and prophetical knowledge will be revealed as to the timing of Jesus' return in the last days. Cf. Dan. 12:9.
1210   The purpose of the light is so that people cannot see the very face of God (TH). Cf. John 6:46.
1211   It is not clear what Paul is exactly referring to here in what has been entrusted to Timothy's care. The possibilities include the gospel, a spiritual gift that was given to Timothy that the elders prophesied about, Timothy's commission as a minister of the gospel etc.

2 TIMOTHY

Introduction

The second letter written by Paul to the young pastor Timothy who was ministering in the ancient city of Ephesus. Ephesus was cradled between two mountains as it slopes down towards the bottom of the city where the harbour, markets and amphitheatre are located.

Paul once again writes to Timothy from prison (2 Tim. 1:16) only two years after his first letter to Timothy in about AD 67. This is Paul's farewell letter and Paul encourages Timothy to remain strong, fearless and to persevere until the end. Paul reminds Timothy that there will be terrible times coming for the church in the last days where all godly standards will be thrown out the window and Christians will surround themselves with what their itching ears want to hear. The theme of apostasy continues as we are reminded of the rebellion of Korah and his associates and also others such as Alexander who have turned away from the faith. This is always an ever-present danger and we need to watch out for man-made myths and deception as we approach the end. Paul tells Timothy that the end of his life is near and that he has fought the good fight and kept the faith right to the end.

1 ⁱThis letter is from Paul, an apostle of Christ Jesus by the will of God. I have been sent to tell others about the promised life that is in Christ Jesus.
²I am writing this letter to you Timothy, my dear son.

Grace, mercy and peace from God the Father and Christ Jesus our Lord.

We must not be ashamed to testify about the Lord Jesus

³I thank God for you, Timothy. I serve God with a clear conscience as my forefathers did. Night and day, I constantly remember you in my prayers. ⁴I remember the tears you had for me—I really wish to see you again so that I might be filled with joy. ⁵I remember also your sincere faith which first lived in your grandmother Lois and in your mother Eunice. I can see that this *faith* lives in you also. ⁶Therefore I would like to remind you to fan into flame the gift of God, which is in you through the laying on of my hands.¹²¹² ⁷For God did not give us a cowardly spirit but one of power, love and good-sense.

⁸So do not be ashamed to testify about our Lord, or ashamed of me his prisoner. But I urge you to join with me in suffering for the gospel by the power of God. ⁹For he has saved us and called us to live a holy life, not because of anything that we have done but because that was his plan from the beginning of time—to show us his grace through Christ Jesus. ¹⁰But this *grace* has now been revealed when our Saviour, Christ Jesus, appeared *on the scene*. He destroyed death and has brought life and immortality to light through the gospel.

¹¹It was for this gospel that God appointed me as a preacher, an apostle and a teacher. ¹²That is the reason why I am suffering the way that I am. But I am not ashamed because I know in whom I have believed¹²¹³ and I am convinced that he is able to keep safe what I have entrusted¹²¹⁴ to him until the day *that he returns*.

¹³Previously you heard from me the pattern of healthy teaching. Keep following this pattern with faith and love in Christ Jesus. ¹⁴Guard the precious truth that has been entrusted to you by means of Holy Breath living in us.

1212 The practice of laying hands on people was common in the early church for several functions, among which are: (1) healing (Mark 8:23); (2) bestowing a blessing (Mark 10:16); (3) making it possible for people to receive the Holy Breath and spiritual gifts (Acts 8.17); and (4) setting people apart for certain functions (Acts 13.3). This last function is in focus in the present context. In the history of the church, the laying on of hands has also become an important part of the rite of ordination, that is, of setting apart certain people for specific church offices (TH).
1213 It is unclear who Paul is referring to here but it could be either Christ or God the Father.
1214 Probably Paul is referring to the gospel here but it could be his ministry too as this is his last letter in the NT and the letter to Timothy here was written just before his death in c. AD 67. We have to entrust what we have done for God to him and to those who come after us.

¹⁵*Timothy*, you may well know that everyone in *Minor* Asia¹²¹⁵ has abandoned me including Phygelus and Hermogenes.

¹⁶I pray that the Lord may show mercy to the household of Onesiphorus because he often cheered me up and was not ashamed of my imprisonment. ¹⁷On the contrary, when he was in Rome, he actually searched hard for me until he found me. ¹⁸I pray that the Lord may grant him mercy on that day! You know very well in how many ways that he helped me in Ephesus.

Enduring hardship like a good soldier of Jesus Christ

2 ¹As for you my son, continue to be strengthened by the grace that comes in Christ Jesus. ²And the things that you have heard me say in the presence of many witnesses, you must pass this on to other qualified men whom you trust so that they, in turn, can teach others.

³Like a good soldier of Jesus Christ, you must endure hardship. ⁴No one serving as a soldier becomes entangled by civilian affairs but he wants to please his commanding officer. ⁵Also, if anyone competes as an athlete, he does not receive the winner's crown unless he competes according to the rules. ⁶The farmer who has worked hard should be the first one to receive a share of the crops. ⁷*Timothy*, you must think about what I am saying, for the Lord will give insight to you in all of this.

⁸Remember Jesus Christ who was raised from the dead and who is a descendant of David. This is my gospel,¹²¹⁶ ⁹for which I am suffering intensely even to the point of being chained like a criminal. But God's word is not chained. ¹⁰Therefore I will endure everything if it will bring salvation and eternal glory that is in Christ Jesus to those whom God has chosen.¹²¹⁷

¹¹Here is a dependable statement:

If we have died with him then we will also live with him.
¹²If we endure to the end then we will also reign with him.
If we disown him then he will also disown us.
¹³If we are not loyal in following Christ he will always remain loyal,
    for he cannot disown himself.

Timothy is a worker approved by God

¹⁴Keep reminding the *Christians in Ephesus* of these things. You must warn

---

1215 This is not the modern-day continent of Asia but the ancient Roman province of Minor Asia (southwestern Turkey). The ancient city of Ephesus was its capital at the time.
1216 Rom. 2:16. This may be a reference to Luke's gospel.
1217 Paul is referring to the Jews here as they were the chosen ones (Eph. 1:4). The Gentiles were included (Eph. 1:13) but the Jews were chosen. Cf. Matt. 22:14.

them, before God, against quarrelling about words because it has no value and it only ruins those who are listening.

¹⁵Do your best to present yourself to God as one approved—a workman who is not ashamed, one who correctly handles[1218] the word of truth. ¹⁶But make sure that you avoid godless chatter which only leads people to become more and more ungodly ¹⁷and their message will spread like gangrene. Among those who have become more and more ungodly are Hymenaeus and Philetus, ¹⁸who have wandered away from the truth. They say that the resurrection has already taken place which is destroying the faith of some *people*.

¹⁹Nevertheless, God's solid foundation stands firm sealed with these inscriptions: "The Lord knows those who are his," and, "Everyone who confesses the name of the Lord must turn away from wickedness."[1219]

²⁰In a large house, there are articles not only of gold and silver but also wood and clay. Some articles are for special use and some for everyday use. ²¹So, if you keep yourself pure then you will be like an article that is reserved for special use, set apart as holy, useful to its owner, having been prepared for every good work.

²²Make sure that you, together with those who call on the Lord with a pure heart,[1220] flee the evil impulses of youth[1221] and pursue righteousness, faith, love and peace. ²³Don't have anything to do with foolish and stupid arguments because you know that they only produce fights. ²⁴The Lord's worker must not fight, instead, he must be kind to everyone, be skilled in teaching and be very patient. ²⁵He must be able to gently instruct those who oppose him, perhaps God will cause them to turn to him leading to a knowledge of the truth. ²⁶Then they will come to their senses and escape the trap of the devil who had taken them captive to do his will.

Godlessness in the last days

3 ¹*Timothy*, know this: There will be terrible times in the last days. ²People will be lovers of themselves, lovers of money, boastful, proud, arrogant, disobedient to their parents, ungrateful, godless, ³without love, unforgiving, slanderous, without self-control, brutal, hateful of what is good, ⁴treacherous,

---

1218   The Greek word here (*ortho-tomeo*) literally means to make a straight cut, to dissect correctly. Interestingly Paul as a tentmaker would know how to cut straight the material (cloth made of goat hair, leather skins) used in tent making. A common error is holding the view that certain portions of the NT including the gospels (particularly Matthew 24) were addressed to the Jews only and not the Christian church.

1219   Cf. Num. 16:5 which refers to the rebellion of Korah, Dathan and 250 other leaders when they rose up against Moses. The rebels were swallowed by the earth and the comparison here is made with the present day false teachers and their ultimate fate. God knows those amongst the Ephesian Christians who really belong to him.

1220   An expression meaning Timothy's fellow Christians.

1221   The primary focus here is on the sexual impulses and passions of youth since Timothy was a young man and these are the sins that often get young people into trouble.

rash, conceited, and lovers of pleasure rather than lovers of God. ⁵They act as if they worship God but in all reality, they do not believe. Make sure that you have nothing whatsoever to do with them.

⁶These *false teachers* are the kind *of men* who worm their way into homes and gain control over weak-willed women, who are burdened by the guilt of their sins and carried away by all kinds of evil impulses. ⁷*These women* are always trying to learn things but they never seem to be able to arrive at the truth. ⁸Just as Jannes and Jambres opposed Moses,[1222] so also these men oppose the truth—men who have corrupt minds and who have failed in their faith. ⁹But they will not get very far because their foolishness will become obvious to everyone just as in the case of Jannes and Jambres.

Final instructions to Timothy from Paul

¹⁰But you have followed my teaching, my way of life, and what my purpose *in life is*. You know about my faith, my patience, my love, my perseverance, ¹¹persecutions, and sufferings. You *also* know what happened to me in Antioch, Iconium and Lystra—the persecutions that I endured out of which all of them the Lord rescued me. ¹²In fact, the truth is that everyone who wants to live a godly life in Christ Jesus will be persecuted. ¹³Evil men will go from bad to worse—they will deceive others and be deceived themselves.

¹⁴But as for you, *Timothy*, make sure that you continue in what you have learned and have become convinced of because you know *that you can trust* those who taught you. ¹⁵You know how from infancy you have known the sacred Scriptures[1223] which are able to make you wise for salvation through faith in Christ Jesus. ¹⁶All Scripture is God-breathed and is useful for teaching, rebuking, correcting and training in righteousness, ¹⁷so that the man of God may be thoroughly qualified and equipped to do every good work.

Paul urges Timothy to keep going in his work for God

4 ¹*Timothy*, in the presence of God and of Christ Jesus who will judge the living and the dead, and in view of his appearing and his kingdom, I seriously urge you *as follows*: ²Preach the word and be ready to do it whether convenient or not. Make sure that you correct, rebuke and encourage, teaching with great patience. ³For the time is coming when men will not be able to bear healthy teaching. Instead, to suit their own agenda, they will gather around them a great number of teachers to say what their itching ears want to hear. ⁴They will turn

---

1222 There is no reference to Jannes and Jambres in the Bible but Jewish tradition says that they were two of the Egyptian magicians who were adversaries of Moses.
1223 I.e. the Jewish sacred writings what we now know as the OT.

away from listening to the truth and rather turn to myths. ⁵But keep a clear head in all situations and endure hardship, doing the work of an evangelist. Carry out fully all the duties of your ministry.

Paul declares that he will soon die

⁶As far as I am concerned, my time *on earth* has almost come to an end like when a drink offering[1224] is being poured out. ⁷I have fought the good fight, I have finished the race, I have kept the faith. ⁸Now there is in store for me the wreath of righteousness, which the Lord, the righteous judge, will award to me on that day. He will give this to not only me but also to everyone who has been eagerly waiting for his appearing.

Paul's final instructions to Timothy

⁹Timothy, do your best to come to me soon, ¹⁰because Demas has loved this world and has deserted me and has gone to Thessalonica. Crescens has gone to Galatia and Titus to Dalmatia. ¹¹Luke is the only one who is with me. Get Mark and bring him with you because he is helpful to me in my ministry. ¹²I am about to send Tychicus to Ephesus.

¹³When you come, bring the coat that I left with Carpus at Troas, and my scrolls, especially the parchments.[1225]

¹⁴Alexander the metalworker[1226] did me a great deal of harm. The Lord will repay him for what he has done. ¹⁵You too should watch out for him because he strongly opposed our message.

¹⁶At my first trial, no one came to my defence. In fact, everyone deserted me. I pray that it may not be held against them. ¹⁷However the Lord stood at my side and gave me strength so that through me the message might be fully proclaimed and all the Gentiles might hear it. I was delivered out of the lion's mouth so to speak. ¹⁸The Lord will rescue me from every evil attack and will bring me safely to his heavenly reign. To him be glory forever and ever. Amen.

Final greetings

¹⁹Give my greetings to Priscilla and Aquila and the household of Onesiphorus. ²⁰Erastus stayed in Corinth and I left Trophimus sick in Miletus. ²¹Do your best to get here before winter. Eubulus sends his greetings to you and so do Pudens, Linus, Claudia and all the brothers.

²²The Lord be with your spirit. Grace be with you.

1224 This refers to when a drink offering is poured out on animal sacrifice. Cf. Num. 15:1–12.
1225 Probably scrolls made from sheepskin.
1226 Literally 'coppersmith' in the Greek but this term was used for those who worked with many different metals at the time.

TITUS

Introduction

Paul wrote this personal letter in AD 65–66 to his young assistant Titus and forms part of the pastoral epistles as it deals with matters relating to church order and ministry. Titus was a Gentile convert and became a close companion of Paul during his ministry.

In this letter Paul discusses the spiritual qualifications needed for those to be selected as elders in the church on the island of Crete. This letter has one important eschatological feature in Tit. 2:13 in that of the 'blessed hope'. The blessed hope is not separate from the glorious appearing but grammatically it has to be one and the same thing thereby negating the pre-tribulation belief that these are referring to two separate events: pre-tribulation rapture and Christ coming in glory.

1 ¹From Paul, a servant of God and apostle of Jesus Christ. I have been sent to *encourage* the faith of those whom God has chosen and to *teach* them to know the truth that leads to godliness. ²*This truth leads to* the hope of eternal life which God, who does not lie, promised before the beginning of time. ³At the appropriate time *God* clearly revealed his word and entrusted me *with his message*. I preach it by the command of God our Saviour.

⁴To Titus, my true son in our shared faith:

Grace and peace from God the Father and Christ Jesus our Saviour.

Titus with the task of appointing elders on Crete

⁵The reason that I left you on the island of Crete was so that you might be able to complete the tasks that have been left unfinished and go ahead and appoint elders in each city as I have instructed you. ⁶To be an elder, a man must be blameless and only have one wife. This man's children must be believers and not wild and rebellious. ⁷For as an overseer in the church it is necessary that he must be blameless in God's work. He must not be arrogant, quick-tempered, a drunkard or a violent man nor a man who is greedy for money. ⁸Rather he must be hospitable, someone who loves that which is good and doing good. He must be self-controlled, upright, holy and disciplined. ⁹He must be someone who holds firmly to the dependable message as it was taught to him in the beginning. In this way he will be able to encourage others through his healthy teaching and correct those who oppose *Christian doctrine*.

¹⁰For there are many rebellious *Christians in Crete*, especially the converts from Judaism,¹²²⁷ who are talking nonsense and misleading others in the process. ¹¹They must be gagged because they are destroying *the faith of* whole households with their teaching. They are teaching things they ought not to teach and they are doing it for dishonest gain. ¹²Even one of their own *Cretan poets, one they consider* a prophet¹²²⁸ has said, "Cretans are always liars, evil beasts and lazy gluttons." ¹³What he said is true. Therefore I say that you must rebuke these *false teachers* sharply so that they will be healthy in the faith. ¹⁴Rebuke them so that they will pay no attention to Jewish myths or to the commands of those who have turned away from the truth. ¹⁵To those who are *inwardly* pure, all things are

---

1227 Literally the circumcision group.
1228 The prophet Paul is referring to is the philosopher Epimenides, who lived in the sixth century BC. According to writings at that time, the Cretans were considered liars because they claimed that the Greek god Zeus, had a tomb in Crete. But Zeus, of course, being the chief of the gods, could not have died! (TH)

ceremonially pure.[1229] But to those who are defiled *inwardly* and do not believe, nothing is pure. In fact both their minds and consciences are defiled. [16]They claim to know God but their actions show that they don't really know him at all. They are detestable, disobedient and unfit for doing anything good.

How to deal with various groups in the church

2 [1]*Titus*, you must teach that which is consistent with healthy doctrine. [2]Teach the older men to be moderate *in all things*, to be worthy of respect and self-controlled. Teach them to have a healthy faith and love for others and to be able to endure *in difficult circumstances*.

[3]Likewise, you are to teach the older women to behave in a holy manner. They must not be slanderers or drink too much wine. But they must teach what is good. [4]Then they can train the younger women to love their husbands and children, [5]to be self-controlled and pure, to be busy around the home, to be kind and to be subject to their husbands so that no one will be able to mock the word of God.

[6]Likewise, encourage the young men *in the church* to be sensible. [7]In all things you must set them an example by doing what is good. When you teach make sure that you show integrity and that you are serious. [8]And when you teach make sure that you speak in a healthy way that cannot be condemned. Therefore those who oppose you may be ashamed because they have nothing bad to say about us *Christians*. [9]Teach slaves to be subject to their masters in all things. They must *make an effort* to please them and not to talk back to them. [10]They must not pilfer from their masters but they must show that they are fully trustworthy. In this way it will make the teaching about God our Saviour more attractive in every way.

The Blessed Hope

[11]For the grace of God has appeared for the salvation of all mankind. [12]By his grace, he teaches us to say "no" to ungodliness and worldly desires. He teaches us to live self-controlled, upright and godly lives in this present age. [13]And in the meantime, we wait for the blessed hope—the appearing of Jesus Christ—the glory of the great God, our Saviour.[1230] [14]He gave himself

---

1229 Here we are given yet another clue as to the heresy that Titus is confronted with in Crete, and that has to do with confusing moral purity with ritual purity, and teaching that moral purity can be achieved through strict adherence to rules, particularly concerning food. In contrast to this, Paul stresses that ritual purity is dependent on moral purity and not the other way around (TH).

1230 Jesus Christ is in apposition to the glory of the great God. In other words, Jesus is the one who will be appearing and in a sense he is the glory of God. God is the Saviour in this verse not Jesus. This verse is not saying that Jesus is God. Cf. Matt. 26:64, Rev. 6:17.

for us in order to set us free from all wickedness and to purify for himself a special people that are his very own and *a people* who are deeply committed to doing what is good.

¹⁵These things, therefore *Titus*, are the things that you must teach. Encourage and rebuke with all authority *as a pastor*. Do not let anyone disrespect you.

The attitude that Christians must have towards the government

3 ¹You must remind the *believers* that they are to be subject to the rulers and authorities. They must be obedient and be prepared to do whatever is good. ²They must not slander anyone but they must be peaceable and courteous and they must show true humility towards all men.

³For we too previously, *before we were Christians*, were foolish and disobedient. We were deceived and enslaved by all kinds of passions and pleasures. ⁴But when the love and kindness of God our Saviour appeared ⁵he in fact saved us, not because of any good deeds that we had done but because of his mercy.[1231] *God* saved us by means of Holy Breath causing us to be regenerated and renewed by washing our lives spiritually clean, ⁶which he poured out on us in abundance through Jesus Christ our Saviour. ⁷He did this so that by his grace, we might be declared righteous and that we might become heirs having the hope of eternal life. ⁸This is a dependable statement.

Instructions for Christians and how they should live

I want you to stress these things so that those people who have trusted in God may be careful to devote themselves to doing good deeds. This will be good and profitable for all concerned.

⁹But you must avoid foolish controversies, genealogies, divisive arguments and quarrels about the Law because these are unprofitable and pointless. ¹⁰Warn a divisive person two times. After that, have nothing to do with him. ¹¹You can be sure that such a man is corrupt and sinful. He is condemned by his own actions.

Final words

¹²As soon as I send Artemas or Tychicus to you, you must do your best to come to me at Nicopolis because I have decided to spend the winter there. ¹³Do your best to help Zenas the lawyer and Apollos in their travels. Make sure they have everything they need. ¹⁴And the Cretan Christians must also learn to spend

---

[1231] The Son of God didn't appear on the earth out of a mercy based on pity but a mercy based on compassion and love. The point is that we didn't deserve his love and compassion. We deserve judgment and death but God instead gives us love and compassion by sending his Son.

their time doing good as well. This is so that they can meet urgent needs and in doing so, not live unfruitful lives.

¹⁵ All those with me send you greetings. Greet those who are our friends in the faith. Grace be with you all.

PHILEMON

Introduction

Philemon is a prison letter. Paul wrote this letter, his shortest, while in prison under house arrest during a two year period in Rome for the first time in around AD 62.

Philemon lived and attended church at Colossae in what we now know as Southern Turkey. All there is now is a great lump of dirt. Philemon was a slave-owner and probably was a convert of Paul's. Paul was writing a letter to Philemon because his slave, Onesimus, had run away to the great city of Rome from Colossae. While in Rome, Paul had come into contact with him and led him to the Lord. They had developed a strong bond of friendship and like Timothy, Paul considered him to be a son in the Lord. Paul sends him back to Philemon because he was his slave but along with him he sends a letter of appeal and this is where we get a hint of how to deal with social justice issues in the church. Paul was helping Philemon to solve his problems.

¹From Paul, a prisoner of Christ Jesus and Timothy our *Christian* brother, *greetings*:

To Philemon, our beloved co-worker ²and to our sister Apphia, and to Archippus, our fellow soldier[1232] and to the church that meets in your home.[1233]

³Grace and peace to you all from God our Father and from the Lord Jesus Christ.

Paul thanks God for Philemon and the Laodicean church

⁴I am forever thankful to God as I remember you in my prayers. ⁵For I have heard about your faith in the Lord Jesus and your love for all of God's holy people. ⁶I pray that the sharing of your faith may be effective as you understand about all the good things that we have in Christ. ⁷Your love has brought me great joy and encouragement because God's holy people have been refreshed through you, brother.

Paul makes an appeal for Onesimus

⁸Therefore even though I could be so bold and command you to do what you should do, in Christ, *I will not do so*. ⁹But I appeal to you out of love. I, Paul, am an old man and also now am a prisoner of Christ Jesus. ¹⁰My appeal is for my son Onesimus. I became his *spiritual* father while I was in prison. ¹¹At one time he was useless to you but now he has become useful[1234] to both you and to me.

¹²I am sending him back to you, and with him goes my heart. ¹³I would have liked to keep him with me so that he could take your place in helping me while I am in chains for the gospel. ¹⁴However I do not want to do anything without your consent, so that any favour you do will be of your own free will and not coerced.

¹⁵Perhaps the reason Onesimus was separated from you for a little while was so that you might have him back for good, ¹⁶no longer as a slave but better than a slave, as a brother. He is very dear to me but even dearer to you, both humanly speaking and as a brother in the Lord.

¹⁷So if you consider me as a partner *in the work, please* welcome him as you would welcome me. ¹⁸But if he has done anything wrong or owes you anything, charge it to my account. ¹⁹I, Paul, am writing this with my own hand. I will pay

---

1232 Not a literal soldier but in a figurative sense of one who is fighting for the Christian cause.
1233 The church here is likely to be the Laodicean church, the supposed missing letter of Col. 4:16. Laodicea and Colossae were neighbouring cities only 16 km apart from each other in the Phrygia region of modern southern Turkey. The Roman city of Hierapolis (modern-day Pamukkale) was also close by (Col. 4:13). The early church largely met in homes and were in effect house churches.
1234 Onesimus means 'useful' in Greek.

it back. (I could say that you owe me your very self.) ²⁰Yes, brother, I do desire this favour from you in the Lord. Make me happy in Christ.

²¹I am sure as I write this to you that you will do so—I know that you will do even more than I ask. ²²And one more thing: please prepare a room for me because I hope to be restored to you as an answer to all of your prayers.

²³Epaphras, my fellow prisoner in Christ Jesus, also sends you greetings. ²⁴And Mark, Aristarchus, Demas and Luke, my fellow workers, also send you greetings.

²⁵The grace of the Lord Jesus Christ be with your spirits.

HEBREWS

Introduction

No one knows who authored the letter to the Hebrew Christian believers but it was written around AD 67–69. One of the likeliest contenders for authorship is Paul. This letter reads more like a sermon and was written to the first century Jewish believers who were undergoing intense persecution and discouragement. They were being tempted to revert to their old religion, *religio licita* (the legal religion) which was approved by the Roman Empire supposedly after the fire of Rome in AD 64. This temptation for Jewish believers to revert was intense because if they did revert it would mean an end to their persecution.

Similarly, in today's church as we get closer and closer to the final days of the tribulation period, we are faced with increasing persecution and pressures from the world.

The letter to the Hebrews encourages us to press on to the end without compromise and to not fall away. Who else do we turn to? There is no other answer except Jesus. Many scholars hold to the view that those who fall away were not true believers to begin with but the Book of Hebrews seeks to prove that true believers can fall away and that the doctrine of OSAS does not hold true. Hebrews affirms that apostasy is possible and the author seeks to encourage the Jewish Christians of the first century by reminding them of the great faith of the heroes of old throughout the ages, since creation, up to the church age.

God speaks through his Son

1 ¹In the past God spoke to our forefathers through the prophets often and in various ways. ²But towards the end of those days[1235] he has spoken to us by his Son whom he appointed as heir of all things and through whom he made the universe. ³God's glory shines through the Son who is the exact representation of his being. Everything is sustained by his powerful word. After he had provided purification for sins, he sat down at the right hand of the Majestic One in heaven.

The Son of God is superior to angels

⁴This shows that the Son is far superior to the angels just as the name he has inherited is superior to theirs.[1236] ⁵For God never said to any of his angels,

"You are my Son. Today I have begotten you."[1237]

Psalm 2:7

Nor did God ever say about any angel,

"I will be his Father and he will be my Son."

2 Samuel 7:14

⁶And when God was about to bring his firstborn into the world, he said,

"All of God's angels must worship him."

Psalm 97:7

⁷And when God spoke about the angels he said,

"He made his angels as the winds—his servants like a flame of fire."

Psalm 104:4

⁸But when God speaks about the Son he says,

"Your throne, O God,[1238] will last forever and ever.

1235   This refers to the end of the days of the prophets from Moses to John the Baptist. The author of Hebrews is not saying that the 1st century were the last days as we think of it today.
1236   In Hebrew thought, a name was not just a means of identification but it referred to someone's whole nature and personality. Here the emphasis is also on the title that was given to Jesus (TH).
1237   "Begotten" (Gk: *gennao*) here means the male role in causing the conception and birth of a child and the issuing forth out of himself. It also means when a king brings out his son before the people to proclaim him as king along with his father as David did with Solomon (1 Kings 1:32-34). This verse could have a dual meaning referring to the issuing forth out of the Father at the beginning and also the public proclamation of Christ as God's Son. This verse is not referring to Jesus' human begetting (Matt. 1:20) even though the verb is the exact same Greek root *gennao*. The preincarnate Christ was begotten (issued forth from the Father) at the very beginning (Col. 1:15,18, 1 John 2:14).
1238   The Son of God is referred to as God confirming his ontological equivalence to the invisible Yahweh.

> You will rule with righteousness.
> ⁹You love what is right and you hate wickedness.
> Therefore God your God, has set you above your companions by
> anointing you with the oil of joy."
>
> Psalm 45:6–7

¹⁰God also said about him,

> "In the beginning, O Lord, you laid the foundations of the earth and with
> your own hands you made the heavens.
> ¹¹They will perish but you will remain. They will all wear out like a
> a piece of clothing.
> ¹²You will roll them up like a coat and they will be changed like a change
> of clothes.
> But you will remain the same and your years will never come to an end."
>
> Psalm 102:25–27

¹³For to which of the angels did God ever say,

> "Sit at my right hand until I make your enemies as a footstool for your feet."
>
> Psalm 110:1

¹⁴*What then is the purpose of the angels?* Are they not all ministering spirits sent to serve those who are about to inherit salvation?[1239]

Drifting away from God

2 ¹Therefore we must pay more careful attention to what we have heard so that we do not drift *away from God*. ²*Previously*, the message spoken by angels was seen to be reliable and every time someone violated or disobeyed they received their just punishment.[1240] ³How, then, shall we *now* escape *punishment* if we ignore such a great salvation? The Lord himself first announced this salvation and those who heard him confirmed it to us. ⁴While this was happening God added to their witness with signs, wonders and various miracles distributing Holy Breath according to his will.

1239 This has eschatological implications indicating that angels will be helping God's holy people to inherit salvation in the sense of making it through the Great Tribulation and into the Millennial Kingdom. The intent is clearly in the future referring to when Christ brings salvation to those who are waiting Cf. Heb. 9:28

1240 This is referring to when the Jews disobeyed the Law of Moses in that there were serious consequences.

Jesus made a little lower than the angels

⁵God has not put angels in charge as rulers over the *new* world to come of which we are speaking about. ⁶Instead it is said somewhere in the Scriptures,

> "What is mankind, O God, that you are even giving him a second thought or the son of man that you even care about him?
> ⁷You made him a little lower than the angels and you crowned him with glory and honour.
> ⁸You put everything under his feet."
>
> Psalm 8:4–6

For when God put everything under him, he left nothing that is not subject to him. Yet at the present time we do not see everything subject to him. ⁹But we do see Jesus, who was made a little lower than the angels, who is now crowned with glory and honour because of the death he suffered. This is so that by the grace of God he might experience death for everyone's *benefit*.

¹⁰It was very fitting that God, who made all things and through whom everything owes its ongoing existence, should make the founder of their salvation, *Jesus*, perfect through suffering in order that he might bring many sons to glory.[1241] ¹¹Both the one who makes men holy and those who are made holy come out of the same man.[1242] Therefore *Jesus* is not ashamed to call them his brothers. ¹²*Jesus* says *to God*,

> "I will declare your name to my brothers.
> In the middle of the church,[1243] I will sing hymns to you."
>
> Psalm 22:22

¹³He also says,

> "I will put my trust in God."[1244]
>
> Isaiah 8:17

And again he says,

> "Here I am with the children that God has given to me."
>
> Isaiah 8:18

1241 When referring to "bring many sons to glory" it refers to the transformation of the believer into God's likeness. An appropriate quote by author F F Bruce: "Sanctification is glory begun and glory is sanctification complete."
1242 Both Jesus and all of mankind have the same ancestor—Adam.
1243 Cf. Acts 7:38.
1244 Proof here that Jesus like all of us lived the life of faith by trusting in God.

¹⁴Since these children have flesh and blood, Jesus himself shared in their humanity likewise so that by his death he might destroy him who holds the power of death—that is the devil. ¹⁵He became like them that he might free all those whose lives were held in slavery by their fear of death. ¹⁶For surely *the fear of death* is of no concern to angels but it concerns Abraham's descendants. ¹⁷For this reason Jesus had to be made like his human brothers in every way in order that he might become a merciful and loyal high priest in his service to God so that the sins of the people could be forgiven. ¹⁸And because he himself suffered when he was tempted he is able to help those who are being tempted.

Jesus is superior to Moses

3 ¹Holy brothers *in Christ,* you also share in the heavenly calling. Therefore fix your thoughts on Jesus, whom we confess is sent by God and is our high priest. ²God appointed him and he loyally did what he was asked to do just as Moses loyally led God's holy people. ³Jesus has been found worthy of greater honour than Moses just as the builder of a house has greater honour than the house itself. ⁴After all, every house is built by someone but God is the builder of everything. ⁵Moses was loyal as a servant in God's household and he spoke about things that God would say in the future. ⁶But Christ was loyal as a son over God's household of which we are a part of if we keep up our courage and hope of which we boast about.

A warning against unbelief

⁷So as the Holy Breath says,

"Today, if you hear God's voice, ⁸do not harden your hearts as you did
in the rebellion during the time of testing in the desert.[1245]
⁹This is where your ancestors tested and tried me although for 40 years
they saw what I did for them.
¹⁰That is why I was angry with that generation and I said, 'Their hearts
are always going astray and they have not known my ways.'
¹¹I was angry and made a solemn promise that they shall never enter
the land of my rest.'"[1246]

Psalm 95:7–11

¹²Beware brothers, that none of you has a sinful, unbelieving heart that

---

1245 The author is reminding the Hebrew Christians of the time when their ancestors rebelled after leaving Egypt and they did not enter into the Promised Land because of unbelief. (Cf. Num. 14:29–43). Cf. Heb. 10:26–27.

1246 The ultimate implication of rest here and in chapter 4 is the final eschatological rest that believers will have in the Millennial Kingdom (Cf. Isa. 62:6–7).

apostatizes[1247] from the living God. [13]But instead, encourage one another daily until that day which is called "today"[1248] so that none of you may be hardened by the deceitfulness of sin. [14]We have become partners with Christ if we hold firmly till the end the confidence we had in the beginning [15]when *that day* is proclaimed,

> "Today, if you hear God's voice, do not harden your hearts as you did in the rebellion."
>
> Psalm 95:7–8

[16]Who were the people who heard yet rebelled? Was it not all those whom Moses led out of Egypt? [17]Who was God angry with for 40 years? Was it not those who sinned and whose bodies fell *dead* in the desert? [18]Who was God speaking about when he solemnly promised that they would never enter his rest? Wasn't it those who disobeyed? [19]So we see that they were not able to enter in because of their unbelief.

An eschatological rest is coming for God's holy people

4 [1]Therefore since the promise of entering *God's* rest is still open, let us be afraid—very afraid, lest some of you are found to have fallen short *of that promised rest*. [2]For we heard the good news[1249] *about this* just as they also did.[1250] But the message they heard did not benefit them because they did not really believe it. [3]We who have believed are entering that rest just as God has said,

> "I was angry and made a solemn promise that they shall never enter the land of my rest."
>
> Psalm 95:11

Although 'work' came into being because of the overthrow of the world.[1251] [4]For somewhere in the Scriptures God has spoken about the seventh day as follows, "On the seventh day God rested from all his work." [5]And again in the quote above God says, "They shall never enter *the land of* my rest."

1247 To abandon a former relationship or association, or to dissociate (a type of reversal of beginning to associate) – to fall away, to forsake, to turn away (Louw, J, & Nida, E, *Greek-English Lexicon of the New Testament based on Semantic Domains* (1988), 34.26).

1248 "Today" is the very day that Israel and believers finally enter into the millennial rest after the tribulation so the command is that we must encourage each other continually to not fall away because of unbelief.

1249 This does not refer to the good news of Jesus Christ but the good news that one day man will receive a future eschatological rest.

1250 Caleb and Joshua told the people the good news that the Promised Land awaited them, a land of milk and honey and that they should take possession of it. Cf. Num. 13:30

1251 The overthrow of the world refers to the overthrow of God's established order when Adam sinned. And because Adam sinned he was cursed and subsequently he and all his descendants had to toil to produce food (Gen 3:17–19). In the Millennial Kingdom, we will have 'rest' from the curse.

⁶However some are allowed to enter, in spite of those at an earlier time who heard the good news but did not enter in because of their disobedience. ⁷Therefore God appointed another day calling it "Today" when a long time later he spoke in a Psalm of David as it was said before,[1252]

"Today, if you hear God's voice, do not harden your hearts as you did in the rebellion."

Psalm 95:7–8

⁸For if Joshua had brought them to a place of rest, David[1253] would not have spoken about another day after these. ⁹Therefore *we conclude that* there still remains a Sabbath-rest[1254] for the people of God. ¹⁰For anyone who enters God's *future* rest also rests from his own work just as God did from his *on the seventh day of creation*. ¹¹Let us therefore, make every effort to enter that future rest so that none of us will fall as they did *long ago* because of their disobedience.[1255]

Jesus is a great high priest like Melchizedek

¹²The Word of God[1256] is alive and active, sharper than any double-edged sword, even able to penetrate until the distribution of life and breath, both joints and marrow.[1257] *He* is the judge of the thoughts and intentions of the heart.[1258] ¹³Nothing in all creation is hidden from him. All things are uncovered and have been exposed before his eyes to whom we must give account.

¹⁴Therefore since we have a great high priest, Jesus, the Son of God, who has gone through the heavens, let us hold firmly to the faith we profess. ¹⁵For we have a high priest who is able to sympathise with our weaknesses and we have someone who has been tempted in every way just like us and yet was without sin. ¹⁶Let us therefore confidently approach God who shows grace. We will receive mercy and grace from him and he will help us in our time of need.

5 ¹Every high priest is chosen from among men and is appointed on their

---

1252 Joshua and Caleb urged the Israelites to enter into the Promised Land.
1253 The actual Greek here is 'he' but it is God speaking through David in Psalm 95.
1254 The implication here is that there is a future eschatological seventh Sabbath day rest lasting 1000 years.
1255 The Israelites fell dead in the desert and didn't enter in because they refused to listen to the good news preached by Caleb and Joshua about the Promised Land upon their return from spying out the land.
1256 The Word of God is personified here hence the capitalisation. The question remains who is the Word of God? The only possibility is Jesus because John 1:1,14 and Rev. 19:13 tell us that a title and name of Jesus is the 'Word of God'.
1257 The Word of God—Jesus, is able to penetrate our very thoughts and attitudes through the word. He will continue to do this until the resurrection (distribution of life and spirit and joints and marrow). A precedence of this type of language is set in Eze. 37:1–14 which talks in a similar colourful way when expressing the resurrection of Israel.
1258 Cf. Rev. 2:23

behalf in the things of God to offer gifts and sacrifices for sins. ²And since the high priest himself is weak *in many ways,* he is able to be gentle with those who are ignorant and wandering away *from the faith.* ³This *weakness* is why the high priest has to offer sacrifices for his own sins as well as for the sins of the people.

⁴No one takes this honour of becoming the high priest upon himself. He must be called by God, just as Aaron was. ⁵So Christ also did not take upon himself the glory of becoming high priest. But *God* said to him,

"You are my Son. Today I have begotten you."¹²⁵⁹

Psalm 2:7

⁶And *God* says in another *Psalm,*

"You are a priest throughout the age¹²⁶⁰ like Melchizedek."

Psalm 110:4

⁷During the days of his flesh,¹²⁶¹ *Jesus* prayed and pleaded with loud cries and tears to the one who could save him from death. And he was heard because he was deeply respectful. ⁸Although being The Son, *Jesus* learned obedience from what he suffered.¹²⁶² ⁹Once Jesus was made perfect, he became the source of eternal salvation for all who obey him. ¹⁰He was declared by God to be high priest like Melchizedek.

Warning against apostasy

¹¹There is a lot to say about him¹²⁶³ but it is quite difficult for me to explain because you have become lazy in your understanding. ¹²In fact, by now you should have become teachers but you need someone to teach you the fundamentals of God's word all over again. You need milk, not solid food! ¹³Anyone who is drinking milk is still an infant and does not know the difference between right and wrong. ¹⁴But solid food is for the mature one, who by constant use has trained himself to distinguish between good and evil.

6 ¹Therefore let us move forward and leave behind the basic teachings about

---

1259	Cf. Heb. 1:5 footnote.
1260	Interesting subtle change in terminology here which is commonly translated as 'forever' in most English translations. This phrase however more likely means 'in this present age'. This has the astounding implication that Christ is a priest only in this present age until when his enemies are placed under his feet (become his footstool) at the end of the Great Tribulation in Heb. 10:12-13. Same in Heb. 6:20, 7:24, 7:28.
1261	Has the implication here that there was a time previously when Jesus was not in the flesh—the preincarnate Christ. Before the days of his flesh, Christ is referred to as being the Son of God whereas after upon becoming human, he referred to himself as being the Son of Man.
1262	Jesus suffered in the Garden of Gethsemane (the olive press).
1263	I.e. Christ, as the preincarnate Son of God and as the Son of Man in his incarnate form.

Christ and go on to maturity. Let's not lay again the foundation of changing our ways about acts that just lead to death and the foundation of faith in God.[1264] ²Also let us leave the teaching about baptisms,[1265] the laying on of hands,[1266] the resurrection of the dead and eternal judgment. ³We will do this God permitting.

⁴So, it is impossible for those *believers* who have once been enlightened, who have already tasted the heavenly gift, who have received their share of Holy Breath, ⁵who have tasted the goodness of God, and the powers of the coming age, ⁶to bring them back to where they can turn to him again having already abandoned *their faith*.[1267] This is because they would be crucifying the Son of God all over again and subjecting him to public shame.

⁷Land that absorbs the rain often falling on it and subsequently produces a crop is useful for those who are farming it. It receives a blessing from God. ⁸However land that produces thorns and thistles is worthless and is in danger of being cursed *by God*. In the end it will be destroyed by fire.

⁹However even though I am speaking like this dear friends, I am not worried about you. There are things that point to your salvation. ¹⁰For God is not unfair. He will not forget your work and the love you have shown him as you have helped his people and as you continue to help them. ¹¹We would like each of you to show this same devotion to the very end in order to make your hope sure. ¹²We do not want you to become lazy but to imitate those who through faith and patience are inheriting the things *that God has* promised.[1268]

Christ our refuge

¹³When God promised Abraham, he took an oath by himself because there was no one greater for him to swear by.[1269] ¹⁴He said, "I will surely bless you and multiply you."[1270] ¹⁵And so Abraham waited patiently and received what was promised.

¹⁶When as human beings we swear by something we usually swear by

---

1264 The two foundational truths that we first learn is about repentance and faith.
1265 Note that "baptisms" is in the plural. We are physically baptised (immersed) by water but also we are baptised (immersed) into the body of Christ upon conversion (Rom. 6:3). It may also refer to the teaching about John's baptism as well.
1266 Paul and the Apostles laid hands on men such as Timothy thereby imparting spiritual gifts (2 Tim. 1:6). The author of Hebrews here is probably referring to the basic teaching of spiritual gifts.
1267 Clearly this is talking about those who have truly repented and put their faith in Christ. The author lists five evidences of the believer's conversion and is saying that there is no way back for that person who abandons his faith in Christ.
1268 As descendants of Abraham by faith we have been promised to be co-heirs with Christ in the Millennial Kingdom (Gal. 3:29, Rom 8:17). In a sense all believers in Christ are in the process of inheriting the promises as we are being sanctified.
1269 Gen. 22:16.
1270 Gen. 22:17–18.

someone greater than ourselves. The oath confirms what was said and so puts an end to all argument. ⁱ⁷And because God wanted to make it very clear to the heirs of the promise that he wouldn't be changing his mind, he confirmed it with an oath.¹²⁷¹ ¹⁸God did this so that by two unchangeable things (which thereby makes it impossible for God to lie), we—having fled *for refuge*¹²⁷²—may be greatly encouraged to take hold of the hope that lies ahead of us. ¹⁹We have this hope as an anchor to the soul which is firm and secure.¹²⁷³ This hope enters the inner sanctuary behind the curtain. ²⁰Jesus is a precursor¹²⁷⁴ entering on our behalf becoming a high priest throughout the age like Melchizedek.

Melchizedek is the Son of God

7 ¹This Melchizedek was the king of Salem¹²⁷⁵ and priest of the Most High God. He met Abraham upon his return from defeating the kings and blessed him.¹²⁷⁶ ²Abraham gave him a tenth of everything. Melchizedek's name means "king of righteousness" and "king of Salem" means "king of peace". ³Melchizedek had no father or mother and was without genealogy.¹²⁷⁷ He had neither a beginning of days¹²⁷⁸ nor end of life but having been made like the Son of God he stays a priest right through *to the end*.¹²⁷⁹

1271 Paul makes it clear in Gal. 3:26-29 that Christians also inherit the promises made to Abraham which also includes the hope of possession of the land in Israel.
1272 This is in the past tense indicating that the author is drawing a comparison to a situation in Israel's past where there were six designated cities of refuge. Interestingly the exact same language is used to describe when those who had accidentally killed someone could flee to the closest city in Israel for refuge (Josh. 20:1-9). Offenders could be safe in a city of refuge as long as they remained in the city until the death of the current high priest. Similarly because Christ is our high priest in this present age the only condition to be met for our salvation to be secure and assured is that we must remain in the place of refuge—Christ. There is an application for the followers of Jesus in the end days who are told to 'flee for refuge' at the midpoint of the 70th week. Cf. Matt. 24:15-16, Rev. 12:6, Luke 21:36.
1273 Christ Jesus is our hope (1 Tim. 1:1). Author F F Bruce says, "The figure of the anchor is not pressed; all that is meant is that we are moored to an immoveable object—and that immovable object is the throne of God....Abraham rested his hope in the promise and oath of God; but we have more than that to rest our hope upon: we have the fulfilment of his promise in the exaltation of Christ" (Bruce, F F, *The Epistle to the Hebrews (NICNT)* (1990)).
1274 Most English translations translate this as 'forerunner' meaning someone who goes in ahead or in advance of others for their benefit.
1275 An old word for the city of Jerusalem. 'Salem' means peace. This title is applied to him before even the city of Jerusalem existed.
1276 This was the defeat of four kings in Gen. 14:17-20.
1277 This is very significant because every great man in the OT has their ancestry identified. It was especially important that the priests be able to prove their ancestry otherwise they weren't allowed to be priests. In Neh. 7:64, the returning priests who couldn't find their family records and prove their ancestry were excluded from the priesthood and were considered unclean.
1278 The sense here is that Melchizedek was always a fully grown man and didn't have a beginning as in a baby or have an ending as an old man. The Son of God was issued forth out of God in the fullest sense, divine and unique, neither young or old. The Son of God was appointed or set up 'from eternity, from the beginning, before the world began' (Prov. 8:23).
1279 Although translated as 'perpetuity' or 'forever' in many English translations, the actual Greek word used here means 'carry-through'. So the sense is that Melchizedek remains a priest and this will be 'carried through' until there is no longer any need for him to be a priest. Jesus Christ continues to be

⁴Just think how great Melchizedek was. Even the patriarch Abraham gave him a tenth of the plunder he received from battle! ⁵Now the Law requires that the descendants of Levi who become priests to collect a tenth from the people *of Israel* who are their brothers. This even though their brothers are also descended from Abraham. ⁶Melchizedek was not descended from Levi and yet he collected a tenth from Abraham and blessed him who had received the promises. ⁷There is no doubt that the person who blesses is greater than the one who receives the blessing.

⁸In the situation of the *Levitical* priests, a tenth is collected by men who eventually die but as for *Melchizedek* it says[1280] that a tenth was collected by a man who lives now.[1281] ⁹One might even say that Levi, whose descendants collect the tenth, also paid the tenth when Abraham paid it to Melchizedek. ¹⁰This is because even though Levi had not yet been born, he was in the body of his ancestor Abraham when Melchizedek met him.[1282]

Jesus, the new high priest, is superior

¹¹The Law that was given to the people was based on the Levitical priesthood. And so if perfection was possible through the Levitical priesthood why then was there still a need for another priest to come, one just like Melchizedek rather than Aaron? ¹²For when there is a change of the priesthood there must also be a change of the law. ¹³Jesus, of whom we are speaking about, belonged to a different tribe and no one from that tribe has ever served at the altar. ¹⁴It is well known that our Lord descended from Judah yet Moses did not mention this tribe when he spoke about priests.

¹⁵And this is even more evident since another priest like Melchizedek has arisen ¹⁶who has not become a priest by meeting the physical requirement of belonging to the tribe of Levi but by the power of a life that is indestructible. ¹⁷For it is testified about him,

---

a priest until the time when his enemies are made his footstool at the beginning of the Millennial Kingdom (Heb. 10:12-13). He is waiting for this time which is at the beginning of the Sabbath-rest. So, essentially Melchizedek and Christ can be considered to be the same person.

1280 Referring to Gen. 14:18-20.

1281 The Greek literally says, "he lives". The grammar demands that Melchizedek was alive when the writer wrote Hebrews. In other words, Melchizedek is alive essentially saying that Christ and Melchizedek can be considered to be the same person.

1282 The writer's argument here is that even though the Levites habitually collected tithes from the other Israelite tribes, one can't think that they were greater than Melchizedek because they were mortal. Not only was Melchizedek alive at that very time, he also collected tithes from the Levites through Abraham because it is seen that they were in Abraham's genitals or loins and so if that is the case it's as if they were also paying tithes to Melchizedek. In other words the lesser Levite priests were paying tithes to the greater priest (Melchizedek). Therefore the conclusion is that Melchizedek was greater than all hence he must be Christ.

"You are a priest throughout the age like Melchizedek."

Psalm 110:4

¹⁸The old requirement about the priesthood has been annulled because it is weak and useless. ¹⁹For the Law could make nothing perfect and now a better hope is introduced by which we can draw near to God.

²⁰Furthermore this *better hope* was *introduced* with an oath. Others became priests without any oath ²¹but *Jesus* became a priest with an oath when God said to him,

"The Lord has made a solemn promise and will not change his mind:
'You are a priest throughout the age like Melchizedek.'"

Psalm 110:4

²²Because of this oath, Jesus has become the guarantee of a better covenant.[1283]

²³There have been many of those other kinds of priests, since death prevented them from continuing *in office*. ²⁴However because Jesus continues throughout the age his priesthood does not change. ²⁵And so this means that he is able to save completely anyone who comes to God through him because he always lives to intercede for them.

²⁶Such a high priest meets all of our needs. *Jesus* is holy, blameless, pure, having been separated from sinners and exalted high above in the heavens. ²⁷And unlike the other high priests, he does not need to offer sacrifices day after day, first for his own sins and then for the sins of the people. He sacrificed for their sins once and for all when he offered up himself. ²⁸The Law appoints men as high priest who are weak *and imperfect* but when God made the promise with the oath which came after the law, it appointed the Son who has been made perfect throughout the age.

Jesus' ministry in the heavenly temple

8 ¹The whole point of what I am saying is that we have a high priest who sat down at the right hand of the throne of the Majesty in the heavens. ²He is a minister of the holy things, in the true tabernacle set up by the Lord, not by man.

³For every high priest is appointed to offer both gifts and sacrifices and so it was necessary for this one also to have something to offer. ⁴Now, if he were on earth he would not even be a priest for there are already men who offer the gifts prescribed by the law. ⁵The ministry that these men perform is a copy and

---

1283   Cf. Gal. 4:24 footnote for an explanation of covenant.

shadow of what is in heaven. This is why Moses was warned when he was about to build the tabernacle. *God said to him,* "See to it that you make everything according to the pattern shown to you on the mountain." ⁶But now, *Jesus* has been given a superior ministry to theirs just as the covenant of which he is mediator is superior to the old one because the new covenant is established on better promises.

The new covenant is superior

⁷If there had been nothing wrong with the first covenant, there would have been no need for another. ⁸But God found fault with the people and said,

"The days are coming, says the Lord, when I will make a new covenant
> with the people of Israel and with the people of Judah.
⁹It will not be like the covenant I made with their ancestors when I took
> them by the hand and led them out of Egypt. They did not
> continue in my covenant and so I disregarded them.
¹⁰Now, this is the covenant I will make with the people of Israel in the
> following days, says the Lord:
I will put my laws in their minds and write them on their hearts. I will be
> their God and they will be my people.
¹¹No longer will a man teach his neighbour or tell his brother saying,
> 'You must know the Lord.'
For they will all know me from the least of them to the greatest.[1284]
¹²For I will forgive their wickedness and will remember their sins no more."[1285]

Jeremiah 31:31–34

¹³By saying this covenant was 'new,' God has made the first one obsolete and what is obsolete and aging will soon disappear.[1286]

The old covenant

9 ¹The first covenant had rules for worship and an earthly sanctuary.[1287] ²A tent was set up. In the first room called the Holy Place there was the lampstand,[1288] the table and the consecrated bread. ³Behind the second curtain was a room called the Most Holy Place ⁴in which was the golden altar

---

1284 Obviously this has not occurred yet but will be finally fulfilled upon the return of the Messiah when all of Israel will repent and realise and know that Jesus is Lord (Rom. 11:25–32).
1285 This is not that God literally forgets but that he chooses not to recall or think about again.
1286 This came to be true in just a few short years after this letter was written because in AD 70 the temple in Jerusalem was completely destroyed by the Roman Army.
1287 Literally 'holy place' meaning the entire place of worship.
1288 The seven-branch menorah.

of incense[1289] and the gold covered ark of the covenant. This ark contained the gold jar of manna, Aaron's staff that budded and the stone tablets of the covenant.[1290] ⁵Situated above the ark were the cherubim—signs of God's presence, with their wings covering the place of atonement. But it is not possible to discuss everything in detail now. ⁶And when everything is arranged like this then the priests go into the first room every day to perform their duties. ⁷But only the high priest enters the second room and that only once a year.[1291] He always enters with blood which he offers for himself and for the sins the people committed in ignorance.

⁸The Holy Breath was showing here that the way into the Most Holy Place has not yet been opened as long as the first room still stands.[1292] ⁹All of this is an illustration for the present time indicating that the gifts and *animal* sacrifices being offered were not able to clear the conscience of the worshipper to make him perfect. ¹⁰They are only a matter of food and drink and various purification ceremonies. These are all outward rules which apply only until the time when the new order is established.

The new covenant

¹¹However now Christ has become high priest of the good things to come having entered a more perfect tent that is not man-made and not a part of this creation. ¹²He did not enter by means of the blood of goats and calves but he entered the Most Holy Place once and for all by his own blood thereby setting us free forever.[1293] ¹³The *priests* sprinkled the blood of goats and bulls and the ashes of a heifer on the people who are ceremonially unclean and this purifies their bodies to make them outwardly clean.[1294] ¹⁴Since this is true, how much more, then, will the blood of Christ cleanse our consciences from dead works! By *the power of* the eternal Breath *of God*,[1295] he offered himself so that we may serve the living God.

¹⁵For this reason Christ is the mediator of a new covenant so that those who

---

1289   The golden altar of incense was in fact kept just outside the Most Holy Place. Its use however did pertain to the first room because on the Day of Atonement, the high priest would use the hot coals from this altar to burn incense before the mercy seat on the ark of the covenant.
1290   The Ten Commandments were written on these two slabs of stone (Exo. 32:15, Deut. 10:1).
1291   This was on Yom Kippur—Day of Atonement—Tishrei 10.
1292   The people would not be able to see the high priest enter into the inner room (Holy of Holies) where the ark of the covenant was because their view would have been obstructed by the first outer room.
1293   This is the phrase 'eternal redemption'. Cf. Gal. 3:13.
1294   The purpose of this sprinkling of blood and scattering of ashes was to put people back into a state in which they could once again legally take part in temple worship. It has nothing to do with the inward conscience.
1295   This speaks to the eternality of the Breath of God (Holy Spirit).

have been called *by God* may receive the promised eternal inheritance. This is possible because his death sets people free from their sins committed under the first covenant.[1296]

[16]In the case of a will, it is necessary to prove the death of the one who made it [17]because a will only takes effect when the person has died. It never takes effect while that person who made it is still living. [18]This is why even the first covenant was inaugurated by means of blood. [19]For once Moses has proclaimed every commandment of the Law to all the people, he took the blood of calves together with water, scarlet wool and branches of hyssop, and sprinkled all the people.[1297] [20]He said, "This is the blood of the covenant which God has commanded you to keep."[1298] [21]In the same way he sprinkled with the blood both the tent and everything used in worship. [22]In fact, the Law requires that nearly everything be purified with blood for there can be no forgiveness without the shedding of blood.

Christ's death takes away sins

[23]It was necessary therefore for the copies of the heavenly things to be purified in this way but the heavenly things must be purified with better sacrifices than these. [24]For Christ did not enter a man-made sanctuary that was only a copy of the true one but he entered heaven itself where he now appears for us in God's presence. [25]Nor did he enter heaven to offer himself again and again, the way in which the high priest enters the Most Holy Place every year with blood that is not his own. [26]*If that were the case* then Christ would have had to suffer many times since the overthrow of the world.[1299] But now he has appeared once for all at the end of the ages to do away with sin by sacrificing himself. [27]And just as man is destined to die once and after that face judgment by God [28]so Christ was sacrificed once to take away the sins of many people. He will appear a second time not for sin but to bring salvation to those who are waiting for him.[1300]

1296 Christ's atonement was retroactively applied to all OT believers. They are cleansed by means of the New Covenant which enables them and NT believers to receive all the good things to come described in Heb. 9:11. This is the Land promised to Abraham and his descendants (Gal. 3:29).
1297 This took place at Mt. Sinai in Exo. 24:6–8.
1298 Compare this to when Jesus said, "This is my blood of the new covenant which is poured out for many for the forgiveness of sins" when talking to his disciples at the Last Supper in Matt. 26:28.
1299 The significant Greek word which is typically translated as 'foundation' or 'creation' in most translations is from *kataballo* which is from *kata* and *ballo*; meaning to throw down. Strong's 2602. The "overthrow of the world" occurred when Adam and Eve listened to Satan and ate the fruit from the Tree of the Knowledge of Good and Evil. The overthrow of the world refers to the overthrow of God's established order when Adam sinned.
1300 Salvation here means deliverance in an eschatological sense. When Christ appears at his second coming we will be transformed receiving our new bodies thereby bringing salvation to completion.

The Law is only a shadow of the good things that are coming

10 [1]The Law is only a shadow of the good things that are coming and not the realities themselves.[1301] These sacrifices are done year after year through to the end but for this reason the Law can never make perfect those who come *to God*. [2]For if the Law was able to *perfect them* then the worshippers would have been cleansed and they would no longer have felt guilty for their sins. All sacrifices would have stopped being offered. [3]As it is though, the sacrifices are an annual reminder to the people of their sins.[1302] [4]For it is impossible for the blood of bulls and goats to take away sins.

[5]Therefore, when Christ entered into the world, he said *to God*,

"You do not want *animal* sacrifice and offerings but you prepared for me a body.
[6]You are not pleased with burnt offerings and sin offerings.
[7]Then I said to you, 'Here I am—I have come to do your will, O God.
It is written about me in the scroll.'"

Psalm 40:6–8

[8]In the passage above Christ says, "You did not want animal sacrifices and offerings or burnt offerings and sin offerings and you were not pleased with them either." This was even though the Law required them to be made. [9]Then he said, "Here I am, I have come to do your will." He abolished the first to establish the second.[1303] [10]And because he did God's will, we have been made holy through the offering of his own body once for all.

[11]Day after day every priest stands and performs his religious duties frequently offering the same sacrifices but it is never able to take away sins.[1304] [12]But when this priest had offered one sacrifice, he sat down at the right hand of God through the age [13]where he now waits until his enemies will be placed

---

1301   The feasts contained in the law are only a rehearsal of the future prophetic calendar. Three feasts are yet to be fulfilled prophetically: Feast of Trumpets (Yom Teruah); Day of Atonement (Yom Kippur); and Feast of Tabernacles (Sukkot). The seven appointed feasts were to be proclaimed as sacred assemblies (days of celebration and worship)(miqra) but which can also mean 'a rehearsal'. They were a rehearsal of the good things to come.
1302   Specifically each year on the Day of Atonement.
1303   Jesus abolished the first covenant according to the Levitical priesthood and established the new covenant.
1304   Day after day for over 1500 years, thousands of priests have stood and performed their duties but they were never able to take away sins. However the one man Jesus after offering only one sacrifice was able to sit down—something that the priests could never do and never did. There were no seats in the temple or tabernacle.

under his feet.[1305] [14]By his one sacrifice, Jesus has perfected through the age those who are being made holy.[1306]

[15]The Holy Breath also testifies to us about this. First he says,

[16]"This is the covenant I will make with them[1307] after that time says the Lord. I will put my laws in their hearts and I will write them on their minds."

Jeremiah 31:33

[17]Then he added,

"I will remember their sins and lawless deeds no more."

Jeremiah 31:34

[18]So when these things have been forgiven an offering for sin is no longer needed.

Spurring one another on toward love and good works

[19]Therefore *Christian* brothers, we can have every confidence to enter the Most Holy Place by the blood of Jesus. [20]A new and living way has been opened for us through the curtain—that is, his body.[1308] [21]And since we all have a great priest over the house of God,[1309] [22]let us draw near to God with a sincere heart and a sure faith having our hearts purified from a guilty conscience and with bodies washed with pure water.[1310] [23]Let us hold firmly to the hope we profess without wavering, because we can trust God to keep his promise. [24]And let us consider how we may spur one another on toward love and good works. [25]Let us not give up meeting together as some are in the habit of doing but encouraging one another especially as you see the Day of the Lord approaching.

1305 Cf. Psa. 110:1. This has the implication that Jesus is the priest sitting at the right hand of the Father only until the end of the age when his enemies will be finally defeated. After that Jesus begins his reign as king and his priesthood is officially finished (Rev. 11:15).
1306 All who trust in the sacrifice that Jesus made at Calvary have in effect been made perfect provided they are presently continuing in the faith. This will continue until the very end of this age.
1307 Heb. 8:10 quote identifies 'them' as the people of Israel.
1308 The way is opened through the sacrifice of Jesus' body on the cross.
1309 Probably referring to the heavenly temple rather than the temple in Jerusalem.
1310 The author may be drawing a comparison of Christian baptism to the washing done by OT priests.

A warning not to keep on sinning

²⁶If we intentionally keep on sinning after we have received the full knowledge of the truth then there is no sacrifice for sins left.*¹³¹¹* ²⁷All that is left is a terrible expectation of judgment and a raging fire that will consume those who oppose *God*. ²⁸Anyone who rejected the Law of Moses died without mercy on the testimony of two or three witnesses. ²⁹Therefore how much worse do you think someone deserves to be punished who has trampled on the Son of God and who has treated as an unholy thing the blood of the covenant that made him holy and who has insulted the Breath of grace? ³⁰For we know God says, "It is my job to avenge, I will repay," and "The Lord will judge his people." ³¹It is a terrifying thing to fall into the hands of the living God.

The Antichrist is coming and he will not delay

³²You *Jews* must remember how in those earlier days after you had been enlightened when you endured a great struggle despite suffering. ³³At times you were publicly exposed to insult and persecution and at other times you stood alongside those who were being treated *badly* likewise. ³⁴You sympathised with those in prison and joyfully accepted the confiscation of your property, because you knew that you yourselves had a better and longer lasting possession.

³⁵Therefore do not throw away your confidence because it will be greatly rewarded. ³⁶You will need to persevere so that when you have done the will of God you will receive what is promised. ³⁷For there remains a short time,

"The one coming will come and will not delay.*¹³¹²*

³⁸But my righteous one will live by faith.*¹³¹³*

But if he shrinks back, I will not be pleased with him."*¹³¹⁴*

Habakkuk 2:3-4

³⁹But we are not a people who shrink back and are destroyed but we believe and are saved.

1311 This is addressed to believers not unbelievers and is saying that deliberate, habitual sin eventually leads to a loss of salvation. It would be hard to see how a person who deliberately keeps on sinning can still have a belief in God.

1312 This does not refer to the second coming of Christ, but the coming of the Antichrist. It is a quotation from Hab. 2:2-3 (LXX). The 'coming one' in this context refers back to Hab. 1:5-11, a prophecy of the Antichrist and the end times Babylonians. Habakkuk was instructed to write down the vision for the benefit of believers in the last days so that they may 'flee' at the proper time (LGV).

1313 Traditionally this verse was used in the reformation to mean that we do not come by works but by faith which is an application but not the correct interpretation. The verse refers to those who survive in the Tribulation and make it to the resurrection. In other words great faith will be needed.

1314 If a man falls away (shrinks back) in the Great Apostasy (2 Thess. 2:3) then God will not be pleased.

The ancient heroes of the faith

11 ¹Now faith is a guarantee[1315] of the things that are hoped for—evidence of the things that cannot be seen. ²This is what people in the olden days were commended for.

³By faith we understand that the universe was formed at God's command so that what is seen was made out of what is not visible.

⁴By faith Abel offered a better sacrifice than Cain. By faith he was commended as a righteous man because God approved of his offerings. And he still speaks even though he has died.[1316]

⁵By faith Enoch was taken from this life so that he did not experience death.[1317] He could not be found because God had taken him away. Before he was taken *by God* he was commended as one who pleased God. ⁶It is impossible to please God without faith because anyone who comes to him must believe that God exists and that he rewards those who seek him.

⁷By faith Noah, when he was warned about things not yet seen,[1318] because he regarded and respected God, built an ark to save his family. He condemned the world and so he became an heir of righteousness that comes by faith.

The faith of Abraham

⁸By faith Abraham obeyed God and went to a place even though he did not know where he was going. He would later receive this place as an inheritance. ⁹By faith *Abraham* made his home in the promised land like a stranger in a foreign country. He lived in tents as did Isaac and Jacob who also inherited the same promise. ¹⁰For *Abraham* was looking ahead to the city with foundations whose designer and builder is God.[1319]

1315 The Greek word *hypostasis* here was a word often used in legal documents for title deeds of a piece of property (TH).

1316 Abel's blood still speaks in a metaphorical sense in that it remains that God will take vengeance upon all murders at some point in time. This is a reference to Abel's righteous blood crying out from the ground (Gen. 4:10). Abel is considered the father of all of the martyrs of all ages.

1317 Some see Enoch as a picture of the rapture of the church or as one of the two witnesses in the end times because it seems to say that he didn't die. But Heb. 11:13 says that all these people were still living by faith when they died. Also, Rom. 5:12 says that everyone dies because everyone sins. The word for death in v. 5 and v. 13 are two different words meaning two different things. In the Greek v. 5 says *thanatos* and v. 13 says *apethanon* the process where the body dies. In Greek thinking *Thanatos* was the god who was responsible to transport a soul to Hades (Rev. 20:13). Enoch did in fact die but he did not 'experience death'—he was taken straight there because he pleased God by his life. In other words, Enoch was not transported by *Thanatos* but God took him to himself immediately thereby bypassing *Thanatos*.

1318 Noah had never seen rain before the flood.

1319 The newly restored heavenly Jerusalem (Heb. 12:22, Rev. 21:2). This city does not come down out of heaven but is heavenly in the sense that it has a heavenly quality. This millennial city will be elevated and raised above the hills, the chief among mountains (Gal. 4:26, Isa. 2:2–3).

¹¹By faith Sarah herself a barren woman, received the ability to conceive¹³²⁰ even though she was well beyond *child bearing* age since she trusted God to keep his promise. ¹²And even though Abraham was as good as dead, from this one man came descendants as numerous as the stars in the sky and as countless as the sand on the seashore.

¹³All these people *previously mentioned* were still living by faith when they died.¹³²¹ They did not actually receive the things promised but they only saw them from a distance. They openly admitted that they were foreigners and exiles on the earth. ¹⁴Now when people say such things it means that their eyes are fixed upon their *true* homeland. ¹⁵For if they had meant the particular country that they had left behind, they would have had plenty of time to return. *But they did not return.* ¹⁶Instead, they were longing for a better country—a heavenly one. And so God is not ashamed for them to call him their God because he has prepared a city for them.

¹⁷By faith Abraham, when God tested him, offered Isaac as a sacrifice. Even though Abraham had received the promises he went about sacrificing his one and only son.¹³²² ¹⁸God had said to Abraham, "It is through Isaac that you will have descendants." ¹⁹Abraham reasoned that God would be able to raise Isaac from the dead and figuratively speaking, Abraham did receive him back from the dead.

The faith of Isaac, Jacob and Joseph

²⁰By faith Isaac blessed Jacob and Esau with regards to the things to come.¹³²³ ²¹By faith Jacob, when he was dying, blessed each of Joseph's sons and worshipped *God* as he leaned on his walking stick. ²²By faith Joseph, when his end was near, spoke about the exodus of the Israelites from Egypt and gave instructions about what was to be done with his bones.

The faith of Moses

²³By faith Moses' parents hid him for three months after he was born because they could see that he was a beautiful child and they were not afraid to disobey the king's edict.¹³²⁴

²⁴By faith Moses, when he had grown up, refused to be known as the son of

---

1320   Literally 'the overthrowing of the seed'.
1321   This includes Enoch (v. 5) whom many assume did not die but remained alive in heaven.
1322   The term *monogenes* here is not the same as used in Heb. 1:5 although translated as 'begotten' in both places in many older English translations (Heiser, Michael S, *The Unseen Realm* (2015), pp. 36–37). Isaac was unique from Ishmael and the others in the sense that he was the son of promise. He was one of a kind because he was promised.
1323   The things to come specifically concerns the Abrahamic promises about inheriting the Land which was denied Esau.
1324   Pharaoh had made an edict that all male babies were to be killed (Exo. 1:15–17).

Pharaoh's daughter. ²⁵Instead he chose to be mistreated along with the people of God rather than to have the enjoyment of sin for a little while. ²⁶He held the view that to suffer insult for the sake of the Messiah was better than the treasures of Egypt because he was looking ahead to his reward.[1325]

²⁷By faith Moses left Egypt and he wasn't afraid even though the king was angry for he persevered as though he had seen the unseen God. ²⁸By faith Moses established the Passover and ordered the sprinkling of blood on the doorposts so that the destroyer would not kill the firstborn sons of Israel.

The faith of the Israelites after the Red Sea

²⁹By faith the people of Israel passed through the Red Sea as if they were walking in dry land but when the Egyptians attempted to do the same they were drowned.

³⁰By faith the walls of Jericho fell after the people had marched around them for seven days.

³¹By faith the prostitute Rahab, because she welcomed the spies, was not killed with those who were disobedient.

³²And what more should I say? I do not have time to tell you about Gideon, Barak, Samson, Jephthah, David, Samuel and the prophets. ³³By faith they conquered realms, administered justice and received what God promised. They shut the mouths of lions, ³⁴quenched fierce fires and escaped being killed by the sword. They were weak but became strong, they were mighty in battle and routed foreign armies. ³⁵By faith women received back their dead relatives who were raised back to life.

Others, refusing to be freed, were tortured to death in order to be raised to a better life. ³⁶Some others again were mocked and flogged while still others were chained and put in prison. ³⁷They were stoned and some were sawn in two. They were put to death by the sword. They went about in sheepskins and goatskins, destitute, persecuted and mistreated. ³⁸The world was definitely not worthy of these men. They wandered as refugees in deserts and mountains, living in caves and holes in the ground.

³⁹These people were all commended *by God* for their faith yet none of them received what had been promised. ⁴⁰God was thinking of something better—for them and us, so that together with us they would be made perfect.[1326]

1325   This proves that Moses knew about Christ and he even prophesied about him (Deut. 18:15–19, John 5:46, Acts 3:22–23).
1326   We will all together inherit the Land originally promised to Abraham.

The great cloud of witnesses

12 ¹Therefore since we are surrounded by such a great cloud of witnesses *who have previously demonstrated their faith,*[1327] let us remove everything that is in the way and especially sin that holds onto us so tightly. *Instead,* let us run the agonising race lying ahead of us. ²And let us fix our eyes on Jesus, the one who is the pioneer and the finisher of the faith, who for the joy set before him endured the cross and disregarded its shame. He is now seated at the right hand of the throne of God.

God disciplines those whom He loves

³Think about what the Lord went through and how he had to endure so much opposition from sinful men. Do this so that you do not get weary and become discouraged.

⁴In your struggle against sin, you have not yet resisted to the level of being killed. ⁵Maybe you have forgotten the encouragement which comes from God when he says the following,

> "My Son, do not think lightly of it when the Lord disciplines you and do not be discouraged when he rebukes you.
> ⁶For the Lord corrects those whom he loves and he punishes everyone whom he accepts as a son."
>
> Proverbs 3:11–12

⁷Therefore you must endure hardship as though you are being disciplined for God is treating you as sons. For what son is not disciplined by his father? ⁸If you are not disciplined (and everyone is disciplined), then you are illegitimate children and not really God's sons.[1328] ⁹Furthermore, we have all had human fathers who disciplined us and we respected them for it. How much more then should we submit to the spiritual Father and live! ¹⁰Our human fathers disciplined us for a little while as they thought best but God disciplines us for our good that we might share in his holiness. ¹¹No discipline seems pleasant at the time but it is painful. Later on however, it results in righteousness and peace for those who have been trained by it.

1327 These people are those mentioned in the previous chapter who have died in the faith. It's not that those who have died are looking down from heaven watching the progress of Christians who are alive on the earth but that their testimony of faithfulness is recorded in the Scriptures.
1328 If you are not disciplined then this is evidence that you are not truly saved.

Warning to believers to stand firm in the trouble to come

[12]Therefore straighten the weak arms and the paralysed knees.[1329] [13]Make straight paths for your feet so that the lame may not stray but rather be healed.

[14]*In light of this* make every effort to live in peace with all men and to be holy. Without holiness no one will see the Lord. [15]See to it that no one falls away from the grace of God and that no bitter root grows up to cause trouble because many may be defiled as such.[1330] [16]Make sure that no one is sexually immoral[1331] or is godless like Esau, who for a single meal sold his inheritance rights as the oldest son. [17]Afterwards, as you all know, when Esau wanted to inherit the blessing *from his father*, he was rejected. There was no opportunity for him to change his mind even though he sought the opportunity with tears.

The climax of the whole letter

[18]You have not come to what can be touched, to Mount Sinai with its blazing fire, to darkness, gloom and storm as did the people of Israel. [19]You have not come to a trumpet blast or to the sound of a voice. When the people heard the voice they begged not to hear another word [20]because they couldn't bear to hear the command which said, "If even an animal touches the mountain, it must be stoned to death or shot with an arrow." [21]The situation was so terrifying that Moses said, "I am trembling with fear."[1332]

[22]But you have come to Mount Zion, to the heavenly Jerusalem,[1333] the city of the living God. You have come to thousands upon thousands of angels in joyful assembly. [23]You have come to the church of the firstborn,[1334] whose names are written in heaven. You have come to God, the judge of all men and to the spirits of righteous men made perfect.[1335] [24]You have also come to Jesus the mediator of a new covenant whose shed blood is better news than the blood of Abel.[1336]

1329   The author quotes Isa. 35:3–4 about Christ's coming kingdom which was an exhortation to endure in light of Christ's Kingdom which is about to appear. During the tribulation period the persecution and situation will be so tough that it will be as if we are paralysed and it will be very hard to stay on track. We must not fear because the Lord is coming soon.
1330   A warning to Christians to not fall away during the tribulation period and make sure that no bitterness crops up between fellow believers because this will affect many during this time and many will fall away (Matt. 24:10,12).
1331   Covers all general sexual immorality here such as sex before marriage and adultery.
1332   In other words, the Jewish Christians of the 1st century are no longer under the Mosaic system anymore which commanded that the Jews worship God in fear.
1333   New Jerusalem which is in heaven and will come down to the earth at the beginning of the coming Millennial Kingdom (Rev. 21:2).
1334   The church of Jesus Christ who is the firstborn over all creation (Col. 1:15).
1335   The OT and NT believers who have previously died and who will be resurrected at the rapture of the church at the end of the Great Tribulation known as the first resurrection.
1336   Abel's sacrifice of the blood of animals only meant a covering of sin whereas the good news of Jesus Christ meant that sin could be completely paid for by his blood sacrifice on the cross.

²⁵Therefore make sure that you do not refuse him who speaks. For if the people did not escape *judgment* when they refused to listen on earth, then how much less will we escape, if we turn away from him who warns us from heaven? ²⁶His voice shook the earth but now he has promised, "Once more I will shake not only the earth but the sky[1337] as well." ²⁷The words "once more" indicate the removing of created things that can be shaken so that the things that cannot be shaken may remain.

²⁸Therefore, let us be thankful because we are receiving entry into a realm that cannot be shaken. And so let us worship God in a way that is acceptable to him with reverence and awe ²⁹for our God is an all-consuming fire.

Final instructions

13 ¹Make sure that you keep on loving each other as Christian brothers. ²Do not forget to show hospitality for by doing so some people have entertained angels without knowing it.[1338]

³Remember those who are in prison as if you were their fellow prisoners. Remember those who are being mistreated as though you yourselves are being mistreated.

⁴Marriage is to be honoured by all ensuring that husbands and wives are faithful to each other. God will judge adulterers and those who are into pornography.

⁵Keep your lives free from the love of money and be content with what you have because God has said,

"I will never leave you.
I will never abandon you."[1339]

Deuteronomy 31:6,8

⁶*Because God has said this* we can say with confidence,

"The Lord is my helper
I will not be afraid.
What can man do to me?"

Psalm 118:6

1337 Cf. Hag. 2:6, Rev. 6:13. The word for heaven or sky here is in the singular.
1338 Showing hospitality to angels will become more commonplace in the last days as the angels are ministering spirits to help believers transition through the Great Tribulation into the Millennial Kingdom (Heb. 1:14).
1339 God will never initiate a separation however if we depart from him, he will depart from us (1 Chron. 28:9; 2 Chron. 15:2; Ezra 8:22; 2 Tim. 2:12–13).

⁷Remember *the example of* your leaders, who spoke the word of God to you. Think back on how they lived and died and imitate their faith. ⁸Jesus Christ is the same yesterday, today and forever. ⁹Do not be swept away by all kinds of strange teachings. Your inner strength[1340] comes from grace not by which foods are kosher or not. This does not help anyone following such rules.

¹⁰The priests who serve at the tabernacle[1341] have no right to eat at the altar that we have.[1342] ¹¹For the high priest carries the blood of animals into the Most Holy Place as a sin offering, but the bodies are burned outside the camp. ¹²Therefore Jesus also suffered outside the city gate in order to purify the people from sin with his own blood. ¹³Let us, then, go to him outside the camp and share in the shame that he bore. ¹⁴For we do not have an enduring city now but we are looking for the city that is to come. ¹⁵Therefore let us continually offer to God a sacrifice of praise which is the fruit of our lips, confessing the name *of Jesus*. ¹⁶And you must not forget to do good and to share with others for God is pleased with such sacrifices.

¹⁷You must obey your leaders and submit to their authority for they are keeping watch over you as men who must give an account *to God of their ministry*. Obey them so that their service will be a joy, not a burden, which would be of no benefit to you.

¹⁸Please keep praying for us. We are sure that we have a clear conscience. We desire to do well in all things. ¹⁹An urgent prayer point: Please pray that we can reconnect soon.

Closing prayer and final personal words

²⁰May the God of peace, who brought back from the dead our Lord Jesus, the great Shepherd of the sheep, as the result of the blood of the eternal covenant, ²¹equip you with every good thing that you need to do his will. May he work in us to do what pleases him through Jesus Christ, to whom be glory forever and ever. Amen.

²²*Christian* brothers, I beg you to accept the challenge contained in this short letter that I have written to you. ²³I *also* want you to know that our brother Timothy has been released *out of prison*. If he arrives soon, I will come with him to see you all.

²⁴Make sure that you greet all your leaders and all of God's holy people. The believers from Italy send you their greetings.

²⁵May God's grace be with you all.

1340 Literally 'heart'.
1341 This equally implies the Jewish temple as well.
1342 This has nothing to do with the Lord's Supper/communion or that Christians make sacrifices on altars. The implied contrast here is between the rules about food and the Christian sacrifice which is one of praise to God as in v. 15. The OT priests were not allowed to eat the sacrifice for sins on the altar—they had to burn this sacrifice outside the camp (Lev. 16:27).

JAMES

Introduction

James is considered to be a general letter because it is addressed to the wider audience of the Jewish Christians who were scattered outside the land of Israel—the twelve tribes of the diaspora. It was one of the earliest letters written around AD 45–49 by James, the half-brother of Jesus and leader of the Jerusalem church. One of the reasons for the early date of the letter is that James refers to the meeting place as the synagogue in Jam. 2:2. According to the Jewish historian Josephus, James was martyred at Jerusalem in AD 62.

James wrote his general letter to encourage the Jewish believers to live by faith and that good deeds and works should be an outcome of that faith. He covers a wide variety of practical topics all related to living a genuine Christian life.

1

¹From James,[1343] a servant of God and of the Lord Jesus Christ.

To the twelve tribes dispersed among the nations.[1344]

Greetings.

Faith and wisdom

²My *Christian* brothers, consider it to be pure joy whenever you face different kinds of trials. ³For you know that the testing of your faith results in endurance. ⁴But let endurance develop fully so that you may be mature and perfect, lacking in nothing.

⁵If any of you is lacking wisdom, then you should ask God and it will be given to you because He gives generously to everyone who asks without finding fault. ⁶But when you ask you must believe and not doubt because if you doubt you will be like a wave in the sea, blown and tossed about by the wind. ⁷The person who doubts should not think that he will receive anything from the Lord, ⁸for he is in two minds and unstable in everything that he does.

Comparing rich Christians with poor Christians

⁹If a *Christian* brother finds himself to be in humble circumstances *with few possessions* then he should rejoice in his exalted position. ¹⁰However the rich brother should rejoice in the fact that God will *eventually* humble him because he will pass away like a wild flower. ¹¹For the sun rises with scorching heat and withers the plant. Its flower falls off and its beauty is destroyed. In the same way, the rich man will fade away even while he goes about his business.

Difference between trials and temptations

¹²Blessed is the man who perseveres under trial because when he has passed the test, he will be rewarded victorious with eternal life that God promised to those who love him. ¹³And when a man is tempted he should not say, "God is tempting me." For God cannot be tempted by evil nor does he tempt anyone. ¹⁴However each person is tempted when by his own evil desires he is lured and

---

1343   The author of this letter, James, is generally regarded as being the half-brother of Jesus and the leader of the Jerusalem church.
1344   This is most likely a letter written from James to Jewish Christians who were scattered or dispersed amongst the nations because of the persecution of the early believers from the Jewish leaders in Jerusalem and surrounds. The word "dispersed" is the word *diaspora* in the Greek which is also used in English nowadays and has broadened in its meaning to describe any peoples who have been dispersed from their original homeland. Originally it was only used of the Jews living outside their homeland and in the context of this letter by James it is addressed to the dispersed Jewish Christians in the Roman Empire.

drawn away. ¹⁵Then after desire has been conceived, it gives birth to sin, and sin when it is fully grown gives birth to death.

¹⁶My dear *Christian* brothers, do not be deceived! ¹⁷Every good and perfect gift is from above. It comes down from the Father *who created* the heavenly lights.¹³⁴⁵ He does not change like shifting shadows. ¹⁸God chose to give us *new* birth through the word of truth¹³⁴⁶ so that we might have first place amongst everything that he created.

Listening to and obeying God's word

¹⁹My dear *Christian* brothers, take note of this: Everyone should be quick to listen, slow to speak, and slow to become angry, ²⁰for when a man is angry, this does not produce the kind of good life that God *wants for us*. ²¹Therefore rid yourselves of every kind of filthy behaviour and evil that still remains in you, rather humbly accepting the word of God planted in you which is able to save you.

²²Do not just be hearers of the word *of God*, but be doers of the word as well otherwise you are just deceiving yourselves. ²³Anyone who listens to the word *of God* but does not do what it *actually* says is like a man who looks at himself in the mirror ²⁴and then immediately forgets what he looks like after going away. ²⁵But the man who looks intently into the perfect law that gives freedom¹³⁴⁷ and continues to do so not forgetting what he has heard but does what it says, this man will be blessed in what he does.

²⁶If anyone considers himself to be religious¹³⁴⁸ and yet does not keep a tight rein on his tongue, he is deceiving himself and his religion is effectively useless. ²⁷However the religion that God our Father approves of as pure and undefiled is this: to look after orphans and widows in their distress and to keep oneself from being corrupted by the world.¹³⁴⁹

Warning against playing favourites

2 ¹My *Christian* brothers, as believers in our glorious Lord Jesus Christ, I urge you not to play favourites. ²Suppose that a man comes into your synagogue wearing a gold ring and expensive clothing and a poor man wearing grungy-looking clothes also comes in. ³Now what if you show special attention to the

---

1345 I.e. the sun, moon and stars.
1346 I.e. the gospel.
1347 James, being a Jew, takes a Jewish slant on the gospel of Jesus Christ by referring to it as the perfect law that gives freedom as in Matt. 5:48.
1348 This is the only place in the NT where the word "religious" is used. It is an outward expression of pious and careful observance of ritual and liturgical practices. In this context James is asking the question of his readers, "Do you think that you are following God properly?"
1349 Obviously this is not a full and exhaustive list of qualities that constitutes true piety but James mentions two things that are important representing social concern and moral purity.

man wearing expensive clothing and say to him, "Here's the best seat in the house for you," but you say to the poor man, "Stand over there" or "Sit down here on the floor by my feet?" ⁴Isn't that discrimination? Are you not being inconsistent and judging others with malice?

⁵Listen to me my dear *Christian* brothers! Has not God chosen the poor people of the world to be rich in faith and to take their place where he reigns. He has promised this place to those who love him? ⁶However you have disrespected the poor. Is it not the rich people who are overpowering you and dragging you into court? ⁷Are they not the ones who are blaspheming the good name of him[1350] to whom you belong?

⁸If you really are keeping the royal law found in the Scripture which says, "Love your neighbour as yourself," you are doing great. ⁹However if you are playing favourites then you are sinning and the Law condemns you as a lawbreaker. ¹⁰For whoever keeps the whole Law and yet he fails at just one point he is guilty of breaking every law. ¹¹For he who said, "Do not commit adultery," also said, "Do not murder." If you do not commit adultery but do commit murder, you have become a lawbreaker.

¹²Therefore you must speak and act as people who will be judged by the law that gives freedom. ¹³For whoever is not merciful will be judged without mercy. Mercy triumphs over judgment.

Faith and actions

¹⁴My *Christian* brothers, what good is it if a man claims to have faith but has no actions *to back it up*? Can this kind of faith save him? ¹⁵Let's suppose that a *Christian* brother or sister has no clothes and is lacking in food ¹⁶and then one of you says to them, "Go, I wish you all the best. Make sure that you keep warm and well fed," but then you do nothing about their physical needs. What good is that? ¹⁷So in the same way, faith without actions to back it up is *a dead faith*.

¹⁸But someone will *no doubt* say, "You have faith; I have actions." My answer to that is, "Show me how you can have faith without actions. Instead, I will show you my faith by my actions." ¹⁹You believe that there is one God. Excellent! Even the demons believe that and they shudder *with fear at the thought*.

²⁰You are so foolish! Do you want me to give you proof that faith without actions is useless? ²¹God regarded our father Abraham as righteous because he offered his son Isaac on the altar. ²²Can you see that his faith and actions worked together and that his faith was made complete by what he did? ²³And so the Scripture was fulfilled that says, "Abraham believed God, which was counted

---

1350   I.e. Christ.

as righteousness." And so he was called God's friend. ²⁴Therefore you must see that a person is declared righteous by what he does and not by faith alone.

²⁵It was the same with the prostitute Rahab who was regarded as righteous for what she did when she gave lodging to the *Israelite* spies and then sent them off *safely* in a different direction. ²⁶So then, as the body without the spirit is dead, also faith without actions is dead.

Controlling what we say

3 ¹My *Christian* brothers, not many of you should presume to be teachers *of the word* because you will be aware that we who teach will be judged more strictly *than the rest*. ²*As Christians* we all make mistakes. If anyone never makes a mistake in what he says, he is a perfect man able to keep a tight rein on his whole body. ³When a bit is put into the mouth of a horse to make them obey us, we can turn the whole animal. ⁴Take the example also of ships. Although they are large and driven by strong winds, they are nevertheless steered by a very small rudder enabling the one steering the ship to direct it wherever he wants it to go. ⁵And so it is with our tongues. It is a very small part of the body but it makes such large boasts.

Just consider how a large bushfire is set on fire by a small spark. ⁶The tongue is also in a way like a fire. It is a world of evil among the parts of the body. It corrupts the whole person and sets the whole course of his life on fire and is itself set on fire by hell itself.[1351] ⁷All kinds of wild animals, birds, reptiles, and creatures of the sea are being tamed and have been tamed by mankind ⁸but nobody has been able to tame the tongue. It is evil and uncontrollable, full of deadly poison.

⁹With the tongue we praise our Lord and Father, and yet with it, we also curse men who have been made in God's image. ¹⁰Out of the same mouth come praise and cursing. My *Christian* brothers, this should not happen! ¹¹Can fresh water and salt water come up out of the same bore? ¹²Brothers, can a fig tree bear olives or a grapevine bear figs? Neither can a saltwater bore produce fresh water.

True wisdom

¹³Who among you is wise and really understands? Let him show it by his good life, by his deeds done in humility that comes from wisdom. ¹⁴However if you are one to harbour intense jealousy and are narcissistic in your ambitions, do not lie by boasting about your supposed wisdom. ¹⁵Such "wisdom" does not originate from heaven but is worldly, unspiritual, and demonic. ¹⁶For wherever

---

1351   Cf. Matt. 5:22 footnote.

there is jealousy and narcissism, there you will find disorder and every evil practice. ¹⁷But the wisdom that comes from heaven is firstly pure, then peace-loving, considerate, submissive, full of mercy, and good fruit. Such wisdom is impartial and not hypocritical. ¹⁸Peacemakers who sow peace harvest righteousness.

Submitting to God

4 ¹What is causing you to fight and quarrel amongst yourselves? ²You are wanting something but you are not getting what you want. You are killing each other and you are coveting what others have but you cannot have what you are wanting. You do not have it because you are not asking God. ³And when you do ask *God*, you do not receive it because you are asking for the wrong reasons so that you may spend what you get on your own pleasures.

⁴Stop fooling around behind God's back!¹³⁵² Don't you know that friendship with the world is like hatred towards God? Anyone who chooses to be a friend of the world becomes an enemy of God. ⁵The Scripture says for good reason that God is extremely jealous for the spirit that he has placed in us."

⁶However the grace that God gives is even greater. That is why the Scripture says,

"God opposes the proud man but he gives grace to the humble."

Proverbs 3:34

⁷Therefore submit yourselves to God. Resist the devil and he will flee from you. ⁸Draw near to God and he will draw near to you. Wash your hands, you sinners, and purify your hearts, you double-minded.¹³⁵³ ⁹Be sorrowful, mourn, and weep.¹³⁵⁴ Let your laughter turn to mourning and your joy into gloom.¹³⁵⁵ ¹⁰Humble yourselves before the Lord and he will lift you up in honour.

¹¹My *Christian* brothers, do not speak evil of each other. Anyone who speaks evil against his brother or judges him is speaking evil of the Law and is judging the Law.¹³⁵⁶ And when you judge the Law, you are not keeping it but sitting in

---

1352 Literally here the Greek is 'You adulteresses!'
1353 The priests in Israel had to wash their hands and feet before they were allowed to perform any ceremonial duties (Exo 30.20). Ceremonial washing of hands was also practiced at the time of Jesus by zealous Jews like the Pharisees (Mark 7:3–4). These actions were often used figuratively for the removal of moral defilement. And this is obviously the sense intended here by James. When he calls for his readers to wash their hands, he wants them to do right deeds (TH).
1354 Mourning and weeping here are signs of true repentance because of the sinful condition we find ourselves in.
1355 Turning from one state of mind to another gives the picture of a true change of mind needed for repentance.
1356 The law demands that a believer love his fellow believer not speak evil against him (Jam. 2:8).

judgment on it. [12]There is only one Lawgiver[1357] and Judge—the one who is able to both save and destroy.

Boasting is wrong

[13]Now listen up, those of you who say, "Today or tomorrow we will go to a particular city and stay for a year or so where we will do business and make some money." [14]You don't even know what will happen tomorrow. You are just a puff of smoke that appears for a moment and then disappears. [15]Instead you should be saying, "If it is the Lord's will, we will live and do this or that." [16]But as it is you arrogantly boast. All such boasting is evil. [17]Anyone then, who knows the good *acts* he must do and does not do it, is guilty of sin.

A warning to the rich

5 [1]Now listen up, you rich men! Cry and howl because of the miseries that will come upon you. [2]Your wealth has become rotten and your *expensive* clothes have become moth-eaten. [3]Your gold and silver have corroded and their corrosion will be used as evidence against you and consume your flesh like fire. You have stored up treasure in these last days. [4]Look! You failed to pay the workers any wages who mowed your fields and their complaints cry out. The cries of the harvesters reach the ears of *God*, the Lord of hosts.[1358] [5]Your lives on the earth have been lived in luxury and indulgence. In effect, you are fattening yourselves just as cattle are fattened for a day that they will be slaughtered. [6]You have condemned and murdered the innocent man who does not resist you.

Be patient until the Lord's coming

[7]Therefore my *Christian* brothers, you must be patient until the Lord's coming. Look at the example of the farmer. He waits for the land to yield its valuable crop and patiently waits for the early and latter rain. [8]You too must be patient and have courage because it will not be long until the Lord comes.

[9]Do not complain against each other, *Christian* brothers, or you will be judged. The Judge is standing at the door! [10]Brothers, take the prophets, who were an example of patience when suffering evil yet spoke in the name of the Lord. [11]We consider those who persevere as blessed. You have heard of Job's perseverance and have seen the end result of what the Lord *provided*.[1359] The Lord is full of mercy and compassion.

[12]Above all, my *Christian* brothers, do not swear, either by heaven or earth

---

1357 Jer. 9:13, Psa. 9:21 (LXX)
1358 "Hosts" here is literally the Greek word *Sabaoth* which means the heavenly armies.
1359 The Lord abundantly blessed Job because he endured. Cf. Job 42:10–17.

or anything else. Let your "yes" be yes and your "no" be no, lest you come under judgment.

A call to prayer

¹³Is anyone among you in trouble? Then he should pray. Is anyone happy? Then he should sing songs of praise. ¹⁴Is anyone among you sick? Then he should call for the elders of the church to pray over him and anoint him with oil in the name of the Lord. ¹⁵This prayer of faith will make the sick person well and the Lord will raise him up. If he has sinned then he will be forgiven. ¹⁶Therefore confess your sins to each other and pray for each other so that you may be healed. The prayer of a righteous man is both powerful and effective. ¹⁷Elijah was an ordinary man just like us. He prayed with determination that it would not rain and it did not rain for 3 ½ years. ¹⁸He prayed again and the heavens opened and it rained and the earth produced its crops.

¹⁹My *Christian* brothers, if one of you should wander from the truth and someone should bring him back ²⁰then remember this: Whoever turns a sinner from the error of his ways will save him from death and cover over a multitude of sins.[1360]

1360 James implies here that it is not only possible for a Christian to wander from the truth or backslide but to completely fall away. If someone can turn him from the error of his ways then that person has saved him from being spiritually and eternally separated from God.

1 PETER

Introduction

Peter wrote this letter in about AD 60 with the assistance of his scribe Silas (1 Peter 5:12) which is the reason that Peter's first letter is in fluent Greek in comparison to his second letter. This letter is addressed to the Jewish diaspora scattered throughout Minor Asia (Turkey) including Cappadocia with its myriad of volcanic tuff 'fairy castles' which persecuted peoples including Jews made homes in to avoid Roman persecution in the first century. The theme of 1 Peter is suffering for Christ where the word actually occurs at least 17 times. The Christian life is one of suffering because we live in a pagan and antagonistic world towards Christianity. This will only get worse as we head towards the final cataclysmic end. Peter encourages the scattered believers throughout the first century Roman Empire to persevere in their faith until the end.

1 ¹From Peter, an apostle of Jesus Christ, to God's chosen exiled people of the diaspora[1361] who are living in Pontus, Galatia, Cappadocia, Asia[1362] and Bithynia.[1363] ²You have been chosen according to the foreknowledge of God the Father, and you were made a holy people by *his* Breath to obey Jesus Christ and be purified by his blood.

May grace and peace be multiplied to you all.

Jesus is a sure and certain hope

³Blessed be the God and Father of our Lord Jesus Christ! Because of his great mercy, he has given us new birth by raising Jesus Christ from the dead. This causes us to be full of hope. ⁴He has also given us an inheritance that can never perish, spoil or fade away. He is keeping it in heaven for you. ⁵And because of your faith, the power of God guards you until the coming of the salvation that is ready to be revealed in the last time. ⁶You should be glad about these things, though at present for a short time you might be suffering from all kinds of trials. ⁷The purpose of these trials is so that your faith might be proved genuine. Even gold which can be destroyed is purified by fire but your faith is of far greater worth than gold. The result is that you will receive praise, glory and honour at the revelation of Jesus Christ. ⁸And although you have not seen him, you love him and even though you do not see him right now, you believe in him and are filled with an inexpressible and glorious happiness. ⁹You are very happy because you are receiving the goal of your faith, the salvation of your souls.[1364]

¹⁰The prophets carefully searched *the Scriptures* and investigated about this salvation thoroughly and they prophesied about this gift *of salvation* that was coming to you. ¹¹They tried to find out the exact time and circumstances

---

1361 A Greek word originally referring particularly to the nation of Israel which had been scattered throughout the ancient world. The ten northern tribes of Israel were exiled and taken away by the Assyrians in the eighth century BC. Nowadays this term can be used to refer to any dispersed or scattered people from their homeland. Because Peter wrote this letter c. AD 60-63 in the 1st century to the 'diaspora' it is more than likely Peter was writing to the scattered Jewish believers at the time as opposed to the Gentile church. This is also supported by the fact that Peter addresses the recipients of this letter as a 'chosen people' (Amos 3:2), a holy nation and a royal priesthood (Exo. 19:6). These are all references to Israel. Peter's primary goal was to reach the Jews while Paul's primary goal was to reach the Gentiles (Gal. 2:1–10). If this is the case then why would Peter write a letter addressed to Gentile believers? It is my conclusion that this letter should be reckoned against the backdrop that it is primarily for Jewish believers. But it must also be acknowledged that Gentile believers are also considered to be amongst 'the chosen' as well because they have been grafted into the tree upon salvation. The church does not replace Israel but together both Jew and Gentile are being built together to become a spiritual house or holy temple in the Lord (Eph. 2:21).
1362 This does not refer to the modern continent of Asia as we know it but to the western coast of modern-day Turkey encompassing the ancient cities of Ephesus, Smyrna and Miletus.
1363 Collectively all these regions were part of what became to be known as Asia Minor (Turkey).
1364 Notice here in this verse that salvation is being received in a present tense but there is also the aspect that salvation will only be complete at the end of time when Jesus comes back.

to which the Breath of Christ in them was referring to when it predicted the sufferings that Christ would experience and the wonderful things[1365] that would follow. ¹²*God* revealed to these *prophets* that they were not serving themselves but you when they spoke. They spoke of things that have now been told to you by those who have preached the gospel to you by means of Holy Breath having been sent from heaven. Even the angels would really like to understand these things.

God wants his people to live holy lives

¹³Therefore, set your minds ready for action. Be self-controlled and set your hope fully on the blessing *of salvation* which will be given to you at the revelation of Jesus Christ. ¹⁴As obedient children *of God*, you must not conform to the evil desires you had when you lived in ignorance. ¹⁵But just as *God* who called you *to salvation* is holy, so you must be holy in all that you do. ¹⁶For it is written *in the Scriptures*, "Be holy because I am holy."[1366]

¹⁷Since you call God, "Our Father" when you pray to him, knowing that he is totally impartial when he judges each man's work, live the rest of your lives here on earth with a deep awe and respect for God. ¹⁸For you know that your freedom from your former empty way of life from your ancestors was not paid with perishable items such as silver or gold. ¹⁹But it was paid with the precious blood of Christ, a lamb without blemish or defect. ²⁰Christ was known previously even before the overthrow of the world[1367] but was only revealed in these last times[1368] for your sake ²¹and it is through Christ that you believe in God. God is the one who raised him from the dead and glorified him and so, therefore, your faith and hope are in God.

Believers must love each other

²²Now since you have purified[1369] yourselves by obeying the truth and have come to have a genuine love for your fellow believers, make sure that you love

---

1365 This is literally the plural 'glories' in the Greek possibly indicating a series of victories or triumphs that followed Christ's sufferings on the cross. It may include his resurrection, exaltation to the Father's right hand, the gift of the Spirit to the church, the salvation of Gentiles with the Jews and his final return in victory on the Day of the Lord.

1366 This is a reference primarily to Israel (Lev. 11:44, 45; 19:2). Peter is reminding these scattered Jewish believers to be holy just as God reminded Israel to be holy after he rescued them out of Egypt. Two rescue missions pictured here: Salvation out of enslavement to Egypt and salvation out of sin. Therefore the exhortation is to be holy because of what he has done for us.

1367 Peter's point here is that Christ, the Son of God, was even known by Adam and Eve just before sin entered into the world.

1368 "Last times" here refers to the period beginning with the birth of Jesus extending to his second coming. A similar expression appears in Heb. 1:2.

1369 This meant ritual purification in the OT but in this context it refers to a moral and spiritual purification which is to be understood that the believers came to be delivered from the power of sin as they came to understand and obey the truth about Jesus Christ.

one another sincerely from the heart. ²³For you have been born again, not from seed that perishes but through the imperishable seed of the Word of God which is both living and everlasting. ²⁴For *the Scriptures say,*

> "All men are like grass and all their glory is like the flowers in the field.
> The grass withers and the flowers fall off.
> ²⁵But the word of the Lord endures forever."

Isaiah 40:6–8

This word is the good news that was preached to you all.

The Lord is building a spiritual house

2 ¹Therefore you must rid yourselves of all malice, deceit, hypocrisy, jealousy and every kind of bad language. ²You must crave pure spiritual milk like newborn babies so that *as you drink this milk* you may grow up in your salvation. ³For you have now discovered that the Lord is good.*¹³⁷⁰*

⁴As you keep coming to *the Lord,* who is the living Stone—rejected by men but precious and chosen by God, ⁵you also, like living stones, are being built into a spiritual house and a holy priesthood. You offer spiritual sacrifices acceptable to God through Jesus Christ. ⁶For in the Scriptures it says,

> "See, I lay a stone in *the city of* Zion, a chosen and precious cornerstone.
> The one who trusts in him will never regret it."

Isaiah 28:16

⁷Therefore to you who believe, this stone is precious. But to those who do not believe,

> "The stone that the builders rejected has become the cornerstone.
> And a stone that causes men to stumble and a rock that makes them fall."

Psalm 118:22

⁸Another *Scripture* says,

> "A stone that causes men to stumble and a rock that makes them trip."

Isaiah 8:14

They stumble because they disobey the message, which is what God meant for them.*¹³⁷¹*

1370　This is a quote from Psa. 34:8. In the Greek it is literally, "you have now <u>tasted</u> that the Lord is good." Some scholars think that this a reference to communion because Psalm 34 was considered to be a communion hymn in the early church.

1371　This is a difficult verse because it appears to be supporting hyper-Calvinism in saying that God

⁹But you *Israelites* are *God's* chosen race, a royal priesthood, a holy nation, a people¹³⁷² belonging to God. This was so that you might declare the wonderful acts of him who called you out of darkness and into his wonderful light. ¹⁰Once you were not a people, but now you are the people of God. Once you had not received mercy, but now you have received mercy.¹³⁷³

How Christians should live in the community

¹¹Dear friends, I encourage you as foreigners and exiles¹³⁷⁴ that you must abstain from the desires and passions of the old nature, the flesh, which war against the soul. ¹²You must live such good lives among the Gentiles that though they accuse you of being evildoers, they may see your good deeds and so glorify God on the Day of his visitation.¹³⁷⁵

¹³You must submit yourselves for the Lord's sake to every authority instituted among men. That is whether it be to the Emperor¹³⁷⁶ as the supreme authority *of the empire,* ¹⁴or to governors who have been appointed by *the Emperor* to punish evildoers and to praise those who do the right thing. ¹⁵For it is God's will that you should silence the ignorant talk of foolish men. ¹⁶You should live as free men but do not use your freedom as a cover for evil. Rather live as slaves of God. ¹⁷You must show proper respect to all mankind. Love the brotherhood of believers, fear God and honour the Emperor.

---

chooses some to stumble and disobey the message of the gospel. Rather, it is possible to see this verse in this light: if man chooses to disobey the message then it is a foregone conclusion and God's will that they will stumble. In other words it is not that God preordains some men to make it and others not to make it (stumble) but that it is his plan for men to stumble <u>if</u> they reject the gospel. Difficult verses like this must be taken into context with the rest of Scripture that say that God desires all men to be saved (1 Tim. 2:4) and none to perish (2 Pet. 3:9).

1372 The word for people here is *laos*, a term used for Israel in the OT to describe its intimate relationship with God (TH).

1373 This is from Hos. 1:9, 10; 2:23. In Hos. 1:10, God called Hosea's son *Lo-Ammi* (not my people) due to his rejection of the northern kingdom of Israel because of their rebellion and idolatry. But in v. 11 we see that God does not forget his promise to Abraham and in spite of Israel's sin, God would eventually bring all twelve tribes together again into one nation. This promise begins with the ministry of the end times Elijah and is ultimately fulfilled when Christ comes to reign in the future millennial kingdom. This makes so much sense considering that Peter is writing to Jewish Christians of the diaspora and encouraging them that God is fulfilling his promise despite the persecution they are experiencing in foreign lands. This does not mean that Gentile Christians are any less though because they too are part of the commonwealth of Israel and being built together with Israel into one spiritual house (Eph. 2:19–22). It is my opinion that 1 Pet. 2:9–10 should not be interpreted as referring to Gentile believers but instead Jewish Christian believers of the diaspora. In support of this is the fact that Christians aren't a nation or a race but a multitude of believers of every race and nation.

1374 A reminder that the Jewish Christians to whom this letter is addressed to, are living as the diaspora in Minor Asia as detailed in 1 Pet. 1:1.

1375 The Day of his visitation is the Day of the Lord when he returns to usher in the new millennial kingdom which I believe is exactly six thousand years after creation.

1376 This is literally 'king' in the Greek but Peter is referring to the Emperor (Caesar) of the Roman Empire at the time, Nero. Nero reigned as Emperor from AD 37–68.

Christ's example of suffering

¹⁸Household servants, you must submit to your masters with all due respect. Don't just submit to those masters who are good and considerate but you must also submit to those who are harsh. ¹⁹For it is commendable if a man endures the pain of unjust suffering because he is conscious of God. ²⁰How would it be to your credit if you receive a beating for doing something wrong and enduring it? But if you suffer for doing good and you endure it then this is commendable before God. ²¹It was to this *kind of suffering* that God called you to because Christ suffered for you. He thereby left you an example so that you must follow in his footsteps. ²²*The Scriptures speak about Christ as follows,*

"He committed no sin and there was never a lie upon his lips."

Isaiah 53:9

²³When *Christ* was insulted, he never retaliated. When he suffered, he made no threats. Instead, he entrusted himself to the one who judges rightly. ²⁴*Christ* himself bore our sins in his body on the tree. He did this so that we might die to sins and live good lives. By his wounds, you have been healed.[1377] ²⁵For you were like sheep going astray[1378] but now you have returned to the Shepherd and Protector of your soul."

Instructions in how wives and husbands are to treat each other

3 ¹In the same way[1379] *that servants are to be submissive to their masters,* wives are to be submissive to their husbands. This is so that if any of them are not believers, they may be won over without words by the behaviour of their wives ²when they see how pure and reverent your conduct is. ³Your beauty is not about the outward appearance such as hairstyle,[1380] the wearing of gold jewellery and the latest fashion trends. ⁴Instead your beauty should be about your inner self, consisting of an unfading beauty of a gentle and quiet spirit. This is of great worth in God's sight. ⁵For this is the way the holy women of the past who put their hope in God made themselves beautiful. They submitted themselves to their husbands, ⁶like Sarah, who obeyed Abraham and called him, "master."[1381] You are her daughters[1382] if you do what is right and do not give way to fear.[1383]

1377 Peter is quoting Isa. 53:5.
1378 Peter is quoting part of Isa. 53:6.
1379 This is almost certain referring back to 1 Pet. 2:18.
1380 This is literally 'braided hair' as this was the latest trend by Greco-Roman women in the 1st century AD where they intertwined their braids with chains of gold or strings of pearl.
1381 This is the Greek word *kurios* which also means 'lord'.
1382 A Semitic idiom meaning, "you are like Sarah".
1383 Possibly the fear here is referring to fear of their husbands.

⁷Husbands, in a similar manner you are to be considerate of your wives as you live with them. She is weaker than you and so you are to treat her with respect. She is an heir with you of the gracious gift of life. In this way, nothing will hinder your prayers.¹³⁸⁴

Instructions in how Christians are to treat each other

⁸In concluding you are all to be of one mind. Be sympathetic of each other and love each other as brothers should, also being compassionate and humble¹³⁸⁵ in attitude. ⁹Make sure that you do not repay evil with evil or insult with insult. But rather repay insult with blessing because you were called to do this so that you may inherit a blessing. ¹⁰For the *Scripture* says,

"Whoever loves life and would like to see good days, he must keep his tongue from evil and his lips from deceitful speech.
¹¹He must turn away from evil and do good and he must seek peace and pursue it.
¹²"For the Lord watches over good people and he listens to their prayers, but the Lord opposes those who like to do harm."

Psalm 34:12–16

Suffering for doing good

¹³Will anyone harm you if you are keen to do good? ¹⁴But even if you should suffer for doing what is right, you are blessed. Do not be afraid of them nor be troubled.¹³⁸⁶ ¹⁵But in your hearts acknowledge Christ as Lord. Make sure that you are always ready to give an answer to everyone who asks for the reason that you have hope. ¹⁶But do this with gentleness and respect. In doing this keep a clear conscience, so that those who speak woefully against your good conduct in Christ may be ashamed of themselves. ¹⁷It is *actually* better, if it is God's will, to suffer for doing good than for doing evil.

¹⁸For Christ also suffered for sins once, a good man for the guilty, in order to bring you to God. He was put to death physically yet having been made alive in spirit, ¹⁹in that *state*, he also went and preached to the spirits in prison.¹³⁸⁷ ²⁰Long

---

1384 The inference here seems to be that if husbands do not treat their wives properly and the relationship is broken then the husband's prayers will not be heard. In other words, a person's relationship with God is dependent on his relationship with others.
1385 Interestingly humility was not considered to be a virtue in the Hellenistic period.
1386 Cf. Isa. 8:12. Peter here is quoting Isaiah who was telling Israel not to be afraid of the King of Assyria but to fear God only. Assyria was the quintessential enemy of Israel in the OT. Its capital was Nineveh. At one stage they did repent when the prophet Jonah finally went there and declared that they would be destroyed if they didn't repent of their evil ways (Jonah 3:4–10).
1387 These spirits were the billions of people in Noah's day who did not listen to Noah's preaching

ago in the days of Noah, while the ark was being built, God waited patiently for these *people*[1388] but they were unconvinced. Only a few people were saved in the ark, eight in total, and they were saved through the water. ²¹And *in a way* this water symbolises baptism which now saves you also—not that the water removes dirt from the body but it is a promise of a good conscience towards God. It saves you because of the resurrection of Jesus Christ. ²²He has gone into heaven and is at the right hand of God with angels, authorities and powers in submission to him.

Living in a new way

4 ¹Therefore since Christ suffered *physically* in his body, equip yourselves also with the same attitude.[1389] For he who has suffered in his body is finished with sin.[1390] ²As a result then, you must live the rest of your earthly lives controlled by the will of God not by evil human desires. ³For you have spent enough time in the past doing what the Gentiles like to do—indecent sexual depravity, lust, drunkenness, orgies, drinking parties and detestable idolatry. ⁴They think it is strange that you do not participate with them into the same reckless and wild living and so they profane *the name of God* because of you. ⁵But they will have to give account to *God* who is ready to judge the living and the dead. ⁶This is the reason that *Christ* preached the gospel to those who are now dead[1391] so that they might be judged, as everyone is judged yet that they may live as God does, in spirit.

---

for one hundred years when he warned of coming judgment by a future worldwide flood. They remained unconvinced and didn't enter into the ark instead dying and being imprisoned in Hades. The big question here is what did Christ preach to these spirits in prison. If the gospel of grace been it means that these people effectively had a second chance of salvation after their death. If it was a proclamation of victory of what Jesus had achieved by his death then it was an explanation of sorts why they found themselves in this 'hell hole'. The same word used for preaching here is used in Rom. 10:14 and Acts 13:24.

1388 This refers back to the spirits who are now imprisoned after they died in the flood.
1389 What is the same attitude that Christians must have? We must resign ourselves to the fact that this life will indeed bring suffering on some level and that we must be ready to suffer as Christ suffered. One may draw the conclusion that suffering ultimately helps us to have victory over sin.
1390 This is probably a proverbial saying meaning that he who has suffered physically ceases from sinning because he no longer has the desire to keep sinning because of its deleterious effects.
1391 This probably refers to those spirits in prison in 1 Peter 3:19 when Christ proclaimed victory of the gospel.

Believers must use their gifts to serve each other

⁷The end of all things has drawn near.*¹³⁹²* Therefore be clear-minded and self-controlled so that you can pray. ⁸Above all else, you must love each other sincerely, because love covers over a multitude of sins. ⁹Be hospitable to each other without complaining. ¹⁰Each person should use whatever gift he has received in order to serve others. This is being a good steward of God's grace in its various forms. ¹¹And if anyone speaks, he should speak as one speaking the very words of God. If anyone serves, he should serve with the strength that God provides. This is so that in all things God may be praised through Jesus Christ. To him be the glory and the power forever and ever. Amen.

Christians will suffer just as Christ has suffered

¹²Dear friends, do not be surprised at the fiery ordeal that you are suffering through as though something strange was happening to you. ¹³But be glad that you are sharing in the sufferings of Christ, so that you may be full of joy when his glory is revealed. ¹⁴And if you are verbally abused because of the name of Christ, you are *in fact* blessed, for the glorious Breath of God is resting on you.*¹³⁹³* ¹⁵If you do *have to* suffer then it should not be as a murderer or thief or any other kind of criminal or even as a busybody *meddling in other people's affairs*. ¹⁶However, if you are suffering as a Christian, do not be ashamed, but praise God that you bear the name *of Christ*. ¹⁷For now is the time for judgment to begin with the household of God.*¹³⁹⁴* And if it begins with us, what will be the outcome for those who do not obey the gospel of God? ¹⁸*The Scriptures* say,

> "If it is difficult for good people to be saved then what will become of the ungodly and the sinner?"
>
> Proverbs 11:31

¹⁹Therefore those who are suffering according to God's will should commit themselves to their trustworthy Creator and continue to do good.

1392 It was the belief of the early Christians that they expected the world to come to an end perhaps very soon in the next day or month but very certainly in their own lifetime.

1393 It was part of Jewish eschatological belief that in the last days the Spirit of God will be given to God's holy people. Cf. Joel 2:28 (TH). Persecution was a sign that God's Spirit was upon them furthermore confirming the belief at the time that they were in the last days.

1394 Peter is somehow linking the persecution that the Jewish believers were experiencing in Asia Minor with the impending judgment of the end times (Luke 21:12–19). This stands to reason because the early 1st century believers were of the view that the return of Christ was extremely imminent (1 Pet. 4:7).

Instructions to the elders and young men of the church

5 ¹As an elder myself, I appeal to the elders among you. I am a witness of Christ's sufferings and I will share in the glory that is about to be revealed. I appeal to you ²to tend to God's flock which has been entrusted to you. You are to take care of the flock not because you have to but because you are willing as God wants you to. Do this, not being greedy for money but being eager to serve, ³not being overbearing to those entrusted to you, but being examples to the flock. ⁴And when the Chief Shepherd appears,[1395] you will receive the wreath of glory that is unfading.[1396]

⁵Young men, in the same way,[1397] you must submit to those who are older.

Instructions to the whole church

All of you clothe yourselves with humility towards one another, because *as the Scriptures say,*

"God opposes the proud but he gives grace to the humble."

Proverbs 3:34

⁶Humble yourselves, therefore, under God's mighty hand so that he might lift you up in due course. ⁷Commit all you worries to him because he cares for you.

⁸Make sure that you are alert and watching! Your enemy the devil is prowling around like a roaring lion looking for those whom he might devour. ⁹Resist the devil and remain firm in the faith. You know very well that your brothers *in Christ* throughout the world are undergoing the same kind of sufferings.

¹⁰And the God of grace, who called you to his eternal glory in Christ, will himself restore you, confirm your faith, strengthen you *mentally* and give you a firm foundation. But you must suffer for a little while first. ¹¹To him be the power forever and ever. Amen.

1395   It was the belief of the early church that Christ, the Chief Shepherd, would appear very soon even while these elders were still serving in their role at the time.

1396   This is derived from the Greek word *amaranth* which is the nutritious modern-day pseudo-cereal grain. The Greek word *amarantos* here means 'unfading'. This is because the amaranth flower does not generally wither and the reddish colour of the flower never seems to diminish even after it has died. It is also commonly known as 'pigweed'.

1397   This refers back to 1 Peter 3:1, 7 which reminds the readers of the general theme of submission.

Final greetings

¹²With the help of Silas whom I regard as a loyal brother *in the Lord*, I have written this short letter. I want to encourage you all and solemnly declare that *what I have written* concerns the real grace of God. Stand firmly in this *grace*.

¹³And the church in Babylon[1398] here, chosen just like you, sends you her greetings, and so does my *young helper*,[1399] Mark.[1400] ¹⁴Greet one another with a loving embrace.[1401]

Peace be to all of you who are in Christ.

1398 It is not clear which Babylon Peter is referring to. The choices include the real Babylon of Mesopotamia in the Middle East, another real Babylon in Egypt, symbolic Babylon meaning any place of exile, or Rome.
1399 Literally 'son'. But Mark wouldn't be Peter's literal son but 'son in the Lord' so to speak.
1400 This is possibly John Mark who was Paul's young companion on his first missionary journey to Asia Minor (Acts 12:12).
1401 Literally 'kiss'.

2 PETER

Introduction

As indicated by the title, the author of this letter is Simon Peter written around AD 66–67 shortly before his martyrdom in Rome. The writing style in his second letter is a lot different than his first letter supposedly because he didn't have the help of Silas in this letter. In this letter, Peter reminds his readers not to be scoffers and that the Day of the Lord is coming soon. Here Peter repeats the Old Testament formula that a day is like a thousand years and a thousand years like a day. This reminds us that God will only contend with man for 6000 years or six prophetic days until Jesus returns again. Peter warns against false teachers as in his first letter.

1

¹From Simeon[1402] Peter, a servant and apostle of Jesus Christ, to those who through the goodness of our God and Saviour Jesus Christ have received a faith as precious as ours.

²May grace and peace be multiplied to you all through the knowledge of God and Jesus our Lord.

Make your calling and election certain

³*Christ* through his divine power *as God* has given us everything that we need for life and godliness which is possible because we have come to know God. He is the one who has called us to share in his glory and excellence. ⁴In this way *God* has given to us very important and precious promised gifts so that through these *gifts* you might be able to share in the divine nature *of God* and be free of the corruption of the world caused by evil passions.

⁵Therefore for this very reason you must all make a concerted effort to supplement your faith with moral excellence and to moral excellence, knowledge, ⁶and to knowledge, self-control and to self-control, perseverance and to perseverance, godliness ⁷and to godliness, a *mutual* brotherly love and to brotherly love a love *for others*.[1403] ⁸For if you possess these qualities in abundance, they will enable you to be effective and productive in your knowledge of our Lord Jesus Christ. ⁹But if anyone does not have them, he is blind, being short-sighted and forgetful that he has been cleansed from his past sins.

¹⁰Therefore *my Christian* brothers,[1404] be very eager to make your calling and election certain.[1405] For if you do these things, you will never fall *away from the faith*. ¹¹Furthermore you will receive a rich welcome into the eternal reign of our Lord and Saviour Jesus Christ.

¹²Therefore I intend to keep reminding you of these things, even though you already know them and have been firmly grounded in the truth.[1406] ¹³I think that it is the right thing to refresh your memories as long as I am still living in this tent—my body. ¹⁴I know that I shall be leaving this bodily tent very soon as our

---

[1402] Simeon is the Hebrew variant of the Greek form Simon. This is possibly used in this letter to reinforce the Jewish nature of the letter as it is clear that the audience of this letter is the same Jewish audience of the first letter (2 Peter 3:1).

[1403] Interesting to note that the list starts with faith and ends with love—the two bookends!

[1404] This letter is addressed, like 1 Peter, to the scattered Jewish believers of the diaspora abroad in Asia Minor (Turkey). Peter has in mind his Jewish brothers who believe in Jesus Christ.

[1405] Election is the prior decision to select someone from a wider group (for example, God selecting Israel out of the nations to be his people), while call is the actual process of inviting potential elected individuals to share in the privileges and responsibilities of their election. Gentiles become part of the elect of the commonwealth of Israel as they respond to the invitation or call of the gospel.

[1406] Peter is referring back to his first letter. Many of the themes that Peter discussed in his first letter are raised again in his second letter to the Jewish Christians.

Lord Jesus Christ has made clear to me. ¹⁵I will make every effort to see to it that after I am gone, that you will always be able to remember these things.[1407]

The apostles were eyewitnesses of Christ's glory

¹⁶We[1408] did not follow cleverly invented stories when we told you about the power and coming of our Lord Jesus Christ, but we actually saw him and his majesty with our own eyes.[1409] ¹⁷Jesus received honour and glory from God the Father when there was a voice coming to him from the Majestic Glory, saying, "This is my Son, my Son whom I love. I am very pleased with him." ¹⁸We ourselves heard this voice coming from heaven when we were with him on the holy mountain.[1410]

¹⁹Therefore we are even more confident of the word of the prophets of old. You would do well to pay attention to it as you would to a light shining in the darkness until the day dawns and the morning star rises in your hearts. ²⁰Most important is that you must understand that no prophecy of Scripture[1411] is according to one man's own interpretation. ²¹For no prophecy ever had its origin in the will of man, but men spoke from God as they were moved by Holy Breath.

Warning about false teachers

2 ¹There were however false prophets that appeared among the people, just as there will be false teachers among you. They will secretly introduce destructive heresies and they even deny the Master who had set them free.[1412] In doing so they bring swift destruction upon themselves. ²Many people will follow their immoral lifestyle and will bring the way of truth into disrepute.[1413] ³These false teachers will take advantage and profit from you with made-up stories because they are greedy. For a long time now their Judge and Destroyer has been ready and wide awake to judge and punish them.

⁴For God did not spare the angels when they sinned but sent them to Tartarus,[1414] where they are kept chained in darkness waiting for judgment.

1407 "These things" refers to the content of Peter's letters.
1408 This is Peter and the other apostles excluding the readers of the letter.
1409 Peter is referring to when the three disciples saw Jesus on the mountain of his transfiguration.
1410 Cf. Matt. 17:1.
1411 This refers to the OT and in particular prophecy in the OT.
1412 This implies that the false prophets were previously saved (redeemed).
1413 This is saying that many in the Christian community will follow the immoral lifestyle of the false teachers and so outsiders will blaspheme or ridicule the Christian way of life.
1414 In classical Greek mythology *tartarus* was an abyss under the earth reserved for the punishment of rebellious gods and human beings. There is a Greek legend to the effect that the Titans, ancient giants, were imprisoned in Tartarus. This legend forms the background for the reference in 1 Enoch regarding fallen angels taking human wives and thus giving birth to evil giants (TH). According to Greek mythology, Hades is the underworld in its entirety whereas Tartarus is one of the realms within Hades. It may well be that Tartarus is the same abyss mentioned in Rev. 9:1–11 out of which

⁵God did not spare the ancient world when he brought the flood on its ungodly people, but he protected Noah, who was a preacher of righteousness, and seven others. ⁶God condemned the cities of Sodom and Gomorrah by reducing them to ashes. He made them an example of what is going to happen to the ungodly. ⁷He rescued Lot, a good man, who was worn down by the lack of moral restraint by evil men. ⁸For that good man lived day in and day out amongst them and he was tormented in his soul as he heard and saw their evil deeds. ⁹Therefore the Lord surely knows how to rescue godly men from trials and to keep the wicked under punishment until the day of judgment.[1415] ¹⁰This is especially true of those who chase after the lustful excesses of the human nature and those who despise authority.

These *false teachers* are reckless and arrogant, not afraid to insult even heavenly beings. ¹¹Yet even angels, though they are stronger and more powerful *than these men*, do not bring slanderous accusations against such beings in the presence of the Lord. ¹²But these men blaspheme in matters they do not understand. They are like wild animals acting only by instinct, born only to be captured and killed. They will be killed like wild animals.

¹³Indeed, these *false teachers* will be paid back with harm for the harm that they have done themselves. They take pleasure in having wild parties in broad daylight. They are like blots and blemishes causing you disgrace because they party wildly while eating with you. ¹⁴They always have wandering eyes waiting to commit adultery. They are always looking for opportunities to sin. They prey on weak *Christians*. They are experts in greed—they are cursed. ¹⁵They have left the straight path and have gone astray. They have followed the way of Balaam, the son of Beor, who loved the money he received from doing the wrong thing. ¹⁶But *Balaam* was scolded by his donkey for his wrongdoing which spoke with a man's voice and restrained the prophet acting like a madman.

¹⁷These false teachers are like dry bores that have no water and like dry storms that contain no moisture. *God* has reserved the blackest darkness for them. ¹⁸For they speak bombastic nonsense, appealing to the carnal[1416] desires of the sinful human nature, enticing *recent converts* who are in the process of escaping from those living in error.[1417] ¹⁹They promise the *recent converts*

---

is released a demonic horde of locusts at the sound of the fifth trumpet.
1415   The Day of Judgment is the final day on earth as we know it, referred to in the OT as the Day of the Lord, during which time God will judge all nations and bring punishment on the wicked (TH).
1416   Cf. 1 Cor. 3:1 footnote.
1417   How do the false teachers use bombastic nonsense to entice new Christians? It seems in their teaching they have justified indulgence in immoral acts by presenting these sexual acts as legitimate expressions of Christian freedom. And since this kind of life characterizes those who belong to pagan religions, those who are most easily affected by this attitude are the new converts (TH).

freedom, but they themselves are actually slaves of depravity. A person is a slave to whatever conquers him. ²⁰If these *recent converts* have escaped the corruption of the world by knowing our Saviour Jesus Christ but then become entangled and overcome by sin again, then they are worse off at the end than they were at the beginning. ²¹It would have been better for them not to have known the *Christian* way of life than to have known it and then subsequently turn their backs on the holy commandment[1418] that was given to them. ²²The proverbs are true that speak of these *false teachers*: "A dog returns to its vomit," and "A pig that is washed goes back to wallowing in the mud."[1419]

The Lord is coming back

3 ¹Dear *Christian* friends, this is now my second letter to you. I have written both of these letters as reminders in order to stimulate you to have clean thinking. ²Please remember the words spoken in the past by the holy prophets and the command from us, the apostles of the Lord and Saviour.

³The first thing that you must understand is that in the last days scoffers will come who are controlled by their own evil desires. They will scoff at you by ⁴saying, "What of the promise that he would come? Ever since our ancestors died,[1420] everything goes on as normal as it has since the beginning of creation."[1421] ⁵But what these *scoffers* lose sight of is the fact that long ago, the heavens existed and the earth was formed by the word of God. The earth emerged out of water and through the water. ⁶Then later by these very same waters, the world at that time was flooded and destroyed. ⁷By the very same word of God, the present heavens and earth are reserved for fire. They are being kept for the day when the ungodly will be judged and destroyed.

⁸But you must not forget this one thing, dear friends: With the Lord, a day is like a thousand years and a thousand years like a day.[1422] ⁹The Lord is not slow

---

1418 The body of Christian teaching as a whole emphasising on moral and ethical standards.
1419 The message of both proverbs is clear: the false teachers had once become clean through the forgiveness of their sins, but they have now gone back to wallow in the immorality and wickedness that characterized their pagan past (TH). The dog and pig were both unclean animals to the Jew.
1420 This possibly means, ever since the first generation of Christian ancestors had died because Peter wrote this letter some 35 years or so after the death of Christ.
1421 Peter predicts that in the last days, the dominant thought will be evolution. This is the evolutionary concept of 'uniformitarianism' which says the same natural laws and processes that operate in the universe now have always operated in the universe in the past and apply everywhere in the universe. It includes the gradualistic concept that 'the present is the key to the past' and is functioning at the same rates resulting in the earth being nearly 5 billion years old. However, evolution, the theory, is only 200 years old. The term 'uniformitarianism' was coined by William Whewell in the 1800's (Van Kampen, Robert, *The Sign* (2000), p. 171).
1422 Cf. Psa. 90:4. The psalmist (Moses) also says that 1000 years is like 'a watch in the night'. A watch lasted for 4 hours equal to ⅙ of a 24 hour day. This is the mathematical key to understanding that God will only contend with man for six days or six millennia (6000 years). Gen. 6:3 says that God

in concerning his promise, as some may see it. *No, he is patient with you all not wanting anyone to perish but for everyone to turn to God.*[1423]

[10] But the Day of the Lord will come unexpectedly as when a thief comes. Then the heavens will disappear with a crackling roar and the elements will melt and be destroyed in the heat. Everything that is in the earth will no longer exist.

[11] Since everything will be destroyed in this way, what kind of people should you be? You should be living holy and godly lives [12] as you anticipate and eagerly wait for the coming day of God. This is the day in which the heavens will burn up and be destroyed and the heavenly bodies will melt in the heat. [13] But in keeping with God's promise we are waiting for new heavens and a new earth where righteousness dwells.[1424]

Patience is needed for the Lord to return

[14] So my friends, as you wait for these things to occur, you must strive to be found spotless, blameless and at peace with him. [15] Keep in mind though that our Lord's patience means salvation. This is just as our dear brother Paul also wrote to you with the wisdom that God gave to him. [16] In fact, Paul writes the same way in all of his letters concerning these matters.[1425] His letters do contain some things that are indeed difficult to understand and unlearned and weak people twist his teachings as they do the other Scriptures. They do this to their own destruction.

[17] Therefore dear friends, since you already are aware of this, you must be on your guard so that you may not be carried away by the error of men who lack moral restraint. [18] But keep growing in the grace and knowledge of our Lord and Saviour Jesus Christ. To him be glory both now and forever! Amen.

---

would only strive with man for a further 120 years before the flood but it likely has a secondary interpretation meaning 120 Jubilee cycles (120x50=6000 years). The Jubilee year is the 50th intercalated year after seven sabbatical cycles. God would cause the land to produce enough crops to last for three years (Lev. 25:20–22). Cf. Isa. 37:30—sign to King Hezekiah during the Assyrian invasion.

1423   I.e. In the EDV, 'repentance' is translated as turning away from sin and/or turning to God.
1424   Cf. Rev. 21:1 footnote.
1425   The total collection of Paul's letters is at least 13, possibly 14 letters including Hebrews.

1 JOHN

Introduction

Five books are identified with the Apostle John: a gospel; three letters and the Book of Revelation. Although John does not identify himself as the writer of this letter, many second century witnesses affirm that John, one of the original twelve followers of Jesus, was the writer. The date of writing is around AD 85–90 just before the Book of Revelation. The recipients of this letter are undesignated and there are no greetings or specific locations, persons or events in this letter which would help to identify these facts. However the most likely location is that John wrote this letter from his residence in Ephesus to a number of churches in the local area in which he had apostolic authority over.

The big issue in this letter that John addresses is the problem of false teaching and the imposter Gnostic assemblies in the province of Asia Minor. He addresses the heresies that denied Jesus is the Messiah, that Jesus not only just appeared human but he actually came in the flesh, and that holiness was not necessary in the Christian life. John calls these false teachers "antichrists" (1 John 2:18) but also this is the only mention in the NT of the eschatological Antichrist or beast to come.

John uses his typical key words of "light", "truth", "believe", "born of God", and "eternal life" which helps to further prove that this letter was indeed written by the Apostle John himself.

The apostles were eye-witnesses

1 ¹We proclaim to you the one who existed from the beginning,[1426] the one whom we have heard and have seen with our eyes. We saw him and our hands have touched him—he is the Word of Life.[1427] ²Indeed the *Word of* Life was made visible and we have seen him and we testify to this fact. We proclaim to you the eternal *Word of* Life who was with the Father and was made visible to us. ³We proclaim to you all what we have seen and heard so that you also may have fellowship with us. And our fellowship is with the Father and with his Son, Jesus Christ. ⁴We write these things to you so that your joy may be complete.

God is light

⁵This is the message we have heard from him and declare to you all: God is light and in him there is no darkness at all. ⁶If we say that we have fellowship with *God* yet we walk in the darkness, then we are lying and we are not acting in the truth. ⁷But if we walk in the light, as he is in the light, then we have fellowship with one another, and the blood of Jesus his Son cleanses us from all sin.

⁸If we claim to be without sin then we are deceiving ourselves and we are not being truthful to ourselves. ⁹If we continue to admit to our sins,[1428] *God* can be relied upon to be fair and he will forgive us our sins and will cleanse us from all wrongdoing. ¹⁰If we say that we have not sinned then we are making him out to be a liar which means that his word is not in us.

Jesus Christ advocates for us

2 ¹My dear children, I am writing this letter to you in order that you will not sin. However if anybody does sin, we have one who advocates for us to the Father—Jesus Christ, the Righteous One. ²He atoned for our sins by his sacrifice and not only for ours but also for the sins of the whole world.

³And if we continue to obey *Jesus'* commands[1429] then we can be sure that we have really come to know him. ⁴The one saying, "I know him," but does not do what *Jesus* commands is a liar and is not being truthful to himself. ⁵However the one who obeys his word, God's love has been perfected in him. This is how

---

1426 This refers to the beginning of creation. Gnosticism denied the pre-existence of Christ, but here John says that Jesus existed from the beginning.
1427 A title of Christ. Cf. Heb. 4:12.
1428 By admitting to God that we still continue to sin, we are showing our humility before God and our fellow-man. This does not refer to 'confessing' each and every sin to God as a prerequisite to forgiveness because that is an impossibility. We'll never remember every sin we commit. One reason is because we often sin without realizing it. The Psalmist said, "But who can discern their own errors? Forgive my hidden faults" (Psa. 19:12).
1429 Jesus outlined his commands in the Sermon on the Mount (Matt. 5–7).

we can be sure that we are in him. ⁶If we claim to be remaining in *Jesus* then we must walk as he walked.

The new command

⁷Dear friends, the command I am writing to you about is not a new one but an old one which you had from the beginning. This old command is what you have in fact already heard. ⁸Yet the command I am writing to you about, is *in a way*, new. Its truth is seen in *Jesus* and in you because the darkness is fading away and the true light is already shining.

⁹Anyone claiming to be in the light but hates his brother, is still in the darkness. ¹⁰Whoever loves his brother lives in the light and there is nothing in him to cause him to be offended. ¹¹But whoever hates his brother is in the darkness and walks around in darkness. He does not know where he is going because the darkness has blinded him.

¹²I am writing to you, my dear children,*1430* because your sins have been forgiven through the name of *Jesus Christ*.*1431*

¹³I am writing to you, fathers, because you have known him who has existed since the beginning.*1432*

I am writing to you, young men, because you have overcome the evil one.

I am writing to you, my dear children, because you have known the Father.

¹⁴I am writing to you, fathers, because you have known him who has existed since the beginning.

I am writing this to you, young men, because you are strong, and the word of God lives in you and you have overcome the evil one.

¹⁵You must not love the world or anything in the world. If anyone loves the world then the love of the Father is not in him. ¹⁶For everything in the world—the desire of the flesh, the desire of the eyes, and the pride that comes in life, does not come from the Father but from the world. ¹⁷The world and its desires are passing away but the one who does the will of God lives forever.

Warning against many antichrists

¹⁸My dear children, we are in the last hour.*1433* You have heard that

---

1430 John addresses the church as a whole and then proceeds to address two age-groups. No recipients are listed in this letter from the Apostle John but most likely is that John wrote from his residence at Ephesus to a number of churches in the province of Asia over which he had apostolic oversight. This is most likely a circular letter.

1431 The Greek verb *apheontai* (have been forgiven) is in the perfect tense indicating that an action or event completed in the past (Christ's payment for sin on the cross) has relevance for the present situation (believers are presently forgiven of their sins). Cf. 1 John 1:7.

1432 In the beginning was the Word (i.e. Jesus).

1433 Obviously this does not refer to an hour (60 minutes) but it is a Hebrew way of saying that we are in

Antichrist[1434] is coming, but I say to you that many antichrists[1435] have come which is how we know that it is the last hour. [19]These *antichrists* went out from among us but they were not of us. For if they were truly of us they would have remained with us.[1436] But the reason that they left was so that it could be seen that none of them belonged to us.

[20]But you have an anointing[1437] from the Holy One[1438] and so all of you know the truth. [21]I am not writing to you because you do not know the truth but I am writing to you because you do know it and because you also know that no lie ever results because of the truth. [22]Who then is the liar? It is the man who denies that Jesus is the Messiah. Such a man is the antichrist—he denies the Father and the Son. [23]The *assembly* denying the Son does not have the Father but whoever acknowledges the Son has the Father also.

[24]Make sure that what you have heard from the beginning remains in you. If it does, you will also remain in the Son and in the Father. [25]And this is what he promised us—eternal life.

[26]I am writing these things to you about those who are trying to lead you astray.[1439] [27]As for you, you have received an anointing from Christ. This anointing remains in you and you do not need anyone to teach you. He teaches you about all things and what you have been taught is true not false, so make sure that you remain in *Christ*.

[28]My dear children, continue on in him so that when he appears we may be confident and unashamed at his coming. [29]You know that Christ is righteous. Therefore you should also know that the *assembly* that does what is right has been born of *God*.

The true assembly versus the Gnostic assembly

3 [1]Look how truly great is the love that the Father has given to us in that we should be called the children of God as in fact we are. The reason that the world does not know us is that the world has never known him. [2]My dear friends, we are now God's children and what we shall be is not yet clear. But we know that

---

the very last days of the age as we know it. In modern parlance we are '100 seconds to midnight!'
1434   This is the only place in the NT where the term 'Antichrist' is used to describe the coming beast of the abyss in the last 3 ½ years of this age. 'Anti' means 'instead of' or 'against' not false (*pseudo*).
1435   This refers to the false teachers and imposters whom John and his readers had been fellowshipping with in the churches.
1436   This verse proves that OSAS is incorrect. When a person comes to Christ they must remain and continue on in their faith until the very end. In John's language they must learn to be overcomers.
1437   A commissioning or empowering using oil. Literally means 'to pour ointment on'. Christ is the Anointed One because he was specially commissioned to do his Father's work.
1438   I.e. Jesus.
1439   I.e. Gnosticism.

when *Christ* appears, we shall be like him for we shall see him as he is. ³And the *assembly* who has this hope in *Christ* purifies itself, just as he is pure.

⁴But the *assembly* who practices sin also breaks the law. In fact, sin is lawlessness. ⁵And you all know that *Christ* appeared so that he might take away our sins and that in him is no sin. ⁶No *assembly* who *truly* abides in him keeps on sinning but the *assembly* that continues to sin has neither seen him or has known him.

⁷My dear children, do not let anyone lead you astray. The *assembly* that does what is right is righteous, just as *Christ* is righteous. ⁸The *assembly* which does what is sinful is of the devil, because the devil has been sinning from the beginning. The reason the Son of God appeared was to destroy the works of the devil. ⁹The *true assembly*, because it has been born of God will not continue on sinning because his seed[1440] remains in it. It cannot go on sinning because it has been born of God. ¹⁰Therefore this is how we know who the children of God are and who the children of the devil are. The *assembly* who does not do what is right is not born of God nor is anyone who does not love his brother.

Loving one another

¹¹The message that you have all heard since the very beginning is that we must love one another. ¹²Do not be like Cain who was of the evil one and murdered his brother.[1441] Why did he murder him? It is because his own actions were evil and his brother's were righteous.

¹³Do not be surprised, *Christian* brothers, if the world hates you. ¹⁴We know that we have passed from death to life *proven* by the love that we have for the brothers. The one not loving *his brother* remains in death. ¹⁵The *assembly* who hates his brother is a murderer and you all know that no murderer has eternal life in him.[1442] ¹⁶This is how we know what love is: *Jesus Christ* laid down his life for us. And so we ought to lay down our lives for our brothers. ¹⁷If anyone has

---

1440 Gk: *sperma*. Sperm contains non-material information in the physical medium of the DNA that is transferred from father to child when they are conceived so that the child by nature is a product of his/her parents hence the idiom, 'like father, like son'. This does not mean that God has a physical sperm/seed literally dwelling in believers but it is talking about the spiritual or non-material information of God's nature that abides in those who are born again. For further study read Dr. Werner Gitt's book, *In the beginning was information*.

1441 This is a genitive construction with the possibility that Cain was the literal child of the devil/serpent. Because Cain and Abel were twins (Gen. 4:1), there is a theory that Cain is the result of a union between the serpent and Eve and Abel the result of the union between Adam and Eve. Paul describes Eve as being completely seduced by the serpent (2 Cor.11:3, 1 Tim. 2:14). In Gen. 3:20, Eve is described as being the 'mother of all the living' whereas Adam is never described as being the 'father of all the living'. Cf. John 8:44. Furthermore later rabbinic texts claim that Cain's father was a bad angel, even the devil himself (Keener, Craig S, *IVP Bible Background Commentary* (1993)).

1442 Hate is closely related to murder with hate being the first step. Cf. Matt. 5:21.

material possessions and sees his brother in need but has no pity on him, how can the love of God be in him? ¹⁸My dear children, let us not love *just* with words or talk but with actions and in truth.

¹⁹This then is how we know that we belong to the truth and how we can have assurance of his presence *in our lives*: ²⁰When our hearts condemn us *of our sins* God is greater than our hearts and he knows everything.[1443] ²¹My dear friends, if our hearts do not condemn us, then we can approach God with confidence. ²²And we receive from him anything that we ask for because we obey his commands and do that which pleases him. ²³And this is his command: We must believe in the name of his Son, Jesus Christ and we must love one another just as he commanded us. ²⁴And those who obey his commands abide in him and he in them. And this is how we know that he abides in us: he has given his Breath to us.

Testing the spirits

4 ¹My dear friends, do not believe everyone who claims to have the Breath *of God* but test the spirits to see whether the spirit they have is of God or not. This is because many false prophets have gone out into the world. ²This is how you can recognise the Breath of God: Every spirit that acknowledges Jesus Christ as having come in the flesh is of God.[1444] ³But anyone who denies that Jesus Christ has come in the flesh is not of God. This is the spirit of the Antichrist which you have heard is coming and even now is already in the world.[1445]

⁴My dear children, you are from God and you have overcome these *false prophets* because the one who is in you is greater than the one who is in the world. ⁵They are of the world and therefore speak from the perspective of the world and the world listens to them. ⁶However we are of God and whoever knows God listens to us but whoever is not of God does not listen to us. This is how we can know the spirit of truth and the spirit of delusion.

God is love

⁷My dear friends, we must love one another for love comes from God. The *assembly* who loves has been born of God and knows God. ⁸And whoever does not love does not know God because God is love. ⁹This is how God showed his

---

1443 I.e. When we are weighed down by sin, we are reassured that God is present because his mercy is greater than our conscience.
1444 John is countering the false teaching of the Gnostics which said that Jesus did not come in the flesh because they believed that the flesh was inherently evil. The goal of Gnosticism was to escape the body and so death was not enemy but release.
1445 We don't have to wait for the final Antichrist to be revealed at the halfway point of the 70th week for the diabolical consequences of his reign of terror. It is already at work and he will be the final culmination of all the work that is being done in preparation for his arrival. Evil and wickedness is gaining traction as we move closer to the final 3 ½ years. Cf. 2 John 7.

love for us: He sent his one and only[1446] Son into the world that we might have life through him. ¹⁰This is love: not that we loved God but that he loved us and sent his Son as an atoning sacrifice for our sins.

¹¹My dear friends, since God so loved us, we also ought to love one another. ¹²No one has ever seen God. However if we love one another God lives in us and his love is perfected in us.[1447]

¹³By this we know that we live in him and he in us, because he has given his Breath to us. ¹⁴Furthermore we have seen and testify to the fact that the Father has sent his Son to be the Saviour of the world. ¹⁵If anyone acknowledges that Jesus is the Son of God, then God lives in him and he in God. ¹⁶And we have known and have believed the love that God has for us.

God is love. Whoever continues to live in love lives in God and God in him. ¹⁷And so in this way, love is made perfect in us so that we can have confidence on the day of judgment. We can have confidence because we live in this world as did Christ. ¹⁸There is no fear in love, but perfect love drives out fear because fear has to do with punishment. The one who fears has not been perfected in love.

¹⁹We love because he first loved us. ²⁰If anyone says that he loves God yet he hates his *Christian* brother then he is a liar. For anyone who does not love his brother whom he can see with his eyes, how can he love God whom he has not seen? ²¹Christ has given this command to us: Whoever loves God must also love his brother.

Overcoming the world

5 ¹The *assembly* that believes that Jesus is the Messiah has been born of God and every one of them which loves the Father loves the one he begat as well. ²This is how we know that we love the children of God: we love God and carry out his commands. ³How do we love God? We obey his commands and really his commands are not too much trouble. ⁴For the *assembly* that has been born of God overcomes the world. We are victorious in overcoming the world when we *exercise* our faith. ⁵Who keeps on overcoming the world? It is only him who keeps believing that Jesus is the Son of God.

1446 This is the Greek adjective *monogenes* derived from *monos* meaning 'only' and the noun *genos* meaning 'kind, class'. The term literally means 'one of a kind' or 'unique'. Many of the older English translations translate this as 'begotten' which is incorrect. (Heiser, Michael S, *The Unseen Realm* (2015), pp. 36–37) Cf. Heb. 11:17.
1447 The world should see the evidence of God in us by seeing the love that we have for each other.

Life is in the Son

⁶Jesus Christ is the one who came by both water[1448] and blood.[1449] He did not come by water only but by water and blood. The Breath of God is the one testifying to this because the Breath is the truth. ⁷For there are three witnesses: ⁸The Breath, the water and the blood and all three are in agreement.

⁹If we accept man's testimony then how much greater is the testimony of God which he has given about his Son? ¹⁰Anyone who believes in the Son of God *knows* in his *heart* that this testimony is true. Anyone who does not believe God has made him out to be a liar because he has not believed the testimony God has given about his Son. ¹¹This testimony says that God has given to us eternal life and this life is in his Son. ¹²He who is having *fellowship with* the Son has the life but the one not having *fellowship with* the Son of God does not have the life.

Assurance of salvation

¹³I wrote these things to you who believe in the name of the Son of God so that you may know that you have eternal life. ¹⁴We can approach God with confidence knowing that when we ask anything according to his will that he hears us. ¹⁵And if we know that he hears us we can be sure that we can have what we ask for, whatever it is.

¹⁶If you see your *Christian* brother commit a sin that is not mortal in the sense that it leads to death[1450] then you should pray and God will grant him life.[1451] This applies to those who have not committed a mortal sin[1452] but there is such a thing as a mortal sin that does lead to death. Now, I am not saying that you should pray about that *sin*. ¹⁷All wrongdoing is sin and there are many sins that do not lead to death.

¹⁸We know that the *assembly* having been born of God does not continue on sinning. The one who was begotten out of God keeps the *assembly* safe and the evil one cannot harm it. ¹⁹You and I know that we are of God even though the whole world is under the control of the evil one. ²⁰And we also know that the Son of God has already come and he has given to us understanding so that we can know the true and genuine God. We live in union with the true God and in union with his Son, Jesus Christ. This is the true God[1453] and eternal life.

²¹Dear children, you must keep away from false idols.

1448 Water refers to Jesus' baptism at the River Jordan at the beginning of his ministry.
1449 Blood refers to Jesus' blood shed at his crucifixion at the end of his ministry.
1450 Eternal or spiritual death.
1451 Eternal life.
1452 There is a sin so serious that it leads to an eternal death sentence and a person who commits this sin is beyond recovery. The only sin which meets this criteria is unbelief resulting in the abandonment of faith.
1453 John is saying that the Father is the true God, not Jesus in this context.

2 JOHN

Introduction

Five books are identified with the Apostle John: a gospel; three letters and the Book of Revelation. Although John does not identify himself as the writer of this letter, the writer identifies himself as 'the elder', a title of honour probably given to John during the last two decades of his life. The recipient of the letter is "the chosen lady and her children", probably a metaphorical reference to a local church and its members. This letter is written in the same timeframe as John's other two letters around AD 85–95.

Once again John addresses the issue of false teaching and denounces it as in 1 John. Paul commends the "chosen lady" for walking in truth and in love, favourite subjects for John. 2 John is the shortest book in the NT.

¹From the elder,[1454]

To the chosen lady and her children,[1455] whom I truly love. And not just me but everyone who knows the truth love you, ²because the truth lives in us and will be with us forever.

³Grace, mercy and peace shall be with us from God the Father and from Jesus Christ, the Father's Son, in truth and love.

⁴I was very happy to hear that some of your children are living in truth just as the Father has commanded us to do.[1456] ⁵However now dear lady, I am not writing you a new command but one we have had from the beginning. I am asking that we love one another. ⁶And this is love, that we live in obedience to his commands. As you have heard from the beginning, his command is that you live being *grounded* in love.

⁷Many deceivers have gone out into the world—these men have not acknowledged that Jesus Christ came in the flesh. Such a person is the deceiver—the antichrist.[1457] ⁸Watch out that you[1458] do not lose what you have worked for so that you may be rewarded in full. ⁹The *assembly* which goes beyond and does not continue in the teaching of Christ does not have God. However the *assembly* which continues in the teaching has both the Father and the Son. ¹⁰If anyone comes to you and does not bring this teaching, do not receive him into your house[1459] or welcome him. ¹¹Anyone who welcomes him shares in his wicked work.

¹²I have much to write to you all about but I do not want to use pen and paper.[1460] Instead, I am hoping to visit you and talk with you face to face which would make us both happy.

¹³The children of your chosen sister[1461] send their greetings.

1454 Here John the Apostle refers to himself as the elder indicating that he wrote this letter towards the end of his life.
1455 Probably a metaphorical reference to a local church and its members.
1456 Apparently some of the congregation were living in truth whilst some were living in error. In other words, the implication is that there was a church split with dissension.
1457 This is not referring to the final end-times Antichrist, the beast of Revelation. I believe what John is saying here is that people who do not acknowledge that Jesus was the promised Messiah or Christ have the spirit of the final Antichrist and Deceiver (Satan) similar to 1 John 4:3.
1458 TR (KJV, NKJV) has the 1st person plural 'we' indicating John and his helpers instead of 'you'. In other words this verse indicates that we must be diligent in not falling away thereby losing one's salvation because of the deception mentioned in the previous verse.
1459 In context this probably refers to the home assembly as the early church met in houses but a modern-day application would be receiving Mormons or Jehovah's Witnesses into one's home.
1460 Literally papyrus and ink.
1461 The phrase refers to the members of a sister church, the congregation from which John is writing.

3 JOHN

Introduction

Five books are identified with the Apostle John: a gospel; three letters and the Book of Revelation. As in John's second letter, he identifies himself as "the elder". This personal letter is addressed to a loyal believer named Gaius, probably a member of one of the local churches in Asia Minor where John lived. Late in the first century, itinerant ministers would travel from city to city and were put up by believers in their homes. John wrote to commend Gaius for his faithful hospitality and support.

This letter gives an important insight into the features of the early church. In John's second letter, he urges that hospitality and support not be given to untrustworthy ministers whereas in this letter, John commends the support and hospitality of trustworthy travelling ministers.

¹From the elder,

To dear Gaius,¹⁴⁶² whom I truly love.

²My dear friend, I pray that you are going well and that you are in good health—I know that you are keeping well mentally. ³It gave me great joy to have the *Christian* brothers come and tell me about your loyalty to the truth and how you continue to live in the truth. ⁴I have no greater joy than to hear that my children¹⁴⁶³ are living in the truth.

⁵My dear friend, you are so loyal in the work you do for the brothers even though they are strangers to you. ⁶They have told the church *here* about your love. Please send them on their way in a manner pleasing to God.¹⁴⁶⁴ ⁷For it was for the sake of the Name¹⁴⁶⁵ that they went forth taking nothing from the Gentiles. ⁸We must show hospitality to such men so that we may work together for the truth.

⁹I did *in fact* write a letter to the church, but Diotrephes, who loves to be in charge,¹⁴⁶⁶ does not receive us. ¹⁰So if and when I do come, I will call him out on what he is doing and the malicious gossip *being spread* about us. And not satisfied with that, he refuses to welcome the brothers. He also stops those who want to do so and forces them out of the church.

¹¹My dear friend, do not imitate what is evil but imitate that which is good. Anyone who does what is good is of God. Anyone who does what is evil has not seen God.¹⁴⁶⁷

¹²Everyone speaks well of Demetrius¹⁴⁶⁸ even the Truth itself. We also speak well of him and you know that our testimony is true.¹⁴⁶⁹

¹³I have much more to write to you about but I do not want to use pen and ink. ¹⁴I am hoping to see you soon and we will speak face to face.

Peace be with you. The friends here send their greetings. Greet the friends there by name.

1462   This letter is addressed to Gaius, a very common name, who apparently is a very good friend of John's. There is no reason to link him with the Gaius's mentioned in Acts 19:29, 20:4, 1 Cor. 1:14 or Rom 16:23.
1463   Not John's physical children but his children in the faith so to speak.
1464   In other words, help them with money, food and provisions to make their journey easier.
1465   This refers to the Tetragrammaton (Yahweh) although no Jew knows exactly how to pronounce this. 'Yahweh' and 'Jehovah' are Christian inventions. In daily conversation, most Jews use the name 'HaShem' which literally translates to 'The Name' in reference to his true name.
1466   Apparently Diotrephes was a kind of gate-keeper not allowing any instruction or influence into his church.
1467   An idiom meaning that this person does not have an intimate relationship or fellowship with God.
1468   Demetrius was probably the messenger sent by John to deliver this letter to Gaius, since his initial letter sent to the whole assembly was rejected by Diotrephes.
1469   There are three witnesses giving testimony to Demetrius: everyone, the Truth (Holy Breath) and the writer himself which is in accordance with the rule of the Jewish Law quoted in 1 John 5:8. A matter is established by two or three witnesses (Deut. 19:15).

JUDE

Introduction

Jude identifies himself as being the brother of James. Jude is probably Judas, the half-brother of Jesus along with James (Matt. 13:55). Jude wrote his letter around AD 70–80 placing it as the second last book in the NT canon of Scripture. Jude wrote his letter to believers warning them against false teachers urging them to defend the faith.

Interestingly Jude mentions that these false teachers are 'twice dead' which means that they once believed but have turned away from the faith having gone back to being dead again. One can only be 'twice dead' if one can apostatize and lose one's salvation which turns OSAS on its head. Another interesting verse is v. 9 which mentions that the devil and Michael the Archangel disputed over the dead body of Moses. This has interesting implications in that the dead body of Moses seems to be very important, I believe, in the final days when Jesus mentions that the location of 'the' dead body or carcass marks the gathering point for the rapture just before Jesus returns in victory. It is a missing piece making the letter of Jude very important.

¹ This letter is from Jude, a servant of Jesus Christ and a brother of James.*1470* To those who have been called and who are loved by God the Father and kept by Jesus Christ.

² Mercy, peace and love be yours in abundance.

Watching out for false teachers in the church

³ Dear friends, although I was very eager to write to you about the salvation we have in common, I felt compelled to write about another matter: I urge you to defend the faith that was passed down once and for all to God's holy people.*1471* ⁴ For certain men have secretly slipped in amongst you who were written about long ago and rightly condemned. They are godless men who change the grace of our God into an excuse for indecent sexual depravity and they also deny Jesus Christ our only Master and Lord.

How God deals with those who rebel

⁵ Even though you already know all of this, I want to remind you that Jesus*1472* rescued his people out of Egypt but later destroyed those who did not believe. ⁶ Remember also the angels who did not keep their own sphere of authority but abandoned their own home.*1473* The Lord has kept these ones in darkness, bound with everlasting chains for judgment on the great day.*1474* ⁷ In a similar way, Sodom and Gomorrah and the surrounding cities gave themselves up to sexual immorality and perversion in a like manner to these *angels*. They serve as an example of those who suffer the punishment of eternal fire.

⁸ In the very same way, these *godless* men*1475* are just dreamers, living immoral lives because they reject authority and insult celestial beings. ⁹ For even Michael the archangel, when he was disputing with the devil about the body of Moses, did not dare to bring a blasphemous accusation against him.*1476* Rather he said, "The

---

1470 Likely the half-brother of Jesus along with James (Matt. 13:55).
1471 This means that the faith was given only once, and that when it was handed down, it was complete, and therefore it should be handed down to future generations without any change. The false teachers were changing the message.
1472 The oldest MSS have 'Jesus' here whereas some have 'Lord'.
1473 This almost definitely refers to Gen. 6:1-4 which says that the sons of God (watcher angels—1 Enoch 8) took the daughters of men as wives which was a sexual perversion producing the Nephilim or giants. This was probably the reason for Noah's flood.
1474 Cf. 2 Pet. 2:4.
1475 The false teachers referred to in v. 4.
1476 The story about Michael and the devil fighting over the body of Moses is not found in the OT, which simply states that the burial place of Moses is not known by anyone (Deut. 34.6). However, in a composition called *The Assumption of Moses* (written about the 1st century AD), it is related that, when Moses died, Michael was given the task of burying the body. The devil, however, claimed power over the body, since he was lord of the material order. When Michael refused to hand the body over, the devil threatened to accuse Moses of being a murderer for having killed the Egyptian (as recorded in Exo. 2.12). Michael, however, did not respond by rebuking the devil, but simply

Lord rebuke you!" ¹⁰However these men attack with insults anything that they do not understand. They do however have the understanding of wild animals knowing only the natural instincts which results in them being punished. ¹¹Disaster is coming to them! They have followed Cain's way.[1477] They have rushed for profit into Balaam's error[1478] and they will be destroyed like Korah when he rebelled.

¹²These *godless* men are like partially submerged jagged rocks at your love feasts. They eat with you without the slightest fear and are like shepherds who take care only of themselves *and not their sheep*. They are like clouds without rain, blown along by the wind. They are like trees that should be bearing fruit in season but do not. They will be uprooted—twice dead.[1479] ¹³These men are also like the wild waves of the sea, churning up the foam of the shameful deeds.[1480] They are like wandering stars for whom the blackest darkness has been reserved forever.[1481]

¹⁴Enoch, seventh in line from Adam, prophesied about these men when he said, "Look, the Lord is coming with thousands upon thousands of his holy ones ¹⁵to judge everyone and to convict all the ungodly acts they have done in the ungodly way. He will judge all of the harsh words ungodly sinners have spoken against him."[1482] ¹⁶These men are whingers and faultfinders living only to gratify their own desires. They boast about themselves and flatter others for their own advantage.

---

proceeded to bury Moses with his own hands (TH). Why is the body of Moses so important? It may have implications for the location of the rapture of Christians at the end of the seven year tribulation because in response to the disciple's query "Where, Lord?" in Luke 17:37, Jesus replied the vultures/eagles will gather or circle where the dead body is. I believe this is a veiled reference to Moses' dead body being the location for the rapture point somewhere on Mt Nebo. If the devil could claim the dead body then the rapture could be blocked and his ultimate defeat ten days later at the final battle at Jerusalem could be avoided.

1477 In 1st century Jewish thought, Cain was the epitome of self-interest, treachery and materialism.

1478 Balaam was a false prophet and teacher who misled the youth of Israel for his own gain when he received a bribe from Balaak (Num. 22–24).

1479 Having returned to the state they were in before they became Christians, they are in a sense twice dead, the first death being the time before they accepted the Christian message and the second time because they have reverted back to their former state. These people will be uprooted because they are fruitless like the tree that bears no fruit—useless.

1480 When the sea is stormy and wild, foam typically washes up on the shore which contains dirt, muck. In the same way these godless men are scattering their abominations everywhere resulting in confusion of Christians and the Christian message.

1481 In the ancient world the planets were always a mystery because of their irregular movements, which seemed to violate the orderly rules of movement in space. These irregular movements were explained as originating from the disobedience of the angels who controlled these planets, and who were punished by imprisonment (TH). The point here of course is that false teachers and godless men have strayed off course like the planets appear to.

1482 Jude is quoting from the apocryphal book 1 Enoch. This book was widely accepted by Jews and Christians alike and was even considered as authoritative by some church authorities in the second century AD. Cf. Rev. 1:4 footnote.

Jude warns Christians

¹⁷But my dear friends, remember what the apostles of our Lord Jesus Christ foretold. ¹⁸They said to you, "In the last days there will be scoffers who will follow their own ungodly desires." ¹⁹These are the men who divide you. They follow mere natural instincts and do not have *God's* Breath.

²⁰But you, my dear friends, build yourselves up in your very holy faith, praying as *God's* Breath leads. ²¹Keep yourselves in God's love as you wait for the mercy of our Lord Jesus Christ to bring you into eternal life. ²²Be merciful to those who doubt ²³and snatch others from the fire *as it were* and save them. To others show mercy, mixed with fear even hating the clothing stained by corrupted flesh.[1483]

Benediction

²⁴To him who is able to keep you from falling and to present you faultless before his glorious presence with great joy ²⁵and to the only God and Saviour may there be glory, majesty, power and authority both now and forever. Amen.

[1483] Here we more than likely have a figure of speech known as hyperbole, or exaggeration. The idea seems to be that these people are so sinful and so evil that even the very clothes they wear are affected and defiled (TH).

REVELATION

Introduction

The Book of Revelation was written by the Apostle John in about AD 96 and was the last book written as part of the NT. The seven first century churches are located in modern-day Turkey and so they were seven actual churches. But they also represent a prophetic look at the seven kinds of churches in existence in the end times. A template into how the reader is to divide the Book of Revelation is given in Rev. 1:19. It is a prophetic and futuristic account with ties to many books of the OT including Ezekiel, Daniel, Joel, Zephaniah and Zechariah to name but a few.

The book has a heptatic structure (meaning seven). The three sets of seven judgments that John has a vision of do not occur sequentially except within their own series. The scroll (seven seal judgments) covers the entire eschatological scenario from Rev. 6:1 to Rev. 22:9 with the trumpet judgments happening in the same timeframe. The seven bowls of wrath judgments however occur just before the Day of the Lord. The number seven occurs 54 times in the book and it refers to completeness or totality.

The prophecies in the book are sometimes hard to understand and often have speculative and varied interpretations none greater than those who try to calculate a known historical figure with the number 666. Speculation has ranged from Antiochus Epiphanes in the second century BC to Nero in the first century, Teitan (from Irenaeus), Adolf Hitler and King Charles III. You will find my conclusions in the various footnotes.

There are many views in how to interpret eschatology, the main ones being pre-millennial, amillennial, and post-millennial. Personally I take a pre-millennial, post-tribulational view of the end times which you will find supported in many of my comments. The prophecies in this book are yet to be fulfilled and Jesus is returning for a second time at the end of the 70th week to usher in his millennial reign—that is good news indeed!

1 ¹This is the revelation of Jesus Christ which God gave him so that his servants can learn about the things that must take place quickly. He made it known by sending his angel to his servant John ²and he reported all that he saw. It is a message from God and a recording of the true events as revealed by Jesus Christ. ³Blessed[1484] is the person who reads the words of this prophecy and those who hear it and retain what is written in it because the time is near.

To the seven churches

⁴From John[1485] to the seven churches[1486] in Asia:[1487] Grace and peace to you all from him who is, and who was, and who is to come. Grace and peace also comes from the seven spirits[1488] before his throne ⁵and from Jesus Christ, who loyally reveals the truth about God. He is the firstborn *Son*, the first one to be raised out of death and he is the ruler over all the chiefs and kings of the earth.

To him who loves us all and has freed us from our sins by his blood ⁶and has made us to be a people under his rule—priests, so that we may serve his God and Father. To him be glory and power forever and ever. Amen.

⁷Look! He is coming in the clouds. Every person will see him, including those who pierced him.[1489] All the peoples of the earth will mourn because of him. So shall it be! Amen.

⁸The Lord God said, "I am the Alpha and the Omega, the one who exists now, the one who has always existed and the one who will always exist. I am the Almighty.

Someone resembling a man

⁹I, John, your *Christian* brother and follower of Jesus, I also share in the tribulation with you all and am patiently waiting for God's reign to come as you are. I was sent to the island of Patmos[1490] because I was preaching the word

---

1484 The first in a series of seven blessings in the Book of Revelation. The number seven is a recurrent theme in the book. Cf. Rev. 14:13 for the second blessing.
1485 The Apostle John written in AD 96 from visions received while exiled on the island of Patmos off the southern coast of modern-day Turkey.
1486 The seven churches represent a cross-section of churches in Minor Asia in the 1st century but possibly also a cross-section of all churches throughout the church age and in the very last days.
1487 Asia here is the region of southwestern modern-day Turkey known as Asia Minor.
1488 The seven spirits here are likely the seven archangels who minister before the throne of God listed in the apocryphal book 1 Enoch 20:1–8: Gabriel; Michael; Raphael; Uriel; Racquel; Remiel; and Saraquel. David E Aune in his Revelation commentary believes this is the correct view. Enoch is quoted in Jude 14. Cf. Rev. 3:1.
1489 This is a quote from Zech. 12:10 and reflects the idea that those responsible for Jesus' death, either the Jewish religious leaders in Jerusalem or the Roman authorities responsible for the piercing of his side. It may be all of them as well.
1490 The island of Patmos was a small island about 100 km southwest of Ephesus in the Aegean Sea that was a Roman penal colony at the time.

of God and the truth about Jesus. ¹⁰On the Lord's Day,¹⁴⁹¹ I was in spirit *form* when I heard behind me a loud voice that was as loud as a trumpet. ¹¹The voice said, "Write everything that you see on a scroll and send it to the seven churches: to Ephesus, Smyrna, Pergamum, Thyatira, Sardis, Philadelphia and Laodicea."

¹²I turned around to see the person who was speaking to me and having turned around I saw seven golden lampstands. ¹³Amongst the lampstands was someone resembling a man who was dressed in a long robe reaching down to his feet and with a golden sash around his chest. ¹⁴His head and hair were white like wool, as white as snow and his eyes were like blazing fire. ¹⁵His feet were like fine shining bronze as in a glowing furnace, and his voice was like the sound of raging waters. ¹⁶In his right hand, he held seven stars and out of his mouth came a sharp two-edged sword. His face was like the sun shining at full strength.

¹⁷When I saw him, I lay face down at his feet *and did not move* as though I was dead. Then he placed his right hand on me and said, "Do not be afraid. I am the first and the last. ¹⁸I am the living one. I was dead and now I am alive forever and ever! And I hold the keys of Death and Hades.¹⁴⁹²

¹⁹"Therefore you must write down what you have seen and what will be after this.¹⁴⁹³ ²⁰The mystery of the seven stars that you saw in my right hand and the seven golden lampstands is this: The seven stars are the angels of the seven churches; the seven lampstands are the seven churches.¹⁴⁹⁴

To the church at Ephesus

2 ¹"To the angel¹⁴⁹⁵ of the church in Ephesus¹⁴⁹⁶ write this:

1491 Most likely this means the first day of the week, Sunday, the day that the Lord was resurrected. A few translations translate this as 'Day of the Lord' which appears to be a mistranslation. Pre-tribbers use this to support the view that the Day of the Lord begins at the beginning of the last seven year tribulation period and continues on for a period of time.

1492 Literally this is *Thanatos* and *Hades* who are two Greek gods. In Greek mythology, *Thanatos* was the Grim Reaper or personification of death itself whereas *Hades* was the god of the underworld. Whereas *Thanatos* was a minor Greek figure, *Hades* in contrast was the boss. *Thanatos* was like a courier transporting the dead to *Hades*, the underworld. *Hades* or the Hebrew equivalent, *Sheol*, were sometimes pictured as underground cities with locked gates preventing the dead from leaving. So in effect what Jesus is saying here is that he has the authority and power to open and shut these gates because he holds the keys.

1493 This verse probably gives a template into how the reader is to divide the Book of Revelation: what John saw and then the interpretation of that particular symbol or vision. This interpretation is from the original Hebrew MSS of Revelation (Sodot). *The Pulpit Commentary* and *Exegetical Helps on Revelation* allow this view also.

1494 There were many other churches in the region including Miletus, Colossae, and Hierapolis but the seven churches of Revelation in Asia Minor seem to be a representation or prototype of the seven kinds of churches in existence throughout the church age with a particular focus on the last seven years before Christ returns. Some commentators say that the seven churches represent a kind of prophetic timeline starting with Ephesus in the 1st century and Laodicea in the 21st century.

1495 This is *angelos* ('angel' in English). It simply means messenger and could either refer to an angel or an actual human messenger such as a pastor who took the letter to the church.

1496 Ephesus (modern-day Efesus) was probably the mother church where all the others were planted

These are the words of him who holds the seven stars in his right hand and walks among the seven golden lampstands: ²I know the kind of life you have lived, your hard work and your perseverance. I know that you do not tolerate evil men and that you have tested those who claim to be apostles, but they are not because you have found them out to be lying. ³You have persevered and have endured hardships for my name's sake and have not grown tired.

⁴Yet I do hold this against you: You have forsaken your first love. ⁵Never forget the height from which you have fallen! Turn from your sins and do the things that you did at first. If you do not turn from your sins, I will come to you and remove the lampstand from its place.[1497] ⁶But you have this in your favour: You hate the practice of the Nicolaitans,[1498] which I also hate.

⁷He who has an ear, let him hear what the Holy Breath is saying to the churches: To him who overcomes, I will give him the right to eat from the tree of life, which is in the paradise[1499] of God.

To the church at Smyrna

⁸"To the angel of the church in Smyrna[1500] write this:

These are the words of him who is the first and the last, the one who died and came back to life. ⁹I know the tribulation you are going through and that you are poverty-stricken yet *really*, you are *spiritually* rich. I know that those who falsely accuse you say they are Jews[1501] yet they are not *Jews in the true sense*. In fact, they belong to the synagogue of Satan. ¹⁰Do not be afraid of what you are about to suffer. Watch out! The devil is going to put some of you in prison

---

	from and was a Roman city with a population of 200,000 to 300,000 people.
1497	This means that Christ will come and remove the community of believers from that place. Interestingly the ancient city of Ephesus was one of only three cities in the ancient world to have street lighting in its harbour street. However Ephesus gradually declined in importance after the nearby Cayster River silted up despite constant dredging. The modern-day shoreline is now 5 km away from the original harbour. Although Ephesus still retained its importance to Christianity for a few centuries, it was completely abandoned by the 15th century thereby seemingly fulfilling this prophecy. They had lost their first love—Christ!
1498	What was the practice of the Nicolaitans? Probably came from Nicolas in Acts 6:5 who was the sole Greek of seven deacons in the Jerusalem church. Supposedly he was the originator of an early heresy named after him. He started a teaching which sought to compromise between Christianity and certain pagan practices such as freedom to commit sexual immorality. Nicolas apostatised from the Apostolic faith by embracing the teachings of Plato and blending this with Christianity.
1499	Originally this word is an ancient Persian word meaning a 'walled garden' like a fruit orchard. It became a way for speaking about heaven and is transliterated from Persian to Greek now English.
1500	Smyrna (modern-day Izmir) is a Turkish city by the coast.
1501	There was a large population of Jews in Smyrna but John (being a Jew himself) was probably referring to Christians as being the true people of God.

to test you all[1502] and you will suffer persecution for ten days.[1503] Be loyal *to the Lord*, even to the point of death and I will reward you victorious with eternal life.

¹¹He who has an ear, let him hear what the Holy Breath is saying to the churches: He who overcomes will not be hurt at all by the second death.

To the church at Pergamum

¹²"To the angel of the church in Pergamum[1504] write this:

These are the words of him who has the sharp, double-edged sword. ¹³I know where you live—Satan has his throne there yet you remain true to my name. You did not abandon your faith in me even when Antipas, my loyal witness, was killed there *in Pergamum*, where Satan lives.[1505]

¹⁴Nevertheless, I do have a few things against you: You have people there who hold to the teaching of Balaam, who taught Balak to entrap the Israelites to sin by eating food sacrificed to idols and to commit sexual sins. ¹⁵Likewise you also have people there who hold to the teaching of the Nicolaitans. ¹⁶Change your mind! Otherwise, I will soon come and I will fight against them with the sword that comes up out of my mouth.

¹⁷He who has an ear, let him hear what the Holy Breath is saying to the churches: To him who overcomes, I will give some of the hidden manna.[1506] I will also give to him a white pebble[1507] with a new name written on it which is only known to him who receives it.

To the church at Thyatira

¹⁸"To the angel of the church in Thyatira[1508] write this:

1502   The test could be dual fold. For the devil's purposes he would like the church of Smyrna to renounce their faith whereas God perhaps will be testing the genuineness of their faith.
1503   Cf. https://luke21.com.au/the-ten-days-of-persecution.
1504   Pergamum (modern-day Bergama) was an important religious centre. Asclepius—the ancient Greek god of healing was worshipped nearby. When the kingdom of Pergamum became part of the Roman Empire in 133 BC, the city of Pergamum became the capital of the province of Asia. It was in Pergamum that the process of turning animal skins into parchment was developed; the word 'parchment' is derived from the name Pergamum. There was a huge library of some 200,000 volumes housed in Pergamum second only to Alexandria in northern Africa.
1505   According to some sources, Antipas the Bishop of Pergamum was martyred in the hollow bronze bull on the altar of Zeus in Pergamum. He refused to worship the Roman Emperor.
1506   This simple promise reflects a popular Jewish belief that the jar full of manna that had been stored in the Covenant Box (Exo. 16:32–34; Heb. 9:4) was believed to have been hidden by Jeremiah in a cave on Mount Nebo after the destruction of the temple (2 Mac. 2:4–8). It would remain there until the Messianic age, when God would once more feed the people with it (TH).
1507   In the ancient Greek courts, judges would acquit a person by throwing a white pebble into an urn and convict a person by throwing in a black pebble. So a white pebble would seem to indicate a vote of acquittal (Cockburn, Sir A J E, *Stories from Greek history* (1923), p. 41).
1508   Thyatira (modern-day Arkhisar) was an industrious city famous for its dyeing and manufacture of woollen goods. It was not a poor place but valued prosperity and equal opportunity. Nonetheless it was probably the least important of the seven cities. It was southeast of Pergamum, halfway between

These are the words of the Son of God, whose eyes are like blazing fire and whose feet are like fine shining bronze. ¹⁹I know all about your hard work, your love and faith. I also know how you serve one another, how you are persevering and that now you are doing more than you did at first *when you started to believe.* ²⁰But I do have this against you: You allow that woman Jezebel¹⁵⁰⁹ *in your midst*, the one calling herself a prophetess. She teaches and misleads my servants into sexual immorality and to eat food sacrificed to idols.¹⁵¹⁰ ²¹I have given her time to turn away from her sexual immorality but she is unwilling. ²²And so I will throw *this Jezebel* onto *her* sickbed and she will really suffer along with those who commit adultery with her unless they turn to God. ²³I will strike her followers dead. Then all the churches will know that I am someone who knows the thoughts and intentions of everyone. I will repay each of you according to your works. ²⁴Now to the rest of you in Thyatira, the ones who do not hold to her teaching and have not learned Satan's so-called deep secrets as it were, I won't burden you with anything else. ²⁵But you must hold on firmly *to your faith* until I come.

²⁶To him who overcomes and does my will to the end, I will give my authority over the nations—

²⁷'He will rule them with a rod of iron, shattering them like ceramic pots.'

Psalm 2:9

I will give the same authority just as I have received from my Father. ²⁸I will also give him the morning star.¹⁵¹¹ ²⁹He who has an ear, let him hear what the Holy Breath is saying to the churches.

---

      it and Sardis. Thyatira's most prominent citizen was Lydia (Acts 16:14).
1509 Jezebel here is a metaphor for wickedness and evil. She is the epitome of the wicked woman.
1510 The same false teaching as that of the Nicolaitans for the churches of Ephesus and Pergamum.
1511 The morning star is probably the planet Venus, a symbol of victory and domination. Victorious Roman generals built temples in honour of Venus, and the sign of Venus was on the standards of Caesar's legions. The meaning here is that it is a reward for being victorious.

To the church at Sardis

3 ¹"To the angel of the church in Sardis[1512] write this:

These are the words of him who has the seven spirits of God and the seven stars.[1513] I know all about your hard work. You have a reputation of being alive but in fact, you are dead. ²Wake up! Strengthen what you still have before it dies completely. For I have found that what you have done so far is not yet perfect in God's view. ³Therefore remember the teachings you have received and heard. Turn from your sins and obey these teachings. If you do not wake up, I will come like a thief and you will not know at what time I will come to you.

⁴However there are a few people in Sardis who have not dirtied their clothes. They will walk with me dressed in white for they are worthy. ⁵To him who overcomes, he will be dressed in white like them. I will never blot out his name from the book of life[1514] but I will acknowledge his name before my Father and his angels. ⁶He who has an ear, let him hear what the Breath *of God* is saying to the churches.

To the church at Philadelphia

⁷"To the angel of the church in Philadelphia[1515] write this:

These are the words of him who is holy and true, he who holds the key of David.[1516] What he opens no one can shut and what he shuts no one can open. ⁸I know your works. Look! I have set before you an open door that no one can shut.[1517] I know that you do not have a lot of strength yet you have kept my word

---

1512 Sardis (modern-day Sart) was south of Thyatira, and was the ancient capital of the Lydian empire in western Turkey. It was on the Royal Road during Persian rule which became the most important link between the West and the East. The first coins known to man were minted and made at Sardis.

1513 In 1 Enoch 48:2–10 God is referred to as the 'Lord of Spirits' several times whereas here Jesus is the 'Lord of Spirits'. Cf. Rev. 4:5. The seven spirits of God are a heavenly reality while the seven stars are a symbol of that heavenly reality (Aune, David E, *52a Word Biblical Commentary Revelation 1–5* (1998), p. 219).

1514 The book of life is a metaphor for eternal life. Ancient Israel had a roll of citizens (Isa. 4:3) and Athens and some other Greek cities had the custom of erasing from the rolls the names of citizens executed by the state. Cf. Psa. 69:28, Rev.20:12, Rev. 22:19.

1515 There are very few ruins in Philadelphia (modern-day Alashehir) to speak of. The region was in a fertile valley where some of the best grapes in Asia Minor grew. Philadelphia was famous for its wine. The city must have been somewhat prosperous because it was known as "Little Athens" during the Roman period and also after an earthquake in AD 17. The city was a border city but it had no natural defences. There was probably not a particularly large number of Christians in this place.

1516 A symbol of authority probably referring to David's promised future Messianic kingdom.

1517 This means that there is some sort of opportunity or open door for the Philadelphian church that isn't available for the others. What that opportunity is, is not clear. Some commentators think that it is the opportunity to preach the gospel and others say that no one will be able to stop them from entering into the Messianic kingdom. It is interesting, however, that the Philadelphian church receives the best commendation and seems to be the only church that will be protected from the

and have not denied my name. ⁹Listen! I will make those who belong to the synagogue of Satan, those who claim to be Jews but are not, I will make them come and prostrate themselves¹⁵¹⁸ before you. I will make them acknowledge that I have loved you. ¹⁰Since you have kept my instruction to endure patiently, I will also keep you *safe* within¹⁵¹⁹ the hour of trial¹⁵²⁰ that is going to come upon the whole world to test the inhabitants of the earth.

¹¹I am coming soon. Hold onto what you have so that no one will take away your reward of victory. ¹²To him who overcomes, I will make him a pillar in the temple of my God. Never again will he leave it. I will write on him the name of my God and the name of the city of my God (the New Jerusalem coming down out of heaven from my God) and my new name. ¹³He who has an ear, let him hear what the Breath *of God* is saying to the churches.

To the church at Laodicea

¹⁴"To the angel of the church in Laodicea¹⁵²¹ write this:

These are the words of the Amen, The Loyal, The True Witness and The Beginning¹⁵²² of God's creation: ¹⁵I know your works, that you are neither cold nor hot.¹⁵²³ I wish you were either one or the other! ¹⁶So, because you are lukewarm and neither hot nor cold, I am about to spit you out of my mouth. ¹⁷You say, 'I am rich and well off. I do not need anything.' But you do not realise how pathetic, pitiful, poor, blind and naked you really are. ¹⁸I advise you to buy from me gold refined in the fire so that you might be rich. Buy also white¹⁵²⁴ clothes

---

	tribution period seeming to indicate that their passage into the Messianic kingdom is assured.
1518	An act of submission meaning that they have been defeated.
1519	The small Greek preposition, (*ek*) is very important here. It means out from the middle of. In other words, it demands that you have to be in the trial before you can be taken out of it. It doesn't demand that this church will escape the seven year tribulation period altogether. Supporting this is Robert Mounce who says in his commentary on this verse, "It is precisely because the church was faithful to Christ in time of trial that he in turn will be faithful to them in the time of their great trial" (Mounce, R H, *The Book of Revelation (NICNT)* (1997)). Jesus also said, "I am not asking that you take them out of the world but that you protect them from the evil one" (John 17:15). It is preservation in the trial that is taught.
1520	I.e. the last 3 ½ years—the Great Tribulation. Cf. Rev. 14:7.
1521	Laodicea, south of Philadelphia, was famous for its wealth. It was a city situated where three highways converged famous for its textiles and particularly its black wool. This brought a wealthy banking sector. They also had a medical school that was famous the world over for its manufacture of ear and eye ointments. They produced it in tablet form and shipped it the world over. Laodicea also lay on a fault-line so earthquakes were common in this area. Cf. Col. 2:1 footnote.
1522	"The Beginning" is a title of Christ (Cf. Col. 1:18).
1523	A judgment on the church's spiritual condition likened to their distance from the source of the cold refreshing waters of Colossae and the hot healing waters of Hierapolis. They were not fulfilling any useful purpose neither being refreshing or healing rather it was a 'lukewarm' church.
1524	White here probably symbolises spiritual purity.

to wear so you can cover your shameful nakedness and ointment for your eyes so that you can see.[1525]

[19]Those whom I love, I correct and discipline. So be enthusiastic and turn from your sins. [20]Listen up! I stand at the door and knock. If anyone hears my voice and opens the door, I will come in and eat with him and he will eat with me.[1526]

[21]To him who overcomes, I will give him *the honour* to sit with me on my throne, just as I overcame *the enemy* and sat down with my Father on his throne. [22]He who has an ear, let him hear what the Breath *of God* is saying to the churches."

John sees the throne room in heaven

4 [1]After these things I saw a door in heaven which was open. And the man with the voice I had first heard speaking to me like a trumpet said, "Come up here and I will show you what must happen after this." [2]Immediately I was in spirit *form* when there in front of me was a throne in heaven with someone sitting on it. [3]The one who was sitting there had the appearance of jasper[1527] and carnelian.[1528] Surrounding the throne there was a rainbow *glowing* like an emerald.[1529] [4]Also surrounding the throne were 24 other thrones and seated on them were 24 elders.[1530] They were dressed in white and had golden wreaths[1531] on their heads. [5]And from out of the throne, flashes of lightning came forth, sounds and the rumbling sound of thunder. In front of the throne, seven torches

---

1525 The three things they are advised to buy will meet their pitiable condition of poverty, blindness, and nakedness (TH).
1526 Often this verse is interpreted as being that Jesus is asking the individual to open the door of his heart to be invited in as an offer of salvation. But the context is clearly not Jesus pleading with an individual to be saved, rather He's seeking admittance to a church! Jesus is standing outside of the church and knocking. The Laodicean church had shut the door on Jesus as they were quite self-sufficient. This was borne out when the city was destroyed in AD 60 by an earthquake. They were so wealthy and self-sufficient that they had no need of funds from Rome to rebuild.
1527 Jasper (SiO_2) is semi-precious silica stone which is opaque and has vitreous or glass like appearance perhaps resembling a diamond. It portrays God's absolute purity and perfection. Jasper was the first gem on the Jewish high priest's garment and could be either green, red, yellow or brown.
1528 Carnelian (SiO_2) is a ruby red semi-precious gemstone portraying God as our redeemer. Carnelian was the last gem on the Jewish high priest's garment. Jasper and carnelian reinforce the image that God is the first and the last.
1529 The point of comparison is not the colour of an emerald but its brilliance. A rainbow when viewed from the air is a circle not the normal arch that is seen when one is on the ground.
1530 There is no consensus amongst scholars as to the identity of the 24 elders. The possibilities are heads of the twelve tribes and the twelve apostles. In Judaism there were twenty-four priestly courses so it may be a symbol for continuous 24-hour worship, day and night, with 24 hours in a day being the most common use of the number. It suggests fullness of time.
1531 Wreath – '*stephanos*'. Roman magistrates wore golden wreaths as crowns, as a symbolic testament to their lineage back to Rome's early Etruscan rulers.

were burning.[1532] These are the seven spirits of God.[1533] ⁶Also in front of the throne there was something that looked like a sea of glass, like crystal.[1534]

And in the centre, around the throne on each of its sides, there were four living creatures. They had many eyes in the front and the back. ⁷The first living creature was like a lion, the second was like an ox, the third had a face like that of a man and the fourth was like a flying eagle.[1535] ⁸Each of the four living creatures had six wings and was covered with eyes all around and even having eyes under their wings. Day and night they never stopped saying,

> "Holy, holy, holy is the Lord God Almighty, who was and is and is to come."

⁹And whenever the living beings give glory, honour and thanks to him who sits on the throne, the one who lives forever and ever, ¹⁰the 24 elders lay face down before the one who sits on the throne and worship him who lives forever and ever. They cast their victor's wreaths before the throne and say,

> ¹¹"Worthy are you, our Lord and God, to receive glory, honour and power.
> For you created all things and by your will they were created and came into being.

John sees a scroll and the Lamb in the throne room[1536]

5 ¹I saw in the right hand of him who sat on the throne, a scroll with writing on both sides.[1537] It was sealed with seven seals.[1538] ²And I saw a powerful angel announcing in a loud voice, "Who has the authority to break the *seven* seals and open the scroll?" ³But no one in heaven or on earth or under the earth[1539]

1532   The seven torches are an allegorical representation of the seven spirits which we saw previously in Rev. 1:4 and 3:1 which are the seven archangels. In early Judaism angels were thought to be made of fire.
1533   Cf. Rev. 1:4 footnote.
1534   Gen. 1:7 speaks of two waters: one above the firmament and one below. Yahweh sits enthroned over the flood (Psa. 29:10). There were two waters and God's throne was thought to sit upon the heavenly sea. It speaks of the transcendence of God, his separation from the created order.
1535   The four living creatures are cherubim (Eze. 1:5, 10:20). Because of their close proximity to God, they represent the holiness and glory of God.
1536   A scene very similar to the one in Dan. 7:9–14.
1537   A scroll was a document made of sheets of parchment or papyrus that were pasted together in one long strip and then rolled up like a tube, and usually tied, or else sealed, as this scroll was. This scroll was most likely an 'opisthograph' which means that it had writing on both sides (Eze. 2:9–10). The scroll represents the entire seven-year eschatological scenario from Rev. 6:1 through to 22:9, with words of lament and mourning and woe. Some also maintain that it could represent Christ's title deed to planet earth (Jer. 32:8–15).
1538   The seals were usually small pieces of wax applied to the scroll in order to keep it closed and its contents secret. They also identified the author of the scroll and could not be broken except by someone who had the authority to do so (TH).
1539   In other words, no one was found in the entire cosmos or universe.

had *the authority* to open the scroll or to even look in it. ⁴I, John, wept and wept because no one was found who had the authority to open the scroll or read its *contents*. ⁵Then one of the elders said to me, "Do not cry! Look! The Lion of the tribe of Judah, the Root of David, has been victorious. He is able to open the scroll and its seven seals.

⁶Then I saw a lamb standing in the centre of the throne which was surrounded by the four living beings and the elders. It looked like it had been slaughtered. It had seven horns and seven eyes.[1540] They are the seven spirits of God who have been sent out to all parts of the earth.[1541] ⁷The Lamb[1542] came and took the scroll from the right hand of him who sat on the throne. ⁸And when he had taken it, the four living beings and the 24 elders lay down before the Lamb. Each one had a harp and they were holding golden bowls full of incense, which are the prayers of God's holy people.[1543] ⁹And they sang a new song:

"You are worthy to take the scroll and to open its seals because
    you were slaughtered.
With your blood, you purchased men for God from every tribe and
    language, people group and nation.
¹⁰You have made them to be a gathering of kings and priests to serve
    our God and they will reign on earth.

¹¹Then I looked and I heard the voice of many angels numbering thousands upon thousands and ten thousand times ten thousand. They surrounded the throne together with the living beings and the elders.[1544] ¹²In a loud voice they all sang:

"Worthy is the Lamb, who was slaughtered.
He is worthy to receive power and wealth, wisdom and strength, honour,
    glory and praise!"

¹³Then I heard every creature in heaven and on earth and under the earth and on the sea and everything that is in them, singing:

1540 In the Bible a horn is a symbol of strength and power whilst the eyes represent the ability of God to see and know everything (TH).
1541 The seven eyes are the seven spirits of God or the seven archangels: Gabriel; Michael; Raphael; Uriel; Racquel; Remiel; and Saraquel. Cf. Rev. 1:4 footnote.
1542 The Lamb is Christ Jesus hence the capitalisation.
1543 Cf. Rev. 8:5.
1544 John describes the precise order surrounding the throne of God. First it is the innermost throne, then the four living beings, next the 24 elders and lastly the myriad of angels.

"To him who sits on the throne and to the Lamb, let there be praise and honour and glory and power forever and ever!"

¹⁴The four living beings said, "Amen," and the elders lay face down and worshipped *God and the Lamb.*

The first six seals are opened in the throne room

6 ¹I was watching as the Lamb broke open the first of the seven seals.[1545] Then I heard one of the four living beings say in a voice as loud as thunder, "Come!" ²I looked and there right before me was a white horse. Its rider was holding a bow and he was given a victor's crown. He rode out like a conqueror searching for victory.[1546]

³When the Lamb broke open the second seal, I heard the second living being say, "Come!" ⁴Then another horse came out, a fiery red one. Its rider was given the power to take peace away from the earth so that people should slaughter each other. He was given a large sword.[1547]

⁵When the Lamb broke open the third seal, I heard the third living being say, "Come!" I looked and right before me was a black horse. Its rider was holding a pair of scales[1548] in his hand. ⁶Then I heard what sounded like a voice among the four living beings, saying, "A day's ration of wheat for a denarius coin[1549] or three day's ration of barley for a denarius coin. Do not damage the oil and the wine!"

⁷When the Lamb broke open the fourth seal, I heard the voice saying, "Come!" ⁸I looked and right before me was a speckled and strong horse![1550] Its

---

1545   Do all seven seals need to be broken before the scroll can be read? Bible commentator John F Walvoord says Roman law required a last will and testament to be sealed seven times, as illustrated in the wills of Caesar Augustus and Emperor Vespasian. However it is the unsealing, not the reading of the scroll, that unleashes each judgment one by one.

1546   The first four seals almost certainly parallel Matt. 24:4–8 and the 'beginning of birth pains'. You will notice in the Matthew passage that there are four 'birth pains' which match up with the four riders here in Revelation chapter 6. The rider of the white horse is thought by many Bible scholars to be the Antichrist starting his activity at the beginning of the seven years. But in my view this is not possible because the Antichrist is not revealed until he comes up out of the abyss at the fifth trumpet judgment at the halfway point some 3 ½ years later (Rev. 9:1–11). It is more likely to be a personification of the condition of deception that prevails on the earth at the start of the seven year tribulation period. This is also supported by Matt. 24:4 when the first thing that Jesus says to his disciples is to watch out for deception.

1547   A short sword (or dagger) used for cutting and stabbing (Louw, J, & Nida, E, *Greek-English Lexicon of the New Testament based on Semantic Domains* (1988) 6.33).

1548   This is a balance scale. Ancient balance scales often consisted of a rod held by a cord in the middle and with pans attached to both ends. Weights could be placed in one pan, while the item to be weighed would be placed in the other (Louw, J, & Nida, E, *Greek-English Lexicon of the New Testament based on Semantic Domains* (1988) 6.214).

1549   One denarius coin was the amount paid for one day's wage. It was a small silver coin.

1550   Original Hebrew MSS (Sodot) has speckled and strong horse. Cf. Zech. 6:3.

rider was named Death. Hades was following close behind him. They were given power over a quarter of the earth to kill through war, famine and pandemic under *the authority of* the beasts of the earth.

⁹When *the Lamb* broke open the fifth seal, I saw under the altar[1551] the souls of those who had been slaughtered because of the word of God and the testimony they had maintained. ¹⁰They called out in a loud voice, "Master, the one who is holy and true, how long until you judge the inhabitants of the earth and punish them for killing us? ¹¹Then a white robe was given to each of them and they were told to wait a little while longer. They were to wait until the complete number of their fellow servants and brothers were killed as they had been.

¹²I watched as *the Lamb* broke open the sixth seal.[1552] There was a huge earthquake. The sun turned black like *mourning clothes*[1553] and the whole moon turned blood *red*. ¹³The stars in the sky fell to earth as when unripe *fruit*[1554] falls from the tree when shaken by a strong wind. ¹⁴The sky receded like a scroll rolling up. Every mountain and island was removed from its place.

¹⁵Then the kings of the earth, the elite, the generals, the rich, the influential people and every slave and every free man hid in the caves and among the rocks of the mountains. ¹⁶They called to the mountains and the rocks, "Fall on us and hide us from the face of him who sits on the throne and from the wrath of the Lamb! ¹⁷For the great day of their[1555] wrath has come and who is able to withstand it?"

1551 This altar appears to be the heavenly equivalent of the altar in front of the Jewish temple where animal sacrifices were made. Their blood was typically poured out at the base of this brazen altar perhaps indicating that it is as if the blood of the Tribulation martyrs is similarly poured out at the base of the heavenly altar.
1552 The sixth seal consists of such great cosmic signs that it signals a complete breakdown of the elements of the universe meaning the return of Christ.
1553 This is literally sackcloth made of hair—a coarse black garment worn in times of mourning.
1554 This is literally when unripe figs drop from the fig tree. Unripe figs usually grow in the winter and fall off in the spring.
1555 Both Yahweh and Jesus descend to earth on the great day of their wrath (Matt. 26:64).

The 144,000 from the twelve tribes of Israel

7 ¹After this[1556] I saw[1557] four angels standing at the four corners of the earth.[1558] They were holding back the four winds[1559] of the earth to prevent any wind from blowing on the land, sea or any tree. ²Then I saw another angel coming up from the horizon in the east. He had the seal[1560] of the living God and he called out in a loud voice to the four angels who had been given the power to harm the land and the sea. ³*The angel said,* "Do not harm the land or the sea or the trees until I[1561] have marked the foreheads of the servants[1562] of our God with a seal."[1563] ⁴Then I heard someone telling me the number of those who were marked with a seal. It was 144,000 from all the tribes of Israel.[1564]

1556   "After this" does not mean that the events in chapter 7 occur chronologically after the sixth seal judgment. It refers to what John saw next in his vision. Chapter 7 should not be seen as an event in sequence in between the sixth and seventh seals as on a timeline but merely as an interlude in concepts and visions. Western writers typically record their stories or accounts in a chronological fashion as a series of consecutive events that occur one after the other. This style of writing is called 'step logic' as events are recorded step by step. In the Hebrew way of thinking passages aren't grouped by chronology but in other ways such as the subject at hand. This style of writing is called 'block logic'. This is important because the temptation in the Book of Revelation is to see the seal, trumpet and bowl judgments as being 21 judgments all in a sequence or steps one after the other spanning seven years. Rather, a better way of seeing the Revelation is in the context of 'block logic' with many of the judgments occurring concurrently. Chronology is appropriate within the blocks but not outside of them.

1557   In the vision, the 144,000 are protected and sealed <u>before</u> the start of Daniel's 70th week (seven-year tribulation). John has a vision of the redeemed in the 70th week including the 144,000 sealed Israelites and the tribulation saints who have rejected the mark of the beast and who are martyred throughout this time.

1558   The earth is considered to be a vast square surface with four corners. The number 'four' signifies universality as in the four directions of the compass.

1559   The four winds seem to correspond to the first four horsemen who are identified in Zech. 6:5 as being four spirits (strong winds).

1560   The seal referred to here is not the same wax seal referred to in chapters 5 and 6 which are broken by the lamb. Rather the seal here is an instrument that marks or stamps a figure, number or name upon an object or a person. Kings often had seals on their rings known as 'signet rings'.

1561   This is actually an exclusive "we" here in the Greek so the four angels are not included in the marking process. Having the pronoun 'I' makes this point clearer even though others would be included in the process.

1562   The servants here are masculine in gender in the Greek and as servants they have a ministry or purpose to fulfil during the first half of the 70th week. Their purpose is obscure but many commentators say that their purpose is to evangelise the world. Their purpose in my view is to not only evangelise but to prepare the Christian world to be ready to flee at the halfway mark. They will be sealed for this purpose in order to protect them. They will form the core of the woman of Revelation 12 but will invite those who are willing, to join them in their flight to the mountains as in Exo. 12:38 when a large 'mixed multitude' fled Egypt with the Israelites in their flight into the wilderness. Only those who are like the five wise virgins will have the faith to make this journey, first to Judea and then to Jordan.

1563   The seal is the name of the Lamb and his Father (Rev. 14:1).

1564   Interestingly the order of the twelve tribes is not in the birth order and does not include Dan and Ephraim. When taking the meanings of each of the names from the book of Genesis in this particular order in John's revelation a meta-narrative (bigger story) message is derived which speaks from the perspective of a woman. This woman is the same woman as in Revelation 12, the believers who are take refuge in the wilderness for time, times and half a time. The bigger story is as follows:
   "I will <u>praise the Lord</u> because the Lord <u>has seen</u> my misery and a <u>troop</u> is coming. I am happy because the daughters will <u>call me blessed</u>. I have had a great <u>struggle</u> but God has <u>caused me</u>

⁵From the tribe of Judah,¹⁵⁶⁵ there were 12,000 who had the seal together with 12,000 from each of the tribes of Reuben,¹⁵⁶⁶ Gad,¹⁵⁶⁷ ⁶Asher,¹⁵⁶⁸ Naphtali,¹⁵⁶⁹ Manasseh,¹⁵⁷⁰ ⁷Simeon,¹⁵⁷¹ Levi,¹⁵⁷² Issachar,¹⁵⁷³ ⁸Zebulun,¹⁵⁷⁴ Joseph¹⁵⁷⁵ and Benjamin.¹⁵⁷⁶

The large crowd in white robes

⁹After this I looked and there right before me was a crowd so large that no one was able to count it! There were people from every nation, tribe, people and language and they were standing before the throne and in front of the Lamb. They were wearing white robes and were holding palm branches¹⁵⁷⁷ in their hands. ¹⁰They called out in a loud voice, "Our God and the Lamb is the one who has saved us and our God sits on the throne."

¹¹All the angels were standing around the throne, the elders and the four living beings. They lay face down before the throne and worshipped God. ¹²They said, "Amen! Praise and glory, wisdom and thanks, honour, power and strength be to our God forever and ever. Amen!"

¹³Then one of the elders asked me, "These who are dressed in white robes— who do you think they are and where did they come from?"

¹⁴I replied, "Lord, I don't know but you do." And he said to me, "These are the ones who are coming out of the great tribulation.¹⁵⁷⁸ They have washed their robes and made them white in the blood of the Lamb. ¹⁵That is why they stand

---

to forget all my troubles. The Lord has heard that I am not loved, now at last my husband will become attached to me. God has rewarded me, God has presented me with a precious gift. And God will add to me his son, the son of (his) right hand." The 144,000 from all the tribes of Israel are a part of the woman but they are the rest of the woman's offspring who give this message. Their initial role in the first 1260 days is to urge and encourage the church (the ten virgins) during the first half to heed the warning, to wake up and 'become ready' with oil in their lamps, and to be ready to flee to the wilderness when the time comes at the halfway mark.

1565 Leah said of Judah, "This time I will praise the Lord." (Gen. 29:35)
1566 Leah said of Reuben, "It is because the Lord has seen my misery." (Gen. 29:32)
1567 Leah said of Gad, "A troop is coming." (Gen. 30:11 YLT)
1568 Leah said of Asher, "I am happy for the daughters will call me blessed." (Gen. 30:13 NKJV)
1569 Rachel said of Naphtali, "I have had a great struggle with my sister…" (Gen. 30:8)
1570 Joseph said of Manasseh, "God has made me forget all my troubles…" (Gen. 41:51 NLT)
1571 Leah said of Simeon, "Because the Lord heard that I am not loved…" (Gen. 29:33)
1572 Leah said of Levi, "Now at last my husband will become attached to me…" (Gen. 29:34)
1573 Leah said of Issachar, "God has rewarded me…" (Gen. 30:18)
1574 Leah said of Zebulun, "God has presented me with a precious gift." (Gen. 30:20)
1575 Rachel said of Joseph, "May the LORD add to me another son." (Gen. 30:24)
1576 Rachel first named her son Ben-Oni meaning, "son of my trouble." But his father (Jacob) named him Benjamin meaning, "son of my right hand." (Gen. 35:18)
1577 Palm branches indicate joy and happiness.
1578 The Great Tribulation is specifically the last 1290 days (time, times and half a time) of the last seven years of the Christian age. These are most likely the tribulation martyrs who lose their lives for refusing to take the mark of the beast. This occurs because of their laziness and reluctance to flee to the place of refuge in time, i.e. the five foolish virgins.

before the throne of God and serve him day and night in his temple.*¹⁵⁷⁹* He who sits on the throne will protect them with his presence. ¹⁶Never again will they be hungry or thirsty. The sun will not beat down upon them nor any scorching heat. ¹⁷For the Lamb at the centre of the throne will be their shepherd. He will lead them to places where fresh pure water is flowing. And God will wipe away every tear from their eyes."*¹⁵⁸⁰*

8 ¹When the Lamb broke open the seventh seal, there was silence in heaven for about half an hour.*¹⁵⁸¹*

*The seven trumpets*¹⁵⁸²

²Then I saw the seven angels*¹⁵⁸³* who were standing in the presence of God and there were given to them seven trumpets.*¹⁵⁸⁴*

³Meanwhile another angel who had a golden bowl came and stood at the altar. He was given a lot of incense to offer together with the prayers of all of God's holy people*¹⁵⁸⁵* on the golden altar in front of the throne. ⁴The smoke of the incense together with the prayers of God's holy people went up before God from the angel's hand. ⁵Then the angel took the bowl, filled it with *burning coals* from the altar and threw its *contents down* upon the earth.*¹⁵⁸⁶* And so followed thunder, rumblings, flashes of lightning and an earthquake.

⁶Then the seven angels who had the seven trumpets prepared themselves to blow them.

⁷The first angel blew his trumpet and there came hail and fire mixed with blood and it was thrown down upon the earth. A third of the earth was burned up, a third of the trees were burned up and all the earth's *vegetation*¹⁵⁸⁷ was burned up.

1579 There is no temple in the city because God and the Lamb are its temple (Rev. 21:22).
1580 A figure of speech indicating that God will remove every source of pain and sorrow.
1581 The chapter divisions are arbitrary divisions and so here the main division is better served at v. 2. Since the sixth seal concerns the second coming of Christ then the seventh seal would indicate the Day of the Lord and the very end. Silence for half an hour indicates the demand for silence as the Judge of all the earth is about to appear and preside. Scripture interprets Scripture as follows: "Be silent before the Sovereign LORD, for the day of the LORD is near" (Zeph.1:7 NIV). "The LORD is in his holy temple; let all the earth be silent before him" (Hab. 2:20).
1582 The seven trumpets begin a new sequence of judgments which overlap the seal judgments. The opening of the seventh seal does not initiate the seven trumpet judgments.
1583 The definite article "the" here infers that these angels are known and not seven random angels or messengers. They are likely the seven spirits (archangels) who stand before God referred to in Rev. 1:4, 3:1, 4:5 and 5:6 also known as 'The Angels of the Presence' who are believed to be continually in God's presence. Gabriel is one of those who stand in the presence of God (Luke 1:19).
1584 Trumpets were used mainly in war or religious situations and could either be a ram's horn (shofar) or a metal instrument such as a bugle.
1585 The prayers of God's holy people are considered to be offerings to God. The incense is added to make the prayers acceptable to God (TH).
1586 It appears that the catalyst for the trumpet judgments, like for the seven seal judgments, is the prayers of God's people. Cf. Rev. 5:8b.
1587 Literally all the green grass was burned up.

⁸The second angel blew his trumpet and something like a huge mountain on fire was thrown into the sea. A third of the sea turned into blood. ⁹A third of the living creatures in the sea died and a third of the ships were destroyed.

¹⁰The third angel blew his trumpet and a great asteroid, burning like a torch,[1588] fell from the sky on a third of the rivers and on the underground water. ¹¹The name of this asteroid is Wormwood.[1589] One-third of all the waters *of the earth* turned into wormwood and many people died from the waters that had become bitter.[1590]

¹²The fourth angel blew his trumpet and the sun, moon and stars were struck so that they did not shine for one-third of the time. And so one-third of the day did not have light and likewise for the night.

¹³Then I looked and heard an eagle[1591] that was flying in mid-air and it called out in a loud voice saying, "Disaster! Disaster! Disaster[1592] to the inhabitants of the earth, because of the remaining trumpet blasts about to be blown by the three angels."

The fifth trumpet (first disaster)

9 ¹The fifth angel blew his trumpet and I saw a star that had fallen from the sky to the earth. The star[1593] was given the key to the shaft of the abyss.[1594] ²When the star opened the abyss, smoke rose from it like the smoke rising from a gigantic furnace. The sun and the sky were darkened by the smoke from the abyss. ³And then out of the smoke locusts[1595] descended upon the earth and they were given power like that of scorpions of the earth *to sting people*. ⁴They were told not to harm the grass on the earth or any plant or tree, but

---

1588 Cf. Rev. 4:5 footnote.
1589 The name of the star derives from its effect on the water; it turned the water sour and bitter, so that it killed many of those who drank it. Wormwood itself is a bitter drug, made from an aromatic plant (*Artemisia absinthium*) and is highly toxic. Insecticides were made from it but it derives its name from the practice of brewing the leaves in a tea, for people and animals as a worming medicine (TH, Warner, Tim, *LGV* Rev. 8:11 footnote 111).
1590 It appears that not everyone who drank the bitter wormwood water died. Maybe only those with a poor or weakened immune system.
1591 KJV here has 'angel' but most translations have 'eagle'.
1592 The three 'disasters' correspond to the fifth, sixth and seventh trumpet judgments to complete the series. The first four trumpet blasts invoke a judgment primarily on the earth's environment whereas the final three blasts begin at the midpoint of the tribulation period and primarily affect mankind himself.
1593 The star is spoken of as being a living being. In Job 38:7 stars are spoken of as if they were living beings. The star here is almost certainly Satan because of the similarity of how Jesus spoke about Satan falling like lightning from heaven in Luke 10:18. Jesus also said that he gives the disciples authority to trample on snakes and scorpions which is almost certainly a metaphor for demons.
1594 The abyss is a very deep hole under the earth which is the place in the depths of the earth where the demons are imprisoned until their final punishment. It is also where the end times beast will appear from.
1595 The prophet Joel spoke of locusts as being instruments of God's wrath or anger in the end times before the Day of the Lord (Joel 2:1–11). These locusts seem to be demonic beings.

only those people who did not have the seal of God on their foreheads. ⁵They were not given the power to kill these people, but only to torture them for five months. The pain caused by the torture is like the pain caused by a scorpion sting. ⁶During those five months, men will seek death but they will not find it. They will want to die but death will elude them.

⁷The locusts looked like horses prepared for battle. On their heads, they were wearing something like wreaths of gold¹⁵⁹⁶ and their faces resembled human faces. ⁸Their hair was like women's hair and their teeth were like lion's teeth. ⁹They had breastplates of iron and the sound of their wings was like the sound of many chariots with horses running into battle. ¹⁰They had tails and stings like scorpions, and with their tails, they were capable of hurting people for five months.¹⁵⁹⁷ ¹¹The angel of the abyss was their king¹⁵⁹⁸ ruling over them whose name in Hebrew is 'Abaddon' and in Greek, 'Apollyon.'

¹²The first disaster is over but two more disasters are yet to come.

The sixth trumpet (second disaster)

¹³The sixth angel blew his trumpet and I heard a voice coming from the four horns¹⁵⁹⁹ of the golden altar that stands before God. ¹⁴The voice spoke to the sixth angel who had the trumpet, "Release the four angels who are bound at the great river Euphrates." ¹⁵The four angels were released *as instructed* for they had been kept ready for this very hour, day, month and year to kill one-third of mankind. ¹⁶The number of the mounted troops was 200 million. Someone told me their number.

¹⁷The horses and riders I saw in my vision¹⁶⁰⁰ looked like this: Their breastplates were fiery red, dark blue¹⁶⁰¹ and yellow like sulphur. The heads of the horses resembled the heads of lions and out of their mouths came fire, smoke and sulphur. ¹⁸These three plagues of fire, smoke and sulphur that came out of the horses' mouths killed one-third of mankind. ¹⁹The power of the horses was

---

1596 A wreath here probably symbolising a victor's crown.
1597 The torment is restricted to a period of five months which is equivalent to the life cycle of the locust. Typically locusts appear in the dry season which corresponds from spring through to late summer. The fifth trumpet judgment occurs at the midpoint of the 70th week just before the Feast of Passover around the Feast of Purim which is around the time that locusts would begin to appear in Israel.
1598 Locusts lead a kind of double life. The locust normally enjoys a quiet, solitary life, slowly and inconspicuously munching on grass like the grasshopper. But their appearance and behaviour changes upon swarming operating as a single cohesive unit almost like they have a leader or 'king' over them. They develop strong wings and an insatiable hunger, and become 'gregarious', hoarding together in giant swarms as big as 10 km x 10 km, and as dense as 50 locusts per cubic metre.
1599 The horns of the golden altar of incense are the four corners. They project up from the altar at each corner and are in the shape of horns thereby giving rise to the name the four horns.
1600 This is the only place in the entire Book of Revelation that the word "vision" is used.
1601 Literally 'hyacinth' which was a dark blue flower.

in their mouths and tails. Their tails were like snakes having heads with which they inflict injury.

²⁰The rest of mankind who were not killed by these plagues still did not turn to God regarding their evil actions. Instead, they did not cease worshipping demons and idols of gold, silver, bronze, stone and wood. These are *inanimate objects* that cannot see, hear or talk. ²¹Neither did these people turn away from their murders, their drug use,[1602] their sexual immorality or their stealing.

John eats the scroll given to him by the Messenger

10 ¹Then I saw a different powerful Messenger[1603] coming down from heaven. He was wrapped in a cloud wearing it like a robe. He had a rainbow above his head and his face was *shining* like the sun. His legs were like columns of fire. ²He was holding a small scroll which was lying open in his hand. He placed his right foot on the *surface of the* sea and his left foot on the *dry* land.[1604] ³He gave a loud shout like the roar of a lion. When he shouted, the seven thunders spoke. ⁴As the seven thunders spoke, I was about to write *what was being said* when a voice from heaven said, "Seal up what the seven thunders have said and do not write it down."[1605]

⁵Then the Messenger whom I had seen standing on the *surface of the* sea and the land raised his right hand to heaven.[1606] ⁶And he took an oath *in the name* of him who lives forever and ever, the one who created the heavens and all that is in them, the earth and all that is in it and the sea and all that is in it and he said,

---

1602 The Greek word here is *pharmakon* and is often translated as 'sorceries', 'witchcraft' or 'magic'. But this Greek word is where we get the modern-day word 'pharmacy' which literally means drugs. Drug use has reached epidemic proportions in these last days of the church and it seems only appropriate that the meaning could well be that people at the end are totally absorbed by the use of drugs and are not willing to give up that sinful lifestyle. In the day, drugs were often used by sorcerers and witches etc.

1603 The Greek word is *angelos* here which simply means 'messenger' but often translated as angel. This angel or messenger appears to be Jesus because of the description given in v. 1. Ezekiel had a similar vision in Eze. 1:26–28.

1604 The Messenger (Jesus) has one foot on the dry land and one foot on the surface of the earth's oceans indicates that this message is for the whole earth.

1605 It does not mean that John himself will reveal what the seven thunders said at a later time implying that he is one of the two witnesses. Rather Mounce in his commentary on this verse favours the explanation that the seven thunders, like the seals and trumpets, formed another series of warning plagues. He says, "The adamant decision of the human race not to repent (Rev. 9:20–21) would render another series useless. In the verses that immediately follow, an angel under oath will declare that there shall be no further delay (vv. 5–7), so possibly it was too late to record any further warnings." Furthermore he says, "In this context, to seal up means not to disclose. John seals up what the thunders said by not writing them down. What was said is not to be made known to the churches. In Dan 12:4 the prophet is told to 'close up and seal the words of the scroll until the time of the end' (cf. Dan 12:9). In contrast, what the thunders said is never to be revealed" (Mounce, R H, *The Book of Revelation (NICNT)* (1997)). This aligns with what Jesus said in Matt. 24:22 that the days have been cut short for the sake of the elect.

1606 This is the gesture of someone making a vow or promise to God in heaven.

"There will be no more delay. ⁷However in the days before the seventh angel is about to blow his trumpet, the mystery of God¹⁶⁰⁷ will be accomplished as he announced to his servants, the prophets."

⁸Then the voice from heaven that I had heard previously, spoke to me once more and said, "Go and take the scroll that lies open in the hand of the Messenger who is standing on the sea and land."

⁹So I went to the Messenger and asked him to give me the small scroll. He said to me, "Take it and eat it. It will be bitter in your stomach but in your mouth, it will be as sweet as honey." ¹⁰I took the small scroll from the Messenger's hand and ate it. It tasted as sweet as honey in my mouth but once I had eaten it, it became bitter in my stomach.¹⁶⁰⁸ ¹¹Then they¹⁶⁰⁹ told me, "You must prophesy again against many peoples, nations, languages and kings."¹⁶¹⁰

The two witnesses

11 ¹I was given a long cane as a measuring rod and I was told, "Go and measure the temple of God¹⁶¹¹ and the altar. Also, count the number of worshippers in it.¹⁶¹² ²But do not include the outer court in your calculations because it has been given to the Gentiles who will trample on the holy city for 42 months.¹⁶¹³

1607   To keep the consistency of the Bible the mystery of God is the gospel—Jesus Christ revealed. Cf. Col. 2:2–3. At this point in time in the period before the seventh angel sounds the seventh trumpet, the final opportunity for those on the earth to repent and turn to Christ will occur.

1608   The Lord also told Ezekiel in Eze. 3:1–3 to eat a scroll which was sweet as honey in the mouth. This indicates that the contents of the scroll and message is one of destruction and judgment but God causes it to be as sweet as honey to the prophet himself. The scroll most likely outlines what God plans to do before his Son returns and is installed as King on Mt. Zion (Psa. 2:4–7). Even though John is the one who receives the scroll, it is a vision and the prophet concerned is most likely one of the two witnesses or both.

1609   God and his Son, Jesus, giving the instruction to John to prophesy in his vision.

1610   Some, including early Christian writers, understand from this passage that John himself will be raised from the dead in the last days and be one of the two witnesses. But seeing as John died after writing Revelation, it would be impossible for him to die twice, once as the Apostle John and then again as one of the two witnesses because man is only destined to physically die once (Heb. 9:27). John saw only a vision. One of the witnesses will be a contemporary man in the spirit of Elijah just as Jesus said in Matt. 11:14, "if you are willing to accept it, John the Baptist is Elijah who was prophesied to come." The prophet Malachi prophesied that Elijah would return before the Day of the Lord (Mal. 4:5). The other witness is possibly a man in the spirit of Moses.

1611   This is the temple in Jerusalem. This indicates that there will be a Jewish temple rebuilt before the commencement of the final 70th week or the last seven years. It could be bricks and mortar or perhaps just some temporary tent-like structure as well. There is much controversy as to where exactly this temple will be located and whether it will be a God ordained temple or an idolatrous temple. Contemporary Jews believe that the final temple will definitely be located on the current temple mount area above the Western Wall area perhaps adjacent to the Dome of the Rock or instead of it. Another possibility is that the temple will be measured out and confirmed by the two witnesses at the start of their ministry to the south at the original temple site located in the old city of David a few hundred metres from the Jerusalem city southern wall south of the Dung Gate. We will have to wait and see. Cf. http://www.askelm.com

1612   The worshippers are Jews as only Jews are allowed in or around the temple.

1613   These 42 lunar months will occur in the second half of the tribulation because the beast will stop

³I will give power to my¹⁶¹⁴ two witnesses and they will prophesy for 1260 days and they will be clothed in sackcloth."¹⁶¹⁵

⁴These two *men* are the two olive trees¹⁶¹⁶ and the two lampstands¹⁶¹⁷ who stand before the Lord of the earth. ⁵If anyone tries to harm *the two witnesses* then fire¹⁶¹⁸ comes from their mouths and consumes their enemies. So this is how anyone who wants to harm them must die. ⁶These men have the power to shut up the sky so that it will not rain during the time that they are prophesying. They also have the power to turn the waters into blood and to strike the earth with every kind of plague¹⁶¹⁹ as often as they want.

⁷Now when the *two witnesses* have finished their testimony, the beast coming up out of the abyss will make war with them and will overpower and kill them.¹⁶²⁰

	the sacrifices at the halfway point according to Dan. 9:27. The two witnesses prophesy in the first half for exactly 1260 days whereas 42 months is the length of time that the beast will be in authority until the seventh trumpet when the kingdom of the world becomes the kingdom of the Lord and Christ (Rev. 11:15).
1614	Jesus talking here describes the 'two witnesses' as 'my two witnesses'. Many think that one of the witnesses will be Elijah himself returning to earth because he did not die. However, he was seen with Moses and Jesus in spirit form on the Mount of Transfiguration in Matt. 17:3 and wrote a letter to King Jehoram apparently after he had already departed (2 Chron. 21:12–15). Elijah, like Moses had an unusual end to his life. It may be that Elijah was translated more 'laterally' by the chariot of fire to another place on earth just as Philip was in Acts 8:39–40, and lived out the rest of his days in hiding. Most likely the 'last days Elijah' will be an ordinary man (Jam. 5:17–18) who will minister in the power and spirit of Elijah just as John the Baptist did (Matt. 11:14).
1615	The sackcloth was coarse cloth, usually made of goat's hair, which was worn as a sign of mourning, and which shows that the message of the two witnesses, or prophets, is to be one of doom and destruction, and a call for people to repent while there is still time (TH).
1616	A clear reference to Zech. 4:1–14 where the two olive trees, on either side of the lampstand, are the two men chosen and anointed by God to serve him, the Lord of the whole earth. In that context, the two olive trees provide a continual source of oil to the lampstand so that it can keep burning. In the same way the two witnesses will provide oil (Holy Breath) to the end time's church during the first half of the tribulation. This will be a time that much encouragement and instruction will be needed for the church as it sees persecution and also warning to escape to the mountains (Jordan) when the time comes.
1617	Lampstands represent churches in the Book of Revelation (Rev. 1:20). In the Zechariah passage there is only one lampstand but here there are two lampstands possibly referencing the only two churches out of the seven in the end times that do not receive any criticism or correction—Smyrna and Philadelphia. In other words they keep their testimony either by martyrdom (Smyrna) or escape (Philadelphia).
1618	Cf. Jer. 5:14. It is possible that the fire coming out of the two witnesses mouths is the Word of God and that their enemies are the wood that is consumed by their fiery words.
1619	This literally means a widespread contagious disease in its narrowest meaning but it could be referring to a more generalised suffering. The verse reminds the reader of the plagues of Egypt.
1620	The beast (Antichrist) comes up out of the abyss at the sound of the fifth trumpet blast (Rev. 9:1–11) which is at the mid-point of the seven year tribulation period. The use of the present participle and not the aorist (a completed action in the past) indicates that it is likely that the beast immediately makes war with the two witnesses. In other words the first thing on the beast's agenda will be to wage war against the two witnesses and the Jews and their temple. The beast first sets up the Abomination of Desolation on the extremities of the temple but it could take some time to overthrow or bring low the sanctuary due to the resistance of the Jews and their newly built temple and sacrificial system (Dan. 8:11). A precedence of this type of Jewish resistance was set in AD 70 when Roman General Titus took five months to completely conquer the city of Jerusalem from

⁸Their bodies will lie in the street of the great city which is figuratively called Sodom and Egypt where their Lord was also crucified.[1621] ⁹For three and a half days men from every people group, tribe, language and nation see their corpses[1622] and their corpses are not permitted to be put into a tomb.[1623] ¹⁰The inhabitants of the earth rejoice greatly over them and celebrate by sending each other gifts because these two prophets had tormented those who dwell on the earth.

¹¹But after the three and a half days God breathed life into them and they stood up causing great fear amongst those who were watching them. ¹²Then they heard a loud voice from heaven saying to them, "Come up here." And so they went up to heaven in a cloud while their enemies looked on.

¹³At that very time a major earthquake struck and a tenth of the city[1624] collapsed. Seven thousand people were killed in the earthquake and the survivors were terrified. They gave glory to the God of heaven.[1625]

¹⁴The second disaster has passed and the third disaster is coming soon.

The seventh trumpet (third disaster)

¹⁵The seventh angel blew his trumpet and there were loud voices in heaven which said, "The realm of the world is now the realm of the Lord and his Messiah and he will reign forever and ever." ¹⁶The 24 elders who were seated on their thrones before God, lay face down and worshipped him. ¹⁷They said,

> "We give thanks to you Lord God Almighty, the One who is and who was
> > because you are exercising your great power and have begun to reign.
> ¹⁸The nations were angry and your fury has come.[1626]
> It is the time for the dead to be judged and to reward your servants the
> > prophets and your people and all those who revere your name,

---

Passover in April AD 70 to early September because of the fierce resistance of the Jews for their city and temple (https://biblehub.com/library/schaff/history_of_the_christian_church_volume_i/section_38_the_jewish_war.htm). This could also equate to the five month period mentioned in Rev. 9:5 which is the length of time after the abyss is opened when the demonic locusts torment those who do not have the seal of God on their foreheads. This period could also be when an enforcing of the mark of the beast occurs.

1621 John clearly identifies the city as Jerusalem. The two witnesses are Christians because the verse clearly says 'their Lord'. The Jews do not identify with Jesus Christ.

1622 TR (KJV, NKJV) has 'corpses' as in the plural whereas Westcott and Hort (critical text) on which most modern translations are based have the singular 'corpse'. Interestingly all modern English translations translate this in the plural despite the Greek critical text saying otherwise.

1623 Normally the Jewish custom was that a dead person was to be buried on the same day that the death occurred or within 24 hours at most.

1624 I.e. Jerusalem.

1625 The survivors give glory to God in repentance and acknowledgment of his great power.

1626 The time for the 'seven bowls of God's anger' (Rev. 16:1) has now come with the unveiling of the seventh trumpet. Cf. Psa. 2:1 (LXX).

both small and great alike.

The time has come for destroying those who destroy the earth."[1627]

[19] Then God's temple in heaven was opened and I saw his ark of the covenant within. Then there were flashes of lightning, rumblings, claps of thunder, an earthquake and a great hailstorm.

The church escapes to a safe place in the desert

12 [1] A great sign appeared in the sky: a woman[1628] clothed with the sun and with the moon under her feet and a wreath consisting of twelve stars on her head.[1629] [2] She was pregnant and cried out in pain as she was about to give birth. [3] Then another sign appeared in the sky: an enormous red dragon[1630] with seven heads and ten horns and seven royal crowns on his heads.[1631] [4] His tail swept a third of the stars out of the sky and threw them down to the earth.[1632] The dragon was standing in front of the woman who was about to give birth. He was waiting to devour her child, the moment he was born.

[5] She gave birth to a son, a male child, who will rule all the nations with a rod of iron.[1633] However, her child was snatched up to God and his throne.[1634] [6] The

---

1627 This does not mean those who destroy the environment but rather those who have exterminated people. This would include those who have engaged in ethnic cleansing. The original 'destroyers' in the 1st century would have been the Roman Empire.

1628 Ancient Christian writers understood the woman to be the loyal church. The woman here is true Israel which consists of all believers including the loyal church, those who listen to the warning to flee when the time is right. Cf. Gal. 3:29 footnote. Loyal believers will have safe refuge for time, times and half a time (1290 days) in southern Jordan. For further information see Luke 21 article titled, "Who is the woman of Revelation 12?" and tribulation timeline.

1629 The sign is an astronomical sign which gives us the exact date of Jesus' birth on Rosh Hashanah, 3 BC. Cf. Matt. 2:1 footnote.

1630 A monstrous legendary beast conceived as being an enormous winged serpent or lizard.

1631 Interestingly the largest of the 88 constellations in the night sky is Hydra, a serpentine water monster in Greek and Roman mythology. It lies adjacent to the constellation, Virgo, the virgin.

1632 Stars are often angels in the Bible. A commonly accepted interpretation here is that Lucifer took one third of the angels with him in his primordial rebellion after the creation of the universe. However the position of this verse places it firmly after the conception of Jesus Christ so there is some doubt on this. Verse 3 says that the seven heads have seven crowns (diadems) whereas Rev. 13:1 says that ten crowns (diadems) are on the ten horns. Crowns (diadems) are a metonym (figure of speech) representing kings.

1633 This idiom was first used in Psa. 2:9 and its meaning is that Jesus will rule with complete authority and his enemies will be completely defeated. This will occur in the millennial kingdom starting when he returns to the earth. It will be possible for people to sin in the millennial kingdom but there will be no delay in justice but judgment will be swift.

1634 The male child is Jesus who ascended into heaven after his resurrection.

woman fled into the desert where she has a place, having been prepared for her by God for 1260 days[1635] so that they[1636] can take care of her there.

⁷Then war broke out in heaven. Michael[1637] and his angels fought against the dragon and the dragon and his angels fought back. ⁸But he was not strong enough and they lost their place in heaven. ⁹The great dragon was thrown down out of heaven. The dragon is that ancient serpent[1638] called the devil or Satan who leads the whole world astray.[1639] He was thrown down to the earth and his angels with him.

¹⁰Then I heard a loud voice in heaven say, "God's salvation has now come and God is now demonstrating his power and rule as king. His Messiah is now showing all his authority. For the accuser of our brothers, who accuses them before our God day and night, has been thrown down *to the earth*. ¹¹They overcame him by the blood of the Lamb and through the truth that they proclaimed. They did not love their lives even when they were faced with death. ¹²Therefore rejoice, all of you who live in heaven. But it is disastrous for all you who live on the earth and in the sea because the devil has gone down to you. He is furious because he knows that his time is short."

¹³When the dragon saw that he had been thrown down to the earth, he pursued the woman who had given birth to the male child. ¹⁴*God* gave the woman the two wings of a great eagle[1640] so that she might fly to the place prepared for her in the desert, where she would be taken care of for a time, times and half a time.[1641] There she will be *safe* from the face of the serpent. ¹⁵Then the serpent spewed out a river of water from his mouth so that it would overtake the woman

---

[1635] The 1260 days refers to the duration of the two witnesses' ministry in the first half not the duration of time that the woman will be kept safe (Rev. 11:3). That time is indicated by v. 14 (time, times and half a time). The Greek verb tenses indicate that the place is held ready for 1260 days before the woman flees.

[1636] "They" are unknown agents but the closest antecedents are the two witnesses. Angels are also commanded to look after those who take refuge in the shelter of the Most High (Psa. 91:11–12).

[1637] Michael was the guardian angel and protector of Israel (Dan. 10:21).

[1638] The serpent in Gen. 3:1 was a real animal. Satan entered into the body of the most clever of all the beasts of the field in order to deceive Eve. Martin Luther states it this way: "Let us therefore, establish in the first place that the serpent is a real serpent, one that has been entered and taken over by Satan..." (https://www.answersingenesis.org/angels-and-demons/satan/was-satan-the-actual-serpent-in-the-garden/) Henry Morris says that there is, "no reason why we should not assume that, in the original creation, the serpent was a beautiful, upright animal with the ability to speak and converse with human beings" (Morris, Henry, *The Genesis Record* (1976), p. 109).

[1639] Cf. Matt. 4:10 footnote.

[1640] Cf. Exo. 19:4. Almost this exact same phrase was used of the Israelites when they escaped from the clutches of the Pharaoh of Egypt some 3500 years previously. The two wings of a great eagle represents supernatural help possibly the two witnesses who would lead the woman into the safe place and care for her there with the help of angels. The desert refuge is in southern Jordan because of Dan. 11:41 which states that only Edom, Moab and Ammon will escape the Antichrist.

[1641] This is an ancient way of saying 3 ½ years. It is first seen in Dan. 7:25.

and sweep her away with the torrent.[1642] [16]But the earth helped the woman by opening its mouth and swallowing the river that the dragon had spewed out of his mouth. [17]The dragon was furious at the woman and went off to make war with the rest of her descendants—those who obey the commandments of God—those who hold to the truth that is in Jesus.[1643]

The seven headed beast system

13 [1]I stood on the seashore and I saw a beast rising up out of the sea.[1644] It had ten horns and seven heads with ten royal crowns on its horns.[1645] On each head, there was a blasphemous name. [2]The beast I saw looked like a leopard[1646] but had feet like those of a bear[1647] and a mouth like that of a lion.[1648] The dragon gave the beast his power and his throne and great authority. [3]One of the heads of the beast seemed to have had a fatal wound but the fatal wound had been healed.[1649] The whole world was astonished and followed the beast. [4]Everyone worshipped the dragon because he had given his authority to the beast. They also worshipped the beast asking *themselves*, "Who is like the beast? Who can make war against it?"

The two human beasts

[5]A mouth was given to the beast to make proud boasts and to insult God.[1650]

1642 A flood or torrent of water is often a metaphor for a large army (Dan. 9:26, 11:22).
1643 These are the rest of the church who have not proceeded to the place of refuge in the desert.
1644 The sea represents the nations. Cf. Rev. 17:15.
1645 The beast rising up out of the abyss has ten horns or ten kings with crowns meaning that they have authority and power as kings whereas the ten kings of the fourth beast (Mystery Babylon (NWO) – Dan. 7:8,24) are not crowned meaning that they don't have authority but are waiting for the Antichrist to rise. Then three of these original kings are subdued and the Antichrist installs his own ten kings. They then have the power and authority to reign for one hour during the last 42 months of the 70th week symbolised by the crowns.
1646 In Dan. 7:6 the beast's body is the leopard, the modern equivalent being Germany. Germany has a tank called the leopard tank and in World War II, Germany conquered parts of France using tanks extremely quickly with a military technique which came to be known as blitzkrieg (lightning attack). In Dan. 7:6 the leopard has four heads. The spots of the leopard could possibly mean the different EU nations. Germany and France are the 'engine' of the E.U. underpinning its foundation.
1647 The bear in Dan. 7:5 is Russia (its national symbol). The three ribs in Russia's mouth could be three territories that Russia conquers including Ukraine. The bear tears its foes apart with its feet.
1648 The lion in Dan. 7:4, a symbol of royal power, represents Great Britain whose national symbol is the lion. It is the premier monarchy in the world with its head being King Charles III. Charles is known as the 'godfather of climate change' and initiated 'Terra Carta' in 2021, a take-off of Magna Carta. Terra Carta is a global sustainability initiative with ten guiding articles.
1649 The seven heads represent seven kings or leaders of Gentile world empires who have oppressed the Jews since ancient Egypt. The particular head here that has a fatal wound has to be one of the former seven kings. My conclusion is the Nazi dictator, Adolf Hitler – the seventh head. He will rise and the healing of his fatal wound along with his resurrection will astonish the world. Adolf Hitler died on April 30th 1945 due to a self-inflicted gunshot to the head. Cf. Rev. 17:9–11.
1650 The beastly system of the previous verses is personified by giving it a mouth to speak and now the beast (the seven headed system) has become the beast (the human Antichrist) also known as the 'first beast' (vv. 12,14). In the preface of Hitler's *Mein Kampf* manifesto, he says, "I know that fewer

It was given authority to act as it wished for 42 months. ⁶It spoke and uttered blasphemies against God. It blasphemed his name, his dwelling place and all those who live in heaven. ⁷God allowed it to make war against God's holy people and to conquer them. It was also given the authority over every tribe, people group, language and nation. ⁸All the inhabitants of the earth will worship *the beast*—he whose name has not been written in the Lamb's book of life. The Lamb was slaughtered because of the overthrow of the world.[1651]

⁹"He who has an ear let him hear.[1652] ¹⁰If anyone is meant to be taken captive then he will be taken captive. If anyone kills with the sword then he must be killed by the sword. This then means that God's holy people must endure and keep the faith."[1653]

¹¹Then I saw another beast rising up out of the land.[1654] It had two horns like a lamb but it spoke like a dragon. ¹²It exercised all the authority of the first beast on his behalf. It forced the land and its inhabitants to worship the first beast, the one whose fatal wound had been healed. ¹³The second beast performed great and miraculous signs, even causing fire to come down from heaven to the land in full view of people. ¹⁴And it deceives the inhabitants of the earth because it was given the power to perform these signs on behalf of the first beast, telling them to set up an image in honour of the beast who was *fatally* wounded by the sword[1655] and yet came back to life. ¹⁵The second beast was allowed to give life to the image of the first beast so that the image was able to speak and cause everyone who did not worship it to be put to death.[1656]

¹⁶*The second beast*[1657] also forced everyone, small and great, rich and poor, free

---

people are won over by the written word than the spoken word and that every great movement on this earth owes its growth to the greatest speakers, not the greatest writers." Cf. Dan. 11:32,36.

1651   The reason that the Lamb (Christ) was slain is that Satan overthrew or overcame the world by his deception of Eve at the very beginning a few days after creation. The significant Greek word which is typically translated as 'foundation' or 'creation' is from *kataballo* which is from *kata* and *ballo*; meaning to throw down. Strong's 2602. The overthrow of the world occurred when Adam and Eve listened to Satan and ate the fruit from the Tree of the Knowledge of Good and Evil.

1652   Vv. 9–10 are marked in red as Jesus' words as it is a formula often used by Jesus in addressing the seven churches and when he spoke to Peter at his arrest not to resist or draw weapons (Matt. 26:52).

1653   This is directed at the woman's fellow offspring (the elect) who ignored the call to flee to safety at the mid-point of the tribulation (Rev. 12:17). This remnant will be faced with the mark of the beast and so this is a warning not to resist with weapons but to submit to arrest and imprisonment, without trying to escape their God-given destiny. They will have to accept their destiny in that they missed the safe place and they need to keep believing and not lose their hope even though they face imprisonment or martyrdom.

1654   This beast is the false prophet (Rev. 19:20) and it appears that he comes from the land of Israel.

1655   Likely a figure of speech (synecdoche) where sword represents all categories of weapons. Cf. Matt. 26:52. For example, "The citizens were all put to the sword" is a synecdoche in which the term 'sword' stands in for the entire category of weapons used to kill.

1656   Cf. Dan. 3:3–6.

1657   It is possible in the Greek that it could be read that the image of the beast forced everyone to take the mark of the first beast because it simply uses the neuter pronoun 'it'. However translators invariably

and slave, to receive a mark[1658] on[1659] his right hand or his forehead. [17]Therefore no one was able to buy or sell unless he had the mark, the name of the beast or the number of its name.[1660] [18]You must be wise if you are to figure this out. If anyone has insight let him calculate the number of the beast for it is the number of a man. Its number is 666.[1661]

The Lamb and the 144,000 singers

14 [1]Then I looked and I saw the Lamb standing on Mt Zion and with him were 144,000[1662] *men* who had his name and his Father's name written on their foreheads.[1663] [2]I heard a sound from heaven which was like the roar of a lot of water and that of thunder. It sounded like harpists playing their harps. [3]They[1664] were standing before the throne and singing a new song. The four living creatures and the elders were also there. No one was able to learn the song except for the 144,000 *men* who had been purchased from the rest of the people on earth. [4]These are those who were not defiled with women for they have kept themselves *sexually pure*.[1665] They are devoted to the Lamb following him where he goes. They have

---

prefer to translate it as the second beast.

1658 The issue of what this mark actually is has been the subject of much debate with bible scholars over the years. Almost certainly the mark (*charagma*), is an engraving, scratch, etching or branding like on horses and cattle etc. Interestingly *charagma* comes from the Greek word *charax*, which means 'a palisade, a stake' (*Thayer's Lexicon* (2011), Strong's G5482).

1659 KJV has 'in' here. The mark could possibly be something internal.

1660 The Greek makes it clear that there are three possibilities not two: the beast's mark or logo, the beast's name or the beast's number (666). One must ensure that one avoids all three.

1661 The number of the beast has caused much controversy over the years with many Bible scholars using Gematria (substituting letters for numbers) to solve the riddle of the 666 meaning. John indicates that wisdom is required to solve the riddle but as yet no one can be sure until the beast arises. Early church father Irenaeus, raises one possibility of the name of the beast being 'Titan' (Teitan) calculating his number as 666 using Gematria in his book *Against Heresies* (Book V, Chapter 30.3). The only name in the entire Bible associated with 666 is Adonikam in Ezra 2:13. The sons of Adonikam numbered 666 and the name means 'risen master'. Interestingly the beast arises out of the abyss (Rev. 11:7) and proclaims himself to be God (2 Thess. 2:4). Adolf means 'noble wolf'. Perhaps the beast is the noble wolf of old who rises from the dead and becomes master of the world and takes on a new name, Adonikam. So, when Adolf Hitler rises from the dead as the beast and forces his mark upon the entire world, every one of his 'sons' will be the '666 people'—literally his descendants by their own choice. Tim Cohen in his book, *The Antichrist and a Cup of Tea* suggests that 'Prince Charles of Wales' adds up to 666 in both English and Hebrew Gematria. The problem with King Charles being the Antichrist is that the beast is not revealed until the 5th trumpet judgment at the half-way point of the 70th week.

1662 There is no definite article (the) indicating that these are specifically the 144,000 referred to in Rev. 7:4, however the number clearly links the two passages. In chapter 7, the 144,000 Israelites are sealed at the beginning of the 70th week whereas here the 144,000 are standing on Mt. Zion with the Lamb seven years later at the end.

1663 The names could be the abbreviated names of the Father יהוה (YHWH – tetragrammaton) and the Lamb Χς (Chi, sigma-Christos) which could also be the seal on the foreheads of the servants in Rev. 7:3. (Aune, David E, *52b Word Biblical Commentary Revelation 6–16* (2013), pp. 804–805).

1664 Probably an angelic choir and orchestra.

1665 The identity of these 144,000 is revealed as being those who kept themselves sexually pure which probably means they kept themselves spiritually pure and undefiled by their complete devotion to God and their refusal to worship idols. Often in the Old Testament idolatry is compared to sexual

been purchased from the rest of the human race and are the first ones to be offered to God and the Lamb. ⁵They have never lied and they are faultless.

Three angels have a message for the world

⁶Then I saw another angel flying in the air high above with an eternal message of the gospel to proclaim to all peoples living on the earth—to every nation, tribe, language and people group. ⁷He said in a loud voice, "Fear God and give him the glory because the time for him to judge has now come. Worship him who made the heavens, the earth, the sea and the underground water."

⁸A second angel followed and said, "Fallen! Fallen is the great *city of Babylon*.¹⁶⁶⁶ She made all the nations drink the wine of her sexual sins."¹⁶⁶⁷

⁹A third angel followed them and said in a loud voice, "If anyone worships the beast and its image and receives its mark on the forehead or the hand, ¹⁰he too will drink the wine of God's fury which has been poured full strength into the cup of his anger. This person will be tormented with burning sulphur¹⁶⁶⁸ in the presence of the holy angels and of the Lamb. ¹¹The smoke of the fire that torments them rises forever and ever. There is no rest day or night for those who worship the beast and its image or for anyone who receives the mark of its name."¹⁶⁶⁹ ¹²This means that God's holy people who obey his commandments and loyally follow Jesus must endure patiently.

¹³Then I heard a voice from heaven say, "Write: Blessed¹⁶⁷⁰ are the dead who die in the Lord from now on."¹⁶⁷¹

---

immorality. Most commentators favour this spiritual understanding of the text. They have a role as being singers after the return of Jesus following the pattern David established, arranging choirs and instrumentalists to offer continual praise outside the 'Tabernacle of David' which temporarily housed the ark of the covenant (1 Chron. 15:16). Singers and choirs will have their place at the dedication of the New Jerusalem and the millennial temple (Eze. 40:44 NKJV).

1666 The ancient Mesopotamian city of Babylon was a world empire political and religious capital. It was renowned for its luxury and moral corruption. In the 1st century AD the city of Rome was the quintessential Babylon. In Rev. 17:18 it is almost certain that 'Mystery Babylon' is identified as being the city of Rome – the great city that rules over the kings of the earth. Rome was known as the 'Eternal City'. Rome was considered to be the pinnacle of society. In Revelation chapter 18 the city of Rome does not seem to continue to fit the description of 'Babylon the Great'. The question here is what city is the second angel referring to? The choices are ancient Babylon located in modern-day Iraq, Rome, Jerusalem and a modern-day equivalent such as New York. My preference is New York as it is the political and financial capital of the greatest hegemony of the modern-day world. Cf. Rev. 18 where the fall of 'Babylon' is described in greater detail.

1667 The fact that the fall of Babylon is mentioned here in chapter 14 but isn't described in more detail until chapter 18 proves that the Revelation is not written in a chronological and sequential order.

1668 Sulphur burns with intense heat igniting at very high temperatures greater than 200°C.

1669 There is perpetual torment for those who worship the beast and take his mark. This flies in the face of annihilation or conditional immortality which believes that this punishment will have an end date and is only for a time after which they will be destroyed.

1670 This is the second blessing in the Book of Revelation. Cf. Rev. 16:15 for the third blessing.

1671 This probably refers to those who have not abandoned their faith but have persevered to the end.

The *Holy* Breath says, "Yes, indeed! They will enjoy rest from all their hard work *on earth,* for a record of what they did will go with them."

The harvest of the righteous and the wicked

¹⁴I looked and there right before me was a white cloud with someone seated on the cloud. He resembled the Son of Man¹⁶⁷² with a golden wreath on his head holding a sharp sickle¹⁶⁷³ in his hand. ¹⁵Then another angel came out of the temple *in heaven* and called out in a loud voice to the man sitting on the cloud. He said, "Take your sickle and reap the earth for the time for reaping is here and the harvest is ripe." ¹⁶So the man who was seated on the cloud swung his sickle over the earth and the earth was harvested.¹⁶⁷⁴

¹⁷Then another angel came out of the temple *in heaven* and he too had a sharp sickle. ¹⁸Yet another angel again came from the altar who was responsible for the fire *of the altar* and he called out in a loud voice to the angel who had the sharp sickle. He said to him, "Take your sharp sickle and gather the clusters of grapes from the earth's vine because its grapes are ripe."¹⁶⁷⁵ ¹⁹The angel swung his sickle on the earth, gathered the grapes and threw them into the great winepress of God's wrath. ²⁰They were trampled in the winepress outside¹⁶⁷⁶ the city and blood came out of the winepress coming up as high as the horses' bridles.¹⁶⁷⁷ The blood went for a distance of 1600 stadiums.¹⁶⁷⁸

1672   This is a way of referring to the Messiah (Christ) and was originally used by Daniel in Dan. 7:13.
1673   A sickle is a blade, with a handle, that is usually curved and is used to cut grain plants or grass.
1674   This harvest is the so-called 'rapture'—a harvest of the believers.
1675   The grapes represent the wicked of the earth and refers to the final battle at the very end of the tribulation period. Cf. Joel 3:13.
1676   Joel 3:12 gives the hint as to the exact location of the winepress where the nations will be judged—the Valley of Jehoshaphat, which means "the LORD judges." Joel 3:14 also calls it the "valley of decision" (i.e. God's decision).
1677   The inference is that the blood splashed up as high as the horses' bridles (about 1.5 m high).
1678   The stain of blood will be seen flowing down the winepress for a great distance possibly beginning at Megiddo in the north, winding its way down the Jordan River to the Dead Sea. Cf. Midrash Lamentation Rabbah 2:2:4. 1600 stadiums is equivalent to about 300 km.

Seven angels with seven plagues

15 ¹I saw another incredible and astonishing sign in heaven. I saw seven angels with the seven last plagues.[1679] These are the seven last plagues because with them God's fury will be complete.

²Furthermore I saw what looked like a sea of glass mixed with fire. Standing on the sea of glass, holding harps given to them by God, were the overcomers, those who had victory over the beast, his image and *did not take* the number of his name. ³They were singing the song of Moses, the servant of God, and the song of the Lamb:

> "How incredible and astonishing are your works, Lord God Almighty.
> How right and true are your ways, King of the nations.
> ⁴All people will fear you, O Lord, and bring glory to your name for you alone are holy.
> All nations will come and worship you because your righteous works have been revealed."

⁵After this I looked and saw that the temple (tabernacle of the testimony)[1680] in heaven was opened. ⁶The seven angels with the seven plagues then came out of the temple. They were dressed in clean, shining linen and were wearing golden sashes around their chests. ⁷Then one of the four living beings gave seven golden bowls to the seven angels. These bowls were filled with *the wine of* God's fury.[1681] He lives forever and ever. ⁸The temple was filled with smoke from the glory of God and his power. No one could enter the temple until the seven plagues of the seven angels were completed.

1679 These are the seven last plagues also known as the "seven bowls of wrath". There are many plagues and judgments before these last ones during the seven-year tribulation as well as every kind of plague issued by the two witnesses (Rev. 11:6). The pre-trib theory believes the church is removed before the entire tribulation while pre-wrath says the church cannot be present on the earth during the seven trumpet judgments and seven bowls of wrath with the church being raptured afterwards approximately one year before the end at the sixth seal. I believe this is incorrect because of a misunderstanding of 1 Thess. 5:9 where Paul says that God did not appoint believers to suffer wrath. The seven seals, seven trumpets and seven bowls of wrath however present no problem to God as he is more than able to protect his people from wrath and plagues as he has demonstrated in history when he protected the Israelites from the plagues of Egypt despite his people living very close in the land of Goshen. God made a distinction between Israel and Egypt and is more than able to protect his holy people (Exo. 8:22–23, 9:4,26) in times of trouble.

1680 The ancient tabernacle was a "Tent of the Testimony" (Num. 17:7, 18:2) because it contained the two tables of testimony brought down from Mt. Sinai by Moses (Exo. 32:15, Deut. 10:5), (Mounce, R H, *The Book of Revelation (NICNT)* (1997)).

1681 Cf. Rev. 14:10.

The seven bowls of God's anger

16 ¹Then I heard a loud voice coming from the temple *in heaven* saying to the seven angels, "Go and empty the seven bowls of God's anger on the earth."

²The first angel went and emptied his bowl on the land and horrible and foul-smelling ulcers broke out on the people who had the mark of the beast and worshipped his image.

³The second angel emptied his bowl on the sea and it turned into blood like that of a dead man[1682] and every living thing in the sea died.

⁴The third angel emptied his bowl on the rivers and underground water and they turned into blood. ⁵Then I heard the angel in charge of the waters address God saying, "Your punishments are right, O Holy One, the one who is and was. ⁶For they have shed the blood of your people and the prophets. You have given them blood to drink *instead of water*. They are getting what they deserve." ⁷I heard *a voice from* the altar respond, "Yes, Lord God Almighty, true and right are your judgments."

⁸The fourth angel emptied his bowl on the sun and God allowed the sun to scorch people with fire. ⁹People were seared by the intense heat and they cursed the name of God who had control over these plagues. But they refused to turn to God and acknowledge his greatness.

¹⁰The fifth angel emptied his bowl on the throne of the beast and all the places under its rule were plunged into darkness. People were biting their tongues in agony ¹¹and cursed the God of heaven. They cursed God because of their pains and sores but they refused to turn from their evil ways.

¹²The sixth angel emptied his bowl on the great river Euphrates and so its water dried up to prepare the way for the kings from the east.[1683] ¹³Then I saw three unclean spirits that looked like frogs. They were coming out of the mouth of the dragon, out of the mouth of the beast and out of the mouth of the false prophet. ¹⁴They are spirits of demons performing amazing signs. They go out abroad to the rulers and kings of the whole world to gather them for the battle on the great day of God Almighty.[1684]

¹⁵"Look out, I am coming like a thief! Blessed[1685] is he who remains awake

---

1682 The blood of a corpse is dark and coagulated. This is very similar to the plague on Egypt in Exo. 7:20–21.
1683 This is the region where the Tigris and Euphrates river system runs for over 2700 km from the mountains of Turkey to the Perisan Gulf supporting over 60 million people. Interestingly in the last decade or so there has been decreased rainfall in the region. In the end it will completely dry up in preparation for the oriental armies of the east to approach Israel for the final battle of the ages in Jerusalem.
1684 I.e. Judgment day right at the very end.
1685 This is the third blessing in the Book of Revelation. Cf. Rev. 19:9 for the fourth blessing.

and keeps his clothes with him so that he may not walk around naked and be ashamed when he is seen."[1686]

[16]Then he[1687] gathered the kings to the place that in Hebrew is called Har-Magedon.[1688]

[17]The seventh angel emptied his bowl into the air and out of the temple came a loud voice from the throne saying, "It is over!" [18]Then there came flashes of lightning, rumblings and peals of thunder and a severe earthquake. There has never been an earthquake as powerful as this since the human race has existed on the earth. It was an absolute mega-quake. [19]The great city[1689] split into three parts and all the cities of the nations collapsed. (God remembered Babylon the Great and how he would make her *drink* the wine from his cup—the cup filled with his furious anger.[1690]) [20]Every island disappeared and the mountains vanished. [21]Huge hailstones from the sky, weighing some 40 kg or more, fell onto people. They cursed God because of the plague of hail and because it was such a terrible plague.

Mysterious Babylon the prostitute and the beast

17 [1]One of the seven angels who had the seven bowls came and said to me, "Come with me and I will show you the punishment of the great prostitute who sits on many waters.[1691] [2]With her the kings of the earth have committed

---

1686   In v. 15, Jesus is referring to a Jewish temple idiom referring to when the captain of the temple (Acts 4:1) would do his nightly rounds. At night guards were placed in 24 stations about the temple gates and courts. Each guard consisted of ten men so all up there were 240 Levites and 30 priests on duty, keeping watch. If the captain (the thief in the night) found any guard asleep when on duty he was beaten or his garments were set on fire possibly leaving him naked and ashamed. The point is that as Christians, we are also on watch. We do not know when the captain (Jesus) will come like a thief in the night and we don't want to be ashamed that we are caught napping. Cf. Edersheim, A, *The Temple, It's Ministry and Services* (1994), pp. 111–112.

1687   It is God himself who gathers the world's armies to Armageddon for the world's final assault on Jerusalem.

1688   Har-Magedon ("Armageddon" in most translations) is a direct transliteration from the Hebrew har mo'ed and literally means the 'mountain of assembly' not the 'mountain of Megiddo' as in most translations. As Zec. 12:11 points out, Megiddo is a plain and not a mountain. The archaeological site of Megiddo is an archaeological tell (an artificial mound of dirt created by successive layers of building and occupation over millennia) and not a geographical mountain. Effectively the great final battle of the ages occurs at Jerusalem at the mountain of assembly (Mt. Zion/temple mount) as indicated by Zec. 14:2. Cf. Heiser, Michael S, *The Unseen Realm* (2015), pp. 368–375.

1689   More than likely Jerusalem is referred to here from Rev 11:8.

1690   The timing is important to get right here. Babylon would already be destroyed because this was the seventh bowl of God's fury occurring right at the end of the tribulation period. Chapters 17 and 18 describe this event—the destruction of 'Babylon the Great' in more detail. God was recalling that he would destroy her too in the future because this revelation of God to John occurred in the 1st century AD.

1691   This refers to a city which is situated near rivers and water. In 17:18 John specifies this woman/prostitute clearly as being the city of Rome. Here however the city is described as being located next to a lot of water.

adultery. The inhabitants of the earth were intoxicated with the wine of her adulteries."

³Then the angel carried me away, in spirit *form*, into a desert where I saw a woman sitting on a scarlet beast that was covered with blasphemous names. The beast had seven heads and ten horns. ⁴The woman was dressed in purple and scarlet and she was glittering in gold, precious stones and pearls. She held a golden cup in her hand, filled with abominable things and the filth of her adulteries.[1692] ⁵A mysterious title was written on her forehead:

> Babylon[1693] the Great, the mother of prostitutes, the source of every filthy and detestable thing on the earth.

⁶I saw that the woman was drunk with the blood of God's holy people. These were the ones who bore testimony to Jesus. When I saw her I was beyond astonishment.

⁷Then the angel said to me, "Why are you astonished? I will explain to you the mystery of the woman and of the beast she rides that has seven heads and ten horns." ⁸The beast that you saw once existed, now doesn't and will come up out of the abyss and then go to its destruction.[1694] The inhabitants of the earth will be astonished (the ones whose names have not been written in the book of life because of the overthrow of the world) when they see the beast because it once existed, now doesn't and yet will exist again.[1695]

⁹"You must be wise to figure this out. The seven heads are seven mountains[1696] on which the woman sits. ¹⁰They are also seven kings.[1697] Five have fallen, one

---

1692 Like the OT prophets, John speaks of idolatry as sexual immorality and describes nations that try to lead God's holy people into idolatry as fornicators and whores (TH).

1693 Babylon is a code word in the Bible for the enemies of God and his people. Ancient Babylon was known for its idolatry and originates from 'Babel' which symbolises unified false religion, sorcery, astrology and rebellion against God. In this chapter Babylon is almost certainly referring to Rome and its idolatry but 'Babylon the Great' seems to be appropriate for the modern-day Rome, New York. In the Bible, the metaphor of Babylon seems like it can be applied to several different cities including Jerusalem (Zech. 2:7), Rome (1 Pet. 5:13) and also modern-day New York (Rev. 18).

1694 This verse indicates that the beast (Antichrist) will be a known historical person who will be resurrected. When the world sees this familiar figure of history they will be absolutely astonished.

1695 This statement about the coming beast is a mockery of the description of God in Rev. 1:8. It really means someone who once lived and is dead now. It reflects an epitaph often used in the ancient Greek and Latin world: 'I was not, I became, I am not'. David E Aune says if this parody is to have any force, it must refer to a person who both died and returned from the dead (or was expected to do so) (Aune, David E, *52c Word Biblical Commentary Revelation 17–22* (1998), pp. 939–940).

1696 Mountains are symbolic of kingdoms in the Bible. Cf. Psa. 97:5, Dan. 2:35, Mic. 1:4.

1697 The word means 'kings' and not 'kingdoms' however the best fit still seems to be seven leaders or dictators of seven Gentile kingdoms that have oppressed Israel and the Jews. These seven are in order: Egypt, Assyria, Babylon, Persia, Greece, Roman Empire, and Nazi Empire. In the time that John wrote this in c. AD 96, five Gentile kingdoms were in the past, the Roman Empire was still in

exists now and the other one has not yet come. But when *the seventh king* does come, he[1698] will only remain for a little while. ¹¹The beast who once existed and now doesn't is an eighth king. He belongs to one of the seven *kings* and is going to be destroyed.[1699]

¹²"The ten horns you saw are ten kings who have not yet begun to rule. They will be given authority to rule as kings along with the beast for a very short amount of time. ¹³These ten kings have one mind and they will give their power and authority over to the beast.[1700] ¹⁴They will wage war against the Lamb but the Lamb together with his called, chosen and loyal followers, will overcome them because he is Lord of lords and King of kings."

¹⁵Then the angel said to me, "The waters you saw, where the prostitute sits, are people groups, multitudes, nations and languages.[1701] ¹⁶The beast and the ten horns you saw will hate the prostitute. They will bring her to ruin and leave her naked. They will eat her flesh and burn her with fire. ¹⁷For God has put it into their hearts to accomplish his purpose by agreeing to give the beast their power to rule until God's words are fulfilled. ¹⁸The woman you saw is the great city that rules over the kings of the earth."[1702]

Babylon the Great is destroyed in one hour

18 ¹After this I saw another angel coming down from heaven. He had great authority and the earth was lit up by the splendour of his glory. ²He shouted out with a mighty voice:

"It has fallen! Babylon the Great has fallen!"[1703]

---

	power and the Nazis were yet to come but only in existence for twelve years from 1933–1945.
1698	The pronoun "he" is also present in the Greek and proves that the beast is a man.
1699	This verse tells us that the beast will be the eighth king (world power) who will come from one of the previous seven kingdoms. He must be a historical person who comes back to life who was a leader or dictator from one of the seven Gentile world powers. The choices are further limited because we know that the beast will be a person who was fatally wounded by a weapon but is healed upon his resurrection (Rev. 13:3,14). Adolf Hitler killed himself by first swallowing a hydrogen-cyanide capsule and then shooting himself in the head with his own pistol at 3:30 pm, 30th April 1945 thereby qualifying himself to be the beast of the end times.
1700	The ten kings here are equivalent to the ten toes of the giant statue of Nebuchadnezzar's dream described in Dan. 2:42–44 and the ten horns of Dan. 7:7,24. Initially the ten kings are part of the Babylonian prostitute system (NWO) and then morph into rulers in the beast's kingdom for the final 3 ½ years.
1701	New York and the U.N. seem to perfectly fit the description here where all the nations regularly gather in a building that sits near the water on Manhattan Island. The name Manhattan comes from the Munsi language of the North American Lenape meaning 'island of many hills'.
1702	This also definitely refers to the city of seven hills—Rome but also to New York (the new Rome). Paul Strathern sees the hegemonic link between Rome and New York when he states that after WWII, "The *Pax Americana* prevailed, in much the same way as the *Pax Romana* had done nearly two millennia previously." (Strathern, Paul, *Ten Cities That Led The World* (2022), p. 175).
1703	This is what is called the 'prophetic past tense' – announcing a future event in the past tense as if it

She has become a home for demons and a prison for every evil spirit.
It has become a prison for every unclean and repulsive bird.[1704]
³This is because all the nations have drunk the wine of her sexual
   immorality.
The kings of the earth have committed sexual sin with her and the
   businessmen of the world have grown rich from her excessive
   luxuries."

⁴Then I heard another voice from heaven saying:

"Leave Babylon now, my people, so that you will not share in her sins.
Leave Babylon now so that you will not receive any of her plagues
⁵for her sins are piled up to heaven and God has remembered her crimes.
⁶Treat her exactly as she treated others.[1705]
Pay her back double for what she has done.
Mix for her a cup of wine twice as strong as the cup she has mixed for others.
⁷You must give her as much torture and grief proportional to the glory
   and luxury she allowed for herself.
For in her heart Babylon boasts saying, 'I sit as queen. I am not a widow
   and I will never need to mourn.'[1706]
⁸Therefore in one day plagues, death and mourning will overtake her.
She will be consumed by fire for mighty is the Lord God who judges her.

⁹"When the kings of the earth who committed sexual sin with her and lived in luxury because of her see the smoke coming from the burning *city*, they will cry and mourn over her. ¹⁰They will stand at a great distance *from the city* terrified by her great suffering. They will cry out saying, 'Oh dear, what a pity for such a great city. What a disaster for such a powerful city as Babylon! In just one hour your punishment has come.'

---

      has already occurred (TH).
1704 The picture here is of a city that has become desolate and deserted where only birds and bats roam. This picture is also typical of descriptions of ancient Babylon, Nineveh and Edom in the OT. The repulsive birds possibly refer to bats as bats were considered as birds back in the day that this was written. Unclean birds are those birds that are considered unclean under the Jewish Law. Unclean birds could not be eaten as they were non-kosher.
1705 It is not exactly clear to whom God (the voice from heaven) is commanding to repay Babylon for her sins. The likelihood is that it is either the ten kings of Rev. 17:16 or an angel or angels. Even though the citizens of Babylon themselves are being addressed in v. 4 it is not likely that the voice is commanding the citizens of Babylon to punish themselves so it must be one of the other two choices.
1706 In other words she has complete authority and is not subject to anyone else including a husband—a complete boast about her control over her subjects.

¹¹"The businessmen of the world will cry and mourn over *Babylon* because there is no one buying their merchandise anymore—¹²merchandise of gold, silver, precious stones and pearls, fine linen, purple cloth, silk, scarlet cloth, every kind of scented wood, every kind of article made of ivory, costly wooden articles, bronze, iron, marble, ¹³cinnamon, spices, incense, myrrh, frankincense, wine, olive oil, fine flour, wheat, cattle, sheep, horses, chariots and slaves (human beings).

¹⁴"The businessmen will say, 'All the good things you craved for have gone. All your riches and shiny things have vanished into thin air, never to be recovered.' ¹⁵The businessmen who got rich from doing business with her will be standing at a great distance and will be terrified by her great suffering. They will cry and mourn ¹⁶saying:

"'What a disaster! How disastrous for such a great city!
It was a city dressed in fine linen, purple and scarlet clothing.
It glittered with gold, precious stones and pearls.
¹⁷In one hour such great wealth has been entirely destroyed.'

"Every sea captain and all who travel by ship, the sailors and all who earn their living from the sea will stand at a great distance ¹⁸and cry out as they see the smoke coming from her burning. They will say, 'Was there ever a city like this great city?' ¹⁹They will throw dust on their heads, crying and grieving saying:

"'What a disaster! How disastrous for such a great city!
It was a city from which all those who owned ships on the seas became
    rich through her wealth!
In one hour she has been completely ruined!
²⁰Rejoice, all of you who live in heaven! Rejoice, people of God, apostles
    and prophets!
For God has passed judgement on Babylon for the way she has treated you.'"

²¹Then a powerful angel picked up a boulder the size of a large millstone and threw it into the sea and said:

"The great city of Babylon will be thrown down with violence likewise,
    never to be found again.
²²The sound of harps, musicians, flutes and trumpets will never be heard
    in you again.

No tradesmen will ever work in you again.
The sound of the mill grinding grain will never be heard in you again.
²³The light of a lamp will never shine in you again.
The happy voices of the bridegroom and bride will never be heard in you again.
For your city's businessmen were the global elite and by your
    pharmaceutical sorcery all nations were deluded.
²⁴In the city was found the blood of prophets and God's holy people.
    She is responsible for the killing of people all over the earth.

Great joy over the destruction of Babylon the Great

19 ¹After these things I heard a loud voice in heaven that sounded like the roar of a great crowd of people crying out:

"Hallelujah![1707] Salvation and glory and power belong to our God.

²His judgments are true and just. For he has condemned the great
    prostitute who corrupted the earth with her immorality.
He has punished her, avenging the lives of his servants."

³And again they said:

"Hallelujah! The smoke from the burning of that city rises forever and ever."

⁴The twenty-four elders and the four living beings lay face down and worshipped God, who was seated on the throne. And they said:

"Amen, Hallelujah!"

⁵Then a voice came from the throne, saying:

"Praise our God, all you—his servants, those of you who fear him,
    from the least important to the most important."

The wedding feast of the Lamb

⁶Then I heard what sounded like a vast crowd of people, similar to the sound

---

1707   This comes from two Hebrew words: *halal* meaning 'praise' and *jah*, a contraction of 'Yahweh' or 'Lord'. Therefore it means Praise the Lord! This word only occurs four times in the NT, all in this passage.

of the roar of rushing waters and like the loud claps of thunder and they were saying:

> "Hallelujah! Our Lord God Almighty reigns.
> ⁷We must all rejoice and be glad and give him the glory!
> For the wedding of the Lamb has arrived and his bride has made herself ready.
> ⁸God has given to her fine linen, bright and clean that she may wear it.
> (Fine linen represents the good deeds of God's holy people.)

⁹Then he[1708] said to me, "Write this down: 'Blessed[1709] are those who have been invited to the wedding feast of the Lamb.'[1710] These are the true words of God."

¹⁰*At this pronouncement,* I laid face down to worship him but he said to me, "Do not worship me! I am a fellow servant just like you and your fellow brothers who hold to the truth about Jesus. You must worship God! For the spirit of prophecy is ultimately about the truth in Jesus."[1711]

The second coming of Jesus Christ on a white horse

¹¹Then I saw heaven open and there was a white horse with a rider called Loyal and True. When he judges and makes war he does it fairly. ¹²His eyes shone like blazing fire and he had many crowns on his head. He has a name written on him that no one knows except himself. ¹³He is dressed in a robe that is covered in blood. His name is the Word of God. ¹⁴The armies of heaven were following him, riding on white horses and dressed in fine linen—white and clean. ¹⁵Out of his mouth comes a sharp sword with which he strikes down the nations. He will shepherd them with a rod of iron. He treads the winepress of the furious anger of God Almighty. ¹⁶On his robe and on his thigh he has written:

KING OF KINGS AND LORD OF LORDS

¹⁷Then I saw an angel standing in the sun and he cried out in a loud voice to all the birds flying high overhead saying, "Come and gather together for the great feast of God.[1712] ¹⁸Come, so that you may eat the flesh of kings, generals,

---

1708   The identity of the speaker is not immediately apparent but v. 10 tells us that it is probably the bowl angel of Rev. 17:1.
1709   This is the fourth blessing in the Book of Revelation. Cf. Rev. 20:6 for the fifth blessing.
1710   Cf. Luke 13:29.
1711   In other words John is instructed that he shouldn't be worshipping the bringer of the message, the angel, but it is all about the content of the message. It's all about Jesus and what he has done so worship God.
1712   This feast refers to the aftermath of the battle of Armageddon. The strewn bodies from the battle will be so numerous that it will require a multitude of birds to clean up the battlefield.

soldiers, horses and their riders and the flesh of all people, free and slave, from the least *important* to the most *important.*"

¹⁹Then I saw the beast and the kings of the earth and their armies gathered together to make war against the rider on the horse and his army. ²⁰But the beast and the false prophet who had performed the miraculous signs on behalf of it were both captured. With these signs, the false prophet had deluded all of those who had received the mark of the beast and worshipped its image. The two of them were thrown alive into the fiery lake of burning sulphur.[1713] ²¹The rest of the soldiers were killed with the sword that came out of the mouth of the rider on the horse. The birds were all completely satisfied with the flesh *of the soldiers* that they had eaten.

The dragon is chained for a thousand years

20 ¹After these things I saw an angel coming down out of heaven and he was holding the key to the abyss and a heavy-duty chain. ²The angel seized[1714] the dragon—the ancient serpent who is the devil or Satan, and he bound him. The dragon remained bound for a thousand years. ³The angel threw him into the abyss and locked and sealed it over him to keep him from deceiving the nations anymore until the thousand years were over. After that, *Satan* must be set free for a short time.

The first resurrection saints will serve as priests of God

⁴Then I saw thrones on which were seated those *people* who had been given the right to judge. They were the souls of those who had been beheaded because of their testimony for Jesus and the Word of God. They had not worshipped the beast or his image and had not received his mark on their foreheads or their hands. They came *back* to life and ruled with Christ for a thousand years.[1715] ⁵(The remaining dead people did not come back to life until the thousand years

---

1713 Eze. 39:11 says Gog (Antichrist) will be buried in the Valley of Hamon Gog. However Isa. 14:16–20 says of the man who shook the earth (Antichrist) that even though he will initially be dumped in a mass grave with the others after the final battle and thrown out like a worthless branch, he will be denied a proper burial for he has destroyed the land. It is then that he and the false prophet will be the first two cast alive into the Lake of Fire.

1714 The verbs "seized", "bound" and "threw" (vv. 2–3) are all written in the aorist indicative form indicating a completed action in the past however this is likely a prophetic past tense similar to Rev. 18:2. Much of the Book of Revelation is written in this style announcing future events in the past tense as if they had already occurred.

1715 This gives the impression that only the tribulation martyrs will be resurrected but they are part of a much larger group who have died in Christ throughout the ages. Cf. 1 Thess. 4:16–17.

were over.) This is the first resurrection.[1716] ⁶Blessed[1717] and holy are those who take part in the first resurrection because the second death[1718] has no power over them. However, they will *serve* as priests of God and of Christ and they will reign with him for the thousand years.[1719]

Satan's ultimate destiny finally arrives

⁷When the thousand years are complete, Satan will be released from his prison. ⁸Then he will go out and deceive the nations in the four corners of the earth, Gog and Magog,[1720] to gather them for battle. They will be as numerous as the sand on the seashore. ⁹They marched across the breadth of the earth and surrounded the camp of God's holy people, the city that he loves.[1721] But fire came down from heaven and consumed them. ¹⁰The devil, who had deceived them, was thrown into the lake of burning sulphur. This is where the beast and false prophet had been thrown. They will be tormented day and night forever and ever.

The great white throne judgment

¹¹Then I saw a great white throne and the one sitting on it. Heaven and earth fled from his presence and there was no place for them. ¹²I saw the dead, both important and unimportant and they were standing before the throne and books were opened. Another book was opened—the book of life. The dead were judged according to their works as recorded in the books.[1722] ¹³The 'Sea' released the dead *people* that were in her and 'Death' and 'Hades' released the dead *people* that were in them.[1723] Each person was judged according to their works. ¹⁴Then

---

1716 This 'first resurrection' statement refers back to the last statement in v. 4 and not what is in the parentheses. So, in other words, by implication, those who come back to life after the thousand years are the 'second resurrection'. This effectively rules out a pre-tribulation rapture because this is the first resurrection and it clearly occurs after the appearance and defeat of the devil at the time of his binding when he is thrown into the abyss. Note: The first resurrection includes Christ and all of God's people in the OT including those who rose from the tombs at Christ's resurrection (Matt. 27:52–53). Christ and those who rose from the tombs earlier are the firstfruits similar to the wave offering offered at the Feast of Firstfruits as a sample of what was to come (Lev. 23:9–11).
1717 This is the fifth blessing in the Book of Revelation. Cf. Rev. 22:7 for the sixth blessing.
1718 I.e. eternal death in the lake of fire.
1719 Believing Jews and Gentiles are being built up into a royal priesthood. Cf. 1 Pet. 2:5.
1720 There are two different Gog and Magog battles referring to two different times and events. The Ezekiel 38–39 reference clearly refers to the Battle of Armageddon but this passage refers to a short period after the 1000 years. The duplicated use of the names Gog and Magog here is to show that it demonstrates the same rebellion and antagonism towards God as in Ezekiel 38–39. For example, the name 'Jezebel' has become a metaphor for someone who has a 'Jezebel spirit' in that they exhibit similar characteristics to the original Sidonian princess who was married to King Ahab.
1721 Jerusalem.
1722 These ones are part of the second resurrection. Their only hope is to have their names written in the book of life. The Bible however clearly demonstrates that no man is saved by his works but God does give all men a fair trial.
1723 This statement has its origins in ancient Greek mythological thinking as to the three locations where they thought the dead were. The three regions were ruled by the three Greek gods/goddesses

'Death' and 'Hades' were thrown into the lake of fire. The lake of fire is the second death. [15]If anyone's name was not found written in the book of life, they were thrown into the lake of fire.

God now dwells with man

21 [1]Then I saw a new[1724] heaven and a new earth because the first heaven and the first earth had passed away and there is no more ocean.[1725] [2]I saw the holy city, New Jerusalem, coming down out of heaven from God, made ready like a bride beautifully dressed for her husband. [3]I heard a loud voice from the throne saying, "Now the tent[1726] of God is with men and he will make his home with them. They will be his people and God himself will be with them and be their God. [4]He will wipe away every tear from their eyes and there will be no more death or mourning or crying or pain for the old order of things has passed away."

[5]He who was seated on the throne said, "I am refreshing all things! Write this down for these words can be trusted and are true."

[6]He said to me, "These words have come to pass and it is complete. I am the Alpha and the Omega, the Beginning and the End. Whoever is thirsty I will allow him to drink freely from the well that gives life. [7]He who overcomes will receive all these things and I will be his God and he will be my son. [8]But the cowardly, the traitors *who have turned their backs on Jesus*, the sexual perverts, the murderers, the sexually immoral, the drug users, the idolaters and all liars—their place will be in the fiery lake of burning sulphur. This is the second death."

---

named here. In Greek mythology, *Thalasa* was the goddess of the sea, *Thanatos* was the god who transported the dead to the world of the dead and *Hades* was the god of the world of the dead. Those who had died at sea were not thought of as going to the world of the dead (*Hades* or *Sheol*—the Hebrew equivalent). So, wherever the dead were situated whether at sea, on the way to the world of the dead or actually already in *Hades*, they would all be released to stand before the great white throne at the second resurrection. In other words, everyone will be judged.

1724 In the Greek, there are two words that can be used to describe something that is new. The first word '*neo*' is used to describe something that is completely new in time and never seen before. For example, a house that is newly restored to its original condition could never be *neo* because it is not new in time. When the house was first built it was *neo*, but now that it is something old being renewed or restored, it would be described as *kainos*. The word that is used here and also in 2 Pet. 3:13 to describe the new heavens and the new earth is *kainos* describing something that is refreshed or renewed. Therefore, here it is not referring to a heaven and earth that are destroyed and then replaced by a heaven and earth that are newly created. It is speaking of the current heaven and earth passing from one condition to another, being qualitatively renewed (*kainos*) to their full glory. Cf. https://www.christianweek.org/new-earth-renewed-earth/

1725 Cf. Parallel passages in Isa. 65:17, 66:22–24 and 2 Peter 3:13 indicate that the renewed heaven and renewed earth refer to the millennial kingdom but the sense here is that the everlasting state is also in view. Cf. Ironside, H. A., *Revelation: An Ironside Expository Commentary* (1920), p. 202. So now John's vision switches back to the beginning of the one thousand year period as opposed to the last verse in chapter 20 which is at the end of the one thousand year period.

1726 In the Greek this is literally 'tabernacle', as in the tabernacle of God with the Israelites in the OT. The implication here seems to be that even in all its renewed splendour, Jerusalem does not fully match or reflect the boundless glory of God.

John has a vision of New Jerusalem

⁹Then one of the seven angels who had the seven last plagues came and said to me, "Come and I will show you the bride, the wife of the Lamb." ¹⁰The angel carried me away in spirit *form* to the top of a very high mountain. There he showed me the holy city, Jerusalem,[1727] coming down from God out of heaven. ¹¹The city shone with the glory of God. Its brilliance was like that of a very precious jewel like a jasper, clear as crystal. ¹²It had a great high wall with twelve gates and twelve angels, one angel *guarding* each gate. On the gates were written the names of the twelve tribes of Israel. ¹³There were three gates on the east, three on the north, three on the south and three on the west. ¹⁴The city's wall had twelve foundations and on them were the names of the twelve apostles of the Lamb.

¹⁵The angel who had spoken with me had a golden measuring rod with which to measure the city, its gates and its walls. ¹⁶The city was laid out like a square with equal sides. He measured the city with the rod and it was found to be 12,000 measures[1728] in length, width and height. ¹⁷He measured the thickness of its wall and according to human measurements which the angel was using it was 144 cubits.[1729]

¹⁸The *city* wall was made of jasper and the city itself of pure gold, transparent like glass. ¹⁹The foundations of the city walls were decorated with every kind of precious stone. The first stone was made out of jasper, the second sapphire, the third chalcedony,[1730] the fourth emerald, ²⁰the fifth sardonyx,[1731] the sixth carnelian, the seventh chrysolite,[1732] the eighth beryl,[1733] the ninth topaz,[1734] the

---

1727 New Jerusalem.
1728 The perimeter of the city is 12,000 of the angel's golden measuring rods. In Ezekiel's vision of the future millennial city he sees each side being 4,500 'measures' (Eze. 48:30–35). Ezekiel's measuring rod was 6 long cubits (12 feet) (Eze. 40:5) whereas the angel's golden rod must have been 9 long cubits (18 feet). The city is a perfect cube and therefore would have a perimeter of about 65 km (16.25 km length, width and height).
1729 A cubit is the distance from the elbow to the fingertips which is about 18–20 inches. The wall was 144 cubits thick which is about 240 feet or 73 m.
1730 Some translations have agate here which has a variety of colours. Perhaps a green coloured stone is meant here.
1731 A variety of onyx, a semi-precious stone perhaps a red coloured stone here.
1732 In today's terminology this is a peridot, a transparent yellowish-green silicate of magnesium. The biblical gem was probably a gold-coloured stone (TH).
1733 A semi-precious blue-green colour-of-sea-water stone which is an ore source of the rare element beryllium which is used in medical and aerospace applications. When the first eyeglasses were constructed in 13th century Italy, lenses were made of beryl (or of rock crystal) as glass could not be made clear enough.
1734 A gemstone ranging in colour from golden brown to yellow in its natural state. It is one of the hardest naturally occurring minerals.

tenth chrysoprase,[1735] the eleventh jacinth[1736] and the twelfth amethyst.[1737] [21]The twelve gates were twelve pearls each gate made of a single pearl. The main street of the city was made of pure gold, transparent as glass.

[22]I did not see a sanctuary in the city because the Lord God Almighty and the Lamb are its sanctuary. [23]The city does not need the sun or the moon to shine on it for the glory of God gives its light and the Lamb is its lamp. [24]The nations will live and exist by its light and the kings of the earth will bring their wealth and riches into it. [25]The city gates will never be shut at any time, day and night, because there will be no darkness there. [26]The treasure and the wealth of the nations will be brought into it. [27]Nothing impure will ever enter it nor will anyone who does anything abominable or deceitful. But only those whose names are written in the Lamb's book of life *will be able to enter the city.*

The river of life

22 [1]Then *the angel* showed me a river of life-giving water which was sparkling like crystal. The water was flowing from under the throne of God and of the Lamb. [2]It continued flowing down the middle of the great street of the city. On each side of the river stood the tree of life, bearing twelve crops of fruit. It yielded fruit every month and the leaves of the tree are for the healing of the nations. [3]No longer will there be any curse. The throne[1738] of God and of the Lamb will be in the city and his servants will serve him. [4]They will see his face and his name will be on their foreheads.[1739] [5]And in *the city* there will be no more need for the light of the sun during the day or no more need for the brightness of the moon for the Lord will be an eternal light for you and God will shine on you.[1740]

[6]The angel said to me, "These words *of the book* can be trusted and are true. The Lord, the God of the spirits of the prophets, sent his angel to show his servants the things that must quickly take place.

1735 The modern stone is an apple-green chalcedony (aka Australian jade), but there is uncertainty about the meaning of the Greek term (*chrysoprase* is a transliteration of the Greek) (TH).
1736 This is a reddish-orange variety of zircon (TH).
1737 A purple or violet semi-precious variety of quartz stone. The ancient Greeks wore amethyst and carved drinking vessels from it in the belief that it would prevent intoxication. Amethyst derived its name from the belief that it protected its wearer from drunkenness.
1738 "Throne" is singular here indicating that the throne of God and the Lamb is the same throne.
1739 It is only through God's only begotten Son, Jesus Christ, that we can approach God, know God, and see God because he lives in unapproachable light (1 Tim. 6:16). The Son is the image of the invisible God (Col. 1:15).
1740 The original Hebrew MSS (Sodot) is followed here.

Jesus is coming quickly

⁷Jesus says, "Pay attention everyone, I am coming quickly! Blessed[1741] is the one who keeps the words of the prophecy in this book."

⁸I, John,[1742] am the one who heard and saw these things. When I had heard and seen them, I lay face down to worship at the feet of the angel who had been showing them to me. ⁹But the *angel* spoke to me saying, "Do not do it! I am just a fellow servant like you and your brothers the prophets and like all those who keep the words of this book. You must worship God!"

¹⁰Then he said to me, "Do not keep the words of the prophecy of this book a secret because the time is near. ¹¹Let him who is evil continue to do evil. Let him who is immoral keep acting immorally.[1743] Let him who is acting the right way continue to keep acting the right way and let him who is holy continue to keep being holy."

¹²Jesus says, "Pay attention everyone, I am coming soon! I have my reward *for you all* with me and I will give to everyone according to what he has done. ¹³I am the Alpha and the Omega, the First and the Last, the Beginning and the End."

¹⁴Blessed[1744] are those who are doing his commandments[1745] so that they may have the right to eat from the tree of life and that they may go through the gates into the city.[1746] ¹⁵Outside *of the city* are the dogs,[1747] the drug takers, the sexually immoral, murderers, idolaters and every one of them who loves to lie and practice falsehood.

¹⁶"I, Jesus, have sent my angel to announce to you these things for the churches. I am the root and the descendant of David[1748] and also the bright morning star."[1749]

1741 This is the sixth blessing in the Book of Revelation. Cf. Rev. 22:14 for the seventh blessing.
1742 John the Apostle, was generally considered to be the youngest of all the apostles and the apostle whom Jesus loved (John 20:2). He is believed to be the author of the Gospel of John, the letters of 1, 2 & 3 John and the Book of Revelation.
1743 It's not that evil or immorality is being encouraged but that every person has a free will and choice to live his life as he or she wants. Michael Heiser says, "…evil is the perversion of God's good gift of free will." (Heiser, Michael S, *The Unseen Realm* (2015), p. 66)
1744 This is the seventh and final blessing in the Book of Revelation. Cf. Rev. 1:3 for the first blessing in the series.
1745 I.e. These are Jesus' commandments as outlined in Matt. 5:21-48, not specifically and necessarily the Ten Commandments.
1746 This seems to imply that not everyone during the millennial kingdom will be able to enter into the city and have access to the tree of life within the city. There will be sinners in the millennial kingdom especially those who have been born during this time. However Jesus will rule with a rod of iron meaning that all rebellion and sin will be dealt with immediately.
1747 The Jews typically called Gentiles, 'dogs'. Cf. Matt. 15:26-27. But perhaps what is meant here is people who act in an ungodly manner like the heathen or Gentiles of old.
1748 This is analogous to the family tree with Jesus both the progenitor and descendant of David. Jesus comes before David yet after him as well. The Son of God is the root and Jesus as the Son of Man is the stem or offshoot of David (Isa. 11:1).
1749 The planet Venus is both the morning star and the evening star depending on the time of the year.

¹⁷The *Holy* Breath and the bride[1750] say *to Jesus*, "Come!" Let everyone who hears this also say, "Come!" Whoever is thirsty, let them come and whoever wishes, let them take the free life-giving water.

A warning to those who read this book

¹⁸I, John, have a warning for everyone who hears the words of the prophecy of this book: If anyone adds anything to them, God will add to them the plagues described in this book. ¹⁹Furthermore if anyone omits any words from this book of prophecy, God will omit his part from the book of life[1751] and from the holy city which are described in this book.

²⁰He who verifies these things says, "Yes, I am coming quickly."
Amen. Come, Lord Jesus.
²¹The grace of the Lord Jesus be with you all. Amen.

As the morning star (Venus) announces the coming day in the early dawn before the sun rises, Jesus at his first coming was the Morning Star being the sign and evidence of a new day or age. But his second coming is as the Sun of Righteousness (Mal. 4:2).

1750 The Holy Breath (Holy Spirit) and the bride of Christ, the wife of the Lamb, the loyal end times church, are anticipating and waiting patiently for the bride's husband, Jesus Christ, to return while residing in the wilderness of southern Jordan. This has a precedent when Rebekah (the bride) and Abraham's (the Father's) chief servant Eliezer (Holy Breath) were afar off and Isaac (the Son) came to meet them (Gen. 24:65). Similarly, they were in the wilderness (the Negev) and Eliezer was with Rebekah as they approached the man in the distance.

1751 Most modern translations have 'tree of life'. Cf. Rev. 3:5.

www.ingramcontent.com/pod-product-compliance
Lightning Source LLC
Chambersburg PA
CBHW040240130526
44590CB00049B/4006